Computer Literacy

BASICS

A Comprehensive Guide to IC³

Connie Morrison
Consultant, Encore
Training, Inc.

Dr. Dolores Wells
Hillsborough Community
College

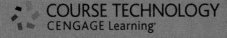

COURSE TECHNOLOGY
CENGAGE Learning

Australia • Brazil • Japan • Korea • Mexico • Singapore • Spain • United Kingdom • United States

COURSE TECHNOLOGY
CENGAGE Learning·

Computer Literacy BASICS: A Comprehensive Guide to IC³, Fourth Edition
Connie Morrison, Dolores Wells

Executive Editor: Donna Gridley

Product Manager: Allison McDonald

Development Editors: Karen Porter, Lisa Ruffolo

Associate Product Manager: Chad Kirchner

Editorial Assistant: Brandelynn Perry

Senior Content Project Manager: Cathie DiMassa

Marketing Manager: Julie Schuster

Manufacturing Planner: Julio Esperas

Production Service: GEX Publishing Services

Text Designer: Shawn Girsberger

Photo Researcher: Abigail Reip

Manuscript Quality Assurance Lead: Jeff Schwartz

Manuscript Quality Assurance Reviewers: John Freitas, Susan Pedicini, Danielle Shaw, Ashlee Welz Smith, Marianne Snow, Susan Whalen

Copy Editors: Michael Beckett, Mark Goodin, Pam Hunt

Proofreaders: Brandy Lilly, Kim Kosmatka, Vicki Zimmer

Indexer: Alexandra Nickerson

Art Director: Faith Brosnan

Cover Designer: Hanh L. Luu

Cover Image: Imagewerks/Getty Images

Compositor: GEX Publishing Services

For product information and technology assistance, contact us at
Cengage Learning Customer & Sales Support, 1-800-354-9706
For permission to use material from this text or product, submit all requests online at **www.cengage.com/permissions**
Further permissions questions can be emailed to
permissionrequest@cengage.com

Hardcover:

ISBN-13: 978-1-133-62973-3

ISBN-10: 1-133-62973-3

Softcover:

ISBN-13: 978-1-133-62972-6

ISBN-10: 1-133-62972-5

Hard Spiral:

ISBN-13: 978-1-133-62971-9

ISBN-10: 1-133-62971-7

Course Technology
20 Channel Center Street
Boston, Massachusetts 02210
USA

Cengage Learning is a leading provider of customized learning solutions with office locations around the globe, including Singapore, the United Kingdom, Australia, Mexico, Brazil, and Japan. Locate your local office at:
www.cengage.com/global

Cengage Learning products are represented in Canada by Nelson Education, Ltd.

To learn more about Course Technology, visit **www.cengage.com/coursetechnology**

Visit our company website at **www.cengage.com**

Any fictional data related to persons or companies or URLs used throughout this book is intended for instructional purposes only. At the time this book was printed, any such data was fictional and not belonging to any real persons or companies.

Windows is a registered trademark of Microsoft Corporation in the United States and other countries.

Please visit **login.cengage.com** and log in to access instructor-specific resources.

Printed in the United States of America
1 2 3 4 5 6 7 16 15 14 13 12

ABOUT THIS BOOK

Computer Literacy BASICS, Fourth Edition, provides complete coverage on computing basics, including computer hardware and components, operating system software, application software, networks, and the Internet. Lessons are organized in three modules, and within each module, concepts and features are introduced in a logical progression to build on previously learned concepts and features. Illustrations provide visual reinforcement of features and concepts, and sidebars provide notes, tips, and concepts related to the lesson topics. Step-by-Step exercises provide guidance for using the features. End-of-lesson projects include a comprehensive review of the lesson content. Teamwork projects, Critical Thinking activities, Online Discovery challenges, and Job Skills projects provide additional practice and require you to apply your problem-solving skills.

The Computing Fundamentals module focuses on hardware and software and how they work together. The lesson activities include exercises that guide students to explore the Windows operating system, change settings, and customize the desktop. Students also learn how to manage files and folders, protect and maintain their computers, and solve computer problems. Hands-on exercises, lesson reviews, and end-of-lesson projects provide students with opportunities to practice and master computing fundamental skills. The module review includes additional review questions and projects.

The Key Applications module focuses on four of the Microsoft Office 2010 applications: Word, Excel, PowerPoint, and Access. The lessons explain the purpose of commonly used software features, and step-by-step exercises demonstrate how to use those features. The end-of-lesson projects provide additional practice to master using those features to complete typical day-to-day tasks at home, school, and work. The module review includes an integrated project which entails using word processing, spreadsheets, presentations, and databases to process information and then share the information with others.

The Living Online module introduces students to communication network fundamentals and the relationships between networks and the Internet. Through hands-on exercises, students learn how to use e-mail software to exchange e-mail messages. They also learn how to use a Web browser to navigate the Internet, visit Web sites, and find information. The final section focuses on how to use computers at work, school, and home. It discusses the risks of working with hardware and software and the standards for using the Internet safely, ethically, and legally. The module review provides a thorough recap of living online concepts and skills.

To complete all lessons and End-of-Lesson material, this book will require approximately 47 hours.

Start-Up Checklist

Hardware

- Computer and processor 500-megahertz (MHz) processor or higher
- Memory: 256 megabytes (MB) of RAM or higher
- Hard disk: 3.5 gigabyte (GB) available disk space
- Display 1024 × 768 or higher-resolution monitor

Software:

- Operating system: Windows XP with Service Pack 3, Windows Vista with SP1, or Windows 7

INSIDE THE BASICS SERIES

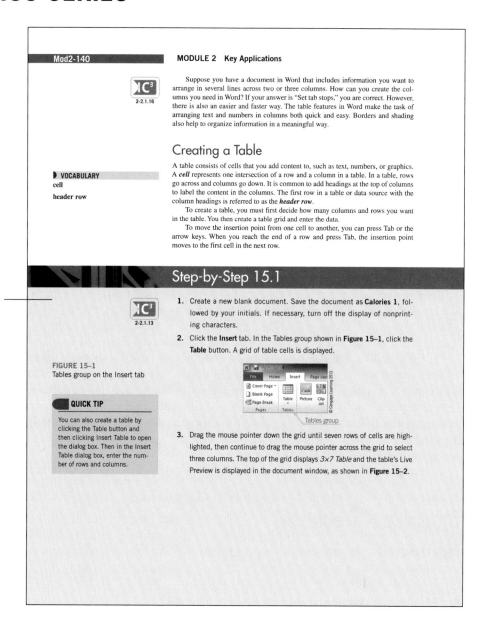

2-2.1.16

Suppose you have a document in Word that includes information you want to arrange in several lines across two or three columns. How can you create the columns you need in Word? If your answer is "Set tab stops," you are correct. However, there is also an easier and faster way. The table features in Word make the task of arranging text and numbers in columns both quick and easy. Borders and shading also help to organize information in a meaningful way.

Creating a Table

A table consists of cells that you add content to, such as text, numbers, or graphics. A **cell** represents one intersection of a row and a column in a table. In a table, rows go across and columns go down. It is common to add headings at the top of columns to label the content in the columns. The first row in a table or data source with the column headings is referred to as the **header row**.

To create a table, you must first decide how many columns and rows you want in the table. You then create a table grid and enter the data.

To move the insertion point from one cell to another, you can press Tab or the arrow keys. When you reach the end of a row and press Tab, the insertion point moves to the first cell in the next row.

▶ **VOCABULARY**
cell

header row

Step-by-Step 15.1

2-2.1.13

1. Create a new blank document. Save the document as **Calories 1**, followed by your initials. If necessary, turn off the display of nonprinting characters.

2. Click the **Insert** tab. In the Tables group shown in **Figure 15–1**, click the **Table** button. A grid of table cells is displayed.

FIGURE 15–1
Tables group on the Insert tab

> **QUICK TIP**
>
> You can also create a table by clicking the Table button and then clicking Insert Table to open the dialog box. Then in the Insert Table dialog box, enter the number of rows and columns.

3. Drag the mouse pointer down the grid until seven rows of cells are highlighted, then continue to drag the mouse pointer across the grid to select three columns. The top of the grid displays *3x7 Table* and the table's Live Preview is displayed in the document window, as shown in **Figure 15–2**.

Step-by-Step Exercises offer "hands-on practice" of the material just learned. Each exercise uses a data file or requires you to create a file from scratch.

Lesson opener elements include the **Objectives,** a list of **Data Files** required for lesson activities, a list of **Words to Know** defined throughout the lesson, and the **Estimated Completion Time**.

End of Lesson elements include the **Summary, Lesson Review Questions, Projects, Teamwork Projects,** and **Critical Thinking, Online Discovery,** and **Job Skills** activities.

iv

Instructor Resources Disk

ISBN-13: 978-1-133-62959-7
ISBN-10: 1-133-62959-8

The Instructor Resources CD or DVD contains the following teaching resources:

The Data and Solution files for this course.

ExamView® tests for each lesson. ExamView is a powerful testing software package that allows instructors to create and administer printed, computer (LAN-based), and Internet exams.

Instructor's Manual that includes lecture notes for each lesson and references to the end-of-lesson activities and Unit Review projects.

Answer Keys that include solutions to the lesson and unit review questions as well as sample solutions for end-of-lesson projects and activities.

Copies of the figures that appear in the student text.

Grids that show skills required for the Microsoft Certification Application Specialist (MCAS) exam, SCANS workplace competencies and skills, and activities that apply to cross-curricular topics.

Suggested Syllabus with block, two quarter, and 18-week schedule

Annotated Solutions and Grading Rubrics

PowerPoint presentations for each lesson.

ExamView®

ExamView®. This textbook is accompanied by ExamView, a powerful testing software package that allows instructors to create and administer printed, computer (LAN-based), and Internet exams. ExamView includes hundreds of questions that correspond to the topics covered in this text, enabling students to generate detailed study guides that include page references for further review. The computer-based and Internet testing components allow students to take exams at their computers, and save the instructor time by grading each exam automatically.

To access additional course materials [including CourseMate], please visit www.cengagebrain.com. At the CengageBrain.com home page, search for the ISBN of your title (from the back cover of your book) using the search box at the top of the page. This will take you to the product page where these resources can be found.

IC³

IC³ stands for the Internet and Computing Core Certification program, a global training and certification program. Completing this program and earning IC³ certification shows that you have the necessary computer skills to excel in a digital world, and are capable of using a wide range of computer technology. IC³ provides three exams: Computing Fundamentals, Key Applications, and Living Online. The skills needed for these exams are valuable to any functional user of computer hardware, software, networks, and the Internet. By passing the three IC³ exams, you give yourself a globally accepted and validated credential that provides the proof employees or higher education institutions need.

SAM 2010   *SÁM*

SAM 2010 Assessment, Projects, and Training version 1.0 offers a real-world approach to applying Microsoft Office 2010 skills. The Assessment portion of this powerful and easy to use software simulates Office 2010 applications, allowing users to demonstrate their computer knowledge in a hands-on environment. The Projects portion allows students to work live-in-the-application on project-based assignments. The Training portion helps students learn in the way that works best for them by reading, watching, or receiving guided help.

- SAM 2010 captures the key features of the actual Office 2010 software, allowing students to work in high-fidelity, multi-pathway simulation exercises for a real-world experience.
- SAM 2010 includes realistic and explorable simulations of Office 2010, Windows 7 coverage, and a new user interface.
- Easy, web-based deployment means SAM is more accessible than ever to both you and your students.
- Direct correlation to the skills covered on a chapter-by-chapter basis in your Course Technology textbooks allows you to create a detailed lesson plan.
- SAM Projects offers live-in-the-application project-based assignments. Student work is automatically graded, providing instant feedback. A unique cheating detection feature identifies students who may have shared files.
- Because SAM Training is tied to textbook exams and study guides, instructors can spend more time teaching and let SAM Training help those who need additional time to grasp concepts

Note: This textbook may or may not be available in SAM Projects at this time. Please check with your sales representative for the most recent information on when this title will be live in SAM Projects.

AUTHOR ACKNOWLEDGEMENTS

This book represents a true team effort, and it was a pleasure working with everyone. My appreciation goes to all the members of the team who made this book possible. I owe special thanks to the following individuals: Donna Gridley, Allison McDonald, and Cathie DiMassa for their direction and support in the development of this book; Karen Porter, for her meticulous editing and valuable input; and Jeff Schwartz and his team, for the thorough quality assurance reviews. I am also very grateful to my family, Gene, Al, Amy, and Chris, for their continued support. — **Connie Morrison**

My love and appreciation goes to: My mom, who taught me humility, forgiveness, love, and compassion; My son Bryan, whom I miss every day; Dave—my best friend, buddy, and pal for his love and support. My appreciation and thanks goes to our entire team for their direction, assistance, support, and help in the development of this book, which made this book possible. Special thanks goes to Lisa Ruffolo, who always was there to answer my questions and make suggestions and to Allison McDonald for her guidance and suggestions along the way. This book truly was a team effort. — **Dolores Wells**

Bring Your Course Back To the BASICS

Developed with the needs of new learners in mind, the **BASICS**, part of the Origins Series, is ideal for lower-level courses covering basic computer concepts, Microsoft Office, programming, and more. Introductory in nature, these texts are comprehensive enough to cover the most important features of each application.

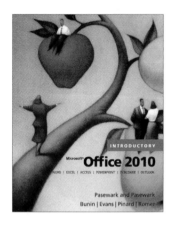

Microsoft Office 2010 Introductory
978-0-538-47539-6

Provide a thorough introduction of the most important Microsoft Office 2010 skills to beginning students with *Microsoft Office 2010 Introductory*, part of the Origins Series. This text includes features that make learning easy and enjoyable, yet challenging for learners. Students will be engaged with activities that range from simulations to case studies that challenge and sharpen problem-solving skills while gaining the hands-on practice needed to be successful computer users.

Microsoft Office 2010 Fundamentals
978-0-538-47246-3

Teach your introductory level class the essentials of the Microsoft Office 2010 software applications with *Microsoft Office 2010 Fundamentals*, part of the Origins Series. This text is ideal for inexperienced computer users who need to learn Microsoft Office 2010 skills for everyday life. Although introductory in nature, this text is comprehensive enough to cover the most important features of Word, Excel, PowerPoint, Access, and Publisher.

Microsoft Office 2010 Fundamentals Projects Binder
978-0-538-47989-9

Offer your students a chance to expand on their Microsoft Office 2010 skills by providing projects for hands-on practice. The *Microsoft Office 2010 Fundamentals Projects Binder* allows students to apply what they've learned and to reinforce their skills in a project-based environment. The variety of real-world projects help prepare students for how they will use their Microsoft Office skills in a professional setting.

CONTENTS

MODULE 1   COMPUTING FUNDAMENTALS

MODULE 2 KEY APPLICATIONS

MODULE 3 — LIVING ONLINE

MODULE I

COMPUTING FUNDAMENTALS

Computer Concepts

LESSON 1   **2 HRS.**
Computers and Computer Systems

LESSON 2   **2 HRS.**
Input, Output, and Processing

LESSON 3   **1 HR.**
Computer Protection

LESSON 4   **1 HR.**
Computer Maintenance

LESSON 5   **1.5 HRS.**
Computer-Related Issues

LESSON 6   **1 HR.**
Software and Hardware Interaction

LESSON 7   **1.5 HRS.**
Software Fundamentals

Introduction to Microsoft Windows

LESSON 8   **1.5 HRS.**
Operating Systems

LESSON 9   **1 HR.**
Windows Management

LESSON 10   **1.5 HRS.**
Operating System Customization

COMPUTING FUNDAMENTALS

Computer Concepts

 LESSON 1
Computers and Computer Systems
| 1-1.1.1 | 1-1.1.3 | 1-1.1.4 |
| 1-1.1.2 | | |

 LESSON 2
Input, Output, and Storage
| 1-1.1.5 | 1-1.1.7 | 1-1.1.9 |
| 1-1.1.6 | 1-1.1.8 | |

 LESSON 3
Computer Protection
| 1-1.2.1 | 1-1.2.3 | 1-1.2.4 |
| 1-1.2.2 | | |

 LESSON 4
Computer Maintenance
| 1-1.2.5 | 1-1.2.6 | 1-1.2.7 |

 LESSON 5
Hardware and Software
| 1-1.2.8 | 1-1.2.9 |

 LESSON 6
Software and Hardware Interaction
| 1-2.1.1 | 1-2.1.2 | 1-2.1.3 |

 LESSON 7
Software Fundamentals
1-2.2.1	1-2.2.5	1-2.2.9
1-2.2.2	1-2.2.6	1-2.2.10
1-2.2.3	1-2.2.7	
1-2.2.4	1-2.2.8	

Introduction to Microsoft Windows

 LESSON 8
Operating Systems
| 1-3.1.1 | 1-3.1.3 | 1-3.1.5 |
| 1-3.1.2 | 1-3.1.4 | |

 LESSON 10
Operating System Customization
1-3.3.1	1-3.3.4	1-3.3.6
1-3.3.2	1-3.3.5	1-3.3.7
1-3.3.3		

LESSON 9
Windows Management
1-3.2.1	1-3.2.4	1-3.2.7
1-3.2.2	1-3.2.5	1-3.2.8
1-3.2.3	1-3.2.6	

LESSON 1

Computers and Computer Systems

■ OBJECTIVES

Upon completion of this lesson, you should be able to:

- Understand the importance of computers.
- Define computers and computer systems.
- Classify computers.
- Use computer systems.
- Identify system components.
- Identify types of storage devices.
- Care for storage media.
- Explore computers in your future.

■ DATA FILES

You do not need data files to complete this lesson.

■ WORDS TO KNOW

arithmetic/logic unit (ALU)

central processing unit (CPU)

circuit board

computer

control unit

data

hard disk

hardware

information

memory

mobile device

motherboard

notebook computer

random access memory (RAM)

read-only memory (ROM)

server

software

supercomputer

tablet PC

USB flash drive

MODULE 1   Computing Fundamentals

This lesson introduces you to computers, starting with a brief history and ending with a look into the future. You will learn how to classify computers and their components and identify and care for storage devices.

Understanding the Importance of Computers

The computer is one of the most important inventions of the past century. The widespread use of computers affects each of us individually and as a society. You can see computers in use almost everywhere! For instance, consider the following:

- Educational institutions use computers to enhance instruction in all disciplines and to provide online instruction.
- Video game systems transport you to an imaginary world.
- Using ATMs, you can withdraw money from your bank account from almost any location in the world.
- On television and at the movies, you can see instant replays in sports or amazing special effects that take you to outer space.
- Mobile computing, text messaging, e-mail, and online audio/video conferencing allow you to communicate with people at almost any location.

As indicated by these examples, you find computers and computer technology everywhere throughout society—from businesses and financial organizations, to home electronics and appliances, and to personal applications such as clothing embedded with iPod controls.

The importance of the computer is not surprising. Many people consider the computer to be the single most important invention of the 20th century. This technology affects all aspects of everyone's daily lives. Computers are no longer bulky machines that sit on desktops—they come in every shape and size and are found everywhere. As more powerful and special-purpose computers become available, society will find more ways to use this technology to enhance everyone's lives. See **Figure 1–1**.

© Andersen Ross/Getty Images

FIGURE 1–1   Students doing online research

A Brief History of the Computer

Computers have been around for more than 60 years. The first computers were developed in the late 1940s and early 1950s. They were massive, special-purpose machines with names like UNIVAC and ENIAC and were designed initially for use by the military and government. These early computers had less processing power than today's iPhone, occupied small buildings or entire city blocks, and cost millions of dollars. Computers in the mid-1950s through early 1970s were somewhat smaller and more powerful, but still were limited in what they could do. They remained expensive, so only major companies and government organizations could afford these systems. See **Figure 1–2**.

FIGURE 1–2   Early computers

In 1971, Dr. Ted Hoff developed the microprocessor. It took visionaries such as Steve Jobs and Steve Wozniak to see a future for the microprocessor and its application to personal computers. Jobs and Wozniak built the first Apple computer in 1976. Shortly thereafter, a second version, the Apple II, was released. It became an immediate success, especially in schools. In 1980, Bill Gates worked with IBM to develop the disk operating system (DOS) for the IBM PC. This computer, introduced in 1981, quickly became the PC of choice for businesses. See **Figure 1–3**.

ABOVE AND BEYOND

The first IBM PC ran on a 4.77 MHz Intel 8088 microprocessor. The PC came equipped with 16 kilobytes (KB) of memory, expandable to 256 KB. The PC came with one or two 160 KB floppy disk drives and an optional color monitor.

FIGURE 1–3   The Apple II and IBM PC

1-1.1.1

Defining Computers and Computer Systems

Throughout a normal workday, millions of people interact globally with computers and other digital devices, often without even knowing it. Doctors, lawyers, warehouse workers, store clerks, homemakers, teachers, musicians, and students—to name a few examples—constantly depend on computers to perform part of their daily duties.

So, what exactly is a computer? What does it really do? A *computer* is an electronic device that receives data (input), processes data, stores data, and produces a result (output).

A *computer system* includes hardware, software, data, and people. The actual machine—wires, transistors, and circuits—is called *hardware*. Peripheral devices such as printers and monitors also are types of hardware. *Software* consists of instructions or programs for controlling the computer. *Data* is text, numbers, sound, images, or video. The computer receives data through an input device, processes the data, produces output (or *information*), and stores the data and information on a storage device. The users, the people who use computers, are also part of the system. See **Figure 1–4**.

▶ **VOCABULARY**

computer

computer system

hardware

software

data

information

U.S. Air Force photo/Senior Master Sgt. Edward E. Snyder

FIGURE 1–4   Using a mobile computer to process data into information

Consider how a store clerk might use a computer system to complete a sale for a customer who has an account at the store:

- *Inputs data*: The store clerk enters the customer's name and scans the barcode of an item into the computer through input devices, such as a keyboard and digital scanner.

- *Processes data*: The computer uses stored instructions to process the data into information.

- *Outputs information*: An output device, such as a monitor or a printer, displays the information.

- *Stores data and information*: The data and information are stored in temporary memory and then on a permanent storage device, such as a hard drive.

This series of steps—input, processing, output, and storage (IPOS)—is often referred to as the information processing cycle. See **Figure 1–5**.

Inputs data	Processes data	Outputs information	Stores data and information
Emmet Bender 20 East Street Tampa, Florida 33222	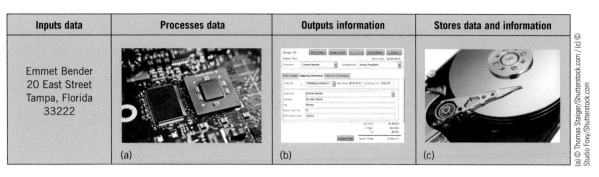 (a)	(b)	(c)

FIGURE 1–5   Information processing cycle

This brief overview of a computer and the tasks you can accomplish with it might make the computer seem very complicated. A computer, however, performs only two operations:

- Arithmetic computations such as addition, subtraction, multiplication, and division, and comparisons such as greater than, less than, or equal to
- Logical operations using logical operators, such as AND, OR, and NOT

Classifying Computers

Computers today come in all shapes and sizes, with specific types being especially suited for specific tasks. Computers are classified as either special purpose or general purpose. *Special-purpose computers* are used mostly to control something else. Tiny chips are embedded in devices, such as a dishwasher, bathroom scale, or airport radar system, and these chips control these particular devices.

General-purpose computers are divided into categories based on their physical size, function, cost, and performance:

- *Desktop computers* and *notebook computers* (also called *laptop computers*) are today's most widely used *personal computers (PCs)*, which are computers designed for one person to use at a time. Most desktop computers are designed so that all components fit on or under a desk. The all-in-one desktop computer is a single-unit desktop. Two popular types of personal computers are the PC (based on the original IBM personal computer design) and the Apple Macintosh. Notebook computers are small personal computers that include a built-in monitor and keyboard. They are designed to be carried from one location to another.

- A *server* generally is used by small to medium-size companies and can support a few users or hundreds of users. Most servers are referred to as network servers or application servers. A computer that delivers Web pages to browsers and other files to applications via the HTTP protocol is considered a *Web server*. A *database server* stores databases and database management systems. A *file server* stores remote programs and data files that are shared by a set of designated users.

- *Mobile devices* generally can fit into the palm of your hand. Examples of mobile devices (or handheld devices) are calculators, smart phones and other cell phones, electronic organizers, handheld games, and other similar tools. Many mobile devices can connect wirelessly to the Internet.

- A *tablet PC* is a personal computer similar in size and thickness to a notepad. You can take notes using a stylus or digital pen on a touch screen. This device functions as your primary personal computer as well as a note-taking device.

ABOVE AND BEYOND

Deep Blue was a chess-playing computer developed by IBM. On May 11, 1997, the machine won a six-game match by two wins to one with three draws against world champion Garry Kasparov.

1-1.1.1

VOCABULARY

special-purpose computer

desktop computer

notebook computer

laptop computer

personal computer (PC)

server

Web server

database server

file server

mobile device

tablet PC

▶ **VOCABULARY**

mainframe computer

supercomputer

embedded computer

ABOVE AND BEYOND

Supercomputers are often used to conduct and test medical experiments.

■ The modern ***mainframe computer*** is a large, expensive computer capable of supporting hundreds or even thousands of users. This type of computer is much bigger than personal computers. Large companies use these to perform processing tasks for many users.

■ A ***supercomputer*** is the fastest type of computer. Government agencies and large corporations use these computers for specialized applications to process enormous amounts of data. The cost of a supercomputer can be as much as several million dollars.

Other types of computer devices include the following:

■ ***Embedded computers*** perform specific tasks and can be found in a range of devices such as digital watches, traffic lights, automobiles, household appliances, and system controllers for high end medical equipment.

■ *Portable music and media players* are usually smaller than a deck of cards. They can store and play back music and video. Examples are MP3 players and portable DVD players.

Today's small personal and handheld computers are more powerful than the mainframes and supercomputers of yesteryear. **Figure 1–6** shows examples of different types of computers.

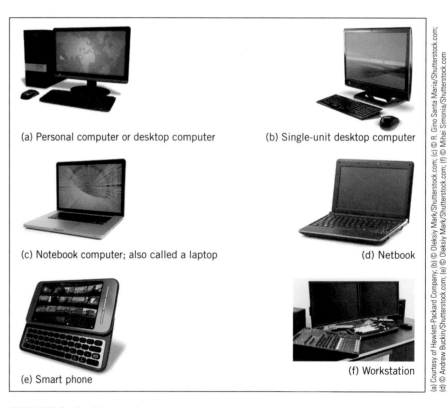

(a) Personal computer or desktop computer

(b) Single-unit desktop computer

(c) Notebook computer; also called a laptop

(d) Netbook

(e) Smart phone

(f) Workstation

(a) Courtesy of Hewlett-Packard Company; (b) © Oleksiy Mark/Shutterstock.com; (c) © R. Gino Santa Maria/Shutterstock.com; (d) © Oleksiy Mark/Shutterstock.com; (e) © Andrew Buckin/Shutterstock.com; (f) © Mihai Simonia/Shutterstock.com

FIGURE 1–6　Types of computers

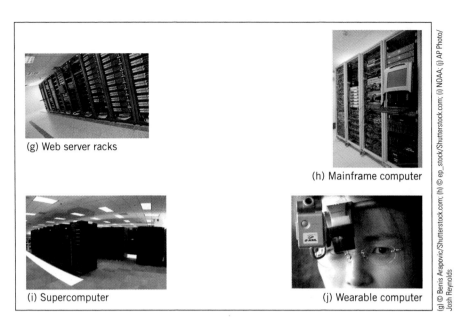

(g) Web server racks

(h) Mainframe computer

(i) Supercomputer

(j) Wearable computer

(g) © Benis Arapovic/Shutterstock.com; (h) © ep_stock/Shutterstock.com; (i) NOAA; (j) AP Photo/ Josh Reynolds

FIGURE 1–6 Types of computers (continued)

Other computer devices include the following:

- *Calculators* are used for performing mathematical calculations.
- *Computer game systems* are specialized computers used to play games. Some of the more popular are the Sony PlayStation, Nintendo Wii, and Microsoft Xbox.

■ *Electronic book readers* enable you to read an electronic version of a traditional print book (see **Figure 1–7**).

FIGURE 1–7   Electronic book reader

Using Computer Systems

Computers are used for all kinds of tasks—to predict weather, fly airplanes, control traffic lights, play games, access the Internet, send e-mail, and so on. You might wonder how a machine can do so many things.

To appreciate how a computer operates requires knowledge of calculus, probability, and statistics—all of which are needed to understand physics and circuit analysis. Most of us, however, do not need this level of comprehension. Instead, we need only a fundamental understanding. Just about all computers, regardless of size, take raw data and change it into information. Recall that computers follow the IPOS procedure—input, processing, output, and storage. For example:

■ You enter programs and data with some type of input device.

■ The computer uses instructions to process the data and to turn it into information.

■ You send the information to some type of output device.

■ You store it for later retrieval.

TECHNOLOGY CAREERS

Computers on the Job

In the past few decades, computers have had dramatic effects on how we live, learn, and work. For example, the kinds of jobs available have changed because of computers. Fifty years ago, only a handful of people were computer programmers, and none were Web designers or software entrepreneurs. Today, nearly all jobs require some computer skills.

Time-consuming, labor-intensive communication tasks that used to require face-to-face meetings, telephone calls, overnight deliveries, or paging through printed materials are now performed quickly and efficiently using Internet browsers and e-mail. Students can participate in distance-learning classes to take courses not available where they live. Even the electric-meter reader and delivery person now carry handheld computers that track a consumer's electricity use or the location of a package. Cashiers use computers for retail sales, and managers use them to update the store's inventory, handle customer calls, and advertise products. All of these advances, now taken for granted by many of us, are recent innovations.

Input, output, and processing devices grouped together represent a computer system. The components that the computer uses to process data are contained within the system case. **Figure 1–8** shows many of these components.

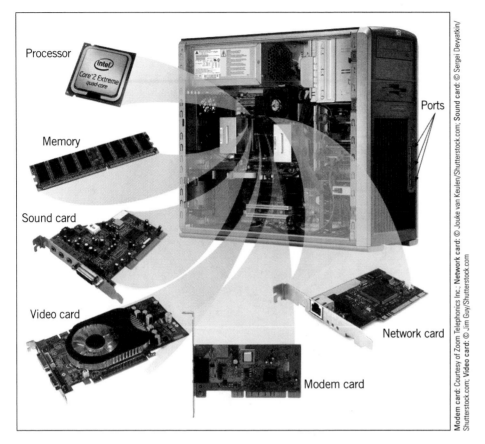

FIGURE 1–8   Computer system components

1-1.1.2
1-1.1.3

▶ **VOCABULARY**

motherboard

circuit board

central processing unit (CPU)

Identifying System Components

The PC system case is the metal and plastic case that houses the main system components of the computer. Central to all of this is the ***motherboard***, or system board, that mounts into the case. The motherboard is a circuit board that contains many integral components. A ***circuit board*** is simply a thin plate or board that contains electronic components. See **Figure 1–9**. The following are some of the most important of these components:

- Central processing unit
- Memory
- Connectors
- Expansion ports and expansion slots

Back panel connectors

Advanced Graphics Port (AGP) slot

PCI bus

Heat sink and CPU

Expansion slots for RAM

Connectors to storage devices

© any_keen/Shutterstock.com

FIGURE 1–9   Motherboard

The Central Processing Unit

The ***central processing unit (CPU)***, also called the microprocessor or central processor, is the brains of the computer. The processor is housed on a tiny silicon chip similar to that shown in **Figure 1–10**. This chip contains millions of switches and pathways that help your computer make important decisions. The switches control the flow of the electricity as it travels across the pathways. The processor knows which switches to turn on and which to turn off because it receives its instructions from computer programs. Programs are a set of special instructions, written by programmers, which control the activities of the computer. Programs also are known as software.

FIGURE 1–10   Microprocessor

Some chip manufacturers now offer dual-core and multicore processors. A *dual-core processor* is a single chip that contains two separate processors, and a *multicore processor* is an expansion that provides for more than two separate processors. These processors do not necessarily double the processing speed of a single-core processor, but do provide increased performance when running multiple programs simultaneously. Microprocessor speed generally is measured in gigahertz (GHz). Speeds for current microprocessors are in the 2 GHz to 4 GHz range.

The CPU has two primary sections: the arithmetic/logic unit and the control unit.

▶ **VOCABULARY**
dual-core processor

multicore processor

arithmetic/logic unit (ALU)

control unit

binary code

The Arithmetic/Logic Unit

The *arithmetic/logic unit (ALU)* performs arithmetic computations and logical operations. The arithmetic computations include addition, subtraction, multiplication, and division. The logical operations involve comparisons—asking the computer to determine if two numbers are equal or if one number is greater than or less than another number. These might seem like simple operations. However, by combining these operations, the ALU can execute complex tasks. For example, a video game uses arithmetic operations and comparisons to determine what appears on your screen.

The Control Unit

The *control unit* is the boss, so to speak, and coordinates all of the processor's activities. Using programming instructions, it manages the flow of information through the processor by controlling what happens inside the processor.

You communicate with the computer through programming languages. You might have heard of programming languages called Java, COBOL, C++, or Visual Basic. These are just a few of the many languages you can use to give instructions to a computer. For example, you might have a programming statement such as *Let X = 2 + 8*. With this statement, you are using a programming language to ask the computer to add the numbers 2 and 8 and assign the calculated value to *X*. However, when you input this instruction, something else has to happen. The computer does not understand human language. It understands only machine language, or *binary code*, which contains only 1s and 0s. This is where the control unit takes over.

Recognizing How a Computer Represents Data

The control unit reads and interprets the program instruction and changes the instruction into machine language. Earlier, this chapter discussed the processor and its pathways and switches. As electricity travels through processor pathways, it turns switches on and off, which represents the 1s and 0s. When electricity is present, it represents a 1. The absence of electricity represents a 0. After changing the instructions into machine language (binary), the control unit then sends out the necessary messages to execute the instructions. A single zero or a single one is called a *bit*, which is the smallest unit of information storage. Eight bits are equal to one byte. A *byte* is a single character, such as a letter or number. See **Table 1–1** for a list of measurement terms. As a comparison, 1 gigabyte (GB) of data is equivalent to about 450 digital songs.

▶ VOCABULARY

bit

byte

QUICK TIP

The Step-by-Step exercises in this book are written for a personal or notebook computer with the Windows 7 operating system. The windows and desktop for earlier versions of Windows are similar. Please make appropriate adjustments if you are using a different Windows version or are working on a network.

TABLE 1–1   Measurement terms

TERM	ABBREVIATION	NUMBER OF BYTES
Kilobyte	K or KB	1024 (approximately 1,000)
Megabyte	MB	1,048,576 (approximately 1 million)
Gigabyte	GB	1,073,741,824 (approximately 1 billion)
Terabyte	TB	1,099,511,627,776 (approximately 1 trillion)

To view an example of a binary number and perform other calculations, use your computer's calculator to complete Step-by-Step 1.1.

Step-by-Step 1.1

1. Click the **Start** button  on the taskbar, point to **All Programs**, click **Accessories**, and then click **Calculator**. The Standard calculator is displayed (see **Figure 1–11**).

FIGURE 1–11
Windows Standard calculator

Menu bar

View menu

Used with permission from Microsoft Corporation

2. Click **View** on the menu bar and then click **Scientific** to display the Scientific calculator. Click **View** on the menu bar and then click **Programmer** to display the Programmer calculator.

3. If necessary, click the **Dec** (decimal) option button. Enter **30** by clicking the calculator numeric buttons. Click the **Bin** (binary) option button to calculate the binary equivalent of 30: 11110.

4. Click the **Dec** option button and convert **1112** to binary. The number 10001011000 is displayed.

5. Click **View** on the menu bar and then click **Date calculation** (see **Figure 1–12**). The dates on your calculator might differ.

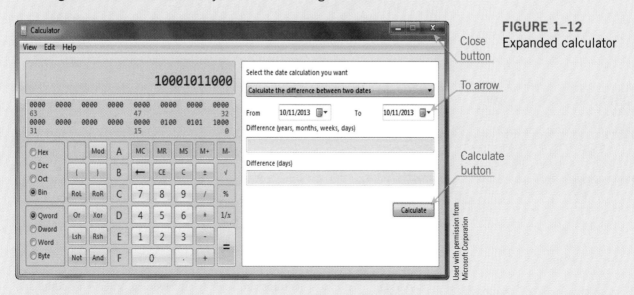

FIGURE 1–12
Expanded calculator

Close button

To arrow

Calculate button

Used with permission from Microsoft Corporation

6. Click the **To** arrow and then select the date of your next birthday.

7. Click the **Calculate** button.

8. What is the difference in months and weeks? What is the difference in days?

9. Click the **Close** button [X] to close the Windows Calculator.

Memory

Memory is where data is stored on the motherboard. Sometimes understanding memory can be confusing because it can mean different things to different people. The easiest way to understand memory is to think of it as either short term or long term. When you want to store a file or information permanently, you use secondary storage devices such as the computer's hard drive or a USB drive. You might think of this as long term memory.

Random Access Memory

You can think about the memory on the motherboard as short term memory. This type of memory is called *random access memory*, or *RAM*. RAM is also referred to as main memory and primary memory. You might have heard someone ask, "How much memory is in your computer?" Most likely, they are asking how much RAM is in your computer. The computer can read from and write to this type of memory. Data, information, and program instructions are stored temporarily within the CPU on a RAM chip or a set of RAM chips, such as those shown in **Figure 1–13**.

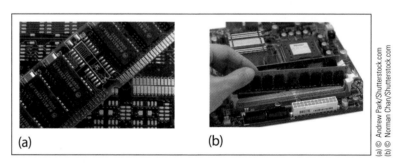

(a)   (b)

© Andrew Park/Shutterstock.com
© Norman Chan/Shutterstock.com

FIGURE 1–13   RAM chips

When the computer is turned off or otherwise loses power, whatever is stored in the RAM memory chips disappears. Therefore, RAM is considered volatile. To understand how RAM works and how the computer processes data, think about how you would use a word-processing program to create an address list of your family and friends:

1. First, you start your word-processing program. The computer then loads the word-processing program instructions into RAM.

2. You input the names, addresses, and telephone numbers (your data). Your data is also stored in RAM.

3. Next, you give your word-processing program a command to process your data by arranging it in a special format, such as alphabetical order. This command and your processed data, or information, now also are stored in RAM.

4. You then click the Print button. Instructions to print are transmitted to RAM, and your document is sent to your printer.

5. Next, you click the Save button. Instructions to provide you with an opportunity to name and save your file are loaded into RAM. The information is now stored in permanent memory at the saved location. After you save your file, you exit your word-processing program and turn off the computer.

6. All instructions, data, and information that you used to create your address list are erased from RAM.

This process is known as the *instruction cycle* or *I-cycle,* and the *execution cycle* or *E-cycle*. When the CPU receives an instruction to perform a specified task, the instruction cycle is the amount of time it takes to retrieve the instruction and complete the command. The execution cycle refers to the amount of time it takes the CPU to execute the instruction and store the results in RAM. Together, the instruction cycle and one or more execution cycles create a *machine cycle*.

For every instruction, a processor repeats a set of four basic operations, which compose a machine cycle: (1) fetching, (2) decoding, (3) executing, and, if necessary, (4) storing (see **Figure 1–14**). *Fetching* is the process of obtaining a program instruction or data item from RAM. The term *decoding* refers to the process of translating the instruction into signals the computer can execute. *Executing* is the process of carrying out the commands. *Storing*, in this context, means writing the result to memory (not to a storage medium).

▶ **VOCABULARY**
instruction cycle
I-cycle
execution cycle
E-cycle
machine cycle
fetching
decoding
executing
storing

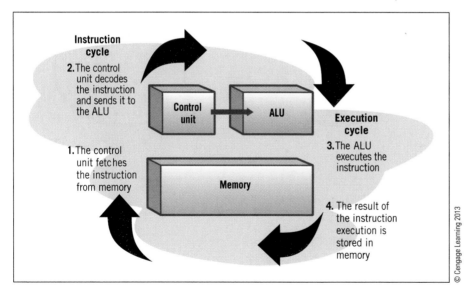

FIGURE 1–14   Processing cycle

Machine cycles are measured in microseconds (millionths of a second), nanoseconds (billionths of a second), and even picoseconds (trillionths of a second) in some of the larger computers. The faster the machine cycle, the faster your computer processes data. The speed of the processor has a lot to do with the speed of the machine cycle. However, the amount of RAM in your computer can also help increase the speed with which the computer processes data. The more RAM you have, the faster the computer processes data. See **Figure 1–15**.

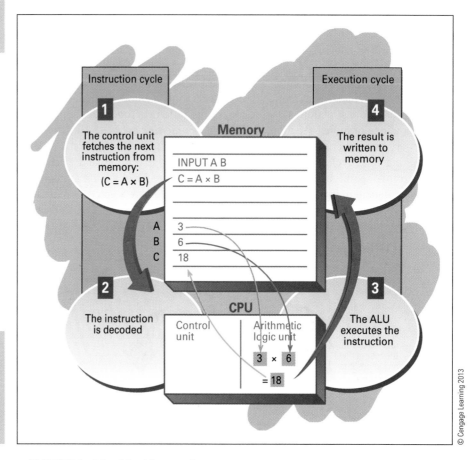

FIGURE 1–15   Machine cycle

Read-Only Memory

Another type of memory you will find on the motherboard is *read-only memory*, or *ROM*, which is permanent storage of data, usually burned onto chips. ROM chips are found throughout a computer system. The computer manufacturer uses a ROM chip to store specific instructions that are needed for computer operations. Because ROM is nonvolatile, these instructions remain on the chip even when the power is turned off. A common ROM chip is the *BIOS ROM*. The computer uses instructions contained on the BIOS ROM chip to start the system when you turn on your computer. A computer can read from a ROM chip, but cannot write or store data on the chip.

1-1.1.4

Identifying Types of Storage Devices

As data is entered in the computer and processed, it is stored in RAM (temporary memory). If you want to keep a permanent copy of the data, you must store it on some type of storage medium. Storage devices are categorized by the method they use to store data. The categories include magnetic technology, optical technology, and solid-state storage.

Magnetic Storage Devices

Magnetic storage devices contain oxide-coated polyester film, usually in the shape of a disk, that has been magnetized to hold data. As the disk rotates in the computer, an electromagnetic read/write head stores or retrieves data in circles called *tracks*. The number of tracks on a disk varies with the type of disk. The tracks are numbered from the outside to the inside. As data is stored on the disk, it is stored on a numbered track. Each track is labeled and the location is kept in a special log on the disk called a *file allocation table (FAT)*. Types of magnetic storage media include hard disks, magnetic tape, 3½-inch disks, and Zip disks.

▶ **VOCABULARY**
track
file allocation table (FAT)
hard disk

Hard Disks

Most *hard disks* (also called hard drives) are used to store data inside the computer, although external (removable) hard disks are also available. Internal hard disks provide two advantages: speed and capacity. Accessing data is faster, and the amount of data that can be stored is much larger than what can be stored on other types of magnetic storage devices. The size of the hard disk is measured in gigabytes or terabytes and can contain several platters (see **Figure 1–16**).

Platter

Spindle

Head

Actuator arm

Actuator

© roadk/Shutterstock.com

FIGURE 1–16   Hard disk

Removable Disks

Removable disks are designed to be removed from the computer without turning off the power. Removable magnetic media are rarely used and include 3½-inch disks and Zip disks. A 3½-inch disk, usually just called a disk, is a flat circle of iron oxide-coated plastic enclosed in a hard plastic case. Although the 3½-inch is the most common size, you might see other sizes. A 3½-inch disk can hold about 1.44 megabytes (MB) of data, or around 690 characters (see **Figure 1–17**). To protect unwanted data from being added to or removed from a disk, write protection is provided. To write-protect a disk, open the write protect window on the disk. A Zip drive looks like a thicker 3½-inch disk but requires a special drive and can hold 100–750 MB of data. Both types of removable magnetic media are practically obsolete since the introduction of USB drives and solid-state storage media, which can store thousands of times more data.

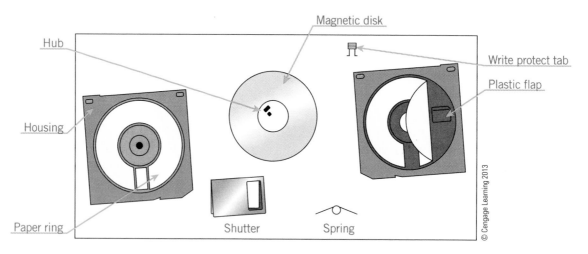

FIGURE 1–17   Parts of a 3½-inch disk

Optical Storage Devices

Optical storage devices use laser technology to read and write data on plastic platters that contain a metal layer, which reflects the laser light back to a sensor in an optical drive (see **Figure 1–18**). The term *disc* is used for optical media. CDs and DVDs are types of optical storage media. Most computers today come equipped with some type of optical storage—usually a dual CD/DVD drive. The technology for CDs and DVDs is similar, but storage capacities are quite different, and several variations exist.

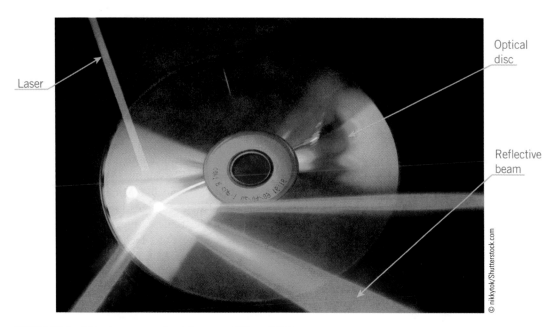

FIGURE 1–18   Laser reads data on a CD or DVD

These storage devices come in the formats listed below:

- *CD-DA*: The compact disc digital audio format is also known as an audio CD; it is the industry-wide standard for music publishing and distribution.

- *CD-R*: The compact disc-recordable format makes it possible for you to create your own compact discs that can be read by any CD-ROM drive. After information is written to this type of disc, it cannot be changed.

- *CD-ROM*: The compact disc read-only memory format can store large amounts of data—up to 1 GB, although the most common size is 650 MB, or about 74 minutes of audio information. A single CD-ROM has the storage capacity of 700 3½-inch disks with enough memory to store about 300,000+ text pages. You can read data from the CD; you cannot store data on a CD unless you are using a writable CD.

- *CD-RW*: The compact disc-rewritable is a type of compact disc that enables you to write onto it multiple times. Not all CD players can read CD-RWs.

- *DVD-ROM*: The digital video disc read-only memory is a read-only DVD format commonly used for distribution of movies and computer games; its capacity ranges from 4.7 GB to 17 GB.

- *DVD-R*: The digital video disc-recordable is similar to the CD-R except it has a much larger capacity; after information is written to this type of disc, it cannot be changed.

- *DVD-RW*: The digital video disc-rewritable stores data using technology similar to that of a CD-RW, but with a much larger capacity.

- *Blu-ray*: Also known as Blu-ray discs (BD), these discs provide more than five times the storage capacity of traditional DVDs. A single-layer disc can hold up to 25 GB, and a dual-layer disc can hold up to 50 GB. This format was developed for storing large amounts of data and to enable recording and playback of high-definition video.

▶ **VOCABULARY**
solid-state storage
USB flash drive

The color of a CD/DVD indicates its quality. It is best to look for a gold or silver CD/DVD. When viewing the color, look at it from the underside of the disk and not from the top. The shelf-life of a CD/DVD is cited as approximately 2 to 25 years or longer. The quality of the storage media and the storage environment affects the shelf life.

Solid-State Storage Media

Solid-state storage, also referred to as removal media, is a nonvolatile, removable medium that uses integrated circuits. The main advantage of this type of storage medium is that everything is processed electronically, and it contains no mechanical parts. Several types of solid-state storage are available. Miniature mobile storage media, for example, are popular solid-state storage devices for cameras, smart phones, music players, and other such electronics. **Figure 1–19** contains an assortment of miniature mobile storage media, most of which are no larger than a matchbook.

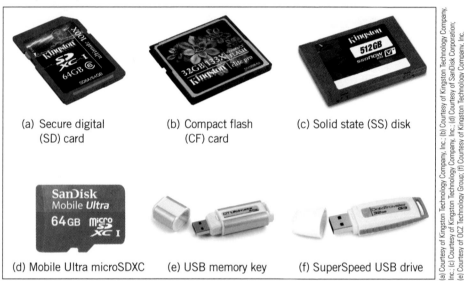

(a) Secure digital (SD) card

(b) Compact flash (CF) card

(c) Solid state (SS) disk

(d) Mobile Ultra microSDXC

(e) USB memory key

(f) SuperSpeed USB drive

(a) Courtesy of Kingston Technology Company, Inc.; (b) Courtesy of Kingston Technology Company, Inc.; (c) Courtesy of Kingston Technology Company, Inc.; (d) Courtesy of SanDisk Corporation; (e) Courtesy of OCZ Technology Group; (f) Courtesy of Kingston Technology Company, Inc.

FIGURE 1–19   Miniature mobile storage media

Another popular solid-state storage medium is the ***USB flash drive***. This small removable data storage device comes in a variety of configurations, such as those shown in **Figure 1–20**. It uses a USB connector to connect to your computer's USB port or other electronic device. Flash drives are also known by other names such as a key drive, thumb drive, jump drive, USB flash memory drive, and USB stick.

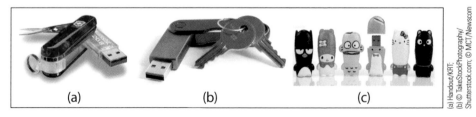

(a)

(b)

(c)

(a) Handout/KRT; (b) © TakeStockPhotography/Shutterstock.com; © MCT/Newscom

FIGURE 1–20   Examples of USB flash drives

Network Drives

A *network drive* can be a hard drive or a tape drive located on a computer other than the user's local system. It is connected to a network server and is available to and shared by multiple users.

Remote storage is used to extend disk space on a server and to eliminate the addition of more hard disks or other storage devices. When the amount of available space on the server falls below a designated level, the remote storage process frees up disk space by moving excess content to an attached storage device. Doing this frees up additional disk space on the specified server. The storage device could be on the same network, a separate network, or on the Internet.

▶ **VOCABULARY**

network drive

remote storage

Caring for Storage Media

Removable storage media require special care if the stored data is to remain undamaged. Here are some safeguards that should be taken:

- Keep away from magnetic fields such as those contained in televisions and computer monitors (magnetic media).

- Avoid extreme temperatures.

- Remove media from drives and store them properly when not in use.

- When handling DVDs and other optical discs, hold them at the edges.

- Never try to remove the media from a drive when the drive indicator light is on.

- Keep discs in a sturdy case when transporting.

Exploring Computers in Your Future

Computers of the future will be more powerful and less expensive than contemporary computers. It is also fair to assume that almost every type of job will somehow involve a computer. With long-distance connectivity, more people will work full-time or part-time from home. See **Figure 1–21**.

FIGURE 1–21 Working from home

A major focus of new types of computers is connectivity, or the ability to connect with other computers. Wireless and mobile devices are now as common as wired desktop machines. Computer literacy, which is the knowledge and understanding of computers and their uses, will become even more important.

SUMMARY

In this lesson, you learned:

- A computer is an electronic device that receives data, processes data, produces information, and stores the data and information.

- A computer derives its power from its speed, reliability, accuracy, storage, and communications capability.

- Computer classifications include personal computers (desktop and notebook), mobile devices, servers, mainframes, and supercomputers.

- Almost all computers perform the same general functions: input, processing, output, and storage. Input, output, and processing devices grouped together represent a computer system.

- The machine cycle is made up of the instruction cycle and the execution cycle.

- The motherboard is the center of all processing. It contains the central processing unit (CPU), memory, and basic controllers for the system. It also contains ports and expansion slots.

- The motherboard contains different types of memory. Random access memory (RAM) is volatile and is used to store instructions, data, and information temporarily. Read-only memory (ROM) is nonvolatile and is used to store permanent instructions needed for computer operations.

- The CPU is the brains of the computer. The CPU has two main sections—the arithmetic/logic unit (ALU) and the control unit. All calculations and comparisons take place in the ALU. The control unit coordinates the CPU activities.

- To maintain a permanent copy of data, you should store it on some type of storage medium. The three categories of storage media are magnetic storage, optical storage, and solid-state storage.

■ LESSON REVIEW

TRUE / FALSE

Circle T if the statement is true or F if the statement is false.

T   F   **1.**   ROM chips are found throughout a computer system.

T   F   **2.**   When data is stored on a disk, it is stored in circles called tracks.

T   F   **3.**   The faster the machine cycle, the faster your computer processes data.

T   F   **4.**   A supercomputer is the slowest type of computer.

T   F   **5.**   The two primary sections of the CPU are the arithmetic/logic unit and the control unit.

MULTIPLE CHOICE

Select the best response for the following statements.

1. A _____ consists of hardware, software, data, and users.

   A. client   C. mobile device

   B. node   D. computer system

2. A _____ is a personal computer you can use to take notes with a stylus or digital pen on a touch screen.

   A. mainframe computer   C. tablet PC

   B. notebook computer   D. mobile device

3. A computer system includes which of the following?

   A. hardware   C. software

   B. data   D. all of the above

4. Random access memory (RAM) is _____.

   A. permanent   C. nonvolatile

   B. volatile   D. the same as ROM

5. The main advantage of _____ storage media is that they process data electronically and contain no mechanical parts.

   A. optical storage   C. 3½-inch

   B. solid-state   D. input

FILL IN THE BLANK

1. The instruction cycle and the execution cycle create a(n) _____ cycle.

2. A computer manufacturer uses a(n) _____ chip to store specific instructions that are needed for computer operations.

3. You can think of RAM as _____-term memory.

4. The _____ unit coordinates all of the processor's activities.

5. Optical storage devices use _____ technology to read and write data.

PROJECTS

PROJECT 1-1

Access the Dell computer Web site at *www.dell.com*. Select the For Home, Laptops or the For Small and Medium Business, Laptops link. Using a spreadsheet program or paper and pencil, create a table that compares three computers. Include the following elements in your table: processor speed, amount of RAM, number of expansion slots, number of USB ports, other ports, and price. Based on your comparisons, write a short paragraph explaining which computer you would purchase and why.

PROJECT 1-2

1-1.1.2

Using the Internet or other resources, research the history of computers. For the first part of this project, find the answers to the following questions: (1) What was the name of the first commercially available electronic digital computer? (2) In what year was the IBM PC first introduced? (3) What software sent Bill Gates on his way to becoming one of the richest men in the world? (4) In what year did Apple introduce the Macintosh computer? (5) What is the name of the first computer game invented? Use your word-processing program to answer each of these questions and provide some additional historical facts.

For the second part of this project, learn about the history of the central processing unit. Launch your Web browser and open the home page for Wikipedia at *www.wikipedia.org*. When the Web site is displayed, enter *CPU* as the search text. On the Central processing unit page, click the History link. Use a presentation program (such as Microsoft PowerPoint) to create a presentation on what you found at this Web site. Find related images and add them to your presentation. Share your presentation with your class.

PROJECT 1-3

Using Google or another search engine, find an image of a computer system with the case removed. Print a copy of the image or capture a screen shot and copy and paste it into a word-processing document. Examine the image and look for the motherboard and the components connected to the motherboard. Locate and identify the number of available expansion slots. Locate the RAM chips. See if you can find the CPU. Can you see the chip itself? What other elements are visible? Using Figure 1-9 as a guide, label each element you locate and provide a brief description of the elements.

TEAMWORK PROJECT

1-1.1.1

Work as a team to gather and analyze research about how people use general-purpose computers. Briefly interview 10–20 people and identify the following information: (1) What types of computers does each person use? (2) What kinds of activities do they perform on each type of computer? Be sure your research covers at least four types of general-purpose computers.

To analyze the results, create a table or spreadsheet listing the types of computers your research identified. Next, use each type of computing activity as a column heading in the table, consolidating similar activities if possible. Enter the number of times each type of computer was used for each type of activity. Create a chart of the results.

CRITICAL THINKING

You are purchasing a new computer and have the option to include a variety of storage devices. Research the storage devices listed in this chapter. Then write a report listing each of the devices you would select for your computer and explain why you would select this particular device.

1-1.1.4

ONLINE DISCOVERY

Google has a feature that lets you search only blogs. This feature, called Blog Search, is located at *http://blogsearch.google.com*. Frequently Asked Questions about Blog Search can be found at *www.google.com/help/about_blogsearch.html*. Access Blog Search and search blogs for three of the following topics: CPUs, computer memory, optical discs, magnetic disks, types of computers, and the future of computers. Write a one-page report or create a three-slide presentation on what you learned. Google also has a Web site where you can start your own blog, located at *https://www.blogger.com*. Recruit two or three teammates and start a blog about your class activities.

JOB SKILLS

Computing jobs are often on the forefront of technology and include Web design, programming, hardware engineering, and software development. Learn about careers in the computer field. Visit a computing career Web site such as *computingcareers.acm.org*, *www.bls.gov/k12/computers.htm*, or *www.sciencebuddies.org/science-fair-projects/science_careers.shtml* (look for the Math and Computer Science section). Identify a job that interests you. Write a one-page report that includes the job title and describes the nature of the work, what types of skills you need to succeed in the job, and the types of organizations that hire people with those skills.

LESSON 2

Input, Output, and Processing

■ OBJECTIVES

Upon completion of this domain, you should be able to:

■ Identify and describe standard and specialized input devices.

■ Identify and describe standard and specialized output devices.

■ Connect input and output devices to a computer.

■ Consider computer performance factors.

■ DATA FILES

You do not need data files to complete this lesson.

■ WORDS TO KNOW

audio input

biometrics

digital camera

expansion slot

FireWire

inkjet printer

input

keyboard

laser printer

modem

monitor

mouse

output

plug and play

pointing device

port

printer

scanner

trackball

Universal Serial Bus (USB)

MODULE 1   Computing Fundamentals

When it comes to processing data, the computer does all of the work. However, it needs help. *Input*, which is data or instructions, must be entered into the computer and then stored temporarily or permanently on a storage media device. To turn the data into information, it must be processed. The central processing unit (CPU), which you learned about in Lesson 1, processes the data. After the data is processed, it is presented to you through an output device.

▶ **VOCABULARY**

input

modem

keyboard

1-1.1.5

Standard Input Devices

Input devices enable you to enter data and commands into the computer. Output devices enable the computer to give you the results of the processed data. Some devices, such as the fax machine and fax modem, perform both input and output functions. You use these devices to send (output) and receive (input) data over communications media. A *modem* is a device that allows one computer to talk to another.

The type of input device you use is determined by the task you need to perform. An input device can be as simple as a keyboard or as sophisticated as devices used for voice or retinal recognition.

Keyboards

The *keyboard* is the most commonly used input device for entering text and numbers into a computer. If you want to use the computer efficiently, you must learn to type. Most of the keyboards provided with desktop computers are enhanced. An enhanced keyboard has 12 function keys along the top, two Alt keys, two Ctrl keys, an Ins key and Delete key, and a set of directional/arrow keys between the typing area and the numeric keypad.

Some keyboards, such as the one shown in **Figure 2–1**, have multimedia hot keys for accessing e-mail and the Internet and adjusting speaker volume. Enhanced keyboards also might provide other features such as a zoom key or slider. This feature makes it easy to zoom in for a closer look at documents, spreadsheets, pictures, maps, and Web pages, for example.

Multimedia hot keys

Zoom key

Courtesy of Logitech

FIGURE 2–1   Enhanced keyboard

Not all keyboards, however, are traditional. Some other popular types of keyboards are:

- *Ergonomic*: This type of keyboard lets you use more natural and comfortable hand, wrist, and arm positions.
- *Cordless or wireless*: This is a battery-powered keyboard that transmits data using wireless technology.
- *Specialized*: This keyboard has specialized keys that represent items such as those used in fast-food restaurants.
- *Security*: This keyboard provides security features such as a biometric fingerprint reader, magnetic stripe, and smart card readers (see **Figure 2–2**).

Biometric fingerprint reader

© MadTatyana/Shutterstock.com

FIGURE 2–2   Keyboard with fingerprint reader

- *Foldable or flexible*: An easily transported keyboard primarily used with mobile devices, this type of keyboard is soft to the touch and is water resistant (see **Figure 2–3**).

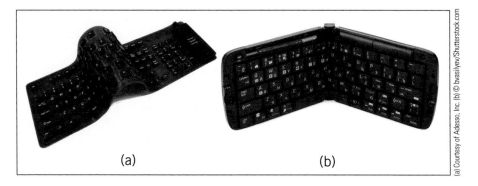

(a)   (b)

(a) Courtesy of Adesso, Inc. (b) © bvasilyev/Shutterstock.com

FIGURE 2–3   Foldable keyboards

■ *Laser virtual keyboard*: Packaged in a case smaller than a soda can, a laser beam generates a full-size laser keyboard. This keyboard easily connects to any personal computer, including Macintosh, BlackBerry or other smart phone, and most other handheld devices (see **Figure 2–4**).

Courtesy of Celluon

FIGURE 2–4   Laser virtual keyboard

Pointing Devices

▶ **VOCABULARY**
pointing device
mouse

A *pointing device* is an input device you use to position the pointer on the screen. The pointer can have several shapes, but the most common is an arrow. You use a pointing device to move the pointer; select objects such as text or graphics; and click buttons, icons, menu items, and links. The following sections discuss various pointing devices.

Mouse

The most common pointing device for personal computers is the *mouse*. It moves on a flat surface and controls the pointer on the screen. The mouse fits conveniently in the palm of your hand. You can use any of the following types of mice:

■ *Mechanical*: This type of mouse has a ball located on the bottom that rolls around on a flat surface as you move the mouse. Sensors inside the mouse determine the direction and distance of the movement. In general, you use a mouse pad with a mechanical mouse.

■ *Optomechanical*: This mouse is the same as a mechanical mouse, but uses optical sensors to detect the motion of the ball.

■ *Optical*: An optical mouse (see **Figure 2–5a**) uses a laser to detect the mouse's movement. Optical mice have no mechanical moving parts. They respond more quickly and precisely than mechanical and optomechanical mice.

■ *Wireless*: A wireless mouse (see **Figure 2–5b**) is a battery-powered device that relies on infrared waves to communicate with the computer.

■ *Trackball mouse*: This is an upside-down mechanical mouse, with the ball on the top (see **Figure 2–5c**).

- *Radio frequency*: This type of mouse is similar to a typical wireless mouse, but uses radio frequency instead of infrared waves (see **Figure 2–5d**).
- *Foldable mouse*: This is a wireless foldable mouse (see **Figure 2–5e**).

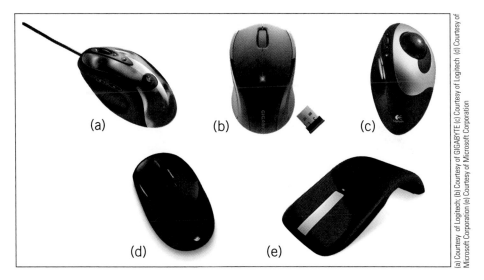

FIGURE 2–5   (a) Optical mouse (b) Wireless mouse (c) Trackball mouse (d) Radio frequency cordless mouse (e) Foldable mouse

Most mice have two or three buttons; many also have a wheel. You use the left button for most mouse operations. Generally, clicking the right button displays a shortcut menu. After you place the on-screen pointer where you want it, press a button on the mouse. This triggers an action in the computer; the type of action depends on the program. Use the wheel to scroll or to zoom a page or image.

You use the mouse in the following ways in many software programs and Web pages:

- *Pointing*: Placing the on-screen pointer at a designated location
- *Clicking*: Pressing and releasing the mouse button to select a specific location within a document
- *Dragging*: Pressing down the mouse button and moving the mouse while continuing to hold down the button to highlight a selected portion of text
- *Double-clicking*: Pressing and releasing the mouse button two times in rapid succession to select a word
- *Triple-clicking*: Pressing and releasing the mouse button three times in rapid succession to select a paragraph
- *Right-clicking*: Pressing the right mouse button to display a menu
- *Rotating*: Rotate the wheel forward or backward to scroll vertically
- *Tilting*: Pressing the wheel right or left to scroll horizontally

Trackball

▶ VOCABULARY
trackball

The *trackball* is a pointing device that works like a mouse turned upside down; the ball is on top of the device. See **Figure 2–6a**. You use your thumb and fingers to operate the ball, which controls the pointer on the screen. A trackball is stationary, making it a good alternative to the mouse when you have limited desktop space. Some trackballs are built into the keyboard (see **Figure 2–6b**).

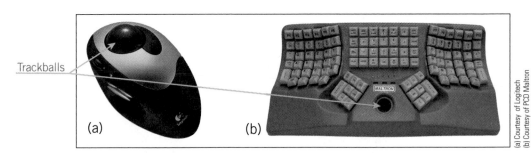

Trackballs

(a)   (b)

(a) Courtesy of Logitech
(b) Courtesy of PCD Maltron

FIGURE 2–6   (a) Trackball on a mouse (b) Trackball on a keyboard

■ **ABOVE AND BEYOND**

A typical wired mouse has a power consumption rating of about 0.5 watts (5 V/100 mA). One hundred milliamperes (mA) is the maximum additional current that a mouse can draw, according to the USB 2.0 specification. In comparison, a wireless mouse uses only a small receiver for power, which draws a maximum of 0.075W.

Touchpad

A common feature on laptop computers is the touchpad, a pointing device with a specialized surface that can convert the motion and position of your fingers to a relative position on screen. Portable media players also include touchpads.

Pointing Stick

Some notebook computers contain a pointing stick, a pressure-sensitive device that looks like a pencil eraser. It is located on the keyboard, generally between the G, H, and B keys. See **Figure 2–7**. You move a pointing stick with the forefinger, while using the thumb to press related keys. In a confined space, many people find a pointing stick more convenient than a mouse. IBM popularized this device by introducing the TrackPoint on its ThinkPad notebooks.

Pointing stick

Courtesy of Hewlett-Packard Company

FIGURE 2–7   Pointing stick

Audio Input

Audio input is sound entered into a computer. Sound includes speech, sound effects, and music. Examples of audio input devices are microphones, CD/DVD players, radios, and other hardware such as electronic keyboards. Voice input is a category of audio input. You can use voice-recognition devices such as microphones to speak commands into the computer and to enter text. The computer must have voice-recognition software installed before you can use a voice-recognition device. Directory assistance is a type of voice-recognition technology, as are devices that disabled persons use to command wheelchairs and other objects to increase mobility.

Standard Output Devices

Output is data processed into a useful format. Output devices display information. Examples of output are printed text, spoken words, music, pictures, video, and graphics. The most common output devices are monitors and printers.

1-1.1.5

Monitors

Desktop computers typically use a *monitor* as their display device. The screen is part of the monitor, which also includes the housing for its electrical components. Screen output is called soft copy because it is temporary.

The cathode ray tube (CRT) was one of the earliest types of computer monitors. See **Figure 2–8a**. CRT monitors are similar to older models of televisions and can display monochrome or color output. A monochrome monitor has a one-color display, which can be white, green, or amber. Color monitors display thousands of colors. Common sizes for CRT monitors are 17-, 19-, and 21-inch, though some are 30 inches or more. CRT monitors are nearly obsolete and have largely been replaced by flat-panel monitors.

Flat-panel monitors come in two varieties: liquid crystal display (LCD) and gas plasma. They take up less space than CRT monitors and are much lighter in weight, though they provide a larger viewing area.

LCD panels produce an image by manipulating light within a layer of liquid crystal cells. See **Figure 2–8b**. LCD panels were originally used on notebook computers and other mobile devices such as cell phones and PDAs. In 1997, several manufacturers started producing full-size LCD panels as alternatives to CRT monitors. LCD panels are now the primary technology for computer monitors, and are usually produced in widescreen sizes, which allow two pages to be displayed side by side in word-processing software. Older LCD monitors do not have a widescreen format, but produce a nearly square screen display.

Gas plasma technology consists of a tiny amount of gas that is activated by an electrical charge. See **Figure 2–8c**. The gas illuminates miniature colored fluorescent lights arranged in a panel-like screen. These monitors have a brilliant color display and are available in sizes up to 60 inches or more. Similar to LCD monitors, gas plasma displays are typically produced in widescreen sizes.

(a)   (b)   (c)

FIGURE 2–8   (a) CRT monitor (b) LCD panel (c) Gas plasma display

Printers

Printers produce a paper copy, or hard copy, of processing results. Printer output is called hard copy because it is permanent. Several types of printers are available, with significant differences in speed, print quality, price, and special features.

When selecting a printer, consider the following features:

- *Speed*: Printer speed is measured in pages per minute (ppm). The number of pages a printer can print per minute varies for text and for graphics. Graphics print more slowly than regular text.

- *Print quality*: Print quality is measured in dots per inch (dpi). The higher the dpi, the better the resolution or print quality.

- *Price*: The price includes the original cost of the printer and what it costs to maintain the printer. You can purchase a good-quality printer very inexpensively whereas a high-output system can cost thousands of dollars. The ink cartridges and toners need to be replaced periodically.

Printers are classified as either impact or nonimpact. Impact printers use a mechanism that actually strikes the paper to form letters and images. Dot matrix printers are impact printers, though they are mostly obsolete. Nonimpact printers form characters without striking the paper. The two most popular types of printers, laser printers and inkjet printers, are examples of nonimpact printers.

Laser Printers

A *laser printer* produces images using the same technology as copier machines. The image is made with a powdery substance called toner. A laser printer produces high-quality output. Laser printers are generally affordable for most consumers. Color laser printers, however, are still expensive, some costing thousands of dollars. **Figure 2–9** illustrates how a laser printer works.

▶ **VOCABULARY**
laser printer

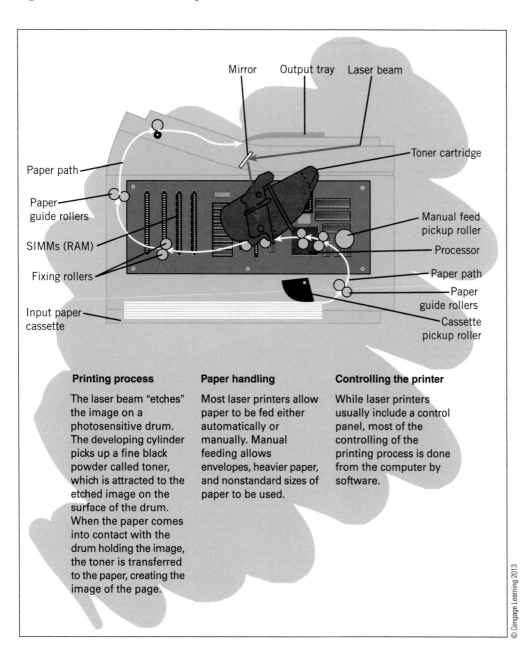

Printing process

The laser beam "etches" the image on a photosensitive drum. The developing cylinder picks up a fine black powder called toner, which is attracted to the etched image on the surface of the drum. When the paper comes into contact with the drum holding the image, the toner is transferred to the paper, creating the image of the page.

Paper handling

Most laser printers allow paper to be fed either automatically or manually. Manual feeding allows envelopes, heavier paper, and nonstandard sizes of paper to be used.

Controlling the printer

While laser printers usually include a control panel, most of the controlling of the printing process is done from the computer by software.

© Cengage Learning 2013

FIGURE 2–9 How a laser printer works

Inkjet Printers

An *inkjet printer* provides good-quality color printing for less expense than a laser printer. **Figure 2–10** shows how an inkjet printer works. Inkjet printing, like laser printing, is a nonimpact process. Nozzles squirt ink as they pass over the media. Unlike earlier versions of the inkjet printer, newer versions can use regular photocopy paper.

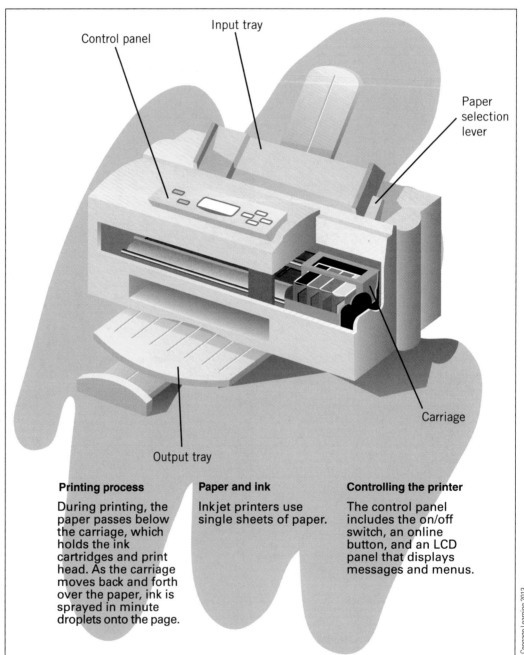

Control panel

Input tray

Paper selection lever

Carriage

Output tray

Printing process

During printing, the paper passes below the carriage, which holds the ink cartridges and print head. As the carriage moves back and forth over the paper, ink is sprayed in minute droplets onto the page.

Paper and ink

Inkjet printers use single sheets of paper.

Controlling the printer

The control panel includes the on/off switch, an online button, and an LCD panel that displays messages and menus.

© Cengage Learning 2013

FIGURE 2–10   How an inkjet printer works

Speakers

Speakers also are a type of output device. Speakers and headsets generate sound, such as music or instructions on how to complete a tutorial. You use headsets or earphones to hear the music or other voice output privately.

Specialized Input Devices

Other input devices are used for specialized applications. The following section describes these input devices.

1-1.1.6

Digital Cameras

The pictures you take with a ***digital camera*** are stored digitally and then transferred to the computer's memory. Digital cameras use a variety of storage media to store the images, including flash memory cards, memory sticks, USB keys, mini-discs, and other solid-state storage devices. After transferring pictures to the computer, you can view them quickly and edit any imperfections with photo-editing software.

▶ **VOCABULARY**
digital camera

Video input is a set of full-motion images captured with a video camera. You can save the video on a storage medium such as a hard drive, CD, or DVD. After saving the video, you can view and edit it. A digital video (DV) camera records video as digital signals; some DV cameras also capture still images. Some are a little larger than a credit card. A PC video camera is a type of digital video camera you can use to send live images over the Internet, make video telephone calls, and send e-mail messages with video attachments. The mini digital camera is small enough to fit in your pocket (see **Figure 2–11a**).

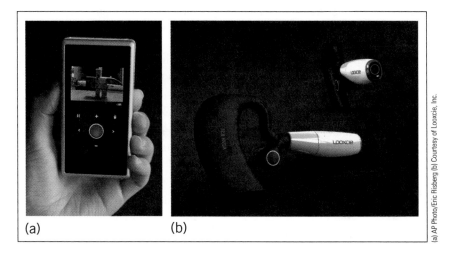

(a)   (b)

FIGURE 2–11   (a) Miniaturized digital video camera (b) Wearable video camera

Webcams are video-capturing cameras connected to computers or to computer networks; they display images through the World Wide Web. Generally, you use Webcams for videoconferencing and communications. You can also use Webcams for security purposes, monitoring both movement and sound. The Looxcie Webcam shown in **Figure 2–11b** is a wearable video camera that stores up to five hours of video. You can use this Webcam to instantly capture and share clips on social networks, and rewind to save the past 30 seconds of action.

Game Controllers

The joystick and wheel are types of pointing devices. You use joysticks and wheels, such as the ones shown in **Figure 2–12**, most often for games. The joystick consists of a plastic or metal rod mounted on a base. You can move the rod in any direction. Some joysticks have switches or buttons that can input data in an on/off response. A wheel is a device you use to simulate driving a vehicle. Most wheels also include foot pedals used for braking and acceleration actions.

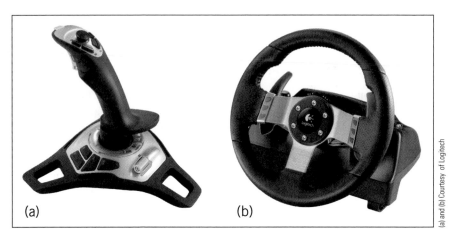

(a)   (b)

FIGURE 2–12   (a) Joystick (b) Wheel

Scanners/Bar Code Readers

Scanners are devices that can change images into codes for input to the computer. Scanners are available in various sizes and types, including the following:

- *Image scanners*: These devices convert images into an electronic form that you can store in a computer's memory. You can then manipulate the images.

- *Bar code scanners*: This type of scanner reads bar lines that are printed on products (for example, in a retail store). See **Figure 2–13a**.

- *Magnetic scanners*: These devices read encoded information on credit cards. The magnetic strip on the back of each card contains the user's encoded account number.

- *Wireless scanners*: These scanners use Bluetooth wireless technology to scan barcode data, such as from a hospital bracelet, and transmit it to a computer. See **Figure 2–13b**.

- *Optical character recognition (OCR) and optical mark recognition (OMR) scanners*: These devices use a light source to read characters, marks, and codes; the data is then converted into a digital format. Banks use OCR technology to scan checks. Commonly known as Scantrons, schools and other organizations use OMR for testing purposes.

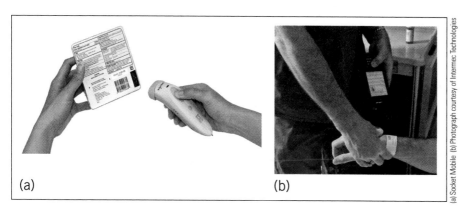

FIGURE 2–13   (a) Optical scanner (b) Bluetooth scanner

Touch Display Screen

The touch display screen, shown in **Figure 2–14**, is a special screen that reacts to direct touches within the display area, usually from a person's finger or hand. You use your fingers to "point" to the desired object to make a selection. You can find these screens in public places such as airports, hotels, banks, libraries, delivery services, and fast-food restaurants. Many mobile devices such as the popular iPhone and iPad products, notebook computers, and desktop computers have touch screens.

FIGURE 2–14   Touch screen

Stylus

A stylus and digital pen are pen-like writing instruments. See **Figure 2–15**. You use these devices to enter information by writing on a screen on a mobile device or using the pen as a pointer.

FIGURE 2–15   Mobile device with stylus

Environmental Probes and Sensors

Environmental monitoring in many industries and companies is a critical component of stabilization in the work area. With a standard Web browser such as Internet Explorer, workers can use environmental probes and sensors to view information such as the temperature and humidity of a remote environment, smoke detector readings, pollution control readings, and so on. A variety of industries, such as farming, tropical fish production, moisture monitoring, and warehouse security, use environmental probes and sensors.

Remote Controls

You use remote controls, also a type of specialized input device, to manage devices such as televisions, lights, and fans. Industry and business also use remote controls for various applications. For example, a construction worker can use a remote control to operate a crane, or a warehouse worker can have a remote control for a product cart.

Security Devices

Consider the following scenario: You are going on a two-week vacation to Ireland and England—you are packed and ready to go, but you do not need a wallet or credit cards. You use your fingerprint as an input device to pay for all of your expenses.

In information technology, *biometrics* is an authentication technique using automated methods of recognizing a person based on a physiological or behavioral characteristic. Biometric devices consist of a reader or scanning device and software that convert the scanned information into a digital format. Additional software then compares the scanned information to a database of stored biometric data.

Biometric technology can identify people based on their fingerprints, face, handwriting, or voice. Other less common techniques use the retina (analysis of the capillary vessels located at the back of the eye), iris (analysis of the colored ring surrounding the eye's pupil), hand geometry (analysis of the shape of the hand and length of the fingers), or vein (analysis of the pattern of veins on the back of the hand and the wrist).

The way biometric technology works, however, is basically the same for all identification techniques:

- *Enrollment*: You enroll in the system by establishing a baseline measurement for comparison.
- *Submission*: You present biological proof of your identity to the capture system.
- *Verification*: The system compares the sample you submitted with the stored sample.

Privacy and civil liberties advocates, however, are concerned about the widespread adoption of biometric systems. They argue that by using biometric data, unauthorized parties can access someone's data without their consent and link it to other information, resulting in secondary uses of the information. This erodes the users' personal control over their private information. On the other hand, biometrics can also be applied to private security. For example, several companies now offer biometric computer keyboards and USB flash drives with fingerprint authentication that can be used for personal applications. (Flash drives were discussed in Lesson 1.) See **Figure 2–16**.

> **VOCABULARY**
> **biometrics**

(a)   (b)

(a) PRNewsFoto/Pay By Touch (b) Courtesy of EnnovaDirect, Inc.

FIGURE 2–16   (a) Biometric keyboard scanner (b) USB fingerprint scanner

Virtual Devices

Similar to the laser virtual keyboard mentioned earlier, virtual devices use the synchronized positioning of light-emitting and sensing devices to detect user input. **Figure 2–17a** shows a virtual computer keyboard and **Figure 2–17b** shows a virtual piano keyboard.

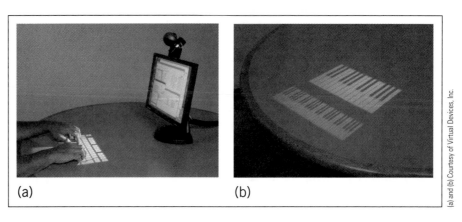

(a)   (b)

FIGURE 2–17   (a) Virtual computer keyboard (b) Virtual piano keyboard

Touch-Sensitive Pads

The touch-sensitive pad on a portable device, such as an iPod, enables you to scroll through a list, adjust the volume, play music, view videos or pictures, and customize settings.

Input Devices for the Physically Challenged

A variety of special input devices are available for the physically challenged. Following are some examples:

- Some keyboards can be operated with one hand or with the feet.
- A program called Camera Mouse enables users to use a Webcam and control the mouse pointer by moving their heads.
- A human-computer interface uses eye control to move a pointer and make selections.
- A joystick computer mouse can be operated with the lips, chin, or tongue for people with little or no head movement.
- Voice input devices allow visually impaired, blind, and physically challenged people to more easily interact with computers.
- A computer display screen is sensitive to human touch and allows the user to interact with the computer by touching an active area or a target, or to control data such as pictures or words on the screen.

Specialized Output Devices

1-1.1.7

Similar to specialized input devices, a variety of specialized output devices are also available:

- *Projectors*: A data projector projects the computer image onto a screen, usually for presentations.

- *Fax machines and fax modems*: These devices transmit and receive documents over a telephone line or through a computer.

- *Multifunction printer*: A multifunction printer combines output options such as printing, scanning, copying, and faxing.

- *Control devices/robots*: The field of robotics is defined as the study, design, and use of robot systems for manufacturing. Typical applications of robots include testing, product inspection, assembly, packaging, and painting.

Specialized Printers

Impact printers, such as the dot matrix and line printer, have been around for a long time. Dot matrix printers transfer ink to the paper by striking a ribbon with pins. The higher the number of pins, the better the resolution or output. The mechanism that actually does the printing is called a printhead. The speed of the dot matrix printer is measured in characters per second (cps). With the reduction in cost of laser and ink jet printers, dot matrix printers are seldom used today. A variation of the dot matrix printer is the line printer. This type of high-speed printer is attached primarily to large computers such as mainframes or midrange servers.

Several other types of specialty printers are available. Some examples are:

- *Thermal*: A thermal printer forms characters by heating paper. The printer requires special heat-sensitive paper.

- *Mobile*: A mobile printer is a small, battery-powered printer, primarily used to print from a notebook computer.

- *Label and postage*: A label printer prints labels of various types and sizes on paper that contains an adhesive on one side; a postage printer is a special type of label printer. This type of printer contains a built-in digital scale and prints postage stamps.

- *Plotters/large-format*: Engineers, architects, and graphic artists use plotters and large-format printers for drawings and drafting output.

Output Devices for the Physically Challenged

Similar to input devices for the physically challenged, output devices are also available. Following are some examples:

■ *Screen magnifiers*: These devices contain a range of magnifications and fonts that enlarge the information displayed on the computer screen (see **Figure 2–18**).

■ *Screen readers*: A screen reader assists people who are visually impaired. A speech synthesizer generally reads the screen content. Some screen readers can also read scanned documents.

■ *Voice synthesizers*: Speech synthesis is the computer-generated simulation of human speech. A voice changes written computer text into synthetic speech. This technology is useful especially for people with limited sight.

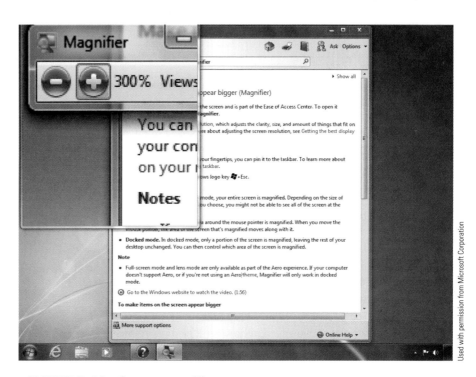

FIGURE 2–18   Screen magnifier

Connecting Input and Output Devices to a Computer

1-1.1.8

Input and output devices must be connected to the computer. Some devices connect to the computer through a physical connection, such as a port. You can plug the cable for a printer into a port located on the back, front, or side of the computer. Some monitors also have ports. Wireless devices connect through infrared or radio waves.

Ports and Connectors

A **port**, also called a jack, is an interface to which a peripheral device attaches to or communicates with the system unit or other peripheral devices. Older peripheral devices use serial and parallel ports to connect to the computer. Serial devices transmit data one bit at a time. Parallel devices transfer eight bits at a time. (Recall that a bit is represented by a 0 or 1. Typically, eight bits make one byte.) Older computers traditionally have at least one parallel port and one serial port, with a printer connected to the parallel port and a mouse connected to the serial port.

A **Universal Serial Bus (USB)** port can connect up to 127 peripheral devices with a single connector and transfer data at rates of up to 200 million bits per second (Mbps). (A bus transfers data between components inside a computer or between computers.) USB replaces the standard serial and parallel ports on today's computers. USB 3.0 is a recent and more advanced version of USB technology, with speeds 40 times faster than that of its predecessors. Personal computers typically have four to eight USB ports on the back, front, or side of the system unit. Using a daisy-chain arrangement or a USB hub, you can use a single USB port to connect up to 127 peripheral devices. A USB hub is a device that plugs into a USB port and contains multiple USB ports into which cables from USB devices can be plugged. USB also supports plug and play and hot plugging. **Plug and play** refers to the ability of a computer system to configure expansion boards and other devices automatically. Hot plugging means you can add and remove devices while the computer is running and have the operating system automatically recognize the change.

Another type of external bus is **FireWire**, also known as IEEE 1394 and IEEE 1394b. The IEEE 1394 bus standard supports data transfer rates of up to 400 Mbps and can connect up to 63 external devices; IEEE 1394b provides speeds up to 3200 Mbps. **Figure 2–19** shows examples of FireWire and USB ports.

ABOVE AND BEYOND

The SuperSpeed USB (USB 3.0) is the most recent version of the USB specification, with ten times the current bandwidth of USB 2.0. Transfer rates are approximately 4.8 Gbits/sec (Gigabits per second) and have been available in commercial products since 2009.

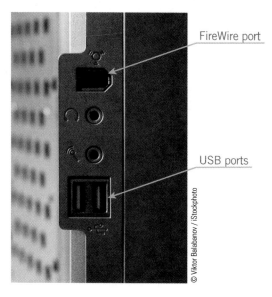

FIGURE 2–19   USB and FireWire ports

In addition to the preceding ports, you might find three additional special-purpose ports on computing devices. These special-purpose ports are:

■   *SCSI*: An abbreviation for Small Computer System Interface, SCSI (pronounced skuzzy) is a standard interface for connecting peripherals such as disk drives and printers.

- *IrDA*: A wireless standard that allows data to be transferred between devices using infrared light instead of cables is called IrDA. Both the computer and the device must have an IrDA port, and the IrDA port on the device must align with the IrDA port on the computer.
- *Bluetooth*: Bluetooth uses radio waves and provides wireless short-range communications of data and voice between both mobile and stationary devices. This technology does not require alignment; it is an alternative to IrDA. See **Figure 2–20**.

FIGURE 2–20   Bluetooth devices

Traditionally, ports were located on the back of the system unit only. With the introduction of portable devices, such as digital cameras and smart phones, computers now also include ports on the front of the system unit. This location provides for easier access.

Expansion slots are openings on the motherboard where an expansion board can be inserted. Expansion boards enhance functions of a component of the system unit or provide connections through a port or other connectors to peripheral devices. Expansion boards are also called adapter cards, expansion cards, add-ins, and add-ons. See **Figure 2–21**.

PC: Courtesy of Hewlett-Packard Company; **iPhone:** © kai zhang / iStockphoto; **Wireless mouse:** © Mau Horng/Shutterstock.com; **Wireless keyboard:** © Chivacat/Shutterstock.com; **Bluetooth headset:** © Dja65/Shutterstock.com; **Inkjet printer:** © Lusoimages/Shutterstock.com; **Mobile phone:** © Pakhnyushchha/Shutterstock.com; **Wireless gamepad:** © CAN BALCIOGLU/Shutterstock.com; **Wireless headphones:** © DUSAN ZIDAR/Shutterstock.com

▶ **VOCABULARY**
expansion slot

Expansion card

Expansion slot

© Andrew Howe/iStockphoto

FIGURE 2–21 Expansion slot and card

Hardware Installation

For most hardware devices to work, they need a set of instructions that communicates with the computer's operating system. This set of instructions is called a driver. The operating system usually includes drivers for popular peripheral devices and performs an automatic plug-and-play installation for newly connected devices.

If the operating system does not contain a driver for the hardware, you must install the driver manually. Usually, the software is included with the hardware device. If an installation disk is not available, the manufacturer's Web site generally provides a downloadable file.

Considering Computer Performance Factors

1-1.1.9

A variety of factors can affect a computer's performance. In Lesson 1, you learned about the central processor, computer memory, and input/output devices. These three components, plus video capability and disk organization, affect the speed at which the computer performs.

The following list provides an overview of the devices that affect computer performance.

1. *Microprocessor*: The architecture of the central processor is the most important processing element. CPUs are classified by generations. The higher the generation, the faster and better the processing speed. Most processors support parallel processing. With this type of processing, while one instruction is being executed, the next instruction is fetched from memory and decoded. Thus, the faster the processor, the more instructions per second it can process.

MODULE 1 Computing Fundamentals

2. *Random access memory (RAM)*: The amount of RAM also helps to speed up the processing cycle and to enhance the computer's performance. When the memory capacity is reached, the CPU stores data on the hard drive. This slows down the processing cycle because it takes longer for the CPU to read from a hard drive than from RAM. To improve computer performance dramatically, increase the amount of RAM on your computer.

3. *Hard disk*: The size and speed of the hard drive also affects a computer's performance. The bigger and faster the hard drive, the faster it can process data. In addition, how the disk is organized is a performance factor. If a hard disk contains many unneeded and outdated files, it takes longer for the computer to find the information it needs.

4. *Video*: The video device connected to the computer can enhance or slow down the computer's performance. Having adequate video memory for the video card allows the processor to perform to its full potential.

Windows 7 provides several options to determine what hardware you have in your computer system. In Step-by-Step 2.1, you learn how to view this information. You might notice abbreviations such as MB or GB, which are units for measuring bytes, and were introduced in Lesson 1.

Step-by-Step 2.1

1. Click the **Start** button ⊕ on the taskbar, and then click **Computer**. The Computer window opens, as shown in **Figure 2–22**.

FIGURE 2–22
Computer window

System properties button

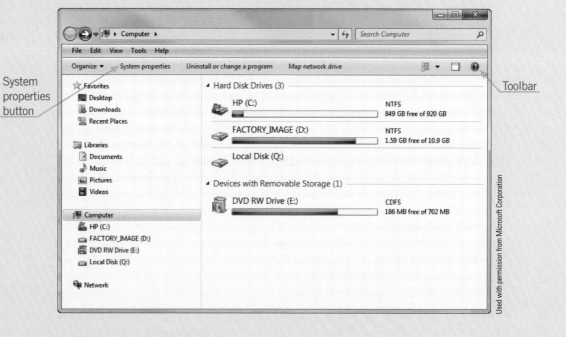

Toolbar

Used with permission from Microsoft Corporation

2. Click the **System properties** button on the toolbar. The System window opens (see **Figure 2–23**). Most likely, your System window will display different system information.

FIGURE 2–23
System window

Change settings link

3. What processor does your computer contain? How much memory (RAM) is in your computer? Does your computer support pen and touch input?

4. Click the **Change settings** link. If a User Account Control dialog box is displayed, click the **Continue** button. The System Properties dialog box is displayed (see **Figure 2–24**).

FIGURE 2–24
System Properties dialog box

Tabs

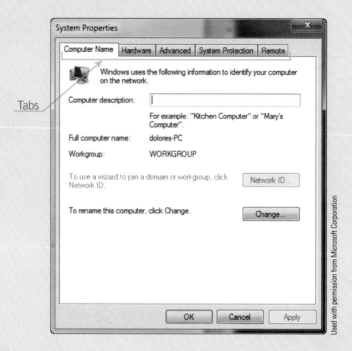

5. Click each tab in the dialog box and read the information it contains. If directed by your instructor, use Notepad or your word-processing program and write an overview of the features in the System Properties dialog box.

6. Click the **OK** button to close the System Properties dialog box, and then close the System window.

ETHICS IN TECHNOLOGY

Computer Viruses

The word *virus* can put fear into anyone who uses the Internet or exchanges disks. How can such a small word cause such fear? It is because a virus can cause tremendous damage to your computer files!

A computer virus is a small software program that spreads from one computer to another and interferes with the operation of the computers. A virus is written to attach itself intentionally to other programs or to disk boot sectors and duplicates itself whenever those programs are executed or the infected disks are accessed. A virus can delete or corrupt data, delete everything on the hard drive, or spread the virus to other programs through e-mail.

Viruses can be stored on your computer for weeks or months and not cause any damage until a predetermined date or time code is activated. They are easily spread by e-mail attachments or downloaded files. Computer viruses can be disguised as attached greeting cards, audio and video files, or as other attachments. Not all viruses cause damage. Some are just pranks; your desktop might display a silly message or animation. Viruses are created by persons who are impressed with the power they possess because of their expertise in the area of computers; sometimes they create them just for fun. To protect your computer from virus damage, install an antivirus software program on your computer and keep it running at all times so that it can continuously scan for viruses.

SUMMARY

In this lesson, you learned:

- Input devices enable you to input data and commands into the computer. The most common input devices are the keyboard and mouse.

- Other types of input devices include the trackball, joystick, wheel, pointing stick, touch display screen, stylus, voice recognition device, touchpad, scanner, digital camera, video camera, and biometric scanner.

- Monitors and printers are examples of output devices. Monitors produce soft copy. Printers produce a paper or hard copy of the processed result.

- Criteria for selecting a printer include speed, print quality, and cost.

- Input and output devices must be connected to the computer. Some input and output devices communicate with the computer through a physical connection. Wireless devices communicate with the computer through infrared or radio waves.

- Peripheral devices can connect to the computer through serial, parallel, and Universal Serial Bus (USB) ports. USB is the current standard and replaces serial and parallel ports.

- FireWire is a type of external bus that can connect up to 63 external devices.

- SCSI, IrDA, and Bluetooth are special-purpose ports.

- A computer's performance is affected by the speed of the processor, the amount of RAM, hard disk size and speed, capability of monitor, and disk organization.

■ LESSON REVIEW

TRUE / FALSE

Circle T if the statement is true or F if the statement is false.

T   F   **1.**   Input devices enable the computer to give you the results of processed data.

T   F   **2.**   A trackball mouse is an upside-down mouse.

T   F   **3.**   The mouse is the most commonly used input device for entering data.

T   F   **4.**   Input and output devices can stand alone—they do not need to be connected to the computer.

T   F   **5.**   Keyboards can be wireless or cordless.

MULTIPLE CHOICE

Select the best response for the following statements.

1. Which of the following types of keyboards is designed to provide users with a more natural and comfortable hand, wrist, and arm position?

   A.   security   C.   ergonomic

   B.   cordless   D.   wireless

2. Which one of the following is a type of scanner that converts graphics into an electronic form?

   A.   image scanner   C.   bar code scanner

   B.   magnetic scanner   D.   OCR scanner

3. Most notebook computers contain a _____.

   A.   pointing device or pointing stick

   B.   media player

   C.   printer

   D.   digital camera

4. _____ produce an image by manipulating light within a layer of liquid crystal cells.

   A.   LCD panels   C.   Scanners

   B.   Gas plasma monitors   D.   CRT monitors

5. Which of the following is a biometric identification scanning technique?

   A.   fingerprint   C.   voice

   B.   face   D.   all of the above

FILL IN THE BLANK

Complete the following sentences by writing the correct word or words in the blanks provided.

1. A(n) _____ is the most widely used device for entering data into the computer.

2. A(n) _____ reads encoded information on the back of credit cards.

3. A person's fingerprint, face, handwriting, or voice can be used for _____ identification.

4. A(n) _____ combines various output options such as printing, scanning, copying, and faxing.

5. A(n) _____ port can connect up to 127 peripheral devices with a single connector.

PROJECTS

PROJECT 2–1

You are in the market for a new keyboard and want to research keyboards before purchasing one. Use Google or another search engine and review several different types of keyboards. Then select two of the keyboards that you would like to test. Describe each keyboard, describing similar characteristics and those that make the keyboards different. Determine which keyboard you would purchase for personal use and explain why you selected it. Press the Print Screen key to capture an image of the keyboard you selected and paste it in a document.

1-1.1.5

PROJECT 2–3

Digital cameras were one of the specialized devices discussed in this lesson. Review the section on digital cameras. Then use Google or another search engine to research digital cameras. Select at least five digital cameras that you would like to purchase. Describe the pros and cons of each camera and then indicate the one you would select to purchase. Explain why you selected this particular camera.

1-1.1.6

PROJECT 2–2

Biometric technology is the automated method of recognizing a person based on a physiological or behavioral characteristic. Use the Internet and other sources to research this topic.

1-1.1.6

1. Use your favorite search engine to search for Web pages discussing biometric technology.

2. Based on your findings, create a document listing the pros and cons of biometric technology. Include your personal opinion about this topic.

3. Submit the document to your instructor as requested.

TEAMWORK PROJECT

This exercise is a role-playing activity to dramatize how a computer works. Select one of the following roles to play: processor, main memory, storage device, or input/output device. Then select a specific task, such as (a) inputting pictures from a digital camera, modifying and viewing the pictures, and outputting and printing the pictures; (b) using word-processing software to create a report on a specified school topic, adding pictures to the report, and then printing copies for all students in the class; (c) using a spreadsheet program to create a worksheet and chart and then print copies for all students in the class; (d) using a presentation program such as PowerPoint to create a presentation with text, images, and video; then display the presentation to the class. Role-play parts of a computer to accomplish the task you select. Be prepared to play these roles in front of the class or your instructor.

CRITICAL THINKING

You want to learn more about how the computer processes data and the factors that control the processing speed. Your instructor thinks this is a great idea and asks you to prepare a report or a presentation on what factors produce the best processors. In the report or presentation, describe processing speed and how to influence and increase the speed.

1-1.1.9

■ ONLINE DISCOVERY

Gmail is a free Web mail service provided through Google. You can use Gmail to communicate with your classmates and instructor for this course. Complete the following steps to create an account.

1. Open your browser and go to *http://mail.google.com/mail/help/open.html.*

2. When the Welcome to Gmail screen is displayed, read the information provided on the page. Then click the **Create an account** button.

3. Type your first and last name and desired user name. Click the **check availability!** button to verify that the name is available.

4. Enter a password for accessing the account. Click the **Password strength** link to have Google assess the security of your password as poor, fair, or strong. Your goal is to create a strong password. It must be a minimum of eight characters. Be sure to write down your password or send the password to yourself in an e-mail. Re-enter the password to verify it.

5. If you are using a school computer or a computer other than your own, do not select the "Stay signed in," "Enable Web History," or "Set Google as my default homepage" check box.

6. Click the **Security question** arrow button, and then select a security question that you are sure to remember. Enter the answer and e-mail the answer to yourself.

7. If you have another e-mail address, you can enter it into the Recovery e-mail text box. However, this is not necessary or required.

8. Select your geographic location, such as United States. You can leave the Birthday field blank.

9. For Word Verification, type the characters displayed on the form.

10. Read the Terms of Service, and then click the **I accept. Create my account.** button.

11. When an Introduction to Gmail page is displayed, read the information on the page and then click **Show me my account**. Sign in to your account using your user name and password.

12. Click the **Compose mail** link and send a message to your instructor and another classmate. List three facts in the message that are related to the topics presented in this lesson. If requested by your instructor, print a copy of your message and submit it to your instructor.

For additional information, see *http://mail.google.com/support/.*

■ JOB SKILLS

In most jobs, particularly if you are working in a large company, managers want their employees' attention, energy, and drive focused on the company and its goals. The employee who is eager, reliable, and willing to do more than the usual tasks generally attracts the attention of managers. In most instances, that employee is more likely to get ahead. Use the Internet or other sources and research "working to get ahead." Write a paragraph or two describing the skills and characteristics successful employees have based on your findings. List the address or addresses of the Web sites where you located your information.

LESSON 3

Computer Protection

■ OBJECTIVES

Upon completion of this lesson, you should be able to:

- Protect computer hardware from theft and damage.
- Safeguard data.
- Identify environmental factors that can damage computers.
- Protect computers from power loss and fluctuation.
- Identify common computer hardware problems.

■ DATA FILES

You do not need data files to complete this lesson.

■ WORDS TO KNOW

backup

data theft

driver

encryption

humidity

ping

power spikes

surge suppressor

uninterruptible power
   supply (UPS)

MODULE 1 Computing Fundamentals

Computers enhance our lives. They make our daily tasks much easier, our work more efficient, our learning more interesting and convenient, and even our game playing more exciting. As computers continue to play a central role in business and our personal lives, protecting computer systems and the information they hold has become increasingly important. This lesson examines how to protect computers and their data from typical dangers.

1-1.2.1

Protecting Computer Hardware from Theft and Damage

Theft of and damage to computer equipment are serious problems that many organizations face. In addition to the capital loss of equipment and the related down time until it is replaced, losing sensitive and confidential information through theft or damage could have long-term consequences. One safeguard you can use to prevent theft in the workplace is to physically secure equipment, especially items such as notebook computers, handheld devices, cell phones, and other transportable devices. See **Figure 3–1**.

© lawyerphoto /Shutterstock.com

FIGURE 3–1 Preventing computer theft

In addition, you can apply the following safeguards to help protect computer hardware from theft:

- If the equipment is located within an office or open lab, use security locks and/or tabs to secure the equipment to the desk or other furniture.
- Attach an alarm that will sound if the equipment is moved from its designated location.
- Mark all equipment with an identification tag or symbol that can be traced easily.
- Insure the equipment. Some insurance policies cover loss due to accidental damage, theft, vandalism, power surges, lightning strike, flood, fire, earthquake, and other natural disasters.
- Use a designated schedule to back up data to a separate system.

ABOVE AND BEYOND

Another type of theft that is sometimes overlooked involves employees accessing a company's computer for personal use. Theft of computer time is a crime committed regularly on the job. Some companies use spyware to monitor employee personal use, though this practice has been challenged in court.

Safeguarding Data

In most instances, hardware can be replaced when it is stolen or damaged. Data, on the other hand, is a critical component of most businesses and is not easily replaced. Many companies protect their data with security devices such as firewalls and intrusion-detection devices. Data thieves, however, also steal laptops and servers. They then use the remote software on the stolen system to connect to the organization's network and bypass the company's security measures. In other instances, ***data theft*** can occur when older systems are discarded and the data is not completely deleted. The risk and severity of data theft is increasing due to four predominant factors:

- The value of data stored on computers
- Massive amounts of confidential and private data being stored
- Increased use of laptops and other mobile devices outside of a secure network
- Increased proficiency of data hackers and thieves

Many businesses and organizations use data encryption to protect their data. ***Encryption*** is a secure process for keeping confidential information private. The data is scrambled mathematically with a password or a password key. The encryption process makes the data unreadable until it is decrypted.

> **▶ VOCABULARY**
> **data theft**
> **encryption**
> **backup**

Data Backup

Even saved data can be lost or corrupted by equipment failure, software viruses, hackers, fire or water damage, or power irregularities. Because data is so valuable, you must back up important files regularly. To back up files, you save them to removable disks or some other independent storage device that you can use to restore data in case the primary system becomes inaccessible. A hard disk crash (or failure) can result in a catastrophic loss of data if it occurs on a critical system and the files have not been backed up properly.

    Backup procedures should place a priority on files that would be difficult or impossible to replace or reconstruct if they were lost, such as a company's financial statements, important projects, and works in progress. Large organizations have secure backup procedures that include a regular schedule for backing up designated files. They store the backup files off site so they will survive intact if the main system is destroyed either by natural disaster or by criminal acts. When flooding is a possibility, it is a good idea to locate computers above the first floor of a building.

> **▤ ABOVE AND BEYOND**
>
> Data backup systems include disk and tape devices that make archive copies of important files and folders. You should back up data to storage media that can be removed and stored in a separate location from your computer.

Identifying Environmental Factors that Can Damage Computers

1-1.2.2

Computers require the right balance of physical and environmental conditions to operate properly. As indicated previously, computer equipment and its data are subject to various types of hazards. These hazards include theft of hardware and data as well as damage caused by improper use. Environmental factors such as temperature, humidity, and electrical fields also can contribute to hardware and software damage. Organizations can prevent many of these conditions through proper planning and by providing employees with appropriate training on how to use and safeguard the equipment. As an employee, you should know how to protect computers from environmental risks.

    The following sections describe environmental factors that are detrimental to computers and how you can control and contain some of these problems.

Temperature

Environmental conditions in a computer room or data center are critical to ensuring that a computer system runs properly and reliably and remains accessible to users. A temperature range of 68 to 75 degrees is optimal for system reliability. The general consensus is that you should not operate computer equipment in a room where the temperature exceeds 85 degrees. A separate thermostat can monitor temperature and humidity levels in a computer room (see **Figure 3–2**).

Courtesy of Sensatronics

FIGURE 3–2   Temperature control

Humidity

▶ VOCABULARY
humidity

A high level of *humidity* can cause computers to short circuit, resulting in the loss of data and damage to hardware. Excessive humidity also can cause components to rust. For example, taking a cold notebook computer from an air-conditioned office into an automobile on a sunny day could create a thin film of condensation covering the entire interior of the laptop. Over time, the condensation can cause hardware problems. Consider the following humidity factors to protect your data and computers:

- For optimal performance, the relative humidity of the computer room should be above 20 percent and below the dew point (which depends on the ambient room temperature).

- Environments that require high reliability should have a humidity alarm that rings when the humidity is out of an acceptable range.

- Some equipment has special humidity restrictions. Generally this information is contained in the equipment manual.

Water Damage

Most computer centers contain some type of sprinkler system. If water sprinklers are activated, newer models of computers most likely will not be damaged, provided that the computer's power is turned off before the water starts to flow. Modern computer systems contain a cut-off device that is triggered if the sprinklers turn on. If the computer does suffer water damage, make sure it is completely dried out before you restore the power. Storage devices and printouts, however, can be damaged or destroyed by water. Other types of water damage may occur from flooding and broken pipes.

Magnetic Fields and Static Electricity

Magnetic fields and static electricity exist wherever electrical current flows. A single spark from static electricity can damage the internal electronics of a computer. Computer technicians have grounding protection on the floor and use a grounded strap on their wrists when they service computers. You should do the same if you need to open a computer case, such as to install a component. Grounding prevents damaging a computer with a static electrical spark. Computer rooms should also have tile floors and antistatic carpet to reduce static electricity.

Data on a hard drive is stored in small magnetic dots on the disk and is therefore sensitive to magnetic fields. To prevent losing data, do not store magnets directly on a computer.

Physical Damage

Most electronic devices can suffer damage from physical contact with other objects. You can prevent physical damage to desktop computers by arranging the equipment so it is stable on a desk or floor and cannot fall or be knocked over. Notebook computers are generally more costly than desktops with similar storage and processing capabilities. They are also more prone to physical wear and tear because they are portable. To help protect the computer and limit the extent of the damage, most portable systems are insulated with shock absorbing material. This reduces damage to internal components if the computer is dropped or subjected to impact with another object. You should take additional steps to prevent physical damage to portable computers by transporting devices with care, such as in padded cases.

Poor Maintenance

One of the best ways to cut down on computer repair is through preventive maintenance. Create a monthly maintenance schedule and follow it regularly to clean equipment and perform tasks to keep computer devices in good working order. For example, if you use a mechanical mouse, you need to remove the ball and clean it periodically. Poorly maintained printers can print pages that are smudged or otherwise difficult to read. Cable connections can be weakened by dust, preventing normal communication with a computer. Damaged cables in general can prevent peripheral devices from communicating with the computer. Lesson 4 covers computer maintenance in detail.

1-1.2.3

Protecting Computers from Power Loss and Fluctuation

One ever-present threat to a computer system is an electrical power failure. A computer needs electricity to operate in general and to store data in particular. An unexpected power outage, for example, can wipe out any data that has not been properly saved.

To safeguard computer systems against power outages, secure electric cords so that they cannot be disconnected accidentally. You also need to protect computers and other electronic devices from *power spikes*, which are short, fast transfers of electrical voltage, current, or energy that can damage computer hardware and software. *Surge suppressors* (see **Figure 3–3**) plug into electric outlets and can protect against power spikes. Some lower end brands of surge suppressors wear out over time, however, and need to be monitored and replaced as necessary.

▶ **VOCABULARY**

power spike

surge suppressor

uninterruptible power supply (UPS)

Courtesy of Monster Cable Products, Inc.

FIGURE 3–3   Surge suppressor

⎯ **WARNING**

Do not plug a laser printer into a UPS. Laser printers need a lot of power when they start a print job, and can damage a UPS or even components connected to it. Instead, plug your laser printer directly into a wall outlet or a surge suppressor.

One option for preventing data loss due to power outages is to install an *uninterruptible power supply (UPS)*. These electrical devices range from basic kits to more sophisticated models designed for desktop computers and networks. The UPS shown in **Figure 3–4** is designed for a single computer. A UPS contains a battery that temporarily provides power if the normal current is interrupted, and generally keeps a computer running for several minutes following a power outage. This additional time provides an opportunity for you to save data and to properly shut down the computer. Most UPS systems now also include a software component that shuts down the computer automatically. The two basic types of UPS systems are standby power systems (SPSs) and online UPS systems. An SPS monitors the electrical power and switches to battery power if it detects a power problem. Depending on the computer system, the switch to battery power can take less than one second. An online UPS constantly provides power, even when the system is using electrical power. In either case, you avoid momentary power lapses.

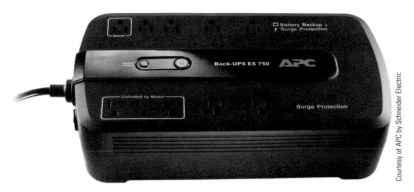

Courtesy of APC by Schneider Electric

FIGURE 3–4   Uninterruptible power supply

Identifying Common Computer Hardware Problems

1-1.2.4

Computer equipment and stored data are subject to computer hardware issues. Some common problems are a failed or "crashed" hard drive, damaged media, printer and monitor problems, loss of network or Internet connectivity, and general failure such as newly installed hardware not working. You can resolve or prevent many of these conditions by proper planning and by receiving appropriate training on how to use and protect the equipment. You can solve many problems on your own, while other problems may require the assistance of a professional.

The following sections provide an overview of common hardware problems and suggestions on how to troubleshoot and resolve them.

Crashed Hard Drive

Crashed hard drives generally are caused by software corruption or hardware defects. Hard drives can stop working if they become overheated, are dropped or shaken, become worn out, or are infected with a virus. Some suggestions to evaluate the condition of the drive are as follows:

- If a boot disk is available, use the disk to determine if the drive is readable. If so, back up the data and reformat the original disk.
- Several software solutions are available; these diagnostic and data recovery programs can locate and recover bad sectors.
- Use a data recovery service.

Damaged Media

Hard disks and other media eventually fail. Hard disks are mechanical devices with moving parts, and inevitably wear out. CDs and DVDs can be scratched, warped, or physically damaged in other ways. Tapes can be harmed by electromagnetic fields. Flash drives can also suffer physical damage, such as from unsafe removal, dust, lint, sun exposure, shock, or force.

Many people assume that information stored on damaged media, such as disks, tapes, or CDs, is unrecoverable. In many instances, however, you can recover the data. The first step is to locate the hardware and damaged media and move it to a secure environment. Secondly, inspect or test the media to determine what type and how much damage has occurred.

The type of damage determines the type of recovery method to use. If the media was damaged by water, do not restart the computer. This could cause a short if even small amounts of water are still in the computer. If the media is wet, do not dry it. Instead, place it in an airtight plastic bag to keep the media wet. If media such as hard disks get wet and then dry out, contaminants remain on the disks. The contaminants degrade the disk, causing it to lose data. If the media was damaged by fire and is still inside a melted computer case, leave it in the case if water or other elements were used to control the fire. The case should be opened by a professional. If the computer was dropped or otherwise physically harmed in some way, do not restart the computer. The read/write heads can be damaged or out of alignment.

Another option is to locate a disaster data recovery company with the knowledge, skills, and equipment necessary to recover data from the computer.

Printer Problems

Printer problems are a frequent problem. Generally, these problems are easily fixed.

Paper jams stop printers from printing a complete file when paper becomes trapped in the printer. Using the wrong type of paper can cause a printer jam, as can wrinkled or torn paper. If the rollers that feed the paper are worn or dirty, they might turn slowly or unevenly and cause a jam. When eliminating a paper jam, always pull the paper in the direction of the paper path. Pulling the paper backward can damage the printer (see **Figure 3–5**).

Courtesy of CLAS Computer Support Group/University of Connecticut

FIGURE 3–5   Paper jam

If ink or toner comes off the paper when touched, look for one of three possible causes. The printer's fuser assembly might be damaged and need to be replaced; the toner cartridge could be defective and need to be replaced; or some toner may have spilled into the printer. If toner has spilled, you need to clean it out of the printer with a dry cloth.

If the printed image is faded, this could indicate one of three conditions: the toner is low, the print density is set too low, or economy mode printing is turned on.

Display Problems

The hardware for your display consists of two elements: the monitor and the video card. It can be more difficult to determine the source of display problems than printer problems, for example, because more hardware is involved (see **Figure 3–6**).

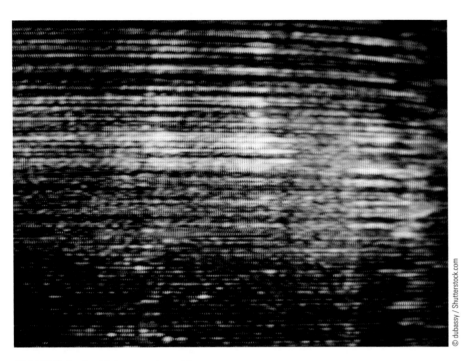

© dubassy / Shutterstock.com

FIGURE 3–6   Video card problem

Consider the following factors as you troubleshoot a display problem:

- Check that the monitor power cord is plugged in and that the monitor cable is connected to the computer.
- Verify that the monitor is turned on and the display settings are correct.
- Update the video driver. The majority of display problems are caused by incorrect, corrupted, or missing video drivers. (See the following section for the definition of a driver.) You usually can upgrade the video driver when you update the operating system; otherwise, visit the Web site for the video driver manufacturer and look for instructions on updating the video driver.

Inoperable Hardware Devices

When a hardware device such as a printer or monitor does not work, it could be a software problem, an electrical problem, or a mechanical problem. A small program called a *driver* instructs the operating system on how to operate specific hardware. As mentioned in the previous section, most display problems are caused by missing or corrupted drivers. Other causes are incorrect installation of the software for the hardware device and hardware failure. Also check the following alternatives:

▶ **VOCABULARY**
driver

- Check the power cord and verify that it is plugged in.
- Verify that the circuit breaker has not tripped.
- Make sure the electrical plug strip, the UPS, or the surge protector are turned on and working properly.

Loss of Network or Internet Connectivity

Local networks and the Internet provide valuable resources for organizations and individuals. Because people depend on these systems, losing connectivity means they cannot communicate or work effectively. Intermittent connectivity and time-out problems can result in poor network performance.

The following are common causes for connectivity problems:

- The network provider's system is not working properly.
- Network adapters and switch ports do not match.
- The network adapter is incompatible with the motherboard or other hardware components.

Some troubleshooting options are:

- Use the DOS *ping* command to test connectivity and isolate hardware problems and any mismatched configurations.
- Verify that other computers on the same network and those plugged into the same switch are also experiencing network connectivity problems.
- If you are using a router, restart the router.
- Check the computer's network card or board and verify it is using appropriate settings as indicated by the manufacturer.
- Try another network cable if you are working on a cabled network.
- If you are using a wireless router within a home, beware of signal interference from other home appliances. Common sources of interference are cordless phones, garage door openers, and microwave ovens. In densely populated areas, a wireless signal from one person's home network may interfere with a neighbor's home network.

The following Step-by-Step exercise shows you how to use the ping command.

▶ **VOCABULARY**
ping

ABOVE AND BEYOND

Connecting computers to a network or the Internet creates opportunities for unauthorized access from outside the network. Software and hardware devices that safeguard a network and provide security from unauthorized entry are called firewalls.

Step-by-Step 3.1

1. Click the **Start** button 🪟 on the taskbar, point to *All Programs*, click **Accessories**, and then click **Command Prompt**. The Command Prompt window appears, as shown in **Figure 3–7**.

FIGURE 3–7
Command Prompt window

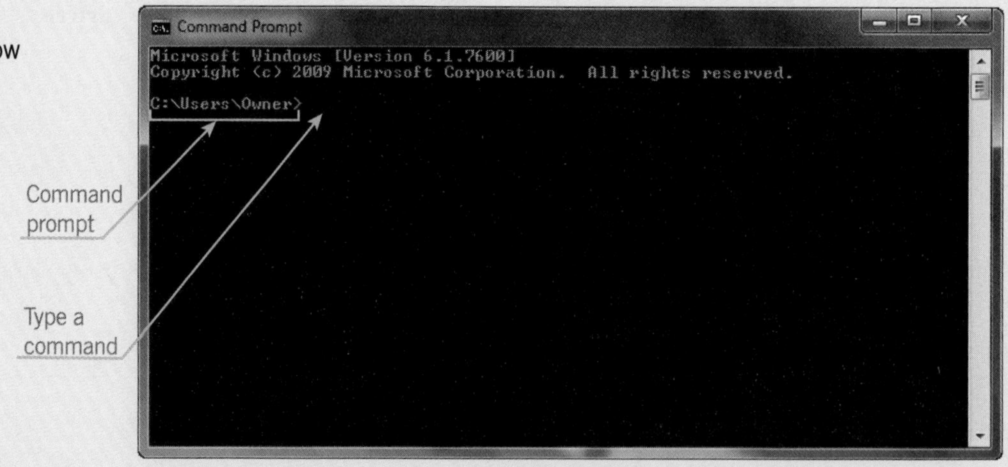

Command prompt

Type a command

2. At the command prompt (such as C:\), type **ping** *Web site address of your school or another Web site address* and then press the **Enter** key.

The results include a series of replies, which indicates the connection is working (see **Figure 3–8**). The time shows the speed of the connection. Your specific results will be different from those in **Figure 3–8**.

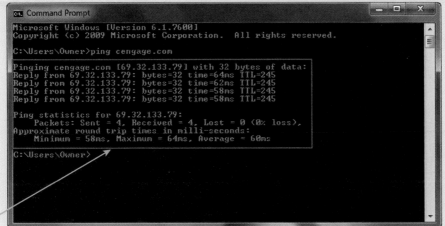

Results of the ping command

FIGURE 3–8
Replies to ping command

Used with permission from Microsoft Corporation

If a "timed out" error instead of a reply is displayed, there is a breakdown somewhere between your computer and the site to which you are attempting to connect.

3. Close the Command Prompt window.

ETHICS IN TECHNOLOGY

The Golden Rule of Computer Ethics

You probably heard the Golden Rule when you were in elementary school: "Do unto others as you would have them do unto you." The Golden Rule applies to computer ethics, too. Would you appreciate it if someone used their computer to cause you financial harm or to ruin your reputation? Of course not, and you should extend the same courtesy to other people. Don't give in to the urge to snoop around in other people's files or interfere with their work by accessing and changing data in files. You wouldn't want someone to mess with your hard work or private files, would you? And if you had spent a few months creating a great computer game, how would you feel if all your friends started passing copies of the game around to all their friends, without even giving you credit for the program, not to mention cheating you out of any potential profit for your work?

If you do write computer programs, think about the social consequences of the programs you write. Don't copy software illegally, and don't take other people's intellectual property and use it as your own. Just because something is posted on the Web does not mean it is "free" for anyone to use. Use your computer in ways that show consideration of and respect for other people, their property, and their resources. Many organizations create a use policy that outlines acceptable behavior for using the organization's computers, including ethical behavior.

SUMMARY

In this lesson, you learned:

- Computer equipment needs to be protected from theft and damage.
- Data should be backed up frequently and consistently to avoid losing important information.
- The right balance of physical and environmental conditions are required for computers to operate properly.
- High humidity, water, and electric/magnetic fields can damage computer equipment.

- Preventive maintenance reduces equipment repair needs.
- Electrical power failure can destroy data and equipment.
- Surge suppressors can protect against power spikes.
- Computer systems are vulnerable to problems such as a crashed hard disk, damaged media, printer and display problems, inoperable hardware devices, and loss of network and Internet connectivity.

■ LESSON REVIEW

TRUE / FALSE

Circle T if the statement is true or F if the statement is false.

T   F   **1.**   One ever-present threat to a computer system is an electrical power failure.

T   F   **2.**   Power spikes are short, fast transfers of electrical voltage, current, or energy.

T   F   **3.**   Crashed hard drives generally are caused by software corruption or hardware defects.

T   F   **4.**   Data theft is decreasing.

T   F   **5.**   The hardware for your display consists of four elements: the monitor, the video card, the controls, and the UPS key.

MULTIPLE CHOICE

Select the best response for the following statements.

1. Generally, a _____ keeps a computer running for several minutes following a power outage.

   A.   driver   C.   backup

   B.   spike   D.   UPS

2. Computer technicians use grounding protection when they service computers to prevent damage from _____ .

   A.   condensation   C.   power surges

   B.   high temperatures   D.   static electricity

3. _____ can protect against power spikes.

   A.   Surge suppressors   C.   Undamaged media

   B.   Video drivers   D.   Network connections

4. A high level of _____ can cause computers to short circuit.

   A.   smoke   C.   dust

   B.   humidity   D.   alarms

5. Most display problems are caused by missing or corrupted _____ .

   A.   surge suppressors   C.   drivers

   B.   network connections   D.   storage media

FILL IN THE BLANK

Complete the following sentences by writing the correct word or words in the blanks provided.

1. One of the best ways to cut down on computer repair is through _____ .

2. Notebook computers generally are more costly than _____ _____ .

3. _____ should be performed on a regular basis for files that would be difficult or impossible to replace.

4. The _____ on a mechanical mouse should be cleaned periodically.

5. Using the wrong type of paper or using wrinkled or torn paper in a printer can cause a _____ .

■ PROJECTS

PROJECT 3–1

1-1.2.2

Your instructor has assigned you to a team responsible for maintaining the school's computer lab. As you learned in this lesson, static electricity can damage computer components. Using the Internet or other resources, research the types of damage static electricity can cause in computers. Also research how to avoid static electricity when you are working in a computer's case, such as installing an expansion board. Complete the following:

1. Use word-processing software to write a one-page report summarizing your research.

2. Be sure to identify the types of damage static electricity can cause and explain how to avoid static electricity.

3. Submit the document to your instructor as requested.

PROJECT 3–2

Your instructor has asked you to draft an acceptable use policy for the school's computer lab. Complete the following:

1. Write a statement that describes appropriate and inappropriate behavior and acceptable and unacceptable use of equipment.

2. Share your statement with your classmates.

PROJECT 3–3

Computer crimes are responsible for the loss of millions of dollars to businesses and individual computer users. Some crimes result in more loss than others. Complete the following:

1. Use the Internet and other resources to locate information on lost revenue and other costs due to computer crimes in the last year and for two previous years. Some search terms that may be helpful are "computer crimes," "computer crime costs," "hackers," "viruses," "data loss," and "software piracy."

2. Use a spreadsheet program to prepare the data, organizing it according to the type of crime, if necessary. Use formulas that will add the totals of each type of crime, if necessary. Use a chart to compare each year's data.

3. Submit the document to your instructor as requested.

■ TEAMWORK PROJECT

1-1.2.1
1-1.2.2
1-1.2.3
1-1.2.4

Working with one or two partners, research three of the hardware and software issues and problems discussed in this lesson. Find information on the Internet that describes each issue and recommends how to troubleshoot the problem to determine its cause. Create a presentation describing the three problems and possible solutions. Share your team's presentation with your class.

CRITICAL THINKING

Use the Internet and other resources to identify early security measures that were used to protect computers and computer data. Describe how these measures counteracted the intrusions made on the computers. Then, visit the Web sites of some companies that now make computer security devices, such as us.kensington.com and www.computersecurity.com. Describe how and why these devices are different. Write a report of your findings.

ONLINE DISCOVERY

Protecting a home network is just as important as protecting a business or company network. An unsecured home network is as vulnerable to unauthorized use and intrusion as networks within small and large organizations. Security measures help prevent unauthorized users from accessing a home network system. Research this issue and then create a document explaining at least three ways you can protect your home network.

JOB SKILLS

Your supervisor has assigned you responsibility for maintaining the company's computer lab. Assume that the lab has 30 networked computers, a server, 2 color inkjet printers, 3 laser printers, and a scanner. Hardware and software needs to be updated and maintained on a regular schedule. As part of this job, one of your tasks is to create a maintenance schedule for the equipment. Use the Internet for research as necessary. Complete the following:

1. Use a spreadsheet program or word-processing software and create a schedule listing required maintenance.

2. Record how often maintenance is scheduled.

3. Submit the document to your instructor as requested.

LESSON 4

Computer Maintenance

■ OBJECTIVES

Upon completion of this lesson, you should be able to:

- Identify maintenance issues.
- Maintain hardware.
- Upgrade and replace hardware components.
- Perform preventive maintenance.
- Request specialized maintenance.

■ DATA FILES

You do not need data files to complete this lesson.

■ WORDS TO KNOW

cable management

cookie

corona wires

defragmentation

ergonomic keyboard

fragmentation

maintenance

Recycle Bin

sector

seek time

touchpad

wireless keyboard

This lesson explores the importance of computer maintenance, the risks of using a computer if the equipment is not properly maintained, and the measures that can be taken to minimize those risks. The type of maintenance needed determines whether the work should be performed by a computer user or someone with expert knowledge.

1-1.2.5

▶ **VOCABULARY**

maintenance

cable management

Identifying Maintenance Issues

Consider the following: To properly maintain a car and have it run smoothly, you change the oil and filter, check the tire pressure, and complete other required maintenance on a regular schedule. A computer is no different; it also requires regular *maintenance*. Sooner or later, you will begin to experience problems with the hardware. For instance, after an extended period of use, the performance of a hard disk can slow or printer problems can occur. The keyboard and the mouse can become sluggish, and the monitor may not work properly. This could be the result of loose or incorrect cables, poor power connections, or other more severe problems.

Managing computer cables is an overlooked problem when maintaining a computer system. Damaged and poorly maintained cables can prevent peripheral devices from communicating with the computer. Unorganized and unprotected cables also can create safety hazards (see **Figure 4–1**).

FIGURE 4–1   Unprotected cables are a safety hazard

Cable management kits and individual cable management products are available online and through most stores that sell computer equipment (see **Figure 4–2**). You use these kits to organize cables and bundle them together.

FIGURE 4–2   Managing cables

Maintaining Hardware

1-1.2.6

One of the best ways to cut down on computer repair is through preventive maintenance performed on a regular schedule. As a general rule, you should clean a computer every three to six months. If it is in a dusty environment, however, you should clean it more often. This section provides guidelines that you easily can put into practice.

Keyboard and Mouse

You should check and clean the keyboard periodically. Dirt, dust, hair, and food particles can accumulate, causing the keys to jam or otherwise malfunction. Many people clean the keyboard by turning it upside down and shaking it. A more effective method, however, is to use compressed air. Every six months, use a can of compressed air to remove the dust from the keyboard (see **Figure 4–3**).

© Lon C. Diehl / PhotoEdit

FIGURE 4–3   Cleaning a keyboard

If you spill a liquid on the keyboard, turn off the computer immediately. Disconnect the keyboard, spray it with water to clean it, turn it upside down and shake to remove the liquid, and then use a cloth to dry it as much as possible. After it is cleaned, leave it upside down and don't reconnect it until after at least 12 hours.

MODULE 1 Computing Fundamentals

A mouse with a ball (which is a mechanical mouse) can be difficult to move if the rollers are clogged. Cleaning mechanical mice often eliminates jerky or erratic movement of the mouse pointer. To clean the rollers, you need to remove the cover of the mouse (see **Figure 4–4a**). Next, remove the ball (see **Figure 4–4b**) to access the rollers. Generally, you will find dirt or hair in the middle of the roller. Remove as much of this debris as possible (see **Figure 4–4c**), clean the ball, and then remove any other debris from the mouse. Finally, reassemble the mouse.

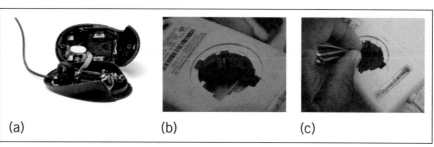

FIGURE 4–4   (a) Removing the cover of a mouse (b) Removing the mouse ball (c) Cleaning debris

Cleaning a printer helps prolong the printer's life. The first step is to check the printer documentation. If this is unavailable, most likely you can find information online. Clean only the parts recommended. Recall that the two more popular types of printers are inkjet and laser. The following general instructions apply to both types of printers:

- Use a cleaner recommended by the manufacturer or a lint-free cloth, and then moisten it with a 50-50 percent solution of water and vinegar. Wring out all excess moisture and thoroughly clean the outside of the printer, making sure that no fluid gets inside the printer.

- Never spray an aerosol directly onto the printer.

- Although not necessary, consider wearing latex gloves to protect your hands from dirt and other debris.

Inkjet Printers

After much usage, small deposits of dry ink accumulate on the print head of an inkjet printer. Eventually, these deposits begin to clog the printer's ink jets and affect the print quality of the document. This also causes streaks and blotchy printing.

Many inkjet printers have a self-cleaning mode that you access through the printer's control panel. If this is not available, use an inkjet cleaning cartridge. This flushes dirt and debris out of clogged printer nozzles. Verify that the cleaning cartridge is approved for your printer.

Dust and ink from inexpensive paper can affect the printer's rollers. Before cleaning inside an inkjet printer, turn it off and unplug it. Let it cool down if necessary. Use a small vacuum to remove the debris.

You can use special cleaning supplies to clean an inkjet printer. Check the printer documentation to verify the correct cleaning supplies your printer needs (see **Figure 4–5**).

WARNING

Most printer manufacturers recommend against using compressed air because the propellant may add moisture to the inside of the printer.

Courtesy of HK Wentworth Limited

FIGURE 4–5   Cleaning supplies for an inkjet printer

Laser Printers

Laser printers should be cleaned when print quality deteriorates or when you change the toner cartridge, which you need to do when the print becomes faint. When you open a laser printer, do not touch anything shiny because it might be hot or contain a charge. To clean the printer, perform the following maintenance tasks:

- Use a printer brush or a good paint brush and a lint-free cloth to clean inside the toner opening.
- Remove paper fragments.
- Use a clean cloth to wipe up any spilled toner and dust.
- Clean the rollers, but don't touch the transfer (sponge) roller.
- Replace the toner cartridge (see **Figure 4–6**).

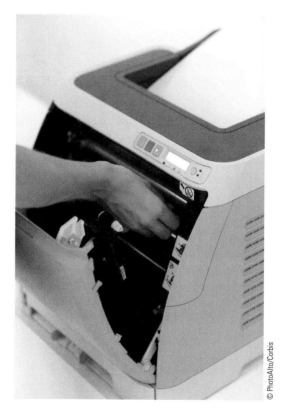

© PhotoAlto/Corbis

FIGURE 4–6   Maintaining a laser printer

⊣▬ WARNING

Exposure to light can damage toner cartridges. After removing a cartridge, always cover it with an extra lint-free cloth or piece of paper.

▶ VOCABULARY

corona wire

Some laser printers contain exposed *corona wires*. These wires are used to generate a field of positive charges on the surface of the drum and the paper. You should not brush or vacuum these wires.

Upgrading and Replacing Hardware Components

At some point, hardware components may be damaged and need to be changed, or output and production needs to be increased. You can make your computer more productive by upgrading various hardware elements. For instance, adding computer memory is often the best value for increasing overall computer performance. Replacing the keyboard and the mouse also can enhance computer performance. The following section describes upgrade options that you can implement.

Computer Memory

One way to measure a computer's power is by its memory capacity. RAM is made up of small memory chips that form a memory module. These modules are installed in the RAM slots on the motherboard of your computer (see **Figure 4–7**).

© gabyjalbert/ iStockphoto

FIGURE 4–7   RAM chips on the motherboard

The hard drive can be compared to long-term memory and RAM to short-term memory. Recall that data stored in RAM is temporary. When the computer is processing data, it reads and writes to RAM. If RAM fills up, the processor continually uses the hard drive to replace old data in RAM with new data. Because hard drive access is considerably slower than RAM, you may notice a processing slowdown when a computer's RAM is overloaded. Congested RAM even can affect the speed of the monitor when the disk operates continuously, writing and copying RAM data out to the disk.

Adding RAM to a computer generally helps increase performance, speed, and usability. However, every system has a maximum amount of RAM that it can support. Check the computer's documentation, or verify with a professional technician prior to purchasing additional memory. Complete the following Step-by-Step exercise to explore the amount of RAM contained in your computer.

Step-by-Step 4.1

1. Click the **Start** button 🪟 on the taskbar, and then click **Computer**. The Computer window opens.

2. Click the **System properties** button on the toolbar to display the System window, shown in **Figure 4–8**. Note the amount of RAM on your computer, which should be listed after "Installed memory (RAM)".

FIGURE 4–8
System window

Performance
Information
and Tools

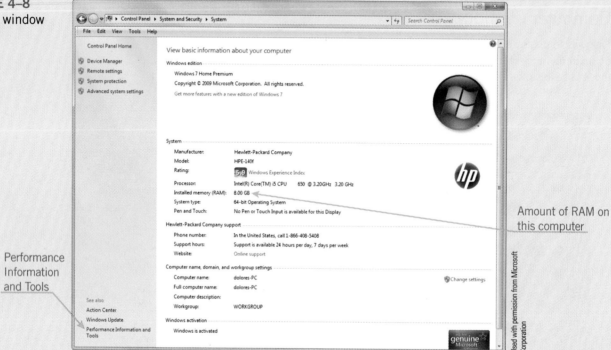

Amount of RAM on
this computer

3. Click **Performance Information and Tools** in the left pane to display the Rate and improve your computer's performance page, shown in **Figure 4–9**. Read the information contained on this page. Write down your computer's base score.

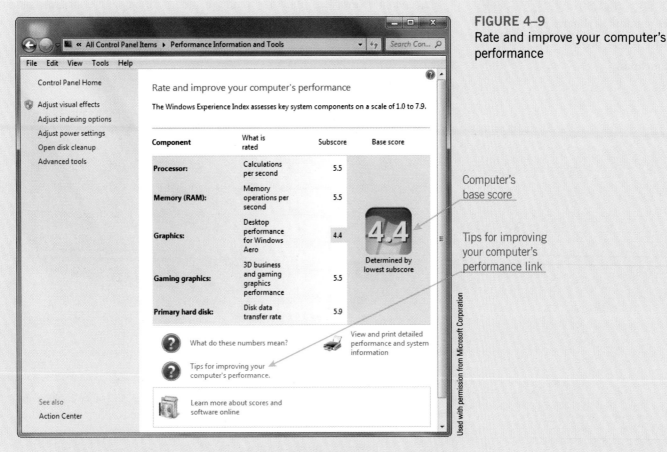

FIGURE 4–9
Rate and improve your computer's performance

4. Click the **Tips for improving your computer's performance** link. Read the information contained in the Windows Help and Support window.

5. List the tasks that you think can help improve your computer's performance.

6. Close all open windows, and then submit your assignment to your instructor.

Keyboards

If a keyboard is no longer working properly even after routine maintenance, you can replace it without replacing any other hardware components. You also might want to replace a keyboard to take advantage of enhanced features. Choosing a keyboard is complicated by the vast range of choices. The person who will use the keyboard should be the one to select it. Design, performance, and comfort should be considered.

▶ **VOCABULARY**

ergonomic keyboard

wireless keyboard

touchpad

Ergonomic keyboards allow for a more natural positioning of your arms and hands. Many ergonomic keyboards have a smaller width, which keeps the mouse closer to you. This reduces your reach and places the mouse in a more accessible position. The ergonomic keyboard shown in **Figure 4–10** also includes a touchpad, which you can use as a pointing device.

Touchpad

FIGURE 4–10   Ergonomic keyboard

A *wireless keyboard* reduces the clutter of unsightly wires and other cable problems and improves mobility. If necessary, you can move around with a wireless keyboard and not be bound to the desk.

Mouse

As with a keyboard, you can replace a mouse without replacing any other computer hardware. Recall from Lesson 2 that a variety of pointing devices are available, including wireless and optical. Some are ergonomic devices such as the one in **Figure 4–11**, which is a wireless ergonomic mouse.

FIGURE 4–11   Wireless ergonomic mouse

A *touchpad* is a pointing device you can use instead of a mouse. These devices sense the position of your finger and then move the pointer accordingly. Most notebook computers contain built-in touchpads, which cannot be replaced or upgraded without replacing the entire computer. However, you can use an external touchpad as an alternative (see **Figure 4–12**).

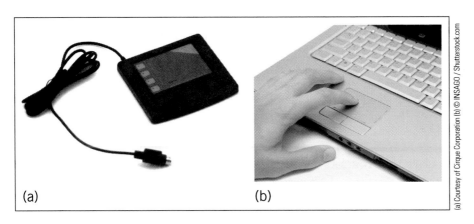

FIGURE 4–12   (a) External touchpad (b) Touchpad built into keyboard

Performing Preventive Maintenance

All computers slow down as you add and delete files, install and uninstall software, and perform normal activities. To eliminate and minimize these problems, Microsoft Windows comes with a set of utilities that perform maintenance tasks. You use these tools to defragment hard drives, empty the Recycle Bin, delete temporary files, and remove cookies. You should run these utilities following a routine maintenance schedule so that the computer can run faster and more efficiently.

Disk Defragmentation

As you use a computer, you add and delete files on the computer's hard disk. When the computer is new (or contains a new hard drive), the operating system, such as Windows 7, writes the file data in a set of side-by-side clusters. As the drive begins to become cluttered and space becomes limited, Windows divides the data for newly created files into sectors. Disk *fragmentation* occurs when data is broken up into many pieces that are not stored close together. The *sectors* are stored in blocks of nonadjacent clusters, thus creating fragmented files (see **Figure 4–13**). This pattern continues until you begin deleting files and adding new ones.

▶ **VOCABULARY**
fragmentation

sector

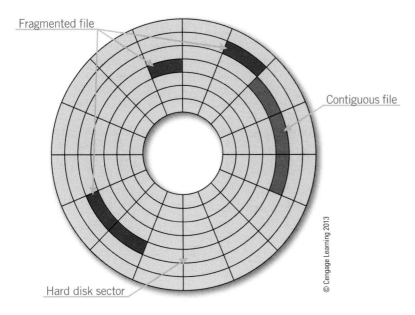

FIGURE 4–13   Fragmented file

MODULE 1 Computing Fundamentals

The computer reads the fragmented file as a single valid file. To do so, the read-write head has to scan multiple parts of the drive which extends disk *seek time.* This can significantly slow the speed of the processing cycle and computer performance. Disk *defragmentation* organizes fragmented files so that all of the file's sectors are stored together. Windows contains a defragmentation utility that reorganizes the contents of the disk to store the pieces of each file contiguously. The defragmentation utility, however, does not work with read-only disks, network drives, or locked drives.

In Step-by-Step 4.2, you run the defragmentation utility. (*Note*: Defragmenting can be a lengthy process. Verify with your instructor if you should complete this exercise.)

Step-by-Step 4.2

1. Click the **Start** button 🌐 on the taskbar, and then click **Control Panel** to display the Control Panel window (see **Figure 4–14**).

FIGURE 4–14
Control Panel

System and Security
category

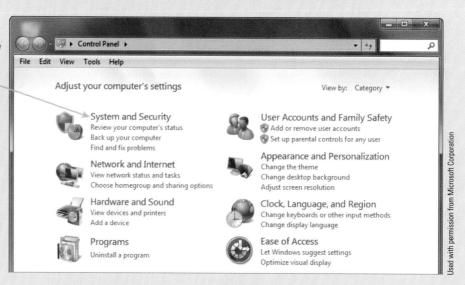

2. Click **System and Security** to display the System and Security window (see **Figure 4–15**).

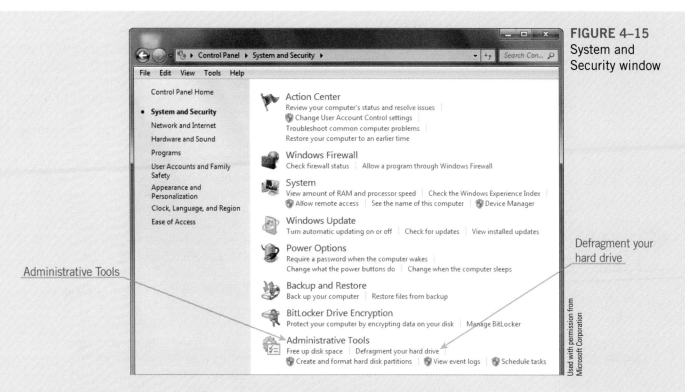

FIGURE 4–15
System and Security window

Administrative Tools

Defragment your hard drive

3. Scroll down, if necessary, to Administrative Tools, and then click **Defragment your hard drive** to display the Disk Defragmenter dialog box (see **Figure 4–16**). (If a User Account Control dialog box is displayed, click **Continue**.)

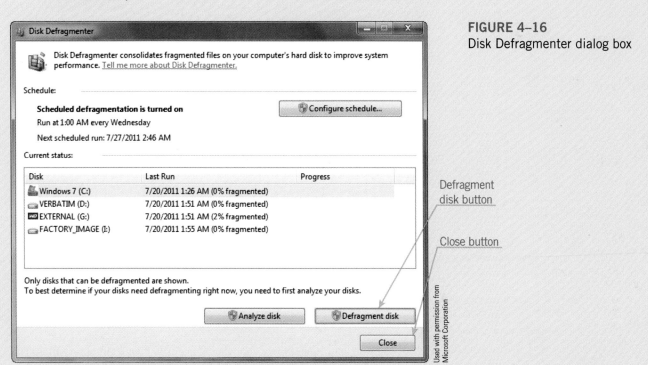

FIGURE 4–16
Disk Defragmenter dialog box

Defragment disk button

Close button

4. If indicated by your instructor, click the **Defragment disk** button. Otherwise, click the **Close** button.

5. Close any other open window.

Recycle Bin

▶ VOCABULARY
Recycle Bin

The Windows ***Recycle Bin*** is a holding area for files and folders before their final deletion from a storage device. Generally, you access the Recycle Bin through an icon located on the desktop. The Recycle Bin contains files that have been deleted from the hard disk, whether accidentally or intentionally. You can open the Recycle Bin to review its contents before permanently deleting the items. Double-click the Recycle Bin icon or right-click the icon and then click Open on the shortcut menu to view the Recycle Bin contents. Right-click an item to display its shortcut menu, which includes commands to Restore, Cut, Delete, or display the item's Properties.

To empty the Recycle Bin and permanently delete the files it contains, right-click the Recycle Bin icon and then click Empty Recycle Bin. A warning box is displayed. Click Yes to continue or No to cancel the command.

To restore a file from the Recycle Bin, open the Recycle Bin to display the list of deleted files. Right-click the name of the file to be restored, and then click Restore. Once a file has been deleted from the Recycle Bin, it cannot be restored.

To modify the Recycle Bin settings, right-click the Recycle Bin icon and then click Properties to display the Recycle Bin Properties dialog box (see **Figure 4–17**). Select the settings that you want to use and then click the OK button.

QUICK TIP

Only files you delete from a hard drive are stored in the Recycle Bin. Removable media, such as USB flash drives, do not typically have Recycle Bins, which means deleting a file on a removable drive permanently deletes the file from the drive.

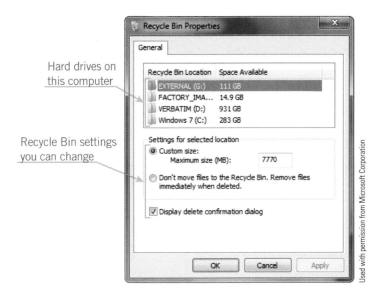

Hard drives on this computer

Recycle Bin settings you can change

FIGURE 4–17   Recycle Bin Properties dialog box

Temporary Files

Various programs, such as those in the Microsoft Office suite, create temporary files. This action is used for the following three reasons:

- To free memory for other programs
- To act as a safety net to prevent data loss
- To print while the computer is performing other tasks

The program determines where and when it needs to create temporary files. The temporary files normally exist only during the current session of the program. When the program is closed through a standard process, the temporary files are closed and then deleted automatically. However, if the computer loses power or the program is not properly closed, the temporary files remain on the hard drive. The following Step-by-Step exercise provides information on how to use a Windows program named Disk Cleanup to delete the temporary files and other files that are not needed.

Step-by-Step 4.3

1. Click the **Start** button  on the taskbar, point to *All Programs*, click **Accessories**, click **System Tools**, and then click **Disk Cleanup** to display the Disk Cleanup: Drive Selection dialog box (see **Figure 4–18**) or, if your computer has only one hard drive, the Disk Cleanup dialog box.

Drives box arrow

Drive C selected

Used with permission from Microsoft Corporation

FIGURE 4–18
Disk Cleanup: Drive Selection dialog box

2. If your computer contains more than one drive or the drive is partitioned, click the **Drives box arrow**, and then select the drive or partition you want to clean. If your computer does not contain more than one hard drive, then skip to step 3.

3. Click the **OK** button. Disk Cleanup scans the selected drive and calculates the amount of space that can be freed up through this process, and then displays the Disk Cleanup for (*your computer name*) dialog box (see **Figure 4–19**).

FIGURE 4–19
Amount of disk space to free

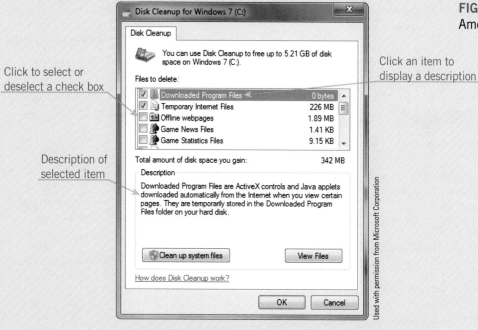

Click to select or deselect a check box

Click an item to display a description

Description of selected item

Used with permission from Microsoft Corporation

Clicking an item in the Files to delete list displays a description of the selection. Click a check box to select the item for deletion. You can use the check boxes to select all of the displayed categories or select specific files to be deleted. Verify that you want to delete the files.

4. Click the **OK** button. The Disk Cleanup dialog box is displayed (see **Figure 4–20**), asking if you want to permanently delete the files.

FIGURE 4–20
Disk Cleanup dialog box

5. To delete the files, click the **Delete Files** button. To cancel the operation, click the **Cancel** button.

Cookies

▶ **VOCABULARY**
cookie

A *cookie* is a small text file that a Web site uses to identify a specific computer. The file is created or updated on your computer's hard drive each time you visit the Web site. Cookies are not a threat to your computer's security. The text file contains a code that identifies you to the Web server each time a Web page is accessed. Primarily, cookies are used to gather information about your surfing habits and for targeted advertising. The following Step-by-Step exercise provides information on how to delete cookies from the hard drive.

Step-by-Step 4.4

1. Click the **Start** button 🔵 on the taskbar, and then click **Control Panel**. Click **Network and Internet** to display the Network and Internet window (see **Figure 4–21**).

FIGURE 4–21
Network and
Internet window

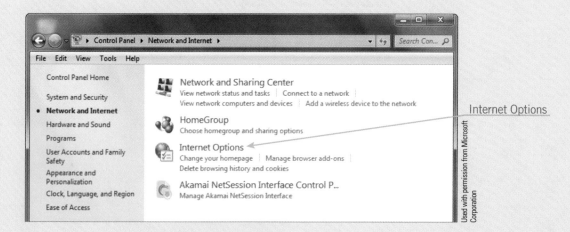

2. Click **Internet Options** to display the Internet Properties dialog box (see **Figure 4–22**).

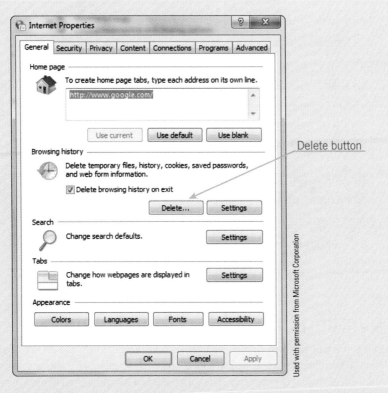

Used with permission from Microsoft Corporation

FIGURE 4–22
Internet Properties dialog box

3. In the Browsing history section of the General tab, click the **Delete** button
    to display the Delete Browsing History dialog box (see **Figure 4–23**).

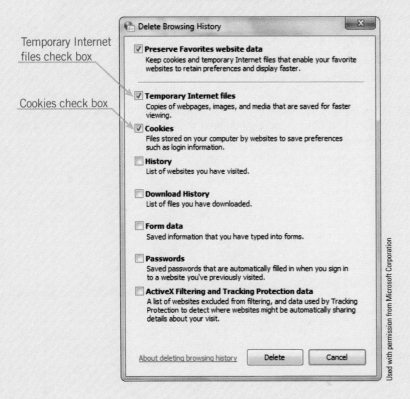

Temporary Internet
files check box

Cookies check box

Used with permission from Microsoft Corporation

FIGURE 4–23
Delete Browsing History
dialog box

4. ***Verify with your instructor before completing this step***. If necessary, click the **Temporary Internet files** check box and the **Cookies** check box to select both check boxes. Make sure the Preserve Favorites website data check box is also selected and that no other check boxes are selected. Click the **Delete** button to close the Delete Browsing History dialog box. If a Delete confirm dialog box is displayed, click **Yes** to delete temporary Internet files and cookies except those for Web sites in your Favorites list.

    Other data you can delete through the Delete Browsing History dialog box includes the history of Web sites you have visited, form data, passwords, and InPrivate Filtering data.

5. Close all open windows.

1-1.2.7

Requesting Specialized Maintenance

Generally, you can perform routine maintenance as discussed in this lesson. However, you should not attempt some maintenance procedures, especially those that involve working with electrical components. The following is a list of internal hardware maintenance or repair that generally should be performed by a computer professional:

- Replacing the power supply or opening the power supply case
- Replacing other electrical components
- Replacing the processor
- Replacing or adding a hard disk
- Replacing or adding additional RAM

Monitors, printers, and scanners are not designed to be opened by the general computer user. If problems are encountered with these devices, they should be worked on by an experienced technician.

Risks of Networked Computing

The security of a computer network is challenged every day by equipment malfunctions, system failures, computer hackers, and virus attacks.

Equipment malfunctions and system failures are caused by a number of factors including natural disasters, such as floods, storms, or fires, and electrical disturbances, such as a brownout or blackout. Server malfunctions or failures mean users lose temporary access to network resources, such as printers, drives, and information.

Computer hackers and viruses represent a great risk to networked environments. People who break into computer systems are called hackers. They gain unauthorized access to systems to steal services and information, such as credit card numbers, test data, and even national security data. Some hackers want to harm a company or organization they do not like or support; sometimes, they do it just for the thrill of being able to get into the system.

People create computer viruses and infect other computers for some of the same reasons. Viruses are very dangerous to networked computers—they usually are designed to sabotage files that are shared.

SUMMARY

In this lesson, you learned:

- A computer requires maintenance on a regular schedule to prevent problems such as the degrading of hard disk performance and monitor trouble.

- Damaged and poorly maintained cables can prevent peripheral devices from communicating with the computer. Unorganized and unprotected cables can also create safety hazards. Cable management should therefore be part of a regular computer maintenance routine.

- To maintain the computer keyboard, use a can of compressed air to remove the dust from the keyboard every six months.

- Clean a mechanical mouse by removing its cover, removing debris from the roller and the ball, and then reassembling the mouse.

- Printer maintenance helps to prevent common printing problems. Many inkjet printers have a self-cleaning mode. If yours does not, use an inkjet cleaning cartridge to flush dirt and debris out of clogged printer nozzles. Clean a laser printer when you change the toner cartridge.

- Adding computer memory (RAM) often provides the best value for increasing overall system performance.

- All computers slow down as you work with them. To improve or maintain computer efficiency, periodically use Windows tools to defragment hard drives, empty the Recycle Bin, delete temporary files, and remove cookies.

- Some maintenance procedures are not suitable for the average computer user and should be performed by a computer professional, such as replacing the power supply or opening the power supply case, replacing other electrical components, including the processor and RAM, and adding an internal hard disk.

■ LESSON REVIEW

TRUE / FALSE

Circle T if the statement is true or F if the statement is false.

T   F   **1.**   Adding RAM to a computer generally helps increase performance, speed, and usability.

T   F   **2.**   Only qualified computer repair specialists should change the toner on a laser printer.

T   F   **3.**   You cannot recover files from the Recycle Bin.

T   F   **4.**   As a general rule, you should clean a computer every three to six months.

T   F   **5.**   Windows includes a disk defragmentation utility.

MULTIPLE CHOICE

Select the best response for the following statements.

1. If a computer loses power or a program is not closed properly, _____ files can remain on the hard drive.

    A.   virus

    B.   temporary

    C.   recycled

    D.   permanent

2. Deposits of dry ink can accumulate on the print head of a(n) _____ printer, causing print quality to deteriorate.

    A.   laser

    B.   default

    C.   inkjet

    D.   network

3. You should check and clean the _____ periodically.

    A.   mouse

    B.   monitor

    C.   keyboard

    D.   all of the above

4. You can use a Windows program called _____ to delete temporary files and other files that your computer does not need.

    A.   Disk Cleanup

    B.   Disk Defragmenter

    C.   Disk Maintenance

    D.   Recycle Bin Cleanup

5. Disk _____ can significantly slow the speed of a computer's processing cycle.

    A.   cleanup

    B.   defragmentation

    C.   maintenance

    D.   seek time

FILL IN THE BLANK

Complete the following sentences by writing the correct word or words in the blanks provided.

1. A(n) _____ is a small text file that a Web site uses to identify a specific computer.

2. A(n) _____ is a pointing device you can use instead of a mouse.

3. Damaged and poorly maintained _____ can prevent peripheral devices from communicating with the computer.

4. Disk _____ organizes fragmented files so that all of the file's sectors are stored together.

5. You can use a can of compressed air to remove the dust from the _____.

■ PROJECTS

PROJECT 4–1

In Step-by-Step 4.4, you explored how to delete cookies and temporary Internet files from your computer. Complete the following to learn more about deleting browsing history:

1. Open the Internet Properties dialog box, and then open the Delete Browsing History dialog box.

2. Click the *About deleting browsing history* link to display a Windows Help and Support topic on browsing history.

3. What types of information does Internet Explorer store when you browse the Web?

4. Summarize two tips Windows Help and Support gives about your browsing history.

PROJECT 4–2

Some people say you should leave your computer on at all times—that turning the computer on and off creates stress on the components. Others argue that computers use a lot of energy, and that computers should be turned off when not in use. Your computer operating system, however, includes power-management settings. Your instructor has requested that you and your team investigate these options.

1. Use Windows Help and Support and prepare a report describing these power-management options.

2. Describe how to create a power plan.

3. Describe how you can change what happens when you press the power button on a mobile PC such as a laptop.

PROJECT 4–3

1-1.2.5
1-1.2.6
1-1.2.7

Printers need more frequent maintenance than most types of electronic devices. Complete the following:

1. Using Google or another search engine, find instructions or tips on maintaining the type of printer you have or use regularly.

2. As you research, identify periodic and occasional maintenance tasks.

3. Note any hazards or cautions you should observe when maintaining a printer.

4. Summarize the maintenance routine and cautions in a one-page explanation.

■ TEAMWORK PROJECT

1-1.2.6

You and your team are responsible for maintaining the computers in your school's computer lab. Work together to create a checklist of tasks that should be performed to maintain the hardware and operating systems of the computers. Be sure to indicate how often each task should be performed.

◼ CRITICAL THINKING

This lesson discussed fragmentation and defragmentation and provides steps for defragmenting a hard drive. Using the Internet and other resources, write a one-page report summarizing your responses to the following:

1. Windows 7 includes a defragmentation tool. Should you supplement that tool with other defragmentation utilities? If so, explain why.

2. How often should you defragment your hard drive? What is a good rule of thumb to follow?

3. Does defragmentation pose any risks to your computer? What can you do to overcome any risks?

1-1.2.6

◼ ONLINE DISCOVERY

Most computer manufacturers provide information on their Web sites about maintaining computer equipment. For example, HP provides a PC Health series of online articles, including one on keeping your hard drive healthy. Dell offers an online article about optimizing your computing. Gateway provides maintenance information online. Explore the Web site of your computer manufacturer to find maintenance information. Use your word-processing program to summarize the advice you found.

1-1.2.5

◼ JOB SKILLS

When you use a computer such as a PC or mobile device on the job, your company owns the computer and trusts you to use it properly. Who should be responsible for maintaining your work computer? Which types of maintenance tasks should you perform? Which types of tasks should your company perform? Who should be responsible for computer problems that result from poor maintenance?

LESSON 5

Computer-Related Issues

■ OBJECTIVES

Upon completion of this lesson, you should be able to:

- Follow the problem-solving process.
- Implement solutions.
- Identify computer issues for consumers.
- Discard equipment responsibly.

■ DATA FILES

You do not need data files to complete this lesson.

■ WORDS TO KNOW

Linux PC

problem solving

support agreement

troubleshooting

useful life

warranty

Sooner or later, you will have a problem with your computer hardware or software. To reach a solution and correct the problem involves a process. **Problem solving** is a systematic approach leading from an initial situation to a desired situation. The process is often subject to some resource constraints, meaning that you usually have a limited amount of time or money to solve the problem. See **Figure 5–1**.

FIGURE 5–1   Solving technology problems

1-1.2.8

Following the Problem-Solving Process

To solve a problem successfully, you must apply a logical plan to act as a guide or road map. The plan helps you in defining the problem, gathering information concerning the problem, identifying possible solutions, and selecting and implementing the best solution. The following steps outline the process you should take to solve problems:

1. Define the problem.

2. Investigate and analyze the problem.

3. Identify possible solutions.

4. Select and implement a solution.

5. Evaluate solutions.

Each step is important in the problem-solving process, also called **troubleshooting**. Complete each step thoroughly before continuing to the next step.

Define the Problem

In the beginning stage, make sure you actually have a problem and identify what it is. Start with the most obvious or simplest possibilities, and continue troubleshooting from there. For example, if you are having trouble sending e-mail, make sure the computer is turned on and connected to the Internet.

Sometimes the problem may not be as obvious as it appears. You must investigate the situation to determine the real issue. Ask questions, use what-if statements, eliminate some facts, include others, clarify the current situation, and identify what the situation should be or what you want it to be. If necessary, make notes or sketches. Collect as much information about the problem as possible. For example, if you are having problems with your computer, describe the system behavior and any error messages you receive. If possible, take a screen shot of the behavior or message by pressing the Print Screen key to store an image of the screen on the Clipboard, opening a program such as Windows Paint or Microsoft Word, and then pasting the image into the file.

Investigate and Analyze the Problem

After you define the problem, you need all the facts. Collect all available data about the problem. Determine why the problem exists and its possible causes. Ask the most basic questions or the ones that are easiest to answer. Continuing with the e-mail example, start with a question such as "What do you see on the screen when you try to retrieve your e-mail?"

Attempt to reproduce the problem, noting what actions you take to do so. For example, if you are having trouble printing a document from your computer, try printing a different document. Then try printing from a different computer, if possible. Also attempt to print a test page using a button or other feature on the printer itself. Investigating the problem in this way helps to narrow the possible solutions. If you can print a test page from the printer, but cannot print at all from any computer connected to the printer, the problem probably involves the connection, such as the cable connecting the printer to your computer or network.

The investigation and analysis step provides information you need to make an accurate decision. Sometimes during this step, you may decide that a problem really does not exist at all or that the problem has an unexpected cause. If there is a legitimate problem, however, your detective work at this stage should provide information that can help you solve the problem.

Identify Possible Solutions

After diagnosing the problem, identify possible solutions. What can you do to solve some or all of the problem? What should you do differently? These are the types of questions that need to be answered as you look for a solution. In exploring possible answers, you may identify more than one solution.

In general, start with the most basic possible solutions or those that are the easiest to try. For example, if you are having trouble with hardware, check to make sure the device is properly connected to a power source. If you are having trouble with a software program, close the program and then restart it.

Select and Implement a Solution

If you identify more than one possible solution, critique and test one solution at a time to determine its likely outcome. Based on this information, choose the solution that provides the best outcome. Avoid combining solutions because you might not know which one solved the problem. If you are not sure about the consequences of your actions, look for help and advice from an expert source, such as hardware or software documentation, information posted on a reputable Web site, technical support personnel, or an experienced colleague or friend. Refer to the notes you took in Step 1 (define the problem) or images you created to accurately describe the problem and any troubleshooting attempts you made.

The next step is to implement the solution, which means you put the solution into action or make the changes that solve the problem. As you did when you defined the problem, take notes about the troubleshooting steps you perform. If the problem recurs, you can refer to the notes to solve the problem again.

Confirm the Solution

After putting the selected solution into place, you need to evaluate its performance. Did it eliminate the problem? Did it accomplish what you need to do? If your answer is yes, you now have a solution to the problem. For example, if your computer was running slowly, did performance return to normal after scanning the computer with antivirus software? If not, you need to return to the previous step to select and try a different solution. If the solution did not work at all, return to the first step, work through your original questions, and determine if you missed a problem or symptom before testing new solutions.

Document the Problem and the Solution

Prepare written documentation describing the problem and the solution. Organize the notes you took during the problem-solving process so you and others can easily refer to the information again. If you discovered a way to avoid or prevent similar problems, begin to follow that practice as soon as possible. For example, if occasional power interruptions cause you to lose work, invest in a UPS (uninterruptible power supply) device and make a habit of backing up your current files at the end of each day.

Keep in mind that solving problems is not a linear process. Instead, you sometimes define the problem, investigate it, and start identifying possible solutions only to determine that you really need to define the problem more clearly. In this case, you take a circular or spiral path, as shown in **Figure 5–2**, rather than a straight path.

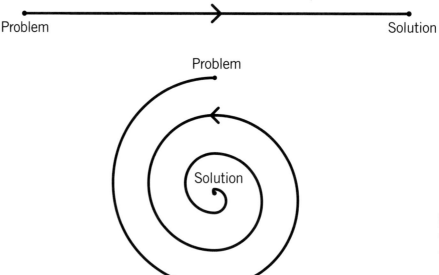

FIGURE 5–2   Following a straight or spiral path to solve problems

ETHICS IN TECHNOLOGY

Who Is Responsible?

Increasingly, computers are used in decisions that affect human lives. Consider medical safety; just about everything in a hospital is linked to a computer. What happens if the computers don't produce the expected results? What happens if they have been programmed incorrectly?

When programmers write a program, they check for as many conditions as possible. They could inadvertently miss a condition, of course. What happens if a computer malfunctions and applies a higher dosage of radiation than the patient needs? What if two medications are prescribed to a patient and the computer doesn't indicate that they are incompatible? Imagine the consequences if someone called for an ambulance and the dispatch system didn't work. It's not always clear who is responsible for these mishaps. Is it the programmer? Is it the company who sold the software or hardware? Is it the person who administered the radiation treatment?

The incidents described here actually happened. These types of ethical issues are being decided in court to determine who has legal responsibility.

Implementing Solutions

Suppose that your printer is not working. The following steps illustrate how to troubleshoot the problem and find a solution. Complete each step fully before continuing to the next step. You can apply these same general steps to other computer-related devices and problems.

1. **Identify the problem.**

The printer is not working. See **Figure 5–3.**

© Nicholas / iStockphoto

FIGURE 5–3   Identifying the problem

2. **Investigate and analyze the problem.**

   Collect all available data and facts regarding the situation. See **Figure 5–4**.

FIGURE 5–4   Analyzing the problem

This step provides information needed to make an accurate decision about how to solve the problem. When analyzing the problem, you want to identify potential causes. Identify the steps you take to create the problem and then reproduce the steps. Write down the steps. Does the problem always occur when these steps are implemented? Review the manual provided for the printer. Most manuals contain a troubleshooting section. A second resource is the Web site of the printer's manufacturer.

3. **Identify possible solutions.**

   Ask questions to identify likely solutions. Is the printer plugged in? Is it turned on? Is it online? Is it beeping? Is it out of ink or toner? Is the print quality low? Does the printer have paper? Is it jammed? Is the cable connected properly? Is the cable in good repair? Have you cleaned the printer recently?

4. **Select and implement a solution.**

   Test all possible solutions until you find one that is likely to work, and then implement the solution.

5. **Confirm the solution.**

Turn off the computer and printer, turn them back on, and then test again.

6. **Document the problem and the solution.**

Describe the symptoms and write down the steps required to resolve the problem. Save the document and print a copy. File the copy or keep it in a notebook.

The following Step-by-Step exercise shows you how to apply the problem-solving process to troubleshoot a problem connecting to the Internet.

Step-by-Step 5.1

1. Click the **Start** button ⊙ on the taskbar, and then click **Control Panel**.

2. Click the **System and Security** link to display the System and Security window. In the Action Center category, click **Troubleshoot common computer problems** to display a list of troubleshooters in the Troubleshooting window. See **Figure 5–5**.

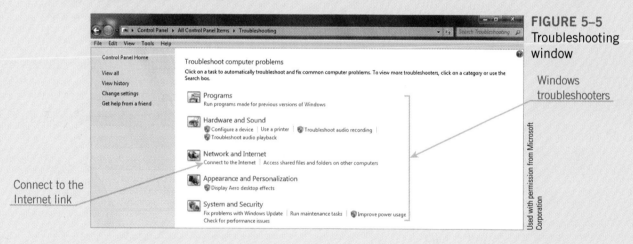

FIGURE 5–5
Troubleshooting window

Windows troubleshooters

Connect to the Internet link

3. In the Network and Internet category, click the **Connect to the Internet** link to start the Internet Connections troubleshooter. See **Figure 5–6**.

FIGURE 5–6
Internet Connections
troubleshooter

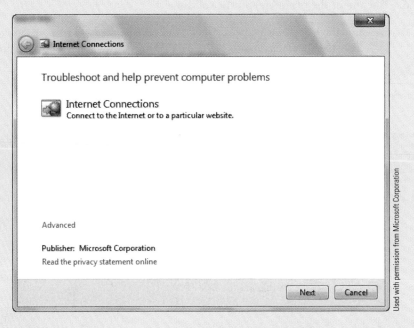

4. Click the **Next** button to start the troubleshooter. Windows attempts to detect the problem, and then displays more detailed problems to solve. See **Figure 5–7**.

FIGURE 5–7
Selecting a problem to solve

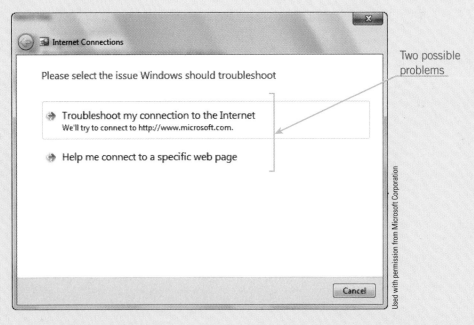

5. Click **Troubleshoot my connection to the Internet**, and then follow the prompts to complete the troubleshooter, exploring additional options as necessary.

6. Use your word-processing program and describe the information Windows provides to help you solve the Internet connection problem.

7. Close all open windows.

Identifying Computer Issues for Consumers

Purchasing, maintaining, and repairing a computer requires considerable research and focused decision making. The following section discusses selecting and purchasing a computer for an organization and purchasing a computer for personal use. See **Figure 5–8**.

FIGURE 5–8   Researching personal computers before purchasing one

Purchasing a Computer

Selecting a computer for an organization or business can be critical to its success and efficiency. The first task is to identify the purpose and tasks for which the computer will be used. Some requirements that are common to most businesses are accounting, budgeting, financial record keeping, correspondence, marketing, and presentations. Companies that specialize in unique and unusual types of businesses also often require specialized applications. To guide purchasing decisions, most organizations have a list of approved computer models and standard software packages.

Purchasing a computer for personal use most often means selecting one that runs the latest version of the Windows or Macintosh operating system. Personal computers are typically used for writing papers or letters, tracking personal finances, playing games, and connecting to the Internet. A Macintosh computer has two primary disadvantages: (1) most new applications are designed for the Windows operating system first, and (2) exchanging data between computers with the Windows operating system and the Mac operating system can sometimes be difficult.

A *Linux PC* is a standard personal computer that runs the Linux operating system. All primary applications, such as word processing, spreadsheets, databases, and so on, are available for Linux. However, the number of software titles for Linux is much lower than for Windows or Macintosh. Linux desktops primarily are popular with the knowledgeable IT professional and the home user with limited funds.

Maintaining a Computer

Similar to your automobile, computers require maintenance on a regular schedule. Generally, routine maintenance can be performed by the average computer user. However, computers can be difficult to use and can break down easily or even arrive damaged from the manufacturer. For these situations, post-sale service and support is critical. Many companies purchase a computer that comes with a parts-and-labor limited warranty that covers the hardware for one to three years.

Warranties

A *warranty* is a written guarantee that a product or service meets certain specifications. It usually explains that if the product or service doesn't meet the specifications, the manufacturer will repair or replace it. Some warranties also list your responsibilities as a consumer, such as to maintain the product according to the manufacturer's guidelines or have it serviced only by a licensed technician. Read the warranty to verify that it does not allow the manufacturer to repair the computer with refurbished or used parts. See **Figure 5–9**.

> **▶ VOCABULARY**
> **Linux PC**
> **warranty**

> **■ ABOVE AND BEYOND**
>
> The standard warranty provided with a computer product is usually sufficient. Some manufacturers and retail services provide extended warranties, which are usually not worth the expense except in certain circumstances. For example, if you are purchasing a notebook computer and plan to travel frequently, an extended warranty on the notebook's display can be a good idea.

FIGURE 5–9   Reading the computer warranty

In addition, look for the following information in a computer warranty:

- Determine if it includes software coverage.
- Check for on-site repair and the length of time it is in force.
- Check the period of free telephone support; look for a minimum of 90 days with no limitations.
- Confirm that technical support is available 24 hours a day, seven days a week.
- Determine if a toll-free number or Web site address is provided.
- Check if the warranty still applies if the computer is used outside the country.

Support Agreements

A computer manufacturer might provide its customers with a *support agreement*, which is a list of services specifically designed to provide assistance to an organization. This allows a company or user to budget for support just like they would for rent or insurance. The terms of service and the assistance to be provided are specified in the agreement. A support agreement can apply to a variety of services, depending on the type of equipment. Generally, these services are determined by a mutual agreement between the company receiving the service and the company providing the support. An example is a support agreement for a company's network. The company providing the support most likely would first provide a free audit of the network. They would then set forth the terms and conditions of the agreement. Some examples of terms could be a fixed cost per hour, remote telephone assistance, in-house assistance, maximum number of hours over a specified time frame, other additional costs, and so on. Most agreements also include information on services not covered.

▶ **VOCABULARY**
support agreement
useful life

ABOVE AND BEYOND

Most computer manufacturers provide extensive help resources online to guide you in solving problems with your computer. Check the manufacturer's Web site before making an expensive technical support phone call.

Useful Life

Useful life is defined as the estimated time period that an asset, such as computer equipment, will be of use to the owner. Depending on the type of company, the time period can vary from one year to five years. A general rule is that the useful life of a computer for a company in the technology industry is two to three years; for developers, two to four years; and for the general public, three to five years. Some businesses consider that the useful life of a computer lasts until it ceases to perform its function.

Depending on the value and condition of the computer, some companies may extend the life of a computer by adding components or upgrading parts of the computer. Other companies may elect to trade in the older equipment.

Discarding Equipment Responsibly

At some point, you need to dispose of or discard computer equipment. Although most consumers dispose of computer systems one at a time, for many companies, discarding equipment can be a major consideration. The U.S. Environmental Protection Agency (EPA) has a Web site containing basic information on the disposal of electronics (*www.epa.gov/osw/conserve/materials/ecycling/basic.htm*). The Web site addresses the mounting problem of computer waste and includes suggestions for reusing equipment. For example, if the equipment is still usable, donate it to agencies such as schools, nonprofit organizations, and lower-income families. The Web site also contains a list of programs that take donations.

If donating is not an option, consider recycling. Many cities and communities provide recycling centers. See **Figure 5–10**. The EPA Web site provides guidelines and assistance to help locate a recycling center. Before donating or recycling, be sure to back up all of your data and then use a utility to wipe or format the hard drive to remove all of your personal data so that no one else can access it.

ABOVE AND BEYOND

If you are replacing one computer system with another, you might not need to discard your monitor if it is working properly. Monitors last longer than CPUs and are often compatible with newer CPUs. Check with your computer provider to determine whether you can use your old monitor with a new system.

ABOVE AND BEYOND

Be aware of the safety concerns regarding recycling computer equipment, which often contains hazardous materials. Most states offer recycling services for components (usually monitors and CPUs) that contain hazardous waste such as lead and mercury. The state services might charge extra to recycle these components because it requires additional effort to remove the harmful substances.

FIGURE 5–10   Recycling computer hardware

© Jyrki Komulainen / Getty Images

TECHNOLOGY CAREERS

Science or Science Fiction?

One way to prepare for a career in a technology field is to watch science fiction movies. How so? New technology often can remind us of gadgets from an old science fiction movie. Some people claim that the resemblance is not because the creators of those fictionalized futuristic shows correctly predicted 21st century trends. Instead, some of the inventors and engineers who create today's technology may be science fiction fans who consciously or unconsciously design their devices to imitate what they saw in the movies or read about in books. For example, a cell phone looks a lot like a "communicator" used on space-ships in 1960s television shows, and the Segway scooter provides individual transportation that is a step toward the personal hovercraft and jetpacks of many tales of the future.

Popular culture has long offered views of a world full of technology, such as those presented in *20,000 Leagues Under the Sea*; *I, Robot;* and *2001: A Space Odyssey*. Many works of science fiction show a respect for real science combined with the imagination to contemplate where it could lead us. Now science imitates science fiction as we enjoy video conference calls, swipe our magnetic identification and cash cards, or pay for goods using only our cell phones.

SUMMARY

In this lesson, you learned:

- Problem solving involves defining a problem and finding a solution.

- The sequence of problem-solving tasks is as follows: defining the problem, investigating and analyzing the problem, identifying possible solutions, selecting and implementing the best solution, evaluating the chosen solution, and then documenting the problem and solution.

- When purchasing a computer for yourself or for an organization, identify the purpose of the computer and the tasks you or others will perform on it.

- Purchasing a computer for personal use most often means selecting one that runs the latest version of the Windows or Macintosh operating system. Computers running the Linux operating system primarily are popular with knowledgeable IT professionals and home users with limited funds.

- Warranties and support agreements help you maintain computer equipment. If a computer fails to perform according to guidelines the manufacturer specifies, the warranty might provide for the repair or replacement of the computer. A computer manufacturer might offer its customers a support agreement, which is a list of services specifically designed to provide assistance to a company or organization.

- When you purchase computer equipment, be aware of its useful life, which is the estimated time period the computer equipment will be of use to you.

- To dispose of computer equipment properly, refer to the guidelines on the EPA Web site and consider donating or recycling the equipment.

◼ LESSON REVIEW

TRUE / FALSE

Circle T if the statement is true or F if the statement is false.

T   F   **1.**   The first step in the problem-solving process is to define the problem.

T   F   **2.**   Combining solutions is the second step in the problem-solving process.

T   F   **3.**   When purchasing a new computer, first determine the brand you want.

T   F   **4.**   Hundreds of software titles are available for the Linux operating system.

T   F   **5.**   If a computer is no longer usable, it should be sent to a recycling center.

MULTIPLE CHOICE

Select the best response for the following statements:

1. The problem-solving process is also called _____.

    A.   recycling   C.   troubleshooting

    B.   investigating   D.   implementing

2. When identifying possible solutions to a problem, start with the _____ possible solutions.

    A.   least obvious   C.   most difficult

    B.   most basic   D.   least likely

3. Review a computer warranty to determine whether it includes _____.

    A.   software coverage   C.   technical support

    B.   on-site repair   D.   all of the above

4. Before donating or recycling computer equipment, you should _____.

    A.   read the warranty   C.   remove all of your personal data

    B.   draft a support agreement   D.   calculate its useful life

5. A possible solution for a nonworking printer is to check if the printer _____.

    A.   is turned on   C.   has a cable connected to the computer

    B   has paper   D.   all of the above

FILL IN THE BLANK

Complete the following sentences by writing the correct word or words in the blanks provided.

1. A(n) _____ is a written guarantee that a product or service meets certain specifications.

2. The third step in the problem-solving process is to identify possible _____.

3. A(n) _____ is a list of services specifically designed to provide assistance to an organization.

4. Some businesses consider that the _____ of a computer lasts until it ceases to perform its function.

5. When you _____ a solution, you put the solution into action or make the changes that solve the problem.

PROJECTS

PROJECT 5-1

In your new job as a technology assistant, you have been asked to present a proposal for purchasing five new computers for the Multimedia department of your company. **1-1.2.9** Assume that the computers will be used for creating videos, advanced presentations, and professional graphics. The current computers in the Multimedia department can handle these tasks, but usually perform slowly. Complete the following:

1. Use the problem-solving process outlined in this chapter to select the type of computer to recommend to the purchasing department. Be sure to consider the processor, hard drive, RAM, USB ports, and video capability.

2. Provide detailed information for each step within the process. The completed report should be one to two pages long.

PROJECT 5-3

When computer manufacturers introduce advancements in hardware technology, they shorten the useful **1-1.2.9** life of computers that consumers and organizations have purchased. Consider how you can extend the useful life of your computer. Use the Internet and talk to other computer owners as necessary to brainstorm a list of possible solutions to this problem. Organize the list in a word-processing document and describe each item. Submit the list to your instructor.

PROJECT 5-2

The question of what to do with used computer equipment is quickly becoming a concern for cities and **1-1.2.9** towns. Complete the following:

1. Using the Internet and other reference materials, research the resources in your city or town for discarding electronic waste.

2. What are the particular problems associated with disposing of computers and other electronic devices? What are the possible solutions? Create a table that lists at least three problems and then suggest at least one solution for each problem. Submit the table to your instructor.

TEAMWORK PROJECT

The sales staff at a computer retailer often argues that an extended warranty covers repairs that the manufac- **1-1.2.9** turer's warranty does not or covers them after the manufacturer's warranty expires. However, most consumer advocacy groups recommend against purchasing an extended warranty. Complete the following:

1. Using the Internet and other sources, research why consumer advocacy groups recommend against purchasing an extended warranty.

2. Prepare a presentation that describes at least three reasons not to purchase an extended warranty.

3. If possible, share your team's presentation with your class.

CRITICAL THINKING

Use the problem-solving steps in this lesson to write a strategy for solving a problem that you or a friend has experienced, or a problem you have heard about in the news. Complete the following:

1. Define the problem, then investigate and analyze it, and identify possible solutions that would use a computer program or some other kind of technology.

2. Choose a solution you think will solve the problem. How will you put the solution into action? What could go wrong with the solution **1-1.2.8** you choose? Would the technology need to be updated in a few years, or would the solution remain useful for a long time? Summarize your troubleshooting process and solution in a written report.

■ ONLINE DISCOVERY

Visit the E-cycling Central Web site at *www.ecyclingcentral. com*. Find the list of questions to ask recyclers, and then answer the following:

1. How should recyclers remove personal data from computer disks?

2. How much of the material that recyclers collect should be recycled rather than disposed or incinerated?

3. How do you know whether a recycler has the proper facilities, training, and equipment to recycle computer equipment?

4. How can you find out whether the recycler exports electronic wastes to other countries?

1-1.2.9

■ JOB SKILLS

Most companies are looking for employees who can solve their problems and help them achieve their goals. Because of this, interviewers often want to know about your problem-solving skills. To answer such a question, avoid generalizations such as "I'm a good problem-solver. I solve problems nearly every day in my current occupation." Instead, tell a story about a specific situation. Complete the following:

1. Identify a time at school or work when you were confronted with a difficult problem. A difficult problem is one that could cause severe consequences if it continues.

2. Describe the problem in a one-page document.

3. Describe specifically what you did to solve the problem.

LESSON 6

Software and Hardware Interaction

■ OBJECTIVES

Upon completion of this lesson, you should be able to:

- Understand how hardware and software interact.
- Explain how a software program works.
- Track software development.
- Compare application software and system software.
- Identify options for software distribution.

■ DATA FILES

You do not need data files to complete this lesson.

■ WORDS TO KNOW

algorithm

application software

beta testing

bundleware

flowchart

inputting

network license

operating system

patch

service pack

single-user license

software

Software as a Service (SaaS)

software development

software license

software piracy

system software

update

upgrade

Web application

Over the last 50 years or so, computer technology has changed the world. Not long ago, the typical worker did not use computers on the job. Customers did not order products online or scan ID cards to receive benefits for frequent shopping. Accounting was done using ledgers. When you think about the recent history of computers, you probably think of innovations in hardware—computers have become smaller and faster. Computer usage has changed just as dramatically. Early computers were used as little more than high-speed calculators. Because computers developed the capacity to do many tasks very quickly, they now have a major influence on the culture and economy. Computers have had such an impact due to the vision and desire of software developers, who created thousands of ways to use computers. They created programs that affect every aspect of your life.

1-2.1.1

Understanding How Hardware and Software Interact

Although software and hardware are clearly distinct parts of a computer system, they often play similar roles and perform similar tasks. Recall that hardware refers to anything you can touch, including objects such as the keyboard, mouse, monitor, printer, chips, disk drives, and CD/DVD recorders. *Inputting* is the process of using an input device to enter data. In Lesson 2, you reviewed input devices. Popular input devices include the keyboard (used for inputting text and numbers), the mouse (used for selecting items on the screen), scanner (used to input images and documents), microphone (used to input sound), and video camera (used to input video).

Using input devices, you interact with software by typing commands such as entering a name for a word-processing document as shown in **Figure 6–1**, selecting an option from a menu, or clicking a button, such as the Save button used in most software programs.

▶ **VOCABULARY**
inputting

ABOVE AND BEYOND

An early computer called the Univac I was a sensation in 1952 when it correctly predicted that Dwight D. Eisenhower would win the presidential election in a landslide victory. The election results were remarkably close to the computer's prediction, but the computer didn't perform a miracle. The programmers who used statistical vote samples (the data) and shrewd analysis techniques (the program commands) deserve the credit for the accurate prediction.

© Yu-Feng Chen/iStockphoto

FIGURE 6–1   Interacting with software

The Role of Software

VOCABULARY
software

You cannot touch software because it has no substance. *Software* (or a program) is programming code written to provide instructions to the hardware so it can perform tasks, such as printing, displaying a Web page or dialog box, or saving a document on the hard disk. Hardware and software interact as a computer processes data. You use input devices—hardware—to enter data. Then specific programmed instructions tell the computer how to process that data—this is the software component that tells the hardware what to do. Finally, other software instructions format the data correctly so you can understand it when you see it on a monitor, print it on a page, or hear it through the speakers.

For instance, a computer programmer might write a program that lets you use the keyboard to access a Web site and then use the mouse to select a music file and download it from the Internet. The software makes it possible to download or retrieve the music file from a server somewhere on the Internet, and other software on your computer allows you to play the music. The CPU, sound card, and speakers in your computer system are hardware devices that function as output devices. Other examples of how data is processed and then sent to an output device are as follows:

- You use a scanner to scan a document and then print a copy (see **Figure 6–2**).
- You create video with your digital video camera and then transfer it from your camera to your computer.
- You use a microphone to create an audio file to accompany a message to your grandmother.

© Pelham James Mitchinson / Shutterstock.com

FIGURE 6–2 Scanning a document

The software provides the instructions on how to accomplish these tasks and where to save the files.

When people have a problem with how their computer is working, they might say, "It's a software problem." This means there is a problem with the program or data, and not with the computer or hardware itself.

A good analogy is a book. The book, including the pages and the ink, is the hardware. The words and ideas on the pages are the software. One has little value without the other. The same is true of computer software and hardware: how the two interact allows us to use the computer to complete tasks.

How a Software Program Works

A computer processes data by applying rules called algorithms. An *algorithm* is a set of clearly defined, logical steps that solve a problem. For example, if you want to explain to someone who has never done laundry how to do it properly, you would explain the process step by step, as shown in **Figure 6–3**.

▶ **VOCABULARY**
algorithm

HOW TO DO LAUNDRY
Collect the clothes that need to be washed.
Separate the clothes into light and dark piles.
Take the light pile to the washing machine and put clothes in the machine.
Add laundry detergent to the washing machine.
Set the dial on the washing machine for the correct size load.
Set the dial on the washing machine for warm wash and warm rinse water.
Turn on the washing machine.
When the cycle has finished, take wash out and put clothes in dryer.
Add a dryer fabric softener sheet to the dryer.
Set dryer cycle to Permanent Press.
Set dryer timer to 40 minutes.
Turn on dryer.
When the cycle has finished, take clothes out.
Fold clothes.
Put away clothes.
Repeat all previous steps with dark clothes.

© Cengage Learning 2013

FIGURE 6–3   An algorithm lists steps required to perform a task

---

If these steps seem like they offer very detailed instructions for performing a simple task, remember that the person you are instructing has no idea how to do laundry. You cannot assume he or she knows anything about it. In the same way, when a programmer writes software instructions for a computer, every step must give explicit instructions. A computer cannot do anything without being instructed how to do it through programmed software commands.

The following is a very simple example of how a programmer would begin to write a software program. After writing an algorithm for solving the problem in plain English (or French, Chinese, or Portuguese, depending on the spoken language of the programmer), the next step would be to rewrite the instructions in a formal programming language. Even then the computer will not understand the instructions; a specialized computer program translates the programming language to machine language that the computer can understand.

To instruct a computer how to perform a simple task such as outputting the average of three numbers, the program must break this down into many steps. For example:

1. Let *A* equal 50.

2. Let *B* equal 144.

3. Let *C* equal 68.

4. Add *A* + *B* + *C*.

5. Let the sum of *A* + *B* + *C* equal *X*.

6. Divide *X* by 3.

7. Let the quotient equal *Y*.

8. Print the text "The average is " followed by *Y*.

Tracking Software Development

Software development is a multistep process that usually begins when someone recognizes a need to perform a task more effectively using a computer. As you have seen, the programmer must first break down the task into an algorithm, or series of steps, that will cover all the actions needed to perform the task. Often the programmer works out the logic for the steps in the algorithm by using a ***flowchart*** that shows different paths the program will take depending on what data is inputted (see **Figure 6–4**).

▶ **VOCABULARY**
software development

flowchart

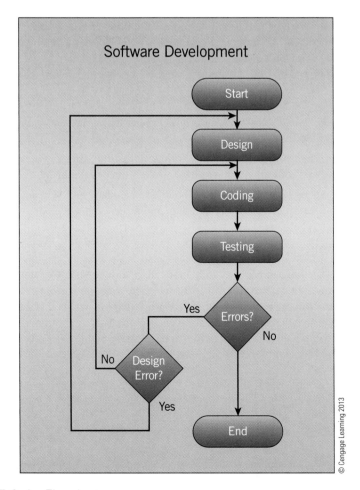

© Cengage Learning 2013

FIGURE 6–4   Flowchart

Next, the programmer writes the steps in a computer programming language, or code, that uses a formal set of terms and syntax, or rules for how the words are used together. The computer takes that code, translates it into language it can understand, and uses the translated commands to execute the program.

This, however, is not the end of the process. Computer programs are written by people, and people can make mistakes. Someone might enter a line of code with a small error in syntax or spelling, producing very different results from what the programmers were expecting. So software development also requires a quality control process that involves running systematic tests, debugging (finding and correcting errors in the code), and *beta testing*, a process that releases commercial software in development to a cross-section of typical users who evaluate the program and report any problems, or "bugs," in the software before it is released to the public.

1-2.1.2

Comparing Application Software and System Software

There are two basic types of computer software: *application software* and *system software*. Application software helps you perform a specific task. System software refers to the operating system and all utility programs that manage computer resources. Figuratively speaking, application software sits on top of system software. Without the operating system and system utilities, the computer cannot run any applications.

Application Software

Application software generally is referred to as productivity software. This type of software is composed of programs designed for an end user. Common application programs are word processors, database systems, presentation programs, spreadsheet programs, and graphic design programs. Some other application categories are as follows:

- *Education, home, and personal software*: Includes reference, entertainment, personal finance, calendars, e-mail, and Web browsers
- *Multimedia software*: Includes authoring, animation, music, video and sound capturing and editing, virtual reality, and Web site development
- *Workgroup computing software*: Includes calendars and scheduling, e-mail, Web browsers, electronic conferencing, and project management

Using Application Software

One of the tasks you can perform with application software is modifying and applying rules to data. In Microsoft Office, for instance, you can customize options that determine how you use each program. In Step-by-Step 6.1, you learn how to customize one feature in Microsoft Word. Complete Step-by-Step 6.1 to modify the Quick Access Toolbar, which is the toolbar that appears to the right of the program icon on the title bar in Microsoft Office programs.

Step-by-Step 6.1

1. Click the **Start** button ⊕ on the taskbar, point to *All Programs*, and then click **Microsoft Office**.

2. Click **Microsoft Word 2010** to open the program and display a new, blank document.

3. Click the **File** tab and then point to the **Options** button (see **Figure 6–5**).

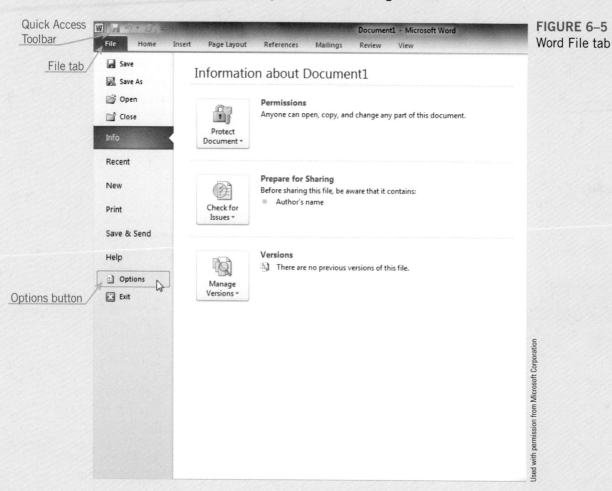

FIGURE 6–5
Word File tab

4. Click the **Options** button to display the Word Options dialog box. Click **Quick Access Toolbar** in the left pane (see **Figure 6–6**). You use the Quick Access Toolbar category of options to add and remove buttons on the Quick Access Toolbar. When you add a command to the list on the right, Word adds a corresponding button to the toolbar.

FIGURE 6–6
Word Options
dialog box

Quick Access
Toolbar category

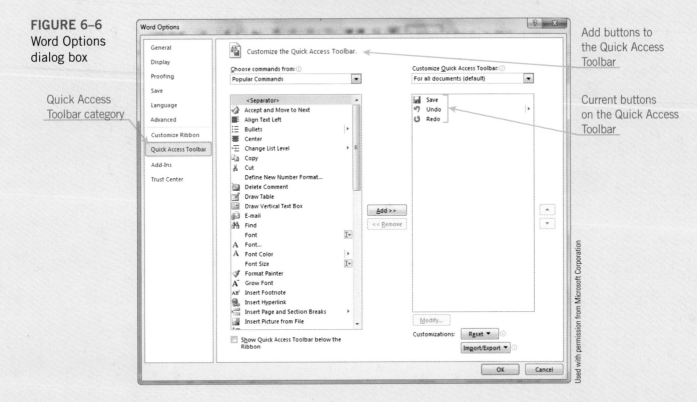

Add buttons to
the Quick Access
Toolbar

Current buttons
on the Quick Access
Toolbar

Used with permission from Microsoft Corporation

5. Review the options in the list of commands on the left, and then click **E-mail** (see **Figure 6–7**).

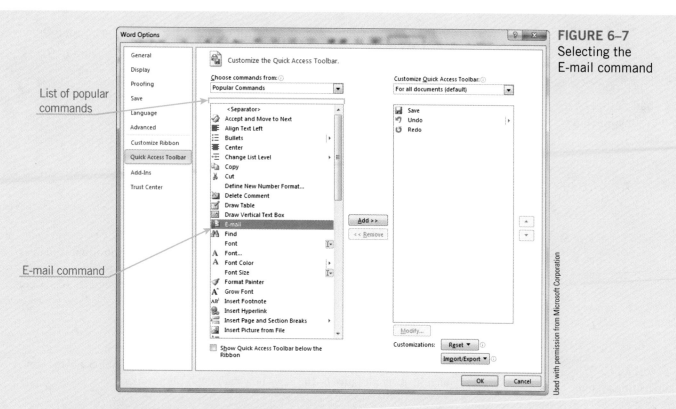

FIGURE 6–7
Selecting the
E-mail command

List of popular
commands

E-mail command

6. Click the **Add** button to add the E-mail command to the Customize
   Quick Access Toolbar list (see **Figure 6–8**).

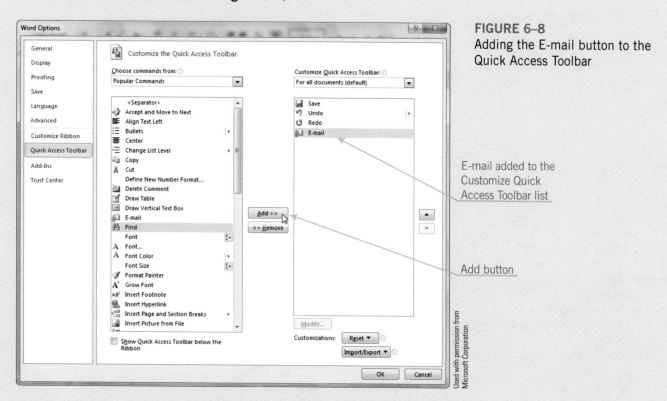

FIGURE 6–8
Adding the E-mail button to the
Quick Access Toolbar

E-mail added to the
Customize Quick
Access Toolbar list

Add button

7. Click the **OK** button to add the command to the toolbar. Your Quick Access Toolbar may have fewer or additional icons (see **Figure 6–9**).

FIGURE 6–9
E-mail button on the Quick Access Toolbar

E-mail button

8. Close all open windows.

System Software

System software is a group of programs that coordinate and control the resources and operations of a computer system. System software enables the many components of the computer system to communicate. There are three categories of system software: operating systems, utilities, and language translators.

Operating Systems

▶ **VOCABULARY**
operating system

Operating systems provide an interface between the user or application and the computer hardware. **Figure 6–10** shows how the relationship works.

FIGURE 6–10   Operating system: Interface between users and computers

ABOVE AND BEYOND

The history of Apple Computer and its founders, Steve Jobs and Steve Wozniak, is a fascinating story. For an overview, check out *http://inventors.about.com/od/cstartinventions/a/Apple_Computers.htm.*

As an interface between you and the hardware, an operating system contains drivers that communicate with the hardware and provides a graphical user interface (GUI) you use to control the computer. An operating system also communicates with applications. A sophisticated operating system such as Microsoft Windows, Mac OS, or Linux includes built-in applications that often include games, basic graphics editors, and e-mail software. Operating systems also communicate with other, more complex applications that are not part of the operating system itself, such as word processors, spreadsheets, and multimedia players. The operating system provides a consistent way for applications to interact with the hardware without having to know all the details of the device or driver.

Utilities and Language Translators

Utilities are programs that help to maintain computer hardware or other software, and usually perform a single task. For example, the disk defragmenting tool used in Lesson 4 is a utility. A language translator, or compiler, is a program that translates computer code written by a programmer into an executable program.

Identifying Options for Software Distribution

1-2.1.3

Software and software licensing options are available through a variety of alternatives and distribution methods; these include single copies for installation on a single-user computer, network versions, and Internet options.

Software Licensing

When you purchase a software program, you are not just purchasing the software—you are purchasing a *software license* that gives you permission to use the program. This *single-user license* gives you the right to install the software on a single computer.

Many companies, government organizations, and educational institutions purchase a *network license*. This type of license gives the organization the right to install a program on a server that can be accessed by a specific number of computers. Some of the benefits include the following:

- If the company purchases a network license instead of multiple single-user copies, the cost per user is lower.

- Most network licenses are offered in five-user increments. Generally the range is from five users to any multiple of five users. Usually, additional licenses can be added at any time.

- Ready-to-use installations can be set up rapidly.

- Standardizing software makes it easier to support.

Software as a Service (SaaS), typically pronounced "sass," is a recently developed software delivery method where an application is licensed for use as a service. The software is provided to customers on demand through the Internet, an intranet, or another network. The demand for SaaS is managed by a company known as an application service provider (ASP). This delivery method provides a more cost-effective alternative than traditional packaged applications. In most instances, you access the product by logging on to the site. SaaS is one of the fastest growing segments of the information technology (IT) industry. Examples of SaaS include Google Docs and Salesforce.com, which is software for tracking sales and customers.

Updating and Upgrading Software

Software development is a continuous process of updating. Users of the program often encounter errors or other problems within the software or discover that some hardware devices may not work properly with the software. When this happens, the software is updated. In most instances, users who purchased the original version of the software can download a fix for the problem. These fixes are called a *patch*, an *update*, or a *service pack*. A software patch is applied over software that you already have installed. An update is a collection of files for revising released software to fix bugs or provide enhancements. A service pack is a collection of updates, fixes, or enhancements to a software program delivered as a single file. Revised versions of software that require patches or updates generally are indicated with numbers such as 1.1 or 1.2 if the modifications are minor.

Some companies also make major improvements to upgrade and modify some of the software's features. This refers to the replacement of a product with a newer version of that same product. In most instances, the modifications generally involve radical changes, so the numbers may be changed to a higher number such as 2.0. *Upgrades* are revised versions of a software program and require the purchase of a newer version of the software.

VOCABULARY

software license

single-user license

network license

Software as a Service (SaaS)

patch

update

service pack

upgrade

ABOVE AND BEYOND

A single-user software license is also called an end user license agreement (EULA). The EULA usually appears as you install the software and gives you the option of accepting or rejecting the agreement. If you accept, you can continue to install the software. If you reject the agreement, the installation does not continue.

Generally, you can download updates and instructions free of charge. Once downloaded, follow the instructions to update the software. Upgrades, on the other hand, might be available for downloading after purchase. Large program upgrades, such as for Microsoft Office, also might be available on DVDs.

More applications are migrating to the Web. These **Web applications** have no installation requirements, can be used on all operating systems, and are accessed through a Web browser over a network such as an intranet or the Internet. Web applications include Web-based e-mail, online calendars, personal information managers, and photo sharing (see **Figure 6–11**). These applications generally are updated online by the company or owner.

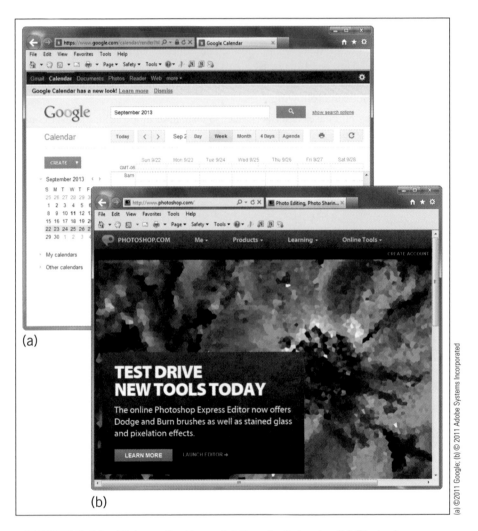

FIGURE 6–11   Web applications: (a) Google Calendar (b) Photoshop.com

In Step-by-Step 6.2, you learn how to access Windows Update information, which provides updates for the Windows operating system. Complete Step-by-Step 6.2 to learn how to apply updates.

Step-by-Step 6.2

1. Click the **Start** button 🌀 on the taskbar, and then click **Help and Support** to open the Windows Help and Support window.

2. In the Search Help box, type **Windows Updates** (see **Figure 6–12**).

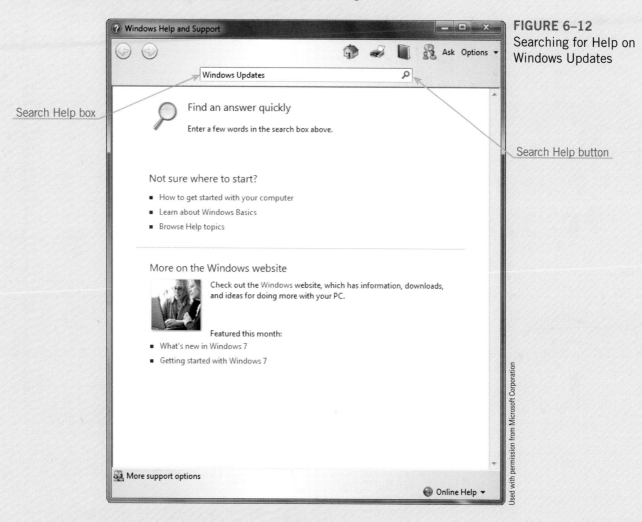

Search Help box

Search Help button

FIGURE 6–12
Searching for Help on Windows Updates

3. Click the **Search Help** button to display the results, and then point to the *Updating your computer* link (see **Figure 6–13**). Your results may differ.

FIGURE 6–13
Results of searching for "Windows Updates"

Updating your computer link

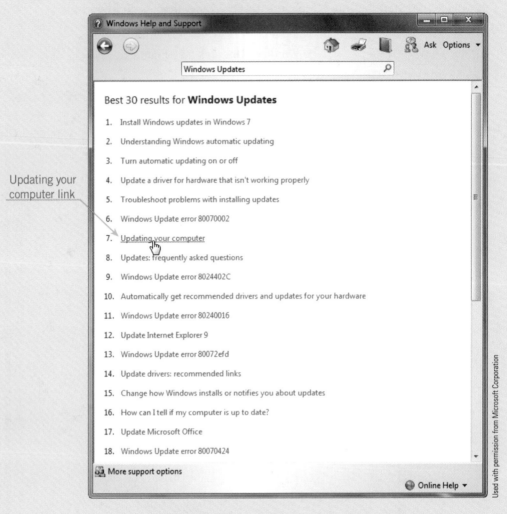

4. Click the **Updating your computer** link to display the Updating your computer page (see **Figure 6–14**).

FIGURE 6–14
Updating your computer page

Updating your computer page

General topics about updating Windows

5. Read the information and then click each of the links to the four general topics about updating Windows (**How can I tell if my computer is up to date?**, **Install Windows updates in Windows 7**, **Get security updates for Windows**, and **Understanding Windows automatic updating**).

6. Using your word-processing program, write a paragraph summarizing the information contained in each of the four general topics.

7. Close all open windows.

Alternative Methods of Software Distribution

Several other methods of software distribution are available. They include the following:

- *Open source*: One or more programmers create a program and make it available to the general public for use without cost; the source code can be modified and redistributed to the software user/developer community.

- *Freeware*: This is copyrighted software given away for free by the author. The author, however, retains the copyright. Code cannot be changed unless it is expressly allowed by the author.

- *Shareware*: This software, often downloadable from the Internet, is usually made available on a trial basis. Most shareware is free for an evaluation period but requires payment if you continue to use it after that.

- *Software bundled with hardware purchases*: Also called **bundleware,** this software is included with the purchase of a new computer.

▶ **VOCABULARY**
bundleware

software piracy

For individual or personal computers, it is the responsibility of the user to verify and use only legitimately licensed software. A network manager's responsibilities are somewhat more extensive. They must verify that the product is used and distributed within the terms of the license and that licensing and maintenance fees are maintained.

As indicated previously, most commercially marketed software is copyrighted. ***Software piracy*** is the unauthorized copying of software. Originally, many software companies attempted to stop the piracy by copy-protecting their software. They soon discovered, however, that this strategy was not foolproof and that software piracy is almost impossible to stop. Many software companies now require some sort of registration that generally includes a license number. This strategy works somewhat, but is not perfect and does not completely stop software piracy.

TECHNOLOGY CAREERS

Software Developer

A software developer maintains and helps develop new application and system software. When you see a software developer job listing, it could include many requirements. A company may be looking for someone to develop software using a particular programming language such as Java, Visual Basic, C, or C++, or a company may be looking for someone to develop add-ons to operating systems programs. This could include enhancements to utility programs, updates to language translators, or new additions to the operating system itself. Many companies seek employees with skills in operating systems such as UNIX and Windows 7.

If you go online to look for software developer jobs, you will find that many of them refer to Oracle, a large information technology software company. Oracle products support database technology, data design and modeling, Web applications, and much more. Salaries and educational requirements for software developers vary significantly. Educational requirements range from some college to a bachelor's or master's degree, sometimes even a Ph.D. Generally, but not always, the more education you have, the higher your starting salary. Most companies require some experience, but a few have entry-level positions.

SUMMARY

In this lesson, you learned:

- Hardware refers to anything you can touch, including objects such as the keyboard, mouse, monitor, printer, chips, disk drives, and CD/DVD recorders. Inputting refers to using an input device to enter data.

- Software is programming code written to provide instructions to the hardware so that you can perform specific tasks. Using input devices, you interact with the software by typing commands, selecting an option from a menu, or clicking a button, for example.

- Hardware and software interact as a computer processes data.

- A computer processes data by applying rules called algorithms, which are sets of clearly defined, logical steps that solve a problem.

- Software development usually begins when someone recognizes a need to perform a task more effectively using a computer. The programmer breaks down the task into an algorithm that covers all the actions needed to perform the task. The programmer often works out the logic for the steps in the algorithm by using a flowchart that shows different paths the program will take depending on what data is inputted.

- The programmer writes the steps in a computer programming language or code that uses a formal set of terms and syntax, or rules for how the words are used together. The computer translates the code into language it can understand, and uses the translated commands to execute the program.

- Software development also requires quality control, which involves running systematic tests, debugging (finding and correcting errors in the code), and beta testing.

- The two types of software are application software and system software. Application software helps you perform a specific task. System software refers to the operating system and all utility programs that manage computer resources.

- Operating systems provide an interface between the user or application and the computer hardware.

- When you purchase software, you are purchasing a license that gives you permission to use the program. A single-user license gives you the right to install the software on a single computer. Organizations using networks can purchase network licenses.

◼ LESSON REVIEW

TRUE / FALSE

Circle T if the statement is true or F if the statement is false.

T   F   **1.**   Freeware is copyrighted software.

T   F   **2.**   Web-based e-mail is considered a type of Web application.

T   F   **3.**   Most computers do not need operating system software.

T   F   **4.**   Application software also is called productivity software.

T   F   **5.**   Technology has not changed much in the past 50 years.

MULTIPLE CHOICE

Select the best response for the following statements.

1. _____ is the process of using an input device to enter data.

   A.   Outputting   C.   Inputting

   B.   Revising   D.   Interacting

2. Web applications are _____.

   A.   upgrades   C.   programs that run on any operating system

   B.   productivity applications   D.   all of the above

3. A computer processes data by applying rules called _____.

   A.   networks   C.   hardware

   B.   applications   D.   algorithms

4. When you purchase software, you are purchasing _____.

   A.   a flowchart   C.   a language translator

   B.   a license   D.   the user interface

5. SaaS is licensed for use as a(n) _____.

   A.   upgrade   C.   service

   B.   patch   D.   all of the above

FILL IN THE BLANK

Complete the following sentences by writing the correct word or words in the blanks provided.

1. Software _____ requires quality control.

2. A(n) _____ is used to show different paths a computer program can take.

3. _____ is programming code.

4. Software _____ is the unauthorized copying of software.

5. Software _____ are revised versions of an existing software program.

■ PROJECTS

PROJECT 6–1

Operating systems can be classified as follows: multiuser, multi-processing, multitasking, multithreading, and real-time. Use the Internet to find information regarding these types of operating systems. Then complete the following list by writing a sentence or two describing each type.

- Multiuser:
- Multiprocessing:
- Multitasking:
- Multithreading:
- Real-time:

PROJECT 6–2

Webopedia provides a complete overview of an operating system. Access this Web site located at *www.webopedia.com/TERM/O/operating_system.html*. Review the information and then write a summary about operating systems, using your Webopedia research and the information contained in your textbook.

PROJECT 6–3

You are part of a team writing the program for an interactive children's game. The object of the game is similar to the poem Jack and Jill. (See *www.poetryfoundation.org/poem/176353* for the complete text.) Your part is to develop the basic flowchart or algorithm for the poem. Complete the following:

1. Identify the steps in the poem.

2. Using the algorithm shown in Figure 6–3 or the flowchart shown in Figure 6–4, write or sketch the steps of the poem.

⬙ TEAMWORK PROJECT

You and two team members have been asked to create a proposal to purchase equipment for a new computer lab for your classroom. Your job is to determine the operating system, the distribution method you will use for software access, and the minimum number of applications you need to accomplish the goals of your computer literacy course. Describe the operating system you will use and explain why your team selected it. Research the distribution method and applications you need, and then organize your findings into a one-page report and a presentation to present to your class.

■ CRITICAL THINKING

As mentioned in this lesson, software piracy is the unauthorized copying of software. Assume that your responsibility is to protect your organization from software piracy. Access the Microsoft Protect Yourself from Piracy Web site at *www.microsoft.com/piracy* and the Webopedia software piracy definition page at *www.webopedia.com/TERM/S/software_piracy.html*. Review the information contained on both of these sites, and then write a report describing these terms: *copy-protecting, shareware, OEM unbundling, counterfeit software,* and *Certificate of Authenticity (COA)*. Describe the approach you would use to protect your organization's software.

■ ONLINE DISCOVERY

Open source, freeware, and shareware are three categories of software described in this lesson. Complete the following:

1. Use the Internet and Web sites such as *download.cnet.com, directory.fsf.org,* and *freewarefiles.com* to find a minimum of two examples of software in each category.

2. Use your word processing program and create a table listing the name of the software program, the Web site address, a short description, and the software category.

■ JOB SKILLS

Computer software engineer is one of the occupations projected to grow the fastest and add the most new jobs during the current decade. You are considering a career as a software engineer and want to learn more about this profession. Using the Internet and other resources, prepare a report of at least one page describing the level of skill and educational requirements required for this type of career. Use a minimum of three Web sites.

LESSON 7

Software Fundamentals

■ OBJECTIVES

Upon completion of this lesson, you should be able to:

- Use word-processing software.
- Work with spreadsheet software.
- Work with presentation software.
- Use database software.
- Work with graphics and multimedia software.
- Use other types of software, including education, entertainment, utility, and miscellaneous programs.
- Select the right software for the task.
- Integrate software.

■ DATA FILES

You do not need data files to complete this lesson.

■ WORDS TO KNOW

bitmapped graphics

cell

database

datasheet

field

multimedia

object

object linking and embedding (OLE)

presentation software

primary key

query

record

table

text editor

utility program

vector graphics

word-processing software

workbook

worksheet

As you learned in Lesson 6, software is divided into two classes: system software and application software. System software consists of low-level programs that interact with the computer at a basic level. Lesson 8 covers system software in detail. Application software (also called end-user software) includes programs such as databases, presentation software, spreadsheets, and word processors. Symbolically speaking, application software sits on top of system software because it cannot run without the operating system and system utilities.

You can purchase application software as individual programs or as a suite. Software suites are groups of related programs that interact nearly seamlessly with each other to make certain tasks easier. A suite generally contains the following four types of programs: word processing, spreadsheet, presentation, and database. Some of the more popular suites are Apple iWork, Corel WordPerfect Office, Google Docs, Microsoft Office, Microsoft Works, and Oracle OpenOffice. Some suites, however, do not include a database program, while others contain add-ons such as Talk (instant messaging) and Calendar (appointment tracking), both part of Google Docs.

1-2.2.1

▶ **VOCABULARY**

word-processing software

Using Word-Processing Software

Word-processing software is a widely used type of application. Primarily, you use this software to create, edit, and print documents and then save them electronically. When creating a document, you easily can correct errors and modify data. In most word-processing programs, you can save the document in a variety of formats including a template, Rich Text Format, plain text format, and as files compatible with earlier versions of the program.

Microsoft Word (see **Figure 7–1**), a word-processing program, includes basic and sophisticated features for creating, editing, formatting, and producing documents. For example, it includes collaboration features that allow you to track the changes made by multiple users. Reviewers can insert their comments within a document. These features are very useful, particularly when two or more people are working on the same project or when instructors need to comment on a student's work.

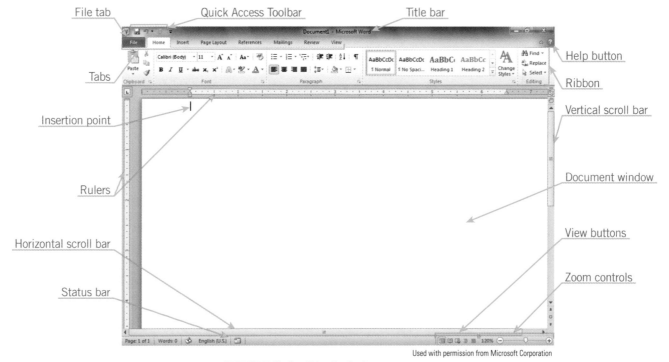

Used with permission from Microsoft Corporation

FIGURE 7–1   Word window

Figure 7–1 shows a blank document opened in Microsoft Word. The following list describes the features displayed in this figure.

■ *Document window*: Area where you type and work with a document.

■ *Help button*: Opens a new window where you can select or search for Help topics.

■ *Horizontal scroll bar*: Moves the page left and right if the page is too wide to fit in the document window.

■ *File tab*: Opens Backstage view, which contains commands tasks such as opening, saving, and printing documents.

■ *Insertion point*: Indicates where characters are entered when you type.

■ *Quick Access Toolbar*: Located in the title bar and contains a repository of the most-used functions; fully customizable.

■ *Ribbon*: Panels that contain command buttons and icons.

■ *Rulers*: Show the positioning of text, tabs, margins, insertion point, and any other elements on the page.

■ *Status bar*: Displays the number of the current page and the total number of pages in the document; also indicates the on/off status of Word features such as spelling and grammar checking.

■ *Title bar*: Displays the name of the program and the name of the document on which you are working; the default name of a document is DocumentX, where X is a number.

■ *Vertical scroll bar*: Moves the page up and down if the page is too long to fit in the document window.

■ *View buttons*: Switch among the following views: Print Layout, Full Screen Reading, Web Layout, Outline, and Draft.

■ *Zoom controls*: Change the magnification of the document so it appears larger or smaller in the document window.

The following basic features in word-processing programs automate the process of creating and editing professional-quality documents:

■ *Accessibility*: Use keyboard shortcuts, size, zoom, color, and sound options.

■ *Copy and paste*: Select and then duplicate a section of text.

■ *Cut and paste*: Select and cut (delete) a segment of text from one place in a document and then insert or paste it somewhere else within the same document or within another document.

■ *Delete*: Select and then delete characters, words, lines, or pages of text.

■ *File management*: Access options so you can create, delete, move, save, and search for files.

■ *Font selection*: Apply font size, font type, color, italics, underline, and bold properties to the text.

■ *Graphics*: Insert pictures, clip art, shapes, SmartArt, WordArt, and other graphical objects.

■ *Page size and size margins*: Define various page sizes and margins; text is readjusted to fit the page.

■ *Print*: Send a document to a printer to produce a hard copy.

■ *Search and replace*: Search for a particular word or phrase; use replace to substitute a character, word or longer text for specified text within the document.

■ *Text insertion*: Insert text anywhere in the document; the inserted text can be copied from another word-processing document, an e-mail message, a Web page, or other document type.

ABOVE AND BEYOND

If your desktop contains a Word icon or an icon for another Microsoft Office program, you can double-click the icon to start the program.

WARNING

As you work in a document, it is a good idea to save it regularly to prevent losing data.

■ *Word wrap*: Automatically moves the insertion point to the next line when one line is filled with text; the text is readjusted if the margins are changed.

Word processors that support these basic features generally are called ***text editors***, whereas word-processing programs that are more robust support additional features. Some of these more advanced features are as follows:

▶ **VOCABULARY**
text editor

■ *Blogs*: Publish blogs directly from the word-processing program.

■ *Footnotes*: Automate the numbering and placement of footnotes.

■ *Headers and footers*: Specify custom text and graphics at the top and bottom of a page.

■ *Macros*: Save a series of keystrokes that represent a series of commands.

■ *Merge*: Merge text from one file into another; useful for generating documents such as mailing labels and then merging them with a form letter.

■ *Page numbering*: Number pages in the format and position you specify.

■ *Reference tools*: Access reference tools such as a spell checker, dictionary, thesaurus, and language translator.

■ *Windows*: Display and edit two or more documents on the same screen.

■ *WYSIWYG*: Work with the document on the screen as it will look when printed; stands for "what you see is what you get".

Microsoft Word also provides other options that you can adjust and configure to suit your working style. You can display these options by clicking the File tab and then clicking the Options button in the left pane. **Figure 7–2** shows an example of options you can modify through the Word Options dialog box. In this figure, the Proofing category is selected.

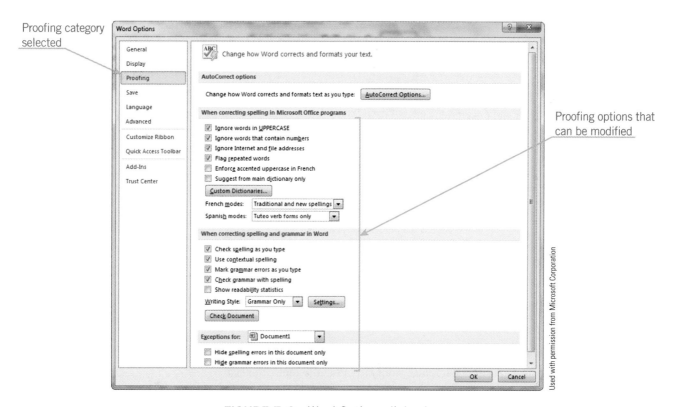

FIGURE 7–2   Word Options dialog box

Working with Spreadsheet Software

A *spreadsheet* is a row-and-column arrangement of data. You use electronic spreadsheet software such as Microsoft Excel to evaluate, calculate, manipulate, analyze, and present numeric data. Calculations are updated automatically, which makes this type of software very effective for tasks such as preparing budgets, financial statements, payrolls, and sales reports, and for managing orders and inventory. You also can use spreadsheet software to make forecasts and identify trends.

A spreadsheet (see **Figure 7–3**) looks much like a page from a financial journal. It is a grid with columns and rows that can contain text, formulas, and numbers (values). This grid in Excel is referred to as a *worksheet*. The terms spreadsheet and worksheet are used interchangeably. When you start Excel, you open a file called a *workbook*. Each new workbook comes with three worksheets, like pages in a document.

1-2.2.2

▶ VOCABULARY

spreadsheet

worksheet

workbook

cell

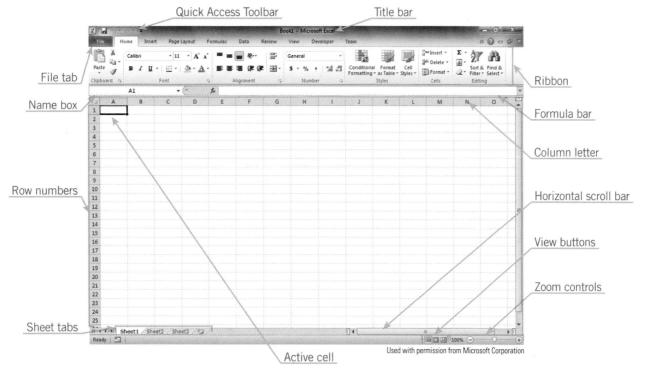

FIGURE 7–3   Excel window

As shown in Figure 7–3, the columns are identified by letters and the rows are identified by numbers. The point at which a column and a row intersect or meet is called a *cell*. Each cell has a name, called the cell reference (or cell address), which is represented by the column letter and the row number. For example, the first cell in a worksheet is cell A1. It is located in column A and row 1. The active cell is the cell where you are working and is surrounded by a thick border. Note that cell A1 is the active cell in Figure 7–3 (as indicated in the Name box) and that 25 rows and the columns A through O are displayed. Some worksheets, however, contain thousands of columns and over a million rows; therefore only a small portion of the worksheet is displayed at one time. Individual worksheets are stored within a workbook. By default, a workbook contains three worksheets named Sheet1, Sheet2, and Sheet3, as shown on the sheet tabs at the bottom of the window. (Sheet is another word for worksheet.)

The basic features supported by most spreadsheet programs are as follows; many of these features are the same as or similar to those contained in word-processing programs:

- *Accessibility*: Use keyboard shortcuts, size, zoom, color, and sound options.
- *Copy and paste*: Select and then duplicate a section of text, formula, number, or other data. When a number or formula is copied from one cell and then pasted into a new cell, the spreadsheet program automatically readjusts the formula based on the new location.
- *Cut and paste*: Select and cut (delete) a segment of text, a number, formula, or other data and then paste (insert) it somewhere else within the same document or another document. If a formula is part of the selection, it is readjusted to apply to the new location.
- *Data filtering*: Locate certain records in a spreadsheet based on selected criteria and then display those selected records.
- *Delete*: Select and then delete numbers, text, formulas, charts, and so on.
- *File management*: Create, delete, move, save, and search for files.
- *Font selection*: Apply font size, font type, color, italics, underline, and bold properties to the data.
- *Formulas*: Use a variety of formulas and functions, including AutoSum, Financial, Logical, Math and Trig, and Statistical functions.
- *Graphics*: Insert illustrations, images, SmartArt diagrams, symbols, special characters, and a variety of graph types into the spreadsheet.
- *Headers and footers*: Specify custom text at the top and bottom of a page.
- *Data entry*: Insert data anywhere in the spreadsheet; the inserted data can be copied from another spreadsheet, an e-mail message, a Web page, or other document type.
- *Macros*: Save a series of keystrokes that represent a series of commands.
- *Merge*: Merge a selection of cells or split merged cells; you can also merge copies of a shared worksheet.
- *Page numbering*: Number pages in the format and position you specify.
- *Print*: Send a document to a printer to produce a hard copy of the worksheet or of the worksheet and chart.
- *Search and replace*: Search for a particular word, phrase, value, formula, and so on; use replace to substitute new data, text, or formulas for others within the document.
- *Reference and editing tools*: Use a variety of built-in editing tools such as a spell checker, thesaurus, grammar checker, and translation tools.
- *Windows*: Display and edit two or more worksheets on the same screen.

The appearance of the spreadsheet is almost as important as the accuracy of the data it contains. You can use formatting to emphasize entries, create a more professional look, and make the information easier to read and understand. In **Figure 7–4**, you can see how graphics and formatting called cell styles can affect the appearance of the data.

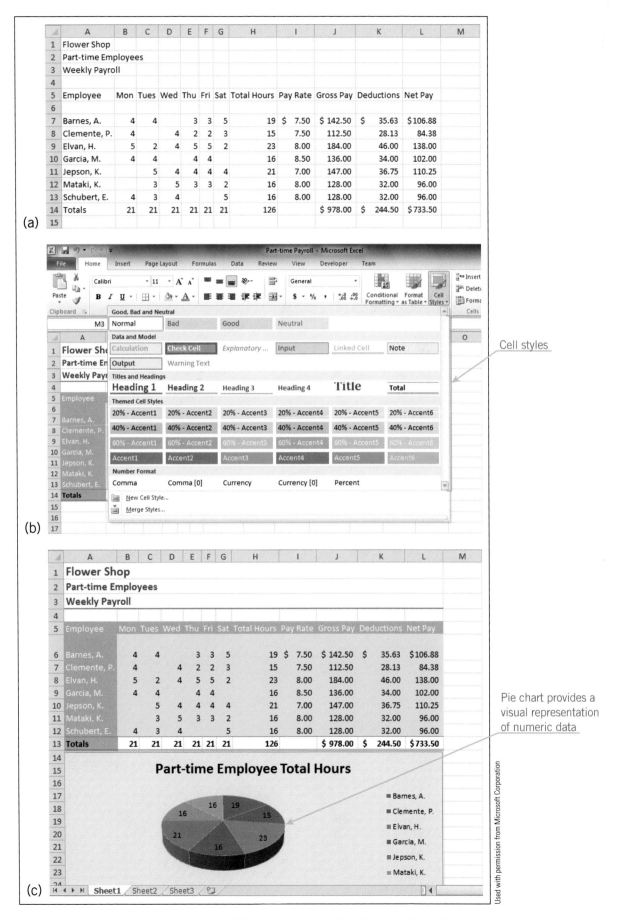

(a)

(b)

(c)

FIGURE 7–4   (a) Unformatted data (b) Cell styles applied (c) Graphic added

In Step-by-Step 7.1, you start Excel and review the commands contained on the Page Layout tab of the Excel Ribbon.

Step-by-Step 7.1

1. Start Excel by clicking the **Start** button 🔵 on the taskbar, pointing to *All Programs*, clicking **Microsoft Office**, and then clicking **Microsoft Excel 2010**.

2. Click the **Page Layout** tab on the Ribbon (see **Figure 7–5**).

FIGURE 7–5
Excel Page
Layout tab

Page Layout tab

3. Review the groups on the Page Layout tab: Themes, Page Setup, Scale to Fit, Sheet Options, and Arrange. Click the buttons in each group and use your word-processing program to summarize the purpose of each button. Submit your summary to your instructor.

4. Close all open windows.

1-2.2.3

▶ **VOCABULARY**
presentation software

Working with Presentation Software

Presentation software is a computer program you use to organize and present information, normally in the form of a slide show. Through the use of sequential slides enhanced with a variety of special effects such as animation, text, graphics, and other features, a presentation is an effective and professional way to communicate topics and ideas. In addition, presentation software provides options for generating notes for the presenter and handouts for the audience. Equipment requirements for the presentation include a projector and computer. Microsoft PowerPoint is the presentation program in the Microsoft Office suite (see **Figure 7–6**).

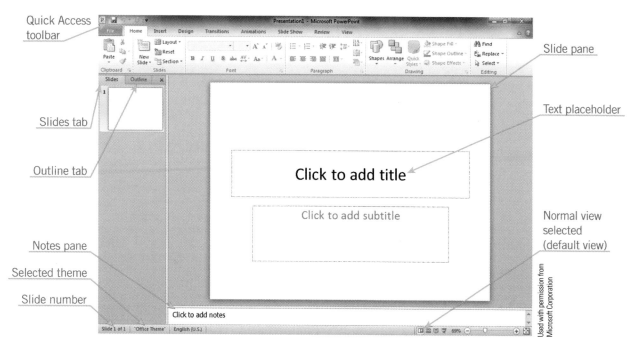

Quick Access toolbar

Slide pane

Text placeholder

Slides tab

Outline tab

Normal view selected (default view)

Notes pane

Selected theme

Slide number

Used with permission from Microsoft Corporation

FIGURE 7–6   PowerPoint window

Besides being excellent for creating on-screen shows, presentation software is also useful in the following scenarios:

- *Self-running presentation*: Job fairs, demonstrations, and conventions are a few examples of where you might see a self-running presentation. When the presentation is completed, it automatically restarts.

- *Presentation broadcasting*: You can use the Web to broadcast your presentation to locations all over the world.

- *Overhead transparencies*: If you do not have access to a computer and projector for your presentation, you can create and print black-and-white or color transparencies. This requires using plastic transparency sheets in your printer.

- *Audience handouts*: Printed handouts support your presentation. Smaller versions of your slides can be printed two, three, six, or nine to a page.

- *PDF document*: Portable Document Format (PDF) is a common format for sharing documents online and through other channels.

Several software companies produce presentation graphics programs. Other than Microsoft PowerPoint—both Macintosh and Windows versions—popular presentation software includes Corel Presentations and OpenOffice.org Impress.

Microsoft PowerPoint comes with a variety of designs, called themes, which you can apply to a presentation. A theme is a predesigned set of fonts, colors, lines, fill effects, and other formatting. PowerPoint also provides transitions, which are animated effects that play between slides. In Step-by-Step 7.2, you start PowerPoint and then review the themes and transitions.

Step-by-Step 7.2

1. Start PowerPoint by clicking the **Start** button 🔘 on the taskbar, pointing to *All Programs*, clicking **Microsoft Office**, and then clicking **Microsoft PowerPoint 2010**.

2. Click the **Design** tab on the Ribbon (see **Figure 7–7**).

FIGURE 7–7
PowerPoint Design tab

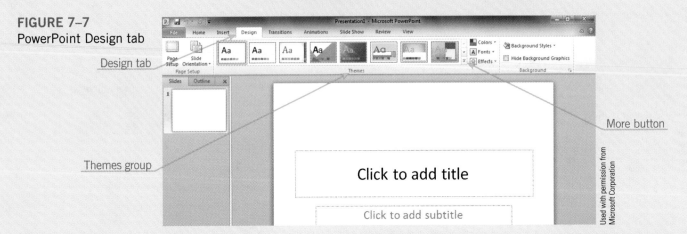

3. Move the mouse pointer over each theme in the Themes group to display a preview and the name of the theme. Click the **More** button to display additional themes in the Themes gallery (see **Figure 7–8**). Click a theme to apply it to the slide.

FIGURE 7–8
Displaying the Themes gallery

4. Click the **Transitions** tab. Click each of the animated transitions in the Transition to This Slide group to play a preview of the transitions.

5. Click the **More** button in the Transition to This Slide group to display the Transitions gallery.

6. Suppose you need to create a presentation about software fundamentals. Use your word-processing program to answer the following questions:

   a. Which theme would you select for the presentation and why?

   b. Which transition would you use and why?

   c. Would you use the same design and transition on each slide? Why or why not?

   d. Submit your assignment to your instructor.

7. Close all open windows.

Effective Presentation Guidelines

You can use graphics, transitions, and other tools to make any presentation more effective and interesting. However, be cautious! Presentation programs contain many features and options, so it is sometimes difficult to avoid getting carried away. Often, the first-time user is tempted to add distracting sounds, animations, and excessive clip art to each slide. Before you create a presentation, therefore, you need to plan and outline the message that you want to communicate. As you develop the outline for your presentation, consider your audience and determine the presentation's purpose, the location in which it will be given, and the equipment you will need.

> **QUICK TIP**
>
> Use photos, clip art, and graphics instead of words for a more powerful presentation.

Follow these guidelines to create an effective presentation:

- Cover one topic per slide.
- Keep the text simple—use the "6 by 6 rule," which is six lines of text, six words per line.
- Use no more than 50 words per slide, including titles and subtitles.

TECHNOLOGY CAREERS

Presentation Expert

Presentations are an organization's most direct communication effort. A good presentation can make a sale, while a bad presentation can prevent a company from landing a contract. As presentations are becoming commonplace, companies are beginning to emphasize the importance of this media.

A growing trend in large companies is to hire a presentation expert to oversee the creation and delivery of presentations within the organization. Depending on the size of the company and the number of presentations required, this person might work alone or as part of a media department. The media department generally functions as a service bureau for the rest of the company. Presentation managers might also be responsible for design. They must stay updated and aware of technological advances in the areas of multimedia. This position often requires additional professional education, such as workshops, conferences, and classes.

Many large companies have a standard set of master slides and templates. All employees are expected to use these standards. The presentation manager might be responsible for creating the masters and templates, and might even be responsible for teaching physical presentation delivery skills or coaching frequent speakers.

Because there are no certifications or degrees for presentation managers, many people employed in this field have graphics design or Web design backgrounds. They might have a four-year degree in a related field such as communications, a two-year degree in design, or a certification that includes design and computer application skills.

MODULE 1   Computing Fundamentals

- Do not clutter your slide with large paragraphs displayed in a small font size. Use short comments and fill in the details orally.

- Use bullets, not numbers, unless providing specific step-by-step instructions. Bullets indicate no significant order, while numbers indicate rank or sequence.

- Use readable typefaces and fonts, such as those provided in PowerPoint themes.

- Choose color carefully.

- Use simple tables to present numbers.

- Add clip art sparingly and only where appropriate.

- Do not try to dazzle your audience with an overabundance of graphics, sound, transitions, and other effects.

1-2.2.4

Using Database Software

Effective information management is the core of a successful business and is important in your personal life. Data is unorganized text, graphics, sound, or video. Information is data that has been organized and processed so that it is meaningful and useful. Most people need a method to store data and convert it into accurate, relevant, and timely information when needed.

Database Software Defined

▶ **VOCABULARY**
database
table

A *database* is a collection of related information organized in a manner that allows for rapid search and retrieval. A database management system (DBMS) is software used to create, maintain, and provide controlled access to data. A table in a database contains the data to organize and is similar to a spreadsheet. Like spreadsheets, database tables are composed of rows and columns. You use both types of software to organize, sort, and calculate data. A database, however, provides additional comprehensive functions for manipulating data. This lesson introduces you to some basic database features for entering, organizing, and reporting data.

Before you begin to design and develop a database, you should do some planning. Consider what data you will include and what information you want to create. After making these decisions, you are ready to begin creating your database.

Database Structure

To use a database program effectively, you first need to understand some basic terminology. In Microsoft Access, a database can consist of one table or a collection of tables. A *table* is composed of columns and rows, referred to as fields and records in Access. **Figure 7–9** shows a sample database table for customers of The Flower Shop. The table is named Customers. The Flower Shop provides wholesale products to florists, so its customers are small flower shop owners or managers.

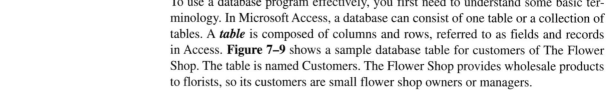

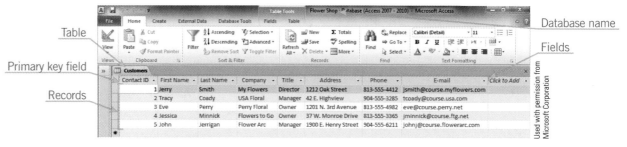

FIGURE 7–9   Records in the Customers table

Parts of the Customers table shown in Figure 7–9 are as follows:

- The rows in the table are called *records*. Each record is a group of related fields, such as all of the information regarding each customer in a customer table.

- The columns in the table are called *fields*. Each field contains a specific piece of information within a record. In the table in Figure 7–9, for example, the Phone field contains the customer's phone number.

- The *primary key*, which is assigned to a field, uniquely identifies each record in a table. It tells the database program how your records are sorted, and it prevents duplicate entries. In Figure 7–9, the primary key is the Contact ID field.

Microsoft Access is one of the most widely used database programs. The Access window is similar to other Microsoft Office 2010 applications in several ways—it displays a title bar, the Ribbon, and a status bar. Unlike Word, Excel, and PowerPoint, however, Access does not have a standard document view. The Access window changes based on the *object* you are using as you work with the database. (An object in Access is a container that you create in the database, such as a table.) Furthermore, many of the Ribbon tabs are unique to Access.

Using the data stored in a table, you can use database software to create queries, forms, and reports. A *query* asks a question about the data stored in the table. The database program searches for and retrieves information from one or more tables to answer the question. You use forms to enter data in a table and reports to print selected data. All of these objects—tables, forms, queries, and reports—are stored in a single file, which is the database.

After you create and save a new database, the next steps are to create fields and then add data to the table. Tables are the primary objects in a database because they contain the data. Most databases contain multiple tables.

Database Tables

Access provides several ways to create a table, including the following:

- Create a new database.
- Add a table to an existing database using the Tables group on the Create tab.
- Create a table by selecting a table template using the Application Parts button in the Templates group on the Create tab.

Creating a table is the first step in a three-step process; adding fields is the second step. The third step is to populate or add records to the table. When editing or adding records to a table, you can create and use a form or use Datasheet view. Views are formats for displaying and working with Access objects. You can display Access tables in the following views.

- *Design view*: Create a table and assign a primary key. Forms, queries, and reports also have a Design view.

- *Datasheet view*: Display a row-and-column view of the data in tables, where you can enter and edit data. A *datasheet* resembles an Excel worksheet. Forms and queries also have a Datasheet view.

When you enter data in a field, it is called an entry. To move from one field to another, you can use the mouse or the keyboard to navigate in the table.

▶ **VOCABULARY**
record
field
primary key
object
query
datasheet

Forms

In addition to adding and viewing records in Datasheet view, you can create and use a data-entry form. A form provides a convenient way to enter and view records in a table. When you create a form, you are adding a new object to the database. You can create a form manually or use the Form Wizard. The wizard asks you questions and formats the form according to your preferences.

Queries

A query enables you to locate records that match specified criteria by providing a way for you to ask a question about the information stored in one or more database tables. The database program searches for and retrieves data from the table(s) to answer your question. Microsoft Access provides four query options:

- *Simple Query Wizard*: Creates a select query from the selected fields
- *Crosstab Query Wizard*: Displays data in a spreadsheet format
- *Find Duplicates Query Wizard*: Locates records with duplicate field values
- *Find Unmatched Query Wizard*: Locates records in one table that have no related records in another table

Suppose, for example, that you want to produce a list of all customers within a specified zip code. When you create a query, you determine what fields you want to display in the query results. Often, you only need to see certain fields in the query results instead of all the fields in the table. In a customer list, for instance, you might want only the customer's last name and the zip code displayed. The order in which you select the fields determines the order in which the information is displayed in the query results.

Reports

Another important feature of database management software is the ability to generate sophisticated reports that show the contents of the database. A report is a database object that allows you to organize, summarize, and print all or a portion of the data in a database. You can create a report based on a table or a query. You can decide what formatting you want to use, such as headings, spacing, and graphics. After the report is generated, you can decide which records you want to include in the report, sort the report, and insert a picture in the report.

Although you can produce a report manually, the Report Wizard, similar to the Form Wizard, provides an easy and fast way to design and create one. The wizard asks questions about which data you want to include in the report and how you want to format the data. An example of a printed report is displayed in **Figure 7–10**.

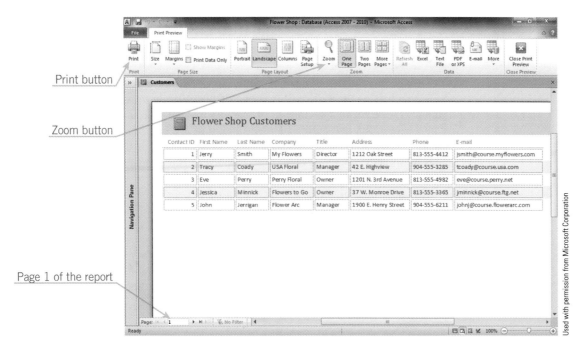

Print button

Zoom button

Page 1 of the report

Used with permission from Microsoft Corporation

FIGURE 7-10   Access report in Print Preview

Online Databases

Entrepreneurs looking to open an online business often want to find an Internet-based database program. Many online databases are dynamic, which means you can change the content frequently.

Using an online database, you can insert new records and modify, delete, and search existing records. You can set up many online databases by uploading a CSV file from Microsoft Excel or Access. A CSV file is a comma-separated value file that can be exported from any spreadsheet or PC database software.

With some online databases, you can create a template for e-mail marketing. Some other features of Web databases are as follows:

- Create and update a contacts list.
- Change photos frequently and update an online catalog.
- Manage and keep your content current.
- Use online documentation.
- Generate formulas and calculated fields to automatically update your data.
- Keep users up to date with the latest information.
- Import and export information easily.

1-2.2.5

Working with Graphics and Multimedia Software

You use graphics and multimedia programs to create and edit images and animation. Most graphics applications fall into one of two main categories: vector or bitmap graphics. A vector image consists of many individual objects, each with properties such as color, fill, and outline. The resolution of a vector image can be adjusted to the highest quality. A bitmap image is composed of pixels in a grid. Each pixel contains information about the color to be displayed. These images have a fixed resolution and cannot be resized without losing image quality.

In addition to graphics such as pictures and photos, media includes audio and video files for playing music and videos. Digital media file types are identified in **Table 7–1**.

TABLE 7–1   Digital media file types

FILE TYPE	MEDIA	DESCRIPTION
FLV	Video	Adobe format for streaming Web video content
GIF	Graphics	Image format for pictures with up to 256 distinct colors
JPG or JPEG	Graphics	Method for compressing graphics files
MOV	Video	File extension for digital video files in QuickTime format
MP3	Audio	Compressed audio format
PNG	Graphics	Bitmapped image format that compresses data
QUICKTIME	Audio and video	Video and audio format that allows for the production of video and multimedia
SWF	Video	Shockwave file format; supports exact positioning of graphical objects
TIF	Graphics	Tagged Image Format; popular among the publishing industry, graphic artists, and photographers for storing images
WAV	Audio	Common audio format

QUICK TIP

Some Web sites offer free clip art that you can download.

Most graphics programs use a variety of tools to create and modify images. The following sections briefly describe types of graphic programs.

Drawing Programs

A drawing program is a graphics program used for creating illustrations. The image is saved in a *vector graphics* format. This allows all individual parts of the picture to be moved, isolated, and scaled independently of the other parts. Because the graphics use mathematical formulas, they can be sized freely without any loss in quality. Resized images will not appear pixelated. Examples of popular drawing programs are Adobe Illustrator and Corel Draw.

Paint Programs

A paint program allows you to simulate painting on the computer through the use of a graphics tablet or a mouse. The images are created with a matrix of picture elements (pixels) and are generated as *bitmapped graphics*. A program called Paint is part of Microsoft Windows. Another popular paint program is Corel Painter. These programs use a variety of tools, such as line, fill, shape, and curve tools (see **Figure 7–11**).

FIGURE 7–11   Image in Paint

Photo/Image Manipulation Programs

You use digital editing software to edit images, photos, and logos. Adobe Photoshop Lightroom is a popular photo management and editing software program (see **Figure 7–12**).

FIGURE 7–12   Photo in Adobe Photoshop Lightroom

Animation Programs

You use animation software to create moving images and 3D graphics. Some of the more popular uses for these programs are online animations and game development. Adobe Flash, 3D Studio Max, and LightWave 3D are examples of this type of software.

Multimedia Programs

Multimedia is defined as the use of text, graphics, audio, and video in some combination to create an effective means of communication and interaction. Some examples of how this software is used are games, interactive presentations, advertisements, screen savers, and interactive books. **Figure 7–13** shows a PowerPoint slide show containing images, video, and sound.

▶ **VOCABULARY**
multimedia

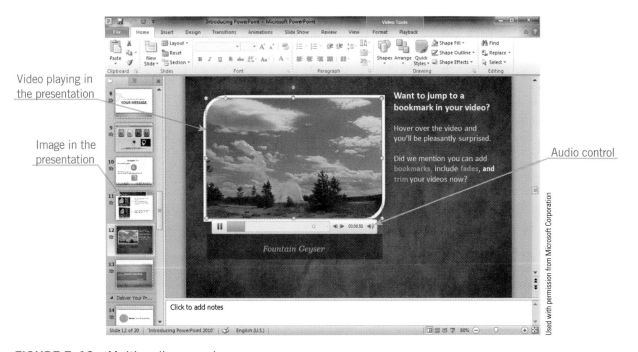

FIGURE 7–13   Multimedia example

Using Other Types of Software

Besides word-processing, spreadsheet, database, and graphics and multimedia software, you can find education and entertainment applications, utility programs, and miscellaneous software such as Web browsers and project management programs. The following sections provide an overview of these types of software.

1-2.2.6

Education and Entertainment Programs

A wide variety of educational programs are available for users of all ages, from 12 months old to adult. Many of these programs are designed to be entertaining as well as educational. The following describes this type of software:

- *Computer-based training (CBT)*: Web-based or computer-based training programs
- *Computer games*: Single-user and multiuser games; combine an educational component with a game format (see **Figure 7–14a**)
- *Audio and video*: Software used to play audio and video; for example, Media Player is audio and video software bundled with Windows
- *Virtual reality*: A technology that lets users interact with a computer-simulated environment (see **Figure 7-14b**)

FIGURE 7–14   (a) Computer game (b) Virtual reality

1-2.2.7

▶ VOCABULARY
utility program

Utility Programs

Utility programs help you perform computer housekeeping chores. You use these programs to complete specialized tasks related to managing the computer's resources, files, and so on. Some utility programs are part of the operating system, and others are self-contained programs. Utility program types include the following:

- *File compression programs*: Compress one or more files to reduce the amount of storage space required. WinZip is a popular file compression program, and Microsoft Windows includes a compression utility.

- *Defragmentation*: Reduce the amount of fragmentation by organizing the contents of the disk to store the pieces of each file contiguously (see **Figure 7–15a**).

- *Antivirus, antiadware, and antispyware programs*: Use these types of software programs to protect against viruses, remove spyware, and prevent adware from playing or downloading advertisements.

- *Backup program*: Create a copy of data on a drive; you should back up your data files on a regular schedule.

- *Single-purpose tools and accessories*: Use widgets or gadgets, mini-applications that provide tools such as a desktop calculator or clock or can access online services or information such as the weather (see **Figure 7–15b**).

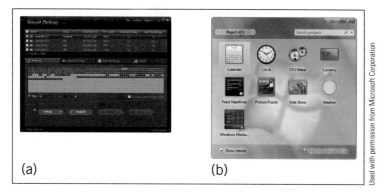

(a)   (b)

FIGURE 7–15   (a) Defragmentation program (b) Windows Gadget gallery

Miscellaneous Software

1-2.2.8

In addition to the programs already described, the following are other types of software:

- *Financial and accounting programs*: Prepare financial statements for stockholders, employees, banks, and owners, for example.

- *Electronic mail*: Send and receive messages on the Internet or through company or individual networks.

- *Chat, messaging, and instant messaging software*: Communicate in real time over the Internet by exchanging text messages.

- *Web browser*: Visit Web sites using programs such as Internet Explorer or Firefox to browse the Web.

- *Computer-aided design (CAD)*: Design houses, buildings, airplanes, and so on; includes the abilities to view a design from any angle and to zoom in and out.

- *Project management*: Plan, organize, and manage resources of the goals and objectives of a specific project.

- *Groupware*: Participate as a member of a workgroup attached to a local area network to organize your activities; also called workgroup productivity software.

- *Web conferencing*: Attend online meetings, share desktop presentations, and use VoIP, whiteboard, and chat, among other features. Popular Web conferencing programs include Adobe Connect Pro, Fuze Meeting, GoToMeeting, and Zoho Meeting.

- *Integrated programs*: Use software such as Microsoft Office or Adobe Design, which contain a collection of programs within a single suite.

- *Specialized software*: Programs such as airline reservation systems, manufacturing-plant automatic/process control, sales force/customer service automation, and school information management are used for specific activities. **Figure 7–16** depicts examples of specialized software.

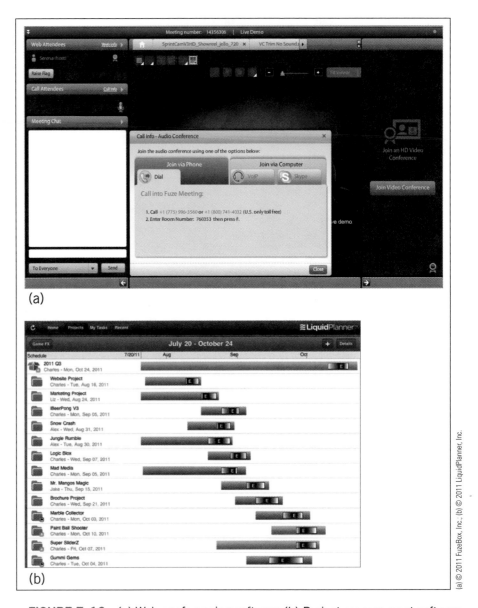

(a)

(b)

FIGURE 7–16   (a) Web conferencing software (b) Project management software

1-2.2.9

Selecting the Right Software for the Task

When selecting a software product for a specific activity, be sure to choose one appropriate for the task. For example, you can create tables using Microsoft Word; however, you also can create tables with a spreadsheet program such as Microsoft Excel or a database program such as Microsoft Access. Identify the end result to determine which program is the most appropriate for creating the table you need.

Another example of incorrectly selecting software is using word-processing software to keep copies of financial records when a spreadsheet or an accounting program would be a better choice.

Integrating Software

As indicated previously, you can use individual programs, such as those in Microsoft Office, to perform common tasks in the workplace, in education, and for personal use. In addition to producing individual documents with these applications, you can integrate data from one program into the other programs. In this context, an object is the data or information that you want to share between the programs. Microsoft Office, for example, provides three methods for inserting objects from one Office document into another Office document: copying and pasting, embedding, and linking. Each method has advantages and disadvantages.

The copy-and-paste process between documents is similar to copying and pasting text or other objects within a single document. Assume that you have a chart or worksheet in Excel and you want to add a copy of it to a Word document. In the Excel document you select and copy the content. Next, you open a Word document, click the location where you want to paste the copied data, and then click the Paste button.

Object linking and embedding (OLE) is a technology developed by Microsoft that lets you create a document or object in one program and then link or embed that data into another program. You can embed or link all or part of an existing file. For example, you can create a form letter using Microsoft Word, link it to an Access database file that contains a list of names and addresses, and then merge the form letter with the names and addresses.

Keeping data current in an embedded object can be difficult if the information changes often. A linked object, on the other hand, retains a connection to the original file, which contains the actual data represented by the linked object. Any changes made to the source file are reflected in the linked object. Assume that you have inserted a linked spreadsheet object into a PowerPoint document. If you modify the spreadsheet data in Excel, the linked spreadsheet object in the PowerPoint document is also modified.

Linking is useful when information is maintained independently. Besides linking objects, you can link an entire file to a file in another program. For example, the Personnel department in a company typically maintains employee records in a database file. Other departments in the company use this data for sending mailings, creating interoffice documents, and so on. A link to the employee records file would verify that the information was current.

Another way to integrate software is to use Internet applications that interact with your desktop or network. Adobe Air applications, for example, can update themselves, exchange items with the system clipboard, use the file system, display native windows and menus, contact a local SQL database, and store encrypted data.

1-2.2.10

QUICK TIP

In addition to embedding and linking Microsoft Office files, you can link a variety of other files, including Adobe and Paint Shop Pro files, video clips, wave sounds, media clips, and others.

▶ **VOCABULARY**
object linking and embedding (OLE)

SUMMARY

In this lesson, you learned:

- You use word-processing software to create, edit, and print documents and then save the documents electronically. When creating a document, you can easily correct errors and modify data.

- A spreadsheet is a row-and-column arrangement of data. You use electronic spreadsheet software to evaluate, calculate, manipulate, analyze, and present numeric data. A spreadsheet updates calculations automatically.

- A database is a collection of related information organized in a manner that provides for rapid search and retrieval. You use database software to create, maintain, and provide controlled access to data.

- A database can consist of one table or a collection of tables, which are composed of columns and rows, and referred to as fields and records. The primary key, which is assigned to a field, uniquely identifies each record in a table. You also can create queries, forms, and reports using database software.

- You use graphics and multimedia programs to create and edit images and animation. Most graphics applications fall into one of two main categories: vector or bitmap graphics.

- Educational and entertainment programs include computer-based training, computer games, audio and video software, and virtual reality software.

- Utility programs help you perform computer housekeeping chores such as managing the computer's resources and files.

- Miscellaneous software includes programs such as e-mail applications, Web browsers, and project management software.

LESSON REVIEW

TRUE / FALSE

Circle T if the statement is true or F if the statement is false.

T   F   **1.**   Word-processing software is ideal for keeping copies of financial records.

T   F   **2.**   Internet Explorer is a Web browser.

T   F   **3.**   In Excel, individual worksheets are stored within a workbook.

T   F   **4.**   Adobe Photoshop Lightroom is a multimedia program.

T   F   **5.**   A database program and a spreadsheet program have the same purpose.

MULTIPLE CHOICE

Select the best response for each of the following statements.

1. Digital editing software is used to edit _____.

   A. images   C. photos

   B. logos   D. all of the above

2. A(n) _____ program creates a copy of data.

   A. backup   C. defrag

   B. utility   D. antiadware

3. _____ software is used to organize and present information in the form of a slideshow.

   A. Spreadsheet   C. Project management

   B. Presentation   D. Groupware

4. A _____ file can be exported from a spreadsheet or database.

   A. CSV   C. CVS

   B. GIF   D. MP3

5. A _____ program contains rows and columns.

   A. multimedia   C. QuickTime

   B. SWF   D. spreadsheet

FILL IN THE BLANK

Complete the following sentences by writing the correct word or words in the blanks provided.

1. Most _____ programs use a variety of tools to create and modify images.

2. A CSV file is a(n) _____ value file that can be exported from any spreadsheet or PC database software.

3. A(n) _____ is composed of columns and rows, referred to as fields and records in Access.

4. _____ software is a computer program you use to organize and present information, usually as a slide show.

5. Columns in a spreadsheet are identified by _____.

■ PROJECTS

PROJECT 7–1

This lesson discussed widgets and gadgets. Complete the following:

2.2.7

1. Use the Internet to research the terms widget and gadget.

2. Locate a minimum of 10 widgets and gadgets. Note the Web addresses of the most useful Web pages.

3. Use your word-processing program to write a short overview of each one. Include the Web site address.

PROJECT 7–2

You can find many graphics programs to suit your needs. Complete the following:

2.2.5

1. Use your favorite search engine to research the topic of graphics programs. Note the Web addresses of the most useful Web pages.

2. Use your word-processing program to list at least five programs, their purpose, and their cost or approximate cost.

3. If you had to select one of these programs to purchase, explain which program you would choose and why. Price is no object.

PROJECT 7–3

This lesson discussed the differences between types of software. Complete the following:

2.2.1
2.2.2
2.2.3
2.2.4

1. Use your word-processing program and create a table with four columns and five rows.

2. Name the columns *Word Processing*, *Spreadsheet*, *Database*, and *Presentation*. Bold the headings.

3. In column 1, list five activities for which you would use a word-processing program; in column 2, list five activities for which you would use a spreadsheet program; in column 3, list five activities for which you would use a database program; and in column 4, list five activities for which you would use a presentation program.

4. Change the text color of the word-processing activities to green, the text color of the spreadsheet activities color to orange, the text color of the database activities to blue, and the text color of the presentation activities to red.

◤ TEAMWORK PROJECT

This lesson discussed specialized software. Interview the technology specialist for your school. Ask questions such as what types of programs are used, how textbooks are ordered, what software is used for class scheduling, how the payroll is handled, what other financial programs are used, and other pertinent topics. As a group, use the answers to the questions to create a presentation to share with your classmates. Integrate a spreadsheet into your presentation that shows the data you used.

2.2.8

■ CRITICAL THINKING

FileMaker Pro, available for both Macintosh and PC, is a database program somewhat similar to Microsoft Access, but does not contain as many advanced features. Instead, it is ideal for small businesses and home users. Use Google or another search engine to research this software and then write a short review of its pros and cons. Explain why and how it is similar to and different from. Also, provide a short overview of FileMaker Pro's reporting and charting capabilities.

 2.2.4

■ ONLINE DISCOVERY

Virtual reality was described in this lesson. One of the online virtual reality Web sites is located in England.

1. Open your browser and then type the Web site address *www .kenmcbride.com/BenCottages/index.html* into the Address bar. Press Enter to display the Benaughlin Cottages Web site located in the United Kingdom. Use the mouse pointer to manipulate and move the screen. Then use your word-processing program to write a minimum 100-word description of this Web site.

2. Use Google or another search engine to look for other virtual reality sites. Locate at least one other site. Then use your word-processing software to list the Web site address and write a short description of the Web site.

 2.2.6

■ JOB SKILLS

People with database development skills and experience with various database programs are in high-demand by employers. Companies of all sizes need skilled professionals to manage everything from planning a new database to managing and supporting existing databases. Use the Internet and research the various database programs, and then list them in a word-processing document. Also research the jobs for database professionals. What skills are necessary for these types of jobs? Is training and certification available? List examples of these training and certification programs.

2.2.4

LESSON 8

Operating Systems

■ OBJECTIVES

Upon completion of this lesson, you should be able to:

- Identify the purpose of an operating system.
- Identify different operating systems.
- Share files on different operating systems.
- Identify user rights.
- Troubleshoot common operating system problems.

■ DATA FILES

You do not need data files to complete this lesson.

■ WORDS TO KNOW

administrative rights

administrator account

driver

embedded operating system

emulation card

file system

handheld operating system

Linux

Mac OS X

operating system (OS)

Palm OS

system administrator

UNIX

Windows Embedded CE

Windows Phone

There are two basic types of software: application software and system software. Fundamental concepts of applications were discussed in detail in Lesson 7. This lesson focuses on system software and how it relates to the operating system and the utility programs that manage computer resources at a low level.

1-3.1.1

Identifying the Purpose of an Operating System

Recall that system software facilitates the use of a computer system. An *operating system (OS)* is system software that enables the computer hardware to communicate and operate with the application software. Without an operating system, a computer cannot function because the operating system manages and coordinates the activities and resources of the computer. For example, operating systems perform jobs such as recognizing input from the keyboard, sending output to the monitor and printer, keeping track of files and directories, and controlling peripheral devices such as the printer, monitor, and keyboard. Manufacturers of peripheral devices, such as printers or monitors, provide programs called *drivers* that the operating system uses to communicate with various hardware devices.

An operating system also manages resources for applications. It provides a consistent way for applications to communicate with hardware so you can print documents on many types of printers, for example. Instead of each application duplicating print settings or learning details about the printer, the operating system handles these tasks. This is why your computer system can use hardware and settings different from another computer, but still reliably run the same applications.

Another way an operating system helps applications is by performing system and file maintenance tasks. For example, the operating system is responsible for such system tasks as preparing the desktop, managing visual and audio effects, handling memory, and maintaining power settings. File maintenance responsibilities are equally important; the operating system controls access to files stored on disks and manages the amount of space the files can use. The way an operating system stores files on disk is called a *file system*. The file system regulates the types of names and other attributes a file can have and organizes the files into folders arranged in a hierarchy, where a main folder can contain subfolders that contain files. The file system allows you to find and retrieve files you store on a computer by keeping track of the files you save and where you save them. The file system also identifies sections of a disk that are not being used.

VOCABULARY
operating system (OS)

driver

file system

QUICK TIP

The Windows and Macintosh operating systems call file containers *folders*, while the UNIX operating system calls them *directories*.

1-3.1.2

Identifying Different Operating Systems

Recall that an operating system provides an interface between the user or application program and the computer hardware. See **Figure 8–1**. The types of operating systems most people use fall into two categories: personal computer operating systems and mobile operating systems.

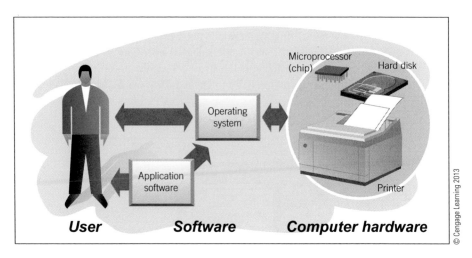

FIGURE 8–1   Operating system

Personal Computer Operating Systems

Several brands and versions of operating system software are available for personal computers. Each is designed to work with one or more particular processors. For example, the Windows operating system is designed to work with an Intel processor or clone. Currently, Microsoft Windows runs on more personal computers worldwide than other operating systems. The most widely used version of Windows is Windows XP, released in 2001. Windows Vista was released in 2006, and Windows 7 was released in 2009. **Figure 8–2** shows the Windows 7 desktop.

FIGURE 8–2   Windows 7 desktop

MODULE 1   Computing Fundamentals

Older Macintosh computers contain a processor manufactured by Motorola. Generally, the Windows operating system does not work with this Motorola processor. Recently, however, Microsoft and Apple released operating systems for use on both platforms. Current Macintosh computers use Intel processors similar to Windows computers. The Macintosh operating system is called *Mac OS X*. **Figure 8–3** shows the Mac OS X Lion.

▶ **VOCABULARY**

Mac OS X

UNIX

Linux

ABOVE AND BEYOND

Macintosh popularized the first graphical user interface; however, Apple did not invent the interface. Xerox Corporation developed the idea of using pictorial icons for a computer interface.

Courtesy of Apple

FIGURE 8–3   Macintosh desktop with windows open

Still another operating system is *UNIX*. This operating system is frequently used by scientists and programmers. UNIX was developed by a group of programmers for AT&T and is considered a multitasking, portable operating system. This means it can run on just about any hardware platform. Some versions of UNIX have a command-line interface, where you enter text commands instead of manipulating objects with a mouse, but most versions provide a graphical user interface such as that shown in **Figure 8–4**. There are several variants of the operating system, such as *Linux* and IBM's AIX.

Courtesy of PR Canonical

FIGURE 8–4   Linux desktop

Both the IBM AIX operating system and Linux are based on UNIX. Linux is an open-source program that is free, and programmers and developers can use or modify it as they wish. Linux has a reputation of being stable and rarely crashing. One Linux user interface is called GNOME (pronounced *gah-NOHM*) and allows the user to select a desktop similar to Windows or Macintosh. GNOME also includes software applications such as word processing, spreadsheet, database, presentation, e-mail, and a Web browser. Even with these included applications, however, the number of available application programs is far fewer than those for Windows or the Mac OS.

Handheld and Embedded Operating Systems

As the interface between hardware and the user, the operating system is responsible for coordinating and managing the activities the device performs. *Handheld operating systems* and *embedded operating systems*, also known as mobile operating systems, are similar in principle to operating systems such as Windows or Linux. These systems, however, are smaller and generally less capable than desktop operating systems.

The diminutive operating systems can fit into the limited memory of mobile and handheld devices, such as smart phones, PDAs, tablet computers, mobile game players, and cameras. Mobile and handheld computers and other devices are used in a variety of application areas, including education, health care, automobile navigation, and for people with disabilities. The more popular handheld computers are those that are specifically designed to provide personal information manager (PIM) functions, such as a calendar and address book. These small devices have plenty of memory to hold software, electronic texts, audio, and video (see **Figure 8–5**).

> **VOCABULARY**
> **handheld operating system**
> **embedded operating system**

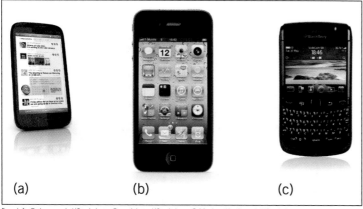

(a) (b) (c)

From left: © thesuperph / iStockphoto; © amriphoto / iStockphoto; © Monique Heydenrych / iStockphoto

FIGURE 8–5 Handheld computers

All of these devices contain an operating system. Operating systems can be categorized by a number of characteristics, including technology, usage, and licensing. In some instances, these categories may overlap. The operating system on most small devices and smart phones resides on a ROM chip. Popular handheld and embedded operating systems include the following:

- *Android*: This is an open-source operating system for mobile devices such as smart phones and tablet computers, and is currently developed by Google. Android is based on a version of Linux.

- *Apple iOS*: This operating system, originally called the iPhone OS, is designed for mobile devices such as the iPhone, iPad, and iPod Touch. You interact with iOS using your fingertips to perform multitouch gestures. The main applications are designed for phone features, e-mail, Web browsing, and media playing.

MODULE 1   Computing Fundamentals

- *BlackBerry*: The BlackBerry operating system runs on handheld devices supplied by Research in Motion (RIM). In addition to phone capabilities, this system also provides services such as multitasking, instant messaging, PIM capabilities, and access to Bluetooth devices.

- *Embedded Linux*: This is a scaled-down Linux operating system used in devices such as mobile phones, media players, PDAs, smart watches, and many other types of devices that require an embedded operating system.

- *Palm OS*: A competing operating system to Windows Mobile, **Palm OS** (also called Garnet OS) runs on Palm handhelds and other third-party devices. Some of the more common built-in applications include an address book, calculator, calendar, contacts, and phone book tools. This OS also includes handwriting-recognition software.

- *Symbian OS*: This is a multitasking operating system designed for smart phones. Some of the more popular features include the capability to send and receive e-mail messages and faxes, maintain contact lists, and browse the Web.

- *Windows Embedded CE*: A scaled-down version of the Windows operating system, **Windows Embedded CE** is designed for devices such as digital cameras, security robots, intelligent appliances, gaming devices, GPSs, media players, and set-top boxes.

- *Windows Phone*: Based on Windows Embedded CE, **Windows Phone** is a mobile operating system that runs on smart phones and other types of handheld computers. Originally called Windows Mobile, this operating system allows you to perform tasks such as accessing e-mail, recording and watching video, exchanging instant messages, reading an e-book, playing games, and managing finances. See **Figure 8–6**.

> ▶ **VOCABULARY**
> **Palm OS**
> **Windows Embedded CE**
> **Windows Phone**

FIGURE 8–6   Smart phones with Windows Phone

1-3.1.3

Sharing Files on Different Operating Systems

In many business, personal, and educational settings, people share files across operating system platforms. A business might have workers using both Macintosh and Windows computers. Depending on the task, artists and designers might use Macintosh computers, while accountants and writers might have PCs. In the classroom, all of the computers might be the same type, but students might have different types of computers at home. These situations require that multiple systems be able to read disks and share files. Hardware and software solutions are available for these problems.

One type of hardware solution is an ***emulation card*** that is added to the motherboard of a computer. These cards enable the computer to run a program that was designed for a different operating system. For example, a card can be added to an older Macintosh that allows it to run Windows programs. Software emulation programs are also available to provide this capability. For example, a Macintosh computer could have software installed that allows it to read disks that were formatted on PCs.

Some file types are readable on different operating systems. One example for word-processing documents is the basic text format (files with a .txt filename extension). This format usually is readable by most word-processing programs on different systems. However, documents saved as .txt files do not retain complicated formatting. Another text format, Rich Text Format (.rtf), does retain more formatting commands, including paragraph breaks, fonts, and styles such as bold and italic. To save a file in text format or Rich Text Format, you use the Save As command in your word-processing program and specifically select Text or Rich Text Format as the file type. These document file types can generally be transferred to other operating systems across a network, to a Linux server, or to a handheld or mobile device (see **Figure 8–7**).

▶ **VOCABULARY**
emulation card

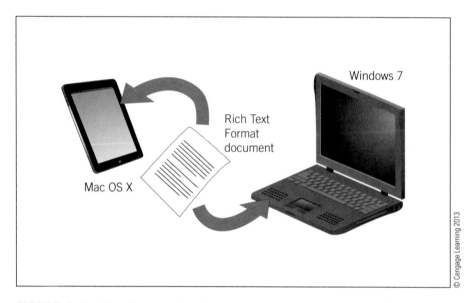

FIGURE 8–7   Transferring files from one operating system to another

If you use the Internet, you regularly share files across different operating systems. Your desktop or laptop computer uses an operating system such as Windows or Mac OS. If you use an Internet service provider to connect to the Internet, you are probably connecting to a UNIX system. If you connect to the Internet using a direct network connection, such as through a school or other organization, you are connecting to computers that use a network operating system. Each operating system provides ways to communicate and exchange information with other operating systems so that you can use more than one operating system simultaneously.

1-3.1.4

Identifying User Rights

An operating system allows you to interact with a computer and take advantage of the computer's technology, but it also sets limitations to protect itself and the data on the computer. The operating system grants permission allowing you to perform some tasks but preventing you from performing others. The tasks you are allowed to perform are defined by your user rights. The system administrator sets the user rights to protect the computer's security. The *system administrator* is a user who has an *administrator account*, which is a local account or a local security group. (An account is a collection of information that determines which files you can access and which settings you use; you access your user account by providing your user name and password.) The administrator account provides unrestricted access to make system-wide changes to the computer, including those that affect other users. Without administrative rights, you cannot make changes such as setting system options, installing software, or modifying passwords.

A typical system administrator has a variety of duties including the following:

- Creating or deleting user accounts on the computer
- Changing account names, pictures, passwords, and other data
- Establishing security access level
- Allocating storage space
- Monitoring systems to prevent unauthorized access and attacks by malicious software

The administrator can grant *administrative rights* to other users, allowing them to make specified types of changes. Without administrative rights, the typical user cannot perform many system modifications, such as installing or deleting software or changing network settings. To have administrative rights, you must know the administrative password. For example, if you want to install software on a computer, the operating system usually asks for the administrative password before it starts the setup process. If you provide the correct password, the operating system continues the installation. If you don't provide the correct password, it stops the setup process.

VOCABULARY
system administrator

administrator account

administrative rights

ETHICS IN TECHNOLOGY

What Is Computer Ethics?

Ethics is the branch of philosophy concerned with evaluating human action, and developing a system or code of morals of a particular religion, group, or profession.

Ethical judgments are no different in the field of computing than they are in any other area. The use of computers can raise many issues of privacy, copyright, theft, and power, to name just a few. For example, many computer professionals condemn hacking into other computers as unethical, while some defend so-called white-hat hackers who breach computer security because they want to gain a deeper understanding of computers and networks.

In 1990, the Institute of Electrical and Electronics Engineers (IEEE) created a code of ethics, and reapproved it in 2006. This code is available at *http://www.ieee.org/about/corporate/governance/p7-8.html*. The Association for Computing Machinery (ACM) also has a code of ethics and professional conduct provided at *www.acm.org/about/code-of-ethics*. This code is considered one of the most definitive sets of ethical standards for computer professionals, and contains 24 statements of personal responsibility. Many businesses and organizations have adopted the IEEE or ACM code to guide their own practices. Remember that they are only codes—not laws. People choose to follow them voluntarily.

Troubleshooting Common Operating System Problems

1-3.1.5

Sooner or later, you will have trouble on your computer that affects the operating system. Examples of these issues are as follows:

- *Incompatibility*: A copy of Quicken for Windows does not run on a computer with a Macintosh operating system. Application software and files need to be compatible with the computer's operating system. Usually, the operating system will not let you install or run an incompatible program. Similarly, an operating system will not let you open a file or use a media device (such as a DVD) if it does not recognize the file or media type.

- *File corruption*: Files can become corrupt as the result of a power failure, turning off the computer without properly shutting it down, a virus, resource conflicts, outdated drivers, bad sectors or lost clusters on the hard drive, bad software installation, and so on. If your operating system is unpredictable, its files might be damaged or corrupted. You can use a system utility that identifies and repairs corrupted files.

- *Disk crashes*: If your system is unstable, programs and even the operating system shut down unexpectedly and you receive error messages when you try to use the operating system and applications. In some instances, restarting, or rebooting, the system can solve the problem. If the problem is more severe, you might need to upgrade or reinstall the operating system.

Microsoft has a number of online tutorials that address Windows 7 performance and maintenance issues. Complete the following exercise to learn about some of these tutorials.

ABOVE AND BEYOND

Sometimes Windows does not boot properly. Instead, a message indicating that you are in safe mode is displayed on the screen. This means that something did not function properly during the boot process. Safe mode provides functionality so you or an expert user can do diagnostic testing.

Step-by-Step 8.1

1. Click the **Start** button on the taskbar, and then click **Control Panel** to open the Control Panel window. See **Figure 8–8**.

FIGURE 8–8
Control Panel window

Used with permission from Microsoft Corporation

2. Click **System and Security** to open the System and Security window. See **Figure 8–9**.

FIGURE 8–9
System and
Security window

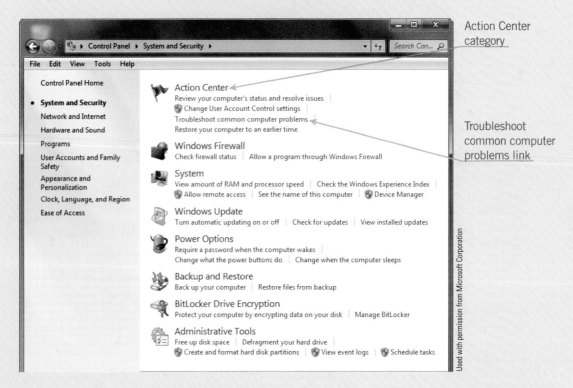

Action Center
category

Troubleshoot
common computer
problems link

3. In the Action Center category, click **Troubleshoot common computer problems** to display the Troubleshooting window. See **Figure 8–10**.

FIGURE 8–10
Troubleshooting
window

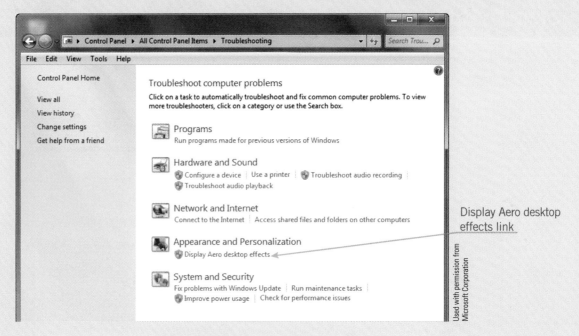

Display Aero desktop
effects link

4. Click the **Display Aero desktop effects** link to start the troubleshooter, shown in **Figure 8–11**.

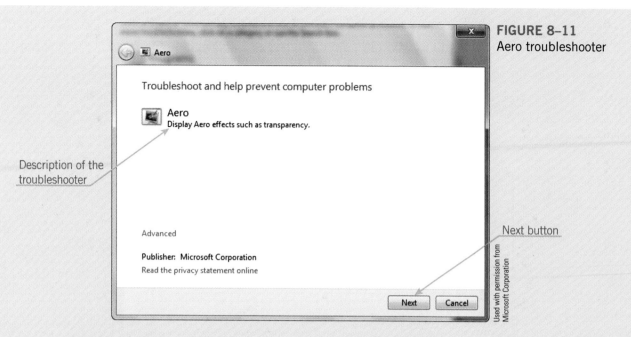

FIGURE 8–11
Aero troubleshooter

Description of the troubleshooter

Next button

Used with permission from Microsoft Corporation

5. Click the **Next** button to have Windows detect problems on your computer.

6. If Windows does not detect any problems, a window opens explaining that Troubleshooting couldn't identify the problem. If Windows does detect a problem, click **Skip this fix**. Click **Explore additional options** to open the Additional Information window. See **Figure 8–12**.

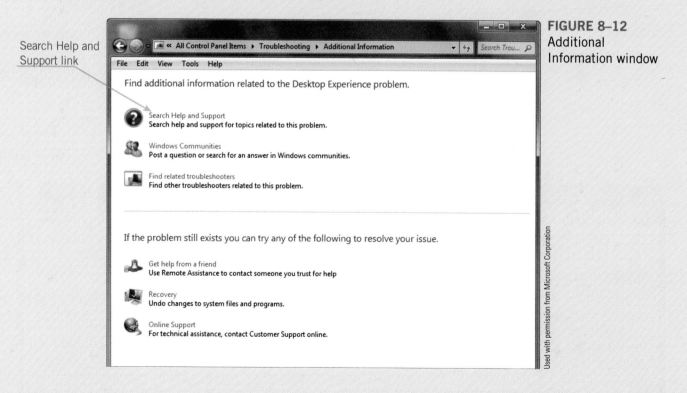

FIGURE 8–12
Additional Information window

Search Help and Support link

Used with permission from Microsoft Corporation

7. Click the **Search Help and Support** link to open a Help window listing topics related to the problem. See **Figure 8–13**. The topics in your window might differ.

FIGURE 8–13
Help topics related to the problem

Select a Help topic to learn more about Aero

8. Select at least one Help topic to learn more about Aero. In a word-processing document, describe Aero and what you need to run it.

9. Submit your word-processing document to your instructor, and then close all open windows.

TECHNOLOGY CAREERS

PC Support Specialist

The PC support specialist provides support for application software and related hardware via telephone, e-mail, online chats, or site visits to computer users.

As a PC support specialist, you need to be knowledgeable about current software and have good oral communication, written communication, and organizational skills. You are required to interact with all departments within the company and with users who have varying skill levels ranging from novice to expert. You might be required to configure and maintain computer systems running Microsoft Windows, Macintosh OS X, or Linux. You might also test new technologies and techniques, develop and follow computer maintenance and backup procedures, manage upgrades and patches to the operating system and other software, and track computer problems and solutions.

A bachelor's degree is preferred for most of these jobs; however, extensive experience performing tasks such as hands-on hardware and software upgrades is also acceptable.

SUMMARY

In this lesson, you learned:

- An operating system is system software that enables computer hardware to communicate and operate with the application software. Without an operating system, a computer would not function because the operating system manages and coordinates the activities and resources of the computer.

- Operating systems provide a consistent way for applications to communicate with hardware without duplicating settings or learning details about the hardware. They also perform system and file maintenance tasks.

- Windows, Mac OS X, and Linux are common operating systems for personal computers.

- Handheld and embedded operating systems, also known as mobile operating systems, are similar in principle to operating systems such as Windows or Linux. These systems, however, are smaller and generally have fewer capabilities than desktop operating systems.

- To share files across operating system platforms, you can use solutions involving hardware, software, and data. For example, saving data or work files in the Rich Text Format means that most other operating systems can read the file.

- An operating system sets limitations to protect itself and the data on the computer. The operating system grants permission to you to perform some tasks but prevents you from performing others according to your user rights.

- The system administrator has unrestricted access to make system-wide changes to the computer, including those that affect other users. Without administrative rights, you cannot make changes such as system modifications, installing software, or changing network settings.

- Typical operating system problems include file incompatibility, file corruption, and disk crashes.

■ LESSON REVIEW

TRUE / FALSE

Circle T if the statement is true or F if the statement is false.

T   F   **1.**   The system administrator generally has an administrator account.

T   F   **2.**   Some file types are readable on more than one operating system.

T   F   **3.**   Handheld computers do not contain an operating system.

T   F   **4.**   An operating system manages resources for applications.

T   F   **5.**   There are five basic types of software.

MULTIPLE CHOICE

Select the best response for the following statements.

1. The way an operating system stores files on disk is called a _____ system.

   A. file

   B. recurring

   C. backup

   D. disk

2. The Macintosh operating system is called _____.

   A. Vista

   B. UNIX

   C. Windows

   D. Mac OS X

3. A(n) _____ card allows a computer to run a program that was designed for a different operating system.

   A. emulation

   B   DOS

   C. replacement

   D. Windows Phone

4. The tasks an operating system allows you to perform are defined by your _____.

   A. password

   B. system administrator

   C. user rights

   D. user interface

5. The _____ operating system was developed by a group of programmers for AT&T.

   A. Apple Macintosh

   B. IBM PC

   C. UNIX

   D. Windows

FILL IN THE BLANK

Complete the following sentences by writing the correct word or words in the blanks provided.

1. Older _____ computers contain a processor manufactured by Motorola.

2. Manufacturers of peripheral devices such as printers or monitors provide programs called _____ that enable the operating system to communicate with hardware devices.

3. The UNIX operating system is considered a(n) _____, portable operating system.

4. Both the IBM AIX system and Linux operating systems are based on _____.

5. Handheld operating systems and embedded operating systems also are known as _____ operating systems.

■ PROJECTS

PROJECT 8–1

1-3.1.5

Windows Disk Cleanup utility helps you free space on your computer by deleting temporary and other unnecessary files from a drive. Complete the following:

1. Use Windows Help and Support and research this utility program.

2. In a word-processing document, explain the purpose of this utility and provide an example of how you would access the program and then use it.

PROJECT 8–2

1-3.1.3

Complete the following:

1. Use your favorite search engine to research information about the BlackBerry Playbook.

2. Assume that you are going to purchase the Playbook and research its features, applications, and accessories.

3. Use your word-processing program to prepare a one-page overview of the Playbook features, applications, and accessories and describe how you could apply these features for personal and business use.

PROJECT 8–3

1-3.1.2

Windows 7 is the most recent operating system developed for the PC, and Mac OS X is the most recent operating system developed for the Macintosh computer. Complete the following:

1. Use your favorite search engine to research information about one of the first operating systems developed for the PC. Also research one of the first operating systems developed for the Macintosh.

2. Use a presentation program to prepare a slide show on the early operating systems for the PC and Macintosh. Be sure to name the operating systems, list the system requirements, list the important features, and provide an illustration such as a screen shot, if possible.

TEAMWORK PROJECT

1-3.1.2

You and two team members have been given the responsibility for purchasing new computers for your company's front office. One team member wants to purchase Apple Macintosh computers with the latest version of the Mac OS X; another wants to purchase PCs with the latest version of Windows; and the third wants to purchase PCs with the UNIX/Linux operating system. The manager has requested that your team do some research and present her with a report so that she can make the best choice. Your report should include the positives and negatives for each of these operating systems. Also include information on how these computers could interact if more than one type of computer was selected.

CRITICAL THINKING

Assume you are a member of a team and your objective is to come up with three ideas on how the Windows 7 operating system can be improved. Provide an overview of your ideas and explain why they would make the operating system better and easier to use.

■ ONLINE DISCOVERY

Android is an open-source operating system for mobile devices such as smart phones. Google released Android under the Apache License, authored by the Apache Software Foundation. A software license sets the terms for using the software. For example, a software license usually defines how many copies of the software a user can make or install. Research the Apache License on at least two Web sites and then answer the following questions:

1. Is the Apache License free?

2. Does the Apache License let users modify the Android software?

3. In what programming language was the Android software developed?

4. What relationship does the Apache License have with the GNU operating system?

5. Provide a brief overview of the information contained on the Web sites you researched. Include the Web site addresses where you located the information.

JOB SKILLS

The Technology Careers sidebar in this lesson describes the job of a PC support specialist. Working as a PC support specialist is a good way to start a career in the computer field. However, this position requires a challenging blend of skills to be successful and earn promotions. As a group or on your own, list the types of skills needed to be an excellent PC support specialist. Organize the skills into categories such as technical knowledge and communication skills. Which are the most important skills for this job? In which areas are your skills the strongest? Where do you need to improve? What parts of this job do you find attractive and why?

⏱ **Estimated Time:**
1.5 hours

LESSON 9

Windows Management

■ OBJECTIVES

Upon completion of this lesson, you should be able to:

- Log on and off the computer.
- Identify desktop elements.
- Manipulate windows.
- Start programs and switch between windows.
- Use desktop folders and icons.
- Manage files.
- Identify strategies for working with files.
- Solve common file problems.

■ DATA FILES

You do not need data files to complete this lesson.

■ WORDS TO KNOW

active window

application file

Computer window

data file

directory

file property

gadget

hidden file

icon

Recycle Bin

shortcut

system file

MODULE 1   Computing Fundamentals

The tools available in the **Computer window** are designed to help you find, view, and manage files easily and effectively. In earlier versions of Windows, My Computer and Windows Explorer were separate programs. In Windows Vista, this program is called Computer and is the same program as Windows Explorer. Windows 7 also merges these tools into one window. All the disk and folder maintenance operations you use with Windows Explorer now are available through the Computer window. In this lesson, you will learn how to use options in the Computer window to manage files and folders.

1-3.2.1

Logging On and Off the Computer

To start Windows, you only need to turn on your computer. Windows automatically starts, and a Welcome message is displayed. After a short time, the Windows logo is displayed. If the computer is set to automatic logon, you are not required to type a user name or password. Otherwise, you log on to Windows by selecting your user name or picture, and then entering a password, if necessary. The next screen that appears is the Welcome screen, followed by the desktop (discussed shortly).

After completing your work, you log off the system to let another user work with Windows. To log off, click the Start button, point to the Shut down arrow button, and then click Log off. You also can end your session by clicking the Start button, clicking the Shut down arrow button to display the Shut down menu, and then selecting an option described in **Table 9–1**.

TABLE 9–1   Ending a Windows session

OPTION	METHOD
Switch user	Click the Switch user command, if necessary press Ctrl+Alt+Delete, and then click the user name to which you want to switch.
Log off	Click the Log off command to close all open programs and the user account; the computer does not shut down but continues running so that another user can log on.
Lock	Click the Lock command to prevent unauthorized users from logging on to the computer.
Restart	Click the Restart command to shut down and then restart the computer.
Sleep	Click the Sleep command to have Windows automatically save your documents and then switch to a low-power state; this option is useful for short intermissions away from the computer.
Hibernate	Click the Hibernate command to have Windows automatically save your documents and then power down the computer; this option is useful for longer intermissions of a few hours or so.
Shut down	Click the Shut down button to close all programs and turn off the computer.

Shutting Down an Unresponsive Application

Sometimes a Windows application stops functioning or does not respond and you cannot close the program or perform any other tasks in Windows, such as turning off the computer. The following Step-by-Step exercise shows how to use the Task Manager to close an unresponsive application or process.

Step-by-Step 9.1

1. Right-click the **taskbar**, and then click **Start Task Manager** or press **Ctrl+Shift+Esc** (press all three keys at the same time) to display the Windows Task Manager shown in **Figure 9–1**. If necessary, click the **Applications** tab, which displays the applications that are currently running.

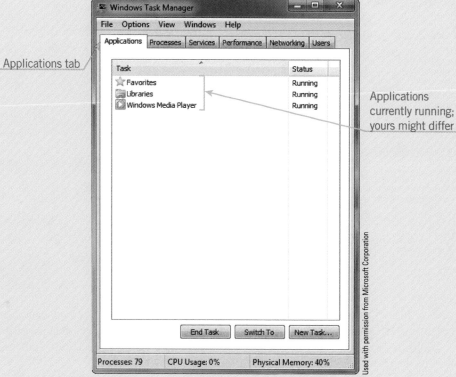

Applications tab

Applications currently running; yours might differ

FIGURE 9–1
Windows Task Manager

Used with permission from Microsoft Corporation

2. Start Microsoft Word. (If it is already running, save and close all documents.)

MODULE 1   Computing Fundamentals

3. In the Windows Task Manager dialog box, click the **Processes** tab shown in **Figure 9–2**, and then click the process you want to close, which is WINWORD.EXE or WINWORD.EXE *32 in this case, the process related to the Microsoft Word application.

FIGURE 9–2
Processes tab in
Windows Task Manager

Processes tab

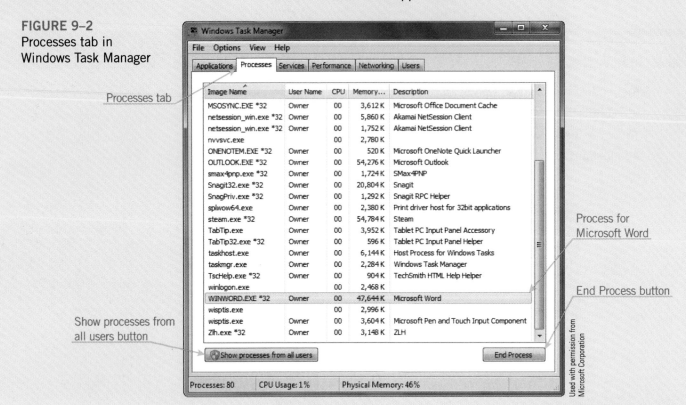

Process for
Microsoft Word

End Process button

Show processes from
all users button

4. Click the **End Process** button. When a message appears requesting confirmation, click the **End process** button in the message box. Leave Windows Task Manager open for the next Step-by-Step exercise.

If an application or process is running in the background, the application or process does not appear on the Applications or Processes tab for the current user. The following Step-by-Step exercise shows you how to reveal the application or process and then force it to close.

Step-by-Step 9.2

1. Start Microsoft Word again.

2. On the Processes tab of the Windows Task Manager dialog box, click the **Show processes from all users** button (shown in **Figure 9–2**) to display processes from all users with an account on the computer (see **Figure 9–3**).

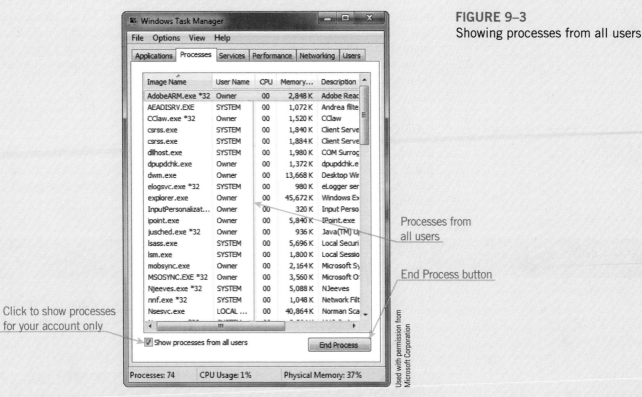

FIGURE 9-3
Showing processes from all users

Click to show processes for your account only

Processes from all users

End Process button

3. Click the application or process that you want to stop, which is WINWORD.EXE or WINWORD.EXE *32 in this case, and then click the **End Process** button to close the selected application or process. When a message appears requesting confirmation, click the **End process** button in the message box.

4. Close Windows Task Manager.

Identifying Desktop Elements

The Windows 7 desktop is the main screen area that you see after you turn on your computer. The objects on the desktop are called *icons*, and simulate a work area in an office. You can place objects on the desktop, and then delete, move, and rename them. You can use icons as shortcuts to start a program, open a window, access a Web site, and perform various other tasks. The *Recycle Bin* is a standard Windows element. The Recycle Bin icon is displayed by default on the desktop when you start your computer for the first time. You use this icon to discard unnecessary items. The Recycle Bin stores the discarded items until you empty it.

The desktop contains three main sections:

1. The taskbar, which is located at the bottom of the screen
2. The Start button, which opens the Start menu
3. The middle section, which contains the desktop background (or wallpaper), open windows, and program and document icons

1-3.2.2

▶ **VOCABULARY**
icon

Recycle Bin

By default, the taskbar displays three program icons you can click to start programs, including Internet Explorer, Windows Explorer, and Windows Media Player. The right side of the taskbar includes the notification area, which displays system status information, including the system date and time, and shortcuts to accessory programs. To the right of the notification area is the Show desktop button (discussed in the "Manipulating Windows" section.)

Customizing the Icons on the Desktop

By default, the Windows 7 desktop displays the Recycle Bin icon only. The Recycle Bin is one of several standard desktop icons. You can display additional standard icons and then modify them as you prefer. Step-by-Step 9.3 shows how to add a standard icon to the desktop and then modify it.

Step-by-Step 9.3

1. Right-click an empty space on the desktop to display a shortcut menu. Click **Personalize** to display the Personalization window shown in **Figure 9–4**.

FIGURE 9–4
Personalization
window

Change desktop
icons link

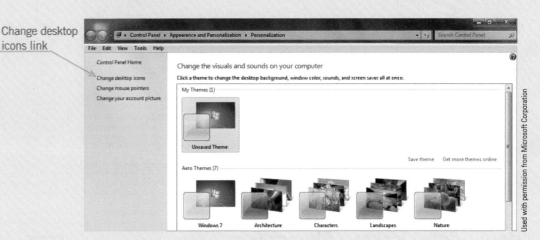

2. Click the **Change desktop icons** link in the left pane to display the Desktop Icon Settings dialog box shown in **Figure 9–5**.

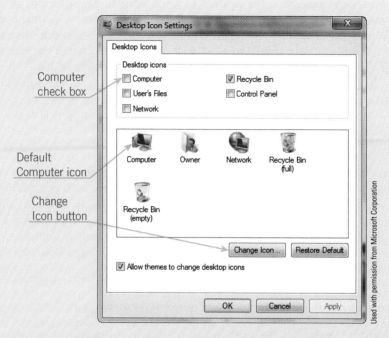

FIGURE 9–5
Desktop Icon Settings dialog box

Computer check box

Default Computer icon

Change Icon button

3. Click the **Computer** check box to display the Computer icon on the desktop.

4. Click the **Computer** icon in the middle section of the Desktop Icon Settings dialog box, and then click the **Change Icon** button to display the Change Icon dialog box shown in **Figure 9–6**.

FIGURE 9–6
Change Icon dialog box

Computer check box is selected

Select a different icon

Current image used for Computer icon

5. With your instructor's permission, select an icon that you prefer for the Computer icon, click the **OK** button to close the Change Icon dialog box, and then click the **OK** button in the Desktop Icon Settings dialog box.

6. Close the Personalization window.

MODULE 1   Computing Fundamentals

Most users generally have a variety of icons located on the desktop that start a program, open a file, and so on. For example, they might have icons that open the following types of windows: program, document, help, games, instructional, folders, mail, and utilities. Each type of window has its own special icon. For instance, folder icons look like file folders and can contain additional folders or files. Microsoft Word has its own designated icon, as does Windows Mail. This standardization of icons helps you easily recognize various programs.

Identifying Other Graphical Elements

▶ **VOCABULARY**
gadget

Besides icons, you also can add other items to the desktop. For example, you can display a *gadget*, which is a small program that performs a limited task, such as displaying current weather information. Windows 7 provides the Gadget Gallery, which has a link to additional online gadgets. To display the Gadget Gallery, you right-click the desktop and then click Gadgets on the shortcut menu. You can drag these gadgets from the Gadgets window to the desktop, and then move them where you like. In **Figure 9–7**, the desktop contains three gadgets—the Clock, CPU Meter, and Weather.

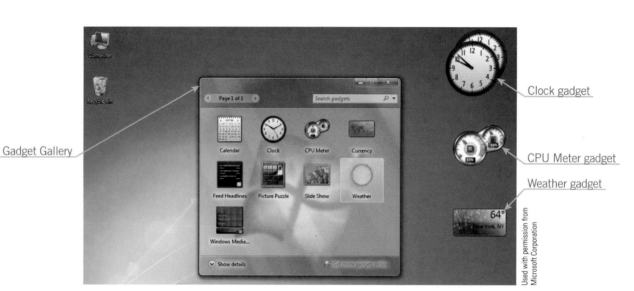

FIGURE 9–7   Windows Gadget Gallery and gadgets

1-3.2.3

Manipulating Windows

When you double-click a desktop icon, a window opens to display folder or program contents. These windows contain standardized tools that let you control the appearance of the windows on the desktop. You use three buttons on a window title bar—the Minimize button, the Maximize/Restore button, and the Close button—to manipulate the way a window is or is not displayed. **Figure 9–8** shows these buttons.

Minimize button | Close button

Restore Down button

Used with permission from Microsoft Corporation

FIGURE 9-8 Window manipulation buttons

- Click the Minimize button to hide the window without closing it; you can display the window again by clicking its button on the taskbar.
- Click the Restore Down button to display the window in less than a full screen. The button in this position becomes the Maximize button after you click the Restore Down button.
- Click the Maximize button to have the window fill the full screen.
- Click the Close button to close the window.

To minimize all open windows at one time using the mouse, click the Show desktop button ▮ on the far right end of the taskbar. Click the button again to reopen all of the windows. To minimize all open windows using the keyboard, press the Windows logo key plus the letter "M".

To resize a window, point to a corner or edge of the window until the pointer changes to a two-headed arrow and then drag. To move a window, drag it by the title bar.

Starting Programs and Switching Between Windows

1-3.2.4

Starting a program in Windows 7 is a simple task. Click the Start button and then click the program name on the Start menu. You also can double-click a program icon located on the desktop. More than one program can be in memory at the same time. When multiple windows are open on your desktop, the one you are working with is called the *active window*. The active window is easy to recognize because its title bar is a different color or intensity. You can make any open window the active window in the following ways:

- If any portion of the window you want to work with is visible, click it. The window moves to the front of the desktop and becomes the active window.
- Click the window's button on the taskbar. If more than one window of the same type is open, such as two Microsoft Word documents, point to the program button, and then click the window you want to display.
- Press and hold down the Alt key; then press Tab. A small window appears in the center of the screen containing icons for all items currently open, including items minimized on the taskbar. Continue holding down the Alt key and then press and release Tab to cycle through the icons. A box surrounds the item's icon and a description appears at the top of the window as it is selected. When the item you want is selected, release the Alt key. That item comes to the front and becomes the active window. This is called the fast Alt+Tab method for switching to a different window.

▶ **VOCABULARY**
active window

ABOVE AND BEYOND

If you are using Windows 7 with an Aero desktop theme, you can use Aero Flip 3D, which previews all the open windows in a 3-D stack. To open Aero Flip 3D, hold down the Windows logo key and then press Tab. Continue holding the Windows logo key and press Tab to cycle through the open windows. To display the window at the top of the stack, release the Windows logo key.

Accessing Online Support

The Help and Support Center provides three options for online help:

- *Windows Remote Assistance*: Remote Assistance is a convenient way for someone you know to connect to your computer from another computer running Windows 7, chat with you, and observe your computer screen as you work. With your permission, you can receive the remote user's keystrokes as if he or she were typing on your keyboard. In this way, you can watch the remote user demonstrate the solution to your problem. In this same category, you also can offer Remote Assistance or invite someone to join a Remote Assistance session.
- *Microsoft Answers*: Post a question or search for an answer in Windows online communities.
- *Microsoft customer support*: Use this service to get support online from a technician who can answer your questions in e-mail, an online chat session, or by phone. This option also gives you access to solution centers and forums that can offer tips and guidelines about working with Windows 7.

To access Help and Support, click the Start button and then click Help and Support.

Identifying the Operating System Version

Microsoft has released many versions of Windows, including Windows XP, Windows Vista, and Windows 7. Windows 7 is available for purchase in three editions: Home Premium, Professional, and Ultimate. Microsoft regularly releases updates for the Windows 7 operating system. It is important to know the version and edition of your software so that you use the correct update. To determine the version and edition of the operating system you are using, complete the following Step-by-Step exercise.

Step-by-Step 9.4

1. Click the **Start** button 🔵 on the taskbar, right-click **Computer**, and then click **Properties** to display the System window. See **Figure 9–9**. The version and edition are displayed in the Windows edition section.

FIGURE 9–9
System window displaying Windows 7 edition

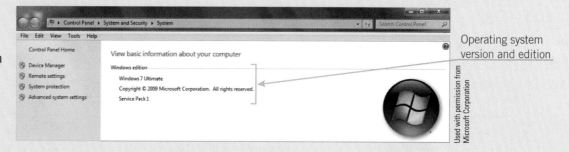

Operating system version and edition

2. Close the System window.

Using Desktop Folders and Icons

1-3.2.5

The first task many people want to complete when they start using Windows is to customize the desktop to better suit how they work. Adding folders, icons, and shortcuts to the desktop helps you to create a personal environment best suited for your particular style and purpose. A *shortcut* is an icon that represents a link to an item, rather than the item itself. Shortcut icons contain arrows. **Table 9–2** provides an overview of how to create and move desktop folders and icons.

▶ **VOCABULARY**
shortcut

TABLE 9–2   Desktop folders and icons

TASK	DESCRIPTION
Create desktop folders	Right-click a blank space on the desktop, point to New, and then click Folder to display a new folder.
Create desktop shortcut	Right-click a blank space on the desktop, point to New, and then click Shortcut to display the Create Shortcut dialog box. Click the Browse button to locate the item, click the item, click OK, and then click the Next button in the Create Shortcut dialog box. Type a name for the shortcut, if necessary, and then click the Finish button.
Delete desktop folders and icons/shortcuts	Right-click the item you want to delete, and then click Delete. The Delete File, Delete Folder, or Delete Shortcut dialog box is displayed. Click Yes to move the file to the Recycle Bin or click No to cancel.
Move and copy desktop folders and icons/shortcuts	Right-click the item you want to move or copy. On the shortcut menu, click Copy to copy the item or click Cut to move the item. Right-click where you want to paste the item, and then click Paste.
Rename desktop folders and icons/shortcuts	Right-click the item you want to rename, and then click Rename. Enter a new name for the item.
Display properties of desktop folders and icons/shortcuts	Right-click the item for which you want to display properties, and then click Properties to display the properties such as the type, location, size, and date of creation in the Properties dialog box.

QUICK TIP

To create a shortcut to a Web page, begin following the instructions for creating a desktop shortcut. Instead of clicking the Browse button to select a file, type the URL of the Web page you want to access, such as *www.microsoft.com*. Click Next, and then complete the remaining instructions.

Managing Files

1-3.2.6

As you have learned, you use folders to organize files on a disk. Folders are represented by icons that look like physical file folders. As you create and use folders and files, they often multiply over time. The Computer window is designed to help you find, view, and manage files easily and effectively. The Computer window gives you control over the organization and management of your files and folders. When you open the Computer window to display the contents of a folder, it is also called a folder window.

MODULE 1   Computing Fundamentals

Displaying Files

The Computer window provides tools you use to search for files and folders and to view details about their contents. Using these tools, you can delete, copy, and move files and folders as necessary. To open the Computer window, click the Start button and then click Computer. If you added the Computer icon to the desktop, you can double-click the Computer icon to display the Computer window (see **Figure 9–10**).

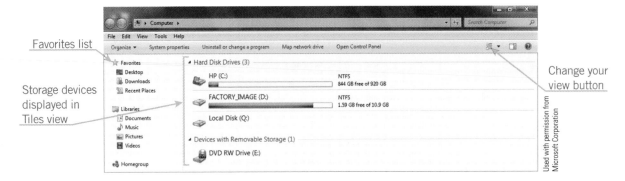

FIGURE 9–10   Computer window

In **Figure 9–10**, the Favorites list is displayed in the left pane and a list of storage devices is displayed in Tiles view in the right pane. The menu bar is also displayed (which you can display by pressing the Alt key). The devices shown in this figure include two local hard drives (C and D), a local disk Q, and a DVD/RW drive. Other storage devices could include USB drives, additional hard drives, remote devices such as those on a network or the Internet, tape back-up drives, and Google's cloud. In **Figure 9–11**, the selected view is Large Icons. Clicking the Change your view button arrow or the View menu, however, provides other view options.

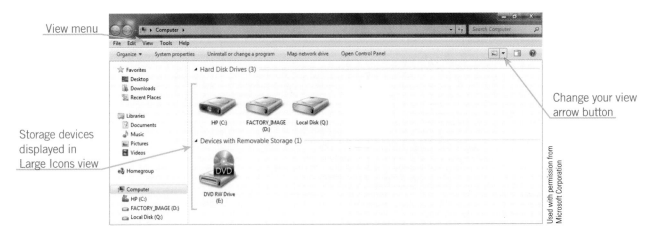

FIGURE 9–11   Computer window in Large Icons view

Windows uses a directory/folder structure to organize and store files. When the right pane of the Computer window contains a folder, you can double-click the folder to display its contents. In the following Step-by-Step exercise, you view the contents of a folder.

Step-by-Step 9.5

1. Double-click the **Computer** icon on the desktop to display the Computer window.

2. Click the **Change your view** arrow button, and then click **Details** to display the window in Details view. See **Figure 9–12**.

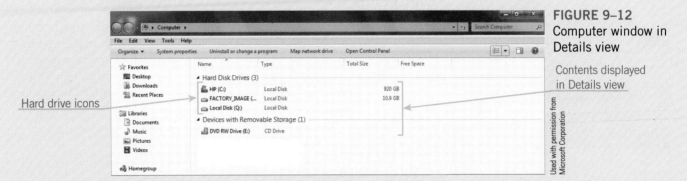

Hard drive icons

FIGURE 9–12
Computer window in Details view

Contents displayed in Details view

Used with permission from Microsoft Corporation

3. Double-click the **Local Disk (C:)** icon or other hard drive icon. Select a folder of your choice and then double-click the folder name to display the contents. Click the **Change your view** arrow button, and then click **Large Icons** to display the window in Large Icons view. **Figure 9–13** shows a folder named *Clock.Gadget* displayed in Large Icons view.

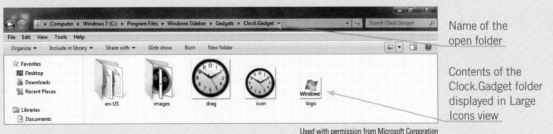

Name of the open folder

Contents of the Clock.Gadget folder displayed in Large Icons view

FIGURE 9–13
Contents of a folder in Large Icons view

Used with permission from Microsoft Corporation

4. Click the **Change your view** arrow button, and then drag the slider from one menu option to another to experiment with the other views.

5. Close any open windows.

Recognizing Types of Files

A computer can contain three types of files: system files, application files, and data files. *System files* usually are found in the Windows or Program Files folder and are essential files necessary for running Windows. An *application file* is part of an application, such as a word-processing program, a graphics program, and so on. A *data file* is one you create when working with an application, such as a document you create when working with Microsoft Word.

▶ **VOCABULARY**
system file
application file
data file

Changing Directory and File Views

A **directory**, or folder, is a container for files and other directories. Windows 7 generally uses the term *folder*, while operating systems such as Linux use the term *directory*. To view the contents of the folder, double-click the folder name. Using the Computer window, you can view files using these options: Extra Large Icons, Large Icons, Medium Icons, Small Icons, List, Details, Tiles, and Content.

Sorting Files

You can use the Computer window to sort files by name, size, type, date, or other characteristics. Sorting creates a list of files organized by that characteristic. Sort any location such as a drive or folder by opening the location in the Computer window, switching to Details view, and then clicking a column heading such as Type to sort the files by that characteristic. In any view, you can right-click the Computer window background, point to Sort by on the shortcut menu, and then click a characteristic such as Type or Date modified.

Creating Folders

You use folders to store, manage, and organize files. To create a folder, go to the location (desktop or another folder) and right-click a blank spot on the desktop or folder window. Point to New on the shortcut menu, and then click Folder. Type a name for the new folder, and then press Enter.

Selecting Files

To select a single file, click the filename or file icon. To select a consecutive group of files, click the first file, hold down the Shift key, and then click the last file. Using the mouse pointer, you can also select a consecutive group of files by dragging the pointer around the outside of all of the items to be included. To select nonconsecutive files, click the first file, hold down the Ctrl key, and then click the next file.

Moving, Copying, Deleting, and Renaming Files

To move a file, select the file and drag it to the new location. Or right-click the file to display the shortcut menu and then click Cut. Access the location where you want to move the file, right-click a blank spot in the folder window to display the shortcut menu, and then click Paste. You can use the same steps to copy a file by clicking Copy instead of Cut. To delete a file, right-click the filename or file icon to display the shortcut menu, and then click Delete. To rename a file, right-click the filename or file icon and then click Rename. Type the new name for the file, and then press Enter.

Retrieving Deleted Files

At some point, you may find that you have unintentionally deleted a file, folder, or other item. If the Recycle Bin has not been emptied and still contains the item, you can restore it. To restore a file, double-click the Recycle Bin to open it. Look through the files and then right-click the filename that you want to restore. On the shortcut menu, click Restore to restore the file to its original location.

▶ **VOCABULARY**
directory

QUICK TIP

You can also sort the icons on the desktop by right-clicking an empty spot on the desktop, pointing to Sort by, and selecting Name, Size, Item type, or Date modified.

QUICK TIP

You use the same techniques to move, copy, delete, and rename folders as you do for files.

ABOVE AND BEYOND

Windows 7 hides filename extensions by default to make the names easier to read. You can still distinguish between a Word document named Budget and an Excel workbook named Budget because the file icons are different.

Emptying the Recycle Bin

Similar to the trash in your home or office, Windows Recycle Bin also needs to be emptied. To empty the Recycle Bin, right-click the Recycle Bin icon on the desktop and then click Empty Recycle Bin. A Delete File or Delete Multiple Items warning box is displayed. Click the Yes button to permanently delete the files contained in the Recycle Bin or click the No button to cancel the command.

Displaying File Properties

File properties are characteristics that help you locate and organize files. The properties provide information about the selected file, such as its creation date, size, and location. You can view file properties for folders, documents, icons, images, and so on. To view the properties of a file, right-click the file, and then select Properties on the shortcut menu to display the Properties dialog box (see **Figure 9–14**). The Properties dialog box can contain a number of tabs: General, Sharing, Security, Details, Previous Versions, Customize, and Compatibility. Most of these tabs contain information about the file. You use the Customize tab to add properties and other information to the file. The Compatibility tab relates to working with Windows.

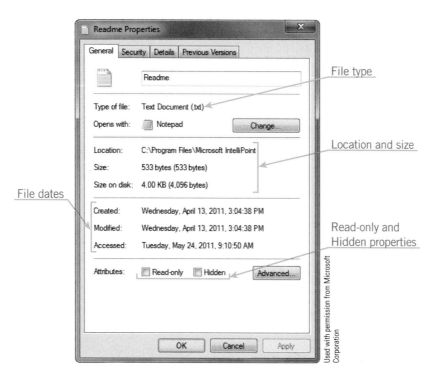

FIGURE 9–14   Properties dialog box for a file

WARNING

If you choose to empty the Recycle Bin, keep in mind that the files are deleted permanently and cannot be restored.

VOCABULARY
file property

ABOVE AND BEYOND

You can also search for programs and files using the Search programs and files text box on the Start menu. Start typing the first few letters of the program or filename, and Windows 7 displays all the files, folders, and programs on your computer with names that match your entry.

Finding Files

The Computer window provides tools to help you search for files and folders, to find details about the contents of the files and folders, and to manage them—deleting, copying, and moving files and folders as necessary. **Figure 9–15** shows the Search text box, which is displayed in a folder window.

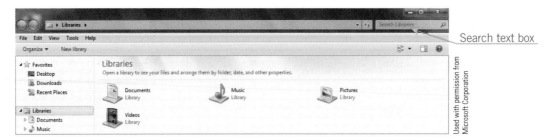

Search text box

FIGURE 9–15   Search text box in a folder window

To find a file or folder using the Search text box, click in the Search text box, and then type a word or part of a word. As you type, the contents of the folder are filtered to include each character you type. When you see the file you want, stop typing.

After you search for a file or folder, the location in the Address box changes to indicate that the window displays search results. See **Figure 9–16**. The lower half of the window also displays other locations you can search. Click the Search text box to display the search filters you can apply to narrow your search.

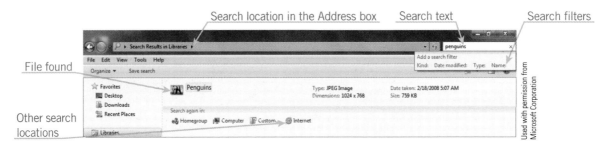

Search location in the Address box   Search text   Search filters

File found

Other search locations

FIGURE 9–16   Search results

TECHNOLOGY TIMELINE

Logical Search Tools

In the 1840s, George Boole, a self-educated mathematician from England, developed ways of expressing logical processes using algebraic symbols. Eventually called Boolean logic, this method uses words called operators to determine whether a statement is true or false. Boolean logic has become the basis for computer database and Web searches. The most common operators are AND, OR, and NOT. These three simple words can be extremely helpful when searching for data. For example, if you search for *railroad AND models*, the results include documents with both words. If you search for *railroad OR models*, the results include documents with either word. Using the OR operator usually finds many more documents than using the AND operator with the same search terms. One way to limit the results is to search for *railroad NOT models*. The results include all documents about railroads but not documents about models.

Displaying and Identifying Hidden Files

A *hidden file* is a file like any other except it is not displayed in a folder window. You can hide a file using the Hidden check box on the General tab of the Properties dialog box for the file. To hide a file, right-click the filename or file icon and then click Properties to display the Properties dialog box. On the General tab, click the Hidden check box (see **Figure 9–17**). To display a hidden file, click the Organize button in the window of the folder containing the file, and then click Folder and search options to open the Folder Options dialog box. Click the View tab, and then click the Show hidden files, folders, and drives option button under Advanced settings. Click OK to apply the settings and close the Folder Options dialog box. To remove the hidden attribute from a file, right-click the filename or file icon and select Properties to display the Properties dialog box. On the General tab, in the Attributes section, deselect the Hidden option.

▶ **VOCABULARY**
hidden file

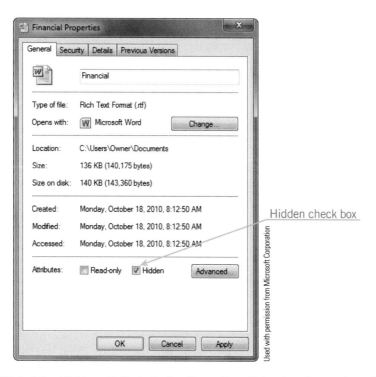

FIGURE 9–17   Hidden attribute in the Properties dialog box for a selected file

Identifying Strategies for Working with Files

1-3.2.7

If you have worked with older versions of Windows, you might be familiar with the file naming convention called "8.3" (pronounced "eight dot three"). The "eight" part means that a filename may be up to eight characters long. The "three" part is an extension (no longer than three characters) to the name. And the "dot" is the period that separates the eight characters from the three characters. Neither spaces nor special characters can be used in this naming system. For example, in the filename *letter.doc*, the name is *letter*, the separator is the standard period, and the extension is *doc*.

Naming and Organizing Files and Folders

Newer versions of Windows, including Windows 7, allow longer names (up to 255 characters) for folders and files, and permit spaces, punctuation marks, and some special characters in the names. Longer names are often easier to remember and help to find files quickly after you create them. For example, you can name a file *Myrtle's Cookies and Cream* instead of an abbreviated name such as *myrtlecc*. In some instances, filename extensions also are longer. Examples include the jpeg extension, which is used for some graphics files, and the html extension, short for Hypertext Markup Language, which is used to designate files in a format used for Web pages. Documents created in Microsoft Office 2007 and later also use four-character filename extensions.

Similar naming conventions also apply to folder names. When you create a new folder (before you click anywhere else or press Enter), simply type the folder name. As you type, your folder name replaces the words *New folder* below the folder's icon. Press Enter to display the new folder name. The folder name should indicate the content of the folder. In general, you should name files and folders using standardized names that are easy to remember and help you stay organized.

You may find that after you have used a folder for a time, you need to rename it. You can rename a folder in four ways:

WARNING

Rename folders that contain data files only. Applications and Windows will not work if they cannot locate a folder using its original name.

- Click the folder in the right pane of a folder window to select the folder, press the F2 key, and then enter the new name in the text box.

- Click the folder to select it, choose Rename from the File menu, and then enter the new name in the text box.

- Right-click the folder name, choose Rename on the shortcut menu, and then enter the new name in the text box.

- Click the folder you want to rename, click the Organize button on the toolbar, click Rename, and then enter the new name in the text box.

Deleting Unneeded Files and Folders

Deleting unused files and folders saves disk space, helps avoid clutter, and enables better access to the hard drive. You can delete a file or a folder in several ways:

- Click the file or folder to select it, and then click Delete on the File menu.

- Click the file or folder to select it, and then press the Delete key.

- Right-click the file or folder, and then click Delete on the shortcut menu.

When you delete a folder or subfolder, you also delete all the files in it. Use extreme caution, therefore, before you delete a folder. To verify that this is what you really want to do, Windows displays a Delete Folder message box. Windows also provides one additional safety net when you are deleting a folder from a hard disk. Folders deleted from a hard disk are transferred by default to the Recycle Bin, from which they can be recovered. However, you cannot recover a folder or a file deleted from an external drive, such as a USB drive, if the drive does not have a Recycle Bin.

Backing up Files and Folders

Occasionally a hard drive fails or a particular file becomes lost or corrupted. To protect these important documents, you should back up files and folders to an external device on a regular basis. Depending on the size of the file or folder, the external device could be a USB drive, a CD, or an external hard drive. Another option is online storage.

Solving Common File Problems

1-3.2.8

Several problems can occur with files. For instance, you may not be able to locate or open a file. Some common problems associated with computer files include the following:

- You cannot find a file because it is hidden. As mentioned earlier, you can view hidden files by clicking the Organize button in the window of the folder containing the file, and then clicking Folder and search options to open the Folder Options dialog box. Click the View tab, and then click the Show hidden files, folders, and drives option button under Advanced settings. Click OK to apply the settings and close the Folder Options dialog box.

- You cannot open a file because it is password protected. To view a password-protected file, you must know the password. Generally, password-protected files are located on a server or on a computer that is used by more than one person.

- You cannot edit a file because it is a read-only file. Read-only files can be read or copied, but they cannot be modified. To make a change in a read-only file, you need to save it with a new filename.

- You cannot access a file. Occasionally, when attempting to open a file, you may receive a "file access denied" message. Generally, this type of file is on a network. In some instances, you might have access to the document but only be able to read and not change it.

- You cannot open a file because it is damaged. When a file is not saved properly, it may become corrupted. This could happen with an intermittent power outage or a hard drive problem. When attempting to open a corrupted file, the Document Recovery task pane may be displayed in the program window. When this happens, there are two possibilities: (a) the program opens the file so you can continue your work, or (b) the Document Recovery task pane displays up to three recovered versions of your document. You can identify a version to keep. In other instances, the file may be damaged and cannot be recovered.

- You cannot open a file in the program that created it. Different file types often are identified by the file extension—the three or four characters separated by a period from the filename. If the file extension is changed or deleted through an error, then the parent program will not be able to open the file. To correct this situation, you must manually change the file extension to the default program extension.

- You cannot save a file because the drive is full. If space is limited on the drive where you want to save a file, first back up the files you need and then delete the files you no longer need to create additional space for new files.

SUMMARY

In this lesson, you learned:

- To start Windows, you turn on your computer, and then, if necessary, log on by selecting your user name or picture and entering a password. To end your Windows session, you can log off and let another user work with Windows by clicking the Start button, pointing to the Shut down arrow button, and then clicking Log off.

- If you are working with an application that does not respond to your actions, you can use the Windows Task Manager to close the nonresponsive application or process.

- The Windows 7 desktop is the main screen area that appears after you turn on your computer. You can place icons on the desktop that are shortcuts to start a program, open a window, or access a Web site, for example. You can also delete, move, and rename the icons on the desktop.

- The Recycle Bin appears on your desktop by default. You use the Recycle Bin to discard unnecessary items, such as folders. The Recycle Bin stores the discarded items until you empty it.

- The desktop contains three main sections: the taskbar, which is located at the bottom of the screen; the Start button, which opens the Start menu; and the middle section, which contains program and document icons.

- You use three buttons on a window's title bar—the Minimize button, the Maximize/Restore down button, and the Close button—to control the way a window is or is not displayed.

- To start a program in Windows 7, you click the Start button and then click the program name. You can also double-click the program icon, which might be located on the desktop. More than one program can be in memory at the same time. When multiple windows are open on your desktop, the one you are working with is called the active window.

- To customize the desktop, you can create desktop folders, add desktop icons or shortcuts, and delete, move, and rename these objects.

- The Computer window is designed to help you find, view, and manage files easily and effectively. Besides displaying files and folders, you use the Computer window to examine file types; change the view of the folder and its files; sort files; manage folders; select, move, copy, delete, and rename files; display file properties; and find files.

- You should take caution when manipulating files by using a standard naming convention to name folders, organizing files and folders logically, deleting unnecessary files, and regularly backing up important files.

- Be aware of common file management problems, including locating files that are difficult to find; learning how to work with attributes to open files that are read-only, hidden, or shared; and naming files to preserve their file extension so they are associated with the appropriate application.

■ LESSON REVIEW

TRUE / FALSE

Circle T if the statement is true or F if the statement is false.

T   F   **1.**   Files and folders should be backed up to an external device on a regular basis.

T   F   **2.**   The Computer window provides tools to help you search for files and folders.

T   F   **3.**   The Help and Support Center provides three options for online help: Windows Remote Assistance, Microsoft Answers, and Microsoft Customer Support.

T   F   **4.**   Windows 7 is available for purchase in six editions.

T   F   **5.**   The Windows desktop is the main screen area that you see after you turn on your computer.

MULTIPLE CHOICE

Select the best response for the following statements:

1. The Windows desktop contains _____ main sections.

   A. four   C. three

   B. six   D. seven

2. The _____ appears on the desktop by default and is used for discarding files, folders, and other items.

   A. Computer icon   C. Gadget Gallery

   B. Recycle Bin   D. Properties dialog box

3. When multiple windows are open on your desktop, the one you are working with is called the _____ .

   A. Computer window   C. working window

   B. active window   D. desktop window

4. The desktop can display which of the following gadgets?

   A. Clock   C. Weather

   B. CPU Meter   D. all of the above

5. You can use the _____ to close an unresponsive application.

   A. Task Manager   C. application toolbar

   B. Restart button   D. Process A button

FILL IN THE BLANK

1. Windows 7 is available for purchase in _____ different editions.

2. Click the _____ button to hide a window without closing it.

3. You can modify the _____ that are displayed on your desktop.

4. A(n) _____ on the desktop is an icon that represents a link to an item.

5. A(n) _____ file is not displayed in a folder window.

◼ PROJECTS

PROJECT 9–1

1-3.2.4

Using your browser, access the following Web site: *http://windows.microsoft.com/en-US/windows7/help/ getting-started.* This Web page contains links to a number of Windows 7 Help pages and how-to videos. Select one of the links and review the Web site content. Then use your word-processing software to list and describe what you learned. Be sure to include the Web site address of the content that you selected.

PROJECT 9–2

1-3.2.7

This lesson discussed techniques for naming and organizing files and folders. Assume you have a new computer and are going to install new files and programs. Data files will include files for your course work. Based on the information in this lesson, complete the following:

1. Describe the naming convention that you would use for files and the naming convention that you would use for folders.

2. Explain why you selected this particular naming convention and how it applies to the organization of your folders and files.

PROJECT 9–3

The Web site located at *http://windows.microsoft.com/ en-US/windows7/help/getting-started* has a number of tutorials about using Windows 7. One of the tutorials focuses on how to change computer sounds. Review the information contained in the "To change a sound scheme" tutorial, and then try the steps yourself on a PC. Use your word processing program to list the steps. Also explain how to preview a sound for a program event. Restore the computer to its original sound scheme when you are finished.

TEAMWORK PROJECT

Windows 7 includes many tools and techniques for finding files. Complete the following:

1. Team up with one or two of your classmates and research the following ways to find files: using the Search text box on the Start menu, using a search box in a folder window, expanding a search beyond a specific folder, using search filters, and saving a search.

2. Create an outline that lists the major steps for finding files. Which method do you recommend when searching for files?

CRITICAL THINKING

Windows 7 includes many accessibility options. Complete the following:

1. Visit the Microsoft Web site at *www.microsoft.com/enable/ products/windows7*.

2. Select three of the Windows 7 accessibility options, and read all the information and view the videos provided about each one.

3. In a word-processing document, describe each option and give examples of how someone could use the option.

ONLINE DISCOVERY

The Windows 7 Forums is a Web site separate from Microsoft that provides news, updates, tutorials, and solutions to problems with Windows 7. Complete the following:

1. Access the following Web site: *www.sevenforums.com/tutorials/ 257-windows-7-tutorial-index.html*.

2. Scroll through the list of tutorials until you find one that interests you.

3. Review the tutorial, perform the steps on a computer, and then write a description of the topic. Explain what you learned and how you can implement it for your own personal use. If necessary, restore the computer to its original state.

JOB SKILLS

Anyone using a Windows PC at their work place needs to know the basics of Windows management. Other types of technology expertise that employers value vary from year to year. Learn about current trends in technology careers by doing some online research. Complete the following:

1. Using your favorite search engine, research trends in technology careers for the current year.

2. Review the trends described on at least three Web sites.

3. Using a word-processing program, list what you see as the top three trends in technology jobs today. Briefly describe each trend.

LESSON 10

Operating System Customization

■ OBJECTIVES

Upon completion of this lesson, you should be able to:

- Use the Control Panel.
- Select Control Panel settings.
- Set up printers.
- Change system settings.
- Install and uninstall software.
- Troubleshoot common software problems.

■ DATA FILES

You do not need data files to complete this lesson.

■ WORDS TO KNOW

Appearance and Personalization category

Clock, Language, and Region category

Control Panel

Ease of Access category

Hardware and Sound category

Mail Setup

Network and Internet category

notification area

Program Compatibility Wizard

Programs category

startup program

System and Security category

System Restore

system setting

User Accounts and Family Safety category

MODULE 1   Computing Fundamentals

Windows 7 provides a number of ways to change system preferences and settings and to install and uninstall hardware and software. You can access most operations through the Control Panel. This lesson focuses on how to use the Control Panel to view and modify preferences.

1-3.3.1

▶ **VOCABULARY**
Control Panel

Using the Control Panel

You use the **Control Panel** to change and customize settings on your computer, such as the desktop, time zone, and account picture. Recall that the left pane of the Start menu includes a list of programs. The right pane has links to some of the more commonly used programs and commands. One of these commands is the Control Panel. To open the Control Panel, click the Start button and then click the Control Panel command on the Start menu (see **Figure 10–1**).

FIGURE 10–1   Control Panel command on the Start menu

Clicking the Control Panel command displays the window shown in **Figure 10–2**.

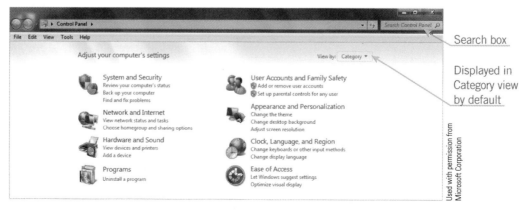

FIGURE 10–2   Control Panel window

The Control Panel is the primary location for all of your operating system configuration needs. The Control Panel opens in Category view by default and displays eight categories. Each category contains a number of tools for customizing or managing your system. Note that in Figure 10–2 a Search box is available that makes it easy for you to locate a specific tool. Begin typing the name of the tool in the Search box to display the tool in the Control Panel window.

This section provides an overview of popular Control Panel tools, including a brief explanation of how to apply these features. In each case, the settings and options on your computer might be different depending on the hardware and software installed.

The *System and Security category* includes settings for a variety of system tasks. This window contains links to all of the tools that are used to perform administrative, system, and security-related tasks. Popular tasks include the following:

- Review the computer's status and resolve issues by troubleshooting common problems
- Check firewall status and view the amount of RAM installed
- Turn automatic updating off and on
- Require a password when the computer wakes
- Back up and restore files from backup
- Free disk space and defragment the hard drive

You also can use the options in this category to check for Windows updates and to view Windows security features. **Figure 10–3** shows a complete list of all of these tools.

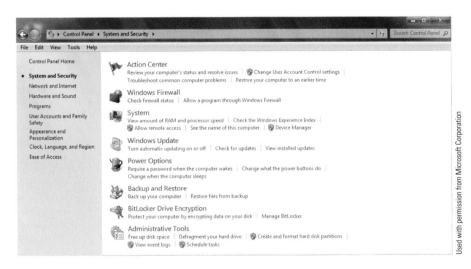

FIGURE 10–3   System and Security window

Used with permission from Microsoft Corporation

▶ **VOCABULARY**
System and Security category

MODULE 1 Computing Fundamentals

▶ **VOCABULARY**

Network and Internet category

Hardware and Sound category

Programs category

The options in the *Network and Internet category* help you to connect to the Internet, view a network and its computers and devices, synchronize with other computers, and perform other networking tasks. Use the options in the Network and Internet window to connect to a network or the Internet. See **Figure 10–4**.

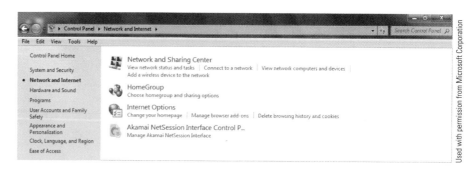

FIGURE 10–4   Network and Internet window

Figure 10–5 provides an overview of the options accessed through the *Hardware and Sound category*, which lets you manage hardware devices such as printers, the mouse, and the keyboard. You also can set power options, adjust and change the sound system, manage audio devices, and set the screen resolution.

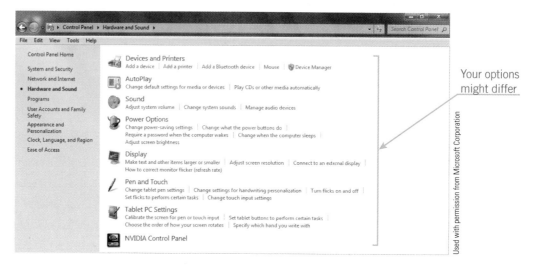

FIGURE 10–5   Hardware and Sound window

The options in the *Programs category* allow you to uninstall a program or view installed updates. See **Figure 10–6**. You also use this window to turn Windows features on and off, activate programs made for previous versions of Windows, and add or uninstall desktop gadgets. Additional gadgets are available online.

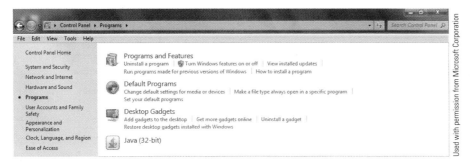

FIGURE 10–6   Programs window

Using the **User Accounts and Family Safety category**, you can change user accounts and passwords, set up parental controls, change a user's online profile, manage Windows credentials, and manage e-mail accounts. See **Figure 10–7**.

▶ **VOCABULARY**

User Accounts and Family Safety category

Appearance and Personalization category

FIGURE 10–7   User Accounts and Family Safety window

The **Appearance and Personalization category** provides options to personalize the desktop by selecting a new color scheme, changing the background, adjusting the screen resolution, and so on. **Figure 10–8** shows the other appearance and personalization options you can modify.

QUICK TIP

You also can change the screen resolution and open the Personalization window by right-clicking the desktop and then selecting Screen resolution or Personalize on the shortcut menu.

FIGURE 10–8   Appearance and Personalization window

MODULE 1   Computing Fundamentals

▶ **VOCABULARY**

Clock, Language, and Region category

Ease of Access category

The *Clock, Language, and Region category* contains options that help you localize your computer. See **Figure 10–9**. For instance, use the Date and Time options to set the time and date, change the time zone, add clocks for different time zones, and add the clock gadget to the desktop. In the Region and Language option, you can change location; the date, time, or number format; and keyboards or other input methods. Clicking the Windows Live Language Setting opens a window with a list of a variety of different language options.

FIGURE 10–9   Clock, Language, and Region window

The *Ease of Access category* helps to make your computer accessible to all users. You can change how your mouse and keyboard work and set up the speech recognition option. **See Figure 10–10.**

FIGURE 10–10   Ease of Access window

If the computer on which you are working is networked, you may not have permission to change all the Control Panel settings. The network administrator can restrict access to settings to prevent unauthorized users from making changes that can affect other users in a network. Examples include creating a new user account or altering regional or language settings. Some hardware settings that control peripherals (such as printers and modems) are allocated through the network and can be protected so that changes made by one user will not affect the entire network.

In Step-by-Step 10.1, you open the Control Panel and then select a new screen saver.

Step-by-Step 10.1

1. Click the **Start** button 🪟 on the taskbar, and then click **Control Panel** to display the Control Panel window.

2. Click the **Appearance and Personalization** category.

3. In the Personalization section of the Appearance and Personalization window, click the **Change screen saver** link to display the Screen Saver Settings dialog box shown in **Figure 10–11**.

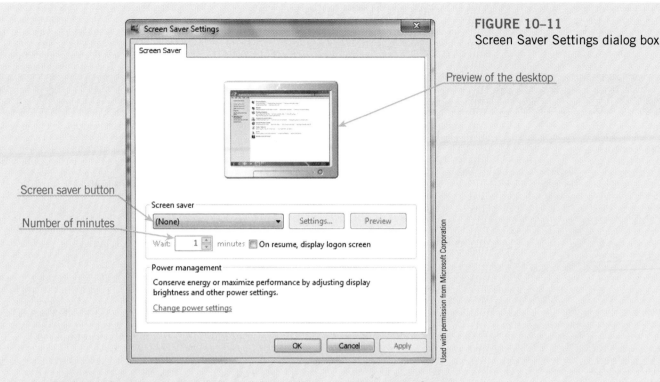

FIGURE 10–11
Screen Saver Settings dialog box

4. Click the **Screen saver** button, and then click a screen saver of your choice, such as Bubbles.

5. Click in the **Wait** text box, and then enter the number of minutes you want the computer to wait before the screen saver starts, such as 5.

6. Click **OK** to accept the settings. Then click the **Back** button until you return to the Control Panel window.

7. Use your word-processing program to open a new document, and then type **Step-by-Step 10.1** at the top of the page. Describe the two changes you made in the Screen Saver Settings dialog box. Save your document using the filename **ic3_ch10**. Keep the document open and leave the Control Panel window open for the next Step-by-Step exercise.

Selecting Control Panel Settings

As noted earlier in this lesson, the Control Panel lets you view and manipulate basic operating system settings and controls. You use some options to change the appearance of the screen or to modify the behavior of input devices. Other options affect various functions such as security or disability settings.

1-3.3.2

Common Control Panel System Settings

The following step-by-step exercises illustrate how to change typical settings such as date and time, display settings, audio volume, mouse and keyboard, disability settings, and security settings.

1-3.3.3

MODULE 1 Computing Fundamentals

Date and Time Settings

In Step-by-Step 10.2, you modify the Date and Time settings.

Step-by-Step 10.2

1. If necessary, display the Control Panel window.

2. Click the **Clock, Language, and Region** link to display the Clock, Language, and Region window. (If necessary, refer to **Figure 10–9** while completing this exercise.)

   The Date and Time category provides the following options: Set the time and date, Change the time zone, Add clocks for different time zones, and Add the Clock gadget to the desktop.

3. Click the **Set the time and date link** to display the Date and Time dialog box shown in **Figure 10–12**. (If a User Account Control dialog box opens, click the **Continue** button and enter a password, if requested.)

FIGURE 10–12
Date and Time dialog box

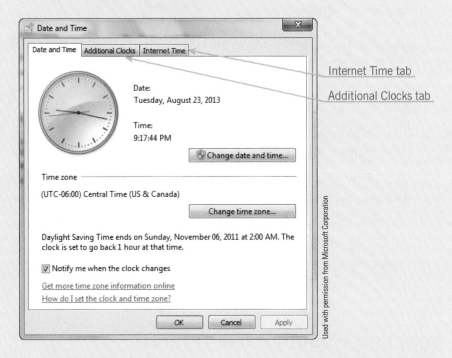

4. Click the **Change time zone** button to display the Time Zone Settings dialog box. If the Automatically **adjust clock for Daylight Saving Time** box is not checked, click the box to insert a check mark. Click the **OK** button to return to the Date and Time dialog box.

5. Click the **Additional Clocks** tab. Note that through this dialog box, you can select additional clocks to display the time in other time zones.

6. Click the **Internet Time** tab as shown in **Figure 10–13**. Note that the computer in Figure 10–13 is set to synchronize with *time.windows.com*. (Your computer might be set to synchronize with a different Web site.)

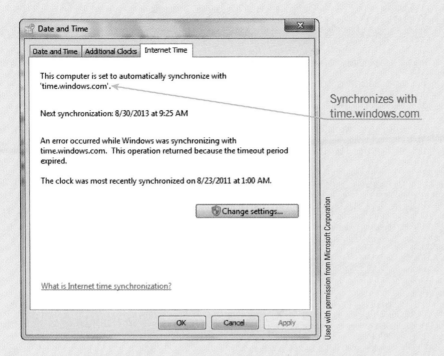

FIGURE 10–13
Internet Time tab

7. Click the **OK** button to close the Date and Time dialog box. Click the **Back** button ⬅ to return to the Control Panel window.

8. If necessary, open your **ic3_ch10** word-processing document. Enter **Step-by-Step 10.2** as a new heading. Then write a paragraph describing what you learned in this exercise.

In addition to using the Control Panel, you also can change some settings by clicking the appropriate icon on the right side of the taskbar, which is called the ***notification area***. If some of the icons are hidden on your taskbar, click the Show hidden icons button ▲ to display the hidden icons. See **Figure 10–14**.

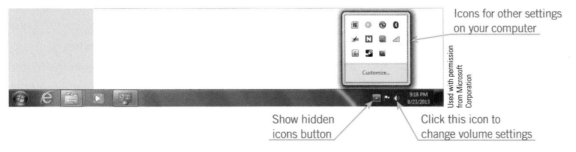

Icons for other settings on your computer

Show hidden icons button

Click this icon to change volume settings

FIGURE 10–14   Notification area of the Windows 7 taskbar

Mouse and Sound Settings

Mouse and keyboard settings also can be changed to meet your particular needs and requirements. In Step-by-Step 10.3, you explore how to change mouse and keyboard options.

Step-by-Step 10.3

1. If necessary, open the Control Panel window, and then click the **Hardware and Sound** category.

2. In the Devices and Printers section of the Hardware and Sound window, click the **Mouse** link to display the Mouse Properties dialog box shown in **Figure 10–15**.

FIGURE 10–15
Mouse Properties dialog box

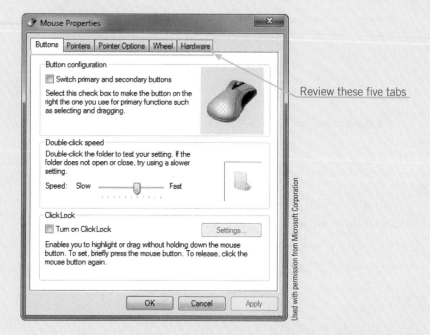

Review these five tabs

Used with permission from Microsoft Corporation

3. Review five of the tabs in the Mouse Properties dialog box: Buttons, Pointers, Pointer Options, Wheel, and Hardware. Click the **Cancel** button to close the dialog box without changing any settings. Return to the Hardware and Sound window.

4. If necessary, open your **ic3_ch10** word-processing document. Enter **Step-by-Step 10.3** as a new heading. Enter **Mouse Properties** as a subheading. Write a short description of each of the five tabs in the Mouse Properties dialog box.

In Step-by-Step 10.4, you explore the sound settings, including playing sounds on speakers, recording sounds with a device such as a microphone, setting system sounds, and working with other communication settings.

Step-by-Step 10.4

1. Return to the Hardware and Sound window, if necessary.

2. Click the **Sound** link to display the Sound dialog box shown in **Figure 10–16**. Review each of the tabs in the dialog box: Playback, Recording, Sounds, and Communications.

FIGURE 10–16
Sound dialog box

3. Click **OK** to close the Sound dialog box. If necessary, open your **ic3_ch10** word-processing document. Enter **Step-by-Step 10.4** as a new heading. Enter **Sound Properties** as a subheading. Write a short description of each of the four tabs in the Sound dialog box.

4. Click the **Back** button ⬅ until you return to the Control Panel window.

5. Click the **Ease of Access** link in the Control Panel window. Review the five options in this window: Let Windows suggest settings, Optimize visual display, Replace sounds with visual cues, Change how your mouse works, and Change how your keyboard works. Then click **Ease of Access Center** to display disability options. Below the **Step-by-Step 10.4** heading in the **ic3_ch10** document, enter **Ease of Access** as a subheading, and then describe the Ease of Access Center options. Save the **ic3_ch10** document.

6. If necessary, click the **Back** button 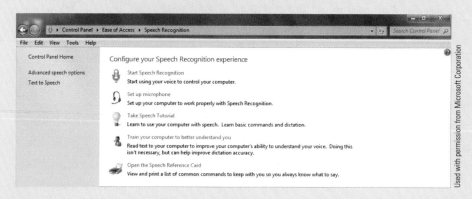 to return to the **Ease of Access** window. Click the **Speech Recognition link** and review the options in the Speech Recognition window shown in **Figure 10–17**.

FIGURE 10–17
Speech Recognition window

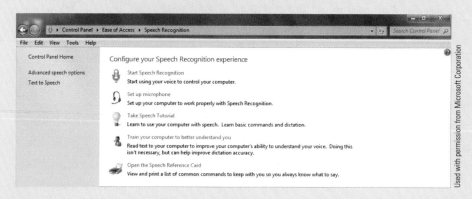

7. Return to the Control Panel window.

Security Settings

Windows contains a number of security options, which can easily be accessed in the Action Center. On the Control Panel Home page, click the System and Security link, and then click Action Center to open the Action Center window. Click Security, if necessary, to display the Security options. The following provides an overview of the Action Center security options.

- *Network firewall*: Monitors the system to verify that a firewall such as Windows Firewall is installed, determines if the firewall should be on or off, and determines if a program should be allowed through the firewall
- *Windows Update*: Turns automatic updating on or off, checks for updates, and views installed updates
- *Virus protection*: Monitors whether antivirus software is installed and up to date
- *Spyware and unwanted software protection*: Monitors the system to verify that antispyware software, such as Windows Defender, is installed and set up to scan the computer
- *Internet security settings*: Includes changing security settings, deleting browsing history and cookies, and managing browser add-ons
- *User Account Control*: Monitors whether User Account Control (UAC) is turned on to notify you when programs try to make changes to the computer
- *Network Access Protection*: Allows network administrators to help protect the security of a network

ETHICS IN TECHNOLOGY

Spyware and Phishing

Many types of software can be harmful to your computer. For example, computer viruses are programs attached to a file and run when you open the file. Spyware is software that secretly monitors your computer activity and collects personal or private information, such as credit card numbers and passwords.

When spyware installs itself on your computer, it can change system settings, interrupt programs, and slow computer performance. Spyware often infects your computer when you visit certain Web sites or download a free program, such as a screen saver or search toolbar.

Occasionally, a type of spyware called adware changes your browser settings to open pop-up ads or divert your browser to Web sites that advertise a product or service. These Web sites might be phishing sites, which attempt to deceive you into revealing personal or financial information. Phishing sites often look like official sites by including logos from reputable businesses, and provide text boxes for entering sensitive information such as account numbers and passwords. Some browsers, including Internet Explorer, include a feature that helps to detect phishing sites. (In Internet Explorer, this feature is called SmartScreen Filter.) Beware of any urgent or exciting but false statements in an e-mail message that want you to react immediately by providing sensitive information. Always make sure you are using a secure Web site when submitting credit card or other confidential information by verifying the address in the Address bar, looking for a Web address that starts with "https", and verifying that a security lock icon appears in the browser's status bar. Some phishing sites can display fake versions of these security devices, so the best advice is to avoid providing any information unless you know or can verify the recipient.

When the status of an Action Center item changes (for example, your antivirus software becomes out of date) Action Center alerts you with a message in the notification area. The status of the item in the Action Center window changes color. For example, red items need urgent attention, while yellow items can be handled at your convenience. You can point to the Action Center icon (a flag) in the notification area to display Action Center messages.

ABOVE AND BEYOND

Windows Vista introduced the Security Center. Windows 7 includes the Action Center instead, which provides security and maintenance options.

Setting Up Printers

You may have access to one or more printers or have several printers installed on your computer. Using the Devices and Printers option in the Hardware and Sound window makes it easy to add or remove printers. The following Step-by-Step exercise shows how to display and update printers.

1-3.3.4

Step-by-Step 10.5

1. If necessary, open the Control Panel window. Click **Hardware and Sound**, and then click **Devices and Printers**. The available printers and fax devices are displayed in the Devices and Printers window, and the toolbar includes buttons for performing common tasks. Click a printer to select it. See **Figure 10–18**. Most likely your list of devices and printers will be different from that in Figure 10–18.

FIGURE 10–18
Devices and Printers window

Add a printer button

Remove device button

Set as the default printer

Used with permission from Microsoft Corporation

2. To add a printer, click the **Add a printer** button on the toolbar to start the Add Printer Wizard. Click **Add a local printer**, and then click **Next** in the next three dialog boxes to review printer information. Click the **Cancel** button to return to the Devices and Printers window.

3. To change the default printer, right-click the printer you want to use as the default, and then click **Set as default printer** on the shortcut menu. Right-click the printer again, and then click the **Printing preferences** on the shortcut menu to display the Printing Preferences dialog box.

4. Review each tab in the Printing Preferences dialog box. If necessary, open your **ic3_ch10** word-processing document. Enter **Step-by-Step 10.5** as a new heading, and then write a short description of each of the three options contained in the Printing Preferences dialog box. Close the Printing Preferences dialog box.

5. To remove a printer, select the printer, and then click the **Remove device** button.

6. In the Address bar of the Devices and Printers window, click **Hardware and Sound** to return to the Hardware and Sound window.

7. Close the Hardware and Sound window.

Changing System Settings

As you have learned, if you have permission within your particular environment, you can use the Control Panel to change your computer's *system settings*, which are the settings that affect the entire computer. When making changes to the settings, however, it is important to understand the effect the change will have on the computer. For example, suppose you incorrectly change the system date or time. This will prevent your documents, e-mails, and other files from displaying the correct date or time. Or, you select a printer not connected to your network or make a change to your Internet connection. This type of change could result in endless hours of trying to resolve the problem. In some instances, you may not be able to make changes. If you are connected to a network, for example, you might not have permission to change specific settings.

When you do make changes, it is a good idea to record the original settings. If the new settings are not correct or need to be returned to the original settings, you have access to these settings.

If you do change a system setting that makes your system unstable, you can use Windows System Restore. *System Restore* creates and saves restore points on a regular basis. If an issue occurs and the system is not working correctly, you can use this feature to return the system files to an earlier point in time. To access System Restore, select the Control Panel and then type System Restore in the search box to start the System Restore Wizard.

1-3.3.5

▶ **VOCABULARY**
system setting
System Restore

◀ **ABOVE AND BEYOND**

Windows sets automatic restore points for system events such as software updates or program installation. You can set a restore point yourself by opening the Control Panel window, clicking the System link in the System and Security category, and then clicking System protection in the left pane. Click the System Protection tab, and then click Create. Enter a description for the restore point, and then click Create.

1-3.3.6

ABOVE AND BEYOND

If a message appears notifying you that you must have administrator rights to install a program, right-click the installation icon for the program, and then click Run as administrator. If the program installs but does not run, right-click the program icon, click Properties, click the Compatibility tab, select the Run this program as an administrator check box, and then try to run the program.

QUICK TIP

Software often includes an uninstall option that you can access by clicking the Start button, clicking the software folder, and then clicking an Uninstall command.

Installing and Uninstalling Software

Your computer most likely has many software programs already installed. Based on the installation media, it may be necessary to make a backup of the program. If the media is on a CD or DVD, most likely a backup is not necessary. The CD or DVD should be stored in a safe place. It also is a good idea to record the product key provided with the installation package. You can write the number on a label and attach it to the CD or DVD. If the software is downloaded from the Internet, then you can make a backup by copying the program to other media such as a CD, a USB drive, or an external hard drive. You also might consider e-mailing to yourself the product key for your software so you have the keys available in a central location.

At some point, however, you will want to install a new program or an updated version (upgrade) of a program you already have. An upgrade generally is not free, but usually costs less than purchasing the software for the first time. If an upgrade is made available, most likely it is to fix problems or to enhance existing features. In some instances, an upgrade may cause compatibility problems if you attempt to install the software on older hardware.

If you register with the software manufacturer, you may be notified of upgrades to the program by e-mail. You also can check the manufacturer's Web site for information about the most recent version of the software. Sometimes minor patches and updated material are offered to registered users at no cost.

Installing new or updated software is a simple procedure that starts by inserting a CD or DVD or by downloading a program from the Internet. Step-by-Step 10.6 provides instructions on installing software from a CD or DVD. Depending on the software, however, the steps may be somewhat different.

Step-by-Step 10.6

1. If you have a disc containing software you have not yet installed on your system, insert the installation disc into the appropriate drive, such as a CD or DVD drive.

2. Most likely an AutoPlay dialog box similar to the one in **Figure 10–19** will be displayed. Click **Run setup.exe**.

FIGURE 10–19
AutoPlay dialog box

Used with permission from Microsoft Corporation

If a dialog box or prompt is not displayed, then complete the following:

a. If necessary, use the Computer window to change to the drive that contains the disc.

b. If necessary, change the View to **Details**.

c. Locate the file named Setup or Install, and then double-click the filename.

d. Generally, an installation wizard is displayed. You might have to click a button to indicate that you agree to the software terms of use. After reading the terms, click the **Yes** or **Continue** button.

3. When the installation is complete, the installation wizard might indicate that the computer needs to restart before the program will be available. If you see this message, verify that all other programs are closed before clicking **OK** or **Finish** to restart the system.

4. After the computer restarts, double-click the **shortcut icon** on the desktop (or locate the name of the program in the All Programs list of the Start menu, and then click the program name).

5. You might be requested to register the program. Registering new software is a good idea, so that you can take advantage of technical support and upgrades offered by the software company. If you have an Internet connection, you can register the program online. If not, click the **Register Later** option to begin using the program.

The same basic instructions apply for installing downloaded software. To install software downloaded from the Internet, complete Step-by-Step 10.7.

Step-by-Step 10.7

1. Download an installation file from a Web site, and then locate the file you downloaded. In many instances, you may need to unzip the file. If you do, right-click the filename, click **Extract All**, select a location for the extracted files, and then click the **Extract** button. If you are using a program such as WinZip, right-click the filename, select **Open with WinZip** or select **Open with** and then select the appropriate program to unzip the file. Make a note of the location of the unzipped files.

2. Locate the unzipped files, and then look for the filename Setup or Install. Double-click the file and follow the prompts to install the software.

3. Use your word-processing software to list the Web site address from where you downloaded the file, the name of the file, and a description of the file you downloaded and how it was installed.

4. Submit a copy of your document to your instructor.

Uninstalling Software Programs

When software programs become outdated or are no longer used, you should uninstall them from the computer's hard drive. Step-by-Step 10.8 provides instructions on how to remove (uninstall) software programs.

Step-by-Step 10.8

1. Open the Control Panel window, and then click **Uninstall a program** in the Programs category to open the Programs and Features window. Wait a moment while Windows 7 compiles a list of installed programs.

2. If necessary, scroll the list to locate the name of the program you want to uninstall. Click the program name to select it. See **Figure 10–20**.

FIGURE 10–20
Programs and Features window

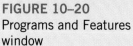
Uninstall button

Selected program

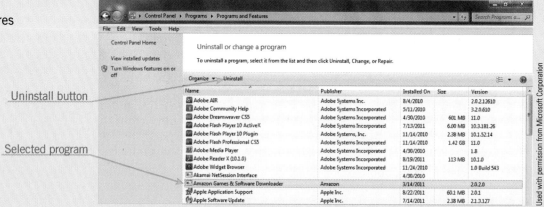

Used with permission from Microsoft Corporation

3. Click the **Uninstall** button or the **Uninstall/Change** button on the toolbar. A dialog box is displayed verifying that you want to remove the program. A User Account Control dialog box might also appear, asking you to verify that you want to continue and to enter a password. Click **Continue**.

4. To remove the program, click the **Yes** button or the **Uninstall** button. Click the **No** button or the **Cancel** button to leave the program installed on your computer. (These instructions might vary depending on the program you are removing.)

You use similar steps to install updates and upgrades to existing programs. An update is a fix for a specific problem in the software. If automatic updating is turned on, updates are installed automatically. Otherwise, to install an update, you need to review and then select the updates from the list that Windows finds for your computer. Optional updates are not installed automatically.

Software as a Service (SaaS)

Recall from Chapter 6 that Software as a Service (SaaS) is a type of software delivery method. The software is provided to customers through the Internet, an intranet, or another network. Bill Gates, founder of Microsoft Corporation, described the software "services wave" as the "next sea change that is upon us." To subscribe to a SaaS application, you must pay a monthly or annual subscription fee, and then access the software online. This eliminates factors such as hardware, installation fees, and upkeep. Some concerns with this model are security of the data, availability of the software program, and control of the data.

Managing User Accounts

Windows 7 has two types of user accounts: standard user accounts and administrator accounts. Standard users cannot install or uninstall applications in the root directory, change system settings, or perform other administrative tasks unless they can provide the correct password for the Administrator account. User Account options are accessed through the Control Panel. Clicking User Accounts and Family Safety opens the User Accounts and Family Safety window. You can click the User Accounts link in this window to perform the following tasks:

- *Change your picture*: Clicking this link lets you select a new picture for your account (see **Figure 10–21**).

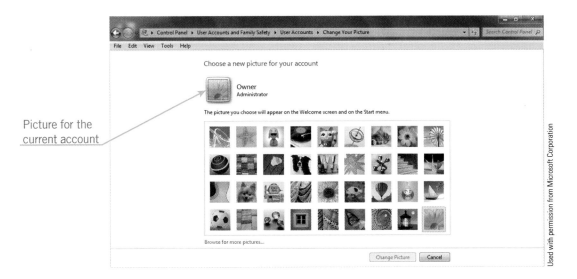

FIGURE 10–21   Change Your Picture window

- *Change your account name*: Clicking this option opens a window and provides a text box for a new account name.

- *Change your account type*: This window provides options to create a Standard user and an Administrator account. Microsoft recommends that everyone using a computer should have a Standard account. Doing so helps to protect your computer because it prevents users from making changes that affect everyone else. Recall that only the Administrator can install software on a computer.

- *Manage another account*: The Manage Accounts window allows the Administrator to select an account and turn it on or off and to make other changes, including changing the account name, picture, and account type; creating a password; and deleting the account. See **Figure 10–22**.

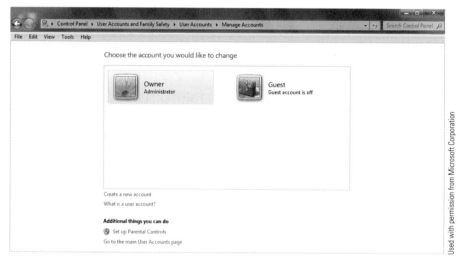

FIGURE 10–22   Manage Accounts window

Mail is an option available in the User Accounts and Family Safety window. Using *Mail Setup*, you can create e-mail accounts and directories, change settings for Outlook files, and set up multiple profiles of e-mail accounts and data files (see **Figure 10–23**).

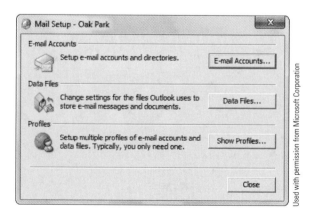

FIGURE 10–23   Mail Setup dialog box

QUICK TIP

To view all Control Panel items, you also can click the arrow button next to "Control Panel" in the Address bar, and then click All Control Panel Items.

To view a complete list of all the tools available in the Control Panel, click the View by button (which displays *Category* by default), and then click Large icons or click Small icons.

Troubleshooting Common Software Problems

1-3.3.7

Generally, software installation is a fairly smooth process. You insert the installation media or unzip the installation file, double-click the setup or install file, and follow the prompts. Occasionally, however, issues occur that prevent the installation for one reason or another. The following list describes some common installation problems.

■ *Install/uninstall software on a network*: Software installation on a network generally is reserved for the administrator or other designated employees. If software is being installed or uninstalled on a computer connected to a network or another computer that does not contain your username or if you are not an administrator, a network policy may prohibit installation rights except for those individuals who have been approved. Contact the administrator or supervisor to resolve the issue.

■ *Defective or lost installation media*: When installing software, you might not always want to install the entire program—you might not need all the features, for example, or have enough disk space. Later on, you might decide to add features and discover that the disk is damaged or missing. If you have registered your software or have proof of purchase, then in most instances you can contact the manufacturer and ask for a replacement disc. Depending on the company, a fee may be charged, or the company may provide the software free of charge.

■ *Installation program will not start*: When you insert the CD or other disk, generally the **Startup program** runs automatically. When this does not occur, use the Computer program to view the CD and search for a file named setup.exe, startup.exe, or install.exe. Double-click this file to start the program. If this does not work, check the information that came with your software or go to the manufacturer's Web site.

■ *Installation stops before completion*: If the program stops responding during installation, most likely there is a problem with the program. The first strategy is to close the program and then restart it. If the program still will not work, there could be issues with your computer or the media could be damaged. Sometimes if you wait, some programs will start responding again. Your next step would be to view the manufacturer's Web site and see if it provides a solution. If not, then contact the manufacturer. If a program fails to start, most likely it means that a problem has occurred in the program itself. If a program freezes, you can press the Ctrl+Alt+Del keys or right-click the taskbar to display a shortcut menu, and then select Start Task Manager. In the Windows Task Manager dialog box, select the process related to the program, and then click the End Process button.

■ *Installed program is not displayed*: The program could be an older version that is not compatible with Windows 7, or a driver could be damaged or needs to be updated. Another possibility is that the executable file that starts the program could have been deleted or damaged. Reviewing the folder that contained the program files would verify if this was or was not the issue. Using the **Program Compatibility Wizard**, you can change the compatibility settings for the program. To access the Program Compatibility Wizard, click Programs in the Control Panel and then click Run programs made for previous versions of Windows.

■ *Installed program fails to work*: Similar issues to those of programs that are not displayed. It could be an operating system compatibility problem, program files could be damaged or deleted, or it could be an incompatibility issue with other programs. Running the Program Compatibility Wizard would eliminate any compatibility issues. If this does not work, the program may have to be uninstalled and then reinstalled.

▶ **VOCABULARY**
Startup program

Program Compatibility Wizard

- *Other programs fail to work after new product is installed*: This could be due to a conflict with another program. Virtualization tools, such as Virtual PC and VMware, are free downloads on the Internet. You can use these programs for compatibility testing. Some Windows 7 background processes also can cause issues. Using the System Configuration Utility (MSCONFIG) can help resolve the background conflicts.

- *Files cannot be read by new application*: Several reasons could account for this issue: a) you might not have permission to access the file; b) the file may be damaged; c) the file could have been created in an older version of the software and the newer version does not read older versions; d) the file does not have the correct extension; or e) the file may be encrypted. To check the file, right-click the filename and then click Properties. Click the General tab and then click Advanced. If the "Encrypt contents to secure data" check box is selected, open the file by using the certificate that was used to encrypt the file.

- *Access to an online application is denied*: Several reasons could account for the denial. The logon could be incorrect or not activated; the site fee could be past due; or the site could be going through an update process. Wait for 10 minutes or so and then try to access the Web site again. Otherwise, contact the Web site through e-mail or telephone to determine the problem.

- *Online application not available*: Several reasons could account for an online application not being available: the Web site could be down or the site could be busy with the maximum number of users. Wait for 10 minutes or so and then try to access the Web site again. Otherwise, contact the Web site through e-mail or telephone to determine the problem.

SUMMARY

In this lesson, you learned:

- You use the Control Panel to change and customize settings on your computer. One popular category is System and Security, which provides settings for a variety of system tasks, such as backup and restore, power options, and Windows Update. Another frequently used category is Appearance and Personalization, which provides options to personalize the desktop by selecting a new color scheme, changing the background, and adjusting the screen resolution.

- You also can change some system and program settings by double-clicking the appropriate icon in the notification area of the taskbar.

- The Action Center provides options to turn a network firewall on or off, set up Windows Update for automatic updating, select programs for virus and spyware protection, set Internet security options, and other security settings.

- When you use the Control Panel to change your computer's system settings, make sure you understand the effect the change will have on the computer. It also is a good idea to record the original settings. If you do make a system change that makes your system unstable, you can use Windows System Restore, a built-in tool that creates and saves restore points on a regular basis.

- You can install software from installation media such as a CD or DVD, or from a file downloaded from a Web site. In either case, you follow similar steps: double-click the setup or install file, and then follow the prompts to install the software.

- To uninstall software, open the Control Panel, and then use the Uninstall link in the Programs category to remove the software from your computer.

- Windows 7 has two types of user accounts: Standard user accounts and Administrator accounts. Standard users cannot install or uninstall applications in the root directory, change system settings, or perform other administrative tasks unless they can provide the correct password for the Administrator account.

- Typical software problems include defective or lost installation media, an installation program that does not start or starts and then stops, an installed program that does not open, and other programs failing to work after a new product is installed.

■ LESSON REVIEW

TRUE / FALSE

Circle T if the statement is true or F if the statement is false.

T   F   **1.**   Mouse and keyboard settings also can be changed to meet your particular needs and requirements.

T   F   **2.**   The network administrator can restrict access to settings to prevent unauthorized users from making changes.

T   F   **3.**   In the Hardware and Sound category, clicking the Mouse link displays the Devices and Printers window.

T   F   **4.**   Printers are part of the Software category.

T   F   **5.**   If you download a zipped file, it is not necessary to unzip it before you can use the files it contains.

MULTIPLE CHOICE

Select the best response for the following statements.

1. The _____ can turn an account on and off.

   A.   system manager   C.   administrator

   B.   passenger   D.   student

2. To view a list of all Control Panel items at one time, you click the _____ button in the Control Panel window.

   A.   Administrative tools   C.   All

   B.   View by   D.   any of the above

3. If a program stops responding during installation, most likely there is a problem with the _____.

   A.   computer   C.   monitor

   B.   program   D.   mouse

4. When you insert an installation CD or DVD into the appropriate drive, generally the _____ runs automatically.

   A.   Programs window   C.   startup program

   B.   screen saver   D.   Administrator account

5. In the Mouse Properties dialog box, you can change _____.

   A.   button configurations   C.   vertical and horizontal scrolling

   B.   pointer options   D.   any of the above

FILL IN THE BLANK

Complete the following sentences by writing the correct word or words in the blanks provided.

1. When a software program becomes outdated, you should _____ it from the computer's hard drive.

2. If your computer system is not working correctly, you can use System Restore to return the _____ _____ to an earlier point in time.

3. In Windows 7, only someone with a(n) _____ _____ can install software on a computer.

4. Using the Program _____ Wizard, you can run programs designed for earlier versions of Windows.

5. If a program freezes, you can press the _____ keys or right-click the taskbar to display a shortcut menu, and then select _____ _____ _____ .

■ PROJECTS

PROJECT 10–1

The Control Panel provides access to information about what's new in Windows 7. Complete the following: 1-3.3.1

1. Open the Control Panel and then display all the Control Panel items using small icons.

2. Click Getting Started, and then review the information displayed in the Getting Started window.

3. Double-click the "Go online to find out what's new in Windows 7" link. Find three features new to Windows 7. Read information or watch videos about these new features, and then close your Web browser. Use your word-processing program to write a paragraph describing them. Explain why you think these features are valuable and how you could apply them.

4. In the Getting Started window, click the Personalize Windows link. Find two ways to personalize Windows that have not been covered in this lesson or in Project 10-2. Add a paragraph to your document describing these features.

5. Submit your document to your instructor.

PROJECT 10–2

Windows 7 lets you select a set of colors and other effects, called a theme, to display on your desktop according to your preferences. Complete the following: 1-3.3.1 1-3.3.2 1-3.3.3

1. Open the Control Panel in Category view, and then click the Change the theme link in the Appearance and Personalization category.

2. Note your current theme, and then review the various themes. Resize the Personalization window to display some of the desktop. If Aero themes are installed on your computer, click an Aero theme to display its effects on the desktop. What are the characteristics of the Aero theme you selected?

3. Select a theme in the Basic and High Contrast Themes section. What theme did you select? What are the characteristics of the theme? If you displayed an Aero theme in Step 2, how does the Basic or High Contrast theme compare to the Aero theme?

4. Restore your original theme, and then click the Desktop Background link to display the Desktop Background window. What is the purpose of this window?

5. Return to the Personalization window, and then click the Window Color link to display the Window Color and Appearance window. What is the purpose of this window?

6. In a word-processing document, provide your written responses to Steps 2–5.

PROJECT 10–3

Many organizations and schools deny access to the Control Panel or to some system settings. Complete the following: 1-3.3.5

1. In a word-processing document, create a table that lists the advantages and disadvantages of providing access to Control Panel settings.

2. Then explain why you agree or disagree with the policy to prevent computer users from changing system settings.

▰ TEAMWORK PROJECT

One of your coworkers is collecting informal inventories of all employees' installed programs. She has requested a list of the software on your computer in the following categories: security, multimedia, and communications. Complete the following:

1. Working with another student, create a table that includes three columns: one listing the program type, another listing the program name, and the third listing the location.

2. In each row, add information about the software installed on your computer in the security, multimedia, and communications categories. For the Location column, identify where you found information about the program.

3. Complete the table using the Control Panel and other resources on your computer.

CRITICAL THINKING

User Account Control (UAC) is a Windows feature that displays confirmation or permission dialog boxes before you perform a task that can affect the entire computer, such as installing or uninstalling software. To complete the task, Windows provides you administrator-level permissions. Some users find these dialog boxes intrusive and turn off UAC, though Microsoft recommends that you leave UAC on to keep your computer secure.

In a paragraph or bulleted list, answer the following question: What are the pros and cons of turning off UAC? Use Help and Support and other resources as necessary to support your answer.

1-3.3.5

ONLINE DISCOVERY

Access Microsoft's Windows 7 Web page at *windows.microsoft.com/en-US/windows/home*. Use the Search tools provided on the Web site to find information about customizing Windows 7. List at least three ways to customize Windows 7 that have not been discussed in this lesson, and then describe each method.

JOB SKILLS

Computer security is a major concern for employers. Knowing how to protect a computer requires thorough knowledge of the computer's operating system. Using online resources such as the Bureau of Labor Statistics (*www.bls.gov*), prepare a document that describes the following information about computer security specialists: job description, responsibilities, education and training, salary, and job outlook.

MODULE 1 REVIEW

Computing Fundamentals

■ REVIEW QUESTIONS

TRUE / FALSE

Circle T if the statement is true or F if the statement is false.

T   F   **1.** Embedded computers perform specific tasks and can be found in a range of devices such as a digital watch.

T   F   **2.** A common feature on laptop computers is the touchpad.

T   F   **3.** The hardware for your display consists of three elements: the monitor, the video card, and the LCD.

T   F   **4.** A cookie is a small text file that is attached to the monitor.

T   F   **5.** Useful life is defined as the estimated time period that an asset, such as a computer, will be of use to the owner.

T   F   **6.** You do not need a license for most software programs.

T   F   **7.** You use electronic spreadsheet software such as Microsoft Excel to create letters, contracts, and other similar documents.

T   F   **8.** An application file and a system file are the same type of file.

T   F   **9.** Windows 7 can be purchased in four different editions.

T   F   **10.** The Control Panel is used to change settings on your computer and to customize the display.

MULTIPLE CHOICE

Select the best response for each of the following statements.

1. Computers have been around for more than _____ years.

   A. 10   C. 25

   B. 32   D. 60

2. _____ produce an image by manipulating light within a layer of liquid crystal cells.

   A. Gas plasma monitors   C. CRT monitors

   B. LCD panels   D. Scanners

3. Many businesses and organizations use _____ to protect their data.

   A. cables   C. encryption

   B. systems   D. static electricity

4. If you spill liquid onto the keyboard, you should _____ .

   A. unplug it or turn it off immediately

   B. spray it with compressed air

   C. turn it upside down

   D. all of the above

5. A list of services designed to provide assistance to a company or an organization is called a _____ .

   A. warranty   C. contract

   B. spreadsheet   D. support agreement

6. The two basic types of computer software are _____ and _____ .

   A. program, application   C. application, system

   B. productivity, application   D. system, networking systems

7. A(n) _____ image is composed of pixels in a grid.

   A. access   C. squares

   B. vector   D. bitmap

8. _____ are programs used by the operating system to communicate with various hardware devices.

   A. Drivers   C. Spreadsheets

   B. Mice   D. Interfaces

9. _____ files are essential files necessary for running Windows.

   A. Database   C. Application

   B. System   D. Data

10. When you insert an installation CD or DVD into the appropriate drive, generally the _____ runs automatically.

    A. Programs window   C. startup program

    B. screen saver   D. Administrator account

FILL IN THE BLANK

Complete the following sentences by writing the correct word or words in the blanks provided.

1. You can think of RAM as _____ memory.

2. When software becomes outdated or is not used any longer, you should _____ it from the computer.

3. A(n) _____ is a row-and-column arrangement of data.

4. _____ software is a computer program you use to organize and present information.

5. The first step in the problem-solving process is to _____ the problem.

6. The _____ operating system is an open source program.

7. _____ software is used primarily to create, edit, and print documents.

8. A(n) _____ is a hardware device that allows a computer to run a program that was designed for a different operating system.

9. A(n) _____ is an icon that represents a link to an item, rather than the item itself.

10. A(n) _____ is a set of clearly defined, logical steps that solve a problem.

■ PROJECTS

PROJECT 1–1

Windows 7 contains a number of enhanced accessibility options and programs. Visit the Microsoft Accessibility page at *www.microsoft.com/enable/products/windows7* and review these options. Describe the purpose of the following tools and the improvements made to them in Windows 7: the Magnifier, On-Screen Keyboard, and Ease of Access Center.

PROJECT 1–2

You are ready to purchase a new computer, but are not sure what operating system you would like to have. Review the three operating systems discussed in Lesson 8 and then select the operating system you would prefer to use. Explain why you selected this particular system and describe at least three features that helped you make this decision.

PROJECT 1–3

Speech Recognition in Windows 7 is an improved feature. This element allows you to use your voice to control the computer. Explore this topic and then prepare a report describing how you can use Speech Recognition to run programs and interact with Windows. Also include information about which languages Speech Recognition supports.

PROJECT 1–4

You and your family have four computers in your house and have decided it is time for a wireless home network. You would like to share files and a printer. In a report of two or three pages, describe the type of equipment you need to set up the network. Also describe the type of software and security you need.

■ SIMULATION

You and a friend started a small computer consulting business. You offer technical support to computer users at home and at work, providing assistance with setting up hardware, troubleshooting problems, and using software effectively.

JOB 1–1

Your first client is a chain of local hardware stores. The president of the chain asks you to research and make suggestions on the upgrade of a new computer system to Windows 7. Right now, all of the company's computers use Windows XP. The typical computer has 1 GB of RAM, an Intel Pentium processor, and about 40 GB of hard disk space. Use the information you have learned in this module for your research, and supplement the information with research on the Internet or from print sources in the library. Prepare a report of three sections. One section should list the benefits of upgrading the system and the equipment that should be purchased. The second section should summarize the drawbacks of upgrading the system. The third section should contain a list of additional components that could be used to further enhance the system.

JOB 1–2

The local high school administrator would like to update the facility's student computer labs. The school has two labs with approximately 60 computers. Some of the computers are five years old, another set is about three years old, and a third set is a year old. The budget for the lab update is approximately $250,000. The school board would also like to purchase a projector with remote controls. Use the Internet and other resources and put together a plan that you and a partner will present to the school board.

■ ONLINE DISCOVERY

If you are looking for the meaning of a particular word, you can type define: in the Google search box followed by the word or phrase for which you are searching. For example, type the following to find the definition of *Internet*: **define: Internet**. If Google has the definition, the word and its definition appear at the top of your search results. If your search contains more than one word, each word appears as a separate link after the words "Search instead for". Click a word to view its dictionary definition.

Use Google's definition feature to find the meaning of the following terms. Define each term in your own words: CAT 6, cloud computing, digital certificate, extranet, IP address, proxy server, public domain, router (in networking), social media, WiMAX.

Finally, add three new words and definitions to the list related to computing. Share these with your classmates.

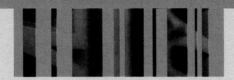

Estimated Time for Module: 23.5 hours

MODULE 2

KEY APPLICATIONS

nonexistent

LESSON 11   1.5 HRS.
Exploring Microsoft Office 2010

Word Processing

LESSON 12   1.5 HRS.
Getting Started with Word Essentials

LESSON 13   2 HRS.
Editing and Formatting Documents

LESSON 14   2 HRS.
Sharing Documents

LESSON 15   1.5 HRS.
Working with Tables

LESSON 16   1.5 HRS.
Enhancing Documents

LESSON 17   1.5 HRS.
Working with Graphics

Spreadsheets

LESSON 18   1.5 HRS.
Getting Started with Excel Essentials

LESSON 19   1.5 HRS.
Organizing and Enhancing Worksheets

LESSON 20   2 HRS.
Creating Formulas and Charting Data

Presentations

LESSON 21   1.5 HRS.
Getting Started with PowerPoint Essentials

LESSON 22   2 HRS.
Enhancing Presentations with Multimedia Effects

Databases

LESSON 23   2 HRS.
Getting Started with Access Essentials

LESSON 24   1.5 HRS.
Managing and Reporting Database Information

KEY APPLICATIONS

 LESSON 11

Exploring Microsoft Office 2010

2-1.1.1	2-1.1.5	2-1.2.2	2-1.2.5
2-1.1.2	2-1.1.7	2-1.2.3	2-1.2.6
2-1.1.3	2-1.1.8	2-1.2.4	2-2.1.16
2-1.1.4	2-1.1.9		

Word Processing

 LESSON 12

Getting Started with Word Essentials

2-1.1.3	2-1.1.7	2-1.2.1	2-1.3.1
2-1.1.5	2-1.1.9	2-1.2.4	2-2.1.16
2-1.1.6			

 LESSON 13

Editing and Formatting Documents

2-1.3.1	2-1.3.6	2-2.1.2	2-2.1.6
2-1.3.2	2-1.4.1	2-2.1.3	2-2.1.7
2-1.3.3	2-1.4.2	2-2.1.4	2-2.1.16
2-1.3.4	2-2.1.1	2-2.1.5	2-2.2.1
2-1.3.5			

 LESSON 14

Sharing Documents

2-1.4.1	2-1.4.4	2-1.4.6	2-2.2.3
2-1.4.2	2-1.4.5	2-1.4.7	2-2.2.4
2-1.4.3			

 LESSON 15

Working with Tables

2-2.1.3	2-2.1.14	2-2.1.15	2-2.1.16
2-2.1.13			

 LESSON 16

Enhancing Documents

2-1.1.8	2-1.4.6	2-2.1.10	2-2.1.16
2-1.2.1	2-2.1.8	2-2.1.11	2-2.2.2
2-1.2.4	2-2.1.9		

 LESSON 17

Working with Graphics

2-1.3.7	2-2.1.6	2-2.1.12	2-2.1.16
2-2.1.5			

Spreadsheets

 LESSON 18

Getting Started with Excel Essentials

2-1.1.1	2-1.1.5	2-1.3.1	2-3.1.2
2-1.1.2	2-1.1.6	2-1.3.2	2-3.1.3
2-1.1.3	2-1.2.4	2-1.3.3	2-3.1.4
2-1.1.4	2-1.2.5	2-3.1.1	

 LESSON 19

Organizing and Enhancing Worksheets

2-1.1.3	2-1.2.4	2-3.1.5	2-3.1.9
2-1.1.5	2-3.1.1	2-3.1.6	2-3.1.10
2-1.1.6	2-3.1.2	2-3.1.7	2-3.2.1
2-1.4.1	2-3.1.3	2-3.1.8	2-3.2.2
2-1.4.2	2-3.1.4		

 LESSON 20

Creating Formulas and Charting Data

2-1.3.2	2-3.1.10	2-3.2.5	2-3.2.8
2-3.1.1	2-3.2.3	2-3.2.6	2-3.2.9
2-3.1.2	2-3.2.4	2-3.2.7	2-3.2.10
2-3.1.4			

Presentations

 LESSON 21

Getting Started with PowerPoint Essentials

2-1.1.1	2-1.2.2	2-4.1.1	2-4.1.7
2-1.1.2	2-1.2.4	2-4.1.2	2-4.1.9
2-1.1.3	2-1.2.5	2-4.1.3	2-4.1.10
2-1.1.5	2-1.3.2	2-4.1.4	2-4.1.11
2-1.1.6	2-1.3.3	2-4.1.5	2-4.1.12
2-1.2.1	2-1.3.5		

 LESSON 22

Enhancing Presentations with Multimedia Effects

2-1.3.7	2-4.1.6	2-4.1.9	2-4.1.12
2-4.1.2	2-4.1.8	2-4.1.11	

LESSON 11

Exploring Microsoft Office 2010

■ OBJECTIVES

Upon completion of this lesson, you should be able to:

- Start Microsoft Office 2010 applications.
- Switch between application windows.
- Close applications.
- Navigate and identify the common elements in application windows.
- Identify the elements in the new Office 2010 user interface.
- Customize the Quick Access Toolbar.
- Open, save, and close documents.
- Use on-screen and online Help features.

■ DATA FILES

To complete this lesson, you will need these data files:

Recycled Vehicles.docx

Recycling.docx

Research (a folder containing Research Report.docx and Research Data.xlsx)

The 3Rs.pptx

Travel Expenses.xlsx

■ WORDS TO KNOW

application window

Backstage view

cursor

document window

file

file compatibility

file extension

folder

I-beam

insertion point

Jump List

minimized

open

path

Ribbon

save

ScreenTip

scroll

shortcut menu

subfolders

2-2.1.16

Microsoft Office 2010 is an integrated software package that enables you to share information between several applications. The applications available in Office are Word, PowerPoint, Excel, Access, Outlook, OneNote, Publisher, InfoPath, Lync, Project, SharePoint Workspace, and Visio. The applications available on your computer depend on which Office suite is installed and the options that were selected during the installation. Microsoft offers several different Office suites, such as Office Professional 2010 and Office Home and Student 2010. Each suite offers a different combination of applications.

Each Office application performs specific tasks. **Table 11–1** provides a brief description of the applications covered in depth in this module: Word, Excel, PowerPoint, and Access, as well as Outlook, which is introduced in the Living Online module of this text.

TABLE 11–1   Microsoft Office 2010 applications

APPLICATION	DESCRIPTION
Access	A database application that enables you to organize, manipulate, and analyze information such as addresses and inventory data
Excel	A spreadsheet application that enables you to work with text, numbers, and formulas to create tables, charts, worksheets, and financial documents
Outlook	An e-mail and scheduling application that enables you to manage e-mail, appointments, tasks, contacts, and events efficiently
PowerPoint	A presentation application that enables you to create multimedia slide shows, transparencies, outlines, and organizational charts
Word	A word-processing application that enables you to create and share documents such as letters, memos, and reports

Starting and Closing Applications

Starting applications, launching applications, and opening applications all have the same meaning. Closing applications and exiting applications also have the same meaning. Not only are the steps for starting and closing all Office applications the same, but the steps will apply to most other applications such as Internet Explorer and Windows Media Player. In Office applications, the File tab in the upper-left corner of the screen replaces the Office Button and the File menu that appear in earlier releases of Office. When you click the File tab, Backstage view is displayed. *Backstage view* provides quick access to common tasks for managing documents, such as saving, opening, and printing.

▶ **VOCABULARY**
Backstage view

application window

Starting Applications and Switching Between Applications

Depending on your computer setup and operating system, you can start most applications by double-clicking the application icon on the desktop or by using the Start button in the lower-left corner of the screen. When an application is started, an application window is displayed. The *application window* serves as the primary interface between the user and the application.

Multiple applications can be open at the same time. A button for each open application appears on the taskbar at the bottom of the screen. Buttons for commonly used applications, such as Internet Explorer and Windows Media Player, may also appear on the taskbar, even if they are not running. To rearrange the order of the buttons on the taskbar, you can drag and drop the application buttons to reposition them. To switch from one open application to another, click the application button on the taskbar.

To display the desktop without closing any of the applications, click the Show desktop button on the right side of the taskbar. The Show desktop button is subtle and transparent, but when you position the mouse pointer over the button, the name of the button is displayed in a small window called a ***ScreenTip***. When you click the Show desktop button, all the open applications are ***minimized***, which means the applications are still running, but the application windows are no longer displayed on the screen. However, the application button is still displayed on the taskbar, and when you click an application button on the taskbar, the application window reopens.

You can view multiple application windows at the same time by changing the layout of the windows on the screen. To access the different window layout options, you right-click the taskbar and select an option from a ***shortcut menu***, which is a list of commonly performed commands from the current window.

▶ **VOCABULARY**
ScreenTip

minimized

shortcut menu

Step-by-Step 11.1

1. Click the **Start** button on the taskbar. Application names may appear in the most frequently used programs list on the Start menu, as shown in **Figure 11–1**.

Frequently used applications

Start button

FIGURE 11–1
Start menu

IC³

2-1.1.1
2-1.1.5
2-1.2.2
2-1.2.3

Used with permission from Microsoft Corporation

2. You can start an application by clicking the application name in the most frequently used programs list on the Start menu, but instead click **All Programs**. A complete list of available programs is displayed.

3. If necessary, click the down arrow on the lower-right corner of the pane to move down through the list. Click the **Microsoft Office** folder. A list of all the programs in the folder is displayed. Click **Microsoft Word 2010** to open the Word application window shown in **Figure 11–2**. The title bar includes the application name.

FIGURE 11–2
Word application
window

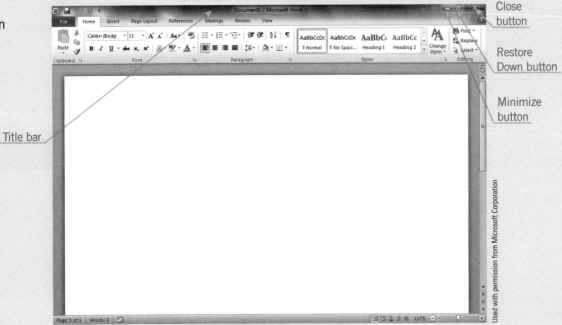

Title bar

Close button

Restore Down button

Minimize button

Used with permission from Microsoft Corporation

4. Click the **Start** button, click **All Programs**, click **Microsoft Office**, and then click **Microsoft Excel 2010**. The application window opens and shows a spreadsheet. Excel is now the active application. The Word application window may no longer be visible on the screen, but Word is still open and running.

5. Click the **Start** button, click **All Programs**, and then click **Microsoft Office**. Right-click **Microsoft PowerPoint 2010**. A shortcut menu is displayed to the right of the application name. In the shortcut menu, position the mouse pointer over **Send to** to display the submenu shown in **Figure 11–3**.

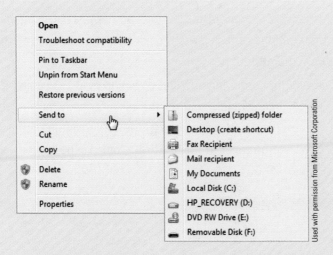

FIGURE 11–3
Shortcut menu with a submenu

6. In the submenu, click **Desktop (create shortcut)**. Then click the **Start** button to close the Start menu.

7. On the rightmost side of the taskbar, position the mouse pointer over the **Show desktop** button (but do not click the button). Then move the mouse pointer away from the Show desktop button, and the Excel window once again is displayed.

8. Click the **Show desktop** button to switch to the desktop and minimize all the running applications. You should see a shortcut icon for PowerPoint as shown in **Figure 11–4**.

FIGURE 11–4
Desktop shortcut icon for Microsoft PowerPoint 2010

9. Double-click the **Microsoft PowerPoint 2010** shortcut button to open the application. A presentation opens. Three applications are now running, and buttons for each of the running applications are displayed on the taskbar as shown in **Figure 11–5**.

Windows Explorer

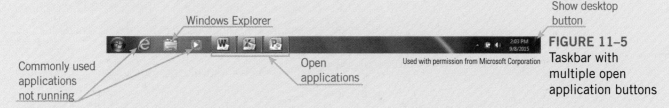

Commonly used applications not running

Open applications

Show desktop button

FIGURE 11–5
Taskbar with multiple open application buttons

10. Click the **Word** button on the taskbar to switch to that application. Then click the **Excel** button on the taskbar to switch to that application.

11. To rearrange the order of the buttons on the taskbar, drag and drop the **Word** button on the taskbar to reposition the button on the right side of the PowerPoint button.

12. To view multiple running application windows at the same time:

   a. Right-click a blank area on the taskbar, and then in the shortcut menu click **Cascade windows**. The three running application windows are arranged from top to bottom on the screen as shown in **Figure 11–6**.

FIGURE 11–6
Cascaded windows

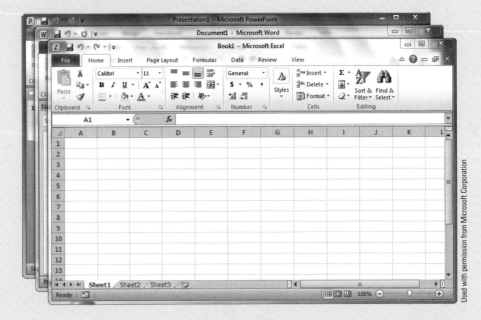

Used with permission from Microsoft Corporation

   b. Right-click a blank area on the taskbar, and then click **Undo Cascade**.

   c. Right-click a blank area on the taskbar, and then click **Show windows stacked**. The three application windows are reduced in size and arranged from top to bottom.

   d. Right-click a blank area on the taskbar, and then click **Undo Show stacked**.

   e. Right-click a blank area on the taskbar, and then click **Show windows side by side**. The application windows are reduced in size and arranged from left to right.

   f. Right-click a blank area on the taskbar, and then click **Undo Show side by side**.

13. Click the **Show desktop** button on the taskbar. Right-click the **Microsoft PowerPoint** shortcut icon, and in the shortcut menu click **Delete**. A dialog box displays an explanation that deleting the shortcut will not uninstall the program. Click **Yes** to move the shortcut to the Recycle Bin.

14. Leave the three applications open for the next Step-by-Step.

Closing Applications and Backstage View

In Backstage view, you can quickly access the Close and Exit commands. The Close command will close the active document. The Exit command will close all active documents and the application. If you attempt to exit an application without saving changes to a document, you will be prompted to save the changes before closing. You can also close the active document and the application by clicking the Close button in the upper-right corner of the application window. However, if multiple documents are open, clicking the Close button will close only the active document.

Step-by-Step 11.2

1. If necessary, start the **Word**, **Excel**, and **PowerPoint** applications. Click the **Word** button on the taskbar to display the Word application window.

2. In the upper-left corner of the application window, click the **File** tab. The commands shown in **Figure 11–7** are displayed in the left pane of Backstage view.

2-1.1.1
2-1.2.5

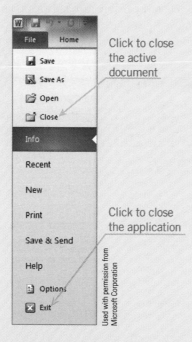

FIGURE 11–7
Backstage view commands

3. Click **Close**. The active Word application window closes, but the Word application is still running.

4. Click the **File** tab, and then click **Exit**. The Word application window closes, and the application is no longer running.

5. You should see the Excel and PowerPoint buttons on the taskbar because those applications are still running. On the taskbar, click the **PowerPoint** button. In the upper-right corner of the application window, click the **Close** button 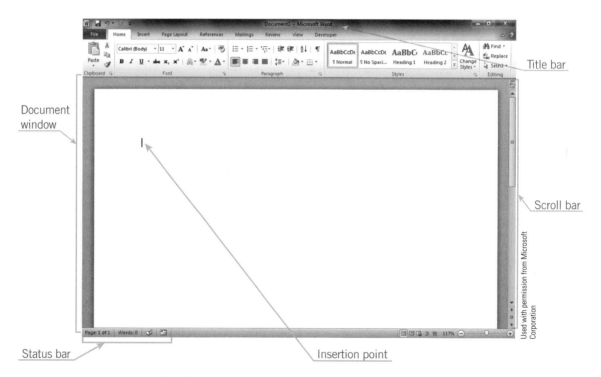. Because only one document is open, the active document and the application both close.

6. The Excel application is still running. If you do not see the Excel application window, click the **Excel** button on the taskbar. Click the **Close** button to close both the active document and the application.

Navigating Application Windows

The application window includes many of the elements of all Windows screens, including the title bar, scroll bars, and the status bar. These elements are labeled in **Figure 11–8**. Most Office applications automatically open a new blank document when the application is started. The *document window* is the area where you enter new text and data or change existing text and data. The Word application window can be resized and moved just like other windows on your screen by using the Minimize, Maximize, and Restore Down buttons.

> **VOCABULARY**
> **document window**

FIGURE 11–8   Word application window

The *insertion point* (often referred to as the *cursor*) is a blinking vertical line that indicates the location in the document where the new text and data will be entered. The arrow keys on the keyboard move the insertion point up, down, left, and right in the document. The Page Up and Page Down keys move the insertion point in bigger increments. To use the mouse to reposition the insertion point, simply move the mouse pointer to the desired location within the document. When positioned within the document window, the pointer changes from an arrow to an *I-beam*, which looks like a capital letter *I*. Position the I-beam over the text in the document where you would like to reposition the insertion point, and then click.

When you *scroll* through a document, you move through the document window on the screen without changing the location of the insertion point. The display on the screen adjusts as you scroll. To scroll, use the horizontal or vertical scroll bars. Another convenient way to scroll, if available, is to use the wheel on the mouse or the trackpad.

▶ **VOCABULARY**
insertion point
cursor
I-beam
scroll

Step-by-Step 11.3

1. Start **Word**. A blank document is displayed in the document window, and the insertion point is blinking.

2. If necessary, click the **Maximize** button to change the size of the window to fill the screen. If the Maximize button is not displayed in the top-right corner of the screen, the document is already maximized.

3. To adjust the size of the window, in the upper-right corner of the window, click the **Restore Down** button ▣. The window size is reduced. Note that when the window is restored down, the Maximize button appears in place of the Restore Down button.

4. Position the mouse pointer over the border on the right side of the window. When the mouse pointer changes to display the Horizontal Resize arrow ⇔, click and drag the border to the left to adjust the width of the window. Then, point to the title bar on the window and click and drag the window to the top of the screen. When you release the mouse button, the window is maximized.

5. In the upper-right corner of the window, click the **Minimize** button ▬ to hide the application window. Notice that the Word button still appears on the taskbar because the application is still running.

6. Click the **Word** button on the taskbar to reopen the application window. The window opens to the previous maximized window size.

7. To return to the previous customized window size, click the **Restore Down** button. Then, click the **Maximize** button once more.

8. The insertion point is still blinking in the document window. Type your first name. Notice that the insertion point moves as you enter text. Press **Enter** five times. Notice that each time you press Enter the insertion point moves farther down in the document window. Type your last name.

IC³
2-1.1.2
2-1.1.3

QUICK TIP

The arrow keys and the Page Up and Page Down keys will not move the insertion point in a blank document. As soon as text and data are added to the document, the keys will perform as described.

9. Press the **Page Up** key. The insertion point moves back to the top of the document window and is now positioned in front of your name.

10. Press the **down arrow** key five times to move the insertion point to the end of your last name. Then press the **up arrow** key five times to move the insertion point to the end of your first name.

11. On the vertical scroll bar at the right side of the document window (see **Figure 11–9**), drag the scroll box all the way down to view the end of the document. Then click the **up** scroll arrow several times until you see your last name in the document window. Note that as you scroll through the document window the insertion point does not move. Scroll to the top of the document window. The insertion point is still positioned at the end of your first name.

FIGURE 11–9
Scroll bar tools

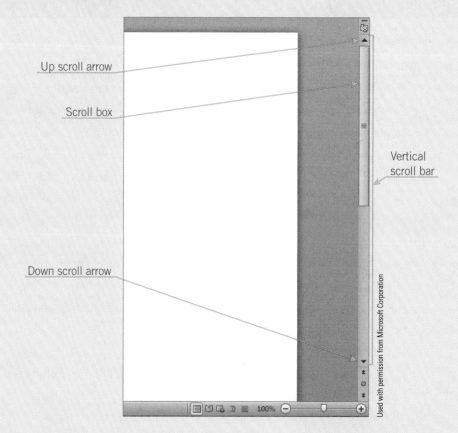

Up scroll arrow

Scroll box

Vertical scroll bar

Down scroll arrow

Used with permission from Microsoft Corporation

12. If there is a scroll wheel on the mouse you are using, move the scroll wheel forward and backward to scroll through the document. Note that the insertion point does not move as you scroll through the document using the scroll wheel on the mouse.

13. If necessary, drag the scroll box to the top of the vertical scroll bar. Position the mouse pointer (I-beam) to the left of the first character in your last name and then click. The insertion point now appears in the new position. Type your middle name or a middle initial, and then press the **spacebar**.

14. Click the **File** tab, and then click **Exit**. When prompted to save changes you made, click **Don't Save**. The document closes, and the application closes.

Using the Office User Interface

The Office applications use a visual design referred to as the Microsoft Office Fluent user interface. There are many features in this new design that make the software more intuitive and easier to use.

Using the Office Ribbon

The **Ribbon** is the blue banner that stretches across the top of the screen, just below the title bar. The Ribbon displays several tabs, including the Home tab, shown in **Figure 11–10**. The Ribbon makes it easy to find commands because related commands and options are organized in groups on each tab. For example, all of the commands for formatting characters appear in the Font group. A dialog box launcher (a small arrow) appears in the lower-right corner of some groups, and when clicked, a dialog box opens with even more options related to the group.

▶ **VOCABULARY**
Ribbon

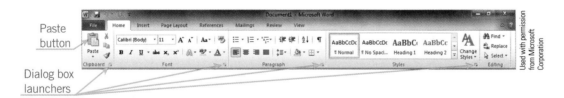

Paste button

Dialog box launchers

Used with permission from Microsoft Corporation

FIGURE 11–10   Home tab on the Ribbon

What makes the Ribbon so unique is that it changes to meet your needs. As you work in a document, the Ribbon adapts by providing appropriate commands and options. For example, if you insert a picture in your document, the Ribbon changes to display tabs related to formatting pictures—hence, the word *fluent* in Office Fluent user interface.

If you do not know the function of a button in any of the groups, position the mouse pointer over the button, but do not click. After a second or two, the name and a description of the command are displayed in a ScreenTip.

If you prefer to use the keyboard instead of the mouse, you can access the tabs on the Ribbon by using keyboard shortcuts that you can display on the Ribbon. Commands can also be accessed with legacy keyboard shortcuts, which have been around for many versions of the application. When a keyboard shortcut is available for the command, the shortcut is included in the ScreenTip.

To maximize the screen space for your document, you can easily minimize the Ribbon by double-clicking one of the tabs. To restore the Ribbon to its original size, you simply double-click one of the tabs.

Step-by-Step 11.4

2-1.1.2

1. Start **Word**. A blank Word document is displayed on your screen.

2. If necessary, click the **Home** tab to make it active. In the Clipboard group, position the mouse pointer over the **Paste** button. Do not click the Paste button. Wait a second or two for the ScreenTip to appear. The ScreenTip provides the button name, a keyboard shortcut, and a description of its function.

3. Click the **Insert** tab on the Ribbon. The groups and options change. Position the mouse pointer over several of the commands on the Insert tab to display their ScreenTips.

4. Click each of the remaining Ribbon tabs to view the groups and commands. You will see that the groups and commands are very different on each tab. Click the **Home** tab.

5. Press **Alt**. Letters for keyboard shortcuts appear under each tab name on the Ribbon. For example, the letter *N* appears under the Insert tab name. Note that more shortcut keys appear in each of the groups. You can press those letters to execute the commands. Press **Alt** again to hide the letters.

6. Press **Alt**, and then press **P** to display the Page Layout tab. Press **M** to display the Margin options. When a command or option is executed, the shortcut keys disappear. Press **Esc** to hide the Margin options. Then press **Alt** once again to hide the keyboard shortcuts.

7. Click the **Home** tab. In the Font group, click the **dialog box launcher** ⬚. The Font dialog box shown in **Figure 11–11** opens.

QUICK TIP

To hide the keyboard shortcuts without executing a command, press Alt, press Esc, or click a different tab name.

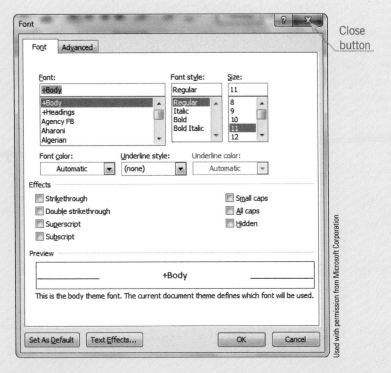

FIGURE 11–11
Font dialog box

8. In the upper-right corner of the dialog box, click the **Close** button to close the dialog box.

9. Double-click the **Home** tab. The groups and command buttons are hidden, and only the tab names are displayed, as shown in **Figure 11–12**.

FIGURE 11–12
Ribbon minimized

10. Click the **Home** tab. All the groups on the Home tab are displayed. Click the **Insert** tab. All the groups on the Insert tab are displayed.

11. Click anywhere within the document. The Ribbon automatically minimizes again. The Ribbon also minimizes when you choose a command or option.

12. Double-click any one of the tabs to maximize the Ribbon. Click anywhere within the document window. The Ribbon is no longer minimized.

13. Leave Word open for the next Step-by-Step.

Customizing the Quick Access Toolbar

By default, the Quick Access Toolbar is positioned above the Ribbon in the upper-left corner of the application window. This toolbar offers quick access to commands you use frequently. The default settings, as shown in **Figure 11–13**, include only three options—the Save, Undo, and Redo or Repeat commands. However, you can customize the toolbar to include the commands you use most often. Keep in mind that the intent of the toolbar is for quick access. If you add too many commands and the toolbar becomes cluttered, it may slow you down.

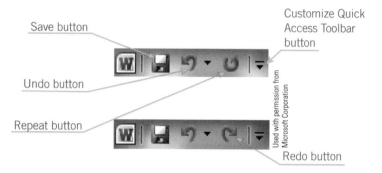

FIGURE 11–13   Quick Access Toolbar

Step-by-Step 11.5

2-1.1.2
2-1.1.4
2.1.1.7

1. If necessary, start **Word**. A blank Word document is displayed on your screen.

2. On the Quick Access Toolbar in the upper-left corner of the screen, click the **Customize Quick Access Toolbar** button ▾. A menu is displayed. The current commands on the toolbar are identified with a check mark.

3. In the menu, select a command that is not already on the toolbar (a command without a check mark.) The new command button is added to the toolbar. Note which command you added to the toolbar.

4. Click the **Customize Quick Access Toolbar** button. At the bottom of the shortcut menu, click **More Commands** to open the Word Options dialog box shown in **Figure 11–14**. In the left pane, the Quick Access Toolbar option is already selected. The buttons currently displayed on the Quick Access Toolbar are listed in the right pane.

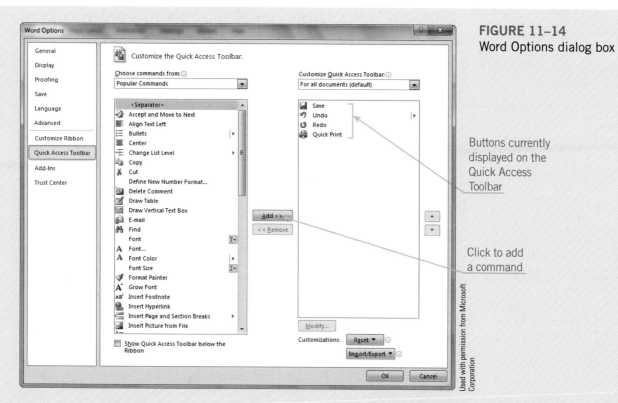

FIGURE 11-14
Word Options dialog box

Buttons currently displayed on the Quick Access Toolbar

Click to add a command

5. In the middle pane, select a command that is not currently displayed on the Quick Access Toolbar. Between the middle and right panes, click **Add** to add the command to the pane on the right. The list in the right pane is updated.

6. In the middle pane, select another command that is not currently displayed on the Quick Access Toolbar, and then click **Add**. Note that the last three commands in the list are the commands that you added to the toolbar.

7. Click **OK** to accept the changes and close the dialog box. The width of the Quick Access Toolbar expands and three new command buttons are now displayed on the right side of the toolbar.

8. Click the **Customize Quick Access Toolbar** button, and then click **More Commands**. In the pane on the right, select the last button in the list.

9. Between the middle and right panes, click **Remove**. At the bottom of the Word Options dialog box, click **OK** to accept the change and close the dialog box. Note that the button is removed from the toolbar.

10. On the Quick Access Toolbar, right-click one of the two remaining new buttons you added to the toolbar. In the menu, click **Remove from Quick Access Toolbar**.

11. Click the **Customize Quick Access Toolbar** button. In the menu, click the last remaining new button you added to the Quick Access Toolbar. The command button is removed from the toolbar.

12. Leave Word open for the next Step-by-Step.

open

file

file extension

folder

subfolders

path

Opening, Saving, and Closing Documents

You use similar procedures to open and save documents in all Office applications. To *open* a document means to load a file into an application. A *file* is a collection of information saved as a unit. Each file is identified by a filename. Remember that the terms *document* and *file* are used interchangeably.

Opening a Document

The Open command in Backstage view, which is accessed using the File tab, enables you to open a file from any available disk and folder. You can also open a document by navigating to the document on the desktop or by using Windows Explorer. Once you locate the file, double-click the filename. If necessary, your computer will start the associated application (such as Word or Excel), and then the document will open.

A *file extension* identifies the type of file. A period separates the filename and the extension. The extension is usually three or four characters and varies depending on the application used to create the document. For example, Word automatically assigns the extension *.docx*, PowerPoint assigns the extension *.pptx*, and Excel assigns the extension *.xlsx*. The *x* in the extensions indicates the XML format. You can quickly identify documents created in versions of these applications prior to Office 2007 because the file extensions created in those applications are *.doc*, *.ppt*, and *.xls*.

A *folder* is a means for organizing files into manageable groups on a designated storage device. All computer files are saved in folders. *Subfolders*, folders within folders, can also be created. The *path* is the route the operating system uses to locate a document. The path identifies the disk and any folders relative to the location of the document. **Figure 11–15** shows two typical paths and identifies the items in the paths. The first example shows a document named Recycled Vehicles.docx saved in a subfolder titled Lesson 11. The Lesson 11 folder is, in turn, stored in a folder titled Data Files for Students, which can be found on the local (this computer's) hard drive—drive C. In the second example, the Word document named Revised Recycled Vehicles.docx is saved in a folder called Solutions, which can be found on a Flash/USB removable memory, which in this example is identified as Removable Disk E.

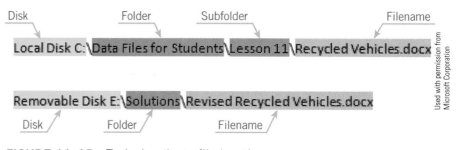

FIGURE 11–15 Typical paths to file locations

Just as you can open multiple applications, you can also open multiple documents within each application. When multiple documents are open within one application, the taskbar displays the documents stacked behind the application button. Point to the application button on the taskbar to display thumbnails of each of the open documents for that application. Then to make a document active, click the document thumbnail. When you right-click the application button on the taskbar, a Jump List is displayed above the button. A ***Jump List*** is a collection of links that provides quick access to files and data. The links displayed in a Jump List vary depending on the application. For example, a Jump List for an Office application provides shortcuts to recently accessed documents. A Jump List for Internet Explorer provides shortcuts to frequently accessed Web sites.

▶ **VOCABULARY**
Jump List

Step-by-Step 11.6

1. If necessary, start **Word**. Click the **File** tab, and then, in the left pane, click **Recent**. In the middle pane, a list of filenames for recently accessed documents is displayed, as shown in **Figure 11–16**. If the document you want to open is in that list, you can click the document filename and the file will open. Do not click any filenames in the Recent Documents list. Also note that in the right pane there is a list of recent locations (disks and folder names) where documents were most recently accessed or saved.

2-1.1.4
2-1.2.2

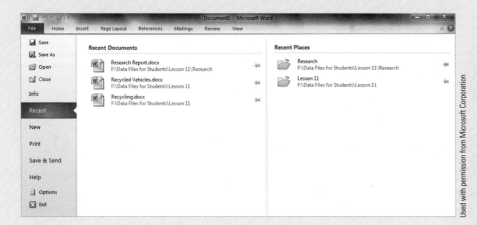

Used with permission from Microsoft Corporation

FIGURE 11–16
Recently accessed files

QUICK TIP

You can control the number of filenames that appear in the Recent Documents list by changing the display settings in the Word Options dialog box. Click File, click Options, and then click Advanced. Scroll down, and under the heading *Display*, change the setting for Show this number of Recent Documents. The maximum number of documents you can display is 50.

2. In the left pane, click **Open**. The Open dialog box appears. Word automatically takes you to the disk and folder of the last file you opened, or to the default folder where Word documents are saved. Your Open dialog box will differ from the one shown in **Figure 11-17**.

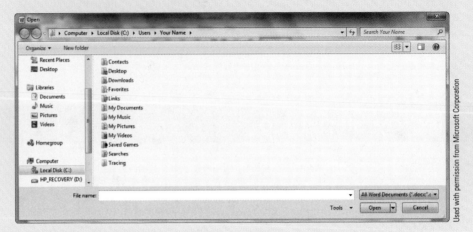

3. Scroll down in the left pane and under Computer, click the disk where your Data Files folder is stored. Then in the right pane, double-click the folder(s) where your Data Files folder is stored. (Your instructor can provide this information.)

4. Double-click the name of the folder containing your Lesson 11 data files. For example, in **Figure 11-18**, the Lesson 11 folder is stored in a folder named Data Files for Students. If necessary, in the lower-right corner of the dialog box, click the **File type** list arrow and select **All Word Documents (*.docx;...)**. In the Lesson 11 folder, you will see a subfolder, Research, and two Word files, Recycled Vehicles.docx and Recycling.docx.

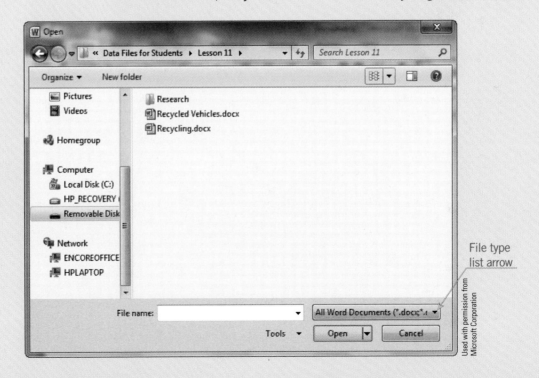

File type
list arrow

5. In the lower-right corner of the dialog box, click the **File type** list arrow, and then click **All Files (*.*)**. The names of all files in the Lesson 11 folder are listed, including those created in applications other than Word. See **Figure 11–19**.

Back button

Forward button

FIGURE 11–19
All files in the Lesson 11 folder

File type list arrow

Used with permission from Microsoft Corporation

6. Click the filename **Recycling.docx** once to select it. At the bottom of the dialog box, click **Open**. The document is displayed in the document window.

7. Click **File** and then click **Open**. The Open dialog box shows the same folder that you last accessed. Double-click the filename **Recycled Vehicles.docx** to open the file.

8. Start Excel. Click the **File** tab, and then click **Open**. Navigate to the disk and folder where your Data Files folder is stored. Open the Lesson 11 folder, and then open the **Research** folder. In the lower-right corner of the dialog box, click the **File type** list arrow, and then click **All Files (*.*)**. Note that there is also a Word file in that subfolder. Also note that the current path for the location of the document is displayed at the top of the Open dialog box.

QUICK TIP

To open multiple documents at the same time, click the first filename in the Open dialog box, hold down Ctrl, and click one or more additional filenames, then click Open.

ABOVE AND BEYOND

To preview a file before opening it, click the Start button and then in the list at the right, click Documents. In the dialog box, click Organize and then point to Layout. If necessary, enable the option Preview pane. When you select a filename, the document will be displayed in the Preview pane. Click anywhere in the Preview pane and scroll through the document.

9. Navigate through the folders:
   a. In the upper-left corner of the dialog box, click the **Back** button ⬅ to return to the list of folders and files in the Lesson 11 folder.
   b. Click the **Back** button again to return to the folder or disk where the Lesson 11 folder is stored.
   c. Click the **Forward** button ➡ to return to the list of folders and files in the Lesson 11 folder.
   d. Double-click the filename **Travel Expenses.xlsx** to open the file.

10. Click the **File** tab, and then click **Recent**. Notice that the document you just opened in Excel, Travel Expenses.xlsx, appears at the top of the Recent Workbooks list. Click the **File** tab to close Backstage view and return to the Excel document window.

11. On the taskbar, click the **Windows Explorer** button 🖼. In the left pane, navigate to the disk where your Data Files folder is stored. In the right pane, navigate to the folder where your Data Files folder is stored. Double-click the **Lesson 11** folder, and then double-click the filename **The 3Rs.pptx**. PowerPoint starts, and the presentation opens.

12. Position the mouse pointer over the **Word** button on the taskbar. Document thumbnails are displayed for the two open documents, as shown in **Figure 11-20**. Note that thumbnails appear when the Windows theme setting is Aero Windows 7. If your Windows theme is not set for Aero Windows 7, you will see a ScreenTip showing the document filename and the application name.

QUICK TIP

You can also navigate to a file or folder by clicking the Start button and then, in the right pane of the Start menu, click Computer.

FIGURE 11-20
Document thumbnails using Aero Windows 7 theme setting

ABOVE AND BEYOND

If the Windows theme is set for Aero Windows 7, you can use Windows Flip 3D to quickly preview all open windows. Hold down Ctrl and the Windows logo key and then press Tab. Flip 3D displays the open windows in a stack. Use the mouse wheel or the trackpad to flip through the stack. Click a window in the stack to show that window, or click outside the stack to close the Flip 3D display. You can also hold down the Windows logo key and then press Tab to flip through the stack one window at a time.

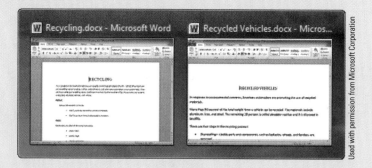

Used with permission from Microsoft Corporation

13. Right-click the **Word** button on the taskbar. A Jump List, similar to the one shown in **Figure 11-21**, appears above the button showing the recent files accessed in Word. Your Jump List may differ. In the Jump List, you can click a link to switch to another document.

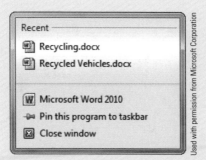

FIGURE 11–21
Jump List for Word

14. Click the **Word** button on the taskbar to hide the Jump List and display the two document thumbnails. Then click the **Recycling.docx** thumbnail. Leave all the documents and applications open for the next Step-by-Step.

Solving Problems with Opening Documents

You may encounter some problems when opening files. The following are descriptions of common problems.

■ There is a problem with file compatibility. *File compatibility* refers to the ability to open and work with files without a format conflict. In most cases, files that were created with an older version of an application can be opened in the newer version of the application. But sometimes, files created in newer applications are not backwards compatible, meaning that they cannot be opened in older versions of the application. Office 2010 files are saved in a new format, and they will not normally open in versions of Office applications prior to Office 2007. Microsoft does, however, provide a free download of compatibility software to enable users with older versions of Office to open, edit, and save files created and saved in the new Office 2010 format.

■ You may also encounter compatibility problems if you are working in a different operating system than the one in which the file was created. For example, if a file was created in PowerPoint on a Macintosh, it may not open in PowerPoint on a PC. This problem generally occurs if you are working with different versions of the software across the different platforms. With a little effort, however, you can usually find a way to open and use almost any file from an Office application.

■ If when you use the Open command from the File tab you do not see the file you are looking for, it could be caused by a number of things. First, you need to verify the document was saved before it was closed. Second, you need to verify you are looking in the right disk and the right folder, as the file you are looking for may be stored in a different location. If the file is stored in a remote storage area or on a network, you must make sure you have access to the storage area or the network. If you are unsure of the location of the file, you can use the Search command, available in the upper-right corner of the Open dialog box, to locate the file. To use the Search feature, you must identify the disk and/or folders in the box to the left of the Search box. Or, you can click the Start button and enter the filename in the Search box.

2-1.2.6

▶ **VOCABULARY**
file compatibility

- The file is in a format that cannot be read by the application you are using. For example, if you attempt to open an Access file using the Open command in Word, you will not see the file listed. You can switch the file type setting within the Open dialog box to display All Files, but that does not necessarily mean that the application you are using will be able to open the file.

- You encounter a corrupted file or a file that will not open. When you attempt to open a file, the application may display an error message as you try to open the file. For example, a virus checker may be stopping you from opening the file. Often a corrupted file may just not open, or it may cause the application to shut down. In these cases, you can try to open the file on a different computer to verify that the file is indeed corrupt and that there is not something wrong with your computer.

Saving and Closing a Document

▶ **VOCABULARY**

save

To *save* a document means to store it on a disk or other storage medium. You can save a document to the hard drive on your computer, to an auxiliary drive or a network location, or to portable media such as Flash/USB removable memory or a writable CD or DVD. A file extension is automatically added to the filename when the document is saved.

To make it easier to find documents, choose filenames with words that help describe the document. The complete path to the file can include up to 255 characters. Filenames cannot include any of the following characters: \ / : * ? " < > | .

You should make a habit of saving frequently and also after making any major changes to your document. The quickest and easiest way to save a document is to click the Save button on the Quick Access Toolbar. When you click the Save button on the toolbar, the document is saved with the same filename and in the same location. If the file does not already have a name, the Save As dialog box will open and you can enter a name for the file. Unless you specify a disk and a folder, the file will be saved to the default location, which is usually in the Documents folder on drive C.

When you change the filename or the location where the file is stored, the original document, with the original name, remains unchanged. When you use the Save As command, you also have the opportunity to change the document format. Each application offers a number of choices for formats to save files in.

To close a document, you can click the Close button in the upper-right corner of the application window. When you point to an application button on the taskbar, thumbnails of the open documents are displayed above the button. You can close a document by clicking the Close button on the thumbnail. Whether you click the Close button in the application window or the Close button on the thumbnail, when you close the last open document, the application closes, too.

Step-by-Step 11.7

2-1.2.4
2-1.2.5

1. If necessary, open the **Recycling.docx**, **Recycled Vehicles.docx**, **Travel Expenses.xlsx**, and **The 3Rs.pptx** documents.

2. On the taskbar, point to the **Word** button. Two thumbnails are displayed above the Word button. Click the **Recycled Vehicles.docx** thumbnail to switch to that document.

3. Click the **File** tab, and then click **Save As**. The Save As dialog box shown in **Figure 11–22** opens. The current path where the file is stored is displayed at the top of the dialog box.

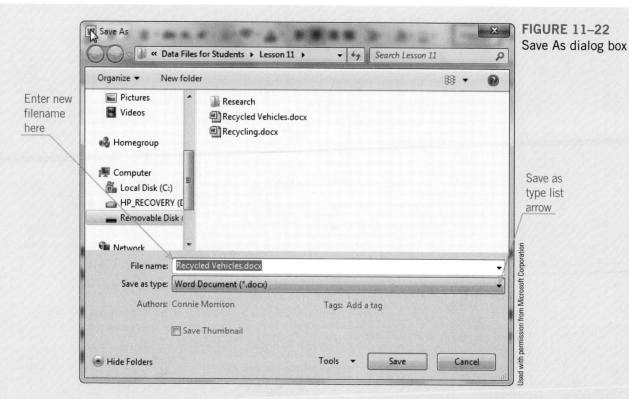

Enter new
filename
here

Save as
type list
arrow

FIGURE 11–22
Save As dialog box

Used with permission from Microsoft Corporation

4. In the left pane, navigate to the disk where you are to save your solution files. In the right pane, navigate to the folder where you are to save your solution files. (Follow your instructor's directions about where to save the files.)

5. If necessary, click anywhere in the **File name** box to select the filename Recycled Vehicles.docx. Type **Revised Recycled Vehicles**, followed by your initials. The selected text is replaced with the new text.

6. The Save as type box shows the default setting Word Document (*.docx), and this setting is correct, so no changes are needed. At the bottom of the dialog box, click **Save**. The document is saved in a new location and with a different filename.

7. On the taskbar, click the **Excel** button to switch to the Travel Expenses document. Click the **File** tab, and then click **Save As**. Navigate to the disk and folder where you are to save your solution files. In the File name box, change the filename to **Updated Travel Expenses**, followed by your initials.

8. In the Save as type box, the default setting for the Excel file format is Excel Workbook (*.xlsx). Click the **File type** list arrow, and in the list click **Excel 97-2003 Workbook (*.xls)**. With this file format, the document can be opened in earlier versions of Excel. Click **Save**. The file is saved with a new filename and in a new location.

9. In the upper-right corner of the application window, click the **Close** button. The spreadsheet window closes, and because it is the only Excel document, the application also closes.

ABOVE AND BEYOND

To create a new folder, in the Save As dialog box, click New folder. The new folder will be added to the folder that is currently open in the dialog box.

10. The Revised Recycled Vehicles document is now displayed on the screen. Scroll down and position the insertion point at the end of the last sentence at the end of the document. Press **Enter** and then type your first and last name. On the Quick Access Toolbar, click the **Save** button to save the changes to the document. The document is saved in the same location (your Solutions folder) with the same filename.

11. Click the **File** tab, and then in the command list click **Close**. The document window closes, but because another Word document is open, the Word application remains open.

12. Click the **File** tab, and then at the bottom of the command list click **Exit**. Both the open document and the Word application close.

13. Position the mouse pointer over the **PowerPoint** button on the taskbar to display the document thumbnail. Then position the mouse pointer over the document thumbnail. A red Close button appears in the thumbnail, as shown in **Figure 11–23**.

FIGURE 11–23
PowerPoint document thumbnail with Close button

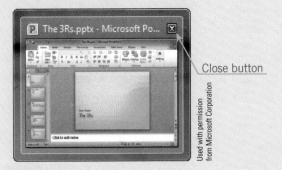

Close button

Used with permission from Microsoft Corporation

14. Click the **Close** button in the thumbnail to close both the PowerPoint document and the application. In the upper-right corner of the Windows Explorer window, click the **Close** button.

Getting Help

The Office applications provide Help features to assist you as you work. You have access to documentation including books and manuals and online help as well. Do not overlook another vital source of help: assistance from others. There may be classmates, instructors, or coworkers who are familiar with the application you are using. Or perhaps your workplace has a help desk. You can communicate with support personnel via phone, e-mail, user groups, and blogs. The key to using these various sources of help is determining what sort of help you need and the quickest or most efficient way to access that help. The idea is to find the assistance you need without in0terrupting or delaying your work.

Whenever you encounter a problem, your first source of help should be the Help features in each Office application. Help is always readily available and is just a few mouse clicks away. For example, you can find out more about most dialog box options by clicking the Help button, which looks like a question mark, on the title bar of the dialog box. This button opens a Help window that provides information about the options available in that dialog box.

Navigating the Help screens is much like navigating a Web page. You can browse the categories presented and click on links to get information about a topic. You can also enter keywords (specific words or phrases) in the Search box. The results for your search will be listed, with links for the most relevant results at the top of the list. Achieving successful search results depends on your ability to identify the keywords that relate to your query. The more search experience you have, the better you will be at recognizing keywords for your searches. To access previous searches, click the Search list arrow.

If your computer is connected to the Internet, you will also have access to all the current Help information available from the Microsoft Office.com Web site or other support specialists. At the Office.com Web site you will find a variety of resources, including tours, slide shows, tutorials, training videos, articles, product user groups, blogs, and the opportunity to chat with Microsoft support personnel. If the word *Offline* appears at the bottom of the Help dialog box, your computer is not currently connected to the Internet, but you can still access Help information from files stored on your computer. You may need to check with your instructor about how to connect to the Internet from your computer.

Step-by-Step 11.8

1. Start **Word**.

2. In the upper-right corner of the application window, click the **Help** button [?]. The Word Help dialog box opens. The dialog box includes a search box and several links for browsing Word Help topics.

2-1.1.8
2-1.1.9

3. If you do not see the Table of Contents pane on the left side of the dialog box as shown in **Figure 11–24**, on the toolbar at the top of the dialog box, click the **Show Table of Contents** button to display the table of contents.

FIGURE 11–24
Word Help
dialog box

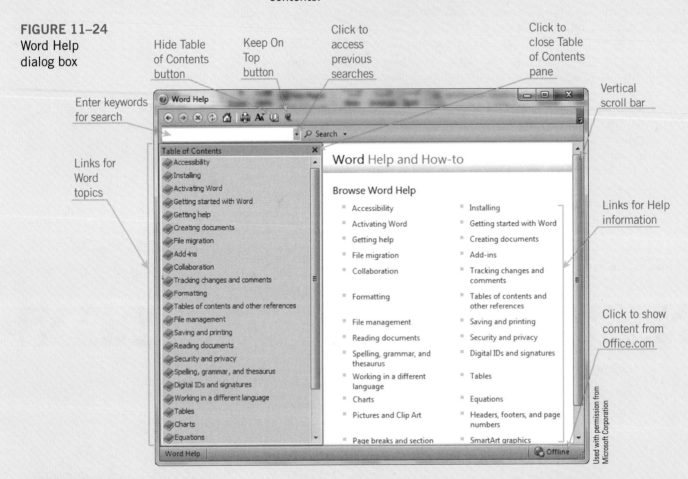

QUICK TIP

To reposition the Help dialog box, drag the title bar. You can also resize the dialog box by dragging one of the borders.

4. In the Table of Contents pane on the left, click **Getting help**. The Table of Contents expands to show more links related to the topic.

5. Under Getting help, click the first link. The links vary depending on whether you have access to information at Office.com. New information is displayed in the right pane.

6. At the top of the Table of Contents pane, click the **Close** button to hide the Table of Contents pane.

7. Position the insertion point in the Search text box. Type the keywords **display recent documents**, and then click **Search**. Articles that may provide relevant information are listed.

8. Click the link **Customize the list of recently used files**. (If your computer is connected to the Internet, you may need to scroll down to see the option in the list.) A new article is displayed.

9. If necessary, use the tools on the vertical scroll bar to scroll down so you can view the information under the heading What do you want to do?. Click the link **Change the number of files that appear in the list of recently used files**. The related section of the article is displayed.

10. If necessary, on the toolbar at the top of the dialog box, click the **Not On Top** button . The Keep On Top button should now be displayed, as shown in Figure 11–24, indicating that the Help dialog box will always be displayed on top of the application window.

11. Drag the Word Help dialog box borders to resize the dialog box so it is a square that covers only about a quarter of your screen. Then position the mouse pointer over the Word Help dialog box title bar, and click and drag the dialog box near the upper-right corner of the screen. You can keep the Word Help dialog box open as you complete the task.

12. Click anywhere in the Word document window. Read and follow the four steps in the Help dialog box. Reposition and/or resize the Help dialog box as needed so you can see the options in the Word Options dialog box.

13. After you complete the fourth step, reposition the Word Help dialog box so you can see the Cancel button at the bottom of the Word Options dialog box. Instead of clicking OK to accept the changes in the Word Options dialog box, click **Cancel** so you do not change the settings.

14. Click the **Close** button to close the Word Help dialog box. Then close Word.

WARNING

When you drag a dialog box or an application window to the very top of the screen, the dialog box or the window is automatically maximized. If the dialog box becomes maximized as you try to reposition it, click the Restore Down button and then try repositioning it again. You can drag the dialog box as far to the right as desired; just do not drag the title bar to the very top of the screen.

NET BUSINESS

Microsoft Office Web Apps are online companions to Word, Excel, PowerPoint, and OneNote that enable you to access documents anytime and anywhere. Regardless of where you are, you can create, edit, save, and share your documents. All you need is a connection to the Web. Office Web Apps provide browser-based viewing in which your document appears similar to how it would appear in the application on your computer, with many of the same editing features available. You can access Office Web Apps through Windows Live, and you can store documents to SkyDrive, a free online storage service from Windows Live. With permission, others can also access your documents at SkyDrive, even if they do not have the Office application installed on their computers.

SUMMARY

In this lesson, you learned:

- You can start an Office application by clicking the Start button on the taskbar and selecting the application from the All Programs menu, or you can double-click the application icon on the desktop.

- Backstage view provides quick access to common tasks for managing documents, such as saving, opening, and printing.

- Common elements found in Office application windows include the title bar, scroll bars, and status bar.

- You can maximize the space for the document window by minimizing the Ribbon.

- You can customize the Quick Access Toolbar by adding or removing command buttons.

- The Open dialog box enables you to open a file from any available disk and folder.

- Problems opening files can involve corrupted data or file compatibility issues, such as trying to open a file in a different application, in an earlier version of an application, or in an operating system other than that used to create it.

- To save a document using a new filename, click the File tab and then click the Save As command.

- To close a document, you can click the Close button in the upper-right corner of the application window, or you can click the File tab and then click the Close command. You can also close a document by clicking the Close button in the document thumbnail that is displayed when you point to the application button on the taskbar.

- Several sources of help are available including application Help features, assistance from others, books and manuals, and online help.

LESSON REVIEW

TRUE / FALSE

Circle T if the statement is true or F if the statement is false.

T   F   **1.**   Office 2010 files will normally open in earlier versions of Office applications.

T   F   **2.**   What makes the Ribbon so unique is that it changes commands and options to meet your needs as you work in a document.

T   F   **3.**   A file is a means for organizing information into manageable groups.

T   F   **4.**   When a keyboard shortcut is available for a command on the Ribbon, the shortcut is included in the ScreenTip.

T   F   **5.**   When you scroll through a document, you move through the document on the screen without changing the location of the insertion point.

MULTIPLE CHOICE

Select the best response for the following statements.

1. The Office application you would use to work with text, numbers, and formulas to create tables, worksheets, and financial documents is _____.

   A. Access

   B. Excel

   C. Outlook

   D. Word

2. A button for each open application appears on the _____ at the bottom of the screen.

   A. Start menu

   B. taskbar

   C. title bar

   D. status bar

3. The _____ is a blinking vertical line that indicates the location in the document where the new text and data will be entered.

   A. insertion point

   B. I-beam

   C. cursor

   D. A or C

4. The _____ is the main window that serves as the primary interface between the user and the application.

    A. application window
    B. document window
    C. desktop
    D. none of the above

5. A(n) _____ is a small window with descriptive text that appears when you position the mouse pointer over a command or control in the application window.

    A. Jump List
    B. I-beam
    C. document thumbnail
    D. ScreenTip

FILL IN THE BLANK

Complete the following sentences by writing the correct word or words in the blanks provided.

1. To save a file with a new filename or to a new location, click the File tab and then click the _____ command.

2. The _____ is the route the operating system uses to locate a document.

3. To view more options in a group on the Ribbon, click the _____.

4. _____ provides quick access to common tasks for managing documents, such as saving, opening, and printing.

5. When an application is _____, the application is still running, but the application window is not displayed on the screen.

6. A(n) _____ identifies the type of file and is automatically added to the filename when the document is saved.

7. A folder stored within another folder is referred to as a(n) _____.

8. _____ is the ability to open and work with files without a format conflict.

9. A(n) _____ is a list of commonly performed commands from the current window.

10. The complete path to the file can include up to _____ characters.

■ PROJECTS

PROJECT 11–1

1. Start Word.
2. Start PowerPoint.
3. Switch to Word.
4. Use the Word Options dialog box to add the Spelling & Grammar command button to the Quick Access Toolbar.
5. Display the keyboard shortcuts on the Ribbon. Use the keyboard shortcut to display the References tab. Then turn off the display of keyboard shortcuts on the Ribbon.
6. Minimize the Ribbon, and then restore it to its original display.
7. Remove the Spelling & Grammar command button from the Quick Access Toolbar.
8. Close Word and PowerPoint.

2-1.1.1
2-1.1.2
2-1.1.4
2-1.1.7

PROJECT 11–2

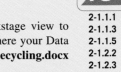

1. Start Word.
2. Use the Open command in Backstage view to navigate to the disk and folder where your Data Files folder is stored. Open the **Recycling.docx** document.
3. Use the Save As command in Backstage view to save the document in a new location with a new filename. Navigate to the disk and folder where your Solutions folder is stored. Change the filename to **Final Recycling**, followed by your initials. Change the file type to **Word 97-2003 Document (*.doc)**.
4. Create a shortcut icon on the desktop to start Excel. Then use the new shortcut icon to start Excel.
5. In Excel, use the Open command in Backstage view to navigate to the disk and folder where your Data Files folder is stored. Open the **Lesson 11** folder, and then open the **Research** folder to open the **Research Data.xlsx** document.
6. Switch to the desktop. Delete the Excel shortcut button.
7. Use Windows Explorer to navigate to the disk and folder where your Data Files folder is stored and open **The 3Rs.pptx** presentation and **Research Report.docx** document, which is stored in the Research subfolder.
8. View all the open documents by cascading the windows. Then undo the cascaded layout.
9. Switch to the **Research Report** document. Use the Save As command in Backstage view to save the document in a new location with a new filename. Navigate to the disk and folder where your Solutions folder is stored. Change the filename to **Research Report Outline**, followed by your initials. Keep the default file format setting.
10. Use the scroll bar tools to move down in the document to view the remaining content on the page.
11. Close the Research Report Outline document. Then close Word and the remaining open document.
12. Close PowerPoint and the open presentation.
13. Close the Windows Explorer window.
14. Close Excel and the open spreadsheet.

2-1.1.1
2-1.1.3
2-1.1.5
2-1.2.2
2-1.2.3
2-1.2.4
2-1.2.5

PROJECT 11–3

1. Start Word.

2. To learn more about customizing the Quick Access Toolbar, open the Word Help dialog box and search for the keywords **quick access toolbar**. In the list of results for the search, click the link **Customize the Quick Access Toolbar**. In the article, under *What do you want to do?*, click the link **Change the order of the commands on the Quick Access Toolbar**. Read the two steps for changing the order of the commands on the toolbar.

2-1.1.1
2-1.1.4
2.1.1.9

3. Leave the Help screen open and on top of the application window. Switch to the Word document. Make note of the order of the buttons on the Quick Access Toolbar.

4. Follow the directions in the Help screen to change the order of the buttons.

5. Move the buttons on the toolbar back to the original order noted above in Step 3.

6. Close the Word Help dialog box, and then close the Word application.

TEAMWORK PROJECT

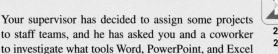

Your supervisor has decided to assign some projects to staff teams, and he has asked you and a coworker to investigate what tools Word, PowerPoint, and Excel offer for collaborative work. Working in pairs, complete the following tasks:

2-1.1.8
2.1.1.9

1. Interview individuals you know who use Word, PowerPoint, and Excel and ask these individuals how they share documents with others, either for work or for personal use.

2. Using the Office Help feature in Word, PowerPoint, and Excel, search for the keyword **collaboration** to get information about features that enable more than one person to work on a document.

3. Browse the Office.com Web site to explore features in the three applications that enable collaboration.

4. Create a new Word document, and save the document as **TP 11-1**, followed by your initials.

5. Make a list of the features in each application that help individuals collaborate in developing documents.

6. Save the changes to the document, and then close the document.

CRITICAL THINKING

CRITICAL THINKING 11–1

You and three other classmates are working on a group project. Sam, one of the group members, created a Word document to draft an outline of the topics to be covered in the project. Sam saved the file on the school network so all group members could access the document. You are having trouble locating the file.

2-1.2.6

1. Create a new Word document, and save the document as **CT 11-1**, followed by your initials.

2. Write a brief summary describing how you would troubleshoot the problem.

3. Save the changes to the document, and then close the document.

CRITICAL THINKING 11–2

Open Word, Excel, and PowerPoint. Stack the windows so you can see the Ribbons in each application window.

2-1.1.1
2.1.1.2
2.1.1.5

1. Create a new Word document, and save the document as **CT 11-2**, followed by your initials.

2. Create a list of the similarities and the differences you see in the Quick Access Toolbars and the tabs on the Ribbons.

3. Save the changes to the document, and then close the document.

4. Undo the stacked layout of the application windows, and then close each of the open applications.

ONLINE DISCOVERY

At the beginning of this lesson, Table 11–1 provides a brief overview of the Office applications covered in this textbook: Word, Excel, PowerPoint, Access, and Outlook. Microsoft offers several more Office applications. Browse www.microsoft.com to learn about other Office applications that are available.

1. Create a new Word document, and save the document as **OD 11-1**, followed by your initials.

2. Create a list of these other Office applications, and include a brief description and explanation of the purpose of each application.

3. Save the changes to the document, and then close the document.

2-1.1.8
2.1.1.9

JOB SKILLS

In exchange for riding privileges, you have agreed to help the owner of a local riding stable with a number of computer-related tasks. The owner has created the following list of tasks she needs to have completed:

A. Schedule regular visits by the vet, keep track of regular chores, and plan activities in the coming months.

B. Prepare a presentation that can be used to train new employees and new riders.

C. Store information on owners, frequent riders, equipment, and employees.

D. Calculate expenses for running the stable as well as income from riders and boarders.

E. Write letters to clients who board their horses at the stable to tell them feed bills will go up at the beginning of the year.

1. Create a new Word document and save the document as **JS 11-1**, followed by your initials.

2. Create a list A through E and write the name of the application you would use to complete each of the tasks described in the list above.

2-2.1.16
2-3.1.10
2-4.1.12

3. Write a brief paragraph describing other jobs you could do for the stable owner.

4. Save the changes to the document, and then close the document.

LESSON 12

Getting Started with Word Essentials

■ OBJECTIVES

Upon completion of this lesson, you should be able to:

- Create a new document.
- Change Word settings.
- Enter text in a document.
- Show nonprinting characters in a document.
- Use the click-and-type setting.
- Change views and magnification in the document window.
- Navigate through a document.

■ DATA FILES

To complete this lesson, you will need these data files:

Interview Questions.docx

Ruts.docx

Super Mart.docx

■ WORDS TO KNOW

default

Normal.dotm template

toggle

word wrap

2-2.1.16

Word is a powerful, full-featured word-processing application. You can use Word to create letters, reports, tables, memos, faxes, blogs, and much more. The Word lessons in this course will introduce you to the commonly used features that enable you to prepare documents efficiently. You will also learn how to change the way the document looks on the screen and how to navigate through a document.

Creating a New Document

▶ **VOCABULARY**
default

Normal.dotm template

When you first start the Word application, a new blank document appears and is automatically titled *Document1*. The blank document is formatted with *default* settings, which are the preset options or variables automatically in effect when the document is created. The default settings for Word documents are stored in the *Normal.dotm template*, a file containing default styles and customizations that determine the structure and page layout of a document. Using the Normal.dotm template greatly increases the speed and efficiency of your work as you do not need to spend time setting up the details of the document formats. Information about overriding the default settings and changing document formats is provided in Lesson 13.

You can open additional documents on top of Document1. All new blank document filenames will be numbered sequentially during the session that Word is open. The filenames for each open document stay the same until you assign a new filename. When the Word application is closed and then reopened, the new blank document filenames begin again with *Document1*.

Step-by-Step 12.1

2-1.2.1

1. Start **Microsoft Word 2010**.

2. Click the **File** tab, and then click **New** to display the Backstage view options shown in **Figure 12–1**. The options in Backstage view will vary, but you should see the Blank document icon, and it should be highlighted. A blank document is displayed in the Preview pane on the right.

Blank
document icon

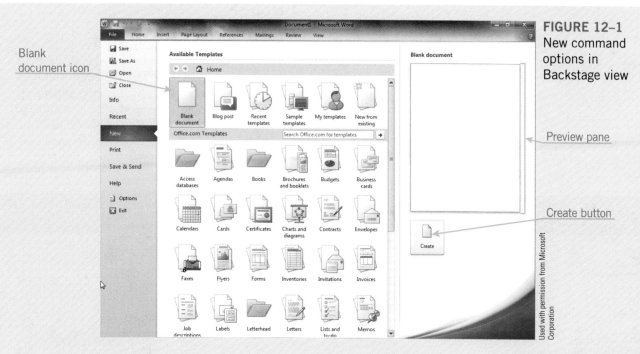

FIGURE 12–1
New command
options in
Backstage view

Preview pane

Create button

Used with permission from Microsoft Corporation

3. Under the blank document in the Preview pane, click the **Create** button. A new document based on the Normal.dotm template opens. Notice that the document title bar shows *Document2*. (If Word was already started when you began this exercise, the document number might be higher than the number 2.)

4. In the upper-right corner of the application window, click the **Close** button to close the current document, which is Document2.

5. Leave the other blank document (Document1) open for the next Step-by-Step.

QUICK TIP

You can also create a new blank document by double-clicking the Blank document icon in Backstage view.

WORKPLACE READINESS

Initiative Is Essential to Success

Are you optimistic and upbeat? Do you generate good energy and good will? Do you perform tasks that need to be completed without being asked? Demonstrating initiative is essential for success. Individuals with strong initiative do not just accept the status quo. They adapt to new situations, and they seek new and challenging work. You can confirm your commitment by taking ownership of your tasks and handling responsibilities with minimum direction and supervision.

Changing Word Settings

As you work with Word, you will begin to recognize "behind the scenes" application settings that are designed to protect your work and improve your efficiency. If you have ever experienced your computer locking up or shutting down while you are working with a document, you know that when you restart an application, one or more of your documents may be recovered. This is because there is a setting to schedule an automatic save of the document information as you work with the document. You can easily customize a setting like this to fit your preferences and meet your needs.

Step-by-Step 12.2

2-1.1.7

1. If necessary, start **Word**.
2. Click the **File** tab. In the left pane, click **Options**. The Word Options dialog box shown in **Figure 12–2** opens.

FIGURE 12–2
Word Options dialog box

Click
to show
the Save
settings

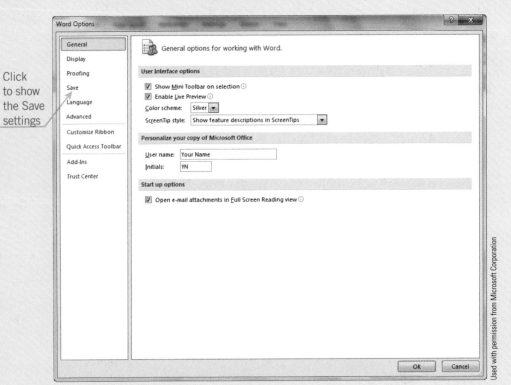

Used with permission from Microsoft Corporation

3. In the left pane, click **Save** to review the Save settings, as shown in **Figure 12–3**.

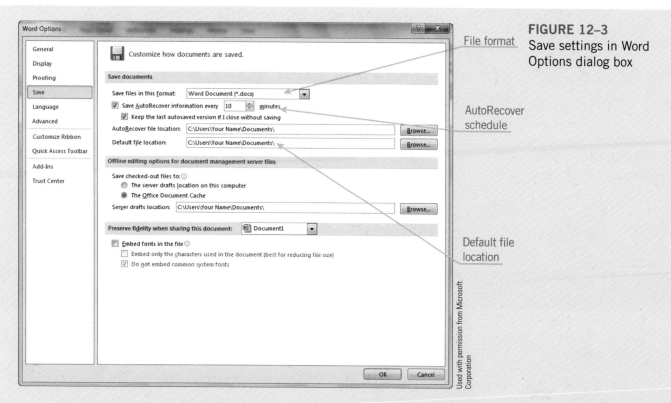

FIGURE 12–3
Save settings in Word
Options dialog box

File format

AutoRecover
schedule

Default file
location

4. Note the file format currently selected under Save documents. The default setting in Word 2010 is to save the document with the file extension *.docx*, indicating the XML format.

5. Click the **Save files in this format** list arrow to view the available settings, but do not make any changes. Click the **Save files in this format** list arrow again to hide the list.

6. Notice there is a setting for saving AutoRecover information. The default setting is every 10 minutes, but your setting may be different. Do not make any changes to this setting.

7. Make note of the setting in the Default file location box. To change this setting, you would click Browse and identify a new path. Do not make any changes to this setting.

8. In the lower-right corner of the dialog box, click **Cancel** to close the dialog box without changing any of the settings.

9. Leave the document open for the next Step-by-Step.

ABOVE AND BEYOND

Users of previous versions of Word are unable to open files saved in the new format, unless they have installed compatibility software. If you often share your documents with users working with previous versions of Word, you should consider changing the file format setting so all documents are saved in the Word 97-2003 (*.doc) format. The drawback to this is that some of the new Word 2010 features are inaccessible in such a document.

Inserting Text and Numbers into a Document

As you enter text in a Word document, the insertion point moves to the right, and the information in the status bar at the lower-left corner of the document window changes to reflect the page number for the current position of the insertion point. The information in the status bar also continually changes to show the current total number of words in the document.

Entering Text in a Document

As you add text to the document, you may see a red or green wavy line under some of the words. Using the default settings, Word automatically checks the spelling and grammar in a document as you are entering the text, and the wavy lines suggest there may be spelling or grammar errors. If you see any wavy lines while entering text in this lesson, ignore them. You will learn more about the spelling and grammar features in Lesson 13.

▶ **VOCABULARY**
word wrap

If the text you are entering extends beyond the right margin, Word will automatically wrap the text to the next line. This feature is called *word wrap*. When you press Enter to start a new line in the document, you create a new paragraph. In a document based on the Normal.dotm template, Word automatically adds extra space after each paragraph, so you do not need to press Enter to create a blank space between paragraphs. The extra space after a paragraph makes the document easier to read. Extra space is also added between the lines within a paragraph.

Step-by-Step 12.3

2-1.2.4
2-1.3.1

1. If necessary, start **Word**, or open a new blank document.

2. Press **Tab**, and then type the sentence below. Notice as you type the text that the insertion point moves in the document window, and when the text expands to the right side of the screen, the text automatically wraps to the next line. Also note that the status bar reflects the number of words in the document.

   `Today, the majority of the American population lives in cities and suburbs. For both recreation and contact with nature, people who live in metropolitan areas depend on parks and recreational paths close to their homes.`

3. Press **Enter** to start a new paragraph.

4. Press **Tab,** and then type the sentence below.

   `Greenways connect parks surrounding and running through metropolitan areas. Sometimes these greenways even link cities together.`

5. Click the **File** tab, and then click **Save As**. The Save As dialog box, similar to the one shown in **Figure 12–4**, will open. Compare the folder structure at the top of the dialog box to the default file location setting that you noted in Step 7 in Step-by-Step 12.2. The path displayed at the top of the Save As dialog box may not be the default file location setting because the path in the dialog box will show the last folder into which a Word file was saved.

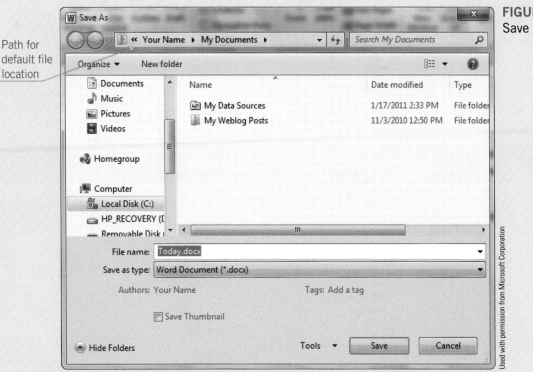

FIGURE 12–4
Save As dialog box

Path for default file location

Used with permission from Microsoft Corporation

6. Navigate to the drive and folder where you are to save your solutions. (Your instructor will provide this information.)

7. In the File name box, replace the existing text with **Recreation and Nature 1**, followed by your initials. Confirm that the Save as type setting is the Word Document (*.docx) format. Click **Save**.

8. Check the word count in the status bar at the bottom-left corner of the window. The word count should be *51*.

9. Leave the document open for the next Step-by-Step.

Showing Characters and Using Click and Type

As you have learned, changing the way a document looks on the screen can make tasks easier. To make editing a document easier, you can also show some special characters. These characters are known as nonprinting characters because, although you can show these symbols on the screen, they do not print.

In the Paragraph group on the Home tab, the Show/Hide ¶ button enables you to toggle the option to show these nonprinting characters. When you *toggle* an option, you alternate between the off and on states by repeating a procedure, such as clicking a button. Nonprinting characters include paragraph markers, blank spaces, page or section breaks, and tab markers. Initially, you may not like showing nonprinting characters while you work with a document, but give it a try. Once you get used to seeing the nonprinting characters on the screen, you will find them very useful as you create and edit the document.

▶ **VOCABULARY**
toggle

Click and type is a Word setting that enables you to quickly position the insertion point within a blank area of a document. When you double-click in a blank space in the document, Word automatically adds blank paragraphs or tabs to position the insertion point where you click. Showing the nonprinting characters can be very helpful when using click and type. When you reposition the insertion point in a blank area of the document, new nonprinting paragraph markers and tab markers indicate how many blank paragraphs or tabs were created to move the insertion point to the new location.

Step-by-Step 12.4

2-1.1.7
2-2.1.6

1. If necessary, open the **Recreation and Nature 1** document from your solution files. Save the Recreation and Nature 1 document as **Recreation and Nature 2**, followed by your initials.

2. On the Home tab, in the Paragraph group, click the **Show/Hide ¶** button ¶ to toggle the feature on. The button will have an orange background when it is enabled.

3. Compare your document to **Figure 12–5**. The nonprinting symbols are identified in the figure. If necessary, scroll up in the document to see the symbols. If you do not see the nonprinting characters on your screen, click the **Show/Hide ¶** button again.

FIGURE 12–5
Nonprinting characters
displayed in a document

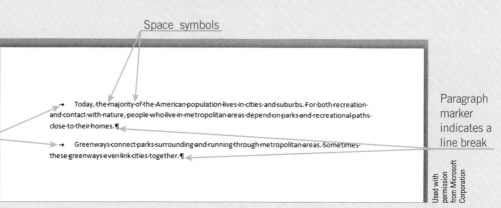

4. Make sure that the click-and-type setting is enabled:
   a. Click the **File** tab.
   b. Click **Options** to open the Word Options dialog box.
   c. In the left pane, click **Advanced**.
   d. In the right pane, below Editing options, make sure there is a check mark in the box for Enable click and type. The option is turned on when there is a check mark in the check box, as shown in **Figure 12–6**.

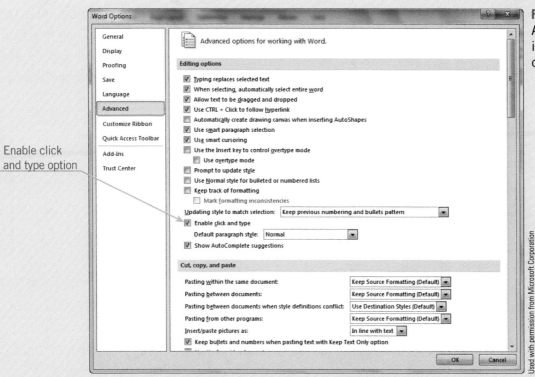

Enable click
and type option

Used with permission from Microsoft Corporation

FIGURE 12–6
Advanced settings
in the Word Options
dialog box

5. Click **OK** to apply the settings and close the Word Options dialog box.

6. Use the scroll bar to move to the bottom of the document. All or most of the document window will be white. Point to the middle of the white area in the document window. The mouse pointer changes to an I-beam, indicating text can be entered in that area of the document. The I-beam is shown in **Figure 12–7**.

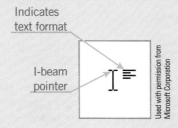

Indicates
text format

I-beam
pointer

Used with permission from Microsoft Corporation

FIGURE 12–7
I-beam in a blank area of
the document

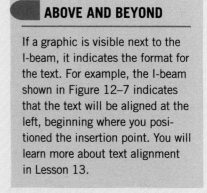

ABOVE AND BEYOND

If a graphic is visible next to the I-beam, it indicates the format for the text. For example, the I-beam shown in Figure 12–7 indicates that the text will be aligned at the left, beginning where you positioned the insertion point. You will learn more about text alignment in Lesson 13.

7. With the mouse pointer positioned in the white area, double-click. The insertion point is now positioned where you clicked. Several new paragraph markers will appear above the new location of the insertion point, as shown in **Figure 12–8**. You may see a tab symbol before the insertion point as is shown in the figure.

FIGURE 12–8
New paragraph markers after insertion point is repositioned using click and type

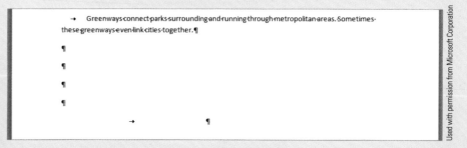

> **QUICK TIP**
>
> When entering numbers in a document, you can use the numbers in the top row on the keyboard or you can use the numbers on the number keypad. If the numbers are not displayed on the screen when you use the keypad, press the Num Lock key on the keypad.

8. Press **Enter**, and then type your first and last names. Press **Enter**, and then type the current date using the *dd/mm/yyyy* format.

9. On the Quick Access Toolbar, click the **Save** button.

10. Close the document, and leave Word open for the next Step-by-Step.

Changing Views and Magnification

Changing the way the document looks on your screen can make working with the document much easier. You can change the way you view your document, and you can also change the magnification to control how much of the document is shown on the screen. The appearance of the document on the screen should be appropriate for the current task.

Changing the Document View

Word offers different options for viewing a document, and you can change the view by selecting options from the Document Views group on the View tab. You can also change the view by clicking one of the view buttons in the status bar in the lower-right corner of the application window.

Each view provides a different way to look at and work with a document. **Table 12–1** describes each of the views. As you work with documents in the different views, you may find that you prefer one view for certain tasks and another view for other tasks.

TABLE 12–1   View options for Word documents

VIEW	DESCRIPTION
Print Layout	The document is displayed on the screen as it will appear when printed. This is the default view in Word.
Full Screen Reading	The screen space is maximized for reading the document. When two pages are shown side by side in Full Screen Reading view, the display of the document appears as though you are reading a book.
Web Layout	The document is shown on the screen as it will appear in a Web browser.
Outline	The document content is shown on the screen in an outline format, which makes it easy to see the structure of the document and to quickly and easily reorganize the content.
Draft	Only the basic document, without elements such as headers and footers, is shown on the screen. The purpose of Draft view is to make the editing process quicker.

Step-by-Step 12.5

1. If necessary, start **Word**. Navigate to the drive and folder where your Data Files folder is stored and open the **Ruts** document. Save the Ruts document as **Getting Through the Ruts 1**, followed by your initials.

2-1.1.5

2. On the Ribbon, click the **View** tab. The Ribbon adapts to show the groups shown in **Figure 12–9**. Note that in the Document Views group the orange background behind the Print Layout button indicates that view is enabled. The document is currently displayed in Print Layout view.

Orange background indicates the view is enabled

Used with permission from Microsoft Corporation

FIGURE 12–9
View tab on the Ribbon

3. In the Document Views group, click the **Full Screen Reading** button. The pages are displayed as in a book. The Ribbon, the scroll bars, and the status bar are hidden. However, a toolbar similar to the Quick Access Toolbar is displayed in the upper-left corner.

4. In the upper-right corner of the screen, click the **View Options** button to display the view menu shown in **Figure 12–10**. If an option is highlighted, the option is already enabled. To enable the three options that are highlighted in the figure, perform the following:

   a. If the Show Two Pages option is not highlighted, click the **option** to enable it. Then click the **View Options** button to reopen the list.

   b. If the Show Printed Page option is not highlighted, click the **option** to enable it. Then click the **View Options** button to reopen the list.

   c. If the Allow Typing option is not highlighted, click the **option** to enable it. Selecting this option will allow you to edit the document in Full Screen Reading view. Then click the **View Options** button to reopen the list.

FIGURE 12–10
View Options menu in Full Screen Reading view

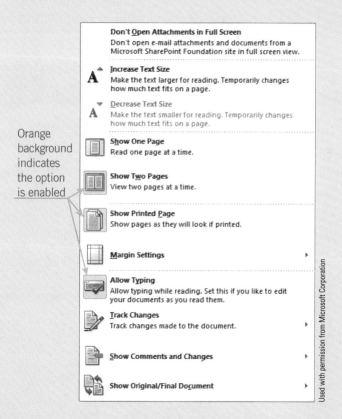

Orange background indicates the option is enabled

Used with permission from Microsoft Corporation

5. After you have confirmed the three options are enabled, click the **View Options** button to close the menu. Your screen should look similar to **Figure 12–11**.

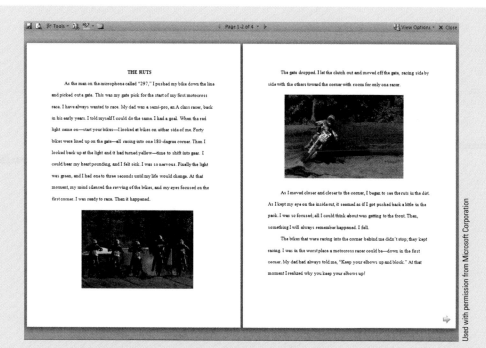

Used with permission from Microsoft Corporation

FIGURE 12–11
Document displayed in Full Screen Reading view

6. To scroll through the pages in Full Screen Reading view, do one of the following:

   a. Press the **up** and **down** arrow keys or the **Page Up** and **Page Down** keys.

   b. Click the **arrows** that appear at the lower corners of the pages.

   c. If your mouse has a wheel, move the scroll wheel on the mouse.

7. Show the first two pages of the document. Position the insertion point in front of the letter *T* in the document title. Type the words **GETTING THROUGH,** and then press the **spacebar** so the revised title reads *GETTING THROUGH THE RUTS*.

8. On the toolbar in the upper-left corner, click the **Save** button to quickly save the changes.

9. In the upper-right corner of the screen, click the **Close** button to close Full Screen Reading view. The document now is displayed again in Print Layout view, the view that was used before Full Screen Reading view. Notice the words you added to the title are still present.

10. In the lower-right corner of the application window, position the mouse pointer over the document view buttons to display ScreenTips for each button, as shown in **Figure 12–12**. Click the **Web Layout** view button 🖳 on the status bar. You will most likely notice a difference in the width of the document and changes to the text wrapping.

FIGURE 12–12
Document view buttons on the status bar

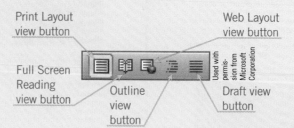

Print Layout view button   Web Layout view button

Full Screen Reading view button   Outline view button   Draft view button

Used with permission from Microsoft Corporation

11. On the status bar, click the **Outline** view button 📃. Notice the Ribbon adapts to display the Outlining tab with tools for navigating and editing the outline. You will have an opportunity to work in Outline view in Lesson 16.

12. On the Outlining tab in the Close group, click the **Close Outline View** button. The Ribbon now shows the Home tab, and the highlighted button on the status bar indicates the document is once again displayed in Print Layout view.

13. Click the **View** tab, and then in the Document Views group, click the **Draft View** button. The white space for the top and left margins is no longer displayed, but the text wrapping does not change.

14. Switch to Print Layout view. Save the changes and leave the document open for the next Step-by-Step.

Changing the Zoom Settings

Zoom options enable you to increase and decrease the size of text and graphics on the screen. You can also show an entire page or multiple pages at the same time. When you open a new document or a saved document, the document window is displayed with the default zoom setting for the current document view. The default settings vary because of the screen size, the screen resolution settings, and the panes displayed on the screen. For example, a page width zoom setting in Print Layout view may be 114%, and a page width setting in Draft view may be 100%.

You can easily change the zoom settings using options in the Zoom group on the View tab, which is shown in **Figure 12–13**. You will also find zoom controls on the right side of the status bar at the bottom of the document window. If your mouse has a scroll wheel, you can use the mouse to zoom in and out.

View and zoom settings are saved with a document, and usually when you open a document, it is displayed in the view and zoom setting in which it was saved. There are, however, two exceptions. If you open a document, change the zoom setting, and then save the document without making any content changes, the zoom settings will not be saved. Also, when you save a document displayed in either Full Screen Reading or Draft view, the document will reopen in Print Layout view.

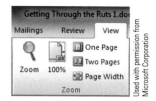

FIGURE 12–13   Zoom group on the View tab

Step-by-Step 12.6

1. If necessary, open the **Getting Through the Ruts 1** document from your solution files. Save the Getting Through the Ruts 1 document as **Getting Through the Ruts 2**, followed by your initials.

2. If necessary, click the **View** tab on the Ribbon, and change the document view to **Print Layout**.

3. On the View tab, in the Zoom group, click the **Zoom** button to open the Zoom dialog box shown in **Figure 12–14**. The Zoom dialog box provides a Preview screen and a text preview panel in the Zoom dialog box so you can preview how the changes you select will appear on the screen. Note that your Percent setting may differ from the one displayed in Figure 12–14.

2-1.1.6

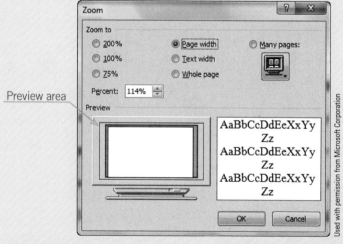

FIGURE 12–14
Zoom dialog box

4. Notice the current setting is Page width. Make a note of the percent that is currently shown in the Percent box. Under Zoom to, click to select the **75%** option, and preview that setting. Note, too, that the Percent box shows 75%.

5. Click to select the **Whole page** option. Notice the percentage changes again.

6. Click to select the **Many pages** option. The percentage will change to 10%, and you will be able to view all the pages in the document at the same time.

7. Click **OK** to accept the change. All four pages of the document are displayed on your screen.

8. In the Zoom group, click the **Page Width** button. The first page of the document should be displayed on your screen.

9. If your mouse has a scroll wheel, press and hold **Ctrl** and roll the wheel toward you to zoom out. Then press and hold **Ctrl** and roll the wheel away from you to zoom in.

10. In the lower-right corner of the application window, zoom controls are displayed as shown in **Figure 12–15**. Position the mouse pointer over the Zoom Out and Zoom In buttons to display the ScreenTips that describe the buttons. Note the current zoom level percentage displayed to the left of the Zoom Out button.

FIGURE 12–15
Zoom controls on the status bar

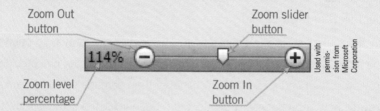

11. Click the **Zoom Out** button twice. Then click the **Zoom In** button three times. Note the changes in the percentages each time you click the buttons.

12. Drag the **Zoom** slider button in the middle to approximately 50%. Then drag the **Zoom** slider button to the right to zoom in to approximately 100%.

13. On the Ribbon, in the Zoom group, click the **Page Width** button.

14. Leave the document open for the next Step-by-Step.

Navigating Through the Document

There are many ways to save time moving through both long and short Word documents, including using the Navigation Pane, scrolling and browsing, and using keyboard shortcuts.

Using the Navigation Pane

When working with long documents, you can easily move through a document by using the Navigation Pane. In the Navigation Pane, you can choose the option to view thumbnails for each page in the document. Each thumbnail is identified with a page number, and the current page is also identified in the status bar. Although most words may be too small to read on a thumbnail, usually graphics or headings will help you identify the page. To go directly to a specific page, click the thumbnail for that page.

Step-by-Step 12.7

1. If necessary, open the **Getting Through the Ruts 2** document from your solution files. If necessary, click the **View** tab.

2. On the View tab, in the Show group, enable the **Navigation Pane** option. The option is enabled when a check mark is displayed in the check box, as shown in **Figure 12–16**. The Navigation Pane is displayed on the left side of the document window.

Click to show
Navigation
Pane

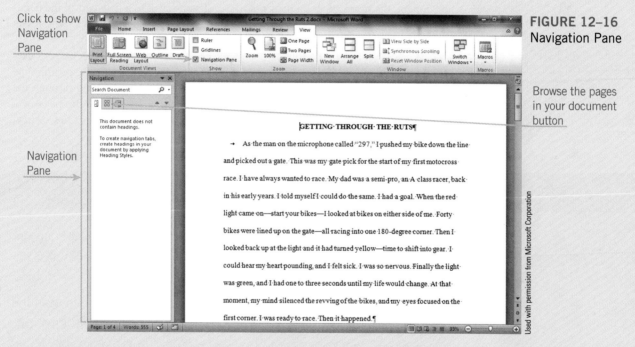

FIGURE 12–16
Navigation Pane

Browse the pages
in your document
button

Navigation
Pane

Used with permission from Microsoft Corporation

3. Under the Search Document box, click the **Browse the pages in your document** button. Four thumbnails are displayed in the Navigation Pane. The page number is shown below the thumbnail.

4. In the Navigation Pane, click the **Page 3** thumbnail. Page 3 is displayed in the document window.

5. In the Navigation Pane, click the **Page 2** thumbnail. Page 2 is displayed in the document window.

6. Leave the document open for the next Step-by-Step.

Scrolling and Browsing

If the location you want to navigate to is currently on the screen, you can simply position the mouse pointer and click. If the part of the document you want to view is currently not visible, you can use the scroll bars to navigate to that part of the document. The scroll bars enable you to quickly move to other areas of the document. If the zoom settings are set for page width (the default setting) or a smaller percentage, the horizontal scroll bar will not appear because the entire width of the document is already visible.

The position of the scroll box on the scroll bar helps you identify what part of the document you are viewing. As you drag the scroll box, a ScreenTip tells you what page you are viewing. As you learned in Lesson 11, when you scroll through a document, the insertion point does not move. If you scroll to a new part of the document and want to reposition the insertion point on that page, then click where you want the insertion point.

When navigating a multipage document, the Go To command can be very useful, because you can go directly to a specific page, a specific line, or a specific type of content in the document. Browsing is another option for navigating through the document. When you browse, you focus on an object such as a specific page or a footnote. To browse, you use the three Browse buttons at the bottom of the vertical scroll bar.

Step-by-Step 12.8

2-1.1.3

1. If necessary, open the **Getting Through the Ruts 2** document from your solution files. If necessary, show the **Navigation Pane**, and click the **Page 2** thumbnail. Also, if necessary, display the **View** tab.

2. On the View tab in the Zoom group, click the **Zoom** button to open the Zoom dialog box. Under Zoom to, select the **200%** option. Click **OK**. The horizontal scroll bar is displayed as shown in **Figure 12–17**.

FIGURE 12–17
Horizontal scroll bar
tools

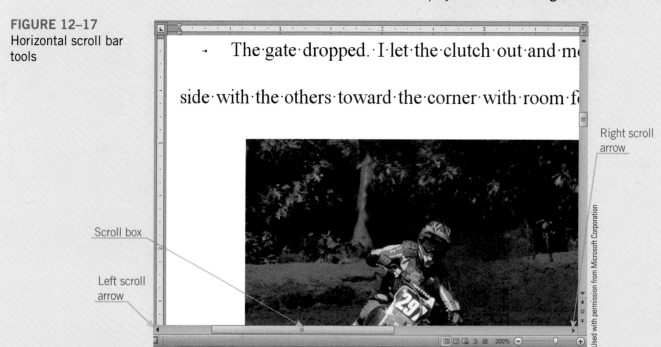

The·gate·dropped.··I·let·the·clutch·out·and·m

side·with·the·others·toward·the·corner·with·room·f

Right scroll arrow

Scroll box

Left scroll arrow

200%

Used with permission from Microsoft Corporation

3. Click the **right** and **left** scroll arrows on the horizontal scroll bar to scroll left and right through the page in the document window. Then drag the scroll box on the horizontal scroll bar at the bottom of the screen to the far right side of the scroll bar.

4. In the Zoom group, click the **Page Width** button to reduce the magnification of the document.

5. If your mouse has a wheel, press and hold **Ctrl** and roll the wheel toward you to scroll down. Then roll the wheel away from you to scroll up.

6. Use the vertical scroll bar tools to show the last sentence in the document. Then use the vertical scroll bar tools to show the beginning of the document. Position the insertion point in front of the document title.

7. At the bottom of the vertical scroll bar on the right side of the screen, click the **Select Browse Object** button, as shown in **Figure 12–18**. A menu of buttons is displayed as shown in **Figure 12–19**. The arrangement of your buttons may differ.

QUICK TIP

When you use the vertical scroll bar, think about moving up and down several floors in a building. To move up or down one or two floors you would likely take the stairs (click the up and down scroll arrows on the scroll bar). To move up or down several floors, you can save time by taking the elevator (drag the scroll box on the scroll bar).

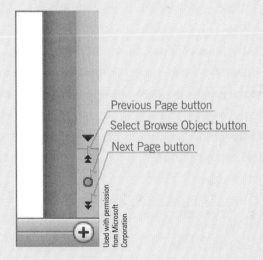

Previous Page button
Select Browse Object button
Next Page button

Used with permission from Microsoft Corporation

FIGURE 12–18
Browse buttons on the vertical scroll bar

Go To button

Cancel

Browse by Page button

Used with permission from Microsoft Corporation

FIGURE 12–19
Select Browse Object button and menu

8. Click the **Go To** button ⟶ to open the Go To tab in the Find and Replace dialog box shown in **Figure 12–20**.

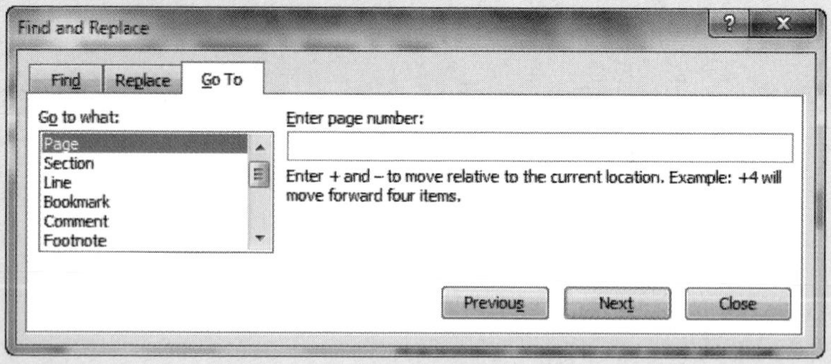

Used with permission from Microsoft Corporation

FIGURE 12–20
Go To tab in the Find and Replace dialog box

9. Under Go to what, click **Line**. Then click the **text box** under Enter page number, and type **33**. At the bottom of the dialog box, click **Go To**. Then click **Close** to close the dialog box. The insertion point is positioned in front of the line of text just above the picture on page 3. In the Navigation Pane, an orange background is displayed behind the page 3 thumbnail, indicating it is the current page. Also, the information on the left side of the status bar also indicates you are viewing page 3 of 4.

10. Click the **Select Browse Object** button, and then click the **Go To** button. Under Go to what, click **Page**. Click the **text box** under Enter page number, type **1**, and then click **Go To**. Close the dialog box. Page 1 is displayed in the document window, and the insertion point is positioned at the top of the page in front of the title. Note there is an orange background behind the page 1 thumbnail and the status bar information indicates you are viewing page 1 of 4.

11. Click the **Select Browse Object** button, and then in the menu click the **Browse by Page** button ⬚. The insertion point moves to the top of the next page. In the Navigation Pane, there is an orange background behind the page 2 thumbnail, and the information on the left side of the status bar also indicates that you are viewing page 2 of 4.

12. On the vertical scroll bar, click the **Previous Page** button to move the insertion point back to the previous page (page 1). Click the **Next Page** button on the vertical scroll bar three times to move the insertion point to the top of page 4.

13. Position the insertion point after the period in the last line of text. Press **Enter**, and type the current date using the *dd/mm/yyyy* format.

14. Save the changes and close the document. Reopen the document. Note that the document is displayed in Print Layout view and the magnification is set at Page Width. Leave the document open for the next Step-by-Step.

QUICK TIP

You can also quickly open the Go To tab in the Find dialog box by pressing Ctrl+G.

Using the Keyboard

If you have good keyboarding skills, using the keyboard to move the insertion point can speed up your navigation. Using the keyboard eliminates the need to move your hand back and forth between the keyboard and the mouse. You can use the arrow keys on the keyboard to move the insertion point one character at a time or one line at a time. If you need to move across several characters or lines, however, using a combination of keys will make the task easier and quicker. **Table 12–2** provides a list of keys and key combinations for moving the insertion point throughout the document.

TABLE 12–2   Keys and key combinations for moving the insertion point

TO MOVE THE INSERTION POINT	PRESS
Right one character	Right arrow
Left one character	Left arrow
Down one line	Down arrow
Up one line	Up arrow
To the end of a line	End
To the beginning of a line	Home
To the next screen	Page Down
To the previous screen	Page Up
To the next word	Ctrl+Right arrow
To the previous word	Ctrl+Left arrow
To the end of the document	Ctrl+End
To the beginning of the document	Ctrl+Home
Down one paragraph	Ctrl+Down arrow
Up one paragraph	Ctrl+Up arrow

Step-by-Step 12.9

1. If necessary, open the **Getting Through the Ruts 2** document from your solution files.

2. Press **Ctrl+End** to move the insertion point to the end of the document. Then press **Ctrl+Home** to move the insertion point to the beginning of the document.

3. Press the **down arrow** key twice to move the insertion point down two lines. Press the **right arrow** key three times to move the insertion point three characters to the right.

4. Press **End** to move the insertion point to the end of the line.

2-1.1.3

5. Press and hold **Ctrl,** and then press the **left arrow** key to move the insertion point to the beginning of the word *motocross.* Continue to hold **Ctrl,** and press the **left arrow** key again to move to the previous word *first.*

6. Press **Home** to move the insertion point to the beginning of the line.

7. Press **Page Down** four times to move down four screens.

8. Press and hold **Ctrl**, and then press the **down arrow** key to move down one paragraph.

9. Close the document and exit Word. If prompted to save changes to the document, click **Don't Save**.

SUMMARY

In this lesson, you learned:

- New blank documents are created based on a template with default settings.

- There are many "behind the scenes" settings in Word that can be changed to meet your preferences.

- Word automatically wraps text to the next line when the line of text extends beyond the right margin.

- Showing the nonprinting characters, such as tab markers, blank spaces, page breaks, and paragraph markers can be very useful as you create and edit a document.

- The click and type setting enables you to position the insertion point in a blank area of a document.

- Word provides several options for viewing a document.

- You can use zoom options to increase or decrease the size of the text and graphics on the screen.

- You can view thumbnails of the document pages in the Navigation Pane to make it easier and faster to navigate through the document.

- You can also use the mouse, the Go To command, the Select Browse Object button, and keyboard shortcuts to navigate through a document.

■ LESSON REVIEW

TRUE / FALSE

Circle T if the statement is true or F if the statement is false.

T   F   **1.** Preset options or variables are automatically in effect when a new blank Word document is created.

T   F   **2.** When you open a saved document, it will always be displayed in Print Layout view.

T   F   **3.** Zoom options allow you to increase and decrease the size of text and graphics for a single page within a document.

T   F   **4.** The Go To command moves the insertion point to a specific page, a specific line, or a specific type of content.

T   F   **5.** The vertical scroll bar includes buttons for browsing objects in the document.

MULTIPLE CHOICE

Select the best response for the following statements.

1. Nonprinting characters include _____.

   A.   paragraph markers

   B.   tab marks

   C.   blank spaces

   D.   all of the above

2. The information in the _____ continually changes to show the current total number of words in the document.

   A.   taskbar

   B.   title bar

   C.   status bar

   D.   Paragraph group on the Ribbon

3. The _____ view allows you to quickly and easily reorganize the content.

   A.   Full Screen Reading

   B.   Draft

   C.   Outline

   D.   Print Layout

4. To move the insertion point to the end of the document, press _____.

   A.   End

   B.   Ctrl+End

   C.   Ctrl+Down arrow

   D.   Shift+Down arrow

5. To change the magnification settings for a document, _____.

   A.   click the Zoom button in the Zoom group on the Ribbon

   B.   use the zoom controls in the status bar

   C.   use the mouse scroll wheel

   D.   any of the above

WRITTEN QUESTIONS

Write a brief answer to the following questions.

1. What is the advantage to using the keyboard to reposition the insertion point in the document?

2. What is displayed in Draft view, and what is the purpose of Draft view?

3. How does using the Normal.dotm template increase the speed and efficiency of your work?

4. What does it mean to toggle an option?

5. Why is the Navigation Pane useful for moving through long documents?

6. Describe how word wrap works.

7. What filename does Word automatically apply when you open a new blank document?

8. What is the purpose of the click-and-type setting?

9. How can the scroll bar help you identify what part of the document you are viewing?

10. How does the AutoRecover setting protect your work?

■ PROJECTS

PROJECT 12–1

1. Start **Word**. If Word is already open, create a new blank document.

2. Type the following two paragraphs.

```
Throughout the twentieth century, shifting
along the San Andreas Faultin California
causednumerous damaging earthquakes. Almost
everyone knows about the San Andreas Fault.

Relatively unknown is the New Madrid Fault in
the central United States. In the nineteenth
century, the New Madrid Fault caused three
of the most powerful earthquakes in U.S.
history. Damage from the earthquake was
reported as far away as Charleston, South
Carolina, and Washington, DC. One earthquake
along this fault line was so powerful that
it caused the Mississippi River to change
course.
```

3. Navigate to your solutions folder, and save the document as **Historic Earthquakes**, followed by your initials.

2-1.1.5
2-1.1.6
2-1.2.1
2-1.2.4
2-1.3.1

4. Switch to **Full Screen Reading** view. If necessary, enable the option **Allow Typing**.

5. Position the insertion point at the beginning of the first word in the document, and type **Historic Earthquakes**.

6. Press **Enter** once to create extra space after the new line of text.

7. Close Full Screen Reading view.

8. Change the Zoom Percent setting to **100%**.

9. Change to **Web Layout** view.

10. Save the changes to the document.

11. Close the document, and leave Word open for the next project.

PROJECT 12-2

1. Open the document **Interview Questions** from the drive and folder where your Data Files folder is stored.

   2-1.1.3
   2-1.1.5
   2-1.1.6
   2-1.3.1
   2-2.1.16

2. Save the Interview Questions document as **Interview Preparation**, followed by your initials.

3. Read each of the questions, choose one to answer. Do not type your response yet.

4. Show the nonprinting characters in the document.

5. Scroll down to the middle of the document. Position the insertion point in the white area about two inches below the last question.

6. Type **Response to Question #x**. Replace the *x* with the question number you chose in Step 3. Press **Enter** to create a new paragraph. Type your response to the question.

7. There should be at least two blank paragraphs between the last question and the response you typed. If necessary, position the insertion point between the last question and the new text you type, and then press **Enter** to add more blank lines.

8. Use the **Go To** command to move the insertion point to the beginning of the first line in the document. Type **INTERVIEW PREPARATION**, and then press **Enter**.

9. Change the magnification to **Page Width**.

10. Save the changes to the document, and close the document. Leave Word open for the next Project.

▶ TEAMWORK PROJECT

Microsoft released the first version of Word for an IBM PC in 1983. The early versions of Word were created for MS-DOS, not Windows. Word made full use of the mouse, but few people used the mouse at this time. They usually accessed the commands by keystrokes, and users often memorized the necessary keystrokes. So, keyboard shortcuts have been around for a long time. You learned several keyboard shortcuts in this lesson, but there are many more.

Choose a partner to help you find keyboard shortcuts for commands related to the following:

- Displaying and using windows

- Using dialog boxes

- Using the Open and Save As dialog boxes

1. Use the Word Help system to learn about keyboard shortcuts for commands related to the above topics.

PROJECT 12-3

1. Open the **Super Mart** document from the drive and folder where your Data Files folder is stored.   2-1.1.3

2. Scroll to the middle of the document until you see the heading *Similarities*.

3. Use keyboard shortcuts to do the following:

   a. Move the insertion point to the end of the document.

   b. Move the insertion point up one paragraph.

   c. Move the insertion point to the end of the line.

   d. Move the insertion point to the previous screen.

   e. Move the insertion point to the beginning of the document.

   f. Move the insertion point down two lines.

4. Use the Go To command to locate line 64. The insertion point should be positioned near the heading *Differences*. Then use the Go To command to locate line 51. The insertion point should then be positioned near the heading *Similarities*.

5. If necessary, show the Navigation Pane. Browse the pages in your document and go to page 1. The first page in the document is a cover page, so it is numbered 0.

6. Using the Navigation Pane, move the insertion point to page 4.

7. Close the document. If prompted to save changes, click **Don't Save**.

2. Try some of the shortcuts described in your list to see if the shortcuts work on your computer.   2-1.1.3

3. Create a new Word document, and save the document as **TP 12–1**, followed by your initials.

4. List three or four shortcuts that you and your partner will most likely use.

5. Save the changes to the document, and then close the document.

6. Demonstrate those shortcuts to others in the class, providing an explanation as to why you and your partner think the shortcuts are helpful.

CRITICAL THINKING

CRITICAL THINKING 12–1

2-1.1.5

In this lesson you explored several different document views. Which of these views do you prefer?

1. Create a new Word document, and save the document as **CT 12–1**, followed by your initials.

2. Write a paragraph describing your view preference, and explain why.

3. Save the changes to the document, and then close the document.

CRITICAL THINKING 12–2

2-1.1.3

In this lesson you explored three methods to navigate through a document: using the Navigation Pane, scrolling and browsing, and using the keyboard. If you need to navigate to a specific page in a document with 10 pages, which method of navigation would you use?

1. Create a new Word document, and save the document as **CT 12–2**, followed by your initials.

2. Write a brief paragraph about which method you prefer, and explain why.

3. Save the changes to the document, and then close the document.

ONLINE DISCOVERY

ONLINE DISCOVERY 12–1

2-1.1.6

In this lesson you explored the options for changing the zoom settings in Word documents. You can also change the zoom settings when you view Web pages. Open your Web browser, and experiment with changing the zoom settings. Compare changing the view of a Web page to changing the view of a Word document.

1. Create a new Word document, and save the document as **OD 12–1**, followed by your initials.

2. Write a brief summary of your findings.

3. Save the changes to the document, and then close the document.

ONLINE DISCOVERY 12–2

2-1.1.9

The arrangement of a standard keyboard on a computer (or a typewriter) is called QWERTY, referring to the first six characters in the top row of letters. But why are the letters on the keyboard not arranged in alphabetical order, or some other logical order? Why QWERTY?

1. Search the Internet to learn the history of the QWERTY keyboard and the Dvorak keyboard.

2. Create a new Word document, and save the document as **OD 12–2**, followed by your initials.

3. Write a brief summary of your findings. Cite your sources by copying the Web page URL and pasting the information at the bottom of the summary.

4. Save the changes to the document, and then close the document.

JOB SKILLS

When you open a Word document attached to an e-mail, the document most likely opens in Full Screen Reading view as a result of default settings. In a discussion with your colleagues, you offered to learn how to change this default setting.

1. Open the Word Options dialog box, and review the settings.

2. Create a new Word document, and save the document as **JS 12–1**, followed by your initials.

3. Write a paragraph describing how you can change the setting so Word documents do not open in Full Screen Reading view when opened from an e-mail attachment. (Do not make any changes to the settings on your computer.)

2-1.1.7

4. Save the changes to the document, and then close the document.

LESSON 13

Editing and Formatting Documents

■ OBJECTIVES

Upon completion of this lesson, you should be able to:

- Delete and insert text using Backspace, Delete, Insert, Overtype modes.
- Undo, redo, and repeat actions.
- Edit text using drag-and-drop editing and the Cut, Copy, and Paste commands.
- Find and replace text.
- Use proofing tools to check and correct spelling and grammar, and use research services.
- Change the character format.
- Format paragraphs with line spacing, alignment, tabs and indents, and bulleted and numbered lists.
- Format documents with margin settings, page orientation settings, and page breaks.

■ DATA FILES

To complete this lesson, you will need these data files:

Carbohydrates.docx

Career Planning.docx

Class Schedule.docx

Expo.docx

Garden.docx

H2O Cove.docx

National Parks.docx

Program Guide.docx

Recommended Diet.docx

Video Replay.docx

Workouts.docx

■ WORDS TO KNOW

alignment

Clipboard

drag-and-drop editing

edit

first line indent

font

format

Format Painter

hanging indent

incremental search

indent

landscape orientation

manual line break

manual page break

margins

points

portrait orientation

select

soft page break

wildcard character

Editing and formatting features give you the ability to refine your documents and determine how they will look on the screen, on the Web, or as printed pages. Word provides many features that enable you to make changes, correct errors, and check the spelling and the grammar in your document.

Editing Documents

When you *edit* a document, you modify or adapt the document and make revisions or corrections. Editing a document involves adding, deleting, changing, or moving text.

Selecting Text

When you *select* text, you identify a block of text you want to edit. The text can be a single character, several characters, a word, a sentence, one or more paragraphs, or even the entire document. Once you select text, you can delete it, replace it, change its appearance, move it, copy it, and so on. You can use the mouse or the keyboard to select text. The quickest way to select text using the mouse is to click and hold the mouse button, drag the mouse pointer over the desired text, and then release the mouse button.

Sometimes it is difficult to select precisely when you are dragging the mouse. **Table 13–1** lists several options for selecting text using the mouse and the keyboard. To deselect the text (remove the highlighting that indicates selection), click anywhere in the document window or press an arrow key. If you accidentally delete or replace selected text, or if you just change your mind, click the Undo button.

TABLE 13–1   Ways to select text

TO SELECT	DO THIS:
Any amount of text	Click and hold the mouse button, drag the mouse pointer over the text, and then release the mouse button
A word	Double-click the word
A sentence	With no other text or objects selected, press and hold Ctrl, and then click anywhere in the sentence
A paragraph	Triple-click anywhere in the paragraph or Double-click in the blank space to the left of the paragraph
An entire document	Press Ctrl+A or Move the mouse pointer to the left of any text, and when the mouse pointer changes to a right-pointing arrow, triple-click
A line	Click in the blank space to the left of the line
Multiple lines	Click and hold the mouse button, and then drag the mouse pointer in the blank space to the left of the lines
One or more characters to the right or left	Press and hold Shift, and then press the right or left arrow key
The end or the beginning of a word	Press and hold Ctrl+Shift, and then press the right or left arrow key
Any amount of text (Click-Shift-Click)	Click where you want the selection to begin, press and hold Shift, and then click where you want the selection to end; everything between the two clicks is selected or Position the insertion point where you want the selection to begin, press F8 to toggle on the select mode, and then use the arrow keys or the mouse to indicate where you want the selection to end (If you don't execute a command such as Delete or applying a format, press Esc to toggle the selected mode off)

Step-by-Step 13.1

1. Start **Microsoft Word 2010**.
2. Open the **Carbohydrates** document from the drive and folder where your Data Files folder is stored. Save the Carbohydrates document as **Revised Carbohydrates 1**, followed by your initials.
3. If necessary, in the Paragraph group on the Home tab, click the **Show/Hide ¶** button to show the nonprinting characters.

2-1.3.2

4. Position the I-beam mouse pointer at the beginning of the first line of text. Click and hold the mouse button and then drag the mouse pointer through the first sentence of text. When all the text in the first sentence is selected, including the period at the end of the sentence, release the mouse button. The sentence is now selected, as shown in **Figure 13–1**.

FIGURE 13–1
Selected text

Selected text

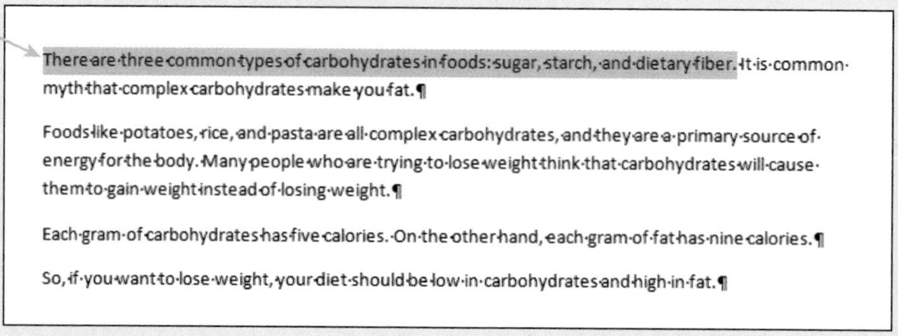

There·are·three·common·types·of·carbohydrates·in·foods:·sugar,·starch,·and·dietary·fiber.·It·is·common·myth·that·complex·carbohydrates·make·you·fat.¶

Foods·like·potatoes,·rice,·and·pasta·are·all·complex·carbohydrates,·and·they·are·a·primary·source·of·energy·for·the·body.·Many·people·who·are·trying·to·lose·weight·think·that·carbohydrates·will·cause·them·to·gain·weight·instead·of·losing·weight.¶

Each·gram·of·carbohydrates·has·five·calories.·On·the·other·hand,·each·gram·of·fat·has·nine·calories.¶

So,·if·you·want·to·lose·weight,·your·diet·should·be·low·in·carbohydrates·and·high·in·fat.¶

Used with permission from Microsoft Corporation

5. Double-click the word **diet** in the last paragraph to select it. Note that the first sentence is no longer selected.

6. Press **Ctrl+A** to select the entire document. Click anywhere in the document window to deselect the text.

7. Click to position the insertion point at the beginning of the second paragraph. Press and hold **Shift**, and then click after the word *rice*. Everything between the two clicks is selected.

8. Continue to hold **Shift** and press the **right arrow** key to extend the selection. Press the **left arrow** key to reverse direction of the selection. Continue to press the **left arrow** key until text in the previous paragraph is selected. Press the **down arrow** and **up arrow** keys to reverse and extend the direction of the selection. Release Shift.

9. Click anywhere in the document window to deselect the text.

10. Position the insertion point at the end of the first paragraph. The insertion point will be displayed between the period and the paragraph marker. Press and hold **Ctrl** and **Shift** and then press **Home**. All of the text from the insertion point to the beginning of the document is selected.

11. Click anywhere in the document window to deselect the text.

◆— **WARNING**

Be cautious when working with selected text. If you press any letters, numbers, or symbols on the keyboard when text is selected, the new keystrokes will replace the selected text. Pages of text can accidentally be replaced with a single character.

12. Practice other methods of selecting text following the instructions in Table 13–1.

13. Deselect the text. Leave the document open for the next Step-by-Step. (If you must close the document, do not save any changes to the document.)

Deleting and Inserting Characters

Editing often involves deleting and replacing existing text. You can quickly delete characters one at a time by using either the Backspace or Delete key. Backspace deletes the character to the left of the insertion point. Delete removes the character to the right of the insertion point. When you hold down either of these keys, the characters will continue to be deleted until you release the key. You can also select characters, words, sentences, or paragraphs and then press Delete or Backspace to delete the selected text.

By default, Word enters text in a document using Insert mode. In Insert mode, when you enter new text in front of existing text, the existing text shifts to the right to make room for the new text. In Overtype mode, new text replaces the existing text. When Overtype mode is activated, Insert mode is turned off. You can activate Overtype mode in the Word Options dialog box, and you can use the Insert key to toggle Overtype mode on and off.

Step-by-Step 13.2

1. If necessary, open **Revised Carbohydrates 1** from your solution files.

2. In the second paragraph, position the insertion point right before the period at the end of the last sentence. Press **Backspace** several times to erase the last four words in the sentence, *instead of losing weight*.

3. In the second paragraph, position the insertion point at the beginning of the word *complex*. Press **Delete** to remove the first letter of the word. Double-click the remaining part of the word to select it, and then press **Delete**.

2-1.3.1
2-1.3.2

4. To make sure Overtype mode is not activated, click the **File** tab, click **Options**, and then click **Advanced**. Under Editing options, make sure there is no check mark for the option Use overtype mode. Also, if necessary, enable the option Use the Insert key to control overtype mode. Compare your screen to **Figure 13–2**. Make note of any changes you make.

FIGURE 13–2
Word Editing options

Enabled

Disabled

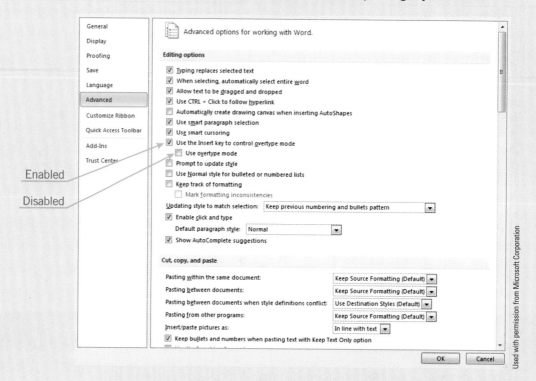

5. Click **OK** to accept the settings and close the Word Options dialog box.

6. In the last paragraph, double-click the word **carbohydrates** to select it, and then type **fat**. The selected text is replaced with the new text.

7. In the last paragraph, double-click the second occurrence of the word **fat**, and then type **complex carbohydrates**.

8. In the first sentence of the second paragraph, position the insertion point right before the first occurrence of the word *and*. Type **bread,** and then press the **spacebar**. Because Insert mode is active, Word inserts the text between the existing characters.

9. Press **Insert** to activate Overtype mode.

10. In the first sentence of the third paragraph, position the insertion point in front of the word *five*. Type **four**. The new text replaces the word *five*.

11. Press **Insert** to toggle off Overtype mode and return to Insert mode.

12. If you made any changes to the settings in Step 4, click the **File** tab, click **Options**, click **Advanced**, and restore the original settings. Then click **OK** to save the changes and close the Word Options dialog box.

13. Save the changes, and leave the document open for the next Step-by-Step.

Undoing, Redoing, and Repeating

Sometimes you may delete or replace text unintentionally. Whenever you perform an action that you want to reverse, you can use the Undo command. If you undo an action and then change your mind, you can reverse the undo action by using the Redo command. You can even undo and redo multiple actions at one time.

There may be times when you want to repeat your last action. For example, you may enter new text in a document and then want to add the same text in other locations in the document. You can use the Repeat command to repeat your last action. The Undo, Redo, and Repeat buttons can be accessed on the Quick Access Toolbar. The Redo button exchanges with the Repeat button on the Quick Access Toolbar when you undo an action.

ScreenTips for the Undo, Redo, and Repeat buttons are conditional and will reflect your recent action. Sometimes an action cannot be reversed, and the ScreenTip for the Undo button displays "Can't Undo." If you cannot repeat the last action, the Repeat button is dimmed and the ScreenTip for the Repeat button displays "Can't Repeat."

Step-by-Step 13.3

1. If necessary, open the **Revised Carbohydrates 1** document from your solution files. Save the Revised Carbohydrates 1 document as **Revised Carbohydrates 2**, followed by your initials.

2-1.3.3

2. Position the insertion point at the end of the document. Press **Enter**, and then type your first and last name.

3. Move the insertion point to the beginning of the document.

4. Position the mouse pointer over the Repeat button on the Quick Access Toolbar to display the ScreenTip *Repeat Typing (Ctrl + Y)* as shown in **Figure 13–3**. Then, click the **Repeat** button. A blank paragraph and your first and last name are inserted at the position of the insertion point.

Repeat button
ScreenTip

FIGURE 13–3
Quick Access Toolbar

5. You change your mind. On the Quick Access Toolbar, position the mouse pointer over the Undo button to show the ScreenTip *Undo Typing (Ctrl + Z)*. Then, click the **Undo** button. The blank paragraph and your first and last names are removed from the top of the document.

6. Click the **Undo** button arrow, and position the mouse pointer over *Typing "bread,"*. All the previous actions above that action in the list will also be highlighted, as shown in **Figure 13–4**. Click **Typing "bread,"**. The last six actions are reversed.

FIGURE 13–4
Multiple actions selected in the Undo list

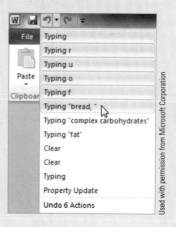

7. On the Quick Access Toolbar, click the **Redo** button to reverse only the last undo. The word *bread*, followed by a comma, is reinserted in the second paragraph.

8. Click the **Redo** button four more times to replace the word *five* with *four*.

9. Click the **Undo** button arrow. The list includes *Typing "bread,"* and *Typing* the letters *f, o, u,* and *r*.

10. Click anywhere in the document window to close the Undo list without reversing any actions.

11. Save the changes, and leave the document open for the next Step-by-Step.

Copying and Moving Text

Selected text can be copied or moved within a document and between documents. For example, you can copy text from an e-mail message to a Word document. There are several ways to copy and move text.

When you use the mouse to drag selected text from the existing location and then drop the selected text in a new location, it is called **drag-and-drop editing**. Drag-and-drop editing makes moving text quick and easy, especially when you are moving the text short distances. You simply drag selected text to the new location and then release the mouse button. You can also copy text using drag-and-drop editing. Hold down Ctrl as you drag, and the selected text will be copied instead of moved.

You can also use the Cut, Copy, and Paste commands to move and copy selected text. When you use the Cut, Copy, and Paste commands, Word uses a feature called the Clipboard. The **Clipboard** is a temporary storage place in your computer's memory. The Clipboard can store data of all Office types, and that data can be inserted into the same document, into other documents in the same application, or into files in other Office programs.

You send selected contents of your document to the Clipboard by using the Cut or Copy commands. The Clipboard stores up to 24 items, which you can view by showing the Clipboard task pane. If you prefer, you can work with the Clipboard task pane open.

▶ **VOCABULARY**
drag-and-drop editing
Clipboard

ABOVE AND BEYOND

Word offers many options for using the Clipboard. Use the Help feature to find out more about the Clipboard and to determine which options best meet your needs.

You can retrieve the contents of the Clipboard by using the Paste command. You can select any one of the items on the Clipboard and paste it, or you can paste all of the items at once. Pasting the contents of the Clipboard does not delete the contents from the Clipboard. Therefore, you can paste Clipboard items as many times as you want. However, when you turn off the computer, the Clipboard contents are erased.

Step-by-Step 13.4

1. If necessary, open the **Revised Carbohydrates 2** document from your solution files. Save the Revised Carbohydrates 2 document as **Revised Carbohydrates 3**, followed by your initials.

2. If necessary, click the **Show/Hide ¶** button to show the nonprinting characters. Triple-click anywhere within the third paragraph to select all the text in the paragraph. Then press and hold **Shift**, and press the **left arrow** key once to remove the paragraph marker from the selection.

3. Point to the selection, and hold down the **left** mouse button. Drag the insertion point to the end of the first paragraph. As you drag the selected text, the insertion point changes to a dotted vertical line as shown in **Figure 13–5**. When the insertion point is positioned at the end of paragraph, release the mouse button. Word automatically adjusts the spacing by adding a blank space between the two sentences.

IC³
2-1.3.2

> **QUICK TIP**
>
> To drag text beyond the current screen of text, drag the pointer toward the top or bottom of the screen. As you hold the pointer at the edge of the screen, the document will automatically scroll in that direction.

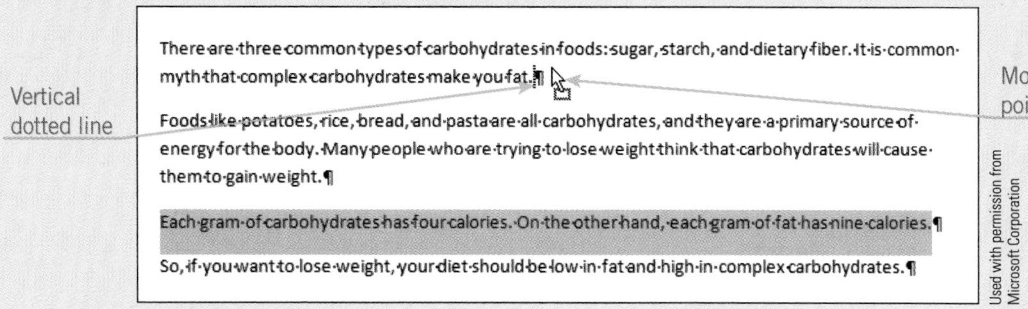

Vertical dotted line

Mouse pointer

FIGURE 13–5
Dragging and dropping to move text

There·are·three·common·types·of·carbohydrates·in·foods:·sugar,·starch,·and·dietary·fiber.·It·is·common· myth·that·complex·carbohydrates·make·you·fat.¶

Foods·like·potatoes,·rice,·bread,·and·pasta·are·all·carbohydrates,·and·they·are·a·primary·source·of· energy·for·the·body.·Many·people·who·are·trying·to·lose·weight·think·that·carbohydrates·will·cause· them·to·gain·weight.¶

Each·gram·of·carbohydrates·has·four·calories.·On·the·other·hand,·each·gram·of·fat·has·nine·calories.¶

So,·if·you·want·to·lose·weight,·your·diet·should·be·low·in·fat·and·high·in·complex·carbohydrates.¶

Used with permission from Microsoft Corporation

4. With the sentence still selected, press and hold **Ctrl** and use the left mouse button to drag the text to the end of the document. As you drag the text, the mouse pointer changes and includes a plus sign as shown in **Figure 13–6**. Release the mouse button. The text is copied to the new location.

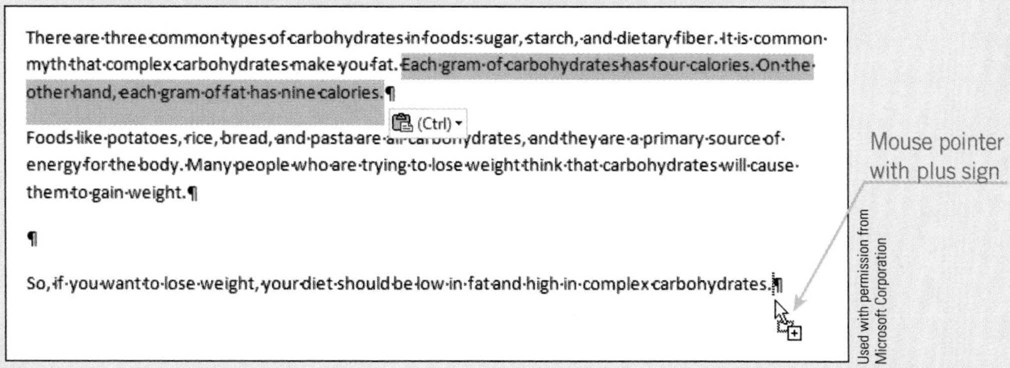

FIGURE 13–6
Dragging and dropping to copy text

There·are·three·common·types·of·carbohydrates·in·foods:·sugar,·starch,·and·dietary·fiber.·It·is·common· myth·that·complex·carbohydrates·make·you·fat.·Each·gram·of·carbohydrates·has·four·calories.·On·the· other·hand,·each·gram·of·fat·has·nine·calories.¶

(Ctrl) ▾

Foods·like·potatoes,·rice,·bread,·and·pasta·are·all·carbohydrates,·and·they·are·a·primary·source·of· energy·for·the·body.·Many·people·who·are·trying·to·lose·weight·think·that·carbohydrates·will·cause· them·to·gain·weight.¶

¶

So,·if·you·want·to·lose·weight,·your·diet·should·be·low·in·fat·and·high·in·complex·carbohydrates.¶

Mouse pointer with plus sign

Used with permission from Microsoft Corporation

5. Click the **Undo** button, and then click anywhere in the document window to deselect the text.

6. On the Home tab, in the Clipboard group, click the **dialog box launcher** to open the Clipboard task pane, as shown in **Figure 13–7**. Your Clipboard may show different items or no items at all. If items appear on the Clipboard, click the **Clear All** button to remove any items from the Clipboard.

FIGURE 13–7
Clipboard task pane

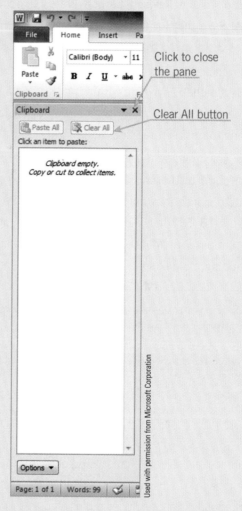

7. Press and hold **Ctrl**, and click anywhere within the last sentence in the document to select the whole sentence. On the Home tab, in the Clipboard group, click the **Cut** button. The selected text is removed from the document and is now stored on the Clipboard and is displayed on the Clipboard task pane.

8. Triple-click anywhere in the second paragraph in the document to select the whole paragraph. In the Clipboard group, click the **Copy** button. The selected text is still displayed in the document, and the selected text is also stored on the Clipboard and it is displayed on the Clipboard task pane. Deselect the text in the document window.

9. Open the **Recommended Diet** document from the drive and folder where your Data Files folder is stored. Press and hold **Ctrl** and press **A** to select the entire document, and click the **Copy** button. The text is stored on the Clipboard.

10. Switch to the **Revised Carbohydrates 3** document, and position the insertion point at the beginning of the second paragraph. In the Clipboard group, click the **Paste** button. At the location of the insertion point, Word inserts the most recent item added to the Clipboard. Notice that the copied text is still displayed on the Clipboard task pane.

11. Open a new blank document, and, if necessary, open the Clipboard task pane. There should be three items on the Clipboard. In the Clipboard task pane, click the **Paste All** button in the Clipboard task pane. All the contents on the Clipboard are inserted at the location of the insertion point. The oldest item on the Clipboard is pasted first. Even though there are three items on the Clipboard, only two paragraphs are displayed in the document because there is no paragraph marker after the *So, if you...* item.

12. Save the new document as **Revised Carbohydrates 4** and then close the document. Also, switch to and then close the Recommended Diet document. If prompted to save changes, click **Don't Save**.

13. In the Revised Carbohydrates 3 document, in the last paragraph, position the insertion point at the end of the last sentence. In the Clipboard task pane, click the **item** that begins *So, if you want to lose weight....* The item from the Clipboard is inserted in the document at the location of the insertion point.

14. In the upper-right corner of the Clipboard task pane, click the **Close** button to hide the pane. Save the changes to the **Revised Carbohydrates 3** document, and then close it. Leave Word open for the next Step-by-Step.

> **QUICK TIP**
>
> You can also access the Cut, Copy, and Paste commands by right-clicking the selected text and choosing the desired command in the shortcut menu that appears. The keyboard shortcut for Cut is Ctrl+X, for Copy it is Ctrl+C, and for Paste it is Ctrl+V.

Finding Text

Scrolling through a long document to locate a specific section of text is time consuming. The Find command makes locating text or formats easier and more efficient. The Find command can be accessed in the Navigation Pane to quickly identify all occurrences of the search words. By default, Word completes an incremental search. In an ***incremental search***, as you begin typing the string of characters to search for, Word highlights the matches for the character string in the document. As the search text is augmented, the matches in the document change.

You can further define the search to find matches for whole words only, or you can search for all occurrences of a specific format in the document, such as all text formatted bold and italic. If you are looking for variations of text, you can use a ***wildcard character***, a keyboard character used to represent one or more characters

> **▶ VOCABULARY**
> **incremental search**
> **wildcard character**

in a search. The question mark (?) searches for a single character; the asterisk (*) searches for a string of characters. For example, when the search text is *b?rn*, matches could include *barn*, *born*, and *burn*. When the search text is *ben**, the matches could include *bend*, *bench*, *Benny*, and *bent*.

Step-by-Step 13.5

2-1.3.4

1. Open the **Workouts** document from the drive and folder where your Data Files folder is stored. Save the Workouts document as **Revised Workouts**, followed by your initials. Scroll down through the document. Note that there are two pages in the document.

2. On the Home tab, in the Editing group on the far right side of the Ribbon, click the **Find** button. See **Figure 13–8**. The Navigation Pane is displayed at the left side of the document window.

FIGURE 13–8
Editing group on the Home tab

Used with permission from Microsoft Corporation

3. In the Navigation Pane, the insertion point is positioned in the Search Document text box, as shown in **Figure 13–9**. Type **workout**. As you enter the search text, incremental matches for the characters are highlighted in the document window. When you finish entering the search text, all the matches in the document window are highlighted. The total number of matches is indicated in the Navigation Pane below the Search Document text box. Also, items showing some of the document content are displayed in the pane so you can see the occurrence of the match in the context of the document.

FIGURE 13–9
Navigation Pane with matches for search text *workout*

Search Document text box

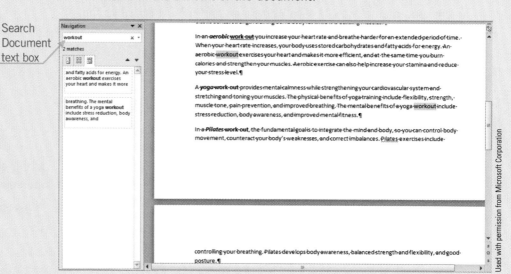

Used with permission from Microsoft Corporation

4. In the Navigation Pane, click the **Next Search Result** button ▼ twice. The second occurrence of the search text is highlighted in the document window. Click the **Previous Search Result** button ▲. The first occurrence of the search text is highlighted.

5. In the Navigation Pane, click the **Browse the pages in your document** button ⊞. Only the page(s) with matches are displayed in the Navigation Pane.

6. In the Navigation Pane, click the **Browse the results from your current search** button ▤. Then click the **Search Document** text box. The current search text is selected. Type **work**. The highlighted matches in the document change, and eight items now are displayed in the Navigation Pane. Note that six of the matches show *work out*, and two of the matches show *workout*.

7. In the Navigation Pane, on the right side of the Search Document text box, click the **Find Options and additional search commands** arrow. In the menu, click **Options** to open the Find Options dialog box shown in **Figure 13–10**. These options enable you to further define your search.

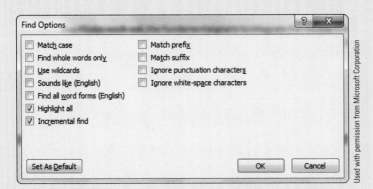

FIGURE 13–10
Find Options dialog box

8. Click the check box next to the **Find whole words only** option to enable the option, and then click **OK**. Click the **Search Document** text box, and then type **work**. Now only six matches are displayed. Note the two occurrences of the word *workout* are not highlighted because the search was for whole words only.

9. Click the **Find Options and additional search commands** arrow. Click **Options**, and enable the **Use wildcards** option. The Find whole words only and Incremental find options are automatically disabled. Click **OK** to save the changes and close the dialog box.

10. In the Navigation Pane, click the **Search Document** text box, type **f?t**, and press **Enter**. Twelve matches are found including *of the, fitness, fits, fat, of time, fatty,* and *benefits*.

11. Click the **Search Document** text box, type **fit***, and press **Enter**. Eight matches are found including *fitness, fits,* and *benefits*.

12. Click the **Find Options and additional search commands** arrow. Click **Options**, and then disable the option **Use wildcards**. Enable the **Incremental find** option, and click **OK**.

13. Close the Navigation Pane. Leave the document open for the next Step-by-Step.

Replacing Text

When you need to replace or reformat multiple occurrences of the same text, you can use the Replace command. The replacements can be made individually, or all occurrences can be replaced at once.

Step-by-Step 13.6

2-1.3.4

1. If necessary, open **Revised Workouts** from your solution files.

2. Position the insertion point at the beginning of the document.

3. On the Home tab, in the Editing group, click the **Replace** button. The Find and Replace dialog box opens, and the Replace tab is displayed as shown in **Figure 13–11**. Notice the word from your previous search is displayed in the Find what text box.

FIGURE 13–11
Replace tab in the Find and Replace dialog box

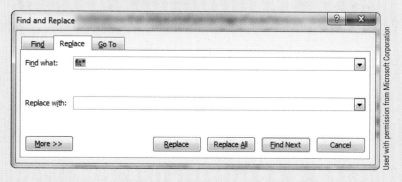

QUICK TIP

You can also open the Find and Replace dialog box by clicking the Find Options and additional search commands arrow in the Navigation Pane, and then in the menu, click Replace. The keyboard shortcut to execute the Find command is Ctrl+F. Use Ctrl+H to execute the Replace command.

4. In the Find and Replace dialog box, click the **More** button for more options, as shown in **Figure 13–12**.

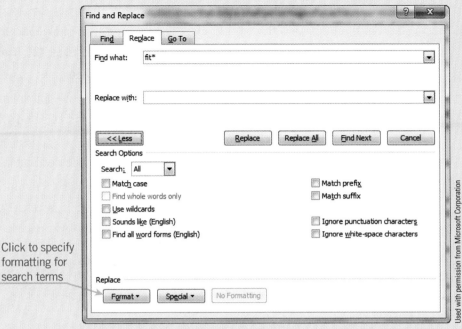

Click to specify
formatting for
search terms

FIGURE 13–12
More options in the Find and
Replace dialog box

5. In the Find what text box, delete any current text, and then type **work out**. With the insertion point still in the Find what text box, click **Format** in the lower-left corner of the dialog box, and then click **Font** to open the Find Font dialog box shown in **Figure 13–13**.

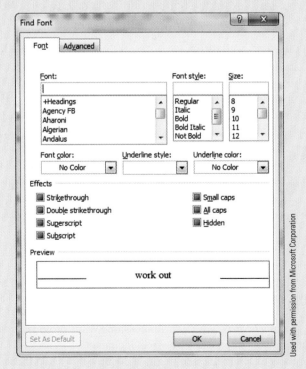

FIGURE 13–13
Find Font dialog box

6. Under Font style, click **Bold**, and then click **OK**. Note that *Font: Bold* is displayed under the Find what text box on the Replace tab. Word will now search for all occurrences of *work out* with the bold format.

7. In the Replace with text box, type **workout**. With the insertion point still in the Replace with text box, click **Format**, and then click **Font**. In the Replace Font dialog box, click **Bold Italic**, and then click **OK**. The search text will be replaced with the new text formatted bold and italic.

8. In the Find and Replace dialog box, click **Find Next**. In the document window, the first occurrence of the bold text *work out* is selected. If necessary, drag the dialog box title bar to reposition the dialog box near the upper-right corner of the screen so you can see the selected match.

9. Click **Find Next** again. No replacements are made in the document, and the next occurrence of the search text is selected. If necessary, drag the dialog box down near the lower-right corner so you can see the selected match.

10. In the dialog box, click **Replace**. The selected text is replaced with *workout*, formatted bold and italic, and the next occurrence of *work out* is selected.

11. In the dialog box, click **Replace All**. Word replaces all occurrences of the search text with the replacement text. A message box opens indicating that three replacements were made. Click **OK** to close the message box.

12. In the Find and Replace dialog box, position the insertion point in the Find what text box. At the bottom of the dialog box, click **No Formatting**. The formats are removed from the Find what text box. Position the insertion point in the Replace with text box, and click **No Formatting** to remove the formats from the Replace with text box.

13. Click **Find Next** once to complete a search without formats. This clears the format settings from the Find what and Replace with text boxes so your next search does not include formats. A message box appears indicating the search item was not found. In the message box, click **No**.

14. In the dialog box, click **Less** to hide the options in the dialog box. Then close the dialog box. Save the changes to the document, and then close the document.

Using the Proofing Tools

An accurate document makes a good impression. Word provides several proofing tools that can help you prepare an error-free document.

Automatically checking the spelling in a document can significantly reduce the amount of time you spend proofreading. When the Proofing option is enabled, as you enter text, Word checks the spelling of each word against its standard dictionary. If Word cannot find the word in its dictionary, it will underline the word with a wavy red line. This does not necessarily mean the word is misspelled. It simply means the word is not listed in Word's dictionary. You can access a shortcut menu to view suggestions for other spellings.

Good proofreading skills also include checking grammar. When you check the grammar in a document, you read for content and make sure each sentence makes sense. Options are also available to automatically check for grammar errors such as incomplete sentences, the wrong use of words, and capitalization and punctuation errors. Possible grammar errors are identified with a wavy green line below a word, phrase, or sentence. You can access a shortcut menu to view suggestions for changes.

The red or green underlines are only visible on your screen. They will not appear when you print the document.

It is common for people to make the same spelling or typing error over and over. For example, you may often enter *hte* instead of *the*. The AutoCorrect feature automatically corrects errors as you enter text, which saves editing time. The AutoComplete feature suggests the spelling for frequently used words and phrases. For example, as you begin to enter the day of the week or the month, AutoComplete provides an option for completing the word for you.

> **QUICK TIP**
>
> The spelling and grammar checkers are helpful tools, but you still need to have a good working knowledge of English grammar and spelling. The spelling and grammar checkers can identify a possible problem, but it is up to you to decide if a change is necessary.

Step-by-Step 13.7

1. Open a new blank document.

2. Type the following text exactly as shown here: **It is beleived**. Then watch the screen as you press the **spacebar.** Word will automatically correct the spelling and change the word *beleived* to *believed*.

2-1.3.5

3. Complete the sentence by typing **the potawatomi indians were originally part of the ancient tribe Anishinabe.**, and then press **Enter**. Notice there are red wavy lines under the words *potawatomi* and *Anishinabe*. Word automatically corrected the capitalization of the word *indians*.

4. Save the document as **Tribes 1**, followed by your initials.

5. Position the mouse pointer over the word *potawatomi* and right-click. A shortcut menu opens and shows alternative spellings at the top of the menu. In the shortcut menu, click the first option, **Potawatomi**. The word in the document is corrected.

6. Right-click the word **Anishinabe**. The spelling you entered is correct, but this word is not included in the Word standard dictionary; that is why the word is flagged. In the shortcut menu, click **Ignore All**. The red wavy line is removed, and the word *Anishinabe* will not be flagged as misspelled if entered again in this document.

7. Position the insertion point at the end of the document, and type **In the early 1700s, lived near Green Bay, Wisconsin.** and then press **Enter**. The entire sentence is underlined with a green wavy line.

8. Position the mouse pointer over any part of the green underlined sentence and right-click. A shortcut menu is displayed, and the words *Fragment (consider revising)* appear at the top of the menu. Click outside the shortcut menu to close it. Position the insertion point in front of the word *lived*, type **they**, and then press the **spacebar**. The green wavy line disappears.

> **ABOVE AND BEYOND**
>
> If you prefer not to have Word check for spelling or grammar errors as you enter text in a document, you can turn off this feature. Click the File tab, click Options, and then click Proofing. Uncheck the options Check spelling as you type and Check grammar with spelling.

> **ABOVE AND BEYOND**
>
> If you want assistance correcting the grammar, in the shortcut menu, click About This Sentence. A Word Help screen will open with suggestions for corrections.

9. Position the insertion point at the end of the document. Slowly type **Sept**. A ScreenTip appears above the four new characters, suggesting the word *September*. Press **Enter** to accept the AutoComplete word. Then press the **spacebar**, and type the current year (for example, *2014*).

10. Press **Enter** to create a new blank paragraph at the end of the document.

11. Save the changes and leave the document open for the next Step-by-Step.

Using the Research Tools

Creating a report often requires research. As you write a report, you may struggle to think of the appropriate word or phrase to make the content easier for the reader to understand. Or, you may want to use a synonym to avoid overusing a word. The commands in the Proofing group on the Review tab provide you quick access to several resources including dictionaries, a thesaurus, translation services, and research Web sites.

How many times have you been required to meet a minimum or maximum requirement for the total number of words in a document? The Word Count command provides statistics about your document that include the number of pages, sentences, lines, and characters as well as how many words are in your document. You can see the current number of words in the document in the status bar at the bottom of the window.

Step-by-Step 13.8

2-2.2.1

You will need access to the Internet to complete all the steps in this exercise.

1. If necessary, open **Tribes 1** from your solution files. Save the document Tribes 1 as **Tribes 2**, followed by your initials.

2. In the second sentence, position the insertion point anywhere within the word *near*. Click the **Review** tab. In the Proofing group, shown in **Figure 13–14**, click the **Thesaurus** button.

FIGURE 13–14
Proofing Group on the Review tab

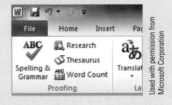

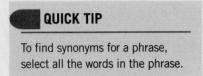

QUICK TIP

To find synonyms for a phrase, select all the words in the phrase.

3. The Research task pane, shown in **Figure 13–15**, opens and shows a list of synonyms for the word *near*.

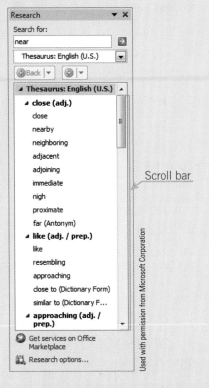

Scroll bar

FIGURE 13–15
Thesaurus search results in Research pane

QUICK TIP

When working offline, the only services accessible in the Research task pane are the thesaurus and the bilingual dictionary that is installed with Office.

4. In the Thesaurus list, scroll down to view the suggested terms below *nearby (adv.)*. Point to *close to (Dictionary Form)*, and then click the **list arrow** as shown in **Figure 13–16**. Click **Insert**. The word *near* in the document is replaced with *close to*.

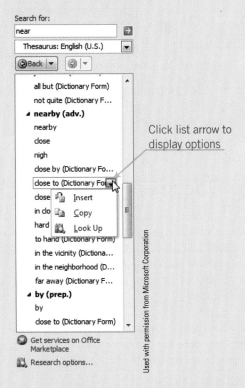

Click list arrow to display options

FIGURE 13–16
Options in the Thesaurus list on the Research pane

5. Select all three lines of text. On the Review tab, in the Language group, click the **Translate** button. In the list of options, click **Translate Selected Text**. The Research task pane changes and shows the translation options.

6. Under Translation, the From box should show *English (U.S.)*. Click the **list arrow** in the To box, and then click **French (France)**.

7. Below Translate the whole document, click the **green arrow** ➡️. When prompted to send the document over the Internet for translation, click **Send**.

8. A window opens in your browser. If necessary, click your browser button on the taskbar to show the translation text.

9. Drag the mouse across the translation text to select the text. (If the original text is displayed when you point to the text, position the mouse pointer at the end of the translation text and drag the mouse pointer to the beginning of the text.) Then press **Ctrl+C** to copy the selected text to the Clipboard.

10. Switch to the **Tribes 2** document. Position the insertion point at the end of the document, right-click, and then in the shortcut menu under Paste Options, click the **Keep Source Formatting** button 📋. The translation text is inserted in the document.

11. At the top of the Research pane, click the **Search for** text box, delete the current text, and then type **Potawatomi**. Click the **list arrow** in the box directly below, and then click **Encarta Dictionary: English (North America)**. A definition of the term is displayed. In the upper-right corner of the Research pane, click the **Close** button to close the pane.

12. On the Review tab, in the Proofing group, click the **Word Count** button. The Word Count dialog box opens, revealing the statistics for the document. Close the Word Count dialog box.

13. Save the changes to the document, close the document, and then close your browser.

QUICK TIP

The translation results may vary depending on the translation service accessed.

Formatting Documents

▶ **VOCABULARY**
format

When you *format* a document, you change the appearance of the text or of the whole document. The formats and design elements used in a document should reflect the purpose of the document and the needs of the reader. Formats can be applied either before or after you enter text in a document.

Word offers a number of formats, including character formats, paragraph formats, and document formats:

- Font styles, text color, and underline are examples of character formats. You can apply more than one character format at a time. For example, you can apply both color and underline formats to characters.

■ A paragraph format is applied to an entire paragraph and cannot be applied to only a portion of a paragraph. For example, you cannot single space part of a paragraph and double space the rest. Word defines a paragraph as any amount of text that ends with a paragraph marker. A paragraph marker is inserted by pressing Enter, which creates a *manual line break*. When you create a manual line break, the new paragraph will include the same paragraph formats as the previous paragraph. Paragraph formats include *alignment* (how the text is positioned between the left and right margins), tabs, and line spacing.

■ Document formats apply to an entire document. For example, paper size and *margins*, the blank spaces around the edges of the page, are document formats. You can position the insertion point anywhere in a document to change the entire document format.

▶ **VOCABULARY**

manual line break

alignment

margins

font

points

Applying Character Formats

Changing the character format can actually make a document easier to read. A *font* is the design of the typeface in your document. Fonts are available in a variety of styles and sizes, and you can use multiple fonts in one document. The size of the font is measured in *points*. The larger the point number, the larger the font size. You can quickly change the appearance of the font by using the command buttons in the Font group on the Home tab. When you open the Font dialog box, more font options are available, and you can make several font changes at one time.

Changing the character format can also set the tone for a document. Consider the purpose of the document when you apply character design elements. While formatting text in all caps can draw the reader's attention, it can also send the wrong message. Some readers may feel text in all caps means that you are yelling at them. Although some font styles and font colors may make the text look pretty or cool, they may also make it harder to read the text.

2-2.1.16

Step-by-Step 13.9

1. Open the **H2O Cove** document from the drive and folder where your Data Files folder is stored. Save the H2O Cove document as **Revised H2O Cove 1**, followed by your initials.

2. Click the **Page Layout** tab. In the Page Setup group, click the **Line Numbers** button, and then click **Continuous** from the list of options. Line numbers will be displayed to the left of each line, which will make it easier to identify the lines of text in the document.

2-1.3.6

3. Select all of the text in line 1. Word is intuitive, and because you selected text, a semitransparent image of the Mini toolbar with common formatting commands appears above the selection. Your screen should look similar to **Figure 13–17**. If you do not see the Mini toolbar, select the text again, and do not move the mouse pointer away from the selection. Position the mouse pointer over the Mini toolbar, and the image will brighten. On the Mini toolbar, click the **Bold** button **B** to apply the bold format. Move the mouse pointer away from the Mini toolbar, and the toolbar disappears.

FIGURE 13–17
Semitransparent image of the Mini toolbar

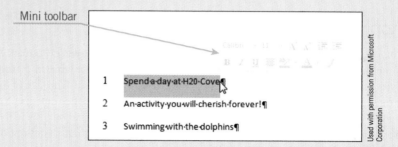

4. Click the **Home** tab. In the Font group, shown in **Figure 13–18**, notice the Bold button is highlighted to indicate that the selected text is formatted bold. With the text still selected, in the Font group, click the **Change Case** button **Aa▾**, and then click **UPPERCASE**.

FIGURE 13–18
Font group on the Home tab

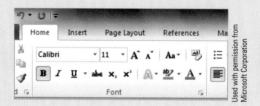

5. Select all of the text in line 2. On the Mini toolbar, click the **Bold** button, and then click the **Italic** button **I**. Also on the Mini toolbar, click the **Font Color** button arrow **A▾**, and click a **red** color.

6. Select the whole word in line 4. In the Font group, click the **Underline** button arrow **U▾**, and then click the last option in the list (the Wave underline). Click the **Underline** button. The underline format you just applied is toggled off. Click the **Underline** button again. The Wave underline option is applied because it is the last underline option used.

7. Drag the mouse pointer to select all of the text in lines 9 and 10. In the Font group, click the **Font** list arrow Calibri to display a list of font options. Position the mouse pointer over one of the font options in the list to show the Live Preview of the new font in the document window, as shown in **Figure 13–19**. Position the mouse pointer over a different font option, and the Live Preview reflects the change in fonts. The text format does not change, however, until you choose a new font style.

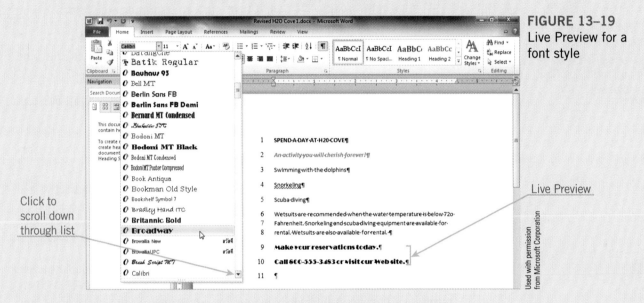

FIGURE 13–19
Live Preview for a font style

Click to scroll down through list

Live Preview

8. Scroll down the list of fonts, and select **Comic Sans MS**. The text in the document changes, and the name of the new font is displayed in the Font box on the Ribbon. With the text still selected, click the **Font Size** list arrow 11. The font sizes are listed in increments. In the size list, click **14** to change the font size to 14 points. With the text still selected, in the Font group, click the **Shrink Font** button A▾ three times to decrease the size by three increments. Then, in the Font group, click the **Grow Font** button A▴ once. The size increases by one increment, and the Font Size box displays the setting *11*.

9. With the text still selected, click the **Font Size** box. The current font size is selected. Type **12**, and then press **Enter**. The font size is changed to 12 points.

10. In line 6, after *72*, select the letter **o**. (*Hint*: Use the arrow keys to position the insertion point in front of the character; then press and hold Shift and press the right arrow key to select the character.) In the Font group, click the **Superscript** button x². In line 1, select the number **2** in *H2O*. In the Font group, click the **Subscript** button x₂.

11. Position the insertion point at the end of the document on line 11. Change the font size to **14**, type **www.H2OCove.net**, and then press **Enter**. A hyperlink format is automatically applied to the URL. Because this document will not be published on the Web, you do not need a hyperlink format. Right-click the **hyperlink**, and then in the shortcut menu click **Remove Hyperlink**.

12. Select the text in line 9. In the Font group, click the **Text Highlight Color** button arrow [aby ⌄], and then click the **Turquoise** color block. The color highlight is applied to the selected text.

13. Click the **Page Layout** tab. In the Page Setup group, click the **Line Numbers** button, and then click **None**.

14. Save the changes, and leave the document open for the next Step-by-Step.

Applying Paragraph Formats

Changing the paragraph formats can also make the document more attractive and easier to read. Paragraph formats include adjusting the blank space between lines of text, aligning text, setting tabs and indents, and adding bullets and numbering. Most of the paragraph formats can be applied using the command buttons in the Paragraph group on the Home tab.

The default line spacing in Word is single spacing. When text is double-spaced, there is a blank line between each line of text, which makes it easier to read. Many reports are formatted with double line spacing. You can also adjust the spacing both before and after the paragraph, which is common in newsletters to help to save space on a page or to make a headline stand out.

Alignment refers to how text is positioned between the left and right margins. Text can be aligned in four different ways: left, center, right, or justified. When the justified alignment is applied, the text is aligned at both the left and right margins and extra space is added between words as needed. The default setting is left alignment. Center alignment is often used for titles, headings, and invitations. Right alignment is often used in tables for dollar amounts and dates. You can quickly apply any of these alignments using the buttons in the Paragraph group on the Home tab.

Step-by-Step 13.10

2-1.3.6
2-2.1.1

1. If necessary, open **Revised H2O Cove 1** from your solution files. Save the Revised H2O Cove 1 document as **Revised H2O Cove 2**, followed by your initials.

2. If necessary, click the **Page Layout** tab. To show the line numbers, click the **Line Numbers** button, and then click **Continuous**. Note that there are 12 lines in the document.

3. Click the **Home** tab. Select all of the text in the document. In the Paragraph group, shown in **Figure 13–20**, click the **Line and Paragraph Spacing** button.

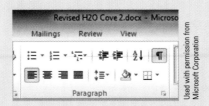

FIGURE 13–20
Paragraph group on the Home tab

4. In the list of options, click **2.0**. All of the lines in the document are now double-spaced. There are still 12 lines in the document, but there is more blank space between the lines.

5. With all of the text still selected, click the **Line and Paragraph Spacing** button, and then click **1.5**. The spacing between lines is reduced to 1½ line spacing, and there is less blank space between each line of text.

6. Position the insertion point in line 9. Click the **Line and Paragraph Spacing** button, and then click **Add Space Before Paragraph**. Extra blank space is added between lines 8 and 9.

7. With the insertion point still positioned in line 9, click the **Line and Paragraph Spacing** button. Note that in the list the next to last option has changed. Click **Remove Space Before Paragraph**.

8. Position the insertion point in line 1. Click the **Line and Paragraph Spacing** button, and then click **Remove Space After Paragraph** at the bottom of the list of options. The extra blank space between lines 1 and 2 is removed. Click the **Line and Paragraph Spacing** button again, and then click **Add Space After Paragraph**.

QUICK TIP

The keyboard shortcut for single-spaced is Ctrl+1. For 1.5-spaced, the shortcut key combination is Ctrl+5, and for double-spaced it is Ctrl+2.

9. In the Paragraph group, click the **dialog box launcher** to open the Paragraph dialog box shown in **Figure 13–21**. Notice that under Spacing, the After box shows *12 pt*. Click the **down arrow** once to reduce the setting to 6 pt. Press **Delete** to remove the number 6, then type **8**. Click **OK** to apply the change and close the dialog box. The space between lines 1 and 2 is adjusted.

FIGURE 13–21
Paragraph dialog box

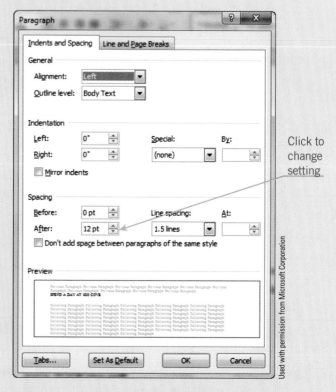

10. With the insertion point positioned in line 1, in the Paragraph group, click the **Center** button. Select all the remaining lines in the document, and then click the **Center** button ≣. All the lines are centered horizontally on the page.

11. Position the insertion point in line 6. In the Paragraph group, click the **Align Text Right** button ≣. The text in all three lines of the paragraph is aligned at the right margin. In the Paragraph group, click the **Align Text Left** button ≣ to move the text back to the left margin. Next, click the **Center** button to center the text between the left and right margins.

12. Select all the text in lines 1 and 2, and increase the font size to **18**. Then select all of the text in lines 3, 4, and 5, and increase the font size to **14**. Deselect the text.

13. Click the **Page Layout** tab. In the Page Setup group, click the **Line Numbers** button, and then click **None**.

14. Save the changes to the document, and then close the document.

Setting Tabs and Indents

Tabs are useful for indenting paragraphs and lining up columns of text. Word's default tabs are set at every half inch. You can, however, set custom tabs at other locations. There are four alignment options and a vertical bar for tabs. **Table 13–2** describes each of the options.

> **ABOVE AND BEYOND**
>
> If you want to set precise measurements for tabs, click the Paragraph group dialog box launcher and then click Tabs to open the Tabs dialog box.

TABLE 13–2   Options for tab settings

TAB SETTING	DESCRIPTION
⌊ Left tab	This is the default tab style. When you begin to enter text at the tab, the text is aligned on the left and extends to the right.
⊥ Center tab	Text is aligned evenly on either side of the tab position.
⌟ Right tab	Text is aligned on the right and extends to the left.
⊥ Decimal tab	Numbers with decimals are all aligned at the decimal point, and text aligns on either side of the tab. A decimal tab can be used to align numbers or text.
❘ Bar tab	This setting does not position the text, but a vertical bar is displayed in the paragraph at the tab position. If the tab is formatted for multiple paragraphs, the vertical bar is displayed in all the paragraphs to create a vertical line along the column of text or numbers.

An ***indent*** is a space inserted between the margin and where the line of text appears. You can indent text from the left margin, from the right margin, or from both the left and right margins. For example, to draw attention to specific paragraphs in a document, you can indent all the lines of the paragraph from the left and right margins. To make a long document with several paragraphs easier to read, you can format a first line indent. In a ***first line indent***, the first line of each paragraph is indented, making it easy for the reader to tell where a new paragraph begins. When creating a bibliography for a report, you need to format a ***hanging indent***, where the first line of text begins at the left margin, and all other lines of the paragraph hang, or are indented, to the right of the first line.

The ruler, which is available from the Show group on the View tab, can be used to quickly set tabs, indents, and margins in your document. The ruler is also a handy reference to see the "true" size of your text and document.

> ▶ **VOCABULARY**
> **indent**
>
> **first line indent**
>
> **hanging indent**

Step-by-Step 13.11

1. Open the **National Parks** document from the drive and folder where your Data Files folder is stored. Save the National Parks document as **Revised National Parks**, followed by your initials.

2. If necessary, show nonprinting characters. Display continuous line numbers.

2-2.1.2
2-2.1.3
2-2.1.4
2-2.1.6

3. To control the formatting marks that are displayed on the screen, click the **File** tab, click **Options**, and then click **Display**. Under Always show these formatting marks on the screen, make sure Show all formatting marks is enabled. Click **OK** to close the Word Options dialog box.

4. Click the **View** tab. If necessary, in the Show group, enable the **Ruler** option. The option is enabled and the ruler is visible when there is a check mark in the box. The horizontal ruler is displayed at the top of the document window, and the vertical ruler is displayed at the left side of the document window.

5. Position the insertion point at the beginning of line 20. Press **Tab** three times. Although they do not appear on the ruler, default tabs are already set for every half inch. The three tab symbols are displayed in the document window.

6. Position the insertion point anywhere in line 3. At the left end of the ruler, click the **tab selector** until the Right Tab symbol ⬑ is displayed, as shown in **Figure 13–22**.

QUICK TIP

You can also show the ruler by clicking the View Ruler button at the top of the vertical scroll bar.

FIGURE 13–22
Tab selector and indent markers on the horizontal ruler

Tab selector   Left indent marker   Right Indent marker

Used with permission from Microsoft Corporation

7. Click the **4-inch** mark on the horizontal ruler as shown in **Figure 13–23**. In line 3, position the insertion point in front of *April 11*, and press **Tab**. The date is now aligned at the right-aligned tab, which was set at the 4-inch mark on the ruler. In line 7, position the insertion point in front of *April 18*. Notice that no tab markers are displayed on the ruler. The tab you set in line 3 was applied to that paragraph only, and that paragraph has only one line of text.

FIGURE 13–23
Tab symbol and indent markers on the ruler

Right tab symbol

Used with permission from Microsoft Corporation

8. Click the **tab selector** until the Center Tab symbol ⬐ is displayed. Then click the **3-inch** mark on the ruler. Press **Tab**. The date is centered at the 3-inch mark on the ruler. Click and drag the **Center Tab** symbol all the way to the left and off the horizontal ruler to remove the tab setting.

9. Select all of the text in lines 7 through 20. Be sure to include the paragraph marker at the end of line 20. Click the **tab selector** until the Right Tab symbol is displayed. Then click the **4-inch** mark on the ruler. The new tab setting is applied to all selected paragraphs. The date in line 7 is aligned with the new tab stop. In line 12, position the insertion point in front of *April 25*, and then press **Tab**.

10. Select lines 3 through 20. Be sure to include the paragraph marker at the end of line 20. Click and drag the **Right Indent** marker △ on the horizontal ruler, and position it at the **6-inch** mark on the ruler.

11. With lines 3 through 20 still selected, click and drag the **Left Indent** marker ▢ on the horizontal ruler to the **1/2-inch** mark on the ruler. Notice that the First Line Indent marker and the Hanging Indent marker also move. See **Figure 13–24**.

First Line
Indent marker

Left Indent
marker

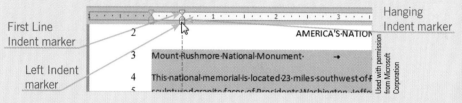

Hanging
Indent marker

FIGURE 13–24
Indent markers on the
horizontal ruler

12. With lines 3 through 20 still selected, drag the **First Line Indent** marker ▽ to the **1-inch** mark on the ruler. The first line of each selected paragraph is indented. Click the **Undo** button.

13. Click and drag the **Hanging Indent** marker △ to the **3/4-inch** mark on the ruler. The Left Indent marker moves with the Hanging Indent marker. All lines except the first line of each paragraph are indented from the left three-quarters of an inch. Deselect the text.

14. Click the **Page Layout** tab, then turn off the display of line numbers. Save the changes to the document, and then close the document.

ABOVE AND BEYOND

When you drag the Left Indent marker, the First Line Indent marker and the Hanging Indent marker also move. To change the margin when the indent markers are positioned with the marker, point to the middle of the margin markers until a two-headed arrow is displayed, and then you can drag the margin marker.

Formatting Bullets and Numbers

Bullets are used to list items when order does not matter—an unordered list. Numbered lists are used to identify steps that should be completed in a specific order, which are often referred to as an ordered list. Bulleted and numbered lists are automatically formatted with a hanging indent. Word automatically calculates the best distance for the hanging indent. You can change the bullet symbol, the number style, or the distance for the hanging indent in the Bullets and Numbering dialog box. When you press Enter to create a new paragraph, the new paragraph will include the same paragraph formats as the previous paragraph.

Step-by-Step 13.12

1. Open **Expo** from the drive and folder where your Data Files folder is stored. Save the Expo document as **Revised Expo 1**, followed by your initials.

2. If necessary, show nonprinting characters. Display the line numbers.

2-2.1.7

3. Select all the text in lines 8 through 15. Click the **Home** tab. In the Paragraph group, click the **Bullets** button arrow ⊞▾. Under Bullet Library, click the **black circle**. Each paragraph in the selection is formatted with a bullet symbol.

4. Select all the text in lines 17 through 20. Click the **Repeat** button on the Quick Access Toolbar. The last action (formatting bullets) is repeated, and bullets are applied to the selected text.

5. Select all the text in lines 22 through 28. In the Paragraph group, click the **Numbering** button arrow ⊞▾. Under Numbering Library, click the second **option** in the first row (1._____, etc.).

6. Deselect the text. In line 28, position the insertion point at the end of the word *Transportation*.

7. Press **Enter**. Word automatically formats the next paragraph with the number 8 and a hanging indent. Type **Water conservation**.

8. Press **Enter**. The next paragraph is formatted for item number 9. Click the **Numbering** button to toggle the option off.

9. Select all the text in lines 22–29. Note that the numbers will not be included in the selection. Click the **Bullets** button. The numbered list is converted to a bulleted list, with the same bullet symbols that were last applied. Deselect the text.

10. Save the changes to the document, and then leave the document open for the next Step-by-Step.

Applying Document Formats

Document formats are applied to an entire document. These formats include layout settings such as margins, page orientation, paper size, and page breaks, and you will look at adjusting these settings in this lesson. More document formats will be covered in Lesson 16. Most of the document formats can be accessed in the Page Setup group on the Page Layout tab.

The margin and page orientation formats you choose should be based on the purpose and content of the document and also on the paper size. If you want more or less content to fit on a page, you can modify the margin settings. The default margin settings are one inch for top, bottom, left, and right margins, but you can easily change those settings.

Portrait orientation formats the content of the document with the short edge of the page at the top. This is the default setting. You can change to *landscape orientation*, which formats the content of the document with the long edge of the page at the top. Your on-screen document accurately reflects the page orientation you choose.

When you fill a page with text or graphics, Word automatically begins a new page by inserting a *soft page break*. You can also break pages manually by inserting a *manual page break*, which forces a page break at a specific location, regardless of how much text or graphics are on the page. The location of a soft page break will change when you add or delete text so that each page remains completely filled with text. A manual page break will remain where you insert it until it is deleted.

▶ **VOCABULARY**

portrait orientation

landscape orientation

soft page break

manual page break

In Print Layout, Outline, and Draft views, the page break is indicated with a dotted line across the page. In Full Screen Reading view the dotted line does not appear, but the pages actually look like separate sheets of paper, so you will clearly see where page breaks are located. In Web Layout view, the document is usually displayed as one long page without page breaks.

Step-by-Step 13.13

1. If necessary, open the **Revised Expo 1** document from your solution files. Save the Revised Expo 1 document as **Revised Expo 2**, followed by your initials. If necessary, show nonprinting characters and line numbering.

2. Position the insertion point at the beginning of line 21. Click the **Page Layout** tab. In the Page Setup group, click the **Breaks** button to show a list of options. Under Page Breaks, click **Page** to create a manual page break. The paragraph and all of the text below the paragraph is now displayed on page 2 of the document.

3. Click the **View** tab. In the Zoom group, shown in **Figure 13–25**, click the **Two Pages** button.

2-1.4.1
2-1.4.2
2-2.1.5

QUICK TIP

The keyboard shortcut for inserting a manual page break is Ctrl+Enter.

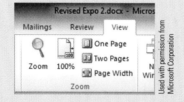
Used with permission from Microsoft Corporation

FIGURE 13–25
Zoom group on the View tab

4. The nonprinting characters reveal a page break, as shown in **Figure 13–26**.

FIGURE 13–26
Manual page break in a document

Manual page break

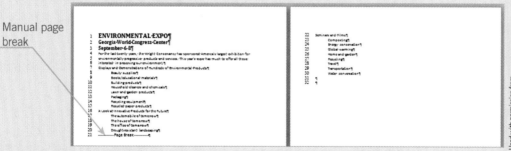
Used with permission from Microsoft Corporation

5. Click the **Page Layout** tab. In the Page Setup group, click the **Size** button to show the page size options. Click the **A5** option. The layout changes in the document window, but the page break does not move.

6. Click the **Size** button again, and then click **Letter 8.5"×11"** to return to the default setting.

7. In the Page Setup group, click the **Orientation** button, and then click **Landscape**. The content still fits on two pages.

FIGURE 13–27
Page Layout settings in Backstage view

8. In the Page Setup group, click the **Margins** button to show the options. Click **Wide**. The margins are adjusted in the document window.

9. Click the **File** tab, and then click **Print**. The Print Preview pane shows the document in landscape orientation. Note that the page orientation, paper size, and margin settings are also displayed as shown in **Figure 13–27**.

Used with permission from Microsoft Corporation

10. Under Settings, click **Landscape Orientation**, and then click **Portrait Orientation**. The Print Preview pane shows the new orientation.

11. When the orientation setting is changed, the Margins setting changes from *Wide Margins* to *Custom Margins*. Under Settings, click **Custom Margins**, and then click **Normal**.

12. Click the **Home** tab. Position the insertion point in front of the page break. Press **Delete** to remove the page break. Then press **Delete** again to remove the blank paragraph that was inserted when the manual page break was created.

13. Click the **View** tab. In the Zoom group, click the **One Page** button.

14. Turn off the display of line numbers. Save the changes to the document, and then close the document. Leave Word open for the next Step-by-Step.

Using Format Painter

When you apply multiple character or paragraph formats to text, and you need to repeat those formats throughout the document, you want the formats to be consistent. You can use the Format Painter button to quickly copy the formatting to other text and objects. *Format Painter* copies and applies font and paragraph formatting as well as some basic graphic formatting, such as borders, fills, and shading, which you will learn more about in Lesson 16.

▶ **VOCABULARY**
Format Painter

Step-by-Step 13.14

1. Open the **Garden** document from the drive and folder where your Data Files folder is stored. Save the Garden document as **Revised Garden**, followed by your initials.

2-1.3.6

2. If necessary, show nonprinting characters. Display the line numbers. Note that Word automatically creates a soft page break to wrap the text to a second page. Manual page breaks are visible when you show nonprinting characters, but no marks are displayed for soft page breaks.

3. Select all the text in line 12. Be sure to include the ending paragraph marker in the selection. Click the **Home** tab. Note that the settings in the Font group indicate that the font is formatted as Cambria, 11 point, and bold. Click the **Underline** button arrow **U ▾**, and you will see that the Wave underline format is highlighted.

4. With the text still selected, on the Home tab, in the Clipboard group, click the **Format Painter** button. The mouse pointer changes to show a paintbrush 📋 when positioned over text.

5. Scroll down to the bottom of page 1. In line 28, click the first word **Tips**. The character formats are applied only to the one word. Also, the mouse pointer no longer displays a paintbrush, so you cannot continue copying the formats.

6. Scroll back to line 12 and select all the text in the line, including the paragraph marker. Double-click the **Format Painter** button. The mouse pointer changes to show a paintbrush, and because you double-clicked the Format Painter button, you now have unlimited opportunities to copy the formats.

7. Scroll down to the bottom of page 1. Click and drag the mouse pointer to select all of the text in line 28. The copied character and paragraph formats are applied to all of the selected text as you drag the mouse pointer.

8. The mouse pointer still displays a paintbrush, so you can continue to use Format Painter. Scroll down to page 2. Click and drag the mouse pointer to select all of the text in line 38.

9. Click the **Format Painter** button. Format Painter is toggled off, and the mouse pointer no longer displays a paintbrush.

10. Scroll to the top of the document. Select lines 3 through 11, including the paragraph markers at the end of the paragraphs. Format the selected text as follows:

    a. Press **Ctrl+J** to justify the alignment of text.

    b. Press **Ctrl+5** to change the line spacing to 1.5 lines.

    c. In the Font group, click the **Font Color** button arrow, and then under Theme Colors click the **Dark Blue, Text 2** color.

    d. In the Paragraph group, click the **Line and Paragraph Spacing** button, and then click **Add Space Before Paragraph**.

11. With the paragraphs still selected, double-click the **Format Painter** button. Then click and drag the mouse pointer over all the text in lines 13 through 27, line 29, and lines 39 and 40. Be sure to select the paragraph markers to make sure both the character and paragraph formats are copied to the selected text. Press **Esc** to toggle off Format Painter.

12. In line 29, double-click the first word **Follow** to select it. Then double-click the **Format Painter** button. Because a paragraph marker is not included in the selection, you have only copied the character formats. Then drag the mouse pointer across the bulleted list and the numbered list to copy the character formats. Press **Esc** to toggle off Format Painter.

13. Select lines 30 through 37 and lines 41 through 46, and apply the **Dark Blue, Text 2** font color.

14. Turn off the display of line numbers. Save the changes, and close the document.

> **QUICK TIP**
>
> You can use Format Painter to copy formats from one Word document to another Word document.

SUMMARY

In this lesson, you learned:

- When you add text while in Insert mode, the new characters are inserted between existing text. When text is entered in Overtype mode, the new text replaces existing text.

- The Undo, Redo, and Repeat commands make editing easy when you make mistakes, change your mind, or repeat actions.

- Selected text can be copied or moved from one location in a Word document to a new location in the same document, to a different Word document, or to another application.

- When you use the Cut, Copy, and Paste commands, Word stores the selected text on the Clipboard.

- The Find command and the Navigation Pane make searching for text easy and efficient. The Replace command can replace multiple occurrences of search text automatically.

- Options can be enabled so that Word checks spelling and grammar as you enter text.

- Font styles, text color, and underline are examples of character formats, and you can apply multiple character formats at the same time.

- Formatting a paragraph for left, center, right, or justified alignment positions the text appropriately between the left and right margins.

- You can use the ruler to format tabs and indents.

- The Bullets and Numbering feature automatically adds and formats bullets and numbers in lists.

- The page orientation determines how the document is printed on the page. Adjusting the margins affects the blank space around the edges of the page.

■ LESSON REVIEW

TRUE / FALSE

Circle T if the statement is true or F if the statement is false.

T   F   **1.**   When you hold down Ctrl as you drag and drop text, the selected text will be copied instead of moved.

T   F   **2.**   Drag-and-drop editing makes moving text quick and easy, especially when you are moving the text short distances.

T   F   **3.**   If you undo an action and then change your mind, you can reverse the undo action by using the Undo command again.

T   F   **4.**   Formats can be applied only after you enter text in a document.

T   F   **5.**   Word defines a paragraph as any amount of text that ends with a paragraph marker.

T   F   **6.**   When an item is pasted from the Clipboard, the item is automatically deleted from the Clipboard.

T   F   **7.**   You can use the Replace command to reformat multiple occurrences of the same text.

T   F   **8.**   Word's default tabs are set at every half inch.

T   F   **9.**   A wavy red line under a word means the word is not listed in Word's dictionary.

T   F   **10.**   The location of a manual page break changes when you add or delete text.

MULTIPLE CHOICE

Select the best response for the following statements.

1.   When searching for text in a document, you can _____.

   A.   search for all occurrences of the search words

   B.   search for whole words only

   C.   search for all occurrences of a specific format

   D.   all of the above

2.   _____ refers to how text is positioned between the left and right margins.

   A.   Line format   C.   Line adjustment

   B.   Alignment   D.   Line spacing

3.   _____ orientation formats the content of the document with the long edge of the page at the top.

   A.   Landscape   C.   Layout

   B.   Horizontal   D.   Portrait

4.   A _____ indent formats the first line of text at the left margin, and all other lines of the paragraph are indented to the right of the first line.

   A.   left   C.   first line

   B.   right   D.   hanging

5.   Paragraph formats include _____.

   A.   adjusting the blank space   C.   margins between lines of text

   B.   tabs and indents   D.   all of the above

FILL IN THE BLANK

Complete the following sentences by writing the correct word or words in the blanks provided.

1. You can store up to _____ items on the Clipboard task pane.

2. In _____ mode, new text replaces the existing text.

3. _____ are the blank spaces around the edges of a page.

4. Word automatically inserts a(n) _____ when a page is full.

5. The size of the font is measured in _____.

6. A(n) _____ is a keyboard character used to represent one or more characters in a search.

7. The _____ feature suggests the spelling for frequently used words and phrases.

8. The _____ feature automatically corrects errors as you enter text.

9. A(n) _____ is a space inserted between the margin and where the line of text appears.

10. _____ will copy and apply font and paragraph formatting.

■ PROJECTS

PROJECT 13–1

1. Open **Video Replay** from the drive and folder where your Data Files folder is stored. Save the Video Replay document as **Revised Video Replay**, followed by your initials.

   2-1.3.2
   2-1.3.3
   2-1.3.4
   2-1.3.5
   2-2.2.1

2. Select the last two lines of text in the document, including the paragraph marker. Cut the selected text to the Clipboard, and then paste the contents at the top of the document.

3. Insert a manual line break at the end of the instructor's name. Type your first and last name, press **Enter**, and then type the current date.

4. Select the first four lines of text, and remove the space after the paragraphs.

5. Select the entire paragraph beginning with the sentence *The debate about*. Change the line spacing to double-spaced.

6. Insert a default 1/2-inch tab at the beginning of the paragraph.

7. One possible grammar error and three possible misspelled words are flagged. Make the necessary corrections.

8. Find the second occurrence of the word *TiVo*. Select the whole sentence with the second occurrence of *TiVo*, and then delete the sentence.

9. Find the word *execute*. Use the Thesaurus to find synonyms for execute, and select a synonym to replace the word.

10. Select the title *My Viewpoint*. Center the title, and increase the font size three increments. Change the text to uppercase.

11. Select the entire line with the instructor name at the top of the document. Delete the sentence. Undo the edit, then redo the edit.

12. Save the changes, and close the document. Leave Word open for the next Project.

PROJECT 13–2

1. Open **Career Planning** from the drive and folder where your Data Files folder is stored. Save the Career Planning document as **Revised Career Planning 1**, followed by your initials.

   2-1.3.4
   2-1.3.6
   2-2.1.7
   2-2.2.1

2. Select the heading *Career Planning*. Change the font style to Cambria, and change the font size to 16 points. Also apply the bold format.

3. Select all three paragraphs with text formatted with the red font color. Apply the numbering format to create a numbered list.

4. Select the first set of blue lines (four lines total), and apply a bullet format.

5. Select the second and third sets of blue lines (each set has three lines total), and use the Repeat button to apply the same bullet format you used in Step 4.

6. Select all the text in the document, and change the font color to Automatic (black).

7. Find all occurrences of *Before you* with a bold format and replace the text with *To* and a bold format. Before closing the Find and Replace dialog box, remove the format from the Find what and Replace with boxes.

8. Change the page orientation to landscape.

9. Save the changes to the document and leave the document open.

10. If you have access to the Internet, translate the document to Spanish (International Sort). Copy the translation text on the Web page. Then open a new blank document and paste the copied contents from the Clipboard using the Keep Source Formatting option.

11. Save the new document as **Revised Career Planning 2**, followed by your initials.

12. Close both documents, and leave Word open for the next Project. Close your browser.

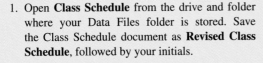

PROJECT 13–3

1. Open **Class Schedule** from the drive and folder where your Data Files folder is stored. Save the Class Schedule document as **Revised Class Schedule**, followed by your initials.

   2-1.3.2
   2-1.3.6
   2-2.1.1
   2-2.1.2
   2-2.1.3

2. If necessary, show nonprinting characters. Display the ruler and the line numbers.

3. Select lines 2 and 3, including the paragraph marker. Format a hanging indent at the 1/4-inch mark on the horizontal ruler.

4. Use Format Painter to copy the formats in lines 2 and 3 to all the other course descriptions (lines 9–10, 16–17, 23–24, and 30–31). Then toggle off Format Painter.

5. Select lines 4 through 7. Move the Left Indent marker on the horizontal ruler to the 1/2-inch mark on the ruler.

6. Use Format Painter to copy the formats in lines 4 through 7 to all the other course descriptions (lines 11–14, 18–21, 25–28, and 32–34). Then toggle off Format Painter.

7. In line 5, select the instructor's name (without the paragraph marker). Copy the selected text to the Clipboard. Then position the insertion point at the end of line 32. Insert a manual line break, and then paste the instructor name.

8. Select all the text and the paragraph marker in line 1. Apply the bold and single straight line underline formats, and add space before the paragraph.

9. Use Format Painter to copy the paragraph formats in line 1 to all the other course titles (lines 8, 15, 22, and 29).

10. Using cut and paste or drag-and-drop editing, reorganize the information so the classes are listed alphabetically by class title.

11. Turn off the display of line numbers. Save the changes, and close the document.

PROJECT 13–4

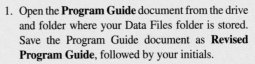

1. Open the **Program Guide** document from the drive and folder where your Data Files folder is stored. Save the Program Guide document as **Revised Program Guide**, followed by your initials.

   2-1.3.3
   2-1.4.1
   2-1.4.2
   2-2.1.4
   2-2.1.5

2. Change the page orientation to landscape. Change the margins to the Wide setting (top and bottom 1 inch and the left and right margins to 2 inches).

3. Center the first seven lines of text, beginning with *Oak Creek Recreation Commission* and ending with *Mt. Washington Recreation Center*.

4. Insert a manual page break in front of the word *Contents*. Then center the paragraph containing the heading.

5. Select all of the text below the *Contents* heading, and then set a right tab at the 6.5-inch mark on the horizontal ruler. Note that the tab has already been entered in front of the page number in each line of text, so the page numbers align on the right side of the document.

6. With the text still selected, remove the space after all the selected paragraphs.

7. Under the *Contents* heading, format the program listings as follows:

   a. Select the first three lines of text below the Contents heading (*Registration*, *Memberships*, and *Hours*). Apply the bold and italic formats, and change the size of the font to 12 points. Then repeat the formatting for the last two lines of text below the *Contents* heading (*Special Events* and *Community Meetings*).

   b. Select each of the headings for each age group (*ELEMENTARY PROGRAMS*, *TEEN PROGRAMS*, and *ADULT PROGRAMS*) and apply bold and underline formatting to the headings (including the page numbers). Change the size of the font to 12 points.

   c. Apply a 1/4-inch left indent to the lists of programs under each age group heading.

8. You decide that the first page could be spread out a little to fill up more of the page. Select all the text on the first page, and increase the font size by two increments.

9. Insert three manual line breaks in front of the first line of text *Oak Creek Recreation Commission*. Insert two manual line breaks in front of *Clifton Community Center*.

10. Save the changes to the document, and then close the document.

TEAMWORK PROJECT

The fonts you use to format a document can be divided into two types: *serif* and *sans serif*. Research these two types of fonts to learn more about them.

1. Choose a partner and together research serif typefaces and sans serif typefaces. Use the Web or other references to read about typography, the art of designing typefaces.

2. When you and your partner have completed your research, work with your partner to create a summary of your findings.

3. Create a new Word document, and save the document as **TP 13-1**, followed by your initials.

4. Type your answers to the following questions in separate paragraphs:

    a. What is a serif?

    b. What is the main difference between a serif font and a sans serif font?

    c. What type of typeface is recommended for body text? Why?

5. After answering each of the questions, select two different portions of the text in the document **2-1.3.6** (such as the title or a paragraph with the answer to a question) and apply a serif font to one portion and a sans serif font to the other selected text.

6. With your partner, compare the different fonts that you have applied and decide which of the fonts is most readable and appropriate for each section of text.

7. Save the changes to the document, and then close the document.

 CRITICAL THINKING

CRITICAL THINKING 13–1

You have been copying multiple items to the Clipboard. You learned in this lesson that there is a limit to the **2-1.3.2** number of items you can store on the Clipboard. What do you think happens when you copy or cut items beyond the limit? Use the Help feature to confirm the answer.

1. Create a new Word document, and save the document as **CT 13–1**, followed by your initials.

2. Write a paragraph describing what happens when you copy or cut items beyond the limit.

3. Save the changes to the document, and then close the document.

CRITICAL THINKING 13–2

If you completed Project 13–4, you had to add blank lines to center the text vertically on the first page of the **2-1.4.2** document. There is another way to center text vertically. Use Word's Help feature to find out how to do this.

1. Create a new Word document, and save the document as **CT 13–2**, followed by your initials.

2. Write a brief explanation of the steps you need to take. Explain what would happen to the second page of the Revised Program Guide document if you followed these steps.

3. Describe at least two other types of documents you could use this feature in.

4. Save the changes to the document, and then close the document.

ONLINE DISCOVERY

Selecting and copying text on a Web page is often similar to selecting and copying text in a Word document. Depending on the browser, you can usually select, copy, and paste Web page content just as you do in Word.

1. In your browser of choice, open a Web page that shows an article with several paragraphs of text.

2. Refer to Table 13–1, and test all the select text options listed in the table, noting whether or not each option works to select text in the Web page.

3. Create a new Word document, and save the document as **OD 13–1**, followed by your initials.

4. Test copying text from the Web page and then pasting the copied text into the Word document. Delete the pasted content.

5. Write a brief summary describing what is similar when selecting and copying text in Word and in a browser.

6. Save the changes to the document, and then close the document.

2-1.3.2

 ## JOB SKILLS

In this lesson you learned to use the proofing tools to help you avoid spelling and grammar errors. Although these features are very helpful, you cannot rely on them to find all errors. You have just prepared a news release for your manager, but before you give your manager access to the document, you want to make sure there are no errors in the document.

1. Create a new Word document, and save the document as **JS 13–1**, followed by your initials.

2. Create a list of steps you will take to proofread the document.

3. Save the changes to the document, and then close the document.

2-1.3.5

LESSON 14

Sharing Documents

■ OBJECTIVES

Upon completion of this lesson, you should be able to:

- Track changes and add comments.
- Show and hide markup and accept and reject changes.
- Customize print settings and properties and pause and cancel print jobs.
- Troubleshoot printing problems.
- Prepare documents for electronic distribution.
- Save documents in PDF or XPS format.
- Send and publish documents.
- Protect documents by restricting access, formatting, and edits.

■ DATA FILES

To complete this lesson, you will need these data files:

Ergonomics.docx

Facilities.docx

Furniture.docx

Safety.docx

Walking.docx

■ WORDS TO KNOW

blog

case sensitive

collating

comment

document management server

duplex printing

encryption

hard copy

markup

metadata

Portable Document Format (PDF)

read-only document

print queue

reverse printing

soft copy

XML Paper Specification (XPS)

The development of a document may involve multiple team members. If you collaborate with others to create or edit a document, you can take advantage of many features in Word that help individuals contribute more effectively to the development of the document.

Revising Documents

In a team effort to create a document, it is common to allow team members to review and edit the document. Tracking changes with revision marks makes it easy to find and identify the source of the edits. Adding comments is another useful feature that allows reviewers to provide feedback and express opinions without changing the content of the document. The revision marks and annotations that appear in a document are referred to as *markup*.

▶ **VOCABULARY**
markup

Tracking Changes

When the Track Changes feature is toggled on, all insertions, deletions, and format changes are indicated with revision marks such as font color, underlines, and balloons in the margins. These revision marks are easy to recognize, and they even identify who made the changes and when the changes were made.

Step-by-Step 14.1

2-2.2.3

1. Start **Microsoft Word 2010**. Open the **Ergonomics** file from the drive and folder where your Data Files folder is stored. Save the Ergonomics document as **Revised Ergonomics 1**, followed by your initials.

2. Confirm that the document is displayed in Print Layout view. Click the **Review** tab. In the Tracking group, click the **Track Changes** button arrow to display the options shown in **Figure 14–1**.

FIGURE 14–1
Tracking group on the Review tab

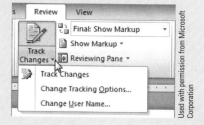

3. Click **Change Tracking Options** to open the Track Changes Options dialog box shown in **Figure 14–2**. Compare your settings, and make changes if necessary, so your settings match the default settings shown in Figure 14–2. Click **OK** to close the dialog box.

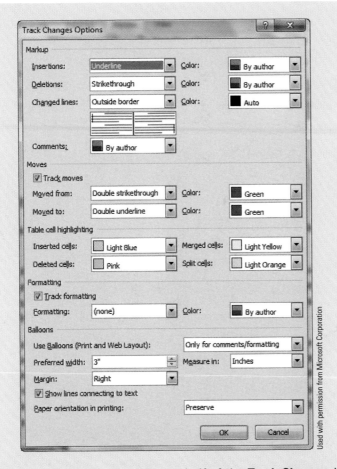

Used with permission from Microsoft Corporation

FIGURE 14–2
Track Changes Options dialog box

4. In the Tracking group, click the top half of the **Track Changes** button to toggle on the feature. The feature is on when the button has an orange highlight. In the fourth paragraph, which begins *With the growing use*, delete the next to last sentence: **The injury is worsened by poor posture.**

5. In the first sentence under the heading *What is Ergonomics?*, position the insertion point after *Ergonomics*. Press the **spacebar**, and then type **(also referred to as human engineering)**.

ABOVE AND BEYOND

To add a Track Changes button to the status bar, right-click the status bar and then click the Track Changes option. You can click the Track Changes button to toggle the feature on and off.

6. Compare the revision marks in your document to those shown in **Figure 14–3**. With default settings, deleted text is identified with a strikethrough and the new text is identified in a different font color and with an underline. A vertical mark in the left margin of the document indicates the lines of text that contain revisions.

FIGURE 14–3
Markup showing deleted and inserted text

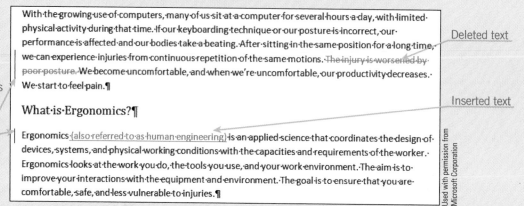

Vertical lines indicate lines with revisions

Deleted text

Inserted text

Used with permission from Microsoft Corporation

7. Position the mouse pointer over the inserted text. A ScreenTip appears showing a user name, a date, and a time. This helps you identify the reviewer who made the change and when the change was made. Next, position the mouse pointer over the deleted text to display the ScreenTip.

8. Click the **Track Changes** button arrow, and then click **Change User Name**. The Word Options dialog box shown in **Figure 14–4** opens. Make note of the user name and the initials. Then change the user name to **Reviewer A** and change the initials to **RA**. Click **OK** to accept the changes, and close the dialog box. This setting change now applies to all Office applications.

FIGURE 14–4
Word Options dialog box

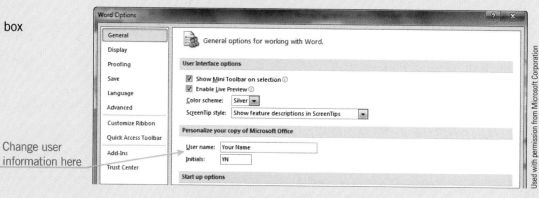

Change user information here

Used with permission from Microsoft Corporation

9. In the fourth paragraph that begins *With the growing use*, double-click the word **growing** to select the word, and then type **increase in**. Markup indicates that the word *growing* is deleted and the new text is inserted. The markup is displayed in a different font color to distinguish that this edit is from a different reviewer. When the ScreenTip appears you will see that the new reviewer name is displayed.

10. In the third paragraph that begins *Did you know...*, select the whole sentence at the end of the paragraph: **There are ways to prevent the discomfort and the painful, long-term injuries.**. Drag and drop the selected sentence to move it to the end of the next paragraph that begins *With the increase in*. At the original location, the edited text is shown in a green font with a double-strikethrough. At the new location, the inserted text is shown in a green font with a double under-line. The green font indicates moved content.

11. At the top of the document, select all the text in the title **COMPUTER WORKSTATION ERGONOMICS**. Using the buttons on the Mini toolbar, apply the bold format **B**, and center the text alignment ☰. Notice that the changes for the character and paragraph formats are identified in balloons in the right margin as shown in **Figure 14–5**. The border color for the balloons matches the color for the markup related to this reviewer.

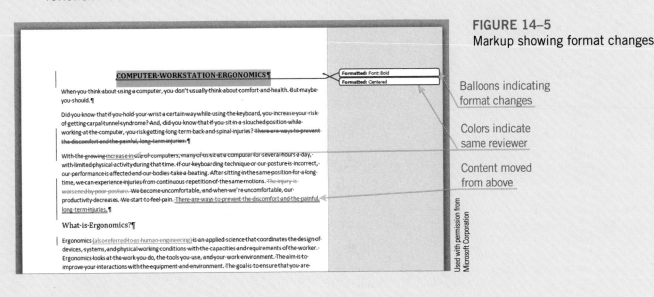

FIGURE 14–5
Markup showing format changes

Balloons indicating format changes

Colors indicate same reviewer

Content moved from above

12. In the Tracking group, click the **Show Markup** button, and then point to *Balloons*. The submenu shown in **Figure 14–6** is displayed. Explore the options:

FIGURE 14–6
Show Markup Balloons options

a. In the submenu, click **Show Revisions in Balloons**. In addition to the balloons for the format changes, new balloons are displayed to identify the moved and deleted text.

b. Click the **Show Markup** button, point to **Balloons**, and in the submenu click **Show All Revisions Inline**. All the revisions are displayed in the lines of text. There is no markup to indicate format changes.

c. Click the **Show Markup** button, point to **Balloons**, and in the submenu click **Show Only Comments and Formatting in Balloons**.

13. Click the **Track Changes** button arrow, and then click **Change User Name**. Change the user name and the initials back to the original setting noted in Step 8 above, and then click **OK**. Click the **Track Changes** button to toggle off the feature.

14. Save the changes, and leave the document open for the next Step-by-Step.

Adding Comments

▶ **VOCABULARY**
comment

A *comment* is a note that the author or a reviewer adds to the document. A comment can be inserted anywhere in a Word document. You can choose how the comments are displayed in the document and whether or not comments will be included when you print the document.

Step-by-Step 14.2

2-2.2.3

1. If necessary, open the **Revised Ergonomics 1** file from your solution files. Save the Revised Ergonomics 1 document as **Revised Ergonomics 2**, followed by your initials.

2. If necessary, click the **Review** tab, and in the Tracking group, toggle on the **Track Changes** feature.

3. Under the heading *What is Ergonomics?*, select the new text you entered: **(also referred to as human engineering)**. In the Comments group, click the **New Comment** button, shown in **Figure 14–7**.

Used with permission from Microsoft Corporation

FIGURE 14–7
Comments group on the Review tab

4. Shading highlights the text you selected, and a line leads to the comment balloon in the margin, as shown in **Figure 14–8**.

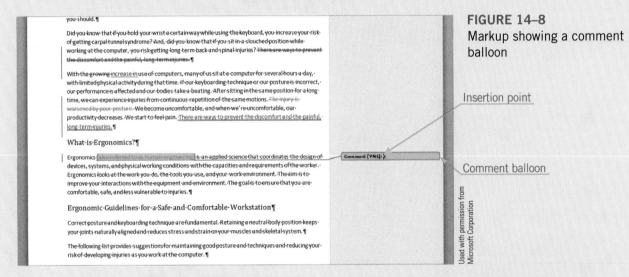

FIGURE 14–8
Markup showing a comment balloon

Insertion point

Comment balloon

Used with permission from Microsoft Corporation

5. The initials at the beginning of the comment text indicate the author of the comment, based on the user information provided in the Word Options dialog box. The number 1 indicates this is the first comment in the document. The insertion point is positioned in the comment balloon. Type **Because it involves human factors, it is often referred to as human engineering.**.

6. Scroll to the bulleted list at the bottom of the first page. In the first bulleted item, position the insertion point after the word *flat*. Click the **New Comment** button, and then type **My keyboarding instructor made us keep our feet flat on the floor!** in the comment balloon. Notice that the comment is automatically numbered sequentially. Because you did not select text, the comment is connected to the word closest to the location of the insertion point.

7. Position the mouse pointer over either one of the comments, and a ScreenTip is displayed showing the reviewer name and the date and time the comment was added to the document.

QUICK TIP

When revisions are set to show inline, the comment reference numbers will appear in brackets in the line of text. To display the comment in a ScreenTip, position your mouse pointer over the comment reference number.

QUICK TIP

When you move or copy text with a comment, the comment markup is pasted with the text.

8. In the Tracking group, click the **Reviewing Pane** button arrow, and then click **Reviewing Pane Vertical**. The changes and comments are now displayed in a pane at the left side of the document as shown in **Figure 14–9**. You can scroll through the list to view the changes, and you can also edit the comments in the Reviewing pane.

FIGURE 14–9
Vertical Reviewing pane

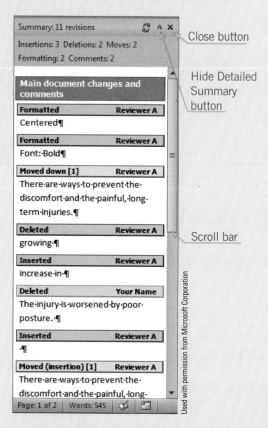

9. Compare your screen to Figure 14–9. At the top of the Reviewing pane is a summary that shows the number of revisions. If you do not see the details about the summary as shown in Figure 14–9, click the **Show Detailed Summary** button.

10. Click the **Hide Detailed Summary** button to hide the summary details.

11. In the Tracking group, click the **Reviewing Pane** button arrow, and then click **Reviewing Pane Horizontal**. The changes and comments are now displayed in the Reviewing pane at the bottom of the document window.

12. In the title bar of the Reviewing pane, click the **Close** button next to the Show Detailed Summary button to close the Reviewing pane.

13. Save the changes to the document, and leave the document open for the next Step-by-Step.

Showing and Hiding Markup

Multiple comments and revisions often clutter the document and make it difficult to read the content. Moreover, if there are multiple users, the revisions may be even more complex to review. You can choose from several options to show the markup. For example, you can choose to show only the edits from a specific reviewer, or you can choose to view only the comments added to the document. To see what the final document will look like, you can hide the entire markup.

There is no limit on the number of reviewers for a document. Word will assign a different color for each of the first eight reviewers. The colors will be reused for additional reviewers beyond the first eight. You can still easily identify reviewers by their initials in the markup ScreenTips.

Step-by-Step 14.3

1. If necessary, open the **Revised Ergonomics 2** file from your solution files.

2. If necessary, click the **Review** tab.

3. In the Tracking group, click the **Show Markup** button. A menu appears, and you can choose the type of revisions you want to review. All types of markup with a check mark will be displayed in the document.

4. Point to **Reviewers** to show the names of the reviewers and their associated colors, as shown in **Figure 14–10**. The default setting displays the comments and changes for all reviewers.

IC³
2-2.2.3

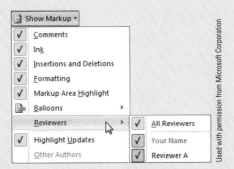

Used with permission from Microsoft Corporation

FIGURE 14–10
Show Markup options with the names of the reviewers

5. Click **Reviewer A** to uncheck that reviewer name. Scroll through the document. Now only the changes and comments from the first reviewer are displayed in the document.

6. Click the **Show Markup** button, point to **Reviewers**, and then click **All Reviewers** to return to the default settings and display all comments and changes.

7. In the Tracking group, in the box displaying *Final: Show Markup*, click the **Display for Review** list arrow, and then click **Final**. The document is displayed on the screen exactly as it will print, with all the revisions accepted and the comments hidden. The markup has not been accepted or removed from the document; it just does not show on the screen.

8. Click the **Display for Review** list arrow again, and then click **Final: Show Markup**.

9. Leave the document open for the next Step-by-Step.

Accepting and Rejecting Changes

After changes and comments are added to a document, the edited document is usually passed on to another person, either the original author or another reviewer, to make a decision about the revisions and comments. That person can decide whether to accept or reject the changes, and he or she can also remove the comments from the document. The Next and Previous buttons in the Comments group help you quickly navigate the comments in the document.

When the edits are complete, you can apply a Marked as Final status. Then when you share the document, those who review the document will know they are viewing the final version. When a document is marked as final, editing is disabled and markup is not visible. The file becomes a ***read-only document***, which permits others to open and view the document, but they are unable to make any changes to the document. Be aware, however, that it is possible for anyone to easily remove the Marked as Final status.

▶ **VOCABULARY**
read-only document

Step-by-Step 14.4

2-2.2.3

1. If necessary, open the **Revised Ergonomics 2** file from your solution files. Save the Revised Ergonomics 2 document as **Revised Ergonomics 3**, followed by your initials. If necessary, click the **Review** tab, and change to **Print Layout** view.

2. Position the insertion point at the beginning of the document. In the Comments group, click the **Next Comment** button. The insertion point moves to the beginning of the text in the first comment balloon.

3. Click the **Next Comment** button again to move to the second comment in the document. In the Comments group, click the **Previous Comment** button to move back to the first comment.

4. Reposition the insertion point at the beginning of the document. In the Changes group, shown in **Figure 14–11**, click the **Next Change** button. The insertion point moves to the first revision in the document, which is the bold format applied to the first paragraph of text.

FIGURE 14–11
Changes group on the Review tab

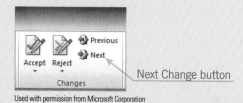

Used with permission from Microsoft Corporation

5. Click the **Next Change** button. The insertion point moves to the second change in the document, which is the center alignment format for the same paragraph.

6. Click the **Next Change** button. The insertion point moves to the text at the end of the paragraph that begins *Did you know.*

7. Click the **Next Change** button. The word *growing* is selected. In the Changes group, click the top half of the **Accept** button ✍. The selected text is deleted, and the next revision is selected.

8. Click the **Next Change** button. The sentence *The injury is worsened by poor posture.* is selected. In the Changes group, click the top half of the **Reject** button ✍ (not the button arrow).

9. Click the **Next Change** button three times. The Next Change command locates the first comment. In the Comments group, click the **Delete Comment** button arrow. Click **Delete All Comments in Document** to remove all the comments.

10. In the Changes group, click the **Accept and Move to Next** button arrow and then click **Accept All Changes in Document**. All revisions are accepted. In the Tracking group, click the **Track Changes** button to toggle off the feature.

11. Click the **File** tab. If necessary, click **Info**. Click the **Protect Document** button. In the submenu, click **Mark as Final**. When prompted to mark the document as final and then save the document, click **OK**. A second prompt appears confirming the Marked as Final status. Click **OK**. Note that the Backstage view now displays a note indicating the document has been marked as final as shown in **Figure 14–12**.

> **QUICK TIP**
>
> If you do not want to review all of the changes and comments in sequence, show the Reviewing pane so you can scroll through the list and quickly locate the change or comment. When you click a comment in the Reviewing pane, the insertion point is moved to that location in the document window.

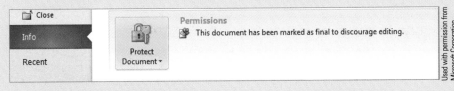

Used with permission from Microsoft Corporation

FIGURE 14–12
Marked as final note in Backstage view

12. Click the **Home** tab. A yellow bar is displayed above the document window and confirms that the document has been marked as final. Also note that the Marked as Final icon 🔖 is shown in the status bar.

13. Select the first word in the document, and then press **Delete**. The selected text is not removed because the document is a read-only document. In the yellow bar above the document window, click **Edit Anyway**. With the first word still selected, press **Delete**. The selected text is removed. Click the **Undo** button on the Quick Access Toolbar.

14. Save the changes to the document, and leave the document open for the next Step-by-Step.

> **QUICK TIP**
>
> Files that have been marked as final in a Microsoft Office 2010 program are not read-only if someone opens it in an earlier version of the Microsoft Office program.

Preparing a Document for Printing

VOCABULARY
hard copy

After the document is finalized, you can prepare a *hard copy*—a printed copy—of the document to share the information. Often, multiple copies are prepared and distributed. Your system may have two or more printers available, including inkjet printers, laser printers, fax programs that also serve as a type of printer, and others. The benefit of having more than one printer to choose from is that different printers offer different features.

Printing a Document

QUICK TIP

When you open a document attached to an e-mail, because of securities settings, you may need to enable editing before you can edit or print the document.

When you click the File tab and then click Print, the print settings are displayed in Backstage view. When you click the Print button at the top of the middle pane, the content in the active window or document is sent directly to the printer, and you will not have the opportunity to change the printing options or printer settings. The default printer options will be applied. If your computer accesses more than one printer, you will want to select the printer you want to use. You can specify the number of copies and the range of pages to print. You can also change the printer settings (such as print quality or the color settings using the Printer Properties link). The options will vary, but most of the print options are similar for all applications. In addition to the print settings, a preview of the print layout is displayed in a pane on the right. If the document has multiple pages, you can use the Previous Page and Next Page buttons to preview each page.

Step-by-Step 14.5

IC³

2-1.4.1
2-1.4.2
2-1.4.3

1. If necessary, open the **Revised Ergonomics 3** file from your solution files.

2. Click the **File** tab, and then click **Print** to show the Print settings in Backstage view as shown in **Figure 14–13**.

FIGURE 14–13
Print settings in Backstage view

Enabled printer

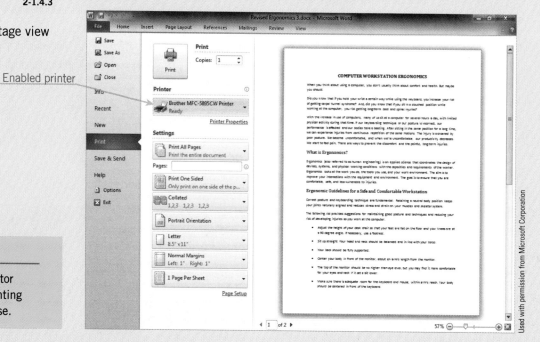

WARNING

Check with your instructor about the policy for printing documents in this course.

3. In the middle pane, under Printer, click the enabled printer name, as shown in Figure 14–13. If your computer is connected to more than one printer, the other printers will be displayed in this list. Click the enabled printer name to close the list without making any changes.

4. At the bottom of the Preview pane, click the **Next Page** arrow to show page 2. Then click the **Previous Page** arrow to show page 1.

5. At the top of the middle pane, change the **Copies** setting to **3**. This setting indicates that three copies will be printed.

6. In the middle pane, under Settings, note that the first setting is *Print All Pages*. Click in the **Pages** box. Type **2**. Note that the setting above now displays *Print Custom Range*. With these settings, you would print three copies of page 2.

7. Delete the numbers in the Pages box. The setting above changes and displays the default setting *Print All Pages*.

8. Under Settings, click **Print All Pages**. In the submenu, click **Print Current Page**. When this option is enabled, the page displayed in the Preview pane is the only page that will print.

9. To print, you would click Print at the top of the middle pane, but there is no reason to print this page of the document. Click the **File** tab to close the Backstage view without printing.

10. Scroll down and select the bulleted list. Click **File** and then click **Print**. Under Settings, click the **Print Current Page** list arrow. In the submenu, click **Print Selection**. To print, you would click Print at the top of the middle pane, but there is no reason to print the bulleted list.

11. At the top of the middle pane, change the Copies setting to **1**. Under Settings, click **Print Selection**, and then click **Print All Pages**. The default settings are restored. Click the **File** tab to close the Backstage view.

12. Deselect the text, and leave the document open for the next Step-by-Step. (If you close the document and are prompted to save changes to the document, click **Don't Save**.)

QUICK TIP

To print a range of pages, use a hyphen to indicate the page range. For example: 2-8. To print multiple pages without printing a full range, use a comma. For example: 2,5,7.

Customizing Print Settings and Properties and Showing the Print Queue

Many people use their default printer settings, and they are not aware of all the additional features and options that are available. Most printers have settings for adjusting the printing speed and the print quality. When working with multipage documents, special features such as reverse printing, collating, and duplex printing are very useful. **Reverse printing** reverses the order of the pages so the last page prints first. When enabled, the **collating** setting prints all of the pages in one copy of the document before printing the next copy so that the printed pages are automatically arranged in the proper order. **Duplex printing** is printing on both sides of the page. Of course, you can manually feed the paper back into the printer to print the back side of the page, but it is very convenient when the printer will do that automatically.

The **print queue** shows information about print jobs that are waiting to print. When you open the print queue, you can see the sequence of the active documents, the document owner, and the number of pages to print. In addition to viewing the status and information about the waiting print jobs, you can also use the print queue to pause, resume, restart, or cancel print jobs.

> **▶ VOCABULARY**
> **reverse printing**
> **collating**
> **duplex printing**
> **print queue**

Step-by-Step 14.6

2-1.4.3
2-1.4.4

1. If necessary, open the **Revised Ergonomics 3** file from your solution files.
2. Click the **File** tab, and then click **Print**.
3. In the middle pane, under Printer, click the **Printer Properties** link to open the Printer Properties dialog box, similar to the one shown in **Figure 14–14**. Property settings will vary depending on the printer selected, but they will most likely include paper size, print quality, and color management.

FIGURE 14–14
Printer Properties dialog box

4. Explore the settings that are available on your printer. If multiple tabs are displayed in the Properties dialog box, view the settings available on each tab.

5. Click **Cancel** to close the Printer Properties dialog box without saving any changes. Do not print the document.

6. On the task bar, click the **Start** button, click **Control Panel**, click **Hardware and Sound**, and then click **Devices and Printers**. Under Printers and Faxes, names of more than one printer may be displayed. A green check mark next to a printer name identifies the default printer. Double-click the name of the default printer. If necessary, click **Display Print Queue** to display a printer dialog box showing the print queue, similar to the one shown in **Figure 14–15**.

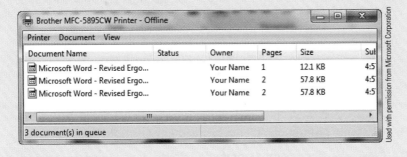

FIGURE 14–15
Print queue with documents waiting to print

7. When you open the print queue immediately after sending a document to the printer, the print queue may already be empty by the time you open it. However, if multiple documents are waiting to print, the print queue will look similar to the one shown in Figure 14–15, which shows multiple documents waiting to be printed.

8. To cancel a print job, you select the job(s) in the list you want to cancel. Because you have not sent a document to the printer, you do not have a document to select, but you can still look at the available commands. In the menu bar of the print queue dialog box, click **Document**. All the commands in your list are dimmed, because you have not selected a document. **Figure 14–16** shows the commands available for a selected document. **Table 14–1** provides descriptions for each of the Document commands.

FIGURE 14–16
Document commands in print queue

TABLE 14–1　Document commands in print queue

OPTION	DESCRIPTION
Pause	Stops the document from being printed, but the document is not removed from the queue.
Resume	Continues the printing process when the selected document was paused.
Restart	Starts the printing process from the beginning for the selected document.
Cancel	Removes the document from the print queue. The current printer job may take a while to cancel, and it may finish printing without canceling, but the remaining jobs in the list will be canceled.
Properties	Shows general information about the document such as size, number of pages in the document, and the date and time the document was sent to the printer. A summary of the printer settings is also available.

9. Close the print queue dialog box and any Control Panel windows.

10. Close the document. If prompted to save changes to the document, click **Don't Save**.

Printing Markup

When you print a document containing markup, you can choose to print the document with or without the markup.

Step-by-Step 14.7

1. Open the **Revised Ergonomics 2** file from your solution files.

2. Click the **File** tab, and then click **Print**. In the right pane, the print preview reveals that the revision marks and comments will also be printed. The document size is reduced so the balloons will also be printed on the same page.

3. In the middle pane, under Settings, click **Print All Pages** to show the list of options shown in **Figure 14–17**. Under Document Properties, click **List of Markup**. This option prints a list of all changes, but the document is not printed. This printed list is very similar to the format shown in the Reviewing pane.

2-1.4.3

FIGURE 14–17
Print options

Used with permission from Microsoft Corporation

4. Under Settings, click **List of Markup**, and then click **Print All Pages** to return to the default settings.

5. Click **Print All Pages**. Under Document Properties, click **Print Markup** to disable the option. Note that the markup is no longer displayed in the Preview pane. Click **Print All Pages**, and then click **Print Markup** again to enable the option and return to the default setting.

6. Click the **Review** tab to close Backstage view without printing.

7. In the Tracking group, click the **Display for Review** list arrow, and then click **Final**. Click the **File** tab, and then click **Print**. Note that the markup is not displayed in the Preview pane so the markup will not print if the document is sent to the printer.

8. Click the **Review** tab. Click the **Display for Review** list arrow, and then click **Final: Show Markup**.

9. Leave the document open for the next Step-by-Step. (If you close the document and are prompted to save changes to the document, click **Don't Save**.)

ETHICS IN TECHNOLOGY

Maintain Integrity When Sharing Documents

Computer use is a privilege, and it imposes certain obligations and responsibilities. The behavior, courtesy, and etiquette expected in verbal and written communications is extended to electronic communications. When sharing documents, users must maintain integrity and discipline themselves to do what is right. It is important that shared documents are maintained in a manner that is accurate and honest.

Only view and edit the files you are authorized to access. Do not move, alter, or delete documents without permission. Respect the property of others. The use of the documents should be limited to the intended objectives, and release of information without permission is unethical. Passwords are used to restrict access, so do not share passwords with those who are not authorized to access the files. To protect confidential information, remove metadata and follow the correct procedures to keep the information secure.

Troubleshooting Common Printing Problems

2-1.4.5

Even when you preview the pages in Backstage view, there are times when the print results do not meet expectations. This could be for a variety of reasons, as shown in **Table 14–2**.

TABLE 14–2   Troubleshooting printer problems

PROBLEM	CAUSE/SOLUTION
The entire document does not print, or some of the document looks blurry and faded	If the colors do not print correctly, the printer may be low on or out of ink or toner.
The document does not look the same as what you see on the screen	Sometimes the font in your document might not be available on the printer you are using. Change the font in your document to a TrueType font, which looks the same on the printed page as it does on the screen, or change the font to one that is available on your printer.
The layout looks wrong	You may be printing a document that was created with a different version of Word or was formatted for different printer settings, such as margins and paper size. Some printers will not print documents with margins less than 0.5". To have Word format the document to your printer's paper size for this printing session only, open the Print dialog box and then show the printer properties. Choose the appropriate paper size, and scale the document to fit the paper size.
Nothing happens	Check the print queue. Your document may be blocked by one or more documents waiting to be printed. Make sure the printer is not out of paper. Make sure the printer is connected to the computer, the printer power is turned on, and the printer is online. Make sure the printer cable is connected to the right port. Check for paper jams. Open the Print dialog box and confirm that the correct printer is shown in the Printer name text box. Run the Windows Printing Troubleshooter. Click the Start button, and then click Help and Support. In the Search box, enter the keywords *printing troubleshooter*, and then select the problem(s) you are having and follow the instructions.
You do not get a printed document, and Microsoft Word itself stops responding	It is likely that the printer driver is not installed or you do not have the correct printer driver. You can try installing an updated printer driver from the printer's manufacturer.

Sharing Files

The use of computers and telecommunications in the workplace has changed how we work. The majority of the information we work with is now generated by e-mail and electronic files. Instead of producing a hard copy of a document, it is now common practice to share a soft copy. A *soft copy* is a digital copy of data, such as a file viewed on a computer's display or shared via an e-mail attachment.

▶ VOCABULARY
soft copy
metadata

Preparing Documents for Electronic Distribution

You may want to control what others can see in the document. For example, you may not want them to see the author of the document or the date the document was created. Information like this is referred to as *metadata*—data that describes other data—and it is still easy to find. Much of this information is automatically updated, and you can remove or manually change some of the information.

Step-by-Step 14.8

2-1.4.6
2-1.4.7
2-2.2.3
2-2.2.4

1. If necessary, open the **Revised Ergonomics 2** file from your solution files. Save the Revised Ergonomic 2 document as **Revised Ergonomics 4**, followed by your initials.

2. Click the **File** tab. If necessary, in the left pane, click **Info**. The document properties are displayed in the right pane as shown in **Figure 14–18**.

FIGURE 14–18
Document properties in Backstage view

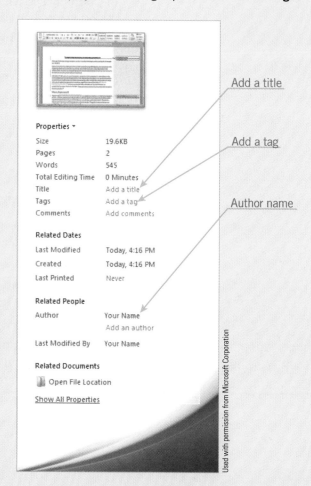

Used with permission from Microsoft Corporation

3. The document properties include the file size, the number of pages and words, and so on. Note the information for the Author and Last Modified By properties on your screen.

4. In the Properties pane, click **545** (the Word count). Word automatically calculates the total number of words, and you cannot change this property.

5. Click **Add a title**. Currently no title has been assigned, but a box is shown, so you can manually update this information. Type **Computer Workstation Ergonomics**.

6. Just below the Title box, click **Add a tag**. Type **safety, comfort, productivity**. These tags will be helpful when searching keywords in documents.

7. At the bottom of the Properties pane, click the link **Show All Properties**. More information about the document is displayed, including the template and boxes to enter information about the status, subject, and more.

8. If necessary, scroll down and then click the link **Show Fewer Properties** to hide some of the property information.

9. In the middle pane, click the **Check for Issues** button, then click **Inspect Document**. When prompted to save changes to the document, click **Yes**. The Document Inspector dialog box shown in **Figure 14–19** opens. Word proposes some features to check.

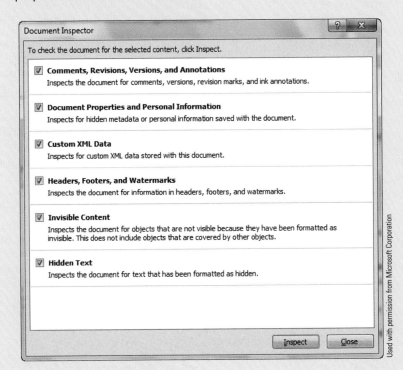

FIGURE 14–19
Document Inspector dialog box

10. At the bottom of the dialog box, click **Inspect**. The inspection results are displayed as shown in **Figure 14-20**.

FIGURE 14-20
Inspection results

11. You want to leave the revision marks in the document, so do not make any changes regarding the markup. However, you do want to remove the personal information, so next to Document Properties and Personal Information, click **Remove All**.

12. Close the Document Inspector dialog box. In the Properties pane, notice that much of the property information has been removed, including the title, the tags, and the names of the author and user who last saved the document. Save the changes to the document.

13. Click the **Home** tab. Notice that except for the moved text, all the markup is the same color throughout the document, and the initials in the comment balloons have changed to *A1* and *A2*. Position the mouse pointer over a markup for a revision in the document. ScreenTips no longer display to provide the name of the reviewer and the date and time of the edits. Removing the personal information made the edits and comments anonymous.

14. Close the document.

Saving the Document in a PDF or XPS Format

When sharing documents with others, you need to consider that not all users will be using Word 2010. Before distributing the soft copy of a document, you may need to save it in a format that enables those working with different applications, platforms, and operating systems to access the file.

The *Portable Document Format (PDF)*, created by Adobe Systems in 1993, is commonly used. To open files in the PDF format, Adobe Reader software must be installed on the computer. Microsoft first included the *XML Paper Specification (XPS)* format in the Office 2007 applications. To open files in XPS format, you must use Microsoft's XPS Viewer, which is installed by default in Office 2010 applications. Both PDF and XPS formats are designed to preserve the visual appearance and layout of each page, and they enable fast viewing and printing. These document formats are especially useful for resumes and newsletters because the appearance and printing of the document will be exactly as intended.

> ▶ **VOCABULARY**
> **Portable Document Format (PDF)**
> **XML Paper Specification (XPS)**

Step-by-Step 14.9

1. Open the **Revised Ergonomic 3** file from your solution files.

2. Click the **File** tab, and then in the left pane, click **Save & Send**. In the middle pane, under File Types, click **Create PDF/XPS Document**. In the right pane, click the **Create PDF/XPS** button. The Publish as PDF or XPS dialog box opens.

3. In the File name box type **Revised Ergonomic 5**, followed by your initials.

4. In the Save as type box, click the list arrow, and then click **XPS Document (*.xps)**. Note that to save a document in the PDF format, you would click PDF (*.pdf). Make sure the Open file after publishing option is enabled as shown in **Figure 14–21**.

2-1.4.6
2-1.4.7

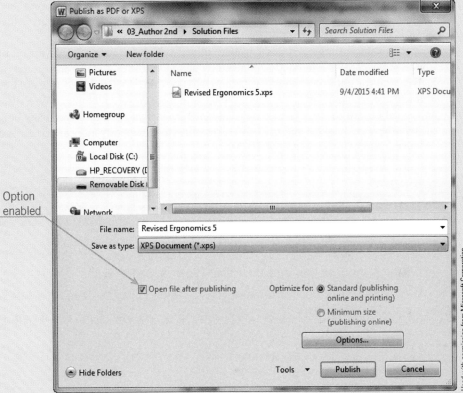

Option enabled

FIGURE 14–21
Publish as PDF or XPS dialog box

Used with permission from Microsoft Corporation

5. Click **Publish**. The document opens in an XPS Viewer window.

6. Drag across some text to select it. Press **Delete**. The read-only format does not allow any changes.

7. Close the XPS Viewer window, and leave the Revised Ergonomic 3 document open for the next Step-by-Step.

Sending and Publishing Documents

When distributing electronic copies of a document, you can choose to attach the document to an e-mail message, create a link in an e-mail message to the current document, attach the document as either a PDF or an XPS file, or send the document as a fax without using the fax machine. Of course, you must be connected to a network or the Internet, and you must have sufficient bandwidth (the speed of data transfer) for transferring the electronic files.

Another way to distribute a document is to publish the document to the Web. To publish the document on the Web, you need a Windows Live account. If you do not have an account, you can sign up for a SkyDrive account for no fee.

You can also share files by saving them to a *document management server*, which is a central location for storing, managing, and tracking files. For example, Windows SharePoint Services is a Web site that provides tools for sharing and updating files and keeping colleagues informed about document status. You can publish the document at the Web site and keep the local document on your computer synchronized with the changes and updates.

Some document management servers also provide features to help organizations manage business processes. Documents are stored in a library, and access to those documents and the rights of users can be controlled. You must have authorization to publish or access files at a Microsoft Windows SharePoint Services Web site. Therefore, using a document management server and new document workspace features is beyond the scope of this lesson.

Publishing to a blog is another alternative. A *blog* (an abbreviated version of the term *Web log*) is a journal maintained by an individual or a group and posted on a Web site for public viewing and comment. Blogs are often referred to as online diaries, and they may include graphics, photos, music, video, and links to Web sites. A typical blog Web site provides links and enables instant feedback, and many blog hosts offer free blog posting services. You must have authorization to access and publish information on a blog Web site.

> **VOCABULARY**
> **document management server**
> **blog**

Step-by-Step 14.10

2-1.4.6
2-1.4.7
2-2.2.3

1. If necessary, open the **Revised Ergonomics 3** file from your solution files.

2. Click the **File** tab, and then click **Save & Send**. In the middle pane, under Save & Send, the Send Using E-mail option is already selected. Note that several options are displayed in the right pane, as shown in **Figure 14–22**.

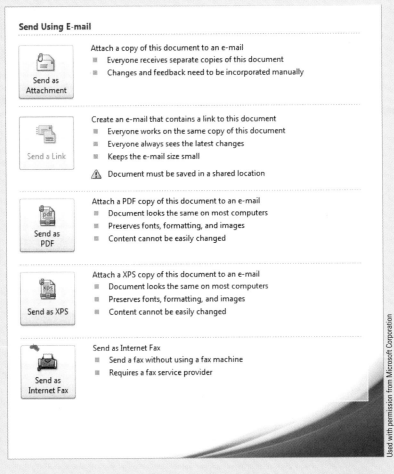

FIGURE 14–22
Send Using E-mail options

Used with permission from Microsoft Corporation

3. In the right pane, click the **Send as Attachment** button. If Microsoft Outlook is your default e-mail application, the Outlook application will open and a new message window opens. If Outlook is not your default e-mail application, most likely your e-mail application will open with a new message form. (If a prompt displays that the mail could not be sent, click OK.)

4. Note that in the message window the Revised Ergonomics 3 document is already attached to the e-mail message and the subject line displays the document filename. Close the message window without saving any changes.

QUICK TIP

Be sure to check if a document is linked with other information sources, such as databases or spreadsheets, to avoid unintentionally sending or publishing information about the linked data.

5. Click the **File** tab, and then click **Save & Send**. In the middle pane, under Save & Send, click **Save to Web**. The information in the right pane adapts, and information similar to what is shown in **Figure 14–23** is displayed. At this point you would sign into your Windows Live account.

FIGURE 14–23
Save to Web options

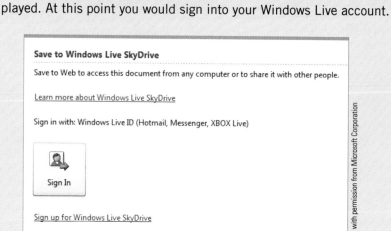

6. Under Save & Send, click **Save to SharePoint**. In the right pane, locations for document management servers are displayed. If your computer is not set up for SharePoint, you will see Browse for a location, as shown in **Figure 14–24**. At this point you would select or navigate to the server space and then click Save As to upload the file to the document management server.

FIGURE 14–24
Save to SharePoint options

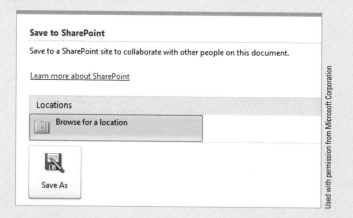

7. In the middle pane, under Save & Send, click **Publish as Blog Post**. In the right pane, the options shown in **Figure 14–25** are displayed. At this point you would click the Publish as Blog Post button. If it is the first time you've posted a blog from Word, you would be prompted to register your blog account.

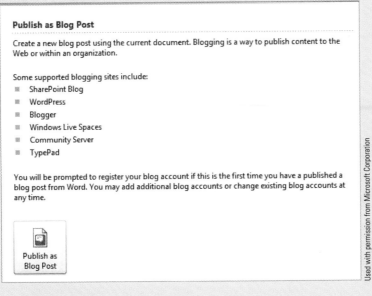

Used with permission from Microsoft Corporation

FIGURE 14–25
Send using Publish as Blog Post options

8. Close the document. If prompted to save changes to the document, click **Don't Save**.

Protecting Documents

If a document contains important or confidential information, you need secure ways to share the information. Word offers features that enable you to control sensitive information and collaborate in confidence.

Restricting Access

The most secure option is to encrypt the document. *Encryption* is a standard method for encoding data. During the process of encryption, a password is assigned, and then all users must enter the password to open the document. If you want to permit some users to modify the encrypted document, you can create a second password that will allow them to edit and save changes to the document. This option limits those who can edit the document.

It is recommended that passwords include a combination of text, numbers, and symbols and be at least eight characters in length—the more characters the better. Passwords are *case sensitive*, which means when entering a password, the upper- and lowercasing of the letters must be identical to the casing of the letters in the assigned password.

▶ **VOCABULARY**
encryption
case sensitive

QUICK TIP

People often choose to use nicknames or commonly used words for their passwords, such as *wildcats* because they are easy to remember. To create a stronger password with a combination of text, numbers, and symbols, replace the vowels with numbers and/or symbols. For example: *w1ldc4t$!.*

Step-by-Step 14.11

2-2.2.3
2-2.2.4

1. If necessary, open the **Revised Ergonomics 3** file from your solution files. Save the Revised Ergonomics 3 file as **Revised Ergonomics 5**, followed by your initials.

2. Click the **File** tab. If necessary, click **Info**. In the middle pane, click the **Protect Document** button, and then click **Encrypt with Password**. The Encrypt Document dialog box opens.

3. Type **#jck0514!** and click **OK**. Then when prompted, type the password **#jck0514!** again and click **OK**.

4. Close the document. When prompted to save the changes, click **Save**. The encryption process is completed.

5. Reopen the **Revised Ergonomics 5** document, using the open password you created in Step 3 above. Users who do not know this password will not be able to open the document. Now that the document is open, you can edit the document.

6. Click the **File** tab, and then click **Save As**. At the bottom of the dialog box, click **Tools**, and then click **General Options** to open the General Options dialog box shown in **Figure 14–26**. Note that the password to open the file is already applied. You can choose to assign one or both passwords. The second password allows users to modify the document. If you choose to use both passwords, make sure the passwords are not the same.

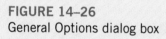

If you forget the password, the file cannot be reopened. When you assign a password to a document, write it down and keep the note in a secure place.

FIGURE 14–26
General Options dialog box

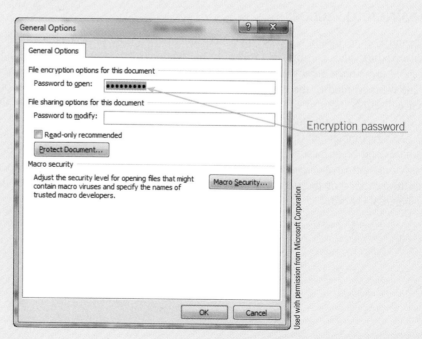

7. In the second password box, type **AEM#1mxB**. Be sure all the letters have the correct casing. The encryption password allows users to open the document. By assigning a second password, users will not be able to modify the document without entering the second password. Click **OK**. When prompted, type the password **AEM#1mxB** and click **OK**.

8. In the File name box, the filename Revised Ergonomics 5 is still displayed. Click **Save**, and close the document.

9. Reopen the **Revised Ergonomics 5** file. When prompted, type the password **#jck0514!** and click **OK**.

10. A second prompt appears indicating that a password must be entered to modify the document. (Users who do not know this password can click Read Only to view the document.) Type the second password **AEM#1mxB**, and click **OK** to open the document with permission to modify the content.

11. To remove the encryption, click the **File** tab, click the **Protect Document** button, and then click **Encrypt with Password**. In the Encrypt Document dialog box, delete all the characters for the current password, and then click **OK**.

12. Close the document. When prompted to save the changes, click **Save**. Then reopen the document. The Password dialog box opens. Even though the document is no longer encrypted, users must still enter a password to modify the document. To remove this password, you would need to open the General Options dialog box and then delete the password characters.

13. In the Password dialog box, click **Read Only**. Select the **document title**, and change the font color to red. Click the **Save** button on the Quick Access Toolbar. The Save As dialog box opens. Click **Save**. A prompt appears indicating that the document is read-only. To save the changes to the document you would need to create a new filename.

14. Click **OK** to close the prompt. Click **Cancel** to close the Save As dialog box, and then close the document without saving the changes.

Restricting Formatting and Edits

Even when you choose to allow others to make revisions and add comments, you can still be selective about who is allowed to make edits as well as the types of edits they can make. After setting the restrictions, you must assign a password to enforce the restrictions.

Step-by-Step 14.12

2-2.2.3
2-2.2.4

1. Open the **Revised Ergonomics 3** file from your solution files. Save the Revised Ergonomics 3 file as **Revised Ergonomics 6**, followed by your initials.

2. Click the **Review** tab. In the Protect group at the far right side of the Review tab, click the **Restrict Editing** button. The Restrict Formatting and Editing task pane shown in **Figure 14–27** appears.

FIGURE 14–27
Restrict Formatting and Editing task pane

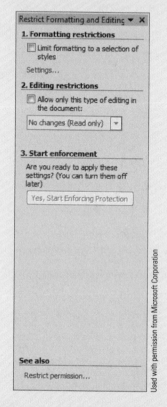

Used with permission from Microsoft Corporation

3. Under 2. Editing restrictions, click **Allow only this type of editing in the document** to enable the option. A check mark appears in the check box when the option is enabled. As shown in **Figure 14–28**, under Exceptions (optional) new options are now displayed, and the current Editing restrictions setting is *No changes (Read only)*.

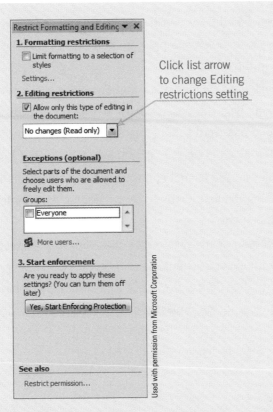

Click list arrow
to change Editing
restrictions setting

Used with permission from Microsoft Corporation

FIGURE 14–28
New Exceptions options in the
Restrict Formatting and Editing
task pane

4. Under Editing restrictions, click the list arrow, and then click **Tracked changes**. Notice that the options in the task pane change again. When the Tracked changes option is enabled, reviewers can make revisions and also add comments to the document.

5. Click the **Editing restrictions** list arrow, and then click **Comments**. New Exceptions options are displayed again. With the Comments option enabled, you can make exceptions and allow specified reviewers to edit all or part of the document.

6. Click the **Editing restrictions** list arrow again, and then click **Filling in forms**. This option allows users to enter information in form fields such as text boxes, check boxes, and lists. When this option is enabled, the exceptions are not available, and users cannot track changes or add comments.

7. Click the **Editing restrictions** list arrow, and then click **No changes (Read only)**.

8. Select the first four paragraphs in the document, (all the text above the heading *What is Ergonomics?*). Then in the task pane, under Exceptions (optional) click **Everyone** to enable the option. Deselect the text. Anyone with access to the document can edit the highlighted paragraphs.

9. Click in the highlighted text. Note that the Everyone check box is enabled. Then click anywhere in the text that is not highlighted. Notice that the check mark is no longer displayed next to the Everyone option. With this setting, no users would be permitted to edit this part of the document.

10. Scroll down and select all the content in the bulleted list. In the task pane, click the **Everyone** option. Deselect the text. Users can edit two regions in the document.

11. In the task pane, under 3. Start enforcement, click **Yes, Start Enforcing Protection**. Type the password **89*A*04*11/** in the first box. Click in the **second password** box, reenter the password, and then click **OK**.

12. Select the heading **What is Ergonomics?**. Note that the Mini toolbar is not displayed. You cannot edit this portion of the document. Try deleting or replacing the text. Formatting and editing is restricted in this portion of the document.

13. At the bottom of the task pane, click the **Stop Protection** button. The Password dialog box opens. To remove the restrictions you must enter a password. Click **Cancel** to close the Password dialog box without making any changes. In the upper-right corner of the Restrict Formatting and Editing task pane, click the **Close** button.

14. Save the changes and close the document.

SUMMARY

In this lesson, you learned:

- Tracking changes with revision marks makes it easy to identify who made the changes and when the changes were made.

- You can choose the markup that you want to appear on the screen and when the document is printed.

- Revisions can be accepted or rejected, and comments can easily be removed from the document.

- Printers provide a variety of settings and options for managing print jobs.

- You can view, pause, and cancel print jobs.

- There are numerous issues to consider when troubleshooting printing problems.

- When preparing documents for electronic distribution, you must choose an appropriate format and you may want to remove metadata.

- Word provides several options for sending and publishing documents.

- You can protect documents by restricting access and by restricting formatting and editing.

LESSON REVIEW

TRUE / FALSE

Circle T if the statement is true or F if the statement is false.

T   F   **1.**   When restricting formatting changes, the setting must apply to the entire document.

T   F   **2.**   A comment can be inserted anywhere in a Word document.

T   F   **3.**   When multiple reviewers have tracked changes in a document, you can choose to show revisions for only one of the reviewers.

T   F   **4.**   When tracking changes, insertions are always red and deletions are always strikethrough.

T   F   **5.**   You can hide all of the markup to see what the final document will look like.

MULTIPLE CHOICE

Select the best response for the following statements.

1. Duplex printing is _____.

   A.   when your computer has access to two printers on the system

   B.   when you apply two or more printing options

   C.   a special printer feature for automatically printing two copies of each page in the document

   D.   a special printer feature for automatically printing content on both sides of the page

2. _____ is invisible data in a document that describes other data.

   A.   Soft copy

   B.   Hidden text

   C.   Metadata

   D.   Transparent text

3. When a document is marked as final, _____.

   A.   the user can view the document but cannot make any changes to the document

   B.   the user must enter a password to open the document

   C.   all personal information is removed from the document

   D.   no more changes can ever be made to the document

4. When you open the printer queue, you see _____.

   A.   the sequence of the active print jobs

   B.   the document owner

   C.   the number of pages to print

   D.   all of the above

5. _____ can be viewed in a balloon in the margin or in the Reviewing pane.

   A.   Insertions

   B.   Comments

   C.   Deletions

   D.   Any of the above

FILL IN THE BLANK

Complete the following sentences by writing the correct word or words in the blanks provided.

1. _____ is a standard method for encoding data.

2. A(n) _____ is a printed copy of a document.

3. A(n) _____ is a central location for storing, managing, and tracking files.

4. A digital copy of data, such as a file viewed on a computer's display or shared via an e-mail attachment, is referred to as a(n) _____.

5. The revision marks and annotations that appear in a document are referred to as _____.

WRITTEN QUESTIONS

Write a brief answer to the following questions.

1. Describe the differences between tracking changes and adding comments in a document.

2. When tracking changes, each of the first reviewers is assigned a different color for markup. When you have nine or more reviewers, the colors are reused. How can you identify reviewers when their markup have the same color?

3. What is the most secure option for restricting access to a document? Explain why.

4. When you restrict edits, what options do you have for controlling the changes that can be made to the document?

5. If you want others to view the document exactly as it appears on your screen, what format should you use when you save the document? Explain why.

■ PROJECTS

PROJECT 14-1

1. Open the **Facilities** file from the drive and folder where your Data Files folder is stored. Save the Facilities document as Revised **Facilities 1**, followed by your initials.

   2-2.2.3
   2-2.2.4

2. Make note of the current user name and initials, and then change the user name to **Senior Manager**, and change the user initials to **SM**.

3. Toggle on the **Track Changes** feature.

4. Add the following three items in the bulleted list, in the correct alphabetical order: **pilates classes**, **strength and conditioning**, and **yoga classes**.

5. Select **pilates** and insert the comment **Should this be initial caps?**.

6. Select the whole sentence at the end of the paragraph beginning *The goal of a rehab facility*. Move the sentence to the end of the paragraph directly above.

7. At the end of the sentence you just moved, insert the new text **both young and old**.

8. Find all occurrences of *rehab* and replace them with **rehabilitation**.

9. Find all occurrences of *clinics* and replace them with **facilities**.

10. Toggle off the Track Changes feature, and then save the changes to the document.

11. Save the document as **Revised Facilities 2**, followed by your initials.

12. Inspect the document and remove the personal information. Do not remove the revision marks and comments. Check the document properties to make sure all the personal information was removed.

13. Close the document, saving changes, but leave Word open.

14. Restore the user name and initials to what they were before you changed them in Step 3.

PROJECT 14-2

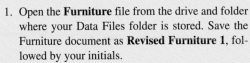

1. Open the **Furniture** file from the drive and folder where your Data Files folder is stored. Save the Furniture document as **Revised Furniture 1**, followed by your initials.

   2-1.4.6
   2-2.2.3
   2-2.2.4

2. Hide the comments in the document.

3. Move to the first revision and reject the change.

4. Move to the second revision and accept the change.

5. Show all revisions inline.

6. Accept all changes in the document.

7. Restore the default settings for showing markup. Change the Show Markup setting so only comments and formatting are displayed in balloons and also enable the option to show comments.

8. Delete all the comments in the document.

9. Toggle off the Track Changes feature.

10. Save the document in the PDF format. Name the file **Revised Furniture 2**, followed by your initials. The document will open in Adobe Reader if the application is installed on your computer.

11. Close the Adobe Reader window. Close the Revised Furniture 1 document and when prompted, save the changes.

PROJECT 14–3

2-2.2.3
2-2.2.4

1. Open the **Walking** file from the drive and folder where your Data Files folder is stored. Save the Walking document as **Revised Walking**, followed by your initials.

2. Protect the document by setting editing restrictions for No changes (Read only). Make exceptions for **Everyone** to edit the last two paragraphs in the document.

3. Enforce the protection by assigning the password **Mac@69MCV8**.

4. Close the Restrict Formatting and Editing pane.

5. Save the changes to the document, and then close the document.

6. Reopen the document and make sure the restrictions are applied as intended. Delete the last paragraph.

7. Save the changes and close the document.

TEAMWORK PROJECT

The document you worked with in Project 14–3 provided information about exercising in both hot and cold weather. Many people have preferences for warm or cool weather for a variety of reasons. Team up with a partner to explore these reasons.

1. With your partner, decide who will take the warm weather topic and who will take the cool weather topic. If both of you prefer the same season, flip a coin to make the decision.

2. Create a new Word document, and save the document as **TP 14-1**, followed by your initials.

3. List the advantages and disadvantages of your chosen climate. If you live in a climate that is more or less warm all year round, use your imagination to list the advantages and disadvantages of cold weather.

PROJECT 14–4

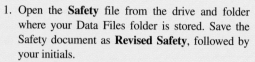

2-1.4.1
2-1.4.2
2-2.2.3
2-2.2.4

1. Open the **Safety** file from the drive and folder where your Data Files folder is stored. Save the Safety document as **Revised Safety**, followed by your initials.

2. Preview the document for printing in Backstage view.

3. Show the document properties in Backstage view. Add the title **Work Place Safety**. Add the comment **industrial ergonomic assessment**.

4. To secure the document and limit access, encrypt the document with the password **BLP9Vj5tm**. To allow options for users to modify the document, create the second password **c4pt44n!**. Save the changes, and close the document.

5. Reopen the document using the encryption password. Then enter the password for modifying the document.

6. Type your first and last name at the end of the document.

7. Save the changes, and close the document.

4. Save the changes to the document.

2-2.2.3

5. Exchange documents and review your partner's list. Track changes and edit the document to include your opinions. Add comments where appropriate.

6. Review the changes and comments your partner added to your document. Accept or reject each revision, and delete the comments. Make any other edits to make your argument stronger.

7. After finalizing your documents, save the changes and share them with each other again and discuss with your partner whose arguments are more persuasive.

CRITICAL THINKING

CRITICAL THINKING 14–1
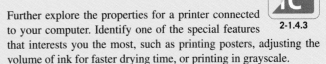

2-1.4.5

If the colors fade or are inconsistent when you print a page, it is possible that the printer is low on ink or toner. The cartridges are an additional expense, however, so you do not want to replace them until they are empty. So, how do you know the amount of ink or toner available in the cartridge(s)? Printers vary, and there is no universal answer for this question.

1. Explore the properties (or preferences) for the printer connected to your computer to locate the estimated levels of ink or toner your printer.

2. Create a new Word document, and save the document as **CT 14-1**, followed by your initials.

3. List the steps that describe how you can check the level of ink or toner for your printer.

4. Save the changes, and then close the document.

CRITICAL THINKING 14–2

2-1.4.3

Further explore the properties for a printer connected to your computer. Identify one of the special features that interests you the most, such as printing posters, adjusting the volume of ink for faster drying time, or printing in grayscale.

1. Examine the feature and options, and use the Help screens to aid you in learning the purpose of the feature.

2. Create a new Word document, and save the document as **CT 14-2**, followed by your initials.

3. Write a short description about the feature, and explain when you would use this feature.

4. Save the changes to the document, and then close the document.

ONLINE DISCOVERY

For several months you have been researching your ancestry, and you would like to share your research data with family members. You plan to e-mail your summary document to all your family members, including grandparents and cousins. Before you send the document you decide to save it in the PDF format for platform neutrality, but to open the file, recipients must have Adobe Reader installed on their computer.

1. Search the Internet for the Adobe Web site and navigate to the Web page where you can find information about downloading the Adobe Reader application.

   2-1.4.4

2. Create a new Word document, and save the document as **OD 14-1**, followed by your initials.

3. Copy the URL into the document. Include the current date.

4. Save the changes to the document, and then close the document.

JOB SKILLS

You share a printer in your work environment, and you sent a document to the printer, but the document never printed. You check the print queue and you see that a document ahead of yours has been paused, which is why your document has not printed. You recognize the name of the owner of the document. You're in a hurry to get the hard copy of the document. What would you do?

1. Create a new Word document, and save the document as **JS 14-1**, followed by your initials.

2. Write a brief paragraph explaining how you would handle this issue.

3. Save the changes to the document, and then close the document.

   2-1.4.7

LESSON 15

Working with Tables

■ OBJECTIVES

Upon completion of this lesson, you should be able to:

- Create a table and insert text.
- Insert and delete rows and columns.
- Adjust column width and row height.
- Use the Draw Table and Eraser tools to create and edit a table grid.
- Format text alignment and direction within a table cell.
- Format borders and shading and apply table styles.
- Sort data in a table.
- Convert text to a table and vice versa.

■ DATA FILES

To complete this lesson, you will need these data files:

Hurricane History.docx

Population.docx

Scores.docx

■ WORDS TO KNOW

ascending order

cell

descending order

gridlines

header row

merging cells

Quick Tables

splitting cells

MODULE 2   Key Applications

2-2.1.16

Suppose you have a document in Word that includes information you want to arrange in several lines across two or three columns. How can you create the columns you need in Word? If your answer is "Set tab stops," you are correct. However, there is also an easier and faster way. The table features in Word make the task of arranging text and numbers in columns both quick and easy. Borders and shading also help to organize information in a meaningful way.

Creating a Table

▶ VOCABULARY

cell

header row

A table consists of cells that you add content to, such as text, numbers, or graphics. A *cell* represents one intersection of a row and a column in a table. In a table, rows go across and columns go down. It is common to add headings at the top of columns to label the content in the columns. The first row in a table or data source with the column headings is referred to as the *header row*.

To create a table, you must first decide how many columns and rows you want in the table. You then create a table grid and enter the data.

To move the insertion point from one cell to another, you can press Tab or the arrow keys. When you reach the end of a row and press Tab, the insertion point moves to the first cell in the next row.

Step-by-Step 15.1

2-2.1.13

1. Create a new blank document. Save the document as **Calories 1**, followed by your initials. If necessary, turn off the display of nonprinting characters.

2. Click the **Insert** tab. In the Tables group shown in **Figure 15–1**, click the **Table** button. A grid of table cells is displayed.

FIGURE 15–1
Tables group on the Insert tab

▶ QUICK TIP

You can also create a table by clicking the Table button and then clicking Insert Table to open the dialog box. Then in the Insert Table dialog box, enter the number of rows and columns.

3. Drag the mouse pointer down the grid until seven rows of cells are highlighted, then continue to drag the mouse pointer across the grid to select three columns. The top of the grid displays *3×7 Table* and the table's Live Preview is displayed in the document window, as shown in **Figure 15–2**.

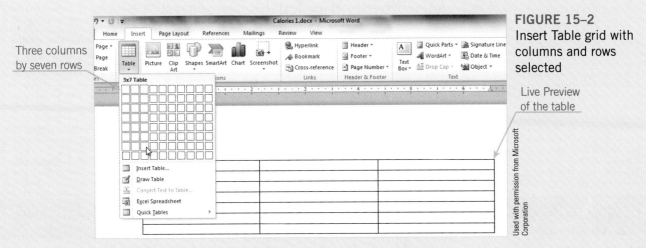

FIGURE 15–2
Insert Table grid with columns and rows selected

Three columns by seven rows

Live Preview of the table

4. With the mouse pointer still positioned over the last selected cell, click. The table is inserted in the document.

5. Because the insertion point is now positioned in a table in the document, the Ribbon adapts to show the Table Tools tabs for formatting and editing tables. Compare your screen with **Figure 15–3**. There are two Table Tools tabs: the Design tab and the Layout tab.

There are two Table Tools tabs

FIGURE 15–3
Table Tools Design tab

6. The insertion point should be positioned in the first cell of the table. Press **Tab** to move the insertion point to the next cell to the right in the same row. Type **20 Minutes**. Press **Tab**, and then type **40 Minutes**.

7. Press **Tab** to move the insertion point to the first cell in the next row.

8. Press the **down arrow** to move the insertion point down to the third row.

9. Enter the remaining data shown in **Figure 15–4**. Use Tab or the arrow keys to move from one cell to another.

	20 Minutes	40 Minutes
Cross-country skiing	192	384
Downhill skiing	144	288
Golf: carrying clubs	132	264
Mountain biking	204	408
Weight lifting	72	144

FIGURE 15–4
Table content for Step 9

10. Save the changes to the document, and leave the document open for the next Step-by-Step.

Modifying the Table Structure

After you create a table, you may decide to change it. For example, you may need to add more rows or delete a column. Word has many features that make these changes easy.

Inserting Rows and Columns

To insert a new row at the end of the table, you can position the insertion point in the last table cell and press Tab. To insert a new row anywhere else in the table, or to insert new columns, you can use the Insert commands on the Table Tools Layout tab.

Step-by-Step 15.2

2-2.1.14

1. If necessary, open the **Calories 1** file from your solution files. Save the Calories 1 document as **Calories 2**, followed by your initials.

2. If necessary, position the insertion point in the last cell in the lower-right corner of the table (*144*). Press **Tab** to create a new row at the bottom of the table.

3. Type the following information in the new row:

   Golf: using a cart   84   168

4. Move the insertion point to any cell in the third row (*Cross-country skiing*). Click the **Table Tools Layout** tab for more table tools, as shown in **Figure 15–5**.

FIGURE 15–5
Table Tools
Layout tab

Rows & Columns group

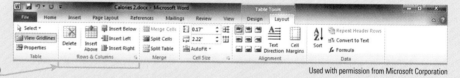

Used with permission from Microsoft Corporation

5. In the Rows & Columns group, click the **Insert Above** button. A new row is inserted above the row where the insertion point is positioned, and the table now has nine rows.

6. Drag across all the cells in the fourth and fifth rows (*Cross-country skiing* and *Downhill skiing*) to select the cells. Click the **Insert Below** button. Because you selected all the cells in two rows, two new rows are inserted below the selection. Click anywhere in the document window to deselect the cells.

7. Type the following information in the sixth and seventh rows:

   Walking: 15 minutes/mile   108   216

   Running: 9 minutes/mile   264   528

8. If necessary, move the insertion point to any cell in the third column (*40 Minutes*). In the Rows & Columns group, click the **Insert Left** button. A new column is inserted on the left side of the column where the insertion point is positioned.

9. Position the mouse pointer above the first row in the first column. When the mouse pointer changes to a down-pointing arrow as shown in **Figure 15–6**, click to select the column. Then click and drag the mouse pointer across to select both the first and the second column.

Mouse pointer

	20 Minutes		40 Minutes
Cross-country skiing	192		384
Downhill skiing	144		288
Walking: 15 minutes/mile	108		216
Running: 9 minutes/mile	264		528
Golf: carrying clubs	132		264
Mountain biking	204		408
Weight lifting	72		144
Golf: using a cart	84		168

FIGURE 15–6
Mouse pointer adapts to select a column

Used with permission from Microsoft Corporation

10. With the first two columns selected, in the Rows & Columns group, click the **Insert Right** button. Two new columns are added to the right side of the second column, and the width of each column is automatically adjusted. In rows 6 and 7, the text within the cells does not fit within the column width, so the text automatically wraps to a new line within the cell.

11. Click in the top cell of the new third column, and type **30 Minutes**. Press the **down arrow** to move down to the fourth row, and type the following numbers to complete the column:

288

216

162

396

198

306

108

126

12. Save the changes, and leave the document open for the next Step-by-Step.

> **QUICK TIP**
>
> You can use the number pad on your keyboard to enter numbers. Make sure that NUMLOCK is turned on.

Deleting Rows and Columns

When you select cells and use Delete to remove content, only the cell contents are removed. The table cell boundaries remain. To remove rows or columns from a table, you must use the Delete commands on the Table Tools Layout tab or in a shortcut menu. When you delete a row or column, the text in the cells is also deleted.

Step-by-Step 15.3

2-2.1.14

1. If necessary, open the **Calories 2** file from your solution files. Save the Calories 2 document as **Calories 3**, followed by your initials. If necessary, show the Table Tools Layout tab.

2. Position the insertion point in the second column of the ninth row (*Mountain biking*), in front of the number 204. Press **Delete** three times to delete the cell contents (*204*).

3. Position the mouse pointer to the left side of the ninth row (*Mountain biking*). The pointer changes to a right-pointing arrow, as shown in **Figure 15–7** . Make sure the pointer on your screen matches the pointer shown in Figure 15–7. With the arrow pointed at the first cell of the ninth row, click the **mouse button** to select the entire row.

FIGURE 15–7
Mouse pointer adapts
to select a row

Mouse pointer

	20 Minutes	30 Minutes			40 Minutes
Cross-country skiing	192	288			384
Downhill skiing	144	216			288
Walking: 15 minutes/mile	108	162			216
Running: 9 minutes/mile	264	396			528
Golf: carrying clubs	132	198			264
Mountain biking		306			408
Weight lifting	72	108			144
Golf: using a cart	84	126			168

Used with permission from Microsoft Corporation

4. With all the cells selected in the ninth row, press **Delete**. The text is removed from all the selected cells, but the cell boundaries remain.

5. The insertion point should be positioned in the first cell in the ninth row. In the Rows & Columns group, click the **Delete** button, and then click **Delete Rows**. The row where the insertion point is positioned is deleted.

6. Select the **ninth row** (*Weight lifting*), click the **Delete** button, and click **Delete Rows**. The cell content and the cell boundaries are removed.

7. Select the **second row** (a blank row), and then drag the mouse pointer down to include the third row (another blank row) in the selection. Right-click the **selection**, and in the shortcut menu click **Delete Rows**.

8. Position the insertion point in the first cell in the first column (a blank cell). Click the **Delete** button, and then click **Delete Cells**. The Delete Cells dialog box opens.

9. Select the **Shift cells up** option, and then click **OK**. The cell is deleted, and the contents of the cells below the deleted cell are shifted up.

10. On the Quick Access Toolbar, click the **Undo** button to restore the blank table cell.

11. Select the **fourth** and **fifth columns** (the two blank columns), click the **Delete** button, and then click **Delete Columns**.

12. With the insertion point positioned anywhere within the table, click the **Delete** button, and then click **Delete Table**. The entire table is deleted.

13. Click the **Undo** button to restore the table.

14. Save the changes, and leave the document open for the next Step-by-Step.

Adjusting Column Width and Row Height

When you create a table grid, Word makes all the columns the same width, and the entire width of the table is based on the current settings for the margins and paper size. You can choose to automatically adjust the width of one or more columns to accommodate the contents within the cells, or you can automatically adjust all column widths at the same time. You can also choose to automatically resize the table to fit in the document window. This is useful because the table width then automatically adjusts when the window size changes.

When the table is first inserted, the height of each row is the same, but when the text wraps to a second line within a cell, the height of all the cells in that row is automatically increased to accommodate the extra line of text.

Step-by-Step 15.4

1. If necessary, open the **Calories 3** file from your solution files. Save the Calories 3 document as **Calories 4**, followed by your initials. If necessary, switch to Print Layout view.

2-2.1.14

2. Click the **View** tab. In the Zoom group, click the **Page Width** button.

3. Position the insertion point in the first cell in the table (a blank cell), and then click the **Table Tools Layout** tab. In the Cell Size group, shown in **Figure 15–8**, note the height of the row displayed in the Table Row Height box.

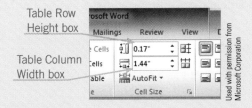

FIGURE 15–8
Cell Size group on the Table Tools Layout tab

4. Move the insertion point to the first cell in the fourth row (*Walking...*). Notice the numbers in the Table Row Height box change to reflect the difference in the height of the row.

QUICK TIP

To automatically adjust the column widths of multiple columns, select the columns and then double-click the right border of one of the selected columns. The width for all selected columns will automatically adjust.

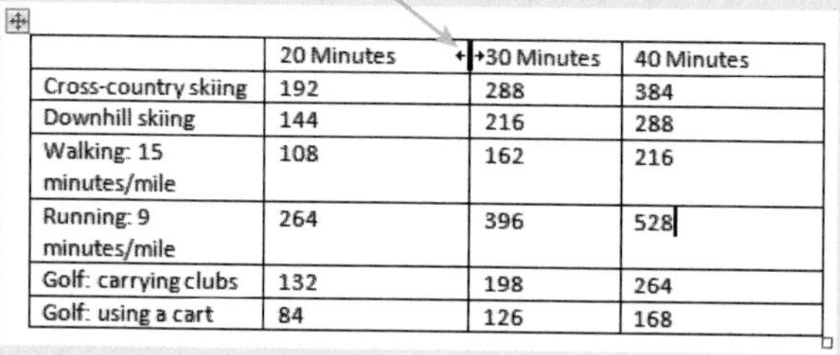

FIGURE 15–9
Mouse pointer adapts to move a column border

5. With the insertion point positioned in the first column, note the width of the column is displayed in the Table Column Width box. Click anywhere in the second, third, and fourth columns. The numbers in the Table Column Width box may vary for each column.

6. Position the mouse pointer over the right border of the second column. The pointer changes to a double-headed arrow as shown in **Figure 15–9**. With the mouse pointer displayed as a double-headed arrow, double-click. The column width is automatically adjusted to the longest line of content in the column, and the extra white space is removed.

Mouse pointer

	20 Minutes	30 Minutes	40 Minutes
Cross-country skiing	192	288	384
Downhill skiing	144	216	288
Walking: 15 minutes/mile	108	162	216
Running: 9 minutes/mile	264	396	528
Golf: carrying clubs	132	198	264
Golf: using a cart	84	126	168

Used with permission from Microsoft Corporation

QUICK TIP

When a table cell is formatted for AutoFit Contents, Word automatically adjusts the cell width each time the cell contents change.

7. With the insertion point positioned anywhere within the table, in the Cell Size group, click the **AutoFit** button. Then click **AutoFit Contents**. The text in the first column no longer wraps within the cells, and the extra white space in the third and fourth columns is eliminated.

8. With the insertion point positioned anywhere within the table, click the **AutoFit** button again, and then click **AutoFit Window**. Extra space is added to all the columns so the table fills the width of the page.

9. Click the **Page Layout** tab, and in the Page Setup group, click the **Orientation** button, and then click **Landscape**. The page width changes, and the width of each column adjusts so the table fills all the space between the left and right margins.

10. Click the **Orientation** button, and then click **Portrait** to return to the original page orientation. Once again, the column widths adjust to fit the page width.

11. Click the **Table Tools Layout** tab. In the Table group, click the **Select** button, and then click **Select Table**.

12. In the Cell Size group, click the **up arrow** in the Table Row Height box to increase the row height to **0.3"**. Deselect the table rows. The row height is increased for all selected rows.

13. Save the changes, and leave the document open for the next Step-by-Step.

Merging and Splitting Table Cells

When you remove the boundary between two cells, it is called *merging cells*. You can merge cells horizontally or vertically. You can merge cells when you want to create a heading to span across two or more columns.

When you convert a cell into multiple cells, it is called *splitting cells*. You can split a cell into two or more rows and/or two or more columns. You can also split a table into two separate tables.

Step-by-Step 15.5

1. If necessary, open the **Calories 4** file from your solution files. Save the Calories 4 document as **Calories 5**, followed by your initials.

2. Position the insertion point in the first row in the table, and then click the **Table Tools Layout** tab. In the Rows & Columns group, click the **Insert Above** button. A new row is added and the four cells in the new row are selected.

3. In the Merge group, click the **Merge Cells** button, shown in **Figure 15–10**. Click in the table to deselect the row. The four cells have merged into a single, wide cell.

IC³
2-2.1.14

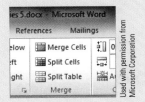

FIGURE 15–10
Merge group on the Table Tools Layout tab

4. Position the insertion point in the new blank row. In the Merge group, click the **Split Cells** button. The Split Cells dialog box opens.

5. Change the number in the Number of columns box to **1**. Change the number in the Number of rows box to **2**. Click **OK**. Click anywhere in the table to deselect the row. You will see that the row is split into two rows.

6. Position the insertion point in the top blank row, and type **NUMBER OF CALORIES BURNED**. Press **Enter**, and then type **Body weight: 150 lbs.**. The height of the cells is automatically adjusted to accommodate the two lines of text. Note all the new text is entered in the same cell.

7. Click in the second row of the table, and then click the **Split Cells** button. Click **OK** to accept the proposed settings of two columns and one row. The row will be split evenly into two cells.

8. Position the mouse pointer over the border that splits the row into two cells. When the pointer changes to a double-headed arrow, drag the border to the left so that it aligns with the first column border, as shown in **Figure 15–11**.

FIGURE 15–11
Drag a cell border to resize the cell

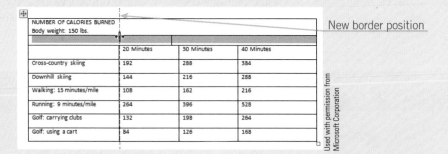

New border position

NUMBER OF CALORIES BURNED Body weight: 150 lbs.	20 Minutes	30 Minutes	40 Minutes
Cross-country skiing	192	288	384
Downhill skiing	144	216	288
Walking: 15 minutes/mile	108	162	216
Running: 9 minutes/mile	264	396	528
Golf: carrying clubs	132	198	264
Golf: using a cart	84	126	168

Used with permission from Microsoft Corporation

9. Click in the cell directly below *Body weight: 150 lbs.* and type **Activity**. Click in the cell directly above the *20 Minutes* column and type **Length of Time**.

10. Position the insertion point anywhere in the seventh row (*Running: 9 minutes/mile*), and then click the **Split Table** button. The rows are now displayed in two separate tables.

11. Click the **Undo** button to return the two tables to one table.

12. Save the changes, and then close the document.

Drawing a Table

There may be occasions when you need to create and customize a more complex table. For example, the table may require cells of different heights or a varying number of columns per row. The Draw Table tool is very useful for creating complex tables. The Draw Table tool enables you to use the mouse to draw the table grid on the screen, the same way you would use a pen to draw the grid on a sheet of paper. When you use the Draw Table tool, the document must be displayed in Print Layout view. The Eraser tool enables you to remove cell boundaries from a table.

Step-by-Step 15.6

2-2.1.3
2-2.1.13
2-2.1.14

1. Create a new blank document. Save the document as **Recycling Rate 1**, followed by your initials.

2. Click the **View** tab. In the Show group, make sure the Ruler option is checked. Then in the Zoom group, click the **Page Width** button.

3. Click the **Insert** tab. Click the **Table** button, and then in the menu below the grid, click **Draw Table**. The mouse pointer changes to a pencil *⌀*.

4. Position the mouse pointer in the upper-left corner of the document near the flashing insertion point. Notice that as you move the mouse pointer, the position of the pencil (mouse pointer) is indicated on both the horizontal and vertical rulers.

5. Position the pointer over the flashing insertion point. Then click and drag the pencil down and to the right. As you drag the mouse, markers on the vertical and horizontal rulers display the table size, as shown in **Figure 15–12**. Release the mouse button when the table (box) is approximately 6½ inches wide by 2½ inches high.

FIGURE 15–12
Creating the outside boundary of a table grid

Pencil

Used with permission from Microsoft Corporation

6. You have created the outside boundary of the table. Note that the Ribbon adapts and now shows the Table Tools Design tab.

7. To create the cell lines inside the table, position the point of the pencil where you want a line to begin and then click and drag to the point where you want it to end. A broken line will follow the mouse as you drag it. Draw all of the lines illustrated in **Figure 15–13**. The four horizontal lines are ½ inch apart, and the three vertical lines are positioned at 1 inch, 4½ inches, and 5½ inches on the horizontal ruler.

Marks on rulers indicate position of boundaries

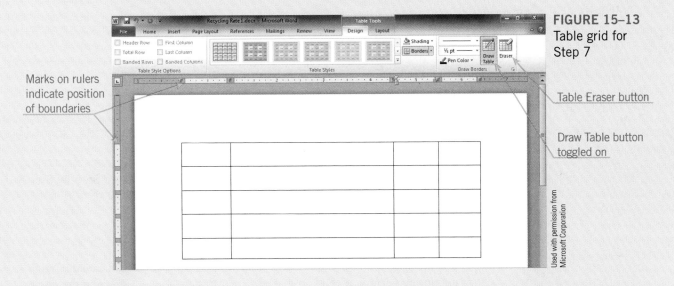

FIGURE 15–13
Table grid for Step 7

Table Eraser button

Draw Table button toggled on

Used with permission from Microsoft Corporation

QUICK TIP

You can also press Esc to toggle off the Draw Table option.

8. On the Table Tools Design tab, in the Draw Borders group, click the **Draw Table** button to toggle off the Draw Table option.

9. In the Draw Borders group, click the **Table Eraser** button. The mouse pointer changes to an eraser ⬭.

10. Position the eraser in the first row on the vertical line between the first and second cells. When the lower corner of the eraser is positioned over the line and you hold down the mouse button, the line appears selected as it does in **Figure 15–14**.

FIGURE 15–14
Eraser tool with selected line

11. Release the mouse button to delete the selected boundary. If the line is not deleted when you release the mouse button, reposition the eraser and try again. The line will only be deleted if the line is selected when you click.

12. Erase two more lines in the first column as indicated in Figure 15–14. Then click the **Table Eraser** button to toggle off the feature.

13. Enter the table text shown in **Figure 15–15**.

FIGURE 15–15
Table content for Step 13

Recycling Rate		2005	2012
PET	Beverage bottles	53%	
	Vegetable oil bottles	15%	
HDPE	Milk jugs	34%	
	Bleach and laundry detergent bottles	16%	

14. Save the changes and leave the document open for the next Step-by-Step.

Formatting Tables

You can make a table easier to read by enhancing its appearance. For example, aligning numbers within a cell can make the data easier to read. Changing the border colors and adding shading to some of the cells can help the reader quickly identify different types of data.

Aligning Data Within Table Cells

The Alignment group in the Table Tools Layout tab provides several commands you can use to align text within the cells. You can align text at the top, center, or bottom of a cell, as well as to the left or right. You can also change the direction of text in a table cell. The direction of the text toggles between three text positions: top to bottom, bottom to top, and horizontal (the default position).

Step-by-Step 15.7

1. If necessary, open the **Recycling Rate 1** file from your solutions files. Save the Recycling Rate 1 document as **Recycling Rate 2**, followed by your initials.

2-2.1.15

2. If necessary, position the insertion point in the table. Then click the **Table Tools Layout** tab.

3. Drag the mouse pointer down the left side of the table to select all the rows in the table.

4. In the Cell Size group, click the **Table Row Height** box, and enter the setting **0.5"**. All the rows are now exactly the same height.

5. All the rows should still be selected. In the Alignment group, click the **Align Top Right** button 🖹 shown in **Figure 15–16**. The text in each cell is aligned at the right side of the cell beginning at the top boundary of the cell.

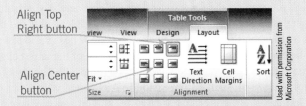

FIGURE 15–16
Alignment group on the Table Tools Layout tab

6. Click the **Align Center Left** button 🖹. The text aligns at the left side of the cells and is centered between the top and bottom boundaries of the cells.

7. Deselect the rows. Point to the cell with *PET*, and drag down to select that cell and the cell below with *HDPE*.

8. With both cells selected, in the Alignment group, click the **Text Direction** button. The text rotates to the right and is displayed from top to bottom.

9. Click the **Text Direction** button again. The text rotates to the right and now reads from bottom to top.

10. Notice that the buttons in the Alignment group are altered to reflect the new text direction. Click the **Align Center** button 🖹. (The button is in the same location shown in Figure 15–16). The text is centered between the left and right and top and bottom boundaries of the cells.

11. Click in the first cell (*Recycling Rate*), and then click the **Align Center** button.

12. Select the last two columns (*2005* and *2012*), and then click the **Align Center Right** button ⊟. The text in the selected cells is aligned at the right side of the cells and centered between the top and bottom boundaries.

13. Click anywhere within the table to deselect the cells. In the Cell Size group, click the **AutoFit** button, and then click **AutoFit Contents**. Your table should look like the table shown in **Figure 15–17**.

FIGURE 15–17
Table with text rotated and aligned

Recycling Rate		2005	2012
PET	Beverage bottles	53%	
	Vegetable oil bottles	15%	
HDPE	Milk jugs	34%	
	Bleach and laundry detergent bottles	16%	

Used with permission from Microsoft Corporation

14. Save the changes and leave the document open for the next Step-by-Step.

Formatting Borders and Shading

As you worked with the Calories and Recycling Rate tables you created in this lesson, the lines you saw on the screen were actually borders. By default, Word formats a ½-point single-line border around all cells in a table. Generally, the default border is appropriate for the tables you create. However, there may be occasions when you want to customize the border and add shading or color to some of the table cells. You may even want to remove the border completely. When you remove the borders from table cells, the boundary lines for the cells still remain. These boundary lines in a table are called *gridlines*. Gridlines are used for layout purposes so you can see the cell boundaries as you work with the table. Gridlines are displayed on the screen, but they do not print.

▶ **VOCABULARY**
gridlines

Step-by-Step 15.8

2-2.1.15

1. If necessary, open the **Recycling Rate 2** file from your solution files. Save the Recycling Rate 2 document as **Recycling Rate 3**, followed by your initials.

2. If necessary, click the **Table Tools Layout** tab. In the Table group, confirm that the View Gridlines feature is enabled. The feature is enabled when the button has an orange highlight.

3. Select all the **cells** in the table. Then click the **Table Tools Design** tab. In the Table Styles group, click the **Borders** button arrow ⊞ ▾, and then click **No Border**.

4. Click in the table to deselect the cells. Your document should now show gridlines that indicate the cell boundaries, as shown in **Figure 15–18**. If you do not see any broken blue lines in your table, click the **Table Tools Layout** tab, and click the **View Table Gridlines** button.

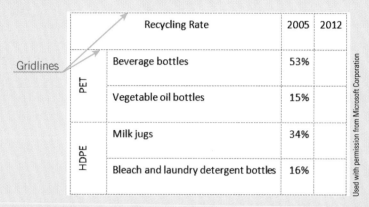

FIGURE 15–18
Table gridlines

5. Select the **first row** in the table. On the Table Tools Design tab, in the Table Styles group, click the **Shading** button arrow. Under Theme Colors, in the second row, select the **Olive Green, Accent 3, Lighter 80%** color. The shading is applied to the selected cells.

6. Select the cells containing *PET* and *HDPE*. Press the **Repeat** button on the Quick Access Toolbar to repeat the format.

7. Select all the cells in the table. In the Draw Borders group, click the **Line Weight** button arrow ½ pt ——— ▾, and then click **¾ pt**. You must change the line weight setting before applying the border.

8. Click the **Pen Color** button arrow. Under Theme Colors, in the first row, select the **Olive Green, Accent 3** color. You must also choose the border color before applying the border.

9. Click the **Borders** button arrow, and then click **All Borders**. The ¾-pt dark olive green border line is applied to all selected cells.

10. Click in the table to deselect the cells. Select all the cells in the first row. Click the **Line Weight** button arrow, and then click **1½ pt**.

11. Position the mouse pointer over the Borders button. The ScreenTip should show All Borders because that was the last border format applied. The pen color is also still set for dark green. Click the **Borders** button. The 1½-pt dark olive green border is applied to all borders of the selected cells.

12. Select the cells containing *PET* and *HDPE*. Repeat the border format.

13. Click in the table to deselect the table cells. Save the changes, and close the document.

14. If you were to open a new document now and click one of the Border button options, the border style, weight, and pen color would be the same as the last border that was applied. Exit the Word application, and then launch the application again. The Border settings are now restored to the default settings.

Applying Table Styles

As you can see, formatting borders and shading can take time. That is why Word provides several table designs that enable you to apply multiple table formats with a single click. These styles are referred to as built-in styles, and the styles include formats for fonts, shading, and borders.

Step-by-Step 15.9

2-2.1.15

1. Open the **Calories 5** file from your solution files. Save the Calories 5 document as **Calories 6**, followed by your initials.

2. Select the first two rows. On the Home tab, in the Paragraph group, click the **Center** button.

3. With the insertion point positioned anywhere in the table, click the **Table Tools Layout** tab, click the **AutoFit** button, and then click **AutoFit Contents**.

4. Click and hold the insertion point in the cell with the data *192*. Drag the mouse down to the last cell in the column and then across to the last cell in the table (*168*). In the Alignment group, click the **Align Top Right** button. Deselect the cells.

5. Click the **Table Tools Design** tab. In the Table Styles group, position the mouse pointer over the second style button, Light Shading (a ScreenTip will show the name *Light Shading*). As the mouse pointer hovers over the style button, the new style's Live Preview is displayed in the document window as shown in **Figure 15–19**.

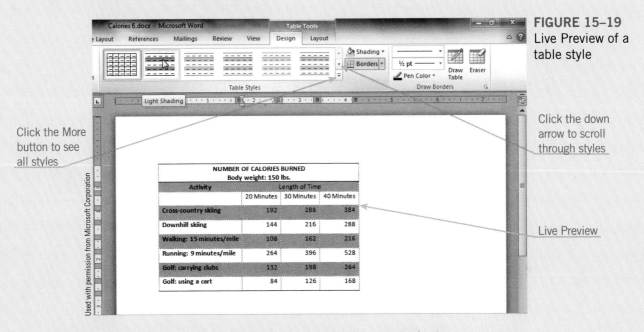

Click the More button to see all styles

Click the down arrow to scroll through styles

Live Preview

Used with permission from Microsoft Corporation

FIGURE 15–19
Live Preview of a table style

QUICK TIP

You can also use the Click-Shift-Click shortcut to select text. Click in the cell with the data *192*, then press and hold Shift and click in the cell with the data *168*.

6. Move the mouse pointer over each of the other styles that appear in the Table Styles group to see the Live Preview of each style.

7. In the Table Styles group, click the **down arrow** to show the next set of styles. Then click the **More** button to show all the built-in styles.

8. Several rows of buttons are displayed, as shown in **Figure 15–20**. In the second row of styles, click the **Light List – Accent 2** table style. The borders and shading are automatically applied to the table.

FIGURE 15–20
Built-in table styles

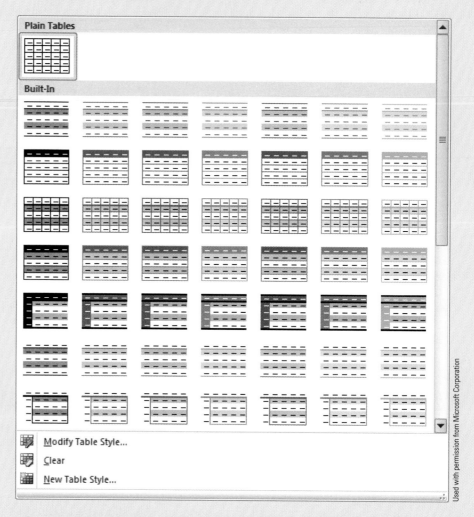

Used with permission from Microsoft Corporation

9. Note that gridlines are displayed for the column boundaries inside the table. The applied built-in table style did not include the column borders. Click the **File** tab, and then click **Print**. In the Preview pane, you can see that the gridlines will not print. Click the **Home** tab to close Backstage view.

10. Select the column headings **Length of Time**, **20 Minutes**, **30 Minutes**, and **40 Minutes**. Apply the bold format. (*Hint*: Click the Bold button on the Mini toolbar.)

11. Save the changes, and close the document.

Using Quick Tables

Word also provides built-in tables, called *Quick Tables*, that include a table grid with sample data and table formats. To save time creating a table, you insert a Quick Table in a document and then you replace the sample data with your own data. You can modify the table structure and styles as needed.

Editing text in the cells of a table is a similar process to entering text in a document. You can enter and delete text, or select and replace the text. The Cut, Copy, and Paste commands are available, and you can also use drag-and-drop editing.

When you show nonprinting characters, you can see that every row ends with a marker. When copying, cutting and pasting, or moving entire rows, these end-of-row markers must be included in the selection for the entire row to be selected.

Step-by-Step 15.10

1. Create a new blank document. Save the document as **Members 1**, followed by your initials.

2. Click the **Insert** tab. In the Tables group, click the **Table** button and then, at the bottom of the menu below the grid, point to **Quick Tables**. The submenu shown in **Figure 15–21** is displayed.

2-2.1.13
2-2.1.15

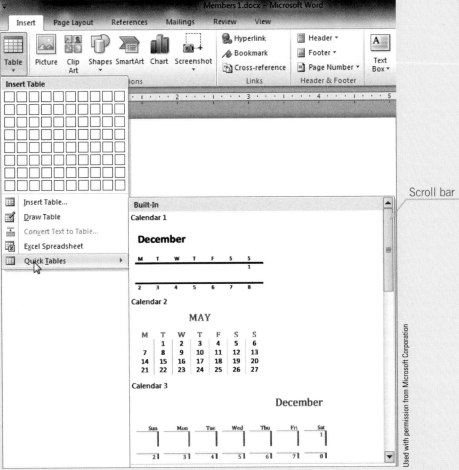

FIGURE 15–21
Built-in menu for Quick Tables

Used with permission from Microsoft Corporation

3. Scroll down and click the **Matrix** Quick Table. A table with sample data is inserted in the document. Select all the rows in the table. Press **Delete** to remove all the text from the cells.

4. Click the **Table Tools Layout** tab. Select the **two columns** at the right side of the table. In the Rows & Columns group, click the **Delete** button, and then click **Delete Columns**.

5. Enter the data shown in **Figure 15–22** to complete the table. You will need to add two new rows at the bottom of the table grid.

FIGURE 15–22
Table content for Step 6

Member Name	# Members in Family	Member #	# Years of Membership
Chang	5	108119	5
Miller	3	107459	7
McGinnis	3	108450	6
Alexander	4	108176	6
Torres	6	107438	7
Castillo	7	107491	7
Rivera	2	108100	6

Used with permission from Microsoft Corporation

6. Select all the cells in the table, click the **Home** tab, and then change the font to **Arial**.

7. Click the **Table Tools Layout** tab. Select the **first column**. In the Alignment group, click the **Align Bottom Left** button ▤. Select the **second**, **third**, and **fourth columns**, and then click the **Align Bottom Center** ▤ button. Deselect the cells.

8. In the last row of the table (*Rivera*), in the second column, select the number **2**, and then type **3**.

9. In the last row of the table, in the fourth column, select the number **6**. Right-click the selection, and then in the shortcut menu click **Copy**. In the second row, (*Chang*), in the fourth column, select the number **5**. Right-click the selection, and then in the shortcut menu, under Paste Options, click the **Keep Source Formatting** 🖊 button.

10. Drag across all the cells in the last row to select all the text. Click the **Home** tab, and then in the Clipboard group click the **Cut** button. Note the cell contents are stored on the Clipboard, but the cell boundaries for the row are still displayed, because you selected and deleted only the cell contents. Click the **Undo** button.

11. In the Paragraph group, click the **Show/Hide ¶** button to toggle on the display of nonprinting characters as shown in **Figure 15–23**.

FIGURE 15–23
Nonprinting characters in a table

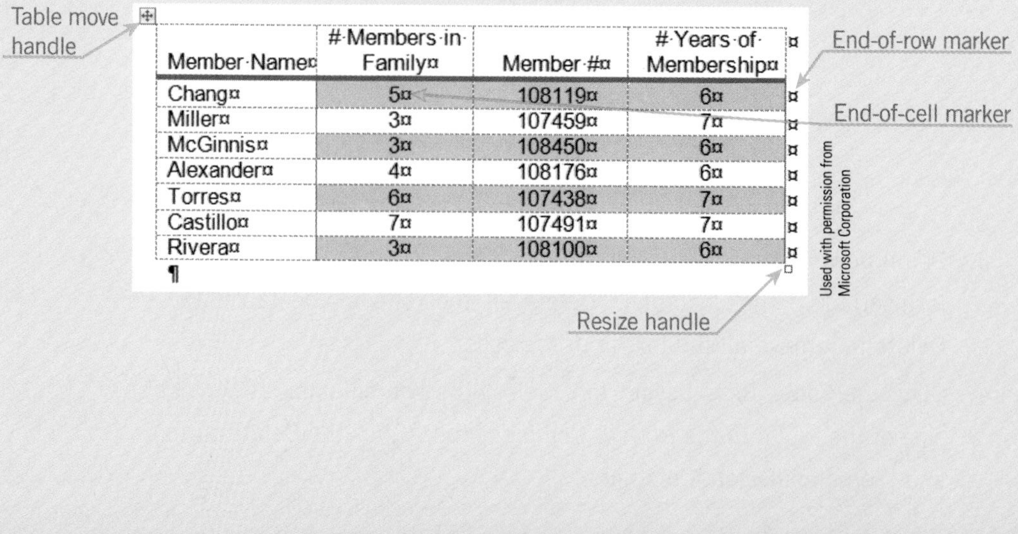

Member·Name¤	#·Members·in Family¤	Member·#¤	#·Years·of Membership¤	¤
Chang¤	5¤	108119¤	6¤	¤
Miller¤	3¤	107459¤	7¤	¤
McGinnis¤	3¤	108450¤	6¤	¤
Alexander¤	4¤	108176¤	6¤	¤
Torres¤	6¤	107438¤	7¤	¤
Castillo¤	7¤	107491¤	7¤	¤
Rivera¤	3¤	108100¤	6¤	¤

¶

Table move handle

End-of-row marker

End-of-cell marker

Resize handle

Used with permission from Microsoft Corporation

12. Position the mouse pointer to the left of the last row in the table (*Rivera*), and then click to select the entire row. The end-of-row marker is included in the selection. Cut the selected content to the Clipboard to remove the entire row. Position the insertion point in the first cell in the first row (*Member Name*). Right-click to show the shortcut menu. Under Paste Options, click the **Merge Table** button ⬚. The *Rivera* row is inserted above the *Chang* row.

13. Select the entire last row (*Castillo*). Then drag and drop the selected cells and position the insertion point to the first cell in the *Miller* row. When you release the mouse button, the *Castillo* row will be displayed above the *Miller* row. Deselect the cells.

14. Save the changes, and leave the document open for the next Step-by-Step.

Aligning and Resizing Tables on the Document Page

To align a table on the page horizontally, you must first select the entire table. Once the entire table is selected, you can format the alignment in the same way you align text paragraphs.

You may have noticed a marker that sometimes appears at the upper-left corner of a table. This marker is the table move handle, and you can drag the marker to reposition the table on the page. You can also use the table move handle to select the entire table.

The resize handle is another marker that sometimes appears in the lower-right corner of a table, and when you drag this marker, you can resize the table.

Step-by-Step 15.11

1. If necessary, open the **Members 1** file from your solution files. Save the Members 1 document as **Members 2**, followed by your initials.

2. With the insertion point positioned anywhere within the table, click the **Table Tools Layout** tab.

3. Move the mouse pointer over the table cells to display the table move handle ⊞ at the upper-left corner of the table as shown in Figure 15–23.

4. Click and drag the table move handle to reposition the table in the lower-right corner of the screen.

5. Move the mouse pointer over the cells again to show the table move handle, and then click the table move handle to select the entire table. Notice the end-of-row markers are also selected.

6. Click the **Home** tab. In the Paragraph group, click the **Center** button. The table is centered horizontally. Deselect the table.

2-2.1.15

7. Point to the lower-right corner of the table. When the resize handle (the small square at the lower-right corner of the table) appears, as shown in Figure 15–23, position the mouse pointer over the handle. The pointer will change to a double-headed arrow. Drag the handle about one inch to the right to increase the width of the table. The table is still centered horizontally.

8. Click the **Table Tools Layout** tab. In the Table group, click the **Properties** button. The Table Properties dialog box shown in **Figure 15–24** opens. Confirm that under Text wrapping, the **Around** option is enabled. You can also select alignment settings in this dialog box.

FIGURE 15–24
Table Properties dialog box

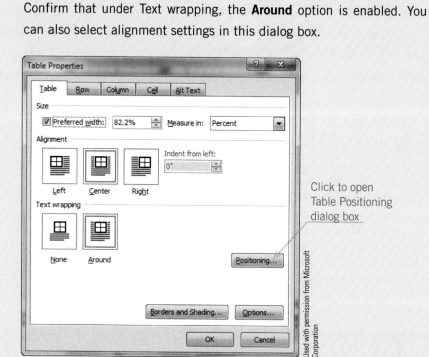

9. In the dialog box, click **Positioning** to open the Table Positioning dialog box shown in **Figure 15–25**. Your settings for Vertical position may differ.

FIGURE 15–25
Table Positioning dialog box

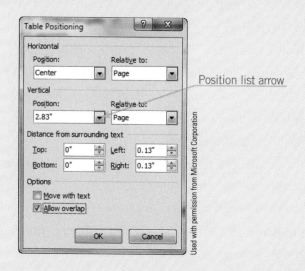

10. Under Vertical, click the **Position** list arrow and then click **Center**. Click **OK**, then click **OK** again to close the Table Properties dialog box.

11. Click the **File** tab, and then click **Print** to preview the document. The table is centered both horizontally and vertically on the page. Click the **File** tab to close Backstage view.

12. Save the changes, and leave the document open for the next Step-by-Step.

Sorting Data in a Table

Tables organize material to make it easier to read, and you have discovered how formatting the table and the characters in the table can add clarity to the information. You can also sort the information in a table on different search criteria to organize the table contents to change the emphasis of the data.

Sorting data in *ascending order* rearranges it into alphabetical order from *A* to *Z*, or numerical order from lowest number to highest number. Sorting data in *descending order* rearranges the data in alphabetical order from *Z* to *A*, or numerical order from highest number to lowest number.

Using default settings, header rows are not included when the data is sorted.

2-2.1.16

▶ **VOCABULARY**
ascending order
descending order

Step-by-Step 15.12

1. If necessary, open the **Members 2** file from your solution files. Save the Members 2 document as **Members 3**, followed by your initials.

2. Note the information in the second row for the *Rivera* member: (3 members in the family, member # 108100, and 6 years of membership).

3. Position the insertion point anywhere in the table, and if necessary click the **Table Tools Layout** tab.

2-2.1.15

4. In the Data group shown in **Figure 15–26**, click the **Sort** button. The Sort dialog box shown in **Figure 15–27** opens.

FIGURE 15–26
Data group on the Table Tools
Layout tab

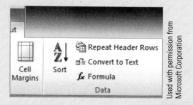

FIGURE 15–27
Sort dialog box

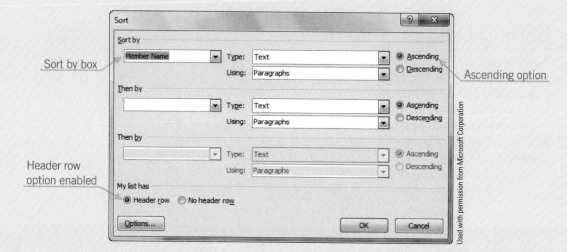

5. Confirm that the Sort settings on your screen match those shown in Figure 15–27. At the bottom of the dialog box, under My list has, the Header row option is enabled. When this option is enabled, column headings are not included in the sort.

6. Click **OK**. The entries in the first column of the table are now displayed sorted in ascending alphabetical order. The related data in the other columns is moved with the member names.

7. Click the **Sort** button again. In the Sort by text box, click the **Member Name** list arrow, and then click **Member #**. The Type text box changes to *Number*.

8. To the right, in the Sort by group, click the **Descending** option, and then click **OK**. The table rows are now arranged so the numbers in the Member # column are in order from the highest number to the lowest number, and the related data in the other columns is moved with the member #.

9. Save the changes, and close the document.

Converting Text to a Table and a Table to Text

Assume that you have already created a multicolumn list using tab settings. You decide that you want to organize the data in a table because it will be easier to format. In Word, it is not necessary to enter all the data again. Word can quickly convert text separated by paragraph markers, commas, tabs, or other characters into a table with cells.

When converting text to a table, Word determines the number of columns needed based on paragraph markers, tabs, or commas, or other characters in the text. Word also provides a command to convert a table to text. When converting a table to text, Word inserts paragraph markers, tabs, commas, or other characters to indicate the column breaks, and you can choose which symbols or characters to use to indicate the column breaks.

Step-by-Step 15.13

1. Open the **Scores** file from the drive and folder where your Data Files folder is stored. Save the Scores document as **Revised Scores 1**, followed by your initials.

2-2.1.13

2. If necessary, show the nonprinting characters. Note that each line includes tab symbols, which organize the data into three columns.

3. Select all the lines of text.

4. Click the **Insert** tab. Click the **Table** button, and then click **Convert Text to Table**. The Convert Text to Table dialog box shown in **Figure 15–28** opens.

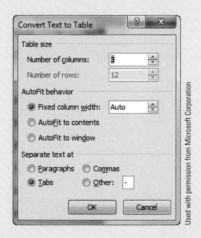

FIGURE 15–28
Convert Text to Table dialog box

5. Under Table size, the number of columns is already set to 3. Under AutoFit behavior, enable the option **AutoFit to contents**. Under Separate text at, make sure the **Tabs** option is enabled.

6. Click **OK**. Click anywhere in the window to deselect the text so you can see the revised content. The selected data is now formatted in table cells.

7. Save the changes to the document.

8. Save the document as **Revised Scores 2**, followed by your initials.

9. With the insertion point positioned anywhere within the table, click the **table move handle** to select the entire table.

10. Click the **Table Tools Layout** tab. In the Data group, click the **Convert to Text** button. The Convert Table to Text dialog box shown in **Figure 15–29** opens. A hyphen, or another character, may be displayed in the Other box.

FIGURE 15–29
Convert Table to Text dialog box

11. Enable the option **Other**. The insertion point is positioned in the Other box, and if a hyphen or other character is displayed in the Other box it will be selected. Press **Shift+8** to replace the hyphen with an asterisk (*). Click **OK**. The columns of text are now separated with an asterisk instead of a tab character.

12. Save the changes, and close the document.

NET BUSINESS

Internet Fraud

Internet fraud refers to any type of scam or hoax that uses one or more components of the Internet, such as e-mail, blogs, or Web sites. The most common types of Internet fraud are auction and retail schemes, business opportunities and work-at-home schemes, identity theft, investment schemes, and credit or debit card fraud. Internet fraud is a federal crime. If you think you have been the victim of Internet fraud, you can file a complaint online at the FBI Web site, *www.fbi.gov*.

White-collar crime refers to a full range of frauds committed by business and government professionals, and Internet fraud is one of the white-collar crimes that the FBI investigates. The Internet Crime Complaint Center (or IC3) is a partnership of the FBI and the National White Collar Crime Center.

SUMMARY

In this lesson, you learned:

- The table feature in Word enables you to organize and arrange text and numbers easily.

- To change the layout of information after you create a table, you can insert and delete rows and columns.

- The AutoFit feature automatically adjusts the width of a column based on the contents of the cells in a column.

- The Draw Table tool and the Eraser tool are especially useful when you need to create a complex table.

- You can format text alignment in table cells the same way you apply those formats in other Word documents.

- Borders and shading greatly enhance the appearance of a table and often make the table easier to read. Word provides several built-in styles to make it fast and easy to apply borders and shading to a table.

- Word provides Quick Tables that are already formatted and contain sample data, so you can quickly create a table.

- You can copy, cut, paste, and move contents within a table.

- You can use the Sort feature to reorganize the table contents to emphasize data in different ways.

- Word can convert text to a table or vice versa.

■ LESSON REVIEW

TRUE / FALSE

Circle T if the statement is true or F if the statement is false.

T   F   **1.**   In a table, rows go down and columns go across.

T   F   **2.**   When you select cells and use Delete to remove content, only the cell contents are removed and the table cell boundaries remain.

T   F   **3.**   Word can create a table from text in which data is separated by paragraph markers, tabs, or commas.

T   F   **4.**   If you do not hide the gridlines in a table, the gridlines will appear in the printed document.

T   F   **5.**   When you remove the boundary between two cells, you are merging the cells.

T   F   **6.**   When a table is first inserted in a document, the height of each row is the same.

T   F   **7.**   When working with a Quick Table, you can replace the sample data, but you cannot change the table structure or the table styles.

T   F   **8.**   To edit text in a table, you can use the Cut, Copy, and Paste commands, and you can also use drag-and-drop editing.

T   F   **9.**   When converting text to a table, Word automatically estimates the number of columns required.

T   F   **10.**   To insert a new row at the end of the table, you can position the insertion point in the last table cell and press Enter.

MULTIPLE CHOICE

Select the best response for the following statements.

1. The _____ option adds extra space to table columns so the table fills the width of the page.

   A.   AutoWidth Column   C.   AutoSize Window

   B.   AutoFit Contents   D.   AutoFit Window

2. When using the mouse to draw the table grid on the screen, the document must be _____.

   A.   in Draft view   C.   in Print Layout view

   B.   at the zoom setting of 100%   D.   in Print Preview

3. If you have already entered the data in a table, you can quickly add predesigned borders and shading by _____.

   A.   using the Table Design command   C.   using the Quick Table formats command

   B.   applying a table style   D.   using the AutoFormat feature

4. Converting one cell into multiple cells is called _____ cells.

   A. splitting   C. combining

   B. merging   D. grouping

5. Use the _____ tool to add cell boundaries.

   A. Remove Border   C. Draw Table

   B. Table   D. Cell Margins

FILL IN THE BLANK

Complete the following sentences by writing the correct word or words in the blanks provided.

1. To reposition a table on the page, you can drag the _____.

2. You can use the _____ tool to remove cell boundaries from a table.

3. The first row in a table or data source with the column headings is referred to as the _____.

4. Sorting text in _____ order arranges numbers from highest to lowest.

5. To resize a table, you can drag the _____.

WRITTEN QUESTIONS

Write a brief answer to the following questions.

1. How do you delete a row from a table?

2. How do borders and shading make a table easier to read?

3. Why might you want to merge cells horizontally?

4. What is the purpose of gridlines?

5. What is the difference between a built-in table style and a Quick Table?

■ PROJECTS

PROJECT 15–1

1. Open the **Population** file from the drive and folder where your Data Files folder is stored. Save the Population document as **Revised Population**, followed by your initials.

    2-2.1.13
    2-2.1.14
    2-2.1.15

2. Position the insertion point at the end of the document, and create a table grid for a 3×6 table (3 columns and 6 rows).

3. Complete the table by entering the data shown in **Figure 15–30**.

	2011	2012
18-24	30,287	28,513
25-34	52,697	44,207
45-54	27,157	40,347
55-64	42,821	50,914
65+	33,640	39,048

Used with permission from Microsoft Corporation

FIGURE 15–30   Table content for Step 3

4. You realize you left out the data for the 35–44 age group. Insert a row in the proper location, and type the following data:

    35–44   23,864   25,890

5. It would be helpful to see the percent change in population. Add a column to the right of the 2012 column, and type the column heading **% Change** in the first row of the new column. Insert the following information in the cells of the new column:

    –5.9
    –16.1
    +8.5
    +48.6
    +18.9
    +16.1

6. Insert a new row above the first row of the table, and then merge all cells in the new row. Type the table title **Population by Age**. Center and bold the contents in the first two rows of the table.

7. In the first cell of the second row, type the column heading **Age**.

8. Automatically adjust the column widths to the content.

9. Select the first two rows, and apply the **Align Center** format. Then select all the data in rows 3 through 8, and apply the **Align Center Left** format.

10. The data in the *% Change* column would look better if the decimal points were aligned. Right-align the numbers (but not the column heading) in this column by applying the **Align Center Right** format.

11. Shade alternate rows of the data beginning with the third row (*18–24*), using a shading color of your choice.

12. Center the table horizontally on the page.

13. Save the changes, and close the document.

PROJECT 15–2

1. Open the file **Hurricane History** from the drive and folder where your Data Files folder is stored. Save the Hurricane History document as **Revised Hurricane History**, followed by your initials.

    2-2.1.13
    2-2.1.14
    2-2.1.15

2. Select only the tabbed data (not the blank line or the source line), and convert the text to a table. Accept the suggested number of columns, select **AutoFit to contents**, and separate the text at tabs.

3. Insert a new row at the top of the table, and then merge all cells in the new row. Type the title **Costliest U.S. Hurricanes**, press **Enter**, and then type **($ in Billions)**.

4. Center the text in the new heading you just entered in the first row by applying the **Align Center** format.

5. Center the data in the Category column by applying the **Align Center** format, and right-align the data in the Damage column by applying the **Align Center Right** format.

6. The data for *Hurricane Andrew* is incorrect. Change the year for Andrew to **1992**.

7. The data in the table is currently arranged in ascending order according to the Year column. Select all the cells with numbers in the Damage column, and sort the data for Column 4 so the storms are listed in order, with the most expensive storm first.

8. You decide the first 10 entries in the table give enough information about the destructive power of hurricanes. Delete the last five rows in the table.

9. Apply a table style that will enhance the table and make it easier to read. If necessary, modify the table style to emphasize all the column headings.

10. Save the changes, and close the document.

PROJECT 15–3

1. Create a new blank document. Save the document as **Order Form**, followed by your initials.

2. Use the Draw Table tool (and the Eraser tool, if necessary) to create the table shown in **Figure 15–31**. (*Hint*: Change the zoom to 50% so you can view most of the page.) The row height should be approximately ½ inch.

3. After completing the grid and entering the text, automatically format the table to fit the window.

4. Select all the cells in the first column, set the text direction as shown, and center all the text vertically and horizontally using the **Align Center** option. Select all remaining cells, and center

all text vertically in the table cells using the **Align Center Left** option.

2-2.1.13
2-2.1.14
2-2.1.15

5. Select the entire table, and set the row height at **0.6"**. If a prompt appears regarding a break between pages, click **OK**.

6. Enhance the appearance of the table by adding or removing borders, adding shading, formatting text, using bold and/or italic, and changing the font size and/or color.

7. Position the table both horizontally and vertically on the page.

8. Save the changes, and close the document.

Customer	Name	
	Address	
	City, State, ZIP	
	Phone	

Clothing	Item #	Color	Size	Qty.	Price	Total

Accessories						

| Thank you for shopping with us! | | | | | TOTAL | |

FIGURE 15–31   Table grid and content for Step 2

PROJECT 15–4

1. Create a new blank document. Save the document as **Workshop Agenda**, followed by your initials.

2. Insert the Matrix Quick Table. Edit the columns and rows, and replace the sample data to create a table that matches the table shown in **Figure 15–32**.

3. Select all the cells, and change the font to **Arial**. Select the column headings, and apply the bold format.

4. Set the page layout to landscape orientation.

5. Select the entire table, and AutoFit the column widths for content. Then with all the table cells selected, use the AutoFit feature to make the table automatically fit the window.

   2-2.1.13
   2-2.1.14
   2-2.1.15

6. Align the text in all cells, except the headings, using the **Align Center Left** format.

7. Align all the text in the header row using the **Align Center** format.

8. Save the changes, and close the document.

Session	Time	Topic	Speaker	Room
1	8:30 a.m. – 9: 45 a.m.	Regulatory Framework	John Preston	Indian
2	10:00 a.m. – 11:45 a.m.	Fact or Fiction?	Jo Ricci	Atlantic
3	1:30 p.m. – 2:45 p.m.	Techniques for Data Collection	Pat Heinreiter	Pacific
4	3:00 p.m. – 4:45 p.m.	Moving Forward	Eli Arnold	Arctic

Used with permission from Microsoft Corporation

FIGURE 15–32   Table content for Step 2

TEAMWORK PROJECT

If you completed Project 15–2, you created a table to organize information about costly hurricanes because of property damage. The data shown in the Hurricane History table was compiled by the National Oceanic and Atmospheric Administration and is current only through 2006. You have probably heard about several powerful and costly hurricanes in the United States. With a partner, find data to update the table with more recent statistics.

1. Create a list of the years from 2006 to the last complete hurricane season (hurricane season begins in June and ends in November, so if you are working on this project before the end of November, do not include the current year in your list).

2. Split the years with your partner so you each have half of them to research.

3. Using Web search tools or other research tools, try to locate a summary of hurricane damage for each year.

4. Open the **Revised Hurricane History** file from your solution files, and save the document as **TP 15-1**, followed by your initials.

   2-2.1.13
   2-2.1.15

5. If any of the years you research total more dollar damage than the hurricanes already listed in the Revised Hurricane History table, insert new rows to add the data you have found.

6. When you have compiled the data, experiment with sorting the rows using different criteria and applying different formats to the header row, borders, cells, and text.

7. With your partner, decide which format presents the data the way you prefer, and then add your names and the current date to the bottom of the document page.

8. Save the changes to the document, and then close the document.

■ CRITICAL THINKING

CRITICAL THINKING 15–1

2-2.1.13
2-2.1.16

The owner of the stable where you ride horses has been complaining about the comings and goings of her part-time staff and unpaid helpers (of whom you are one). She would like a way to keep track of names, phone numbers, what days and hours each helper is scheduled, and hourly pay (if any).

1. Create a new Word document, and save the document as **CT 15-1**, followed by your initials.

2. Use what you have learned in this lesson to create a table layout and design that will help the stable owner organize the information about her staff. Enter several fictitious entries in the table (including yourself) to test your solution.

3. Save the changes to the document, and then close the document.

CRITICAL THINKING 15–2

2-2.1.14
2-2.1.16

In this lesson you learned that the Draw Table and Eraser tools are useful for creating complex table grids. Explore textbooks, journals, magazines, and newspapers to find examples of custom table layouts used to present data. Share these samples with your class, and discuss how drawing a table grid is useful for creating table layouts.

■ ONLINE DISCOVERY

ONLINE DISCOVERY 15–1

2-2.1.15
2-2.1.16

In this lesson, you learned to use tables to organize data in Word. Did you realize that tables are also used to organize Web page content? Open several different Web pages, and identify the table grid used for organizing the content on each page. Be sure to include all Web page elements, such as the Web page title at the top and the menu of links that often appear at the left. You will see that sometimes table border lines are used to enhance the appearance of the page, but in many cases, the table structure is not obvious in the Web page design. (*Hint*: Sometimes selecting all the content on the Web page will help identify the table structure.)

■ JOB SKILLS

JOB SKILLS 15–1

2-2.1.16

If you have ever created a resume, you know how difficult it can be to fit all your work history, educational information, and accomplishments on one page in an appealing format. Have you ever considered using a table grid to organize your information?

1. Create a new Word document, and save the document as **JS 15-1**, followed by your initials.

2. Write a brief paragraph explaining how using a table grid can help you organize the pertinent data for a resume.

3. Save the changes to the document, and then close the document.

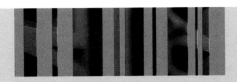

LESSON 16

Enhancing Documents

■ OBJECTIVES

Upon completion of this lesson, you should be able to:

- Create a new document based on a document template.
- Apply and modify styles and create new styles.
- Use built-in building blocks for frequently used text and document parts.
- Insert fields to display the date and time.
- Insert footnotes and endnotes.
- Create and edit hyperlinks.
- Insert symbols and special characters.
- Create custom building blocks.

■ DATA FILES

To complete this lesson, you will need these data files:

Agreement.docx

Debate.docx

Histories.docx

McCabe.docx

Upcoming Events.docx

■ WORDS TO KNOW

blog

boilerplate text

building blocks

character styles

document template

endnotes

fields

footer

footnotes

global template

header

linked styles

Normal template (Normal.dotm)

paragraph styles

placeholder text

style

template

When developing a document, you must keep in mind its purpose and the needs of the reader. By using appropriate design elements, you can publish a professional-looking, effective document. Word provides a number of features to help you easily apply formats to enhance the appearance of the document.

Working with Document Templates

Every Microsoft Word document is based on a **template**, a file that affects the basic structure of a document and contains document settings such as fonts, line spacing, margins, and page layout. Using templates increases the speed and efficiency of your work since you do not need to spend time formatting page layouts and font formats. Templates also help you maintain consistency in the documents you create.

Word has two types of templates. A **document template** contains document settings, content, and formats that are available only to documents based on that template. A **global template** contains document settings that are available to all documents.

Word's default global template, the **Normal template**, is the file Normal.dotm. When you open a new blank document, by default the Normal template provides predefined formats that are already part of the document, such as default settings that affect the page layout, margin settings, paragraph spacing, and font styles. Of course, as you work with a document you often change those default settings.

Create a New Document Based on a Document Template

Creating documents such as fax cover sheets, resumes, and invoices can be time-consuming tasks. Fortunately, Word has predesigned document templates for almost any purpose you can imagine. Depending on your Word installation, many types of document templates may be available to you. Some of the document templates are already installed on your computer and hundreds more are available at the Microsoft Web site Office.com.

Document templates are formatted for a specific purpose, and many of them already contain **boilerplate text**, content that you frequently use in a document for that purpose. For example, if you want to create a fax cover sheet, you can select a fax document template and create a new document based on the template. When the new document opens, the fax form layout is already created, and the document contains boilerplate text such as the sender's company name and address.

Document templates often include **fields** that indicate a location in the document to enter variable data such as the date. **Placeholder text** is displayed in the field and provides guidance for adding text or data to the field. When you click the placeholder text, all the placeholder text is selected, and as you type, the text or data you enter replaces the placeholder text. The field includes codes that automatically format the text or data you enter. Some fields provide a list arrow, and when you click the arrow you can select field content from a predefined list.

Depending on the fields used in the document template, your name or initials may automatically be added to the document. If your name or initials are incorrect, you can enter new text. You can also edit the boilerplate text in the document template; if you choose not to enter text or data into a field, you can delete the placeholder text so it no longer appears in the document. You can easily save a document as a new document template, and you can create a new document based on an existing document.

◗ ABOVE AND BEYOND

To run Word, you must have a Normal template. If the Normal template is deleted, Word will create a new one using the factory defaults.

◗ QUICK TIP

The user name or initials automatically added to a document template are set in Word Options. To change these settings, click the File tab, click Options, and then if necessary, in the left pane click General. If you are using a classroom computer, do not change the Word Options settings without permission.

Step-by-Step 16.1

2-1.2.1
2-1.2.4

1. Launch **Microsoft Word 2010**. Click the **File** tab, and then click **New**. Thumbnails for several templates, similar to those shown in **Figure 16–1**, are displayed in the center pane. Templates already installed are listed under Available Templates. There are several more templates listed under Office.com Templates, but you must be connected to the Internet to download those templates.

Installed templates

Templates that can be downloaded from Office.com

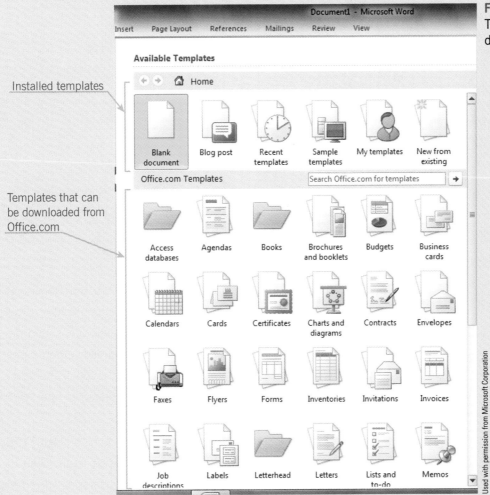

FIGURE 16–1
Thumbnails for available document templates

Used with permission from Microsoft Corporation

2. Under Available Templates, click the **Sample templates** icon. Several thumbnails are displayed. Scroll down to the bottom and select the **Urban Fax** thumbnail. A preview of the document template is displayed in the preview pane as shown in **Figure 16–2**.

FIGURE 16–2
Preview of Urban
Fax document
template

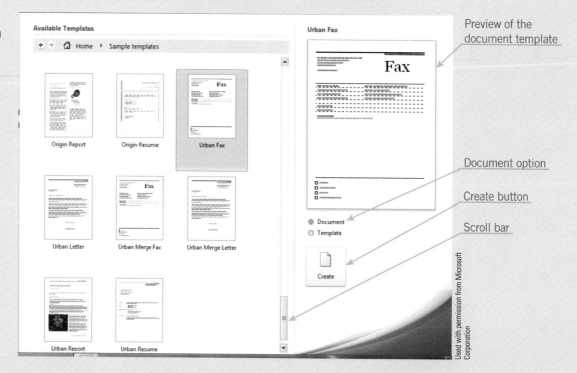

3. Under the preview of the fax cover sheet, make sure the **Document** option is selected. Then click the **Create** button to create a new document based on the document template. A new document opens, and the boilerplate text and fields with placeholder text are already entered in a table format. A company name may be displayed at the top of the form. Also, the FROM field may display the user name stored in the Word Options settings.

4. In the upper-left corner of the form, click the placeholder text **TYPE THE SENDER COMPANY NAME**. (The placeholder text is enclosed in brackets.) When the field is selected, a field tab appears, as shown in **Figure 16–3**. Type **vacation destinations**. The text you enter replaces the placeholder text, and the new text you enter in the field is automatically formatted with a new font style, all caps, and bold.

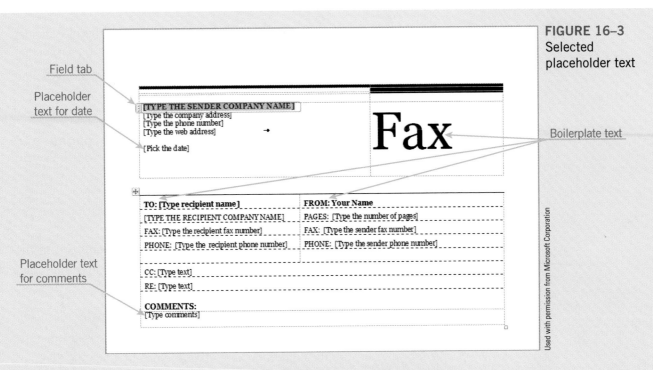

FIGURE 16–3
Selected
placeholder text

Field tab

Placeholder
text for date

Boilerplate text

Placeholder text
for comments

5. Click the placeholder text and enter the data for each of the following fields:

Company address:	**2514 White Bear Avenue North, Saint Paul, MN 55109**
Company phone number:	**612-555-1036**
Company Web address:	**www.vacationdestinations.xyz**
Sender fax number:	**612-555-1040**
Sender phone number:	**612-555-1042**

6. Click the **[Pick the date]** placeholder text. This placeholder also displays a list arrow. Click the **list arrow** to display a calendar similar to the one shown in **Figure 16–4**. Below the calendar click **Today**. The current date is displayed in the field in a predefined format, and every time you open the document the date will be updated.

FIGURE 16–4
Field with date options

7. After RE: (above the bold header COMMENTS), click the placeholder **[Type text]**, and then type **Revised Itinerary**. Then, under COMMENTS, click the placeholder **[Type comments]**, and type the following boiler-plate text:

   `Per your request, we have revised your`
   `itinerary. Please review the attached pages and`
   `let me know if you have any questions or if you`
   `want to make any additional changes.`

   `Best,`
   `Your First Name`

8. Scroll to the end of the document, position the insertion point in the check box to the left of *Please review*, press and hold **Shift**, and then press **X**.

9. The information you have added to the document can be reused in future fax cover sheets whenever a client requests a revised itinerary, so you can save the current document as a template. Click the **File** tab, click **Save As**, and then navigate to the folder where your solution files are stored. In the File name box, type **Revised Itinerary Fax**, followed by your initials. Then click the **Save as type** list arrow, and select **Word Template (*.dotx)**. Click **Save**.

10. Close the document template. Click the **File** tab, and then click **New**. Under Available Templates, click the **New from existing** icon. Navigate to the drive and folder where your solution files are stored, and select the filename **Revised Itinerary Fax.dotx**. Click **Create New**. A new document opens and shows the template boilerplate text.

11. Click the **File** tab, click **Save As**, and navigate to the folder where you save your solution files. In the File name box, type **Carmody Fax**, followed by your initials. Note that the Save as type setting displays Word Document (*.docx). Click **Save**. The file is saved as a new document. Because the template is no longer open, any changes you make will be saved to the document and not to the template.

12. In the second section of the fax form, click the **TYPE THE RECIPIENT COMPANY NAME** placeholder text. Press **Delete** to remove the place-holder text and the field. After CC:, select the placeholder text **Type text**, and then press **Delete**. The placeholder and field are deleted, but the *CC:* boilerplate text remains.

▶ QUICK TIP

You can create a new document based on any existing document. The existing document does not have to be a template file.

▶ ABOVE AND BEYOND

If you save the revised tem-plate file in the My templates folder, you can access the template when you open the New Document dialog box, and then you can create new documents based on that template.

13. Click the placeholder text, and enter the data for each of the following fields. If a user name appears in the FROM field, select the existing text and then type your own first and last name.

Recipient name: **Patrick Carmody**

Recipient fax number: **612–555–9208**

Recipient phone number: **612–555–6442**

Number of pages: **3**

14. Save the changes, and close the document.

WARNING

When exiting Word, if prompted to save changes to the Normal.dotm template, click Don't Save.

Using a Document Template to Create a Blog

A *blog* (an abbreviated version of the term "Web log") is a journal maintained by an individual or a group and posted on a Web site for public viewing and comment. Blogs are often referred to as online diaries, and they may include graphics, photos, music, and video. A typical blog Web site provides links to other Web sites and enables instant feedback or commenting, and many blog hosts offer free blog posting services. The Word New Blog Post template provides the necessary file formats so the blog entry content can be published on the Web. The advantage to posting the blog from a Word document is that you can use Word's photo-editing tools, font formats, and spelling checker.

Completing the process of posting a blog is beyond the scope of this lesson because to post a blog from Word you must have an established and registered blog account with a Microsoft-enabled blog service provider. The following Step-by-Step provides information for those who are using the Blog Post feature for the first time and need to register a blog account. Once the registration is completed, you can use the Publish Blog Post command to post entries directly from a Word document.

▶ **VOCABULARY**
blog

2-1.1.8

Step-by-Step 16.2

1. Click the **File** tab, and then click **New**. Under Available Templates, click the **Blog post** icon, and then in the right pane click the **Create** button.

2. If you have never registered a blog account, the dialog box shown in **Figure 16–5** will appear.

2-1.4.6
2-2.1.16

Used with permission from Microsoft Corporation

FIGURE 16–5
Register a Blog Account dialog box

3. Click **Register Now**. The New Blog Account dialog box shown in **Figure 16–6** opens.

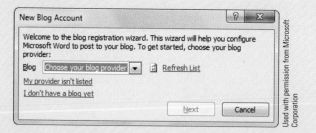

4. Click the **Blog** list arrow to show the blog provider options as shown in **Figure 16–7**.

5. Select one of the providers in the list, and then click **Next**. A new dialog box similar to the one shown in **Figure 16–8** opens.

6. If you have a blog account, you could enter the required information and click OK. Word would then connect to the blog account and a message would be displayed confirming the connection was successful. Click **Cancel** to close the confirmation box.

7. Close the Blog Post document window without saving the changes.

Working with Styles

Another way to quickly and easily change the appearance of document elements is to apply a style. A *style* is a set of formatting characteristics you can apply to characters, paragraphs, tables, and numbered and bulleted lists. When you apply a style, you apply a whole group of formats in one simple step. For example, instead of taking multiple steps to format your title as Arial, 14 point, bold, and center-aligned, you can achieve the same result in one step by applying a title style.

Using styles ensures consistency across multiple documents. Another advantage to formatting your document using styles is that when text is formatted with Word's built-in heading styles you can view, organize, and edit the document content in Outline view.

▶ **VOCABULARY**
style
character styles
paragraph styles
linked styles

Applying Styles and Modifying Style Formats

Styles are included in templates. When a template is attached to the document, you can access all the styles saved in the template. The Normal template contains a set of predefined styles that you can quickly access from the Quick Style gallery in the Styles group on the Home tab. You can apply these styles and modify them. The style changes are applied only to the current document.

The styles provided in the Normal template include character, paragraph, and linked styles. The *character styles* provide text formats such as font name, font size, font color, bold, italic, underline, borders, and shading. The *paragraph styles* provide both text formats and paragraph formats such as line spacing, text alignment, indentation, and tab stops. *Linked styles* provide either text or paragraph formats, depending on the content that is selected when the style is applied. For example, when you select a word or phrase and then apply a linked style, just the text formats of the style are applied. On the other hand, when you click in a paragraph or select an entire paragraph and then apply a linked style, both the text and paragraph formats are applied.

Step-by-Step 16.3

1. Open the **Debate** file from the drive and folder where your Data Files folder is stored. Save the Debate document as **Revised Debate 1**, followed by your initials.

2. Make sure the insertion point is positioned at the top of the document in the title *The Big Debate*. Move the mouse pointer over the styles in the Styles group on the Home tab (see **Figure 16–9**). You can see the Live Preview of the style formats in the document window. Note that in the Live Preview both character and paragraph formats are applied.

2-1.2.1
2-2.1.11

Move pointer over styles to see a Live Preview

Click More button to open the Styles gallery

Dialog box launcher

FIGURE 16–9
Styles group on the Home tab

Used with permission from Microsoft Corporation

3. In the Styles group, click the **More** button to show all the available styles in the Quick Style gallery. Click the **Title** style. The style is a paragraph style so it is applied to all the text in the paragraph where the insertion point is positioned. The font style, font size, font color, and text alignment are modified. On the Ribbon, the Title style is selected in the Styles group, indicating that the style is applied.

4. In the Styles group, click the **dialog box launcher** to open the Styles pane shown in **Figure 16–10**. If necessary, enable the **Show Preview** option to see the previews of the Styles pane. Paragraph styles are marked with a ¶ symbol. Character styles are marked with the character *a*. Linked styles are marked with ¶*a*. The styles listed in the Styles pane are the same as the styles available in the Styles group on the Home tab.

FIGURE 16–10
Styles pane

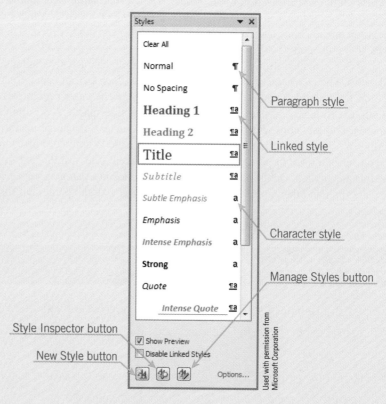

5. If necessary, drag the Styles pane to reposition it so you can use the scroll bar in the document window. In the heading *Background Information*, position the insertion point in the first word **Background**. In the Styles pane, click the **Intense Emphasis** style, which is a character style. The character formats are applied to the current word, but no paragraph formats are applied. At the top of the Styles pane, click **Clear All** to remove all styles from the current word.

QUICK TIP

If your Styles pane does not match the pane shown in Figure 16–10, at the bottom of the pane, click Options. In the Style Pane Options dialog box, make sure the Select styles to show box displays the setting Recommended.

6. With the insertion point still positioned in the *Background Information* heading, apply the **Heading 1** style. The style is a linked style so both character and paragraph formats are applied. To modify the style, select all the text in the heading and apply the **Underline** format. The modification to the style is not permanent; the style change will only apply to this occurrence in this document.

7. Apply the **Heading 2** style to the remaining headings in the document: *Differences*, *Similarities*, and *Conclusion*.

8. On the Home tab, in the Styles group, click the **Change Styles** button. Point to **Colors**, and then under *Built-In* click the **Aspect** built-in color theme. The font colors for the heading styles change, and so the previews of the styles in the Styles pane also change. The styles in the Quick Style gallery on the Ribbon also reflect the new font colors. The modification to the style is not permanent; the style change will only apply to the current document.

9. Position the insertion point at the beginning of the document. Click the **View** tab, and then in the Document Views group click the **Outline View** button. The document is displayed in Outline view, and the Ribbon adapts and displays the Outlining tab shown in **Figure 16–11**.

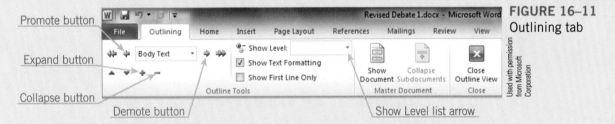

FIGURE 16–11
Outlining tab

Used with permission from Microsoft Corporation

10. On the Outlining tab, in the Outline Tools group, click the **Show Level** list arrow, and then click **Level 2**. All the body text is hidden, and all you see is the text formatted for Level 1 and Level 2 headings as shown in **Figure 16–12**. To show all the body text, click the **Show Level** list arrow, and then click **All Levels**.

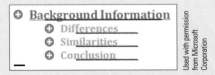

Used with permission from Microsoft Corporation

FIGURE 16–12
Level 1 and 2 headings in Outline view

11. Triple-click the Level 2 heading **Differences** to select the entire section. In the Outline Tools group, click the **Collapse** button. The selected body text is hidden. Drag and drop the heading so it is positioned before the heading *Conclusion*. In the Outline Tools group, click the **Expand** button to show the body text. When the headings are rearranged, the body text moves with the heading.

12. Click anywhere in the Level 2 heading **Similarities**. On the Outlining tab, in the Outline Tools group, click the **Demote** button 🔿 to demote the heading to a lower level (in this case Level 3).

13. Click the **Promote** button 🔹 twice to change the format to a Level 1 heading. Promote the headings **Differences** and **Conclusion** to Level 1.

14. In the Close group, click the **Close Outline View** button. Save the changes, and leave the document open for the next Step-by-Step.

Creating Styles

You can create new styles based on existing styles and formatted text. You can also create new styles using formatting commands or basing the new style on an existing style. After creating a new style, you can add the style to the Quick Style gallery so the style can be accessed on the Ribbon. After creating a new style, you can easily modify the style properties and formats.

You can save modified and new styles to a template so you can access the styles again in the future. Because you most likely share your computer with classmates, in this lesson you will save styles only in the current document.

Step-by-Step 16.4

2-2.1.11

1. If necessary, open the **Revised Debate 1** file from your solution files. Save the Revised Debate 1 document as **Revised Debate 2**, followed by your initials. If necessary, show the **Styles** pane.

2. Select the Level 1 heading **Background Information**. The Heading 1 style was modified in the last Step-by-Step by adding an underline format. To save the modified style for future use, in the Styles group, click the **More** button, and then click **Save Selection as a New Quick Style**. The Create New Style from Formatting dialog box opens.

3. In the Name box, type **My Heading 1**, and then click **OK**. The new style is added to the Quick Style gallery, and it is displayed in the Styles group on the Ribbon and in the Styles pane.

4. Select the heading **Similarities**. Apply the **Italic** format, and change the font size to **16** point.

5. At the bottom of the Styles pane, hover the mouse pointer over the buttons, and click the **New Style** button 🔳. The Create New Style from Formatting dialog box opens. Enter the property settings for the new style:

   a. In the Name box, replace Style1 with **My Heading 2**.

   b. Leave the Style type and Style based on settings as is.

   c. Make sure the options **Add to Quick Style list** and **Only in this document** are enabled.

   d. When your settings match those shown in **Figure 16–13**, click **OK** to save the new style and close the dialog box.

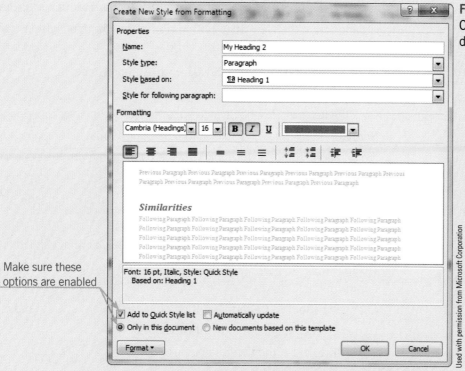

Make sure these options are enabled

FIGURE 16–13
Create New Style from Formatting dialog box

6. In the Styles group, click the **More** button, and then click **Apply Styles** to open the Apply Styles pane, shown in **Figure 16–14**. The current style, My Heading 2, is displayed in the Style Name box.

Style Name list arrow

FIGURE 16–14
Apply Styles pane

7. Leaving the Apply Styles pane open, scroll down in the document, and click anywhere in the *Differences* heading. In the Apply Styles pane, the current style *Heading 1* is displayed. Click the **Style Name** list arrow, and then click **My Heading 2**. The new style is applied to the current text.

8. Scroll down to the last heading in the document, *Conclusion*, and apply the **My Heading 2** style. Then scroll to the top of the document and apply the **My Heading 2** style to the heading *Background Information*. Close the Apply Styles pane.

9. At the top of the document, select the text **By Richard McCabe**. In the Styles pane, click the **New Style** button. Enter the property settings for the new style:

   a. In the Name box, replace *Style1* with **Author Name**, followed by your initials.

   b. Click the **list arrow** for the Style for following paragraph box, and select **Normal**. The Normal character and paragraph formats are applied to the paragraph immediately following the paragraphs with this style.

   c. In the lower-left corner of the dialog box, make sure the options **Add to Quick Style list** and **Only in this document** are enabled.

10. To define the character formats for the new style:

    a. In the lower-left corner of the dialog box, click **Format**, and then click **Font** to open the Font dialog box. If necessary, click the **Font** tab in the dialog box.

    b. Change the font to **Calibri**, and then change the font style to **Italic**.

    c. Under Effects, enable the **Small caps** option.

    d. Click **OK** to close the Font dialog box.

11. To define the paragraph formats for the new style:

    a. Click **Format**, and then click **Paragraph** to open the Paragraph dialog box. If necessary, click the **Indents and Spacing** tab in the dialog box.

    b. Under Spacing, change the Before setting to **10** and leave the After setting as is.

    c. Click **OK** twice to close both dialog boxes.

12. In the Styles pane, point to the **Author Name** style, then click the **Author Name** style list arrow. Click **Modify** to open the Modify Style dialog box.

13. In the Name box, change the style name to **My Author Heading**, followed by your initials. Click **OK**. The new style name is displayed in the Styles pane and in the Styles group, and the text in the document reflects the change in the style format.

14. Close the Styles pane. Save the changes, and leave the document open for the next Step-by-Step.

Using Building Blocks and Data Elements

▶ **VOCABULARY**
building blocks

Building blocks are built-in document parts that are already designed and formatted, enabling you to quickly create a professional-looking document. Word provides several built-in building blocks for frequently used text and document parts, such as predesigned cover pages, headers, footers, and page number formats. Not only do building blocks save you time, but they also ensure consistency in content and formats. The built-in building blocks are stored in the Quick Parts gallery. After inserting building blocks, you can customize the text or document parts, and you can add your own custom building blocks to the gallery.

Creating an effective, professional document also often requires inserting special data elements such as footnotes or endnotes, dates and times, hyperlinks, and copyright and trademark symbols. Word provides quick access to tools that simplify the tasks for adding these elements.

Inserting Page Numbers and Creating Headers and Footers

Page numbers are always helpful when your document has multiple pages. When you insert page numbers in a document, the page number is displayed in a header or a footer. A *header* is information and/or a graphic that is printed in the top margin of the page; a *footer* is information and/or a graphic that is printed in the bottom margin of the page. Your document can have a header, a footer, both, or neither. The advantage of formatting a header or footer rather than just inserting page numbers is that you can include text with the page number.

▶ **VOCABULARY**
header

footer

Step-by-Step 16.5

1. If necessary, open the **Revised Debate 2** file from your solution files. Save the Revised Debate 2 document as **Revised Debate 3**, followed by your initials. If necessary, show the nonprinting characters.

2. Click the **Insert** tab. In the Header & Footer group, shown in **Figure 16–15**, click the **Page Number** button, and then click **Format Page Numbers**. The Page Number Format dialog box opens.

2-2.1.9
2-2.1.10

FIGURE 16–15
Header & Footer group on the Insert tab

3. Under Page numbering, enable the **Start at** option. The setting should change to 1. When your settings match those shown in **Figure 16–16**, click **OK** to accept the change and close the dialog box.

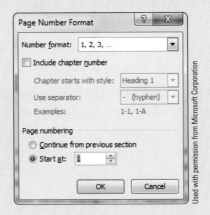

FIGURE 16–16
Page Number Format dialog box

4. Click the **Page Number** button again, and then point to **Bottom of Page**. In the submenu, scroll down through the list to view the available styles. Under Page X of Y, click the **Bold Numbers 3** page number style. If necessary, scroll down to the bottom of the first page. The document window is updated and shows a footer pane at the bottom of the page with *Page 1 of 3* aligned at the right margin.

5. Because the insertion point is positioned in the footer, the document text is dimmed, and the Ribbon adapts and displays the Header & Footer Tools Design tab shown in **Figure 16–17**. Scroll up and down through the three pages in the document. Notice that a header pane is displayed at the top of each page, and the page number is displayed in a footer pane at the bottom of each page.

FIGURE 16–17
Header & Footer group on the Header & Footer Tools Design tab

Header & Footer group

Used with permission from Microsoft Corporation

6. Scroll to the top of the second page, and click anywhere inside the header pane. In the Header & Footer group, on the left side of the Ribbon, click the **Header** button. In the submenu, scroll down, and then click the **Conservative** header style. A header with a field and a bottom line border is inserted in the header pane.

7. Click the placeholder text **[Type the document title]**. A tag labeled Title is displayed at the upper-left corner of the selected field. Type **The Big Debate**. Then click the placeholder text **[Pick the date]**, click the **list** arrow, and click tomorrow's date on the calendar.

8. In the Options group, enable the **Different First Page** check box. Double-click anywhere in the document text. Scroll through the pages. The header and footer panes are now dimmed, and you will see that the header and the footer you just created are displayed on the second and third pages but not on the first page.

9. Position the insertion point at the beginning of the document. Click the **Insert** tab, and in the Pages group at the left side of the Ribbon, click the **Cover Page** button. In the submenu, click the **Conservative** cover page style. A preformatted cover page with several data fields is inserted at the beginning of the document. The document title and date fields already display the information you inserted into the header. Prefilled data for a company name and/or an author name generated from the data in the document properties may also be displayed.

QUICK TIP

To quickly change the cover page design, position the insertion point in the current cover page, click the Cover Page button, and choose a new page design. The text you already entered in the fields is preserved and converted to the new cover page design.

10. At the top of the cover page, right-click the **Company** field, and then click **Remove Content Control**. If necessary, select any remaining text and delete it. If the placeholder was already replaced with prefilled text, you will need to select and delete the text.

11. Below the document title, right-click the **Subtitle** field and then click **Remove Content Control**. Select the name above the date field, and type **Richard McCabe**.

12. At the bottom of the cover page, below the page break code, right-click the **Abstract** field, and then click **Remove Content Control**.

13. Click the **File** tab, and then click **Print**. Scroll through the pages to preview how the pages will print.

14. Click the **Home** tab. Save the changes, and leave the document open for the next Step-by-Step.

Inserting the Date and Time

You can insert a field to show the current date and/or time. By default, the date and/or the time are updated whenever the document is reopened.

The AutoComplete feature can also make entering the current date easy and accurate. When you begin typing calendar terms, such as the month, the day of the week, or the current date, Word shows the complete term in a ScreenTip and you can select the proposed term in the ScreenTip to automatically complete the term.

Step-by-Step 16.6

1. If necessary, open the **Revised Debate 3** document from your solution files. Save the Revised Debate 3 document as **Revised Debate 4**, followed by your initials.

2-2.1.16
2-2.2.2

2. Scroll to the second page, and position the insertion point after *Posted:*.

FIGURE 16–18
Date and Time dialog box

3. Click the **Insert** tab. In the Text group, click the **Date & Time** button. The Date and Time dialog box displays the current date and time in a variety of formats. Under Available formats, click the date format showing the date and time, as shown in **Figure 16–18**. At the lower-right corner of the dialog box, if necessary, enable the **Update automatically** option. Click **OK**. The current date and time is entered as text in your document. Note the time that is currently displayed in the document.

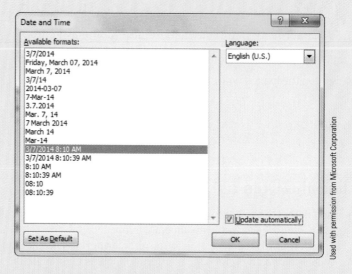

Used with permission from Microsoft Corporation

4. Save the changes, and close the document. Wait at least one minute, and then reopen the document. The time that is displayed in the document is updated.

5. Click anywhere within the date and time to show the field tag. Then double-click the three dots on the left edge of the Update tag to select the tag name and the entire field. Press **Delete**.

6. Type **Wedn**. After you type the letter *n*, the complete spelling of *Wednesday* is displayed in a ScreenTip. Press **Enter** to accept the AutoComplete entry. The full spelling of the word is inserted in the document.

7. Delete the word **Wednesday**.

8. Begin to type the current day of the week. (For example, *Frid.*) When the ScreenTip appears with a complete word, press **Enter**. Type a comma after the current day, and begin typing the current month, and a ScreenTip shows the full date for the Friday in the current week, such as *Friday, March 6, 2014*. Press **Enter** to accept the AutoComplete entry for the full date.

9. Save the changes, and leave the document open for the next Step-by-Step.

Inserting Footnotes and Endnotes

Notes are most commonly seen as references in reports. However, you can also add footnotes to documents to provide additional information or comments for the reader. **Footnotes** are inserted at the bottom of the page on which the note is referenced in the document, and **endnotes** are placed together at the end of the document. Both kinds of notes are linked to an in-text reference symbol—usually a letter or numeral in superscript.

▶ **VOCABULARY**
footnotes

endnotes

Step-by-Step 16.7

1. If necessary, open the **Revised Debate 4** file from your solution files. Save the Revised Debate 4 document as **Revised Debate 5**, followed by your initials.

2-2.2.2

2. Navigate to the heading *Background Information*. In the first line of the third paragraph below the heading, select **Builder's Depot**.

3. With the text selected, click the **References** tab, and then in the Footnotes group shown in **Figure 16–19**, click the **Insert Footnote** button. A superscript numeral *1* is inserted at the end of the selected text.

FIGURE 16–19
Footnotes group on the References tab

4. Compare your screen to **Figure 16–20**. A divider line is created at the end of the document, and the insertion point is positioned next to numeral *1* below the divider line.

Superscript numeral

Divider line

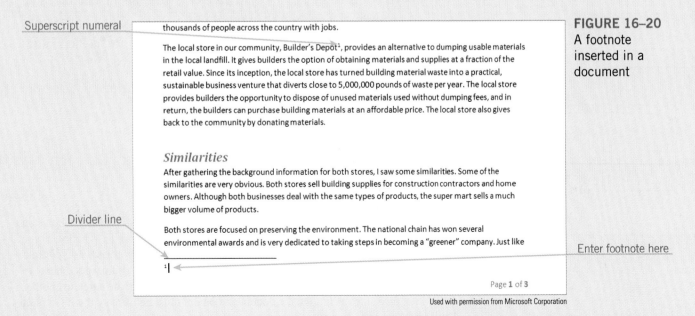

thousands of people across the country with jobs.

The local store in our community, Builder's Depot¹, provides an alternative to dumping usable materials in the local landfill. It gives builders the option of obtaining materials and supplies at a fraction of the retail value. Since its inception, the local store has turned building material waste into a practical, sustainable business venture that diverts close to 5,000,000 pounds of waste per year. The local store provides builders the opportunity to dispose of unused materials used without dumping fees, and in return, the builders can purchase building materials at an affordable price. The local store also gives back to the community by donating materials.

Similarities

After gathering the background information for both stores, I saw some similarities. Some of the similarities are very obvious. Both stores sell building supplies for construction contractors and home owners. Although both businesses deal with the same types of products, the super mart sells a much bigger volume of products.

Both stores are focused on preserving the environment. The national chain has won several environmental awards and is very dedicated to taking steps in becoming a "greener" company. Just like

Enter footnote here

Page 1 of 3

FIGURE 16–20
A footnote inserted in a document

Used with permission from Microsoft Corporation

ABOVE AND BEYOND

To format a footnote with an asterisk or symbol instead of a number, instead of clicking the Insert Footnotes button, click the dialog box launcher in the Footnotes group. Enter the character or symbol in the Custom mark box, and then click Insert.

QUICK TIP

When footnotes are moved or deleted, Word automatically adjusts the reference numbers.

5. Type the following note:

   Builder's Depot was founded in 1995 by a non-profit organization to address the escalating problem of wasteful disposal of usable building materials.

6. Double-click the reference number to the left of the text you just entered. The insertion point moves to the in-text reference symbol.

7. Position the insertion point at the end of the paragraph directly above the paragraph with the new footnote reference. The paragraph ends *country with jobs.*

8. Click the **Insert Footnote** button. A new footnote reference is inserted at the location of the insertion point. Notice that the new reference is numeral *1*. Because the new footnote was inserted ahead of the existing footnote, the existing footnote was renumbered and is now referenced with numeral 2.

9. With the insertion point positioned next to the numeral *1* at the bottom of the page, type the following note:

   The Star Super Store chain is one of the top three home improvement retailers.

10. In the Footnotes group, click the **dialog box launcher** to open the Footnote and Endnote dialog box. Under Location, click **Convert**. When prompted to convert all footnotes to endnotes, click **OK**, and then close the dialog box.

11. If necessary, scroll to the end of the document. The notes are now displayed at the bottom of the third page of the document, and the references numbers are *i* and *ii*. In the endnote at the bottom of the page, double-click the number **i**. The insertion point moves to the first in-text reference symbol.

12. Position the mouse pointer over the superscript numeral *ii*. A ScreenTip will show the text that is displayed in the endnote.

13. Save the changes, and close the document.

Creating and Editing Hyperlinks

A helpful tool on the Insert tab is the Insert Hyperlink button. Usually when you think of a hyperlink, you think about links to Web pages and e-mails. When you type URLs for Web pages and e-mail addresses, Word automatically creates a hyperlink. However, you can also create links to another location in the same document, to another Word document, or to a file in another application. To create a link to another location in the same document, the document content must be formatted with default heading styles or bookmarks.

Step-by-Step 16.8

1. Open the **McCabe** file from the drive and folder where your Data Files folder is stored. Save the McCabe document as **McCabe Bio**, followed by your initials. Close the document.

2. Open the **Revised Debate 5** file from your solution files. Save the Revised Debate 5 document as **Revised Debate 6**, followed by your initials. Show the nonprinting characters.

3. At the top of the second page of the Revised Debate 6 document, select the author name **Richard McCabe**. Click the **Insert** tab. In the Links group shown in **Figure 16–21**, click the **Hyperlink** button.

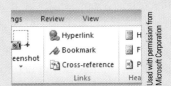

FIGURE 16–21
Links group on the Insert tab

4. Under Link to, make sure that the **Existing File or Web Page** button is enabled. If necessary, in the Look in box, navigate to the folder where you save your solution files. Click the filename **McCabe Bio**. Compare your dialog box to the one shown in **Figure 16–22**.

FIGURE 16–22
Insert Hyperlink dialog box

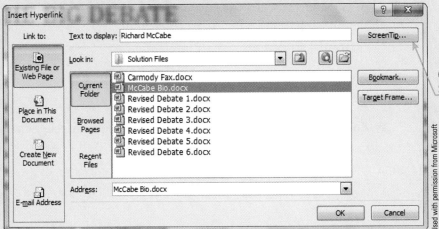

Click to add
ScreenTip to link

5. In the upper-right corner of the dialog box, click the **ScreenTip** button. In the Set Hyperlink ScreenTip dialog box, type **Information about the author**, and then click **OK**.

6. Click **OK** to close the Insert Hyperlink dialog box. A link is created to another document, and the selected text is displayed in a different color indicating the hyperlink format.

7. Position the mouse pointer over the hyperlink text. A ScreenTip appears, showing the text you entered. Press and hold **Ctrl**, and click the **Information about the author** hyperlink to connect to the target. The McCabe Bio document opens.

8. Select all the text in the McCabe Bio document, and copy the selected text to the Clipboard. Close the McCabe Bio document. Position the insertion point at the end of the second endnote in the Revised Debate 6 document. Press **Enter** two times, and then type **About the Author**. Press **Enter**, and then paste the copied text from the McCabe Bio document.

9. Select the heading **About the Author**. Click the **Home** tab. In the Styles group, click the **More** button to open the Quick Style gallery, and then click the **Heading 3** style.

10. Scroll to the top of the second page (page 1) in the document. (The cover page does not have a page number.) Right-click the **Richard McCabe** hyperlink, and in the shortcut menu click **Edit Hyperlink**. The Edit Hyperlink dialog box opens. In the left pane under Link to, click **Place in This Document**. The dialog box adapts to show the headings and bookmarks in the document. Only one heading is displayed because the other headings are formatted with custom styles instead of default heading styles. Under Select a place in this document, click **About the Author**, and then click **OK**.

11. Press and hold **Ctrl**, and then click the **Richard McCabe** hyperlink to make sure the target is the *About the Author* heading at the end of the document.

12. Position the insertion point at the end of the paragraph following the *About the Author* heading. Press **Enter** to create a new paragraph, and then type the following:

    Send your feedback to news@westmorelandtimes.xyz.

13. Press **Enter**. Word automatically creates a hyperlink to the e-mail address. When you click a link to an e-mail address, Word opens an e-mail message form using your default e-mail program.

14. Save the changes, and leave the document open for the next Step-by-Step.

QUICK TIP

If you do not want the hyperlink format applied to the URL or the e-mail address text, click the Undo button or press Ctrl+Z immediately after Word automatically formats the hyperlink. Or, at any time, you can right-click the hyperlink text and in the shortcut menu click Remove Hyperlink.

Inserting Symbols and Special Characters

Sometimes you need to enter special characters or symbols in your document, but the characters and symbols are not available on the keyboard. For example, if you are entering information about copyright, you will likely want to include the copyright symbol. Word provides access to several commonly used symbols and special characters on the Insert tab.

Step-by-Step 16.9

1. If necessary, open the **Revised Debate 6** file from your solution files. Save the Revised Debate 6 document as **Revised Debate 7**, followed by your initials. Show the nonprinting characters.

2. On the last page of the document, position the insertion point at the end of the heading *About the Author*. Press the **spacebar**.

3. Click the **Insert** tab. In the Symbols group on the right side of the Ribbon, click the **Symbol** button. In the submenu, click **More Symbols** to open the Symbol dialog box shown in **Figure 16–23**. Scroll up and down to view the rows of letters and symbols available.

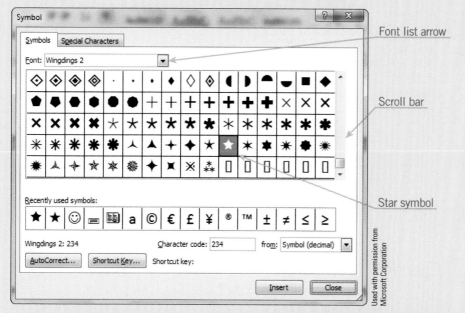

FIGURE 16–23
Wingdings 2 options in the Symbol dialog box

Font list arrow

Scroll bar

Star symbol

4. Click the **Font** list arrow, and scroll down and select **Wingdings 2**. Scroll to the bottom of the list, and select a **star** symbol as shown in Figure 16–23. Then click **Insert**. If necessary, drag the dialog box title bar to move the dialog box to the side of the screen. Note that the selected symbol is inserted at the location of the insertion point.

5. In the dialog box, click **Insert** four more times to add four more stars to the document. Leave the dialog box open.

6. If necessary, reposition the dialog box so you can view the end of the document. Position the insertion point at the end of the hyperlink at the end of the document. Press **Enter**, and type the following, pressing **Enter** after the first line of text:

```
Copyright 2014 The Westmoreland Times
All rights reserved. This material may not
be broadcast, published, rewritten, or
redistributed without written permission.
```

7. In the document window, position the insertion point at the end of the word *Copyright*. Press the **spacebar**.

8. In the Symbols dialog box, click the **Special Characters** tab to show the special characters available. Select the **Copyright** symbol (©) as shown in **Figure 16–24**, and then click **Insert**.

FIGURE 16–24
Special Characters tab in the Symbol dialog box

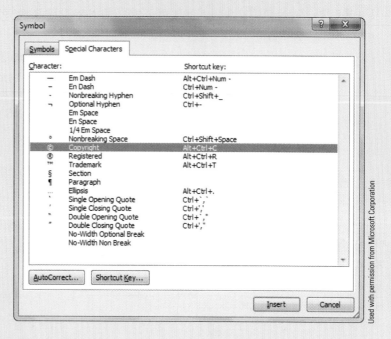

9. Close the dialog box. Save the changes, and close the document.

Creating Your Own Building Blocks

You can also create your own customized building blocks. For example, if you often include a legal disclaimer in documents, you can select the content you want to include (text, formatted text, and/or images), and then save the selected content as a Quick Part. By default, custom Quick Parts are stored in a special template named Building Blocks.dotx, where all the built-in building blocks are stored. Because you may share your computer with classmates, the Quick Parts that you create in this lesson will be removed from the Quick Part Gallery when you complete the Step-by-Step.

Step-by-Step 16.10

2-2.1.16

1. If necessary, open the **Revised Debate 7** file from your solution files. Save the Revised Debate 7 document as **Revised Debate 8**, followed by your initials. Show the nonprinting characters.

2. Position the insertion point in the blank area above the endnote divider line. Type the following paragraph:

   Opinions expressed are those of the columnist and are not necessarily those of The Westmoreland Times.

3. Select the **t**ext you just typed, including the ending paragraph marker. Apply **italic** formatting and change the font size to **10** point.

4. The text should still be selected. Click the **Insert** tab, and in the Text group shown in **Figure 16–25**, click the **Quick Parts** button, and then click **Save Selection to Quick Part Gallery**. The Create New Building Block dialog box opens.

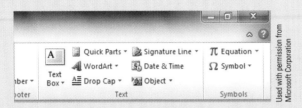

Used with permission from Microsoft Corporation

FIGURE 16–25
Text group on the Insert tab

5. The Name box shows the first words of the selected text. Type **Disclaimer** to replace the existing text.

6. Click in the **Description** box, and type **Disclaimer clause for columnist opinions.**.

7. Note that the setting in the Save in box indicates that the building block will be stored in the default template Building Blocks.dotx. Because you included the paragraph marker in the selection in Step 3, the paragraph formatting will also be stored.

8. When your settings match those shown in **Figure 16–26**, click **OK** to accept the changes and close the dialog box. You just created a building block, and it was saved in the default template Building Blocks.dotx.

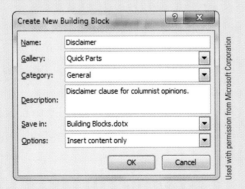

FIGURE 16–26
Create New Building Block dialog box

Used with permission from Microsoft Corporation

9. Deselect the text. Save the changes to the document, and then close the document.

10. Open a new blank document. Click the **Insert** tab. In the Text group, click the **Quick Parts** button, and then click **Building Blocks Organizer**. A dialog box opens and shows all the building blocks available.

11. Under Building blocks, click the **Name** column heading to organize the list in ascending alphabetical order as shown in **Figure 16–27**. Scroll down in the list to view the building block names beginning with the letter *D*. Click the **Disclaimer** building block. The boilerplate text is displayed in the preview pane on the right side of the dialog box.

FIGURE 16–27
Building Blocks
Organizer dialog box

Name column heading

12. At the bottom of the dialog box, click **Insert**. The text is inserted in the document at the location of the insertion point.

13. Click the **Quick Parts** button, and then click **Building Blocks Organizer**. Scroll down and select the **Disclaimer** building block. At the bottom of the dialog box, click **Delete**. When prompted to confirm the deletion of the selected building block, click **Yes**. The building block is removed from the Quick Part gallery.

14. Close the dialog box and then close Word without saving the changes to the document. When you exit Word, you will be prompted to save changes to Building Blocks.dotx. Click **Don't Save**.

WARNING

When you exit a session of Word after creating or deleting a building block, or making changes to a built-in building block, you will be prompted to save the changes to Building Blocks.dotx. When working at a classroom or public computer, do not save any changes without permission.

WORKPLACE READINESS

Dress for Success

Regardless of your employment level or career path, to be effective and project a professional and competent image at work, you need to dress for success. Dressing appropriately will help you gain respect and establish credibility on the job. Every business has its own style, each position has its own status, and workers dress differently for the activities involved in their work. If your employer provides a written dress code, be sure to follow the rules. Many employers, however, do not have established dress standards, so you have to get it right on your own. If in doubt, dress like your boss, or ask a superior for advice.

SUMMARY

In this lesson, you learned:

- Word templates provide a uniform appearance for your documents and can increase the speed and quality of your work.

- You can create predesigned documents by creating a new document based on a template.

- Styles enable you to format document content consistently and efficiently.

- You can apply and modify built-in styles, and you can create new styles.

- Word provides several predesigned building blocks that enable you to create a professional-looking document quickly.

- Several tools are available to insert data elements such as the date and time.

- Word provides features that enable you to quickly format footnotes and endnotes.

- There are several options for creating hyperlinks in Word documents.

- Not all characters and symbols are available on the keyboard, so Word provides numerous symbols and special characters that you can easily insert in a document.

- You can create your own building blocks and add them to the Quick Part gallery.

■ LESSON REVIEW

TRUE / FALSE

Circle T if the statement is true or F if the statement is false.

T F **1.** When you insert page numbers in a document, the page numbers are displayed in a header or a footer.

T F **2.** When you apply a style, you eliminate multiple steps to format the document content.

T F **3.** A template affects document settings such as fonts, line spacing, margins, and page layout.

T F **4.** Building blocks are built-in document parts that are already designed and formatted.

T F **5.** Endnotes are always displayed on the page on which they are referenced.

MULTIPLE CHOICE

Select the best response for the following statements.

1. You can insert hyperlinks in Word documents to create links to _____.

   A. e-mail addresses   C. other Word documents

   B. Web pages   D. all of the above

2. The AutoComplete feature can help you accurately enter _____.

   A. the current day of the week   C. the current calendar date

   B. the current month   D. all of the above

3. Word's Normal template (Normal.dotm) is a _____ template.

   A. global   C. universal

   B. document   D. none of the above

4. Linked styles provide _____.

   A. text formats   C. hyperlink formats

   B. paragraph formats   D. A or B

5. _____ is content that you frequently use in a document.

   A. Prefilled text   C. Boilerplate text

   B. Placeholder text   D. Preformatted text

FILL IN THE BLANK

Complete the following sentences by writing the correct word or words in the blanks provided.

1. When you open a new blank document, by default, the _____ template provides predefined formats that are already part of the document.

2. _____ templates are formatted for a specific purpose, and many of them already contain common document parts.

3. A(n) _____ indicates a location in a document where you can enter variable data, such as an individual's name.

4. A(n) _____ is a journal maintained by an individual or a group and posted on a Web site for public viewing and comment.

5. A(n) _____ is a set of formatting characteristics that you can apply to characters, paragraphs, tables, and numbered and bulleted lists.

WRITTEN QUESTIONS

Write a brief answer to the following questions.

1. What is the difference between a document template and a global template?

2. Why is it beneficial to use templates?

3. What does the term "blog" mean?

4. What is the advantage to using Word's built-in heading styles?

5. What is the advantage to posting a blog from a Word document?

■ PROJECTS

PROJECT 16–1

1. Create a new document based on a sample template already installed. Select the **Apothecary Letter** template.

2. Save the document as **Refund Letter**, followed by your initials.

3. Complete the fields using the following information. If necessary, replace prefilled data with your first and last name.

```
Company Name: Wellington Apartments
Date: Current date
Author name: Your name
Sender company address: 1055 Nowell Road,
                        Raleigh, NC 27607
Recipient name: Mr. Jonas Brzendine
Recipient address:
145 Red Rock Ridge Drive,
Youngsville, NC 27596
Salutation: Dear Mr. Brzendine:
Closing: Best regards,
Sender title: Office Assistant
```

4. Under the salutation, select the placeholder for the body of the letter, and type the following:

Enclosed is a check for your security deposit refund. Also enclosed is a Deposit Settlement Summary detailing the costs deducted from the original security deposit.

If you feel this refund amount is in error, you can make an appeal. All appeals regarding the Deposit Settlement Summary must be in writing and mailed to us within 30 (thirty) days of receiving this settlement check. No explanations will be provided via phone or e-mail; we will respond to all appeals in writing by letter within 30 (thirty) days. Additional information is available at www.wellington.xyz.

5. Position the insertion point at the end of the document, press **Enter** two times, and then type **Enclosures**.

6. Because you entered the company name and address in the letterhead at the top of the document, you do not need the fields below the date. Under the date line, select and delete the name, company, and address for the sender.

7. Select the salutation **Dear Mr. Brzendine:**, and remove the bold format.

8. Save the changes, and close the document.

IC³

2-1.2.1

PROJECT 16–2

1. Open the **Upcoming Events** file from the drive and folder where your Data Files folder is stored. Save the Upcoming Events document as **Revised Upcoming Events**, followed by your initials.

2-2.1.11
2-2.1.16

2. Apply the **Heading 1** style to the heading *The Tenth Annual Antique Fair*.

3. Modify the heading by changing the font to **Comic Sans MS**.

4. Save the modified style as a new Quick Style. Name the new style **My New Style**.

5. Apply the My New Style to the other two headings formatted with the red font.

6. Under each of the headings *The Tenth Annual Antique Fair*, *Railroad Weekend*, and *Horse-Drawn Carriage Rides*, select the three paragraphs and remove the space after the paragraphs.

7. Switch to Outline view. Collapse the body text under the heading *Railroad Weekend*, and then drag and drop the heading so it is at the top of the list before *The Tenth Annual Antique Fair*.

8. Expand the text, and close Outline view.

9. Save the changes, and close the document.

PROJECT 16–3

1. If you completed Project 16–2, go to Step 2. If you did not complete Project 16–2, open the **Upcoming Events** file from the drive and folder where your Data Files folder is stored, and save the Upcoming Events document as **Revised Upcoming Events**, followed by your initials. Then close the document.

2-2.1.11
2-2.2.2

2. Open the **Histories** file from the drive and folder where your Data Files folder is stored, and save the Histories document as **Revised Histories**, followed by your initials.

3. At the end of the document, after *Date Posted:,* insert a field to display the current date using the Month, day, year format (for example: *March 6, 2014*).

4. Select the last paragraph. Format the text with a font of your choice, and if desired, change the font size. Then create a custom style, and name the style **WHS**. Save the new style in the current document only.

5. Save the last paragraph as a building block in the Quick Part gallery. Name the building block **WHS**.

6. Position the insertion point in the blank paragraph at the end of the document, and then type **www.westmorelandhistory.xyz**, and create a hyperlink for the URL.

7. In the middle of the document, select **Upcoming Events**, and then create a link to the document **Revised Upcoming Events** in your solutions folder. Add the ScreenTip: **Click for info about upcoming events.**

8. Remove the custom building block WHS from the Quick Part gallery.

9. Save the changes to the document.

10. Test the hyperlink for Upcoming Events.

11. Close both documents.

PROJECT 16–4

1. Open the **Agreement** file from the drive and folder where your Data Files folder is stored. Save the Agreement document as **Revised Agreement**, followed by your initials.

2-2.1.8
2-2.1.10
2-2.2.2

2. In the first sentence, replace *XXXXX* with the current date, starting with the day, followed by the month, date, and year. (*Hint*: Use the AutoComplete feature.)

3. Create a new footer using the **Alphabet** footer.

4. In the footer pane, replace the Type text placeholder on the left with **Bingham Property Management**. Then double-click anywhere in the document window.

5. In the first paragraph, select **Bingham Property Management**. Insert a footnote: **Bingham Property Management is a subsidiary of Living Solutions, Inc.**.

6. Insert the trademark symbol after *Inc.*

7. Create a cover page using the built-in **Alphabet** style. Type the document title **Lease Agreement**. Remove the subtitle placeholder and field. In the date field, insert today's date. Change the author name to **Bingham Property Management**.

8. Save changes, and close the document.

TEAMWORK PROJECT

Think about the types of documents you create most often. Which would serve you better—a document template or building blocks? Choose a partner to help you with this exercise.

2-1.2.1
2-2.1.16

1. Create a new Word document, and save the document as **TP 16-1**, followed by your initials.

2. Create a list of the types of documents you create most often.

3. Describe the target audience and the content for each of the documents in your list.

4. Considering the document content and the need to create professional-looking documents with consistent information, decide for each document in your list whether a document template or building blocks would serve you best.

5. For each document in your list, describe the content and fields you could include in the document template or in the boilerplate text.

6. Save the changes to the document, and then close the document.

■ CRITICAL THINKING ACTIVITIES

CRITICAL THINKING 16–1

What factors do you think you should consider to create a professional-looking document that makes a good first impression?

2-2.1.16

1. Create a new Word document, and save the document as **CT 16-1**, followed by your initials.

2. Write a brief paragraph explaining what document elements you believe are important for making a good first impression.

3. Save the changes to the document, and then close the document.

CRITICAL THINKING 16–2

Your friend owns a sporting goods business and recently learned how to use the Word document templates.

2-1.2.1

1. Review the templates at Office.com, and create a list of the types of templates that your friend might find useful in the sporting goods business.

2. Create a new Word document, and save the document as **CT 16-2**, followed by your initials.

3. Type a list of your recommendations in a Word document.

4. Save the changes to the document, and then close the document.

■ ONLINE DISCOVERY

Explore Word templates available online, and preview some of the templates in Backstage view. You do not need to download any of the templates.

1. Create a new Word document, and save the document as **OD 16-1**, followed by your initials.

2. Create a list of five or more types of templates that you think you might use in the future.

3. Save the changes to the document, and then close the document.

2-1.2.1

■ JOB SKILLS

1. Open Backstage view, and display the available templates.

2. Browse through the installed templates for a resume template. If you do not see a format that you like, search the Microsoft Office.com Web site and download one that meets your preferences. Remember, you can modify the styles that are in the template.

3. Save the document as **JS 16-1**, followed by your initials.

4. It is important to keep your resume up to date and to have a professional-looking final copy on hand. Enter your personal data in the fields, and approach this project seriously, knowing that you will someday use this resume.

5. Ask a classmate, friend, spouse, or other family member to review your completed resume. Ask them to look for errors and also to provide constructive feedback for improving the resume.

2-1.2.1
2-1.4.6

6. Make the necessary or recommended changes, and when the document is finalized, save the document. If you plan to distribute the resume electronically, save the document in XPS or PDF format to preserve the visual appearance and layout.

LESSON 17

Working with Graphics

■ OBJECTIVES

Upon completion of this lesson, you should be able to:

- Format columns, borders, and shading.
- Insert clip art and pictures.
- Resize, crop, and position graphics.
- Modify graphic colors and apply styles and effects to clip art and pictures.
- Remove the background from a picture and adjust the contrast and brightness.
- Use drawing tools to create your own graphics.
- Use built-in, predesigned, and formatted layouts to create your own graphics.
- Capture a picture of the application screen.

■ DATA FILES

To complete this lesson, you will need these data files:

Begonias.jpg

Biker.jpg

Cycle Tours.docx

Cycling.tif

Dog.jpg

Gardening.docx

Lilies.jpg

Menu.docx

Newsletter.docx

■ WORDS TO KNOW

banner

clip art

crop

desktop publishing

drawing canvas

drawing objects

graphics

manual column break

outcrop

resizing

section

section break

shape

sizing handles

SmartArt

text box

WordArt

Word provides a number of features to add visual interest to documents. The features help you emphasize the content and create an attractive and professional document.

Formatting Columns, Borders, and Shading

VOCABULARY
desktop publishing
section
section break
banner
manual column break

2-2.1.16

Desktop publishing is the process of creating a document using a computer to lay out text and graphics. One common example of desktop publishing is newsletters. Newsletter text is often formatted in multiple columns with headings, borders, and shading, and pictures are often included. All of these enhancements make the articles more appealing and easier to read.

Formatting Text in Columns

A *section* is an area within a document that can have its own separate page formats such as the page orientation, margins, and the number of columns. When you create a new blank document in Word, the document consists of just one section. If you want to change the page formats for one portion of the document you must divide the document into multiple sections by creating a section break. A *section break* controls the section formatting of the text that precedes it. After dividing the document into multiple sections, you can apply different formats in each section. Oftentimes, column headings are formatted as a single-column *banner*, which is a headline that spreads the full width of the page.

By default, all the text you enter in a Word document will be displayed in a single column, approximately six inches wide. Formatting text to display it in multiple columns sometimes saves space on a page, and because the width of the line of text is smaller, the text is often easier to read. Word provides several multicolumn formats, and you can modify these formats to meet your needs. When you format text in columns, the columns are usually balanced so the column heights are approximately equal. There may be occasions, however, when you want to control where text breaks from one column to the next. To adjust where a column ends, you can insert a *manual column break*.

Step-by-Step 17.1

2-2.1.5
2-2.1.6
2-2.1.12

1. Open the **Newsletter** file from the drive and folder where your Data Files folder is stored. Save the Newsletter document as **Revised Newsletter 1**, followed by your initials. If necessary, display nonprinting characters.

2. Triple-click in the paragraph of text under the heading *BENEFITS OF OWNING A PET* to select the entire paragraph.

3. Click the **Page Layout** tab. In the Page Setup group, shown in **Figure 17–1**, click the **Columns** button, and then in the menu click **Two**. Deselect the text.

FIGURE 17–1
Page Setup group on the Page Layout tab

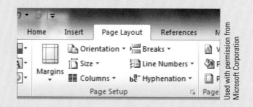

4. Compare your document to **Figure 17–2**. Section breaks divide the document into three sections. The first section contains the heading BENEFITS OF OWNING A PET and is formatted for one column, the text in the second section is formatted for two columns, and the third section is formatted for one column.

BENEFITS·OF·OWNING·A·PET¶ ········Section Break (Continuous) ········

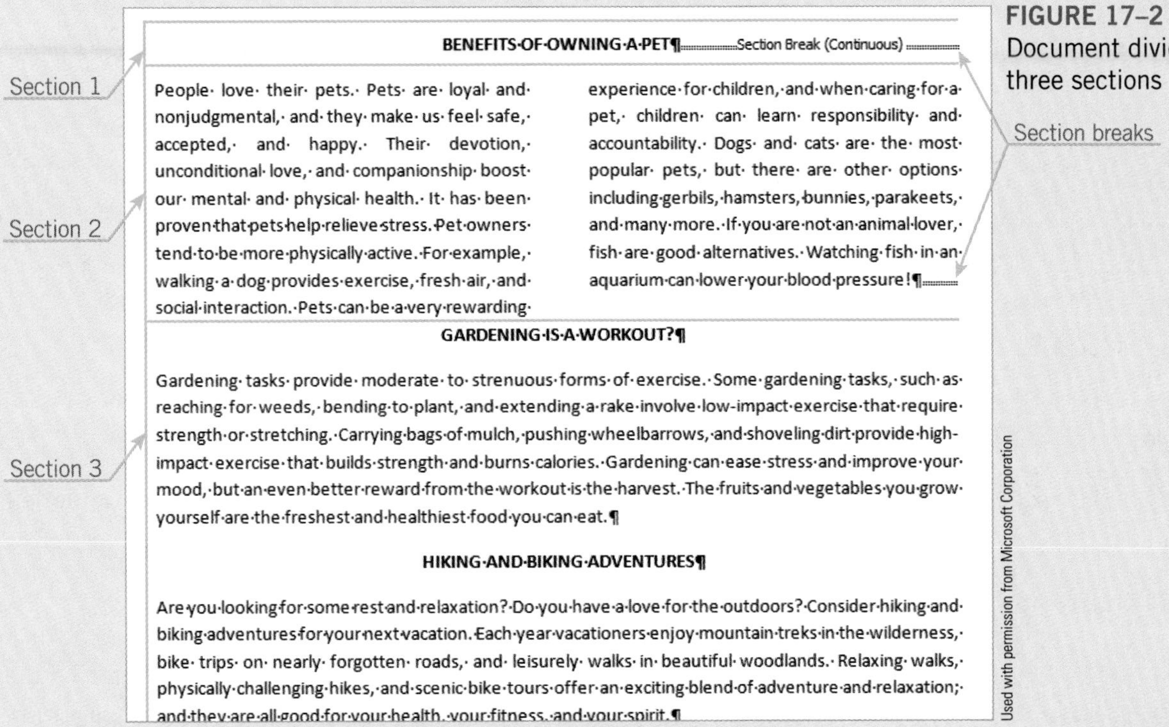

Section 1

Section 2

Section 3

People· love· their· pets.· Pets· are· loyal· and· nonjudgmental,· and· they· make· us· feel· safe,· accepted,· and· happy.· Their· devotion,· unconditional· love,· and· companionship· boost· our· mental· and· physical· health.· It· has· been· proven·that·pets·help·relieve·stress.·Pet·owners· tend·to·be·more·physically·active.·For·example,· walking· a· dog·provides·exercise,·fresh·air,·and· social·interaction.··Pets·can·be·a·very·rewarding·

experience·for·children,·and·when·caring·for·a· pet,· children· can· learn· responsibility· and· accountability.· Dogs· and· cats· are· the· most· popular· pets,· but· there· are· other· options· including·gerbils,·hamsters,·bunnies,·parakeets,· and·many·more.·If·you·are·not·an·animal·lover,· fish·are·good·alternatives.·Watching·fish·in·an· aquarium·can·lower·your·blood·pressure!·¶ ········

GARDENING·IS·A·WORKOUT?¶

Gardening· tasks· provide· moderate· to· strenuous· forms· of· exercise.· Some· gardening· tasks,· such· as· reaching· for· weeds,· bending· to·plant,· and· extending· a·rake·involve·low-impact·exercise·that·require· strength·or·stretching.·Carrying·bags·of·mulch,·pushing·wheelbarrows,·and·shoveling·dirt·provide·high-impact· exercise· that· builds·strength·and·burns·calories.·Gardening·can·ease·stress·and·improve·your· mood,·but·an·even·better·reward·from·the·workout·is·the·harvest.·The·fruits·and·vegetables·you·grow· yourself·are·the·freshest·and·healthiest·food·you·can·eat.·¶

HIKING·AND·BIKING·ADVENTURES¶

Are·you·looking·for·some·rest·and·relaxation?·Do·you·have·a·love·for·the·outdoors?·Consider·hiking·and· biking·adventures·for·your·next·vacation.·Each·year·vacationers·enjoy·mountain·treks·in·the·wilderness,· bike· trips· on· nearly· forgotten· roads,· and· leisurely· walks· in· beautiful· woodlands.· Relaxing· walks,· physically·challenging·hikes,·and·scenic·bike·tours·offer·an·exciting·blend·of·adventure·and·relaxation;· and·they·are·all·good·for·your·health,·your·fitness,·and·your·spirit.·¶

FIGURE 17–2
Document divided into three sections

Section breaks

Used with permission from Microsoft Corporation

5. Triple-click in the paragraph of text under the heading GARDENING IS A WORKOUT?. Click the **Columns** button, and then click **Three**. A new section is created, and the selected text is formatted in three columns of approximate equal width.

6. Position the insertion point at the beginning of the selected paragraph. Type **Yes, with all the bending, stretching, and lifting involved, you can get lots of exercise working in the garden.**. Press the **spacebar**. As you enter the new text, the existing text automatically wraps within the three columns.

7. Triple-click in the paragraph of text below the heading *HIKING AND BIKING ADVENTURES*. Click the **Columns** button, and then click **More Columns**. The Columns dialog box shown in **Figure 17–3** opens.

FIGURE 17–3
Columns dialog box

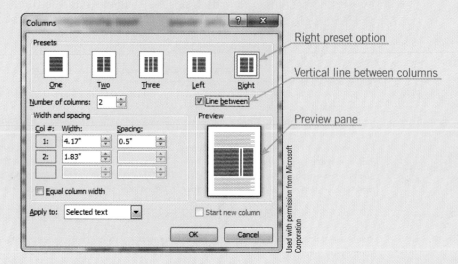

Right preset option

Vertical line between columns

Preview pane

Used with permission from Microsoft Corporation

8. Under Presets, click the **Right** preset option, and below that enable the option **Line between**. (The option is enabled when the box to the left of the option has a check mark.) The Preview pane in the dialog box is updated and shows the new settings.

9. When your dialog box settings match those shown in Figure 17–3, click **OK**. The text is formatted in two columns, with the wider column on the left. Since all of the text fits in the left column no text is displayed in the narrower column on the right.

10. Under the heading *HIKING AND BIKING ADVENTURES*, position the insertion point in front of the sixth line in the left column. The line begins *challenging hikes*. In the Page Setup group, click the **Breaks** button. In the menu, under Page Breaks, click **Column** to create a manual column break. The text following the insertion point is moved to the column on the right, and a vertical line is now displayed between the two columns.

11. Position the insertion point after the paragraph symbol at the end of the three-column article. The insertion point should be flashing in front of the section break as shown in **Figure 17–4**.

▶ **QUICK TIP**

To quickly insert a manual column break, position the insertion point where you want the column to break and then press Ctrl+Shift+Enter.

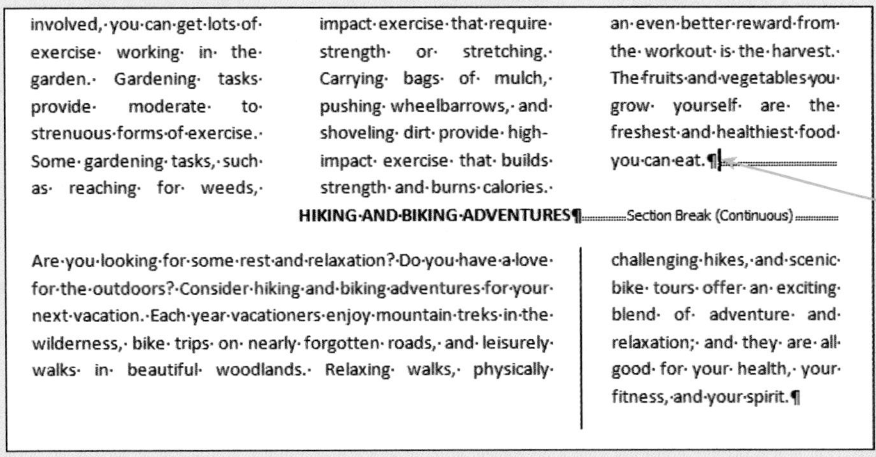

involved,·you·can·get·lots·of· exercise· working· in· the· garden.· Gardening· tasks· provide· moderate· to· strenuous·forms·of·exercise.· Some· gardening· tasks,· such· as· reaching· for· weeds,·

impact·exercise·that·require· strength· or· stretching.· Carrying· bags· of· mulch,· pushing· wheelbarrows,· and· shoveling· dirt· provide· high· impact· exercise· that· builds· strength· and·burns·calories.·

an·even·better·reward·from· the·workout·is·the·harvest.· The·fruits·and·vegetables·you· grow· yourself· are· the· freshest·and·healthiest·food· you·can·eat.·¶

HIKING·AND·BIKING·ADVENTURES¶ ======Section Break (Continuous)======

Are·you·looking·for·some·rest·and·relaxation?·Do·you·have·a·love· for·the·outdoors?·Consider·hiking·and·biking·adventures·for·your· next·vacation.·Each·year·vacationers·enjoy·mountain·treks·in·the· wilderness,· bike· trips· on· nearly· forgotten· roads,· and· leisurely· walks· in· beautiful· woodlands.· Relaxing· walks,· physically·

challenging·hikes,·and·scenic· bike· tours· offer· an· exciting· blend· of· adventure· and· relaxation;· and· they· are· all· good· for· your· health,· your· fitness,·and·your·spirit.·¶

Used with permission from Microsoft Corporation

Insertion point

FIGURE 17–4
Insertion point positioned in front of a section break

12. Press **Delete** to remove the section break. The three-column section becomes part of the section above, and the page setup format changes to a single column, which is the format for the heading *GARDENING IS A WORKOUT?*.

13. Click the **Undo** button to restore the three-column format.

14. Save the changes, and leave the document open for the next Step-by-Step.

Adding Borders and Shading

Borders and shading also can help enhance the appearance of a document such as a newsletter or a flyer. Word offers many options for applying borders above, below, and around paragraphs of text. The borders can be customized by changing the line color, the line style, and the thickness of the line. You can also enhance the document content by adding shading behind the text.

Step-by-Step 17.2

1. If necessary, open the **Revised Newsletter 1** file from your solution files. Save the Revised Newsletter 1 document as **Revised Newsletter 2**, followed by your initials.

2. Position the insertion point anywhere in the heading *BENEFITS OF OWNING A PET*. Click the **Home** tab, and in the Paragraph group shown in **Figure 17–5**, click the **Border** button arrow ⊞▼. In the menu, click **Top Border**. A border line is inserted across the entire top of the paragraph, which extends from the left margin to the right margin.

IC³

2-2.1.16

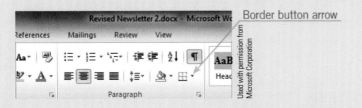

Border button arrow

Used with permission from Microsoft Corporation

FIGURE 17–5
Paragraph group on the Home tab

3. With the insertion point still positioned in the heading *BENEFITS OF OWNING A PET*, click the **Border** button arrow, and then click **No Border**. The border line is removed.

4. With the insertion point still positioned in the heading *BENEFITS OF OWNING A PET*, click the **Border** button arrow. At the bottom of the submenu, click **Borders and Shading** to open a dialog box similar to the one shown in **Figure 17–6**.

FIGURE 17–6
Borders and Shading
dialog box

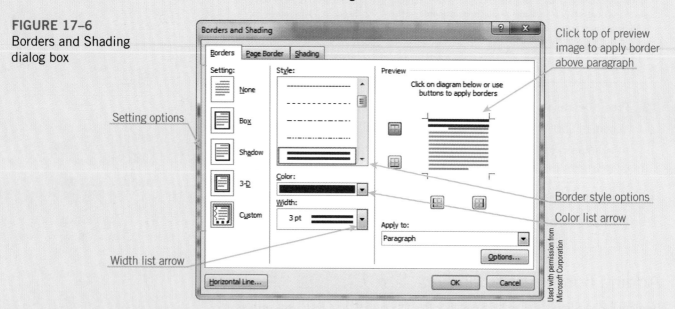

Setting options

Width list arrow

Click top of preview image to apply border above paragraph

Border style options

Color list arrow

5. In the middle pane, scroll down through the Style options, and click the first **border style** with two lines. Click the **Color** list arrow, and then under Theme Colors, in the first row, click the **Dark Blue, Text 2** theme color. (The color name will appear in a ScreenTip.)

6. In the middle pane, click the **Width** list arrow, and then click **3 pt**. The border style formats are displayed in the Preview pane.

7. In the left pane, under Setting, click **None**. The borders are no longer displayed in the Preview pane. Under Setting, click the **Custom** setting option. In the Preview pane at the right, click at the top of the preview image to add a line, as shown in Figure 17–6. The Preview box shows the style, color, and line width for the border at the top of the paragraph.

8. Compare your dialog box settings to those shown in Figure 17–6, and when your settings match, click **OK**. The border is inserted at the top of the paragraph where the insertion point is positioned.

9. Position the insertion point in the heading *GARDENING IS A WORKOUT?*. Click the **Border** button arrow, and then click **Top Border**. The same double-line, blue, 3-point border is inserted at the top of the paragraph.

10. Position the insertion point in the heading *HIKING AND BIKING ADVENTURES*. Position the mouse pointer over the Border button to display the ScreenTip *Top Border*, which is the last border applied. Click the **Border** button to apply the custom top border style you created.

11. Position the insertion point in the first heading *BENEFITS OF OWNING A PET*. Click the **Shading** button arrow. Under Theme Colors, in the second row, click the **Blue, Accent 1, Lighter 80%** color. Because shading is a paragraph format, a blue shade is applied to the entire paragraph where the insertion point is positioned.

12. Position the insertion point in the second heading *GARDENING IS A WORKOUT?*. Note the blue color you just applied is currently displayed on the Shading button. Click the **Shading** button to apply the blue shading.

13. Position the insertion point in the third heading *HIKING AND BIKING ADVENTURES*. Click the **Shading** button to repeat the shading formatting.

14. Save the changes, and leave the document open for the next Step-by-Step.

> **ABOVE AND BEYOND**
>
> To format shading for multiple paragraphs, select the paragraphs before clicking the Shading button.

Inserting and Formatting Graphics

To illustrate an idea presented in a document, or to make a document more functional, you can include *graphics*, which are nontext items such as digital photos, scanned images, and pictures. You can also insert images created or modified in other applications, such as a drawing created in a graphics or drafting program. Graphics created in such a program are saved in a variety of formats, including JPEG (*.jpg), TIFF (*.tif), and bitmap (*.bmp).

> ▶ **VOCABULARY**
> **graphics**
> **clip art**

Inserting Clip Art and Pictures

Clip art is a graphic that is ready to insert in a document. Word has numerous illustrations and photographs you can use that are stored in the Office Collections folder. You can also access clip art that you have saved (in the My Collections folder). If you have an Internet connection open, you can search for clip art at the Microsoft Office.com Web site. Search results appear in the task pane as thumbnails. You can also insert graphics that are stored in other folders. This is called inserting a picture from a file.

Step-by-Step 17.3

2-1.3.7

1. If necessary, open the **Revised Newsletter 2** file from your solution files. Save the Revised Newsletter 2 document as **Revised Newsletter 3**, followed by your initials.

2. Position the insertion point at the beginning of the paragraph under the heading *GARDENING IS A WORKOUT?*.

3. Click the **Insert** tab. In the Illustrations group shown in **Figure 17–7**, click the **Clip Art** button. The Clip Art task pane opens on the right side of the document window.

FIGURE 17–7
Illustrations group on the
Insert tab

4. Position the insertion point in the Search for box as shown in **Figure 17–8**. If there is text in the box, select all of the text. Type **flower**.

FIGURE 17–8
Clip Art task pane

5. Under Results should be, click the **list** arrow to display the list of media file types options shown in **Figure 17–9**. If necessary, click the **+** button to expand the list. Make sure the **Illustrations** and **Photographs** options are enabled. If necessary, disable the Videos and Audio options. When your screen matches the settings shown in Figure 17–9, click the **list** arrow to hide the list of media file types.

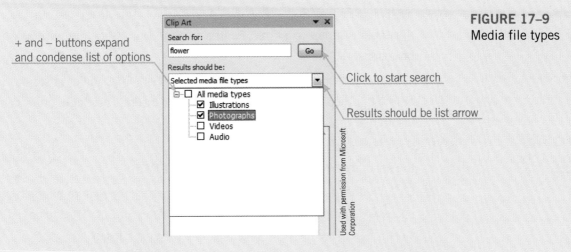

+ and – buttons expand and condense list of options

Click to start search

Results should be list arrow

Used with permission from Microsoft Corporation

FIGURE 17–9
Media file types

6. Under the Results should be box, make sure the **Include Office.com content** option is enabled. Click **Go** to start the search. If you have access to the Internet, the results should show several illustrations and photographs as thumbnails, as shown in **Figure 17–10**. Scroll down through the list to see what is available.

Include Office.com content option enabled

Used with permission from Microsoft Corporation

FIGURE 17–10
Clip Art search results including Office.com content

QUICK TIP

You can also drag and drop
from the Clip Art task pane to
anywhere in your document. Or,
you can click the list arrow on
the right side of the thumbnail
to display a shortcut menu with
options for copying the image,
previewing the properties, and
so on.

7. Disable the **Include Office.com content** option, and click **Go** again. Only two thumbnails are now displayed (one illustration and one photograph).

8. In the Clip Art task pane, click the first thumbnail. The flower illustration clip art is inserted at the location of the insertion point. Close the Clip Art task pane.

9. Position the insertion point at the end of the paragraph under the first heading *BENEFITS OF OWNING A PET*. Click the **Insert** tab. In the Illustrations group, click the **Picture** button. The Insert Picture dialog box opens.

10. Navigate to the drive and folder where your Data Files folder is stored. Select the filename **Dog.jpg**, and then click **Insert**. The Dog picture is inserted at the location of the insertion point.

11. Position the insertion point at the beginning of the first paragraph below the heading *HIKING AND BIKING ADVENTURES*.

12. Click the **Insert** tab. In the Illustrations group, click the **Picture** button. If necessary, navigate to the drive and folder where your Data Files folder is stored. Select the filename **Biker.jpg**, and then click **Insert**.

13. Note that after the Biker picture is inserted the article does not fit on the page, so the picture and the text automatically wrap to a second page. Also note that the last line of text in the left column is spread out because of the column break. The text will be adjusted when the picture is resized in Step-by-Step 17.4.

14. Save the changes, and leave the document open for the next Step-by-Step.

Resizing and Cropping a Graphic

▶ **VOCABULARY**
sizing handles
resizing
crop
outcrop

QUICK TIP

You may find it easier to work
with graphics in a document by
reducing the magnification of the
document. For example, you can
change the zoom of the document view to 75 percent.

Once you have inserted a graphic or picture in a document, there are many ways to manipulate the picture. To work with a graphic, you must select it. You will know it is selected when you see *sizing handles*, eight small circles and squares on the border of the graphic. When a graphic is selected, you can resize, cut, copy, paste, delete, and move it just as you would text.

Resizing stretches or shrinks the dimensions of a graphic. You can resize a graphic just vertically or just horizontally by using one of the square sizing handles on the side of the graphic, but this will distort the image. To change the size of a graphic without distorting the image, you must scale the graphic proportionally by dragging one of the circle corner sizing handles; these change both dimensions of the graphic (height and width) to maintain the proportions of the graphic.

When you *crop* a graphic, you cut off portions of the graphic that you do not want to show. When you *outcrop* a graphic, you add extra white space around the image.

Step-by-Step 17.4

1. If necessary, open the **Revised Newsletter 3** file from your solution files. Save the Revised Newsletter 3 document as **Revised Newsletter 4**, followed by your initials. Click the **View** tab. If necessary, enable the **Ruler** option in the Show group.

2. Click the **Dog** picture. When the picture is selected, the Ribbon adapts to display several more tools. Click the **Picture Tools Format** tab to show the options shown in **Figure 17–11**. Eight sizing handles appear on the outside border of the image. A nonprinting border around the picture is also displayed.

IC³
2-1.3.7

FIGURE 17–11
Picture Tools Format tab and selected object

Shape Height setting

Shape Width setting

Selection handles

Used with permission from Microsoft Corporation

3. Point to the upper-left corner of the selected image. When the pointer changes to a two-headed arrow ⬉, drag the **corner sizing handle** towards the top of the document window. As you drag the sizing handle, you can see the picture size expands proportionally.

4. Click the **Undo** button to restore the original picture size.

5. Point to the lower-right corner of the selected image. When the pointer changes to a two-headed arrow, drag the **corner sizing handle** towards the center of the graphic. Use the rulers at the top of the document window to judge the picture size. When the picture is approximately 2½ inches wide, release the mouse.

6. Click the **flower** illustration to select the graphic object. In the Size group, click the **Shape Height** box down arrow three times to change the height to 1.5". As you change the height setting, the width setting is automatically adjusted.

7. Click the **Biker** picture. In the Shape Height box, select the setting **2.45"**, and type **2**. Then click in the document window. The picture size is adjusted proportionally.

> **ABOVE AND BEYOND**
>
> To change the size of an image to exact measurements, in the Size group on the Picture Tools Format tab, change the settings in the Shape Height and Shape Width boxes.

8. Click the **Dog** picture. If necessary, click the **Picture Tools Format** tab. In the Size group, click the **Crop** button 🖼. The sizing handles change in appearance, as shown in **Figure 17–12**.

FIGURE 17–12
Cropping handles

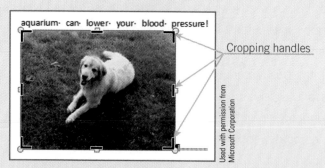

9. Point to the middle cropping handle on the top border, and then drag the **top border** up to outcrop the picture. The cropping line appears as you move the image border. When you release the mouse button, additional white space is added to the picture as shown in **Figure 17–13**.

FIGURE 17–13
Outcropped image

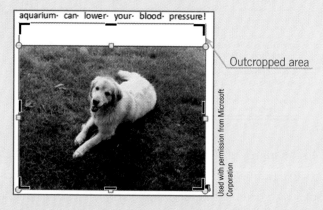

10. The image is still selected and the cropping handles are still visible. Point to the middle cropping handle in the top border, and then drag the **border** down to crop to just below the red ball in the picture.

11. Point to the middle cropping handle on the bottom border, and drag the **bottom border** up to crop the picture just below the dog's paws. When the cropping line on your screen is similar to the one shown in **Figure 17–14**, click outside the picture. The portion of the picture you cropped is gone.

FIGURE 17–14
Cropping lines

12. Click the **Dog** picture. On the Picture Tools Format tab, click the **Crop** button arrow, and then point to **Crop to Shape**. The Shapes menu shown in **Figure 17–15** is displayed. Under Basic Shapes, in the third row, click the **Heart** shape. (A ScreenTip displays the name of the shape.) The image adapts to the new shape.

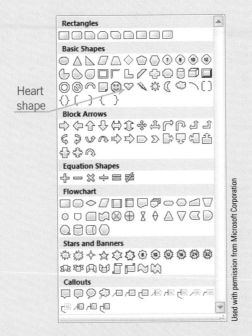

Heart shape

FIGURE 17–15
Shapes menu

Used with permission from Microsoft Corporation

13. Click the **flower** illustration. Click the **Crop** button arrow, point to **Crop to Shape**, and then under Basic Shapes, in the first row, click the **Oval** shape.

14. Save the changes, and leave the document open for the next Step-by-Step.

Positioning a Graphic

By default, when you insert a graphic, Word positions the graphic in the line of text. This means that the graphic is positioned directly in the text at the insertion point. However, you can format the text in the document to wrap around the graphic. A text-wrapping format must be applied to the graphic before you can reposition the graphic in your document. You can then drag and drop the graphic anywhere within the printable area of the page.

Step-by-Step 17.5

2-1.3.7

ABOVE AND BEYOND

When text is wrapped around an image or object, the image is anchored to a paragraph in the document. When nonprinting characters are displayed, you may see the anchor symbol at the beginning of a paragraph. You can drag and drop the anchor symbol to anchor the object to a different location in the document.

QUICK TIP

If you have difficulty positioning the graphics as described in the Step-by-Step, click the Undo button, then click the tool and try again.

FIGURE 17–16
Manual column break

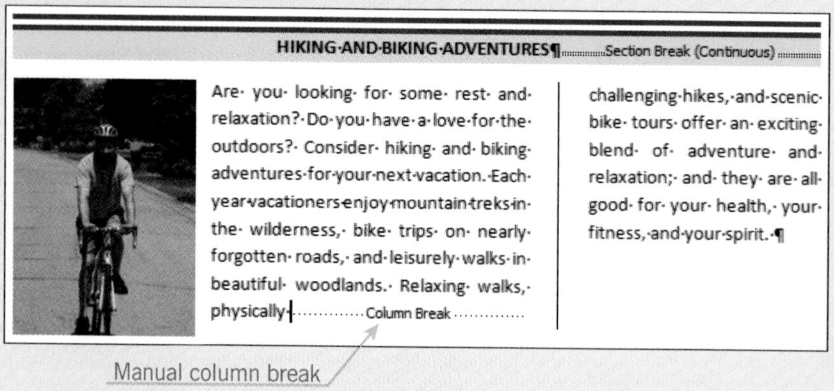

1. If necessary, open the **Revised Newsletter 4** file from your solution files. Save the Revised Newsletter 4 document as **Revised Newsletter 5**, followed by your initials.

2. If necessary, click the **flower** illustration, and then click the **Picture Tools Format** tab. In the Arrange group, click the **Wrap Text** button. Note that at the top of the menu the In Line with Text option is already highlighted. Move the mouse pointer over the other options to see the Live Preview of the other options. Then click **Top and Bottom**.

3. After applying a text-wrapping format to a graphic, you can move the graphic around in the document. Position the mouse pointer over the flower illustration. When the pointer changes to a four-headed arrow ⇱, drag the **graphic** so it is positioned below the text of the third column.

4. Click the **Dog** picture. Click the **Wrap Text** button, and then click **Tight**. Drag the **picture** to the center of the two columns to position the graphic in the center of the article. The text wraps around the heart shape.

5. Click the **Biker** picture. Click the **Wrap Text** button, and then click **Square**. The picture is aligned at the left side of the left column.

6. As noted earlier, the picture affects where the text wraps in the left column, and as shown in **Figure 17–16**, the manual column break now breaks the column in the middle of a line of text.

HIKING·AND·BIKING·ADVENTURES¶ ···········Section Break (Continuous) ··········

Are· you· looking· for· some· rest· and· relaxation?·Do·you·have·a·love·for·the· outdoors?· Consider· hiking· and· biking· adventures·for·your·next·vacation.·Each· year·vacationers·enjoy·mountain·treks·in· the· wilderness,· bike· trips· on· nearly· forgotten· roads,· and· leisurely· walks· in· beautiful· woodlands.· Relaxing· walks,· physically·‖ ···············Column Break ··············

challenging·hikes,·and·scenic· bike· tours· offer· an· exciting· blend· of· adventure· and· relaxation;· and· they· are· all· good· for· your· health,· your· fitness,·and·your·spirit. ·¶

Manual column break

Used with permission from Microsoft Corporation

7. Position the insertion point in front of the column break, as shown in Figure 17–16, and then press **Delete**. The manual column break is removed, and the text from the second column automatically moves back to fill in the first column.

8. Position the insertion point in front of the next-to-last line in the left column that begins *physically challenging*. Click the **Page Layout** tab. In the Page Setup group, click the **Breaks** button, and then click **Column**. The text after the column break automatically flows to the second column.

9. Save the changes, and leave the document open for the next Step-by-Step.

Adjusting Colors and Applying Styles and Effects

You can customize clip art or a photograph by changing its colors. You can match the colors in the current design theme, or you can create your own custom color scheme. Adjusting colors is especially useful if you want to recolor images to match other colors in the document.

To further enhance the appearance of the image, you can apply border styles and other special formats, such as shadows, soft edges, and 3-D effects. You can also add artistic effects to pictures.

Step-by-Step 17.6

1. If necessary, open the **Revised Newsletter 5** file from your solution files. Save the Revised Newsletter 5 document as **Revised Newsletter 6**, followed by your initials.

2. Click the **flower** illustration. Click the **Picture Tools Format** tab. In the Adjust group shown in **Figure 17–17**, click the **Color** button.

FIGURE 17–17
Adjust group on the Picture Tools Format tab

3. As shown in **Figure 17–18**, thumbnails show previews of the flower illustration in a variety of colors with both light and dark backgrounds. In the bottom row, click the second option, **Blue, Accent color 1 Light**.

Blue, Accent color 1 Light option

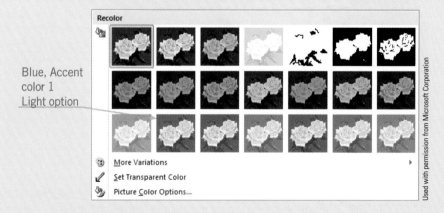

FIGURE 17–18
Thumbnails for recolor options

4. Click the **Dog** picture to select it. Click the **Color** button. Because the image is a photograph and not an illustration, there are also options for Color Saturation and Color Tone. Under Recolor, in the last row, click the second option, **Blue, Accent color 1 Light**. Now the dog and flower images are the same color.

5. Click the **Color** button. Under Color Saturation, click the last option, **Saturation: 400%**.

6. Click the **Undo** button twice to restore the Dog picture to its original colors.

2-1.3.7

7. The Dog picture should still be selected. In the Adjust group, click the **Artistic Effects** button. As shown in **Figure 17–19**, thumbnails show previews of several artistic effects. Move the mouse pointer over some of the thumbnails to see the Live Preview of the artistic effects. Then in the third row, click the second option **Watercolor Sponge**.

FIGURE 17–19
Thumbnails for artistic effects options

Watercolor Sponge option

8. Select the **flower** illustration. In the Picture Styles group, click the **More** button to show all the built-in picture styles shown in **Figure 17–20**. Move the mouse pointer over some of the thumbnails to see the Live Preview of the picture styles. Then in the third row, click the last option, **Snip Diagonal Corner, White**. The picture style is applied to the selected image.

FIGURE 17–20
Built-in picture styles

Snip Diagonal Corner, White option

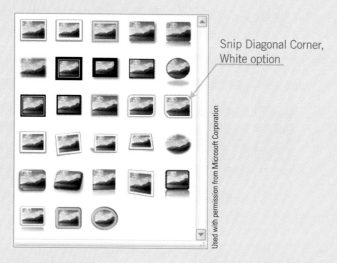

9. Click the **Dog** picture. In the Picture Styles group, click the **Picture Effects** button, and then point to **Glow** to display the options shown in **Figure 17–21**. Move the mouse pointer over some of the thumbnails to see the Live Preview of the glow variations. Then in the last row, click the first option, **Blue, 18 pt glow, Accent color 1**.

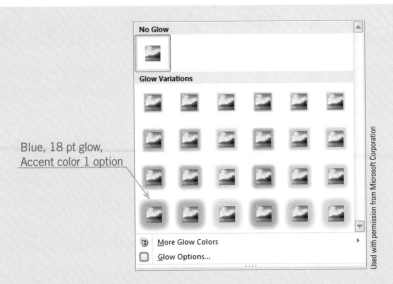

Blue, 18 pt glow,
Accent color 1 option

Used with permission from Microsoft Corporation

FIGURE 17–21
Picture effects options for glow variations

10. The Dog picture should still be selected. In the Picture Styles group, click the **Picture Border** button arrow. Under Theme Colors, in the first row, click the **White, Background 1** color.

11. The Dog picture should still be selected. Click the **Picture Border** button arrow, point to **Weight**, and then click **3 pt**.

12. Save the changes, and leave the document open for the next Step-by-Step.

Removing Backgrounds from Pictures

Sometimes the background colors do not fit the color scheme of the document, or you may just not want to include the background in a picture. When working with illustrations and photographs that have a solid color background, you can hide the background color by making the color transparent. When you enable the Set Transparent Color feature and click a color in the image, all the pixels of that color become transparent.

Word also provides a feature for automatically removing the background colors and images from a picture. When you apply the Remove Background feature, Word automatically suggests the elements to be removed from the image. If you are not satisfied with the results, you can identify the parts you want to keep or remove.

Even after a background has been removed from illustrations and photographs, you can still add effects such as shadows, glows, and reflections to the parts of the picture that are still visible. You can also clarify elements in a picture using contrast controls, and you can lighten or darken the picture b y using the brightness controls.

Step-by-Step 17.7

2-1.3.7

1. If necessary, open the **Revised Newsletter 6** file from your solution files. Save the Revised Newsletter 6 document as **Revised Newsletter 7**, followed by your initials.

2. Select the **flower** illustration. If necessary, click the **Picture Tools Format** tab. In the Adjust group, click the **Color** button, and then click **Set Transparent Color**. The mouse pointer changes to a pen with an arrow ✐. Click the background color in the illustration. All pixels of that color in the image become transparent.

3. On the Quick Access Toolbar, click the **Undo** button to restore the background color.

4. Select the **Biker** picture. If necessary, click the **Picture Tools Format** tab. In the Adjust group, click the **Remove Background** button. The Ribbon adapts to show the Background Removal tab shown in **Figure 17–22**.

FIGURE 17–22
Background Removal tab

5. Note that the picture in the document window now displays a bright background, and a marquee with handles is displayed to indicate what the borders of the image will be after the background is removed. Anything bright pink will be removed. Drag the **middle handle** on the bottom marquee border below the picture border as shown in **Figure 17–23**, and then release the mouse. The marquee is readjusted so the bottom of the bike is included in the picture.

FIGURE 17–23
Readjusting the removal marquee

Drag the bottom marquee border until the crosshair appears below the picture border

6. In the Close group, click the **Keep Changes** button. The picture should now appear as shown in **Figure 17–24**.

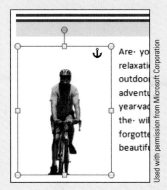

Used with permission from Microsoft Corporation

FIGURE 17–24
Biker picture after background removal

> **QUICK TIP**
>
> Depending on the background elements, you may not be satisfied with the proposed removal. To identify parts of the picture that you do not want removed automatically, click the Mark Areas to Keep button. To identify additional parts of the picture you want to remove, click the Mark Areas to Remove button. The mouse pointer changes to a pencil, and you can drag horizontal and vertical lines to identify the area. To undo any lines you add, click the Delete Mark button.

7. The Biker picture should still be selected. In the Size group, click the **Crop** button, and drag the **middle crop handle** on the top border down to crop the white space at the top of the picture. Then click outside the picture.

8. Select the **Biker** picture, and drag it upward to align with the top of the column. The picture should be aligned to the upper-left corner of the article, with the text aligned to the right side of the picture.

9. The Biker picture should still be selected. If necessary, scroll up so the Biker picture is positioned at the bottom of the document window.

10. On the Picture Tools Format tab, in the Adjust group, click the **Corrections** button. As shown in **Figure 17–25**, options for sharpening and softening the image or changing the brightness and contrast are displayed. Move the mouse pointer over some of the thumbnails to see the Live Preview of the correction options. Then under Brightness and Contrast, in the third row, click the fourth option **Brightness: +20% Contrast: 0% (Normal)**.

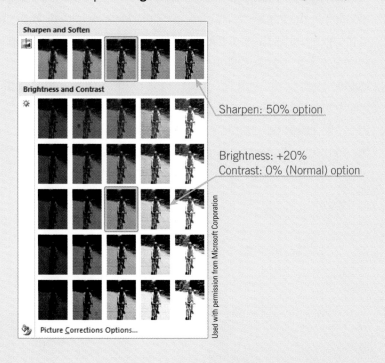

Sharpen and Soften

Brightness and Contrast

Sharpen: 50% option

Brightness: +20% Contrast: 0% (Normal) option

Picture Corrections Options...

Used with permission from Microsoft Corporation

FIGURE 17–25
Corrections options

11. The Biker picture should still be selected. Click the **Corrections** button. Under Sharpen and Soften, click the last option, **Sharpen: 50%**.

12. Save the changes, and leave the document open for the next Step-by-Step.

Creating Your Own Graphics

Sometimes you may need to create your own graphics. For example, you may want to create a fancy title for a document, a map, or an organizational chart. Word offers several tools to simplify these tasks.

Creating WordArt Objects

▶ **VOCABULARY**
WordArt

text box

WordArt is a feature that transforms text into a graphic. The WordArt graphic is created in a *text box,* a drawing object that displays text. Because the text box is a graphic, you can resize and position it like other graphics. Within the text box, you can change the font style, color, and size. To make the text decorative, you can fit the text within a preset shape, apply a gradient file, change the angle of the text, and apply special effects such as text borders and shadows. You can create your own styles, or you can choose from several predefined styles in the WordArt Gallery. Just like other objects, you can resize and reposition the WordArt object in the document.

Step-by-Step 17.8

2-1.3.7

1. If necessary, open the **Revised Newsletter 7** file from your solution files. Save the Revised Newsletter 7 document as **Revised Newsletter 8**, followed by your initials.

2. Position the insertion point at the top of the page. Click the **Page Layout** tab, and in the Page Setup group, click the **Margins** button. At the bottom of the menu, click **Custom Margins**. Under Margins, change the Top margin setting to **1.5** and the Bottom margin setting to **.5**. Click **OK**.

3. Double-click in the white area at the top of the document to position the insertion point in the header pane.

4. Click the **Insert** tab. In the Text group, click the **WordArt** button to open the WordArt gallery shown in **Figure 17–26**.

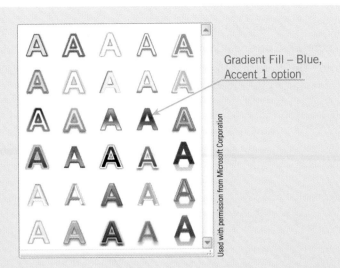

Gradient Fill – Blue,
Accent 1 option

FIGURE 17–26
WordArt gallery

5. In the third row, click the fourth WordArt style option, **Gradient Fill – Blue, Accent 1**. A new text box is displayed in the header section, and the Ribbon changes to show the Drawing Tools Format tab, shown in **Figure 17–27**.

FIGURE 17–27
Drawing Tools Format tab and
WordArt text box

6. The placeholder text *Your text here* is already selected. Type **Health News**. The width of the text box automatically adjusts to fit the new text. Select the new text. Click the **Home** tab, and change the font size to **48** points.

7. Point to the middle sizing handle on the right border of the text box, then click and drag the **handle** to expand the width of the text box to the right margin (where the border line and text end). The text box expands, and the text within the text box is automatically centered.

8. With the text box still selected, click the **Drawing Tools Format** tab. In the Shape Styles group, click the **Shape Fill** button arrow. In the first row under Theme Colors, click the **Blue, Accent 1** color.

9. Select all the text in the text box. In the WordArt Styles group, click the **Text Effects** button, and point to **3-D Rotation**. Move the mouse pointer over some of the 3-D rotation options under Perspective to see the Live Preview.

QUICK TIP

You can also select existing text and click the WordArt button to create a WordArt graphic using the selected text.

10. In the Text Effects menu, point to **Transform** to show the options shown in **Figure 17–28**. Under Warp, in the second row, select the first option, **Chevron Up**. Note that the shape changes, but the effects, including the text, fill color, and line colors remain unchanged.

FIGURE 17–28
Transform options

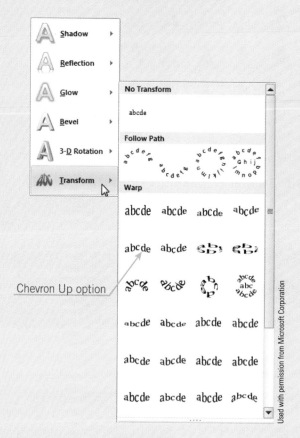

Chevron Up option

11. Click the **Home** tab, and in the Paragraph group, click the **Show/Hide ¶** button to hide the nonprinting characters. Click the **View** tab, and in the Zoom group, click the **One Page** button.

12. Like photographs and clip art, you can position a WordArt object anywhere in the document and wrap text around the object. With the WordArt object selected, click the **Drawing Tools Format** tab, and in the Arrange group, click the **Wrap Text** button, and then click **Square**. Position the mouse pointer somewhere around the border of the WordArt graphic to show the four-headed arrow, and then drag and drop the **WordArt graphic** to reposition it in the middle of the document.

13. Click the **Undo** button. Double-click in the body of the document to close the header and footer panes.

14. Save the changes, and close the document.

Inserting Lines, Shapes, and Text Boxes

You can use *drawing objects*, which are shapes, curves, and lines, to create your own graphic. A *shape* is a predesigned drawing object, such as a star, an arrow, or a rectangle. You can resize and reposition drawing objects the same way you change the size and position of pictures and clip art, and the drawing objects can be changed and enhanced with color, patterns, and borders.

You can copy and paste lines, shapes, objects, and text boxes just like you copy and paste text and graphics. You can even change the direction of the text in the text boxes so the text is displayed vertically. When you are creating a drawing that requires multiple horizontal lines, begin by creating and formatting the first line. Then copy and paste multiple copies of the line in the document window and start building. Not only will you save time, but the objects will be more consistent. If you do not want all the objects to be exactly the same size, you can resize them after you paste them in the document.

▶ **VOCABULARY**
drawing objects

shape

Step-by-Step 17.9

1. Open a new blank document. Show the nonprinting characters and, if necessary, display the ruler. Also, if necessary, change the Zoom setting to **One Page**. Then save the document as **Custom Shapes**, followed by your initials.

2. Click the **Insert** tab. In the Illustrations group, click the **Shapes** button to display the shape tools shown in **Figure 17–29**. Under Lines, click the first shape, the **Line** tool. A ScreenTip displays the name of the tool. The pointer changes to a crosshair ✛ when positioned in the document window.

IC³
2-1.3.7

FIGURE 17–29
Shape tools

Rectangle tool

Oval tool

Used with permission from Microsoft Corporation

3. Point to the paragraph marker, and drag the **crosshair** across the entire width of the document, from the left margin to the right margin. Do not release the mouse button until the line is straight, even, and the length you want. When you release the mouse button, the Ribbon adapts and shows the Drawing Tools Format tab.

4. With the line still selected (the sizing handles on each end of the line indicate that the line is selected), in the Shape Styles group, click the **Shape Outline** button arrow, and then point to **Weight**. Click **3 pt**. The weight of the selected line is now heavier.

5. Notice that the shapes are also available in the Insert Shapes group on the Drawing Tools Format tab shown in **Figure 17–30**. Click the **More** button, and then click the **Line** tool again. Draw a second line, this time drawing the line diagonally across the document window from the left end of the first line to the lower-right corner of the screen. With the second line still selected, click the **Shape Outline** button arrow, and under Standard Colors, click the **Red** color. The color of the line changes.

FIGURE 17–30
Insert Shapes group on the Drawing Tools Format tab

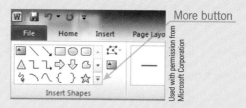

6. In the Insert Shapes group, click the **More** button, and then under Rectangles, click the first shape, the **Rectangle** tool. Position the crosshair just above the horizontal line at the top of the document at about the 2-inch mark on the horizontal ruler. Drag the **crosshair** down and to the right to create a box approximately 4 inches high and 4 inches wide. This box should overlap both the horizontal and diagonal lines.

7. With the rectangle object still selected, in the Shape Styles group, click the **Shape Fill** button arrow, and then under Standard Colors, click the **Green** color. The rectangle object is filled with the green color.

8. In the Insert Shapes group, click the **More** button, and in the Block Arrows section, click the first shape, the **Right Arrow** tool. Begin drawing the arrow in the middle of the green rectangle, and make the arrow wide enough that it extends beyond the right edge of the rectangle and is approximately ¾ inch high.

9. Click the **Insert** tab. In the Text group, click the **Text Box** button. Several built-in text box options are displayed. Below the built-in options, click **Draw Text Box**. In the middle of the green rectangle, on top of the right arrow, draw a box about 3 ½ inches high by 3 ½ inches wide. When you release the mouse button, the insertion point is positioned inside the box. Type your first name in the box.

10. Select the text in the text box, then right-click and use the Mini toolbar to change the font size to **24 pt**. If necessary, click the **Drawing Tools Format** tab. In the Text group, click the **Text Direction** button, and then click **Rotate all text 270°**. Click a blank area in the text box to deselect the text.

11. As you create the objects, they are layered with the most recent objects placed on top. The text box is on top of the arrow, which is on top of the rectangle, which is on top of the diagonal and horizontal lines. The new text box should still be selected. In the Arrange group, click the **Send Backward** button arrow, and then click **Send Backward**. The text box moves backward one layer and is now positioned behind the arrow.

12. With the text box still selected, click the **Send Backward** button arrow, and then click the **Send to Back** button. The name in the text box is no longer visible because the text box is now positioned at the bottom of the stack. Click the **Undo** button.

13. Click the diagonal line to select it. In the Arrange group, click the **Bring Forward** button arrow, and then click **Bring Forward**. The diagonal line moves forward one layer, in front of the rectangle but behind the text box. Click the **Bring Forward** button arrow, and then click **Bring to Front**. The diagonal line is on the top of the stack.

14. Save the changes, and then close the document.

ABOVE AND BEYOND

If time permits, open a new blank document and create more objects. Select the objects and explore the shape styles, shadow effects, and 3-D effects.

Creating SmartArt Graphics

Now that you know how to create text boxes and use the drawing tools, consider how you would create an organizational chart. You would need to create multiple text boxes, arrange and align the boxes to show a hierarchy, connect the boxes with horizontal and vertical lines, and then add text to the boxes. To create an effective illustration would be a tedious task, and you would likely spend a significant amount of time designing and creating the objects. But you can save yourself a lot of time and effort by using SmartArt graphics. *SmartArt* graphics are built-in, predesigned, and formatted layouts that you can use to illustrate concepts and ideas. The graphics are organized in a gallery under eight different categories, and each category includes several layouts. You can see the Live Preview of the layouts to help you choose the graphic that best suits your needs. Once you choose a design, you can focus on the content and quickly produce a professional illustration.

Like the building blocks for headers, the objects in the SmartArt graphics include fields, and you can replace the field placeholder text. The field placeholder text does not print in SmartArt graphics, so if you do not enter data in a field, you do not need to delete the placeholder text. The designs are based on contemporary layouts, and the styles and formats used in the designs are easy to modify.

A SmartArt graphic is inserted in the document in a *drawing canvas* that provides a framelike boundary between the graphic and the rest of the document. Using the drawing canvas is especially helpful if the graphic contains several shapes, because it keeps the shapes together as one object.

VOCABULARY
SmartArt
drawing canvas

Step-by-Step 17.10

2-1.3.7

1. Open a new blank document. Save the document as **Scientific Process**, followed by your initials.

2. Change the Zoom setting to **100%**. Click the **Insert** tab, and in the Illustrations group, click the **SmartArt** button. The Choose a SmartArt Graphic dialog box opens.

3. In the left pane, click **Cycle**. Several new diagrams are displayed in the center pane.

4. Click the first option, the **Basic Cycle** SmartArt graphic. A color preview of the Basic Cycle layout is displayed in the Preview pane, and a description of the layout is included in the Preview pane, as shown in **Figure 17–31**. Click **OK**. The graphic is inserted in the document.

FIGURE 17–31
Choose a SmartArt
Graphic dialog box

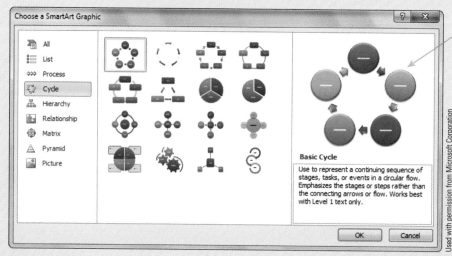

Preview of Basic
Cycle layout

Used with permission from Microsoft Corporation

5. When the SmartArt graphic is selected, the SmartArt Tools Design tab shown in **Figure 17–32** is active. All the objects in the SmartArt graphic are contained in a canvas. Each shape in the graphic includes placeholder text. The Text pane is displayed on the left side of the canvas. (If the Text pane is not displayed as shown in Figure 17–32, on the left side of the SmartArt graphic, click the blue tab with arrows to open the Text pane.)

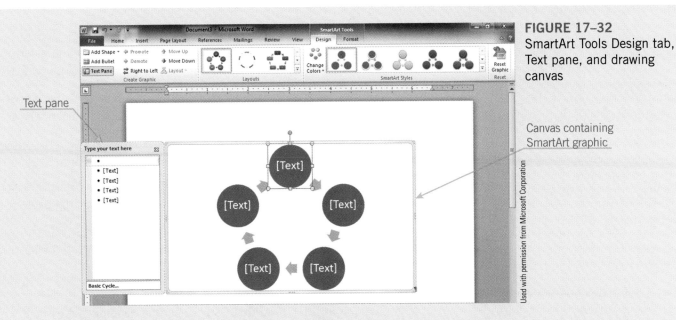

Used with permission from Microsoft Corporation

FIGURE 17–32
SmartArt Tools Design tab,
Text pane, and drawing
canvas

Canvas containing
SmartArt graphic

Text pane

6. Click the field placeholder text in the oval at the top of the canvas, and type **Ask a question**. As you enter the text, the font size adjusts so the text will fit within the oval object. Also, as you enter text in a field, the information in the Text pane is updated. You can choose to enter and edit data in the graphic or the Text pane.

7. Type the text for four more steps (going clockwise in the objects, or top to bottom in the Text pane):

   Form a hypothesis

   Design and conduct an experiment

   Analyze the results

   Draw a conclusion

8. You can easily add or remove objects. Click the **Ask a question** circle object to select it. On the SmartArt Tools Design tab, in the Create Graphic group, click the **Add Shape** button arrow, and then click **Add Shape After**. A new circle object is inserted.

9. The insertion point is already positioned in both the new circle object and in the corresponding new bulleted text box in the Text pane. Type **Observe and gather data**. In the upper-right corner of the Text pane, click the **Close** button to close the Text pane.

10. You realize that the content you entered describes a process, not a cycle. The SmartArt graphic should already be selected. In the Layouts group, click the **More** button, and then click **More Layouts**. In the left pane, click **Process**. Scroll to the top of the center pane. In the third row, click the first option, the **Continuous Block Process** SmartArt graphic. Then click **OK**. The layout changes, but the content remains intact.

11. The graphic should still be selected. In the SmartArt Styles group, click the **Change Colors** button. Roll the mouse pointer over the color options to see the Live Preview of the styles in the document window. A ScreenTip shows the name of each style. Under Colorful, click the first style, **Colorful – Accent Colors**. The colors of the rectangle objects and the arrow change.

12. With the graphic still selected, click the **SmartArt Tools Format** tab. On the right side of the tab, click the **Arrange** button, click **Wrap Text**, and then click **Square**. Now you can reposition the graphic on the page. Point to the drawing canvas border. When the pointer changes to a four-headed arrow, drag the **image** downward towards the center of the page so you can insert a heading above the graphic.

13. Position the insertion point outside the canvas at the top of the document, and type **SCIENTIFIC PROCESS**. Select the **heading** text without selecting the paragraph marker at the end of the text. (*Hint*: Position the insertion point in front of the first letter in the heading. Press and hold Shift and use the right arrow key to select each letter in the heading.) Right-click the selected text, and on the Mini toolbar, change the font size to **18 pt** and center the paragraph.

14. Save the changes to the document and leave the document open for the next Step-by-Step.

Creating a Screenshot

You can use the Screenshot feature to capture a picture of all or part of the application window. For example, you can use the feature to capture the screen of another Word document or of a Web page that is open in a browser. Only windows that have not been minimized in the taskbar can be captured. The Screenshot feature is available in Microsoft Word, Excel, Outlook, and PowerPoint.

ETHICS IN TECHNOLOGY

Web pages often display photos, and computers make it easy to copy and download those images. However, just because information is published on the Internet does not mean that the information is in the public domain and is free. Someone owns the rights to those pictures, and intellectual property law ensures that the owner of the picture is entitled to copyright protection. Before you download or copy images from the Internet, consider how you will use the image. For example, you can copy or download any clip art or photo in the Microsoft Office Clip Art and Media Library without permission and free of charge when you use the images in your own work. However, there are restrictions that prohibit you from selling the image in a product. If you are not sure about how you can use the image, check with the owner.

Step-by-Step 17.11

1. If necessary, open the **Scientific Process** file from your solution files. Change the zoom setting to **One Page**.

2. Close any other Word documents that are open. Then open a new blank document.

3. Click the **Insert** tab. In the Illustrations group, click the **Screenshot** button. A menu displays a thumbnail of the Scientific Process document, as shown in **Figure 17–33**. Note that open documents from other applications, such as Internet Explorer, are also displayed as shown.

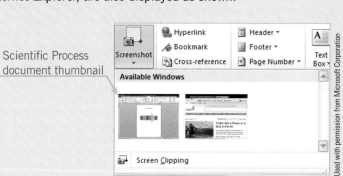

Scientific Process document thumbnail

FIGURE 17–33
Screenshot menu

4. Click the **Scientific Process** document thumbnail. A picture of the Word screen with the Scientific Process document is inserted in the current document.

5. Click the **Insert** tab. Click the **Screenshot** button, and then click **Screen Clipping**. The Scientific Process document is displayed. When the image is dimmed, the mouse pointer changes to a crosshair.

6. Drag the mouse pointer across the dimmed image to create a border around the SmartArt graphic. When you release the mouse button, the full screen image in the current document is replaced with the new clipped screenshot.

7. Save the document as **Diagram Screenshot**, followed by your initials. Then close both Word documents.

SUMMARY

In this lesson, you learned:

- Text can be arranged in a variety of multicolumn formats, all within the same document.

- Borders and shading are effective tools for enhancing the appearance and effectiveness of a document. You can choose from a variety of options for line styles, colors, and shading effects.

- Clip art and pictures help to enhance the appearance and effectiveness of a document.

- You can resize and crop graphics, and you can choose from several options to position the graphic in the document.

- You can further enhance graphics by changing the colors, applying special effects, removing backgrounds, and adjusting the contrast and brightness.

- To add emphasis to your document, you can use the WordArt feature to make text decorative.

- You can create your own graphics using drawing tools, shapes, and text boxes.

- SmartArt graphics are useful in illustrating concepts and ideas.

- The screenshot feature enables you to capture a picture of all or part of the application window.

■ LESSON REVIEW

TRUE / FALSE

Circle T if the statement is true or F if the statement is false.

T F **1.** When you open a new blank document in Word, the document has one section.

T F **2.** You can recolor clip art or a photograph so the colors match those in the current design theme.

T F **3.** A section break controls the section formatting of the text that precedes it.

T F **4.** To reduce or enlarge a graphic proportionally, drag the middle sizing handles on the side of the graphic.

T F **5.** To drop a graphic anywhere within the printable area of the page, the text-wrapping format must be applied to a graphic.

MULTIPLE CHOICE

Select the best response for the following statements.

1. _____ are small squares and circles on the border of a graphic that indicate the object is selected.

   A. Border handles   C. Sizing handles

   B. Crop handles   D. Selection marks

2. To adjust where a column ends, you can insert a(n) _____.

   A. end-of-line break   C. column break

   B. section break   D. manual column break

3. By default, Word inserts graphics _____.

   A. with the text formatted to wrap around the graphic   C. in the line of text

   B. aligned at the left margin   D. at the end of a paragraph

4. When you _____ a graphic, you remove a part of the graphic that you do not want to show.

   A. clip   C. outcrop

   B. crop   D. scale

5. When customizing borders, you can change the _____.

   A. line color   C. thickness of the line

   B. line style   D. all of the above

FILL IN THE BLANK

Complete the following sentences by writing the correct word or words in the blanks provided.

1. The process of creating documents that combine text and graphics is called _____.

2. A(n) _____ graphic is a built-in, predesigned, and formatted graphic layout with fields and placeholders.

3. A(n) _____ is a headline that spans the width of the page.

4. A(n) _____ is a predesigned drawing object.

5. _____ is a feature that enables you to transform text into a graphic.

WRITTEN QUESTIONS

Write a brief answer to the following questions.

1. What is the purpose of dividing a document into multiple sections?

2. What are the benefits of formatting text to be displayed in multiple columns?

3. What happens when you resize a graphic by dragging one of the square sizing handles on the side of the graphic?

4. What features can you use to clarify elements in a picture and lighten or darken the picture?

5. What is the benefit of using the drawing canvas?

PROJECTS

PROJECT 17–1

1. Open the **Menu** file from the drive and folder where your Data Files folder is stored. Save the Menu document as **Revised Menu**, followed by your initials.

    2-2.1.5
    2-2.1.6
    2-2.1.12

2. Select the list below the heading *SUNDAES*. Do not include the blank paragraph above the next heading in the selection. Format the list in two columns of equal width with a vertical line between the columns.

3. Apply the same two-column format to the lists below each of the remaining banner headings: *MILK SHAKES, SPECIALTIES*, and *COFFEE DELIGHTS*.

4. Apply a different shading color to each of the four lists.

5. Apply both borders and shading to the four banner headings. If desired, change the font style, color, and size.

6. Insert manual column breaks as needed so the title and description are displayed in the same column.

7. Insert a WordArt graphic in the header pane. Choose a WordArt style, and enter the text **MENU**. Resize and position the WordArt graphic in the header pane. Change the text color, and add text effects as desired to create an attractive banner at the top of the document.

8. Save the changes, and close the document.

PROJECT 17–3

1. Open the **Gardening** file from the drive and folder where your Data Files folder is stored. Save the Gardening document as **Revised Gardening**, followed by your initials.

    2-1.3.7

2. Position the insertion point in front of the heading *Summer Maintenance*. Insert the picture file **Begonias.jpg** from the drive and folder where your Data Files folder is stored.

3. Crop about 2½ inch from the right side of the photo to remove the dark area in the image. Resize the picture so it is approximately 1½ inches high. Wrap the text square around the picture, and position the picture on the right side of the bulleted list under the heading *Summer Maintenance*.

PROJECT 17–2

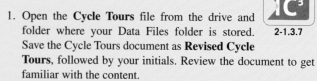

1. Open the **Cycle Tours** file from the drive and folder where your Data Files folder is stored. Save the Cycle Tours document as **Revised Cycle Tours**, followed by your initials. Review the document to get familiar with the content.

    2-1.3.7

2. Select the title **Roundabout Cycle Tours**. Click the **Insert** tab. In the Text group, click the **WordArt** button to create a graphic using the selected text. Choose a WordArt style, and change the font colors and text effects as desired.

3. Format the WordArt graphic to wrap top and bottom, and resize the text box to center it between the left and right margins.

4. Position the insertion point at the beginning of the first paragraph in the body of the document. Open the Clip Art task pane, and search for illustrations or photographs using the keyword **bicycle**. You will need to access Office.com content to get results for the research. If you do not have an Internet connection, insert the picture **Cycling.tif** from the drive and folder where your Data Files folder is stored.

5. Resize and crop the image as needed. Format the image so the text wraps around the object, and position the image as desired in the document. If desired, fit the image to a shape.

6. If desired, recolor the picture to match the WordArt object, or change the color of the WordArt object to match the image.

7. Save the changes, and close the document.

4. Position the insertion point in front of the heading *Preparing for Spring*. Insert the picture file **Lilies.jpg**, which is stored in the drive and folder where your Data Files folder is stored.

5. Resize the picture so it is approximately 1½ inches high. Wrap the text tight around the picture, and position the picture somewhere on the right side of the bulleted list under the heading *Preparing for Spring*.

6. Remove the background from the Lilies picture. Readjust the removal marquee so all three lilies are fully displayed.

7. Reposition the Lilies picture as needed so the text that wraps around the image is easy to read.

8. Save the changes, and close the document.

PROJECT 17–4

2-1.3.7

1. Open a new blank document and save it as **Map**, followed by your initials. Change the page orientation to landscape.

2. Use the Line, Rectangle, and Fill Color drawing tools to create the map shown in **Figure 17–34**. The Rulers on the edges of the screen are included in the figure to help you judge the size and position of the objects. The line weight for the lines representing the four streets is 3 pt.

3. Fill the rectangle with a bright red color.

4. Create four text boxes for the street names:

   a. To create the First Street and Second Street text boxes, draw tall, narrow boxes. Then change the text direction in the text boxes.

   b. Increase the font size to **18** points for the text inside the text boxes. (*Hint*: You can use the Mini toolbar.) Resize the text boxes as necessary.

   c. Remove the outline from the text boxes.

5. Use a shape to create the arrow in the map, and then fill the shape with a bright yellow color.

6. Insert a text box on top of the arrow, and enter the text **One Way**. Format the text box with the Shape Fill setting No Fill, which will allow the arrow color to show in the text box. Also, remove the outline from the text box border.

7. To create the callout that points out the exact address of the red rectangle, click the **Shapes** button, and under Callouts, click the **Line Callout 1** shape tool. Position the mouse pointer above the red rectangle, and drag to the right to create the callout shape. When you release the mouse button, the insertion point will be inside a text box, and you can enter the street address. Remove the fill color and change the font color to **black**.

8. Save the changes, and close the document.

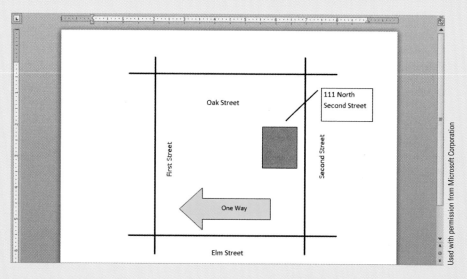

FIGURE 17–34   Map for Project 17–4

PROJECT 17-5

1. Create a new blank document. Save the document as **Organizational Chart**, followed by your initials.

2-1.3.7

2. Create a SmartArt graphic for an organizational chart that shows the hierarchy of the management positions in an organization, using a SmartArt graphic of your choice.

3. Enter the information provided in **Figure 17–35**. To remove an object from the diagram, select the placeholder text box and then delete it. To add the Communications Manager, Production Manager, and General Manager objects, use the **Add Shape Below** command. To add the Public Relations Manager and the Quality Control Manager objects, use the **Add Shape After** command.

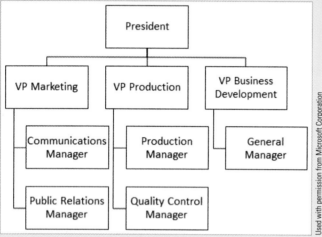

FIGURE 17–35   Data for Project 17–5

4. If desired, change the diagram colors.

5. Save the changes to the document, and then close the document.

TEAMWORK PROJECT

2-2.1.16

Choose a partner, and together gather samples of newsletters, brochures, and flyers. Compare and review the gathered content and list the strengths and weaknesses of the layouts and designs of each document. What elements and attributes are effective; what is ineffective? Share your samples with classmates and discuss the strengths and weaknesses of the layouts and designs.

■ CRITICAL THINKING

CRITICAL THINKING 17-1

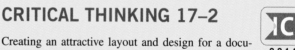
2-2.1.6

If you completed Project 17–1, open the solution file **Revised Menu**. Identify the total number of sections in the document. Check with a classmate to see if the two of you agree on the number of sections in the document.

CRITICAL THINKING 17-2

2-2.1.16

Creating an attractive layout and design for a document can draw attention and make a good first impression. However, even if the layout and design draw attention, if the content is not prepared accurately, the first impression might not be positive.

1. Create a new Word document and save the document as **CT 17-2**, followed by your initials.

2. Create a list of elements that have a negative effect when you review the content of a document.

3. It is a good choice to have someone else proofread your work for errors and provide feedback about the content, layout, and design. Share your list with a partner and ask that person to use your list as a guide for proofreading a document you have created for a class assignment.

4. Save the changes to the document and then close the document.

ONLINE DISCOVERY

In this lesson you worked with pictures saved in the JPEG format (*.jpg). Graphics such as photos and illustrations can be saved in several other formats including TIFF (*.tif), bitmap (*.bmp), and PNG (*.png). The resolution of the image and the size of the file depend on the file format. For example, JPEG images tend to be smaller files than TIFF images.

1. Search the Internet for information to learn more about the four file formats listed above.

2. Create a new Word document and save the document as **OD 17-1**, followed by your initials.

3. Create a list of the file types and explain the benefits of each file type.

2-1.3.7

4. Type a brief summary of when you would use each file format. Be sure to cite your Internet source(s).

5. Save the changes to the document and then close the document.

 JOB SKILLS

In this lesson, you have learned to use several Word features to enhance the appearance of a document. Put your knowledge into practice by designing a newsletter layout and design for your class, school, or workplace.

1. Create a new Word document and save the document as **JS 17-1**, followed by your initials.

2. Enter the following formula to create fake text. Type **=rand(4,7)**. (The number 4 in the equation refers to the number of paragraphs you want to create; the number 7 refers to

the number of sentences in each paragraph. To alter the number of paragraphs and sentences, you can change the numbers in the parentheses.) Press **Enter**, and the random text is inserted in the document.

2-2.1.12

3. Design a layout for the newsletter content using the Word features introduced in this lesson, such as multiple columns, banners, borders, shading, and graphics.

4. Save the changes to the document and then close the document.

LESSON 18

Getting Started with Excel Essentials

■ OBJECTIVES

Upon completion of this lesson, you should be able to:

- Identify the parts of the Excel screen.
- Navigate through a worksheet and a workbook.
- Change views and magnification in the worksheet window.
- Use the AutoCorrect and AutoComplete features when entering data.
- Insert and delete rows, and change column width and row height.
- Copy, clear, move, and delete data.
- Use the Undo and Redo features.
- Use the AutoFill feature to copy and enter data into a range of cells.

■ WORDS TO KNOW

active cell

AutoFill

cell

cell reference

column heading

range

row heading

spreadsheet

value

workbook

worksheet

■ DATA FILES

To complete this lesson, you will need these data files:

Earnings.xlsx

Order Request.xlsx

▶ VOCABULARY
spreadsheet

worksheet

workbook

For hundreds of years, accountants have used spreadsheets to gather, organize, and summarize text and numeric data. A *spreadsheet* is a grid of rows and columns into which you enter text data (e.g., surnames, cities, states) and numerical data (e.g., dates, currency, percentages). Each time one piece of data was changed, paper spreadsheets had to be manually recalculated, which was painstaking and time consuming. Excel is an electronic application designed to replace the paper spreadsheet. When using an electronic spreadsheet, data changes are relatively easy and require far less time. Excel is especially useful when you need to organize and maintain large amounts of data.

Identifying the Parts of the Excel Screen

Excel refers to a spreadsheet as a *worksheet*. The worksheet is always stored in a *workbook* that contains one or more worksheets. When working with large amounts of data, you can organize the data in multiple worksheets and still save all the data in one workbook. In addition, you can have multiple Excel workbooks open at the same time.

The Excel worksheet is divided into columns and rows. Columns of the worksheet appear vertically and are identified by letters at the top of the worksheet window. Rows appear horizontally and are identified by numbers on the left side of the worksheet window. Usually, the top row of a worksheet is used for explanatory text or headings that identify the type of data in each column.

Excel 2010 uses the Microsoft Office Fluent user interface you learned about in Lesson 11, with a Ribbon that adjusts to meet your needs. You will also recognize the Quick Access Toolbar. There are two sets of sizing buttons in the upper-right corner of the window. The top set of sizing buttons controls the application window. The lower set of sizing buttons controls the worksheet window. To maximize the screen space for your worksheet window, you can easily minimize the Ribbon.

Step-by-Step 18.1

2-1.1.1
2-1.1.2
2-3.1.1

1. Launch Excel. Compare your screen with **Figure 18–1**. A new workbook titled *Book1* is opened. Sheet1 appears in the worksheet window. There are two other worksheets in the workbook, Sheet2 and Sheet3, and the tabs for those worksheets are displayed at the bottom of the application window.

Sizing buttons for
application window

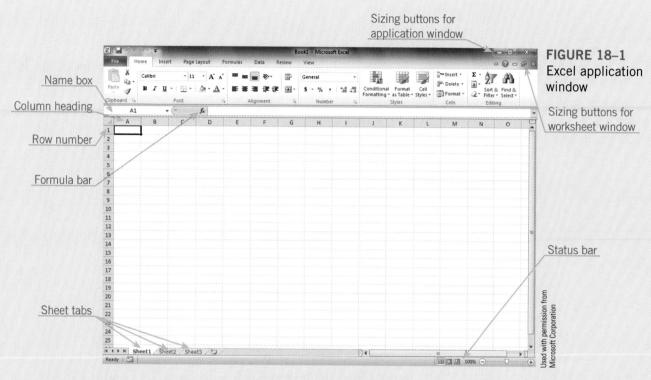

Name box

Column heading

Row number

Formula bar

Sheet tabs

FIGURE 18–1
Excel application
window

Sizing buttons for
worksheet window

Status bar

Used with permission from
Microsoft Corporation

2. Note the various components of the Excel screen and their names. The Ribbon is similar to the Ribbon that appears in Word. Some of the buttons are the same, but there are also many new buttons.

3. Move the mouse pointer over the cells in the worksheet window. When the mouse pointer is within the worksheet cells, it changes to the white plus sign ✚.

4. Position the mouse pointer over the Ribbon. The pointer changes to the normal pointer ↘.

5. Position the mouse pointer over the formula bar. The pointer changes to an I-beam I.

6. On the title bar, in the upper row of sizing buttons, click the **Minimize** button ▭. The application window is minimized. In the taskbar, click the **Microsoft Excel** button to restore the application window.

7. On the title bar, in the lower row of sizing buttons, click the **Minimize Window** button ▭. The worksheet window is minimized, but the Ribbon still appears in the application window. A minimized title bar is displayed in the lower-left corner of the application window as shown in **Figure 18–2**.

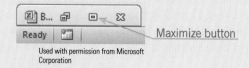

Maximize button

Used with permission from Microsoft
Corporation

FIGURE 18–2
Minimized title bar

8. On the minimized title bar, click the **Maximize** button 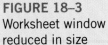, and the worksheet window appears again.

9. In the lower set of sizing buttons, click the **Restore Window** button. The worksheet window is reduced in size, as shown in **Figure 18–3**.

FIGURE 18–3
Worksheet window reduced in size

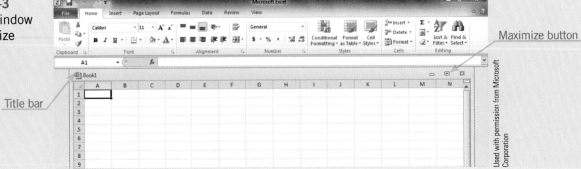

Used with permission from Microsoft Corporation

10. Drag the **Book1** title bar to move the worksheet window around on the screen.

11. In the worksheet window, click the **Maximize** button to maximize the worksheet within the application window.

12. Note the number of rows that are displayed in the worksheet window.

13. In the lower set of sizing buttons, click the **Minimize the Ribbon** button to show more rows in the worksheet. Then click the **Expand the Ribbon** button to restore the Ribbon to the default settings.

14. Leave Excel open for the next Step-by-Step.

QUICK TIP

You can also minimize the Ribbon by double-clicking any one of the Ribbon tabs. To expand the Ribbon, double-click any one of the tabs.

▶ VOCABULARY
cell
cell reference
active cell

2-3.1.2

Navigating a Workbook

A useful workbook has data organized logically in the cells. A *cell* is the intersection of a single row and a single column. The *cell reference* is the column letter followed by the row number (for example, A1 or B4). Before you can enter data into a cell, you must first select the cell. When the cell is selected, a dark border appears around the cell, and the column and row headings for the selected cell are highlighted. You can select a cell using either the mouse or the keyboard. When a cell is selected, it is called the *active cell*. The active cell is identified in the Name box at the top of the worksheet window.

To be useful, the rows and columns in the worksheets must be labeled effectively so you can easily find and identify the data. To move around in a worksheet, you can use the scroll bar features or you can use keyboard shortcuts. Many of the keyboard shortcuts you learned to use in Word move the insertion point in Excel in similar ways. For example, the arrow keys move the insertion point one cell in any direction, and Page Up or Page Down moves the insertion point one screen up or down. **Table 18–1** includes other keyboard shortcuts you can use to move the insertion point in an Excel worksheet.

TABLE 18–1   Keyboard shortcuts for moving the insertion point in Excel

TO MOVE THE INSERTION POINT	PRESS
Right one cell	Right arrow or Tab
Left one cell	Left arrow or Shift+Tab
To the next row	Down arrow
To the previous row	Up arrow
To the first cell in a row	Home
To the beginning of the worksheet	Ctrl+Home
To the last column and row with data in the worksheet	Ctrl+End
To the next screen	Page Down
To the previous screen	Page Up
To a specific cell	F5 (and then enter the cell reference in the Go To dialog box)

Step-by-Step 18.2

1. Click the **File** tab, and then click **Open**. Navigate to the drive and folder where your Data Files folder is stored. Select the filename **Earnings**, and click **Open**.

2. Click the **File** tab, and then click **Save As** to open the Save As dialog box. Navigate to the drive and folder where you save your solution files. In the File name box, type the new filename **Updated Earnings**, followed by your initials. Click **Save**.

3. Cell A1 is the active cell, as shown in **Figure 18–4**. Notice the cell reference *A1* is displayed in the Name box, and the contents of the cell are displayed in the formula bar. Click cell **C5** to select it. The Name box now shows the cell reference *C5*, and the formula bar shows the contents for cell C5.

2-1.1.3
2-1.2.4
2-3.1.1

Name box shows the cell reference

Column letter and row number highlighted for active cell

Active cell

	A1	▾		fx	Emp. #			
	A	B	C	D	E	F	G	H
1	Emp. #	1995	1996	1997	1998	1999	2000	2001
2								
3	1012	$82,313	$79,744					
4	1020	$93,948	$79,797					
5	1030	$82,963	$79,797	$79,027	$82,377	$83,872		
6	1011	$78,566	$80,273					
7	1014	$80,533	$80,293	$81,883				
8	1017	$78,287	$80,740					

FIGURE 18–4
An active cell in a worksheet

Formula bar shows cell contents

Used with permission from Microsoft Corporation

4. Press **Tab** three times to move to cell F5. Then, press **Home** to move to the beginning of the row. Cell A5 is the active cell.

5. Press the **up arrow** to move to cell A4. When you use Tab or an arrow key, the active cell moves to the new location.

6. On the Home tab, in the Editing group shown in **Figure 18–5**, click the **Find & Select** button, and then click **Go To**.

FIGURE 18–5
Editing group on the Home tab

Used with permission from Microsoft Corporation

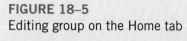
7. The Go To dialog box opens. Under Reference, type **p76**, and click **OK** to move to cell P76, which is now the active cell as shown in **Figure 18–6**.

FIGURE 18–6
Cell P76 selected

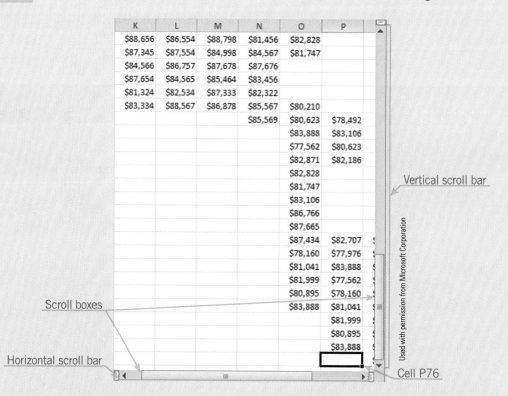

K	L	M	N	O	P
$88,656	$86,554	$88,798	$81,456	$82,828	
$87,345	$87,554	$84,998	$84,567	$81,747	
$84,566	$86,757	$87,678	$87,676		
$87,654	$84,565	$85,464	$83,456		
$81,324	$82,534	$87,333	$82,322		
$83,334	$88,567	$86,878	$85,567	$80,210	
			$85,569	$80,623	$78,492
				$83,888	$83,106
				$77,562	$80,623
				$82,871	$82,186
				$82,828	
				$81,747	
				$83,106	
				$86,766	
				$87,665	
				$87,434	$82,707
				$78,160	$77,976
				$81,041	$83,888
				$81,999	$77,562
				$80,895	$78,160
				$83,888	$81,041
					$81,999
					$80,895
					$83,888

Vertical scroll bar

Scroll boxes

Horizontal scroll bar

Cell P76

Used with permission from Microsoft Corporation

8. On the horizontal scroll bar, drag the **scroll box** to the right so you can see the last cell with data, cell T76. Then click the **scroll up** arrow on the vertical scroll bar to move up one row. The scroll bar changes the view on the screen, but it does not change the active cell.

9. Click above the scroll box on the vertical scroll bar to move up one screen, and then click below the scroll box to move down one screen. Click to the left side of the scroll box on the horizontal scroll bar to move one screen to the left, and then click to the right of the scroll box to move one screen to the right.

10. To navigate back to the beginning of the document, press and hold **Ctrl** and then press **Home**. The active cell is now cell A1.

11. Press and hold **Ctrl** and then press **End** to move to the last cell with data in the worksheet. The active cell is now cell T76.

12. Click the **Sheet2** sheet tab at the bottom of the worksheet window to open the second worksheet in the workbook. The cells in the worksheet are empty. Click the **Sheet3** sheet tab. The cells in the worksheet are empty. Click the **Sheet1** sheet tab to go back to the first worksheet in the workbook.

13. Cell T76 is still the active cell. Press and hold **Ctrl** and then press **Home** to return to cell A1.

14. Leave the workbook open for the next Step-by-Step.

Changing the Workbook View and Magnification

Excel offers several options for viewing a workbook. You can change the view by selecting options from the Workbook Views group on the View tab or by clicking one of the view buttons in the status bar in the lower-right corner of the worksheet window. You can also change the zoom settings to adjust the view on the screen.

Step-by-Step 18.3

1. If necessary, open the **Updated Earnings** file from your solution files.

2. Click the **View** tab. The view commands are in the Workbook Views group, shown in **Figure 18–7**. The current view is Normal, which is the default view.

2-1.1.5
2-1.1.6
2-1.2.5

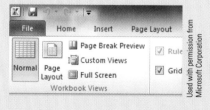

Used with permission from Microsoft Corporation

FIGURE 18–7
Workbook Views group on the View tab

3. Click the **Page Layout** button. The view changes, and the column and row labels are separated from the worksheet cells because these labels will not appear in a printed worksheet. You can see the white margins that will appear when the worksheet is printed.

4. Click the **Page Break Preview** button. When prompted about adjusting the page breaks, click **OK**. Scroll down and you see that the worksheet will print on six pages. You will learn more about working with the Page Break Preview in Lesson 19.

5. Click the **Full Screen** button. The Full Screen view hides the Ribbon, the formula bar, and the status bar.

6. To close Full Screen and return to the previous view, press **Esc** (or you can right-click in the worksheet window and in the shortcut menu, click **Close Full Screen**).

7. On the status bar, click the **Page Layout** view button 🔲 shown in **Figure 18–8** to display the worksheet as it will be printed.

FIGURE 18–8
View buttons and zoom settings on the status bar

Normal view button

Page Layout view button

Page Break Preview view button

Used with permission from Microsoft Corporation

8. On the status bar, click the **Page Break Preview** view button 🔲 to show the page breaks. If necessary, click **OK** to close the prompt about adjusting the page breaks.

9. On the status bar, click the **Normal** view button 🔲 to return to the default view.

10. On the View tab, in the Zoom group shown in **Figure 18–9**, click the **Zoom** button. The Zoom dialog box opens. Click **50%**, and then click **OK**. You can see all the page breaks.

FIGURE 18–9
Zoom group on the View tab

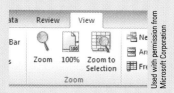

Used with permission from Microsoft Corporation

11. In the Zoom group, click the **100%** button. You can also find zoom controls in the status bar in the lower-right corner of the screen, as shown in **Figure 18–8**.

12. In the lower set of sizing buttons, click the **Close Window** button to close the worksheet window. If prompted to save changes, click **Don't Save**.

Entering Data

You add data to the cells by entering text or a number in the active cell. The text or number is often referred to as a *value*.

Inserting Data

To enter data in a cell, the cell must be active. As you begin entering text, you see the insertion point indicating where the next character of text will appear. By default, Excel shows approximately eight characters in each cell. When text is too long for the width of a cell, it spills over into the next cell if the next cell is empty. If the next cell is not empty, the text that does not fit into the cell is not displayed, but it is still contained within the cell. When you enter more numbers than can fit in the cell, a series of number signs (####) is displayed in the cell.

Step-by-Step 18.4

1. Click the **File** tab. In the left pane, click **New**. In the middle pane, the Blank workbook icon is already selected. In the right pane, click the **Create** button.

2-3.1.3

2. Save the new workbook as **Destinations 1**, followed by your initials.

3. The active cell should be A1. Type **Days**. Notice the text you enter is displayed in both the cell and the formula bar. As new content is entered, the formula bar adapts and shows the three buttons shown in **Figure 18–10**. You will use these buttons in a later step to edit the cell contents.

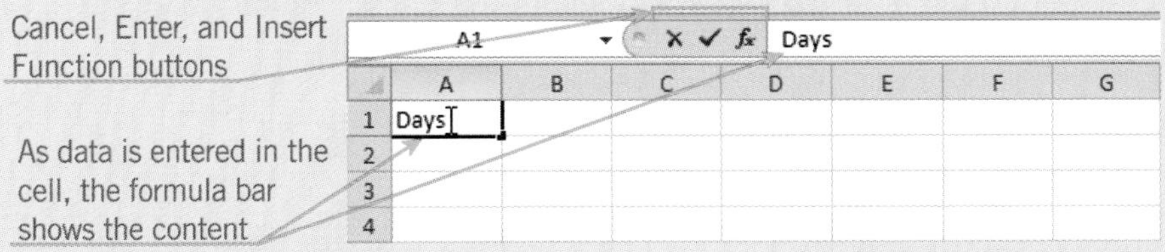

Cancel, Enter, and Insert Function buttons

As data is entered in the cell, the formula bar shows the content

	A	B	C	D	E	F	G
1	Days						
2							
3							
4							

A1 — ✗ ✓ *fx* | Days

Used with permission from Microsoft Corporation

FIGURE 18–10
Formula bar with data entered in the cell

4. Press **Tab**. The insertion point moves to the next cell to the right in the first row, B1.

5. Type **Depart**, and then press **Enter**. The insertion point moves down a row to the first cell in the second row, A2. The default setting aligns text at the left border of the cell.

6. Click cell **C1**, type **Arrive**, and then press **Tab**.

7. Type **Cruise**, and then press **Enter**. The active cell is now C2.

8. Click cell **A1** to select it. *Days* shows in the cell and in the formula bar. To change the text in the formula bar, position the insertion point in front of the word *Days* in the formula bar. Type **Number of**, and then press the **spacebar**. On the formula bar, click the **Enter** button ✔. The change is made in the formula bar and in cell A1. (The Enter button in the formula bar only enters the data. It does not allow for the automatic movement to A2.)

9. Double-click cell **A1**. When the insertion point appears, delete **Number of**, and then type **#**. The edit is made in cell A1 and in the formula bar. Press **Tab**.

10. Press the **right arrow** two times to move to cell D1. The cell currently shows *Cruise*. Type **Destination**, and press **Enter**. The contents of the cell are replaced with the new text you entered, and the cell below, D2, becomes active. Also notice that the new content expands beyond the border of the D column. You will fix that later.

11. Click cell **C1**. It currently shows *Arrive*. Press **F2**. Notice that the insertion point is now positioned at the end of the text in the cell.

12. Press **Backspace** to delete the existing text, and then type **Return**. Press **Enter**. All the contents in the cell are replaced with the new text you entered, and the cell below, C2, becomes active.

13. Click cell **A2**. Enter the following numbers, pressing **Enter** after each number. When you are done, your worksheet should look like the one shown in **Figure 18–11**. The default setting aligns numbers at the right border of the cell.

    4

    5

    7

    10

    7

FIGURE 18–11
Worksheet with data

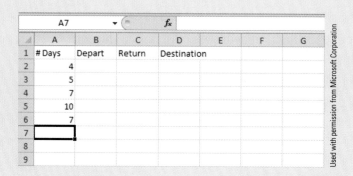

14. On the Quick Access Toolbar, click the **Save** button. Leave the workbook open for the next Step-by-Step.

Using the AutoCorrect and AutoComplete Features

Obviously, to get accurate results, you must enter worksheet data accurately. The AutoCorrect feature in Excel corrects common mistakes as you enter data. For example, if you type *hte*, Excel will automatically change the text to *the*. With the AutoComplete feature, Excel compares the first few characters you enter in a cell with existing entries in the same column. If the characters match an existing cell entry, Excel proposes the existing entry. You can press Enter to accept the proposed entry, or you can continue entering new text.

Step-by-Step 18.5

1. If necessary, open the **Destinations 1** file from your solution files. Save the Destinations 1 workbook as **Destinations 2**, followed by your initials.

2. Click cell **D2**. Type **Caribbean**, and press **Enter**.

3. In cell D3, type **Bahamas and Florida**, and press **Enter**. The contents overlap the right border of the column. The active cell is D4.

4. Type **C**. Notice that Excel suggests *Caribbean* because you entered it earlier in the column. Press **Enter** to accept the proposed text.

5. Type **Alaska**, and press **Enter**.

6. Type **Belize adn**. Then look at the active cell as you press the **spacebar**. Excel automatically corrects the spelling and changes *adn* to *and*.

7. Type **Cozumel**, and press **Enter**.

8. Save the changes, and leave the workbook open for the next Step-by-Step.

2-3.1.2
2-3.1.3

Modifying the Worksheet Structure

Just as you can change a Word table structure, you can change the structure of a worksheet by adding or deleting rows and columns and merging cells. You can also add and delete the worksheets stored within a workbook.

Selecting Multiple Cells in the Worksheet

To select an entire row in a worksheet, click the **row heading**, which is the number at the left of the row. To select an entire column, click the **column heading**, which is the letter at the top of the column. You can also select a row, column, or section of a worksheet by clicking and dragging the mouse to highlight the area you want to select. When you select a group of cells, the group is called a **range**. All cells in a range touch each other and form a rectangle. The range is identified by the cell references of the cell in the upper-left corner and the cell in the lower-right corner, separated by a colon (for example, A1:D4).

> **VOCABULARY**
> row heading
> column heading
> range

Step-by-Step 18.6

2-1.3.2

1. If necessary, open the **Destinations 2** file from your solution files. Save the Destinations 2 workbook as **Destinations 3**, followed by your initials.

2. Click the **column B** heading to select the second column. The column has a dark border, and all the cells in the column are shaded except for the first cell. The lack of shading indicates the first cell is the active cell, as shown in **Figure 18–12**.

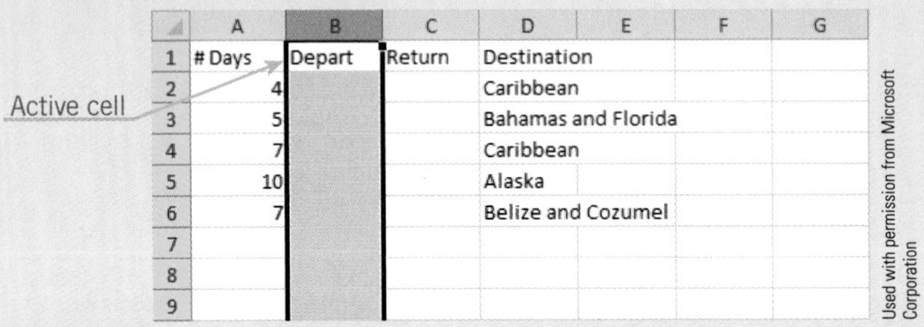

FIGURE 18–12
Selected column

Active cell

	A	B	C	D	E	F	G
1	# Days	Depart	Return	Destination			
2	4			Caribbean			
3	5			Bahamas and Florida			
4	7			Caribbean			
5	10			Alaska			
6	7			Belize and Cozumel			
7							
8							
9							

Used with permission from Microsoft Corporation

3. Click the **row 4** heading to select the fourth row. The entire row has a dark border, and the row number and all the cells in the row are shaded, except for the first cell, A4, which is the active cell.

4. Type **8** and press **Enter**. Notice that this new data replaces the data in the active cell, A4. When you enter data in a selected row or column, the data is entered in the first cell.

5. Point to cell **A1**, and then click and drag the mouse pointer to the right and down to select the range **A1:D6**. Even though some of the content in column D extends beyond the cell borders, as shown in **Figure 18–13**, all of the content is selected.

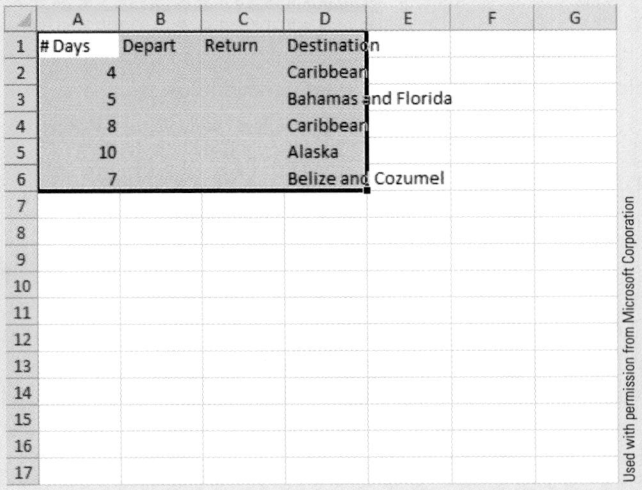

FIGURE 18–13
Selected range of cells

	A	B	C	D	E	F	G
1	# Days	Depart	Return	Destination			
2	4			Caribbean			
3	5			Bahamas and Florida			
4	8			Caribbean			
5	10			Alaska			
6	7			Belize and Cozumel			
7							
8							
9							
10							
11							
12							
13							
14							
15							
16							
17							

Used with permission from Microsoft Corporation

6. Click elsewhere in the worksheet to deselect the range. Click cell **A1**. Hold down **Shift** and click cell **D6**. All cells between A1 and D6 are selected. Click elsewhere in the worksheet to deselect the range.

7. Click cell **A1**. Press and hold down **Shift**, and use the right and down arrow keys to select the range **AI:D6**. Click elsewhere in the worksheet to deselect the range.

8. Save the changes, and leave the workbook open for the next Step-by-Step.

ABOVE AND BEYOND

Instead of holding down the Shift key to select a range of cells, you can press F8 and then press the arrow keys to select the cells. The F8 key enables the Select mode. To turn off the Select mode, press F8 again, or press Esc.

Inserting and Deleting Rows and Columns

When you insert or delete a row or a column in Excel, it affects the entire worksheet. All existing data is shifted in some direction. For example, when you add a new column, the existing data shifts to the right. When you add a new row, the data shifts down a row. To add or delete rows and columns, use the buttons in the Cells group on the Home tab. To insert or delete multiple columns and rows in a single step, select the desired number of columns or rows before executing the command.

Step-by-Step 18.7

1. If necessary, open the **Destinations 3** file from your solution files. Save the Destinations 3 workbook as **Destinations 4**, followed by your initials.

2. Click the **Home** tab, then click any cell in column D. In the Cells group, click the **Insert** button arrow, and then click **Insert Sheet Columns**. A new column is inserted to the left of column D, and the data that was labeled as column *D* is now labeled as column *E*.

3. Click cell **D1**, and type the column heading **Agent**. Press **Enter**, and then type the following list of travel agent initials in cells D2 through D6. Use Excel's AutoComplete feature to complete repeated entries, and remember to press **Enter** after each entry to move to the next cell in the column.

JRK
AMF
JRK
AMF
AMF

2-3.1.4

ABOVE AND BEYOND

If the data in one cell is dependent on the data in another cell, when these cells are adjusted, Excel will keep straight what information is required where. You will learn more about this in Lesson 20.

4. Click cell **C4**. In the Cells group, click the **Delete** button arrow, and then click **Delete Sheet Columns**. The column with the label *Return* is deleted from the worksheet. The content that was in column D and column E is now in column C and column D. If you had selected multiple columns before clicking the Delete Sheet Columns option, all the selected columns would have been deleted.

5. Click any cell in row 6. In the Cells group, click the **Insert** button arrow, and then click **Insert Sheet Rows**. A new row is inserted above the row with the active cell, and row 6 becomes row 7. The existing data shifts down, and the row labels are updated to reflect the change.

6. Click cell **A6**, and type **10**. Click cell **C6**, and type **JRK**. Click cell **D6**, and type **Panama Canal**.

7. Point to the **row 6** heading, and then click and drag down to select rows **6** and **7**.

8. With rows 6 and 7 both selected, in the Cells group, click the **Insert** button. Because whole rows were already selected, you did not need to click the button arrow to select the option to insert sheet rows. Because two rows are selected, two new rows are inserted above the selected rows.

9. Enter the following information in columns A, C, and D of the new rows:

14	AMF	Mediterranean
10	JRK	Caribbean

10. Click the **row 9** heading to select the entire row. In the Cells group, click the **Delete** button. Because you selected the entire row, you did not need to click the button arrow to delete the entire row.

11. Deselect the cells. Save the changes, and leave the workbook open for the next Step-by-Step.

Changing Column Width and Row Height

As you already learned, sometimes the data you enter in a cell does not fit in the column. To accommodate the data, you can widen the column and change the height of a row. There are several options available for changing the cell width and height.

Step-by-Step 18.8

1. If necessary, open the **Destinations 4** file from your solution files. Save the Destinations 4 workbook as **Destinations 5**, followed by your initials.

2. Select cell **A1**.

3. Point to the boundary on the right side of the column B heading. When the pointer changes to a double-headed arrow, as shown in **Figure 18–14**, click and drag the **boundary** to the right. As you drag the boundary, the exact column width appears in a ScreenTip. Release the mouse button when the column width is exactly 11.00 (82 pixels) as shown in Figure 18–14.

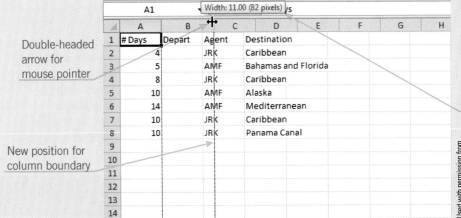

FIGURE 18–14
Dragging a column boundary to change the column width

4. Click the **column D** heading to select the entire column.

5. In the Cells group, click the **Format** button, and then click **AutoFit Column Width**. The column width is automatically adjusted to fit the cell with the most content—in this case, cell D3 with the content *Bahamas and Florida*.

6. Point to the **column A** heading, and then click and drag across the headings to include columns **B** and **C** in the selection.

7. With the three columns selected, position the mouse pointer over the right boundary on the column C heading. When the pointer changes to a double-headed arrow, double-click. The width of each of the three columns is automatically adjusted to fit the contents in that column.

8. Click the **row 1** heading to select the entire row.

9. Click the **Format** button, and then click **Row Height**. The Row Height dialog box opens. Change the row height setting to **25**, and then click **OK**.

10. Click anywhere in the worksheet to deselect the row. Note the change in row 1. The row is now about twice as high as the other rows.

11. Save the changes, and leave the workbook open for the next Step-by-Step.

Editing the Worksheet Data

Sometimes after entering data in a worksheet, you need to reorganize it. You may even want to remove some of the data and not replace it. Or, you may want to move or copy existing data from one location to another.

Clearing, Replacing, and Copying Existing Data

You learned in Step-by-Step 18.4 that you can edit the data directly in the cell, or you can make the necessary changes to the cell contents in the formula bar. To replace cell contents, you can select the cell and enter the new data. The process for deleting data can be as simple as pressing Delete or Backspace. Using these keys, you can clear the cell contents.

Copying data saves you from having to enter the same data into another location. The process, as in all Office applications, is easy. Moving data is similar to copying data, except that you cut the data from one location and paste it in a new location. You can copy or move multiple cells of data at the same time. However, unlike copying or moving data in a Word table, when you paste data to a spreadsheet cell that already contains data, that existing data does not move to make room for the new data. Instead, the existing data in the destination cell is replaced with the pasted data. If you do not want to lose content, you need to copy or move data into empty cells.

The Undo and Redo commands are available on the Quick Access Toolbar. However, the default settings in Excel do not include the Repeat command.

Step-by-Step 18.9

2-1.3.1
2-1.3.2
2-1.3.3
2-3.1.3
2-3.1.4

1. If necessary, open the **Destinations 5** file from your solution files. Save the Destinations 5 workbook as **Destinations 6**, followed by your initials.

2. Click cell **A6**. The cell currently shows *14*. Press **Delete** to remove the contents.

3. With cell A6 still selected, type **10**, and press **Enter**.

4. If necessary, click the **Home** tab. Click cell **A6**. In the Cells group, click the **Delete** button arrow, and then click **Delete Cells**. The Delete dialog box shown in **Figure 18–15** opens. If necessary, click the **Shift cells up** option. Click **OK**. The contents in cells A7 and A8 are shifted one cell up, and cell A8 is now empty. Cell A6 is the active cell.

FIGURE 18–15
Delete dialog box

Used with permission from Microsoft Corporation

5. With cell A6 still the active cell, click the **Insert** button arrow, and then click **Insert Cells**. If necessary, click the **Shift cells down** option. Click **OK**. The contents in cells A6 through A8 are each shifted down one cell, and now cell A6 is empty. Type **14**, and press **Enter**.

6. Click cell **D4**. In the Clipboard group, click the **Copy** button 📑. The contents of the cell (*Caribbean*) are copied to the Clipboard. Also, an animated border (a dotted-line marquee) appears around the selected cell, as shown in **Figure 18–16**.

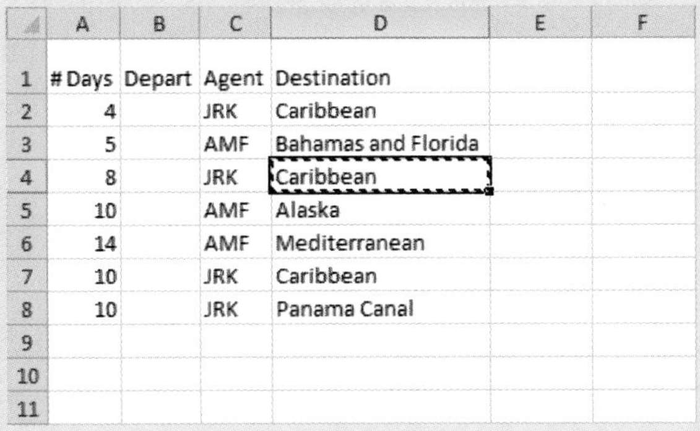

⚠	A	B	C	D	E	F
1	# Days	Depart	Agent	Destination		
2	4		JRK	Caribbean		
3	5		AMF	Bahamas and Florida		
4	8		JRK	Caribbean		
5	10		AMF	Alaska		
6	14		AMF	Mediterranean		
7	10		JRK	Caribbean		
8	10		JRK	Panama Canal		
9						
10						
11						

FIGURE 18–16
Marquee around a selected cell

Used with permission from Microsoft Corporation

7. Click cell **D9**. In the Clipboard group, click the **Paste** button 📋. (Be sure to click the Paste button and not the Paste button arrow.) The copied data is pasted in the destination cell.

8. On the Quick Access Toolbar, click the **Undo** button to undo the Paste action. Click the **Redo** button to reverse the action. Then click the **Undo** button again.

9. The marquee is still displayed around cell D4 to indicate that you can still paste the copied data in other locations. Press **Esc** to remove the marquee around the copied cell.

10. Click cell **B1**. The cell currently shows *Depart*. In the Clipboard group, click the **Cut** button ✂. The contents of the cell are stored on the Clipboard, and a marquee appears around the cell border.

11. Click cell **E1**, and then click the **Paste** button. The contents are cut from cell B1 and moved to cell E1.

12. Click the column **D** heading to select the entire column. In the Clipboard group, click the **Cut** button. Select cell **B1**, and then click the **Paste** button. The entire column is moved, and the AutoFit Column Width format still applies. The contents are moved to column B, and although all the cells are empty, column D still exists.

13. Select rows **4** and **5**. In the Cells group, click the **Insert** button arrow, and then click **Insert Sheet Rows**. Then select rows **9** and **10**. In the Clipboard group, click the **Cut** button. Click cell **A4**, and then click the **Paste** button.

14. Save the changes, and leave the workbook open.

Using the AutoFill Feature to Copy Data

▶ VOCABULARY
AutoFill

Filling data is another method for copying data in a worksheet. The *AutoFill* feature enables you to repeat the same data in a column or row. Using the AutoFill feature is faster than copying and pasting because filling requires only one step. However, the Fill command can only be used when the destination cells are adjacent to the original cell. You can use the mouse to automatically fill data up or down in the same column, or right or left in the same row.

Step-by-Step 18.10

2-3.1.3

1. If necessary, open the file **Destinations 6** from your solution files. Save the Destinations 6 workbook as **Destinations 7**, followed by your initials.
2. Click cell **D1**, type **Vacancy**, and press **Enter**.
3. Cell D2 is the active cell. Type **Yes**, and then press **Enter**.
4. Select the range **D2:D6**.
5. In the Editing group, shown in **Figure 18–17**, click the **Fill** button 📥,
    and then click **Down**. The content in cell D2 is copied and pasted into the cells in the D3:D6 range.

FIGURE 18–17
Editing group on the Home tab

Fill button

Used with permission from Microsoft Corporation

◗ ABOVE AND BEYOND

To quickly fill to the cell on the right, click the destination cell and press Ctrl+R. The contents in the cell at the left are copied to the destination cell. To quickly fill down, click the destination cell and press Ctrl+D. The contents of the cell above are copied to the destination cell.

6. Click cell **D8**, enter **No**, and then press **Enter**.
7. Click cell **D7**. Click the **Fill** button, and then click **Up**. The text is copied from cell D8 and pasted into cell D7.
8. Click cell **C2**. Point to the fill handle, shown in **Figure 18–18**. When the pointer changes to a crosshair ✛, click and drag downward to select the range **C2:C6**. A ScreenTip shows the cell contents (JRK) that will be copied to the range of cells. Release the mouse button, and the contents of C2 are pasted, replacing the contents in cells C3 through C6.

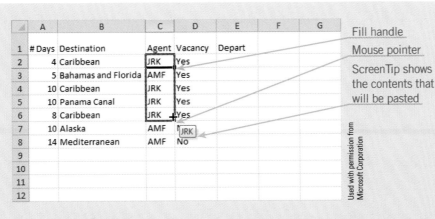

Fill handle

Mouse pointer

ScreenTip shows
the contents that
will be pasted

FIGURE 18–18
Filling down a range of cells

Used with permission from
Microsoft Corporation

9. Deselect the cells. Save the changes, and leave the workbook open for the next Step-by-Step.

Using the AutoFill Feature to Fill in a Series

You can also use the AutoFill feature to automatically fill in a series of numbers and dates. To fill in a series, a pattern must be established in the initial selection of cells. Then when you drag the fill handle, the pattern is continued. When you drag the fill handle down or to the right, the series is continued in ascending order. However, when you drag the fill handle up or to the left, the series is continued in descending order.

Step-by-Step 18.11

1. If necessary, open the **Destinations 7** file from your solution files. Save the Destinations 7 workbook as **Destinations 8**, followed by your initials.

2. Click cell **E2**. Type **3/7**, and press **Enter**. The default setting automatically formats the numbers for the date to appear as *7-Mar*.

3. Type **3/14**, and press **Enter**.

4. You have now established a pattern (every 7 days) for the dates. Select the range **E2:E3**, and click and drag the **fill handle** downward to cell **E8**. When you release the mouse button, the dates for the next five weeks are entered into the cells.

2-3.1.3

5. With the range E2:E8 still selected, in the Editing group click the **Fill** button, and then click **Series**. The Series dialog box opens, as shown in **Figure 18–19**. The settings you see are the settings that you applied when you used the fill handle. When you want to modify the settings, you can click the Fill button and access this dialog box.

FIGURE 18–19
Series dialog box

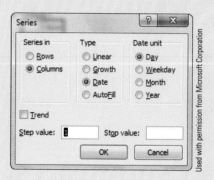

6. Click **Cancel** to close the dialog box without making any changes.

7. Notice the Auto Fill Options button, shown in **Figure 18–20**, is displayed to the right of the fill handle in cell E8.

FIGURE 18–20
After the range of cells is filled

Auto Fill Options button

8. With the range E2:E8 still selected, point to the **Auto Fill Options** button. When the button expands to show a down arrow, click the **down arrow** to open the shortcut menu. The selected option, Fill Series, is the option you want. Click outside the shortcut menu to deselect the cells without making any changes.

9. Save the changes, and close the workbook.

TECHNOLOGY CAREERS

Computer Software Engineers

Computer software engineers evaluate situations, analyze needs, develop software to perform functions, and then verify and test the software to ensure that the requirements are met. They develop many types of software, including business applications, computer games, operating systems, and technical applications used in a variety of industries. They also solve technical problems as they arise. The tasks evolve quickly, so computer software engineers must continually strive to acquire new skills to keep up with changing technology. They must pay attention to detail and have strong problem-solving and analytical skills. Much of the work is part of a team effort, so computer software engineers must be able to communicate effectively with team members and other staff. Job prospects for computer software engineers are excellent. It is one of the fastest growing occupations.

SUMMARY

In this lesson, you learned:

- The Excel application window shows the Quick Access Toolbar, status bar, and other similar features used in other Microsoft Office applications.

- To navigate the workbook, you can use keyboard shortcuts and the scroll bars.

- You can choose from several options to view the worksheet, and you can change the zoom settings to specify the level of magnification.

- To enter data in a cell, the cell must be active. Depending on the width of the column, all the data may not be displayed, but the data is still contained in the cell.

- As you enter data, the AutoCorrect feature automatically corrects some of your keyboarding errors. If the data you are entering matches characters of existing entries in the column, the AutoComplete feature proposes the existing entry to save you time.

- When you insert or delete cells, rows, and columns, all existing data is shifted up, down, left, or right.

- To accommodate the data in a cell, you can widen the column and change the height of a row.

- To reorganize a worksheet, you can add and delete columns and rows; you can also delete, clear, copy and paste, or move the data.

- The Undo and Redo commands are available on the Quick Access Toolbar.

- The AutoFill feature enables you to quickly fill in a series of data.

LESSON REVIEW

TRUE / FALSE

Circle T if the statement is true or F if the statement is false.

T   F   **1.**   You can only have one workbook open at a time.

T   F   **2.**   When you position the mouse pointer over cells in the worksheet, the mouse pointer is shown as a white plus sign.

T   F   **3.**   The worksheet cell labels will not appear in a printed worksheet.

T   F   **4.**   When data is too wide for a cell, the part of the data that does not fit automatically wraps to the cell below.

T   F   **5.**   You can select a cell using either the mouse or the keyboard.

MULTIPLE CHOICE

Select the best response for the following statements.

1. The _____ identifies the column letter and row number.

   A.   active reference   C.   cell position

   B.   cell reference   D.   cell name

2. When a cell is selected, it is called a(n) _____.

   A.   targeted cell   C.   active cell

   B.   selection   D.   cell reference

3. The _____ feature is a quick and easy way to copy data to adjacent cells in a worksheet in a single step.

   A.   AutoComplete   C.   Copy Cells

   B.   AutoFill   D.   AutoSeries

4. By default, Excel shows approximately _____ characters in each cell.

   A.   8   C.   12

   B.   10   D.   18

5. The _____ command automatically adjusts the column width to fit the cell with the most content.

   A.   AutoCell Width   C.   Default Width

   B.   Column Width   D.   AutoFit Column Width

FILL IN THE BLANK

Complete the following sentences by writing the correct word or words in the blanks provided.

1. A(n) _____ is a grid of rows and columns that you enter data in to.

2. The worksheet is always stored in a(n) _____ that contains one or more worksheets.

3. A selected group of cells that touch each other and form a rectangle is called a(n) _____.

4. The _____ feature in Excel corrects common mistakes as you enter data.

5. The text or number in a cell is often referred to as a(n) _____.

WRITTEN QUESTIONS

Write a brief answer to the following questions.

1. What happens when you enter more characters than can fit in a cell?

2. How does the AutoComplete feature work?

3. How do you know when a cell is selected?

4. What happens when you paste new data into a cell that already contains data?

5. Describe three ways to adjust the column width.

PROJECTS

PROJECT 18–1

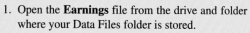

1. Open the **Earnings** file from the drive and folder where your Data Files folder is stored.

   2-1.1.3

2. Create a new blank document in Word. Save the document as **Values**, followed by your initials.

3. Navigate the worksheet to answer the following questions. Create a list in the Word document, and enter your answers.

   a. What is the value in cell O52?

   b. What is the value in cell M49?

   c. What is the value in cell T70?

   d. What is the last cell with a value in column H?

   e. What is the last cell with a value in row 67?

   f. In the range L32:N36, how many of the cells contain values?

4. Save the changes to the Word document **Values**. Close the workbook without saving any changes.

PROJECT 18–2

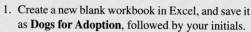

1. Create a new blank workbook in Excel, and save it as **Dogs for Adoption**, followed by your initials.

   2-3.1.1
   2-3.1.2

2. Beginning in cell A1, enter the following data in the cells. Use the AutoComplete feature to save time entering some of the repetitive data.

   2-3.1.3
   2-3.1.4

female	adult	Chocolate Labrador Retriever
male	young	Beagle
male	baby	Brittany Spaniel
female	baby	Saint Bernard
male	young	Terrier
male	young	Yellow Labrador Retriever
female	adult	Brittany Spaniel
female	adult	German Shepherd
male	young	Yellow Labrador Retriever
male	young	Siberian Husky

3. Insert a new column to the left of the current column A, and add the names below.

   Sasha

   Sebastian

   Shaggy

   Lucy

   Blaney

   Chesterfield

   Bailey

   Roxy

   Charlie

   Max

4. Use the AutoFit feature on all the column widths.

5. Add three new rows at the top of the worksheet.

6. In cell A1, type **Adoptable Dogs**.

7. In the third row, enter the following column headings:

Name	Gender	Age	Breed

8. In cell C8, change *young* to **adult**. In cell A1, change *Adoptable Dogs* to **Dogs for Adoption**.

9. Delete row 6.

10. Save the changes, and close the workbook.

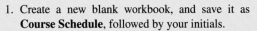
PROJECT 18–3

1. Open the **Order Request** file from the drive and folder where your Data Files folder is stored. Save the Order Request workbook as **Final Order Request**, followed by your initials.

2. Use the AutoFill feature to complete the series of shoe sizes. Fill the series in the range A6:A18 (sizes 7 through 13).

3. Use the AutoFit feature on all the column widths.

4. Edit each of the headings in row 1 so the first letter is capitalized. For example, change *court* to **Court**.

5. Add the following data to the order form:

```
Court:              1 size 9
Cross-training:     1 size 6 and 1 size 8.5
Soccer:             3 size 10.5
Basketball:         4 size 10
Running:            1 size 9.5 and 2 size 12
Walking:            2 size 9
```

6. Insert a new column before the Court column, and then move the column of data for Basketball to the new column B.

7. Delete the empty column G and also column E.

8. Save the changes, and close the workbook.

2-3.1.3
2-3.1.4

PROJECT 18–4

1. Create a new blank workbook, and save it as **Course Schedule**, followed by your initials.

2. In cell B1, type **Monday**. In cell C1, type **Tuesday**. Use the AutoFill feature to copy the series of weekdays to the range D1:F1 (Monday through Friday).

3. In cell A2, type **8:30 am**, and press **Enter**. The default setting will change the number format to 8:30 AM. In cell A3, type **9:00 am**, and press **Enter**. Use the AutoFill feature to copy the series of times to the range A4:A18.

4. Open the Clipboard task pane.

5. In cell B2, type **MATH 111**, and press **Enter**. Select the cell contents, copy the cell contents to the Clipboard, and then paste the contents in cell D2.

6. In cell C5, type **ART 114**. Copy the cell contents to the Clipboard, and then paste the contents in cell E5.

7. In cell C8, type **COMP 201**. Copy the cell contents to the Clipboard, and then paste the contents in cell E8.

8. In cell B7, type **BIOL 105**. Copy the cell contents to the Clipboard, and then paste the contents in cells D7 and F7.

9. In cell B11, type **COMPLIT 110**. Copy the cell contents to the Clipboard, and then paste the contents in cells D11 and F11.

10. In cell F14, type **BIOL LAB**.

11. Your math class also meets on Friday. Click cell **F2**. On the Clipboard task pane, click the **MATH 111** content to paste it in the active cell. Close the Clipboard task pane.

12. Use the AutoFit feature on all of the column widths.

13. Save the changes, and close the workbook.

2-3.1.1
2-3.1.2
2-3.1.3
2-3.1.4

TEAMWORK PROJECT

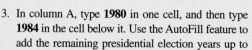

With a partner, explore voting statistics for your state in U.S. presidential elections from 1980 through the most recent presidential election. Follow these steps:

1. Using an almanac or Web research tools, find information on the popular vote for Republican, Democrat, and independent candidates for your state in each election. If there is more than one independent candidate, add together all the votes for all independent candidates. Collect data from 1980 through the most current presidential election. Divide the research assignment evenly so both you and your partner gather the data. For example, you research the election results from 1980 to 1994, and your partner researches the results from 1998 to present.

2. Create a worksheet to compile your data. Save the document as **TP 18–1**, followed by your initials.

3. In column A, type **1980** in one cell, and then type **1984** in the cell below it. Use the AutoFill feature to add the remaining presidential election years up to and including the most recent presidential election.

2-3.1.1
2-3.1.2
2-3.1.3
2-3.1.4

4. Create columns for Republican, Democrat, and Independent candidates. Enter the data you have gathered.

5. Add a column to your worksheet, and title it **Winning Party**. Insert the political party of the candidate who won each election nationally. Use the AutoComplete feature or the AutoFill feature to insert parties if the same party won two or more consecutive presidential elections.

6. Review the data in your completed worksheet, and determine which party won most often in the years you tracked.

■ CRITICAL THINKING

CRITICAL THINKING 18–1

In this lesson you used several keyboard shortcuts to navigate a worksheet.

2-3.1.1
2-3.1.2

1. Create a new Word document, and save the document as **CT 18-1**, followed by your initials.

2. Describe the advantages to using keyboard shortcuts to navigate a worksheet.

3. Save the changes to the document, and then close the document.

CRITICAL THINKING 18–2

In this lesson you learned to use Excel features to organize data.

2-3.1.2

1. Create a new Word document, and save the document as **CT 18-2**, followed by your initials.

2. Write a brief paragraph describing how you can use an Excel workbook to help you organize and maintain some personal data.

3. Save the changes to the document, and then close the document.

■ ONLINE DISCOVERY

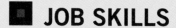

Open the **Earnings** file from the drive and folder where your Data Files folder is stored. Scroll down past row 76. Keep scrolling. The number of rows appears to be endless. Scroll across the worksheet past column T. Keep scrolling. Again, the number of columns appears to be endless. Is there a limit, or can you create an

infinite number of columns and rows? Do some exploring at Microsoft.com, and find out the maximum number of rows and columns that are available in a worksheet. Check with a classmate to see if the two of you agree on the maximum number of rows and columns.

2-3.1.2

■ JOB SKILLS

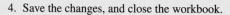

1. Your supervisor at work has asked you to submit a list of dates you are available to work next month, and you realize that you can use Excel to quickly prepare the information.

2. Create a new blank workbook. Save the workbook as **JS 18-1**, followed by your initials.

3. In the worksheet, enter some sample data to indicate dates you are available to work. Be sure to organize the data logically and label the data effectively.

4. Save the changes, and close the workbook.

2-3.1.1
2-3.1.2
2-3.1.3
2-3.1.4

LESSON 19

Organizing and Enhancing Worksheets

■ OBJECTIVES

Upon completion of this lesson, you should be able to:

- Hide, show, and freeze columns and rows.
- Create, rename, and delete worksheets.
- Change the page setup of a worksheet and add headers and footers.
- Customize the print options.
- Apply fonts, alignments, number formats, and conditional formatting to worksheet cells.
- Apply borders, shading, and styles to worksheet cells.
- Sort and filter data in a worksheet.
- Save a workbook in PDF and XPS formats.

■ WORDS TO KNOW

cell style

conditional formatting

filter

footer

freeze

header

header row

sheet tab

split

table style

■ DATA FILES

To complete this lesson, you will need these data files:

Classes.xlsx

Employees.xlsx

Energy.xlsx

Payroll.xlsx

Structures.xlsx

Travel Expenses.xlsx

Tutoring.xlsx

Common uses of spreadsheets include reporting finances, managing expenses and budgets, and tracking student grades. A key feature of Microsoft Excel is how easy it is to organize the data in a worksheet. You can change the appearance of the spreadsheet to emphasize specific data, and you can sort the information to highlight significant data. You will also find it useful to print completed worksheets, and there are many options you can use to make your printed spreadsheets clear, informative, and professional looking.

Managing Worksheets

One of the advantages of working with electronic spreadsheets is that you can keep expanding the rows and columns, and then you can keep adding data. Eventually, though, as the spreadsheet grows in size, locating the data becomes more tedious. In this lesson you will learn how to manage worksheets so you can access data more efficiently.

Hiding and Showing Worksheet Data

▶ **VOCABULARY**
header row

A ***header row*** contains column headings or field names in a data source, such as a table or spreadsheet. In Excel, the header row provides labels that identify the content in the worksheet columns. Effective column headings make it easy to identify information in a worksheet. When navigating through a large worksheet, though, the header row sometimes scrolls out of view, which makes it difficult to continue to identify the data in the cells or locate the correct cell so you can input data accurately. One option to overcome this problem is to change the zoom setting. However, if you need to reduce the magnification significantly, you will not be able to read the data. Another option is to hide some of the rows and columns so you can focus on a particular range of data. When you hide rows and columns, the data remains intact; it is just not visible on the screen.

Step-by-Step 19.1

2-1.1.3
2-1.1.6

1. Open the file **Payroll** from the drive and folder where your Data Files folder is stored. Save the Payroll workbook as **Revised Payroll 1**, followed by your initials.

2. Note that the headings in the header row identify the years from 1995 to 2014. The labels in the first column provide employee numbers.

3. Press **F5** to open the Go To dialog box. Type **k44** and click **OK** to move to that cell. Note that you can no longer see the column headings at the top of the screen, so you cannot identify what year the money was earned.

4. Select the cell range **K44:N49**. Click the **View** tab, and then in the Zoom group shown in **Figure 19–1**, click the **Zoom** button.

FIGURE 19–1
Zoom group on the View tab

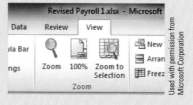

5. Note that the default Zoom setting is 100%. Click to change the magnification setting to **50%**, and click **OK**. If necessary, scroll up to show the top row in the spreadsheet. The content in the cells is much smaller now, but you can see the labels for columns K, L, M, and N, as well as the employee numbers in column A. The row numbers and column letters are highlighted, which makes it easier to identify the employee numbers and years.

6. With the cell range selected, click the **Zoom to Selection** button. The selected cells are magnified and fill the entire document window. Click the **100%** button to reduce the magnification and return to the default settings.

7. Depending on the size of your screen, you may not see the first column that shows the employee numbers, in which case you cannot identify the employee. Press and hold **Ctrl**, and then press **Home** to move back to cell A1.

8. You want to see the earnings for the years 2009 through 2014, so you can hide the columns for 1995–2008. Select columns **B** through **O**. Click the **Home** tab, and then in the Cells group, click the **Format** button to display the menu shown in **Figure 19–2**.

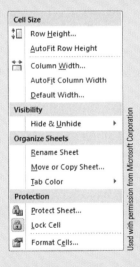

Used with permission from Microsoft Corporation

FIGURE 19–2
Format menu

9. Under Visibility, point to **Hide & Unhide**, and then in the submenu click **Hide Columns**. Column P showing 2009 data is now the second column on the screen, but when you scroll down, you see that no cell contents appear in that column until row 51.

10. You can also hide the rows above row 51. Select rows **2** through **50**. Click the **Format** button, point to **Hide & Unhide**, and then click **Hide Rows**. Now you can quickly access the data for the years 2009 through 2014.

11. Save the changes to the workbook. Then, save the workbook as **Revised Payroll 2**, followed by your initials.

12. Select columns **A** through **U**. Click the **Format** button, point to **Hide & Unhide**, and then click **Unhide Rows**. All 76 rows in the worksheet are now visible again.

13. With the columns still selected, click the **Format** button, point to **Hide & Unhide**, and then click **Unhide Columns**. Deselect the columns. All the cells in the worksheet are now visible.

14. Go to cell **A1**. Save the changes, and leave the workbook open for the next Step-by-Step.

Freezing Rows and Columns

▶ **VOCABULARY**

freeze

split

Another way to keep rows and columns visible as you navigate a worksheet is to freeze them. When you *freeze* columns and/or rows, you lock them so you can keep an area visible as you scroll through the worksheet. By freezing rows and columns, you do not have to hide any data. An alternative way to freeze rows and columns is to *split* a worksheet, which divides the worksheet into two panes. You can split the worksheet horizontally so the panes are displayed on the screen one above the other, or you can split the worksheet vertically so the two panes are displayed side by side on the screen. This way you can show different data in each pane.

Step-by-Step 19.2

)IC³

2-1.1.3

1. If necessary, open the file **Revised Payroll 2** from your solution files.

2. Click anywhere in row **2**. Click the **View** tab, and then in the Window group shown in **Figure 19–3**, click the **Freeze Panes** button. Click **Freeze Top Row**. The top row is now locked, and a thin black border is displayed at the bottom of the row. Scroll down to row 76. Notice as you scroll down through the rows in the worksheet the column headings in the header row do not disappear.

FIGURE 19–3
Window group on the View tab

3. Click anywhere in column **B**. Click the **Freeze Panes** button, and then click **Freeze First Column**. The first column is now locked, and a thick black border is displayed on the right side of the column. Also notice that the border line is no longer displayed below the header row. The first row in the worksheet is unlocked because the command was to lock only the first column.

4. Scroll across the screen to column U. Notice as you scroll across the columns in the worksheet that the first column with the employee numbers does not disappear.

5. Click the **Freeze Panes** button, and then click **Unfreeze Panes**. The column is unlocked.

6. Click cell **B14**. To lock both rows and columns, click the **Freeze Panes** button, and then click **Freeze Panes**. A thick black border is displayed at the bottom of the row above the active cell and on the right side of the column to the left of the active cell. Scroll down and across the worksheet. Column A and rows 1 through 13 are locked.

7. Save the changes to the workbook, and then save the Revised Payroll 2 workbook as **Revised Payroll 3**, followed by your initials.

8. Click the **Freeze Panes** button, and then click **Unfreeze Panes**. Go to cell **A1**.

9. To split the worksheet into two panes, point to the **Horizontal Split** box at the top of the vertical scroll bar shown in **Figure 19–4**.

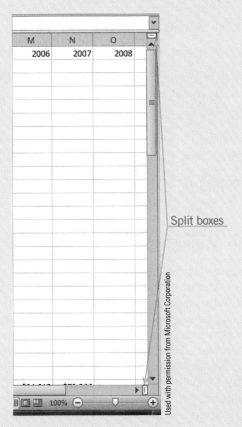

FIGURE 19–4
Split boxes on the vertical and horizontal scroll bars

10. When the pointer changes to a double-headed arrow ⬍, click and drag the **split box** to the bottom of row 10. Release the mouse button.

11. Your screen should look like **Figure 19-5**. Notice there are two vertical scroll bars: one for the top pane and one for the bottom pane. Use the scroll bars, the arrow buttons, or the mouse wheel to navigate in the top pane. Click in the **bottom pane** and scroll. The same content appears in both panes.

FIGURE 19-5
Worksheet split into two panes

Dividing line

Two vertical scroll bars

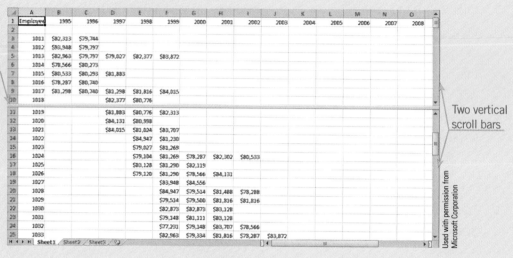

Used with permission from Microsoft Corporation

12. Double-click the **dividing line** to remove it.

13. Point to the split box at the right side of the horizontal scroll bar. When the pointer changes to a double-headed arrow ◀‖▶, click and drag it to the border line between columns B and C to divide the worksheet into two panes, side by side. Scroll through both of the panes.

14. Save the changes to the workbook. Close the workbook and then reopen it. Note that the worksheet is still split into two panes. Leave the workbook open for the next Step-by-Step.

Working with Multiple Worksheets

Excel is useful for organizing data into categories, such as time frames, sales regions, or account names. A workbook can be three dimensional because you have the length, width, and depth. When a single worksheet grows to a large size in length or width, you can organize related information in multiple worksheets, which adds depth.

Compare the workbook to a three-ring binder with tabs. When you need to add a new topic to the binder, you add a new tab to the binder. When you need to add a new category to an Excel workbook, you add a new worksheet to the workbook. At the bottom of the workbook window, a **_sheet tab_** is displayed for quick and easy access to the worksheet. At any time, you can rename the tabs in the binder, and at any time you can rename the sheet tabs in the workbook. A well-organized workbook presents the data logically, and the rows, columns, and worksheets are labeled effectively.

When you no longer need a category, you can remove the information and the tab from a binder. Likewise, when you no longer need a worksheet, you can delete it from the workbook.

You can copy and paste data from one worksheet to another. When you paste content, you can preview the results and choose from several pasting options, which change based on the destination and on the content you are pasting.

▶ **VOCABULARY**
sheet tab

ABOVE AND BEYOND

By default, new blank workbooks include three worksheets. The maximum number of worksheets per workbook is limited by the available memory.

Step-by-Step 19.3

1. If necessary, open the file **Revised Payroll 3** from your solution files. Save the Revised Payroll 3 workbook as **Revised Payroll 4**, followed by your initials.
2. Double-click the **dividing line** to remove the split.
3. At the bottom of the workbook window, click the **Sheet2** sheet tab. The blank worksheet Sheet2 is displayed.
4. At the bottom of the worksheet window, click the **Insert Worksheet** button on the tab to the right of the Sheet3 sheet tab as shown in **Figure 19–6**. A sheet tab for the new worksheet appears to the right of the last sheet tab. Excel automatically assigns the name *Sheet* and a sequential number (in this case *4*) to each new worksheet.

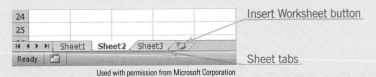

IC3
2-3.1.1
2-3.1.2
2-3.1.4

Used with permission from Microsoft Corporation

FIGURE 19–6
Insert Worksheet button

> **QUICK TIP**
>
> You can also insert a new worksheet by clicking the Insert button arrow in the Cells group and then clicking Insert Sheet. When you use this button, the new sheet tab appears to the left of the active sheet tab.

5. Sheet4 is now the active worksheet. Click the **Home** tab, and in the Cells group click the **Delete** button arrow, and then click **Delete Sheet**. The Sheet4 sheet tab disappears, and the worksheet is removed from the workbook. Right-click the **Sheet3** sheet tab, and in the shortcut menu click **Delete**. The Sheet3 sheet tab disappears, and the worksheet is removed from the workbook.
6. Click the **Sheet2** sheet tab and hold the mouse button. The pointer changes to a sheet, and a down-pointing arrow appears at the upper-left corner of the sheet tab. Drag the **sheet** tab to the upper-left corner of the Sheet1 tab as shown in **Figure 19–7**, and then release. The order of the sheet tabs is rearranged.

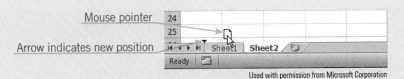

Used with permission from Microsoft Corporation

FIGURE 19–7
Changing the order of worksheet tabs

7. Double-click the **Sheet2** sheet tab. The worksheet name is selected. Type **Current Employees**, and press **Enter**. The sheet tab name is replaced with the new name.
8. Right-click the **Sheet1** sheet tab, and in the shortcut menu click **Rename**. The worksheet name is selected. Type **Earnings**, and press **Enter**.
9. Open the file **Employees** from the drive and folder where your Data Files folder is stored. Select the range **A1:D27**. In the Clipboard group, click the **Copy** button. A marquee surrounds the copied cells.

> **QUICK TIP**
>
> If you delete a tab for a worksheet that contains data, a prompt will appear indicating the worksheet may contain data and asking if you want to permanently delete the data.

10. Click the **Microsoft Excel** button in the taskbar, and switch to the **Revised Payroll 4** workbook. Click the **Current Employees** sheet tab. Click cell **A1**, and then, in the Clipboard group, click the **Paste** button. The copied data from Sheet1 in the Employees workbook is pasted into the Current Employees worksheet.

11. Switch to the **Employees** workbook. Press **Esc** to remove the marquee from the selected cells. Close the workbook without saving any changes.

12. In the **Revised Payroll 4** workbook, deselect the cells, and save the changes to the workbook. Leave the workbook open for the next Step-by-Step.

Formatting the Page Layout

A well-organized worksheet must also have an effective page layout. When a worksheet contains a large amount of data, you can make some adjustments to the page layout so the data is easy to read and access.

Changing the Page Setup

Page Break Preview shows you exactly how the worksheet will be printed. When the worksheet is more than one page in length, Excel determines where to break the page and begin a new one. If you do not like where Excel has split the data between pages, you can create your own page break by dragging the page break to a new location or by selecting a row or cell and inserting a manual page break.

Portrait orientation, the default setting in Excel, formats the content of the document with the short edge of the page at the top. You can change to landscape orientation, which formats the document with the long edge of the page at the top. Another option for page layout is to use the Fit to command to fit the worksheet to a number of pages you designate. The default setting is 100%, and the Fit to command scales the worksheet up or down as necessary.

When you change the page setup settings, the new settings apply only to the current worksheet; they do not apply to all the worksheets in the workbook.

Step-by-Step 19.4

2-1.1.5
2-1.1.6
2-1.4.1
2-3.1.9

1. If necessary, open the file **Revised Payroll 4** from your solution files. Save the Revised Payroll 4 workbook as **Revised Payroll 5**, followed by your initials. Click the **Earnings** sheet tab to make it the active worksheet.

2. Click the **Page Layout** tab, and then, in the Page Setup group shown in **Figure 19–8**, click the **dialog box launcher** to open the Page Setup dialog box, which provides options similar to those in Word. Under Scaling, make sure the Adjust to option is selected and set to 100%. Click **OK** to accept the settings. Click the **View** tab. If necessary, in the Workbook Views group click the **Normal** button.

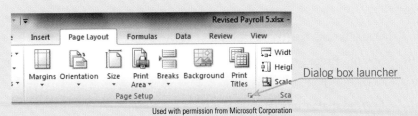

FIGURE 19–8
Page Setup group on the Page Layout tab

3. Scroll down through the worksheet data and you will see black broken border lines below rows 47 and 94. You will also see border lines indicating page breaks to the left of column J and to the left of Column S.

4. On the View tab, in the Workbook Views group, click the **Page Break Preview** button. If the Welcome to Page Break Preview dialog box appears, click **OK**. Broken blue lines, as shown in **Figure 19–9**, indicate borders for the six pages, and the page borders are the same as those that were displayed in Normal view.

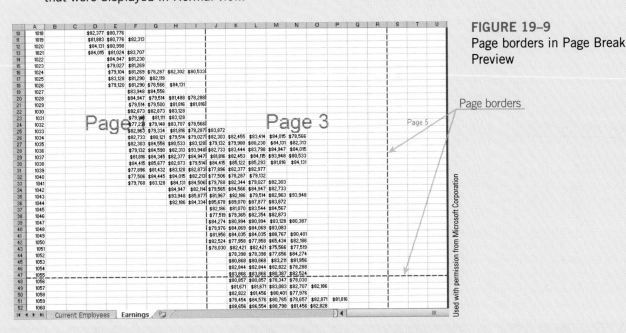

FIGURE 19–9
Page borders in Page Break Preview

5. Click the **Page Layout** tab. In the Page Setup group, click the **Orientation** button, and then click **Landscape**. Scroll down through the worksheet data. Six pages are still displayed on the screen, but the border lines shift for the new page layout.

6. Scroll back to the top of the worksheet. Point to the vertical border between *Page 1* and *Page 4*, and drag the border to the right to include Columns N, O, and P on Page 1. The adjusted vertical border is now displayed as a solid line because you manually created the page break.

7. Select Row **35**. In the Page Setup group, click the **Breaks** button, and then click **Insert Page Break**. A sold black line indicates a manual page break between Rows 35 and 36. On the Quick Access Toolbar, click the **Undo** button.

8. Click cell **J39**. Click the **Breaks** button, and then click **Insert Page Break**. Manual breaks are inserted both above and to the left of the active cell.

9. Click the **Breaks** button, and then click **Reset All Page Breaks** to restore the default page break layout.

10. Click the **dialog box launcher** in the Page Setup group to open the Page Setup dialog box. Under Scaling, click to enable the **Fit to** option. Keep the default setting of 1 page wide, and change the tall setting to **2**. Click **OK**. Now only one page break is displayed, and the worksheet data fits on two pages.

11. Click the **View** tab. In the Workbook Views group, click the **Page Layout** button. In the Zoom group, click the **Zoom** button, click the **50%** option, and then click **OK**. Scroll down to view the worksheet data on two pages.

12. In the Zoom group, click the **100%** button.

13. Save the changes, and leave the workbook open for the next Step-by-Step.

Creating a Header and a Footer

▶ VOCABULARY
header
footer

Headers and footers are a means of providing useful information on a printed worksheet. A *header* is information and/or graphics that are printed in the top margin of a worksheet, and a *footer* is information and/or graphics that are printed in the bottom margin of the worksheet.

You can manually create a header or footer by entering information in the header or footer pane. Fields can be used to automatically insert dates, times, filenames, the file path, the worksheet name, and page numbers. By using fields instead of manually entering the information, the information is always updated automatically. For example, if you use the date field in the footer, whenever you print the worksheet, the footer will include the current date. You can choose from several built-in headers or footers that are constructed using fields, or you can create your own customized headers and footers by inserting the fields yourself.

Step-by-Step 19.5

2-3.1.9

1. If necessary, open the file **Revised Payroll 5** from your solution files. Save the Revised Payroll 5 workbook as **Revised Payroll 6**, followed by your initials. If necessary, click the **Earnings** sheet tab. The worksheet should already be displayed in Page Layout view.

2. Click the **Page Layout** tab. In the Page Setup group, click the **dialog box launcher**. Under Scaling, click the **Adjust to** option, and change the setting to **100%** normal size. Click **OK**.

3. Click the **Insert** tab. In the Text group shown in **Figure 19–10,** click the **Header & Footer** button.

Used with permission from Microsoft Corporation

FIGURE 19–10
Text group on the Insert tab

4. The header pane with three cells (left, middle, right) is displayed at the top of the worksheet. The middle cell of the header pane where it says *Click to add header* is already selected. The Ribbon changes to show the Header & Footer Tools Design tab shown in **Figure 19–11.** (If necessary, click the Header & Footer Tools Design tab to see the options.)

Used with permission from Microsoft Corporation

FIGURE 19–11
Header & Footer Tools Design tab

5. In the Header & Footer group, click the **Footer** button, and then click **Page 1 of ?**. The worksheet view changes to show the bottom of the first worksheet page.

6. At the bottom of the first worksheet, *Page 1 of 6* is displayed in the middle cell of the footer pane. Press the **Page Down** key. The footer for the second page shows *Page 2 of 6*.

7. Scroll to the top of the worksheet, and click in the header pane where it says *Click to add header*.

8. If necessary, click the **Header & Footer Tools Design** tab. In the Header & Footer Elements group, click the **Sheet Name** button. The *&[Tab]* field, which is a code that inserts the worksheet name, is displayed in the cell.

9. Click the **cell** on the right side of the header pane. The worksheet name *Earnings* is displayed in the middle cell. In the Header & Footer Elements group, click the **Current Date** button. The *&[Date]* field is displayed in the cell.

10. Click anywhere in the worksheet. Scroll through the two pages to view the header and the footer.

11. Save the changes, and leave the workbook open for the next Step-by-Step.

Customizing Print Options

Before you send a worksheet to the printer, take the time to see what the printed copy will look like. This gives you one more opportunity to review the page setup and confirm that the information you want to print will be included in the printed copy. For example, you might expect the printed worksheet to look like what you see on the screen. You are accustomed to seeing the worksheet gridlines, row numbers, and column letters. However, when using the default print settings, these elements are not printed.

By default, Excel prints the entire worksheet. If you do not want to print all the worksheet data, you can identify the range you want to print before you choose the Print command. When you create a print area, the print setting is saved with the workbook.

If the worksheet will be printed on multiple pages, you may want to print the row and/or column headings on every page so the user does not need to keep referring back to the first page of the worksheet to identify the cell contents.

You can easily change the print settings using commands in the Page Layout dialog box or in Backstage view.

ABOVE AND BEYOND

Just as you add comments in Word documents, you can also add comments to worksheets. By default, comments added to worksheets are not printed. To print comments, click the dialog box launcher in the Sheet Options group on the Page Layout tab. Then click the Comments box list arrow, and select one of the options.

Step-by-Step 19.6

2-1.4.1
2-1.4.2
2-3.1.9

1. If necessary, open the file **Revised Payroll 6** from your solution files. Save the Revised Payroll 6 workbook as **Revised Payroll 7**, followed by your initials. If necessary, click the **Earnings** sheet tab to make it the active worksheet.

2. Click the **View** tab, and in the Workbook Views group, click the **Normal** button. Select the range **A1:F15**. Click the **Page Layout** tab. In the Page Setup group, click the **Print Area** button, and then click **Set Print Area**.

3. Deselect the cells. The print area is identified with a broken line border around the selected range of cells. Select the range **A17:J25**. Click the **Print Area** button, and then click **Add to Print Area**. Additional data is identified for printing, but the data in row 16 (Employee #1024) will not be printed.

4. Select the range **A28:L31**. Click the **Print Area** button, and then click **Add to Print Area**.

5. Click the **File** tab, and then click **Print**. Only the content in the first print area is displayed on the first page in the Print Preview pane.

6. At the bottom of the Preview pane, click the **Next Page** arrow ▶ to preview the second page. The second print area is displayed on the second page. Click the **Next Page** arrow to preview the third print area on page 3.

7. Note that the gridlines, row numbers, and column letters do not appear in the Print Preview pane. Click the **Page Layout** tab to close Backstage view. In the Sheet Options group, shown in **Figure 19–12**, the check marks indicate that the settings to view the gridlines and headings are enabled. Click the **Print** check boxes under Gridlines and also under Headings so the gridlines and headings will also appear when the worksheet is printed.

Used with permission from Microsoft Corporation

FIGURE 19–12
Sheet Options group on the
Page Layout tab

8. Click the **File** tab, and then click **Print**. Now the gridlines and the row and column headings also appear in the Print Preview pane. Click the **View** tab. In the Workbook Views group, click the **Page Layout** button. The row and column headings are displayed. In the Workbook Views group, click the **Normal** button.

9. Click the **Page Layout** tab. Click the **Print Area** button, and then click **Clear Print Area**. The print area borders are removed from the cells, and the default page break borders are displayed.

10. Because all the pages in the worksheet will be printed, you want the column headings to be printed on each page. In the Page Setup group, click the **Print Titles** button. The Page Setup dialog box shown in **Figure 19–13** opens.

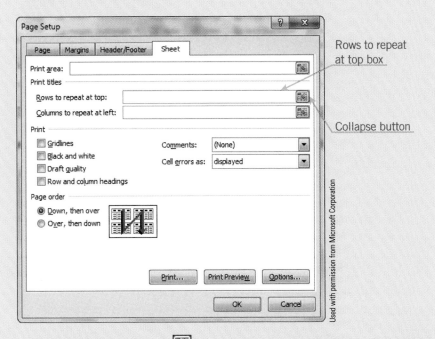

FIGURE 19–13
Page Setup dialog box

11. Click the **Collapse** button ▣ in the Rows to repeat at top box. The dialog box collapses, and the only option visible is the Rows to repeat at top box.

12. In the worksheet window, select row **1**. Note that *$1:$1* is displayed in the Rows to repeat at top box. In the Rows to repeat at top box, click the **Expand** button ▣ to expand the dialog box. At the bottom of the dialog box, click **Print Preview**. Backstage view opens. At the bottom of the Preview Pane, click the **Next Page** arrow to view all the pages. The column headings are displayed at the top of each page.

ABOVE AND BEYOND

You can also quickly access the options to format row and column headings to be printed on each page. In the Page Setup dialog box, under the Print section, enable the Row and column headings check box, and then click OK.

13. In the middle pane of Backstage view, shown in **Figure 19–14**, there are options for changing the worksheet orientation, the page size, the margins, and the scaling. Under Settings, click **Print Active Sheets**. A menu appears with the options to print the active sheets, the entire workbook, or only the current selection. There is even an option to ignore any print areas that have been set.

FIGURE 19–14
Print options in Backstage view

Used with permission from Microsoft Corporation

14. Click the **Home** tab to close Backstage view. Save the changes, and close the workbook.

Formatting the Cell Contents

An effective spreadsheet is well formatted, with consistent formatting of similar elements. Formatting the contents of a cell, like formatting in other Office applications, changes the way it appears. You can control the font styles, sizes, and colors, and you can apply attributes such as bold and italic. Border, color, and shading formats are useful for highlighting important information.

2-3.1.10

When you use the Cut and Copy commands to copy and move all the data in a cell, the formats are also moved or copied. However, when you delete the contents of a cell using the Delete key or the Backspace key, the formats for the cell remain in the cell. Therefore, if you enter new data in the cell, the existing formats will apply to the new contents. To remove the contents and the formats, you need to clear the cell. You can clear the contents and the formats from the cell, clear only the contents, or clear only the formats.

Merging Cells and Changing Font Styles and Sizes

There will be times when you want text to span across several columns. To do this, you can merge cells and combine several cells into a single cell. You can use merged cells to create a title or other informational text for your worksheet.

You learned in Lesson 13 that a font is the design of the typeface. Fonts are available in a variety of styles and sizes, and you can use multiple fonts in one workbook. The font size is a measurement in points that determines the height of the font. Excel automatically changes the row height to fit the font size, but you can also manually set the row height. However, Excel does not adjust the cell width when the font size changes. Bold, italic, underline, and color formats can also add emphasis to the contents of a cell. You can use the Format Painter feature to copy formats.

Step-by-Step 19.7

1. Open the file **Energy** from the drive and folder where your Data Files folder is stored. Save the Energy workbook as **Energy Expenses 1**, followed by your initials.

2. Right-click the **Energy Use** worksheet tab. In the shortcut menu, click **Insert**. In the Insert dialog box, the Worksheet template is already selected. Click **OK**. Double-click the new **Sheet1** sheet tab name, type **Bills,** and then press **Enter**.

3. In cell A1, type **Energy Expenses for 2014**, and then press **Enter**.

4. Cell A2 is the active cell. Enter **End of Billing Period**. Press **Tab**, type **Charges**, and press **Enter**.

5. Select columns **A** and **B,** and double-click the **right border** of the column B heading to use the AutoFit feature to automatically fit the column widths to the cell contents.

2-3.1.3
2-3.1.4
2-3.1.7

6. Select the range **A1:C1**. On the Home tab, in the Alignment group shown in **Figure 19–15**, click the **Merge & Center** button arrow, and then click **Merge & Center**. The three cells are combined into a single cell, and the existing text in cell A1 is centered in this modified cell A1.

FIGURE 19–15
Alignment group on the Home tab

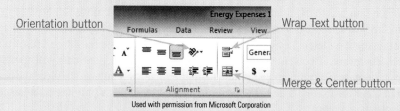

Used with permission from Microsoft Corporation

7. With cell A1 still selected, change the font to **Cambria**, **14 point**. Also, apply the bold format. The height of the cell is increased to accommodate the increased font size.

8. Select the range **A2:B2**. Change the font to **Cambria**, **12 point**, and apply a red font color. The contents in cell B2 now extend beyond column B. Excel does not automatically adjust the column when you change the contents of the column. Use the AutoFit feature for column B.

9. Click cell **B2**, and press **Delete** to remove the contents. With the cell still active, enter **Amount Paid**. Deselect the cell. The new text is formatted in red 12-point Cambria. When you clear the contents of a cell, the formats applied to the contents of that cell are not removed. Apply the AutoFit feature for column B again.

10. Select the range **A2:B2**. In the Editing group shown in **Figure 19–16**, click the **Clear** button. Click **Clear Formats**, and then deselect the cells. The font is restored to the default setting of Calibri 11 point font.

FIGURE 19–16
Editing group on the Home tab

Clear button

Used with permission from Microsoft Corporation

11. Select cell **A2**. Change the font to **Cambria**, **12 point**, and apply the italic format.

12. In the Clipboard group, click the **Format Painter** button. Then click cell **B2** to copy the font formats to the contents in cell B2.

13. Click anywhere in row **2**. In the Cells group, click the **Format** button, and then click **Row Height**. Type **100** in the Row height box, and click **OK**.

14. Save the changes, and leave the workbook open.

Changing Alignment and Wrapping Text in Cells

By default, Excel aligns text at the left of the cell and numbers at the right side of the cell. However, you can also center the cell contents. You can adjust the alignment of the content of a cell vertically as well. Your choices for vertical alignment are top, middle, and bottom. You will find buttons for all of these settings in the Alignment group on the Home tab. You will also find some other interesting options, such as orientating text at an angle within the cell, and decreasing the margin between the edge of the cell and the cell contents. Also, if the text does not fit on one line, you can enable an option to allow the text to wrap to new lines within a cell.

When you move or copy all the data in a cell, the formats are also moved or copied. When you paste cell content that has been formatted, Live Preview shows you what the content will look like after it is pasted. As you preview the results, you can choose from several options in a menu. These menu options change based on the content you are pasting.

Step-by-Step 19.8

1. If necessary, open the file **Energy Expenses 1** from your solution files. Save the Energy Expenses 1 workbook as **Energy Expenses 2**, followed by your initials. If necessary, select the **Bills** sheet tab.

2-3.1.4
2-3.1.7

2. Select the range **A2:B2**. On the Home tab, in the Alignment group, click the **Center** button ▤. Then, in the Alignment group, click the **Middle Align** button ▤. White space now appears above and below the headings in the cells.

3. With the cells still selected, in the Alignment group, click the **Orientation** button ✎▾, and then click **Angle Counterclockwise**. The headings are positioned at an angle within the cells.

4. Explore the other orientation settings by clicking the **Orientation** button and then selecting a new option until you have seen all the orientations in the cell. The last option in the menu opens the Format Cells dialog box where you can change the cell alignment.

5. Click the **Orientation** button, and then click the current highlighted option to toggle the orientation feature off. The cell contents are centered both vertically and horizontally within the cells.

6. Select the range **A2:C2**. In the Cells group, click the **Format** button, click **Row Height**, change the row height to **50**, and then click **OK**. Click cell **C2**, and apply the italic format.

7. With cell C2 selected, in the Alignment group, click the **Wrap Text** button ▤ to apply the format. The feature is highlighted on the Ribbon when enabled. Then, type **Increase/Decrease**, and press **Enter**. As you enter the text, the contents will wrap to a second line inside the cell.

> **QUICK TIP**
>
> The keyboard shortcut Ctrl+1 opens the Format Cells dialog box. You can also access the Format Cells dialog box by right-clicking an active cell or range and then selecting Format Cells in the shortcut menu.

QUICK TIP

If you change your mind after pasting content, at the lower-right corner of the cell, you can click the Paste button arrow and then select a different Paste option.

8. Select cell **B2**. Copy the contents to the Clipboard. Right-click cell **C2**. In the shortcut menu, under Paste Options, point to **Paste Special**. A submenu appears as shown in **Figure 19–17**. Position the mouse pointer over each of the paste options. The results of each paste option are displayed in Live Preview. Under Other Paste Options, click the **Formatting** option. The existing text remains, and the formats from cell B2 are applied. Press **Esc** to remove the marquee.

FIGURE 19–17
Paste options

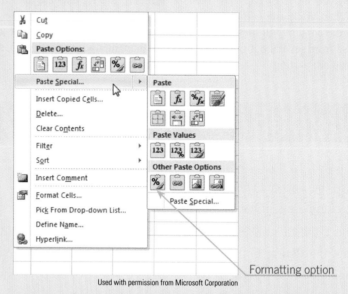

Used with permission from Microsoft Corporation

Formatting option

9. The wrap text format was removed from column C. Cell C2 should still be selected. Click the **Wrap Text** button. Because the font size is now 12 point, the text wraps to a third line. You cannot use the AutoFit feature when the wrap text feature is enabled. In the Cells group, click the **Format** button, and then click **Column Width**. Type **10,** and click **OK**.

10. Save the changes, and leave the workbook open for the next Step-by-Step.

Formatting Numbers and Dates

Generally, numbers are displayed with no formatting and are aligned on the right side of a cell. However, dates are automatically formatted in the default style (such as *20-Jan-14*). You can easily change the format of number data.

Step-by-Step 19.9

2-3.1.5

1. If necessary, open the file **Energy Expenses 2** from your solution files. Save the Energy Expenses 2 workbook as **Energy Expenses 3**, followed by your initials.

2. Click cell **A3**, type **January 20, 2014**, and press **Enter**. In spite of how you entered the date, the default setting shows the date as *20-Jan-14*. And, the data is aligned at the right side of the cell.

3. Type **February 20, 2014**, and press **Enter**. *20-Feb-14* is displayed in cell A4.

4. Select the range **A3:A4**. In the Number group on the Home tab, shown in **Figure 19–18**, click the **dialog box launcher**. The Format Cells dialog box opens showing the Number tab.

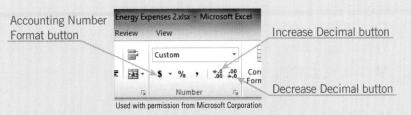

Accounting Number Format button

Increase Decimal button

Decrease Decimal button

Used with permission from Microsoft Corporation

FIGURE 19–18
Number group on the Home tab

5. In the Category list, click **Date** to show the options. In the Type list, click ***Wednesday, March 14, 2001**, and then click **OK**. The content in cells A3 and A4 changes to the new format for the two dates you entered.

6. With the two cells still selected, click the **fill handle** and drag down to cell A14. When you see *Saturday, December 20, 2014* in the ScreenTip on the side of the fill handle, release the mouse button. Automatically fit the width of column A to accommodate its contents.

7. Click cell **B3**, and enter the following data in column B:

    384.83

    290.44

    228.51

    219.44

    135.59

    128.56

    209.31

    246.16

    140.61

    195.11

    224.50

8. Select the range **B3:B14**. (Yes, the last cell in the range is blank. And cell B13 shows *224.5* instead of *224.50*.) In the Number group, click the **Accounting Number Format** button arrow $. Click **$ English (U. S.)**. Cell B13 now shows *224.50*. Notice there is extra white space between the dollar sign and the numbers. With the range of cells still selected, in the Number group, click the **dialog box launcher**. In the Category list, click **Currency**. The Decimal places setting should be 2, and the example should show *$384.83*. Click **OK**.

9. Even though there is no content in cell B14, you applied the format. Click cell **B14**, and type **297.30**. Press **Enter** (or Tab), and the currency format with two decimals is applied to the contents in the cell.

10. Select the range **C3:C14**. In the Number group, click the **dialog box launcher**. Under Category, click **Percentage**. If necessary, change the Decimal places setting to **2**. Click **OK**.

11. Click cell **C3**, and type **10.66**. As you enter the numbers, the percent symbol appears in the cell. Press **Enter**, and continue entering the following data in column C:

    9.55

    10.25

    11.06

    −4.51

    6.92

    8.35

    9.12

    −6.85

    8.35

    −1.19

    −1.25

12. Click cell **C3**, and then in the Number group click the **Decrease Decimal** button 🔽. The number changes to *10.7*. The digit was rounded up to the nearest tenth. Click the **Decrease Decimal** button again. The number is rounded up to *11*.

13. With cell C3 still selected, click the **Increase Decimal** button 🔼 twice to restore the number to two decimal places so *10.66*% is displayed in the cell. Deselect the cell.

14. Save the changes, and leave the workbook open for the next Step-by-Step.

Applying Conditional Formatting

You can quickly identify exceptions or trends in data and unusual cell values by applying conditional formatting. *Conditional formatting* applies designated formats to cells when the cell value meets specified conditions (criteria). You can highlight cell values with borders, shading, and font colors, and you can also use Data Bars, Color Scales, or Icon Sets to help visualize the data. Several built-in rules are available so you can specify criteria based on a comparison operator or criteria based on a cutoff value.

2-3.1.10

▶ VOCABULARY
conditional formatting

Step-by-Step 19.10

1. If necessary, open the file **Energy Expenses 3** from your solution files. Save the Energy Expenses 3 workbook as **Energy Expenses 4**, followed by your initials.

2. Select the range **C3:C14**. On the Home tab, in the Styles group shown in **Figure 19–19**, click the **Conditional Formatting** button, point to **Highlight Cells Rules**, and in the submenu click **Duplicate Values**.

2-3.1.6
2-3.1.10
2-3.2.10

FIGURE 19–19
Styles group on the Home tab

3. The Duplicate Values dialog box opens. Click the **values with** list arrow, and then click **Green Fill with Dark Green Text**. Click **OK**. Deselect the cells. The duplicate values in cells C9 and C12 are highlighted.

4. Select the range **B3:B14**. Click the **Conditional Formatting** button, point to **Top/Bottom Rules**, and then in the submenu click **Above Average**. The Above Average dialog box appears. Leave the settings as is, and click **OK**. Deselect the cells. Excel calculated the average amount for the selected cells and identified five values above average.

5. Click the **Conditional Formatting** button, point to **Clear Rules**, and then in the submenu, click **Clear Rules from Entire Sheet**. All the conditional formats are removed.

⬤ ABOVE AND BEYOND

If the built-in rules for conditional formatting do not meet your needs, you can create your own conditional formatting rules. Choose the New Rule command, and set the formats in the New Formatting Rule dialog box, where you can edit the rule description and customize the formats.

6. Select the range **B3:B14**. Click the **Conditional Formatting** button, and point to **Data Bars**. In the submenu, position the mouse pointer over the thumbnails to preview the results. Under Gradient Fill, click the first option, **Blue Data Bar**. Deselect the cells. The data bars provide a visual for comparing the data in the column.

7. Select the range **A3:A14**. Click the **Conditional Formatting** button, and point to **Color Scales**. In the submenu, position the mouse pointer over the thumbnails to preview the results. Two-color and three-color scales can be used to create a visual of the values, such as the change in seasons. At the bottom of the submenu, click **More Rules** to open the New Formatting Rule dialog box shown in **Figure 19–20**.

FIGURE 19–20
New Formatting Rule dialog box with custom settings

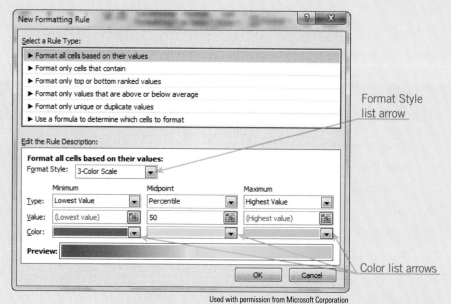

Used with permission from Microsoft Corporation

8. Click the **Format Style** list arrow, and select **3-Color Scale**. Under Minimum, click the **Color** list arrow, and select the standard color **Blue**. Under Midpoint, change the Color setting to the standard color **Yellow**. Under Maximum, change the Color setting to the standard color **Orange**. When your settings match those shown in Figure 19–20, click **OK**.

9. Select the range **C3:C14**. Click the **Conditional Formatting** button, and point to **Icon Sets**. In the submenu shown in **Figure 19–21**, move the mouse pointer over the options to see the Live Preview of the options. Then click the **5 Arrows (Colored)** option. Icons are added to the selected cells to highlight the data.

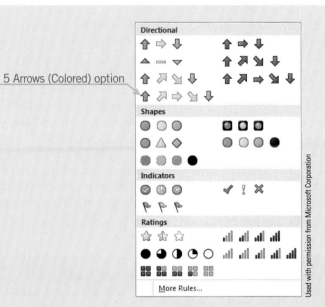

5 Arrows (Colored) option

FIGURE 19–21
Icon Sets submenu

Used with permission from Microsoft Corporation

10. With the range C3:C14 still selected, click the **Conditional Formatting** button, point to **Highlight Cells Rules**, and in the submenu click **Greater Than**. The Greater Than dialog box opens. Type **10.00%,** and then click **OK**. Deselect the cells.

11. Select the range **A3:A14**. Click the **Conditional Formatting** button, point to **Clear Rules**, and in the submenu click **Clear Rules from Selected Cells**.

12. Deselect the cells. Save the changes, and leave the workbook open for the next Step-by-Step.

Adding Shading, Borders, and Styles

You can emphasize important information in a cell, a row of cells, or a column by applying color, shading, or border formats. You can use the Format Painter to copy the format of a worksheet cell without copying the contents of the cell. For example, after applying a date format in one cell, you may format other cells for dates by painting the format.

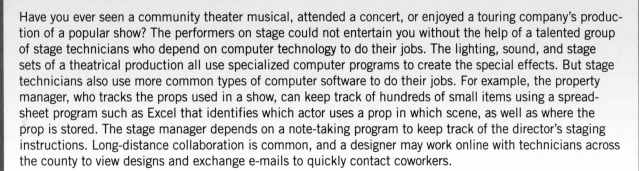

TECHNOLOGY CAREERS

Have you ever seen a community theater musical, attended a concert, or enjoyed a touring company's production of a popular show? The performers on stage could not entertain you without the help of a talented group of stage technicians who depend on computer technology to do their jobs. The lighting, sound, and stage sets of a theatrical production all use specialized computer programs to create the special effects. But stage technicians also use more common types of computer software to do their jobs. For example, the property manager, who tracks the props used in a show, can keep track of hundreds of small items using a spreadsheet program such as Excel that identifies which actor uses a prop in which scene, as well as where the prop is stored. The stage manager depends on a note-taking program to keep track of the director's staging instructions. Long-distance collaboration is common, and a designer may work online with technicians across the county to view designs and exchange e-mails to quickly contact coworkers.

▶ **VOCABULARY**
cell style
table style

ABOVE AND BEYOND

After converting a range of cells to an Excel table, you can manage and calculate the table data independently of any data outside of the table.

A *cell style* is a set of predefined formats you can apply to some of the worksheet data, such as a header row, a cell showing a total, or cells showing the date and time. To apply a cell style, you must first select a cell or a range of cells to be formatted. Excel offers more than 40 styles in the Cell Styles gallery that enable you to apply multiple formats quickly and consistently.

A *table style* is a set of predefined formats that you can apply to all the worksheet data with a single click. When you apply a table style, the selected cells are converted to an Excel table. When you convert a range of cells to an Excel table, you can easily and quickly format the table data. You can choose from 60 table styles in the Quick Styles gallery. If you do not want to work with the data in a table format, you can convert the table to a regular range and the table style format will remain intact.

The cell styles and table styles may override some or all existing formats that you have applied. If desired, you can modify styles after they are applied, and you can save your own customized styles.

Step-by-Step 19.11

2-3.1.6
2-3.1.8

1. If necessary, open the file **Energy Expenses 4** from your solution files. Save the Energy Expenses 4 workbook as **Energy Expenses 5**, followed by your initials.

2. Click cell **A1**. On the Home tab, in the Font group, click the **Fill Color** button arrow. Under Standard Colors, click the **Yellow** color.

3. Cell A1 should still be the active cell. In the Font group, click the **Border** button arrow, and then under Draw Borders, point to **Line Color**. Under Theme Colors, in the first row, click **Dark Blue, Text 2** color. The mouse pointer changes to a pencil.

4. Although Cell A1 is no longer highlighted, it is still the active cell. Click the **Border** button arrow, and then under Draw Borders, point to **Line Style**. In the submenu, click the first **double-line** border style. To apply the defined border, click the **Borders** button arrow, and then click **Bottom Border**. Deselect the cell. A dark blue double line is added to the bottom of cell A1.

5. Click cell **A1**. In the Styles group, click the **Cell Styles** button. (If you do not see the Cell Styles button, click the **More** button in the Styles group.) The Cell Styles gallery of predefined styles, shown in **Figure 19–22**, opens. Move the mouse pointer over the options to see the Live Preview of the styles.

QUICK TIP

When you choose a border line format and the mouse pointer changes to a pencil, you can apply the current border format to one or more of the cells in the worksheet by clicking each cell.

Used with permission from Microsoft Corporation

FIGURE 19–22
Cell Styles gallery

Heading 2 cell style

6. Click the **Heading 2** cell style. Deselect the cell. The border line and shading you applied is replaced with the Heading 2 cell style format. Select cell **A1,** and change the font size to **14 point**.

7. Select the range **A2:C2**. Click the **Cell Styles** button, and then click the **Heading 4** cell style. Deselect the row. The style is applied to row 2. Select cell **C2**. In the formula bar, position the insertion point between / and *D*. Press the **spacebar** and then press **Enter** to control where the line of text wraps in the cell.

8. Click the **Energy Use** sheet tab. Select the range **A1:B13**. In the Styles group, click the **Format as Table** button. The Quick Table Styles gallery shown in **Figure 19–23** opens. In the Medium group, in the first row, click the **Table Style Medium 2** table style, the second option in the first row.

Table Style Medium 2 table style

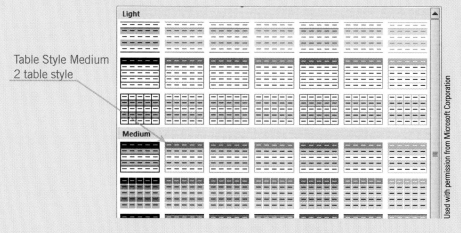

Used with permission from Microsoft Corporation

FIGURE 19–23
Quick Table Styles gallery

9. The Format As Table dialog box opens. The dialog box shows the range of the selection. Make sure the **My table has headers** option is checked so the header rows will show different formats. Click **OK**.

10. The Table Tools Design tab is now displayed on the Ribbon when the table is selected. You can access the Quick Table Styles gallery by clicking the More button in the Table Styles group.

11. Click outside the table to deselect the cells. As shown in **Figure 19–24**, some shading is added to the cells, and the font color in the column headings is changed to white. You will see there are arrows in the header row, as indicated in Figure 19–24. You will learn more about using these AutoFilter arrows in the next section.

FIGURE 19–24
Worksheet data formatted as a table

AutoFilter arrows

	A	B	C	D
1	Date	End Meter Read		
2	1/6/2014	25090		
3	2/3/2014	24541		
4	3/3/2014	23573		
5	4/7/2014	22902		
6	5/5/2014	22229		
7	6/2/2014	21241		
8	7/7/2014	20163		
9	8/4/2014	19278		
10	9/1/2014	18615		
11	10/6/2014	17472		
12	11/3/2014	16104		
13	12/1/2014	17019		
14				
15				
16				
17				
18				
19				
20				
21				
22				
23				
24				
25				

Bills Energy Use eServices

Used with permission from Microsoft Corporation

QUICK TIP

An alternate way to convert table cells back to a normal range is to right-click the table and in the shortcut menu point to Table, and then click Convert to Range. Click Yes to confirm.

FIGURE 19–25
Tools group on the Table Tools Design tab

12. To convert the table back to a range, click anywhere within the table. If necessary, click the **Table Tools Design** tab. In the Tools group, shown in **Figure 19–25**, click the **Convert to Range** button. When prompted to convert the table to a normal range, click **Yes**. The arrows in the column headings disappear, but the shading and font colors remain the same. Also, the Table Tools Design tab disappears.

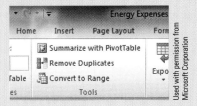

13. Save the changes, and leave the workbook open for the next Step-by-Step.

Sorting and Filtering Data

Worksheets can function as basic databases. You can sort the data and numbers in the columns based on one criteria or on multiple criteria. To sort worksheet data, you must indicate the column you want to base the sort on. If the worksheet has multiple columns of data, you can base the sort on data in as many as three different columns. For example, you can sort the worksheet contents first by the column C data, then by column A data, and then by column B data.

In addition to sorting data, you can filter worksheet data. When you *filter* data, you screen data that matches specified criteria. The data that does not meet the criteria is hidden, and only the data that meets the criteria is shown.

▶ **VOCABULARY**
filter

Step-by-Step 19.12

1. Open the file **Energy Expenses 5** from your solution files. Save the Energy Expenses 5 workbook as **Energy Expenses 6**, followed by your initials.

2-3.2.1
2-3.2.2

2. Click the **Bills** sheet tab. Select the range **B3:B14**. On the Home tab, in the Editing group, click the **Sort & Filter** button. Click **Sort Smallest to Largest** to arrange the data so the lowest amounts paid are at the top of the column. A Sort Warning dialog box opens. Under What do you want to do?, click the **Continue with the current selection** option, and then click **Sort**. The selected data is rearranged in the column, but the associated data in columns A and C do not move. Click the **Undo** button.

3. The range B3:B14 should still be selected. Click the **Sort & Filter** button, and then click **Sort Smallest to Largest**. In the Sort Warning dialog box, leave the Expand the selection option enabled, and click **Sort**. The data in column B is rearranged, and the associated data in columns A and C move with the data in column B. Deselect the data.

4. To sort by multiple criteria, you must open the Sort dialog box. Click any cell containing a value. Click the **Sort & Filter** button, and then click **Custom Sort**. The Sort dialog box shown in **Figure 19–26** opens. By default the My data has headers option is enabled. When this option is enabled, Excel will not include the headers in the sort.

▶ **QUICK TIP**

If your Custom Sort dialog box shows one or more Then by rows, click Delete Level at the top of the dialog box to remove the levels.

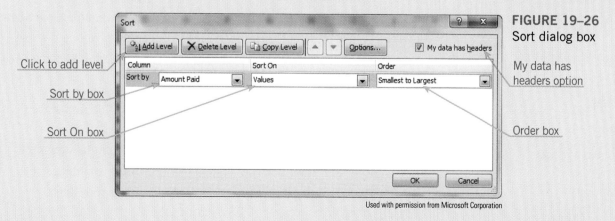

FIGURE 19–26
Sort dialog box

Click to add level

Sort by box

Sort On box

My data has headers option

Order box

Used with permission from Microsoft Corporation

5. Under Column, click the **Sort by** list arrow, and then click **Increase/Decrease**. Under Sort On, the box should already show the option *Values*. Under Order, click the **list** arrow, and then click **Largest to Smallest** to sort the data with the highest value at the top of the column.

6. At the top of the dialog box, click **Add Level**. A Then by box appears under Column, as shown in **Figure 19–27**. Click the **Then by** list arrow, and click **Amount Paid**. The Sort On option should be set to **Values**. Under Order, click the **list** arrow, and click **Largest to Smallest**. With these settings, if two percentages are the same, the order will be determined by the amount paid shown in column B.

FIGURE 19–27
Sort settings for multiple columns

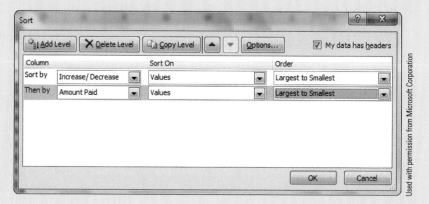

Used with permission from Microsoft Corporation

7. When your settings match those in Figure 19–27, click **OK** to accept the settings. Look at rows 8 and 9. Both rows show *8.35%* in column C, so the order is based on the data in column B. The row with the amount *$209.31* was placed above the row with the amount *$195.11* because the data is arranged from largest to smallest.

8. Click the **Energy Use** sheet tab. If necessary, click any one of the cells containing data. On the Home tab, in the Editing group, click the **Sort & Filter** button, and then click **Filter**. The AutoFilter arrows are displayed in the column heading cells.

9. Click the **AutoFilter** arrow in column A and a submenu opens. Under Date Filters, click the (**Select All**) check box to deselect all the options. Click the **March** check box to filter out all entries that were not in March, and then click **OK**. Only one entry matches the criteria. Notice the row numbers at the left. Rows 2 and 3 and rows 5–13 are hidden because they do not contain data that meets the criteria.

10. Click the **Sort & Filter** button, and then click **Filter** to toggle the AutoFilter feature off. All the rows appear again.

11. Click the **Sort & Filter** button, and click **Filter**. Click the **AutoFilter** arrow in column B, and then point to Number Filters. In the submenu, click **Greater Than Or Equal To**. The Custom AutoFilter dialog box opens.

12. The insertion point is positioned in the first blank box. Click the **list** arrow in the box, and then scroll down the list of all the values in the column. Click **19278**. Your dialog box should look like the one shown in **Figure 19–28**.

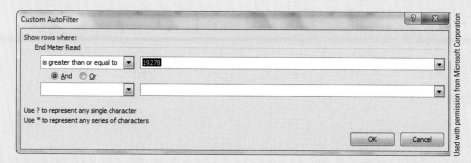

FIGURE 19–28
Custom AutoFilter dialog box

13. Click **OK**. Only those rows with an end meter reading equal to or higher than 19278 appear in the worksheet.

14. Save the changes, and close the workbook.

Saving a Workbook as a PDF or XPS File

If you want to share a workbook, but you do not want the recipient to be able to modify the data, you can save all the workbook data in either a PDF or an XPS file. Both formats preserve the visual appearance and layout of each worksheet, and they enable fast viewing and printing. When the workbook has multiple worksheets with data, each worksheet begins on a new page in the PDF/XPS file.

Step-by-Step 19.13

1. If necessary, open the file **Energy Expenses 6** from your solution files.

2. Click the **Bills** sheet tab. Press and hold **Shift**, and then click the **Energy Use** sheet tab. You do not want to include the eServices sheet tab in the selection, because that worksheet contains confidential information that you do not want to share.

3. Note that the title bar for the Excel window now displays *Energy Expenses 6.xlsx [Group]*. Also, the selected sheet tabs have a white background as shown in **Figure 19–29**.

2-1.2.4

Used with permission from Microsoft Corporation

FIGURE 19–29
Selected worksheet tabs

4. Click the **File** tab, and then click **Save As**. Navigate to the drive and folder where you save your solution files. In the Save as type box, select the **XPS Document (*.xps)** format, and then click **Save**.

5. The workbook opens in the XPS Viewer. Note that the document has two pages. The Bills worksheet data appears on the first page. Scroll down to the second page. The filtered data is displayed on a separate page because it is stored in a separate worksheet.

6. Close the XPS Viewer window. Then close the workbook.

SUMMARY

In this lesson, you learned:

- To keep the header row in view when navigating through a large worksheet, you can change the zoom setting. If that does not work because the worksheet is too large, you can hide some of the rows and columns so you can focus on a particular range of data, or you can freeze some rows and columns.

- You can delete or add one or several worksheets to a workbook, and you can rename each worksheet.

- Headers and footers can be added to worksheets to provide information such as the source and date of the data.

- You can change the page orientation or use the Fit to feature to fit all the data on a specified number of pages.

- You can control the print output by inserting page breaks manually or creating a print area for the worksheet. With the default settings, the gridlines and row and column headings appear on the screen in worksheets but they do not appear when the worksheets are printed. You can change the settings to hide these elements on the screen and/or include them in printed worksheets.

- Before you print, you can preview the worksheet to see what it will look like when it is printed. You can choose

to print the active worksheet only, or you can choose to print all worksheets in the workbook.

- There are many options available for formatting cell contents, including merging cells, changing font styles and sizes, changing the alignment within the cells, and applying number and date formats.

- Conditional formatting enables you to quickly identify exceptions or trends in data as well as unusual cell values.

- To enhance the appearance and highlight data within the worksheet, you can add borders and shading to cells. There are also many predefined styles available that you can quickly apply to give the worksheet a professional look and make reading the data easier.

- To organize worksheet data numerically or alphabetically, you can sort the data based on a single column, or you can sort the data based on multiple criteria. To screen for data that meets certain criteria, you can filter the data.

- To preserve the visual appearance and layout of each worksheet, you can save all the workbook data in a PDF or an XPS file format.

■ LESSON REVIEW

TRUE / FALSE

Circle T if the statement is true or F if the statement is false.

T   F   **1.**   When you save a workbook in the PDF or XPS format, you must save each worksheet as a separate file.

T   F   **2.**   If you do not want to print the entire worksheet, you can identify a print area to customize what appears in the printed document.

T   F   **3.**   With default settings, generally numbers are aligned at the right side of a cell and text is aligned at the left side of the cell.

T   F   **4.**   When you move or copy all the data in a cell, the existing formats are no longer applied to the moved or copied data.

T   F   **5.**   After deleting the contents of a cell using the Delete key or the Backspace key, the existing formats will apply to the new contents when you enter new data in the cell.

T   F   **6.**   When you increase the font size for cell content, you must manually set the row height to accommodate the larger text.

T   F   **7.**   If the worksheet has multiple columns of data, you can base the sort on data in as many as five different columns.

T   F   **8.**   By default, the Wrap Text feature is enabled.

T   F   **9.**   When you apply a table style, the selected cells are converted to an Excel table.

T   F   **10.**   You can quickly identify exceptions or trends in data as well as unusual cell values by applying conditional formatting.

MULTIPLE CHOICE

Select the best response for the following statements.

1. Using default settings, _____ will be printed.

   A.   gridlines   C.   row numbers

   B.   column letters   D.   none of the above

2. To span text across multiple columns, _____.

   A.   merge multiple cells   C.   insert a header row

   B.   split multiple cells   D.   create a header

3. You can insert _____ field in headers and footers.

   A.   a worksheet name   C.   a file path

   B.   a filename   D.   all of the above

4. To sort worksheet data, you must indicate the _____ that you want to base the sort on.

   A.   heading   C.   row

   B.   column   D.   criteria

5. When you _____ data, only the data that meets the criteria will be shown.

   A.   filter   C.   freeze

   B.   conditionally format   D.   none of the above

6. When you use the split box on the vertical scroll bar, _____.

   A.   some of the worksheet data is hidden

   B.   none of the worksheet data is hidden

   C.   the worksheet data is displayed in two panes, side by side on the screen

   D.   the worksheet data is displayed in two panes, one above the other

7. To keep a row and/or column visible as you navigate a worksheet, you can _____ the row and/or column.

    A. highlight   C. freeze

    B. split   D. all of the above

8. The _____ command scales the percentage of magnification of the worksheet.

    A. Size   C. Page Layout

    B. Zoom   D. View Page

9. To switch to a different worksheet in a workbook, click the _____ at the bottom of the worksheet window.

    A. worksheet title bar   C. worksheet tab

    B. worksheet button   D. Excel button

10. If you do not like where Excel has split the data between pages, you can _____.

    A. drag the page break to a new location or insert manual page breaks

    B. change the page orientation

    C. use the Fit to command

    D. all of the above

WRITTEN QUESTIONS

Write a brief answer to the following questions.

1. What are some common uses of spreadsheets?

2. What are the advantages of converting a range of cells to a table?

3. What is the default page orientation in Excel?

4. What is the advantage to using fields instead of manually entering information in headers and footers for dates, times, filenames, and paths?

5. What is the purpose of splitting a worksheet?

■ PROJECTS

PROJECT 19–1

1. Open **Classes** from the drive and folder where your Data Files folder is stored. Save the Classes workbook as **Revised Classes**, followed by your initials.

   2-3.1.5
   2-3.1.6
   2-3.1.7
   2-3.1.9

2. Someone has mistakenly formatted the class numbers with 1000s separators. Use the Clear command to clear formats only from cells B2:B7. Then center all the numbers in the column.

3. Insert a new column to the left of column B. The new column will be very wide since it defaults to the width of the column before it. Do not be concerned. You will adjust the width later. In cell B1, enter the column heading **Fee**.

4. In cell B2, enter **120**. Format this number for Currency with no decimal places, and center the number in the cell.

5. Fill down to cell B7 with the number and format in cell B2. Use AutoFit on the column width.

6. Select the range **D2:G7**, and format the cells so the contents align at the right.

7. Insert a new row above the header row. Merge and center cells A1:H1, and enter the heading **Language Classes**.

8. Change the new heading text to Arial 16 point font. Apply a light olive green shading to the new heading cell.

9. Select the range **A2:H2**. Apply the italic format, and increase the font size to 14 point. Use AutoFit on all column widths.

10. Select the range **A1:H8**. Set the border line color to a dark olive green and the border line style to a single line. Then apply the All Borders format to the range A1:H8.

11. Change the page orientation to landscape.

12. Change the settings so the worksheet row numbers and column letters will be printed.

13. In Backstage view, preview how the worksheet will look when it is printed to make sure it will be printed correctly on the page. Close Backstage view, and make any necessary changes.

14. Save the changes, and close the workbook.

PROJECT 19–2

1. Open **Tutoring** from the drive and folder where your Data Files folder is stored. Save the Tutoring workbook as **Revised Tutoring 1**, followed by your initials.

   2-3.1.5
   2-3.1.6
   2-3.1.8
   2-3.1.9
   2-3.2.1

2. Click cell **A3**, and copy the cell contents to the Clipboard. Select the cell range **A4:A8**, and paste the values and number formatting of the copied cell. Then click cell **A9**, and copy and paste the cell value and formatting in the range A10:A11. Continue to copy the dates to complete the data in column A.

3. Change the format for the range A3:A47 to the 3/14 date format.

4. To make it easier to find information about the students, select the range **A2:H42**, and sort the data in the worksheet using the **My data has headers** option. Create a custom sort, and specify a sort by last name, from A to Z, and then by date, from oldest to newest.

5. Add a custom header to the worksheet that includes fields for the current date at left, the filename in the middle, and the number of pages at the right.

6. Select the cell range **A3:H47**. Apply the **Table Style Medium 11** table style from the Quick Table Styles gallery. Because you did not select the header row cells, there are no headers in the table.

7. Convert the table to a normal range. Use Format Painter to copy the format in cell A3 to the range A2:H2. Then hide row 3.

8. In Backstage view, preview how the worksheet will look when it is printed. Notice it does not fit on one page. Close Backstage view. Scale the page layout so the worksheet fits on one page wide by one page tall. Confirm in Print Preview the worksheet data fits on one page in Print Preview.

9. Save the changes to the workbook. Then save the workbook as **Revised Tutoring 2**, followed by your initials.

10. Change the page layout to landscape orientation. Change the scaling to 120% of the normal size.

11. Insert a manual page break after row 25.

12. Format the worksheet so the column headings in row 2 are printed on the second page. In Backstage view, preview how the worksheet will look when printed.

13. Save the changes, and close the workbook.

PROJECT 19–3

1. Open the file **Structures** from the drive and folder where your Data Files folder is stored. Save the Structures workbook as **Revised Structures**, followed by your initials.

2-3.1.1
2-3.1.2
2-3.1.4
2-3.1.8
2-3.1.9
2-3.2.1
2-3.2.2

2. Rename Sheet1 in the workbook as **Towers**. Rename Sheet2 in the workbook as **Buildings**.

3. In the Towers worksheet, sort the data based on the structure name from A to Z.

4. Sort the data on the Buildings worksheet based on the number of stories from largest to smallest and then based on the year completed from largest to smallest.

5. Insert a new worksheet, and rename the worksheet **Structures**. Arrange the worksheets so they appear in this order: Structures, Buildings, Towers.

6. Copy all the data in the Buildings worksheet. Paste the copied data into cell A1 of the Structures worksheet, using the paste option to keep the source column widths.

7. In the Towers worksheet, copy all the data in the range A2:E21. Paste the copied data into cell A13 in the Structures worksheet, keeping the source column widths. After pasting the new contents, the widths set in Step 6 are adjusted so not all the data is visible.

8. In the Structures worksheet, sort the data based on the height in feet, from largest to smallest.

9. In the Structures worksheet, set the column D width to **7.00**. Set the column E width to **12.00**. Format cells D1 and E1 so the text wraps in the cells.

10. In the Structures worksheet, freeze the top row. Hide column F. Then set the print area for the range A1:E26.

11. In the Buildings worksheet, change the page layout to landscape orientation. Apply conditional formatting to highlight the values for all buildings completed after the year 2000. Format the gridlines and headings to be printed.

12. In the Towers worksheet, filter the data in column C by showing all the text equal to **China**. Format the filtered data as a table, using a table style of your choice.

13. Save the changes. Then save all three worksheets in the XPS format.

14. Close the XPS Viewer window, and then close the workbook.

PROJECT 19–4

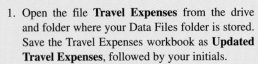

1. Open the file **Travel Expenses** from the drive and folder where your Data Files folder is stored. Save the Travel Expenses workbook as **Updated Travel Expenses**, followed by your initials.

2-3.1.4
2-3.1.5
2-3.1.6

2. Merge and center the range A1:E1.

3. Apply an appropriate cell style to the headings in rows 1 and 2.

4. Format the range B3:D8 using the Accounting format for $ English (U.S.). Remove the decimal places. Then copy the format to cells E3:E8.

5. Enter the following data in column E:

662.16

530.02

329.67

172.41

145.97

11.88

6. In cell C10, type **5/2/14**. Change the date to the **14-Mar-01** format.

7. Select the range **A10:C10**, and format a double-line top border using a color that complements the colors in the cell styles applied in rows 1 and 2.

8. Save the changes, and close the workbook.

TEAMWORK PROJECT

2-3.1.2
2-3.1.6

Worksheets are excellent tools to organize information so you can make easy comparisons between sets of data. For this project, assume you need to set up a home office with new communications equipment. You have a tight budget, so you need several price options for each piece of equipment. With two or three teammates, gather and organize information as follows:

1. As a team, identify a list of six to eight pieces of equipment that a state-of-the-art home office needs. Some of these may be a desktop or laptop computer; an all-in-one printer that includes scanning, copying, printing, and faxing functions; a wireless phone; and so on.

2. Divide the list of equipment among the team members so each teammate is responsible for finding information on at least two items. Using computer catalogs or Web resources, find low-end, moderate, and high-end options for each item. For example, low-end options for a copier would include 10 pages per minute, black-and-white copies, and automatic document feeder. Moderate options for a copier would include 20 pages per minute, color

printing, scanning, and faxing. High-end options would include 30+ pages per minute, sorting, collating, and stapling.

3. Create a worksheet to organize the list of equipment you identify. Save the workbook as **TP 19-1**, followed by a teammate's initials.

4. Create a header row with the column headings **Item**, **Low End**, **Moderate**, and **High End** so you can enter descriptions and prices for each equipment item.

5. Enter the research results in one worksheet. Format the worksheet so you can clearly see all data you have entered. Highlight cells, rows, or columns with color fill, shading, or borders to indicate the items you think are most important.

6. Save the changes to the workbook.

7. Compare your worksheet with other teams in the class to see what equipment items each team considered most important for a home office.

■ CRITICAL THINKING

CRITICAL THINKING 19–1

2-3.1.2
2-3.1.10
2-3.2.10

Worksheets are commonly used to organize and manage expenses. When the data is organized and labeled and formatted effectively, you can identify trends, draw conclusions, and compare and rank data.

1. Open the file **Travel Expenses** from the drive and folder where your Data Files folder is stored. Review the data in the worksheet.

2. Open a new Word document, and save the document as **CT 19-1**, followed by your initials.

3. Write a brief paragraph explaining how you can use the conditional formatting feature to help you draw conclusions about the values in the worksheet.

4. Save the changes to the Word document, and then close the document. Close the workbook file without saving any changes.

CRITICAL THINKING 19–2

2-3.1.2
2-3.1.10

Worksheet data can be very useful, but only if the data is comprehensive and accurate.

1. Open the file **Classes** from the drive and folder where your Data Files folder is stored. Review the data in the worksheet, which provides information about the current number of registrations for each term.

2. Open a new Word document, and save the document as **CT 19-2**, followed by your initials.

3. Write a brief paragraph explaining what additional information could be added to the worksheet to make the data more useful.

4. Save the changes to the Word document, and then close the document. Close the workbook without saving any changes.

■ ONLINE DISCOVERY

There are many Web sites that provide unit converters so you can convert measurements, weights, currency, temperatures, speed, and much more.

1. Search the Internet for *convert feet to meters* to find a site where you can convert feet to meters. Then complete the following steps:

2. If you completed Project 19–3, open your solution file **Revised Structures**. If you did not complete Project 19–3, open the file **Structures** from the drive and folder where your Data Files folder is stored. Save the workbook as a **OD 19-1**, followed by your initials.

3. In the Buildings worksheet (Sheet2), add a new column to the right of column D, and label the new column with the heading **Height in Meters**. Adjust the column width as needed.

2-3.1.4
2-3.2.10

4. Use the online unit converter to convert the data in the Height in Feet column from feet to meters. Enter the conversion results in the new column. Format the cells to show three decimal places.

5. Cite the Web source by typing or copying and pasting the URL in cell A14. Then enter the current date in cell A15.

6. Save the changes, and close the workbook.

■ JOB SKILLS

Your supervisor in the Education Department asks you to revise a worksheet that contains data for tutoring sessions. The data is already entered in a worksheet, but it needs to be organized and formatted so the data is easier to read and access.

1. Open the file **Tutoring** from the drive and folder where your Data Files folder is stored. Save the Tutoring workbook as **JS 19-1**, followed by your initials.

2. Revise the data so that it easier to read and access. Apply formats as desired.

3. Save the changes to the workbook.

2-3.1.1
2-3.1.2
2-3.1.4
2-3.1.10

LESSON 20

Creating Formulas and Charting Data

■ OBJECTIVES

Upon completion of this lesson, you should be able to:

- Understand and create formulas in a worksheet.

- Understand and use relative and absolute cell references.

- Understand and use function formulas to calculate sums, the number of occurrences, averages, and the smallest and largest numbers in a range.

- Use formulas with cell references to connect a worksheet to other worksheets.

- Identify and correct formula errors.

- Create a chart from worksheet data, and interpret data from worksheets and charts.

- Edit chart data, and change chart formats and options.

- Use sparklines to create a visual representation of worksheet data.

■ DATA FILES

To complete this lesson, you will need these data files:

Annual Sales.xlsx
Demographics.xlsx
Gross Profits.xlsx
Mileage Report.xlsx
MPG Report.xlsx

News Data.xlsx
Prices.xlsx
Quality Control.xlsx
Reservations.xlsx

Survey.docx
Tree Sale.xlsx
Utility Bills.xlsx
Weather.xlsx

■ WORDS TO KNOW

absolute cell reference

argument

chart

complex formulas

embedded chart

formula

function formula

mathematical functions

mixed cell reference

operand

operator

order of evaluation

relative cell references

sparkline

statistical functions

One of the primary uses of a spreadsheet is to solve problems that involve numbers. A worksheet is often used to complete complex and repetitious calculations accurately, quickly, and easily. The easiest way to complete these tasks is to use the tools within Excel.

Working with Formulas

Instead of using a calculator to perform mathematical calculations, you can use Excel to perform the calculations. The equation used to calculate values in a cell is known as a *formula*. A formula uses numbers and cell references to perform calculations such as addition, subtraction, multiplication, and division. A formula consists of two components: an operand and an operator. The *operand* is a number or cell reference. The *operator* is a symbol that indicates the mathematical operation to perform with the operands. For example, in the formula =*B5+6*, the operands are B5 and 6; the operator is the plus sign. **Table 20–1** lists some of the mathematical operators used in Excel.

TABLE 20–1   Operators used in Excel

OPERATOR	SYMBOL
Addition	+ (plus sign)
Subtraction	- (minus sign)
Multiplication	* (asterisk)
Division	/ (forward slash)
Percent	% (percent sign)

All Excel formulas begin with the equal sign. This tells Excel that you are entering a formula instead of a numeric value. A formula can be as simple as a single cell reference. For example, if you enter the formula =B3 in cell C4, then cell C4 will show the same contents as cell B3. If you then change the value in cell B3, cell C4 is automatically updated to reflect the change.

Formulas containing more than one operator are called ***complex formulas***. For example, the formula =A4*B5+10 will perform both multiplication and addition. The sequence used to calculate the value of a formula is called the ***order of evaluation***. Multiplication and division are performed before addition or subtraction, and then calculations are performed from the left side of the formula to the right side. You can change the order of evaluation by using parentheses; calculations enclosed in parentheses are performed first. Be sure you position the parentheses correctly when you structure a formula. For example, =8/(4–2) equals 4, while =(8/4)–2 equals 0.

▶ **VOCABULARY**

formula

operand

operator

complex formulas

order of evaluation

QUICK TIP

To create a minus sign in a formula, use the hyphen key in the number row on the keyboard or on the number keypad. You can find all the mathematical operator symbols except percent (%) on the number keypad.

QUICK TIP

When creating formulas, there must be a closing parenthesis for every opening parenthesis. Otherwise, an error message appears when you enter the formula.

Table 20–2 provides examples to demonstrate the order of evaluation.

TABLE 20–2 Examples of order of evaluation

FORMULA	RESULT
=8+4*4	8 + 16 = 24
=8*4+4	32 + 4 = 36
=(8+4)*4	12 * 4 = 48
=8-4/4	8 – 1 = 7
=8/4-4	2 – 4 = -2
=(8*4)-(4/4)	32 – 1 = 31

Computer users often make the mistake of assuming the formula will always deliver correct results. However, computers do not evaluate or assess the worksheet values. The information is simply processed, and the worksheet results are only as good as the data and formulas that are entered. If you input an incorrect formula, or if you input invalid data, the formula produces a false result—often referred to as "Garbage In, Garbage Out" (GIGO).

Creating and Editing a Formula

Generally, cell references are used in formulas rather than the actual value in a cell. That way, if the value in the cell changes, the formula does not need to be updated. There are two ways to enter a cell reference into a formula: you can enter the cell reference, or you can click the cell. When entering the cell reference, the column letter can be entered in either uppercase or lowercase. In the Step-by-Steps in this text, the column letters you will enter are shown in lowercase, while those you click are shown in uppercase.

You can edit a formula the same way you edit text and data in cells.

Step-by-Step 20.1

1. Launch **Microsoft Excel 2010**, and open the file **Prices** from the drive and folder where your Data Files folder is stored. Save the Prices workbook as **Revised Prices 1**, followed by your initials.

2. Click cell **D2**. Type **74.95**, which is the value of the quantity (*5*) times the unit price (*14.99*), and then press **Enter.**

3. Click cell **A2**, type **6**, and press **Enter**. Because the quantity changed, you need to update the line total. Click cell **D2**, type **89.94**, and press **Enter.**

4. The original quantity was correct. Click cell **A2**, type **5**, and then press **Enter.**

2-1.3.2
2-3.2.4
2-3.2.7

5. Instead of updating the line total manually, you can insert a formula that calculates the results and automatically adjusts to changes in the data. Click cell **D2**. Type **=a2*c2**. Compare your screen to **Figure 20–1**. Note that cell A2 has a blue border and cell C2 has a green border. The color of each of those cell borders matches the color of the cell reference in the formula. Also, note that the formula is displayed in both the cell and the formula bar.

FIGURE 20–1
Entering a formula in a cell

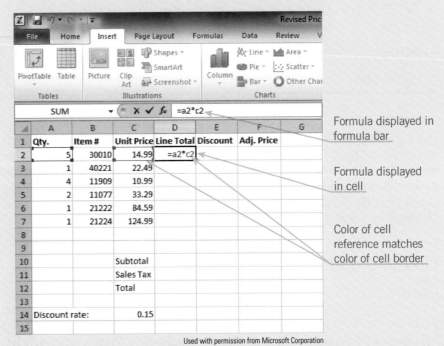

Used with permission from Microsoft Corporation

6. Click the **Enter** button ✔ on the formula bar. Cell D2 is still the active cell, and the formula is displayed in the formula bar. The result of the formula, *74.95,* is displayed in cell D2.

7. Click cell **D2**. To display the formula, the cell must be active; then you can view the formula in the formula bar.

8. Click cell **D3**. Type **=**, and then click cell **A3**. The cell reference A3 is now displayed following the equal sign in both cell D3 and the formula bar.

9. Type *, and then click cell **C3**. Both the cell and the formula bar now show the formula *=A3*C3.*

10. Press **Enter**. The result, *22.49,* is displayed in cell D3. Click cell **D3**. The formula is displayed in the formula bar.

11. Click cell **A3**, and type **10**. Then press **Enter** to change the quantity value. The result in cell D4 changes to *224.90* to reflect the increase in quantity.

12. Click cell **D4**. Type the formula **=a3*c3**, and then press **Enter**. The result *224.90* is displayed in cell D4. This is the same result that is displayed in cell D3 because even though the formula is in row 4, the cell references are for cells in row 3.

13. Click cell **D4,** and press **F2**. Change the *3*s to *4*s in the formula so the formula is *A4*C4*, and press **Enter**. (You can edit the formula either in the cell or in the formula bar.) The result *43.96* is displayed in cell D4.

14. Save the changes, and leave the workbook open for the next Step-by-Step.

Using Relative and Absolute Cell References

By default, when you create formulas, the cell references are formatted as *relative cell references*, which means when the formula is copied to another cell, the cell references will be adjusted relative to the formula's new location. This automatic adjustment is helpful when you need to repeat the same formula for several columns or rows.

There are times, though, when you do not want the cell reference to change when the formula is moved or copied to a new cell. For example, you may be calculating a discount rate on a purchase order. To calculate the discount, the prices should always be multiplied by a fixed amount. To create this formula, you format an *absolute cell reference* that does not change when the formula is copied or moved to a new location. To create an absolute cell reference, you insert a dollar sign ($) before the column letter and/or the row number of the cell reference you want to stay the same. For example, =A1 is a formula with an absolute reference to cell A1.

A cell reference that contains both relative and absolute references is called a *mixed cell reference*. For example, you can have an absolute column reference and a relative row reference. Or, you can have a relative column reference and an absolute row reference. To illustrate, =$A1 is a formula with a mixed cell reference. The column reference is absolute, and the row reference is relative. When formulas with mixed cell references are copied or moved, the row or column references that are preceded by a dollar sign will not change. However, the row or column references that are not preceded by a dollar sign will adjust relative to the cell they are moved to.

▶ **VOCABULARY**
relative cell references

absolute cell reference

mixed cell reference

QUICK TIP

You can use the AutoFill feature to copy a formula to a range of cells.

ABOVE AND BEYOND

You can toggle a cell reference from relative to absolute to mixed. Position the insertion point in or next to the desired cell reference in the formula bar. Each time you press F4, the cell reference will change. For example, the cell reference A1 toggles to A1, then to A$1, then to $A1, and then back to A1.

Step-by-Step 20.2

1. If necessary, open the file **Revised Prices 1** from your solution files. Save the Revised Prices 1 workbook as **Revised Prices 2**, followed by your initials.

2-3.2.3

2. Click cell **D4**. Drag the **fill handle** down to cell D7. When you release the mouse button, results are displayed in each of the selected cells. Using the AutoFill feature, you copied the formula in cell D4 to cells D5, D6, and D7.

3. Click cell **D4**. The formula bar shows *=A4*C4*. *A4* and *C4* are relative cell references.

4. Click cell **D5**. The formula bar shows *=A5*C5*. When you filled the formula down, Excel automatically changed the cell references from *A4* and *C4* to *A5* and *C5*. Click cells **D6** and **D7** to view the relative references in the formulas in each of those cells.

5. Click cell **E2**. Type **=d2*c14**. The cell reference *C14* is an absolute cell reference. Note that cell C14 displays the value *0.15* for the discount rate. Press **Enter**. The result *11.24* is displayed in the cell.

6. Click cell **E2**, and the drag the **fill handle** down to cell E7 to fill down the formula. Then click cell **E3**. The formula bar shows *=D3*C14*. The relative cell reference changed from *D2* to *D3* to show the new row number, but the absolute cell reference to cell C14 did not change.

7. Click cell **C14**, and type **0.10** to change the value. As you press **Enter**, watch the values in column E. The values will change when the new discount rate is entered.

8. Click cell **F2**, type the formula **=d2-e2**, and then press **Enter**. Fill the formula down through cell **F7**.

9. Click the **row 4** heading to select the entire row, and then in the Cells group, click the **Delete** button. Click cell **D6**. The formula has been updated, and the cell references that were for row 7 are now for row 6. Click cell **E6** and note that the absolute reference to cell C14 has been updated to cell C13.

10. Select **row 6**, and then in the Cells group, click the **Insert** button to insert a new row above row 6.

11. Click cell **D7**. The formula has been updated, and the cell references are now for row 7. Click the **Undo** button to remove the blank row.

12. Deselect the cells. Save the changes, and leave the workbook open for the next Step-by-Step.

> **QUICK TIP**
>
> When you insert or delete a new row or column that affects a range of cells identified in a formula, Excel will automatically update the range in the formula to reflect the change(s) in the range.

Using Function Formulas

Obviously a worksheet can contain a great deal of data. The tools within Excel allow you to easily obtain commonly used information from data. For example, if you want to know the average of a set of values, you could use a function formula to perform the calculation. A *function formula* is a special formula that names a function instead of using operators to calculate a result. Excel has more than 300 built-in functions for performing calculations. *Mathematical functions* perform calculations that you could perform using a scientific calculator. *Statistical functions* are functions that describe large quantities of data. For example, a statistical function can determine the average of a range of data. Excel provides other types of functions, including trigonometric and logical functions, which are beyond the scope of this book. **Table 20–3** describes some of the most common mathematical and statistical functions available in Excel. There are several methods for entering functions in the worksheet. You can enter an equal sign, the function name, and the argument. Or, if you want help entering the formula, you can use the buttons on the Ribbon.

> ► **VOCABULARY**
>
> **function formula**
>
> **mathematical functions**
>
> **statistical functions**

TABLE 20–3 Common Excel functions

MATHEMATICAL FUNCTIONS	
=PRODUCT	Multiplies values in the specified cells
=ROUND	Rounds the value to the nearest value in one of two ways: with the specified number of decimal places or to the nearest whole number
=ROUNDUP	Rounds the value up to the next higher positive value (or the next negative value away from zero) with the number of specified decimal places
=ROUNDDOWN	Rounds the value down to the next lower positive value (or to the next negative value toward zero) with the number of specified decimal places
=SUM	Adds the values in the specified range of cells
STATISTICAL FUNCTIONS	
=AVERAGE	Totals the range of cells, and then divides the total by the number of entries in the specified range
=COUNT	Counts the number of cells with values in the specified range
=MAX	Shows the maximum value within the specified range of cells
=MEDIAN	Shows the middle value in the specified range of cells
=MIN	Shows the minimum value within the specified range of cells

Using the SUM Function

Although it is easy to enter a formula, if the formula consists of several cells, it could take you a long time to enter all the cell references. A shortcut for entering cell references is to name a range of cells. The AutoSum feature enables you to quickly identify a range and enter a formula. When you use the AutoSum feature, Excel scans the worksheet and identifies the most logical column or row of adjacent cells containing numbers to sum.

MODULE 2   Key Applications

After identifying the range of cells, the AutoSum feature creates a function formula to calculate the sum of the range. In this case, the function is SUM. The SUM function formula is the most frequently used type of function formula. There are three components of a function formula: the equal sign, the function name, and the arguments. The equal sign tells Excel that a formula follows. The function name tells Excel what to do with the data. The *argument* is a value, a cell reference, a range, or text that acts as an operand in a function formula, and it is enclosed in parentheses after the function name. You will learn about other function formulas in the next section of this lesson. **Figure 20–2** illustrates an example of a formula containing the SUM function. The equal sign indicates that a formula follows. The function name SUM designates that the values of the five cells included in the argument (B4:B8) will be added.

▶ **VOCABULARY**
argument

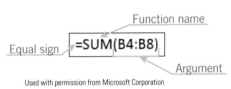

Used with permission from Microsoft Corporation

FIGURE 20–2   Parts of a function formula

Step-by-Step 20.3

2-3.2.5
2-3.2.6
2-3.2.7

1. If necessary, open the file **Revised Prices 2** from your solution files. Save the Revised Prices 2 workbook as **Revised Prices 3**, followed by your initials.

2. Click cell **F9**. Click the **Formulas** tab. In the Function Library group, click the **AutoSum** button shown in **Figure 20–3**.

FIGURE 20–3
Function Library group
on the Formulas tab

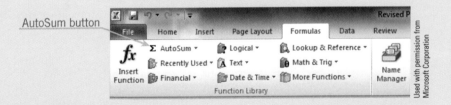

3. As shown in **Figure 20–4**, a marquee is displayed around the cell range F2:F8, and in cell F9 the formula *=SUM(F2:F8)* is proposed. A ScreenTip also appears showing that the formula involves adding numbers. Press **Enter** to accept the formula.

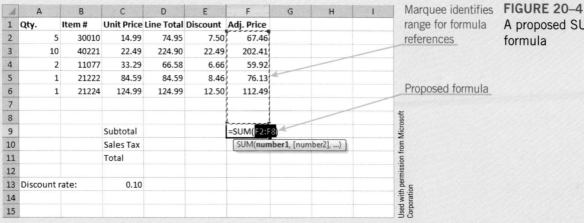

FIGURE 20–4
A proposed SUM function formula

Marquee identifies range for formula references

Proposed formula

4. The result *518.41* is displayed in cell F9. Click cell **F9** to show the formula in the formula bar. Note that the formula is the same as the proposed formula. The cell references in parentheses are relative cell references.

5. Click cell **F10**, type **=f9*(.06)**, and press **Enter**. The result *31.10* is displayed in cell F10.

6. The active cell is F11. Click the **AutoSum** button to add the subtotal and the sales tax. Note the marquee only surrounds cell F10. Point to the sizing handle on either the upper-left or upper-right corner of the marquee, and drag the **top border** of the marquee up to include cell F9 in the selection.

7. When the marquee on your screen matches the marquee shown in **Figure 20–5**, press **Enter**. The result *549.51* now is displayed in cell F11.

▲	A	B	C	D	E	F	G	H
1	Qty.	Item #	Unit Price	Line Total	Discount	Adj. Price		
2	5	30010	14.99	74.95	7.50	67.46		
3	10	40221	22.49	224.90	22.49	202.41		
4	2	11077	33.29	66.58	6.66	59.92		
5	1	21222	84.59	84.59	8.46	76.13		
6	1	21224	124.99	124.99	12.50	112.49		
7								
8								
9			Subtotal			518.41		
10			Sales Tax			31.10		
11			Total			=SUM(F9:F10)		
12						SUM(**number1**, [number2], ...)		
13	Discount rate:		0.10					
14								
15								

FIGURE 20–5
SUM function formula with extended marquee

Selected range for cell references

SUM function formula

8. Click cell **F10**. In the formula bar, position the insertion point after the number *6* in the formula, and type **5**. The formula bar should now show *=F9*(0.065)*. Press **Enter**. The result in cell F10 changes to *33.70*, and the result in cell F11 changes to *552.11*.

9. Cell F11 is the active cell. Click the **Home** tab, and open the **Clipboard** pane. If necessary, clear the contents of the Clipboard.

10. In the Clipboard group, click the **Copy** button. Click cell **A17**, and then in the Clipboard group, click the **Paste** button. The result *0.00* is displayed in cell A17, and the formula *=SUM(A15:A16)* is displayed in the formula bar. This is because you pasted the formula and not the cell value, and the cells referenced in the formula are empty.

11. Click cell **A18**. Click the **Paste** button arrow, and then under Paste Values, click the **Values** button [123]. The result *552.1056* is displayed in cell A18.

12. With cell A18 still active, in the Number group click the **Decrease Decimal** button [.00 / .0] two times so the result that is displayed is *552.11*.

13. Close the Clipboard pane. Save the changes, and then close the workbook.

Using the COUNT Function

The COUNT function is a statistical function that determines the number of cells in the argument range that contain numerical values. It is important to distinguish the difference between the COUNT function and the SUM function. The COUNT function tallies the number of occurrences of numerical data, and the SUM function totals all the numerical data.

Like the SUM function, and several other commonly used functions, you can enter the COUNT function by clicking a button on the Ribbon. Another alternative is to open the Function Arguments dialog box, which is very useful when you use functions that are not as common. The Function Arguments dialog box is useful in the process of building a formula that contains a function. Step-by-Step 20.4 will show you how to access this dialog box and the hundreds of built-in functions that Microsoft offers.

Step-by-Step 20.4

2-3.2.5
2-3.2.7

1. Open the file **Reservations** from the drive and folder where your Data Files folder is stored. Save the Reservations workbook as **Revised Reservations**, followed by your initials.

2. Click cell **B39**, and then click the **Formulas** tab.

3. To calculate the number of Chicken orders, click the **AutoSum** button arrow [Σ ▾], and then click **Count Numbers**. The marquee indicates the B36:B38 range.

4. Click cell **B38**, and then drag up to cell B5 to select the range **B5:B38**. Press **Enter**, and the result *10* is displayed in cell B39.

5. Click cell **C39**. In the Function Library group, click the **More Functions** button. Point to **Statistical**, and a complete list of statistical functions is displayed in a submenu. In the submenu, click **COUNT**. The Function Arguments dialog box shown in **Figure 20–6** opens. A brief explanation of the COUNT function is provided in the dialog box.

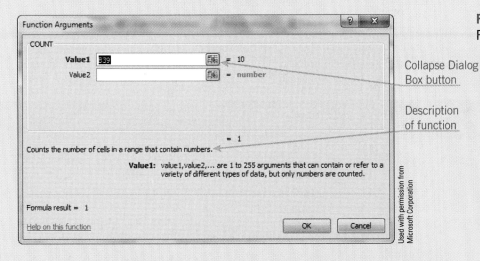

FIGURE 20–6
Function Arguments dialog box

Collapse Dialog
Box button

Description
of function

Used with permission from
Microsoft Corporation

6. A proposed range *B39* is displayed in the Value1 text box, which is obviously not correct.

7. Click the **Collapse Dialog Box** button ▦ at the right side of the Value1 text box. The dialog box minimizes so you can see the worksheet cells, but you can also still see the dialog box title bar and the range of cells for Value1. The proposed formula is also displayed in the formula bar. (If necessary, drag the dialog box title bar to reposition the dialog box on the screen so you can see the formula bar.)

8. Scroll to the top of the worksheet, and then select the range **C5:C38**. The formula in the dialog box is updated and now shows the new range you selected. The formula in the formula bar is also updated.

9. Click the **Expand Dialog Box** ▦ button next to the Value1 text box (or press Enter). The dialog box is maximized. Click **OK**. The dialog box closes, and the result *18* is displayed in cell C39.

10. With cell C39 still active, drag the **fill handle** into column D to fill the function formula across the column. The result 4 is displayed in cell D39. Click cell **D39**. The formula in the formula bar shows =COUNT(D5:D38).

11. Save the changes, and then close the workbook.

> **QUICK TIP**
>
> The intent of the Function Arguments dialog box is to guide you in creating formulas, but sometimes the dialog box can get in the way when you are creating the formula. The collapse and expand features in the Function Arguments dialog box allow you to minimize and maximize the dialog box as you work with it.

Using the AVERAGE, MIN, and MAX Functions

The AVERAGE function is also a statistical function. It calculates the average of the range identified in the argument. For example, the function =AVERAGE(B2,G2) calculates the average of the values contained in cells B2 and G2. Note that in this example, the cell references are separated by a comma instead of a colon. That is because these cells are not adjacent, and only two cells are identified in the range. The comma is used to distinguish the two cell references.

The MIN (minimum) and MAX (maximum) functions are two more statistical functions. The MIN function shows the smallest number contained in the range identified in the argument. The MAX function shows the largest number contained in the range identified in the argument.

Step-by-Step 20.5

2-3.2.5
2-3.2.7

1. Open the file **Weather** from the drive and folder where your Data Files folder is stored. Save the Weather workbook as **Revised Weather**, followed by your initials.

2. Click cell **B11**, and if necessary click the **Formulas** tab.

3. To calculate the average low temperature for the week, click the **AutoSum** button arrow, and then click **Average**. The formula =AVERAGE(B10) is proposed. Click the **formula bar**, and edit the formula so the argument shows the range B2:B8. The revised formula should be displayed as =AVERAGE(B2:B8).

4. Press **Enter** (or click the Enter button on the formula bar). The result 9 is displayed in cell B11.

5. To calculate the average high temperature for the week, click cell **B11**. Drag the **fill handle** to the right to select cell **C11**. The formula is copied to cell C11, and the result 24 is displayed.

6. Click cell **B12**. Click the **AutoSum** button arrow, and then click **Min**. Select the range **B2:B8**, and press **Enter**. The result -2 is displayed in cell B12.

7. Click cell **C12**. Click the **AutoSum** button arrow, and then click **Max**. Select the range **C2:C8**, and press **Enter**. The result 31 appears in cell C12.

8. You realize you entered the formula in the wrong cell. Click cell **C12**, and then click the **Home** tab. In the Clipboard group, click the **Cut** button. Click cell **C13**, and then click the **Paste** button. The formula is moved to cell C13.

9. Click cell **D14**. On the Home tab in the Editing group, click the **AutoSum** button arrow, and click **Max**. Press **Enter** to accept the proposed range *D2:D13*. The result *4.8* is displayed in cell D14.

10. Select the range **B2:B8**. A preview of the Average, Count, and Sum results for the selected range is displayed in the status bar at the bottom of the screen.

11. Click cell **B16**. Click the **AutoSum** button arrow, and then click **Count Numbers**. Select the range **B2:B8,** and press **Enter**. The result *7* is displayed in cell B16.

12. Save the changes, and then close the workbook.

Creating Formulas that Reference Cells in Multiple Worksheets

As you already know, Excel features enable you to work with multiple worksheets (pages) in three dimensions (3D). The 3D reference enables you to access data from three different dimensions in the workbook: length, width, and depth. Length and width refer to the worksheet rows and columns. Depth refers to the ability to connect the worksheets by creating formulas that reference the same cell or range in multiple worksheets. These 3D references are often used in summary worksheets to condense and total data from other worksheets.

Step-by-Step 20.6

1. Open the file **Annual Sales** from the drive and folder where your Data Files folder is stored. Save the Annual Sales workbook as **Revised Annual Sales**, followed by your initials.

2-3.1.1
2-3.2.4

2. Click each sheet tab to view all five worksheets. You will see that the Western worksheet is not complete. The cell contents for the numbers have not been formatted, and the values in the *Difference* column have not been calculated. Also, the Summary worksheet needs to be updated with the Western region data.

3. Click the **Central** sheet tab, and then click anywhere in the cell range B3:D14, where the content is formatted for currency. With a formatted cell selected, double-click the **Format Painter** button.

4. Click the **Western** sheet tab to switch to that worksheet. Drag the mouse pointer to select the cell range **B3:C14**, and copy the number format. Deselect the cells.

5. Click the **Central** sheet tab, and press **Esc** to toggle off the Format Painter.

6. Click cell **D3**. On the Home tab in the Clipboard group, click the **Copy** button. Click the **Western** sheet tab, and select the cell range **D3:D14**. Click the **Paste** button arrow, and click **Paste Special** to open the Paste Special dialog box shown in **Figure 20–7**.

FIGURE 20–7
Paste Special dialog box

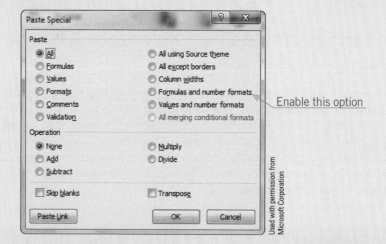

7. Under Paste, enable the option **Formulas and number formats**, and click **OK**. The formula is pasted, and the number formatting is applied to the results.

8. Click cell **B16**. In the Editing group, click the **AutoSum** button. The range B3:B15 should be selected. Press **Enter** to calculate the total goal for the year. Then click cell **B16,** and drag the **fill handle** across cells C16 and D16 to copy the formula. With the range B16:D16 still selected, in the Number group click the **Accounting Number Format** button $, and then click the **Decrease Decimal** button twice to remove the decimal places.

9. Click the **Summary** sheet tab. Click cell **B5**. The formula bar shows the formula =*Southern!B16*. The cell reference *Southern!B16* refers to cell B16 on the Southern worksheet.

10. Click cell **B6**. Type =. Click the **Western** sheet tab, and then click cell **B16**. A marquee surrounds the active cell. Press **Enter**. The value *$402,000* is displayed in cell B6 in the Summary worksheet.

11. Click cell **C6**. Type **=western!c6**. Press **Enter**. The value *$33,879* is displayed in cell C6. Click cell **C6**. You realize you made an error in the formula. In the formula bar, position the insertion point between *C* and *6*, and type **1** so the modified formula is displayed as *=Western!C16*. Press **Enter**. The calculation is updated, and the value *$403,242* is displayed in cell C6.

12. Click cell **D6**. Type **=western!d16**. Press **Enter**. The value *$1,242* is displayed in cell D6.

13. Note that the value in cell C5 is *$373,692* and the value in cell D5 is *$8,692*. Click the **Southern** sheet tab, and then click cell **C8**. Type **32,199**, and press **Enter**. The cell value is replaced, and cells C16 and D16 are updated. Click the **Summary** sheet tab. The values in cells C5 and D5 have automatically been updated to reflect the edits made on the Southern worksheet. Cell C5 now displays *$373,982*, and cell D5 displays *$8,982*.

14. Save the changes, and then close the workbook.

Troubleshooting Common Formula Errors

When Excel cannot properly perform a calculation, an error value appears in the cell where you entered the formula. The error may exist because the cell contains text instead of a numeric value. An error value appears if the cell referenced in the formula contains an error or if a formula tries to divide by zero. An error value also appears if the cell is not wide enough to show the result. There are a number of common errors that occur—and common causes for those errors. **Table 20–4** lists these common errors, their typical causes, and some possible solutions. Fortunately, Excel provides help to solve formula errors.

QUICK TIP

Excel has an AutoCorrect feature that automatically checks a formula for common keyboarding mistakes. Sometimes Excel is able to identify the error. If so, a suggested correction appears in an alert box.

TECHNOLOGY TIMELINE

Did you know that early electronic spreadsheet programs were the "killer apps" for personal computers? Killer applications are computer programs that are so necessary or desirable that they prove the core value of some larger technology, and as a result, they substantially increase the sales of the platform they run on.

VisiCalc is considered to be one of the earliest examples of a "killer app." VisiCalc, originally developed in 1978 for the Apple II computer, was one of the early electronic spreadsheet applications, and it spurred the sale of thousands of Apple II platform computers. In 1983, the Lotus Development Corporation released Lotus 1-2-3, a spreadsheet program, that also offered charts and basic database operations. Shortly after Lotus 1-2-3 was released, the IBM PC became the number-one selling computer. Then in 1985, Microsoft released the first version of Excel for the Mac. Two years later, Microsoft released a new version of Excel to run in the Windows environments. This new version of Excel was one of the first applications that Microsoft introduced to run on the Windows operating system, and therefore, it was also one of the first applications developed for a graphical user interface.

TABLE 20–4   Common errors, their causes, and solutions

ERROR	TYPICAL CAUSE/SOLUTION
#####	**Cause:** Occurs when the column is not wide enough or if a negative date is entered **Solution:** If the column is not wide enough, AutoFit the column or change the number format so the number will fit within the column; negative dates usually occur when there is an incorrect formula calculating a date, so check and correct your date formula
#VALUE!	**Cause:** Occurs when the wrong type of argument or operand is used, which could result from a formula referencing cells with text when the formula requires a number **Solution:** Trace the error to determine the cause and correct it **Cause:** Occurs when a cell reference in the formula refers back to its own cell, either directly or indirectly, creating a circular reference **Solution:** Remove the circular reference or enable repeated recalculations
#DIV/0!	**Cause:** Occurs when a number is divided by zero, which is most often caused by using a cell reference to a blank cell or to a cell that contains a zero **Solution:** Trace the error and correct the reference
#N/A	**Cause:** Occurs when a value is not available to a function or formula, often caused by missing data or by referencing a cell that contains #N/A instead of data (which you can use as a placeholder for data that is not yet available) **Solution:** Trace the error and replace the missing data with a real value **Cause:** Can be caused by giving an inappropriate value for a lookup **Solution:** To resolve, make sure the lookup value argument is the correct type of value—for example, a value or a cell reference, but not a range reference
#REF!	**Cause:** Occurs when a cell reference is not valid, often caused by deleting cells referred to by other formulas or pasting moved cells over cells referred to by other formulas **Solution:** To correct this error, trace the error and then change the formulas; if you notice the error right after deleting or pasting cells, restore the cells on the worksheet by clicking Undo immediately after you delete or paste the cells which caused the error **Cause:** This can also be caused by a link to a program that is not running **Solution:** To resolve the error in this case, start the program the worksheet is trying to link to
#NUM!	**Cause:** Occurs with invalid numeric values in a formula or function, often caused by using an unacceptable argument in a function that requires a numeric argument **Solution:** To correct this, make sure the arguments used in the function are numbers—for example, even if the value you want to enter is $1,000, enter 1000 in the formula **Cause:** This error can also be caused by using a worksheet function that iterates, such as IRR or RATE, and the function cannot find a result **Solution:** To resolve the error in this case, use a different starting value for the worksheet function or change the number of times Excel iterates formulas
#NULL!	**Cause:** Occurs when using a space where it is not appropriate **Solution:** Check for inappropriate spaces in the formula; for example, when referencing two ranges, make sure a comma separates the ranges: =SUM(C1:C5,D4:D5)

Step-by-Step 20.7

1. Open the file **Quality Control** from the drive and folder where your Data Files folder is stored. Save the Quality Control workbook as **Revised Quality Control**, followed by your initials.

2-3.2.8

2. Click cell **E4**. Type **=d4/c4**, and press **Enter**. The characters #### are displayed in cell E4 as shown in **Figure 20–8**.

◢	A	B	C	D	E	F	G
1	QUALITY CONTROL REPORT						
2	Item	Processed	Tested	Flawed		Est. Flawless	
3				#	%		
4	8 oz. jars		2,000	26	####		
5	12 oz. jars		4,500	55			
6	24 oz. jars		3,100	36			
7	32 oz. jars		2,500	16			
8	64 oz. jars		2,750	12			
9							
10							

FIGURE 20–8
Error notification of insufficient space

Used with permission from Microsoft Corporation

3. Double-click the **right border** of the column E label to use the AutoFit feature on the width of column E. Cell E4 now displays *1.30%*. Click cell **E4**, and drag the **fill handle** down to E8.

4. Click cell **F4**. Type **=a4/c4**, and press **Enter**. As shown in **Figure 20–9**, *#VALUE!* is displayed in the cell and there is a small green triangle in the upper-left corner of the cell.

◢	A	B	C	D	E	F	G
1	QUALITY CONTROL REPORT						
2	Item	Processed	Tested	Flawed		Est. Flawless	
3				#	%		
4	8 oz. jars		2,000	26	1.30%	#VALUE!	
5	12 oz. jars		4,500	55	1.22%		
6	24 oz. jars		3,100	36	1.16%		
7	32 oz. jars		2,500	16	0.64%		
8	64 oz. jars		2,750	12	0.44%		
9							
10							

FIGURE 20–9
A formula error notification

Used with permission from Microsoft Corporation

5. Click cell **F4**. An exclamation point within a diamond shape is displayed to the left of the active cell. This is the Error Checking button, which is displayed when a cell may contain a formula error. Point to the **Error Checking** button ⬦, and a ScreenTip that describes the error is displayed.

6. Click the **Error Checking** button. In the menu, click **Show Calculation Steps**. The Evaluate Formula dialog box shown in **Figure 20–10** opens. Under Evaluation, the formula is displayed with the cell values. Now you can clearly see the problem: you are trying to divide text (*oz. jars*) by numbers.

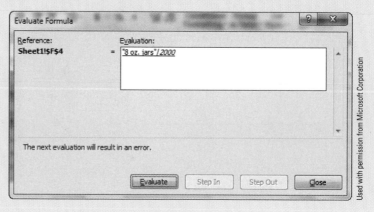

7. Close the dialog box. In the formula bar, change A4 to **F4** so the revised formula is *=F4/C4*.

8. Press **Enter**. A Circular Reference Warning opens and explains that a cell reference in the formula (in this case F4) refers to the cell's own value. Click **OK**. The value *0* is displayed in cell F4. As shown in **Figure 20–11**, in the lower-left corner of the screen, the status bar indicates that the circular reference is the cell reference F4.

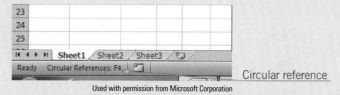

9. Click cell **F4**. Type **=(100%-e4)*b4**, and press **Enter**. The value *0* is displayed in cell F4 because cell B4 has no value. Click cell **F4**, and then fill down the formula to cell F8.

10. Click cell **B4**. Type **200000**, and press **Enter**. The value *197,400* is now displayed in cell F4.

11. Click cell **B4**. In the Number group, click the **Comma Style** button 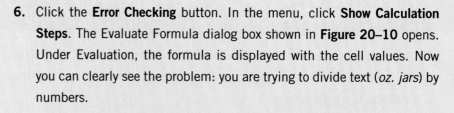, and then click the **Decrease Decimal** button twice. Click the cell **B4** fill handle, and fill down to cell B8. The value *200,000* is now displayed in all the selected cells. In the lower-right corner of cell B8, click the **AutoFill Options** button. The menu shown in **Figure 20–12** is displayed.

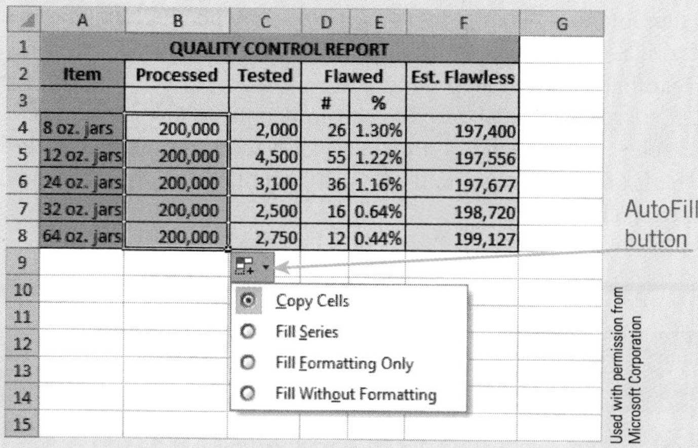

⊿	A	B	C	D	E	F	G
1		QUALITY CONTROL REPORT					
2	Item	Processed	Tested	Flawed		Est. Flawless	
3				#	%		
4	8 oz. jars	200,000	2,000	26	1.30%	197,400	
5	12 oz. jars	200,000	4,500	55	1.22%	197,556	
6	24 oz. jars	200,000	3,100	36	1.16%	197,677	
7	32 oz. jars	200,000	2,500	16	0.64%	198,720	
8	64 oz. jars	200,000	2,750	12	0.44%	199,127	
9							
10			◉ Copy Cells				
11			○ Fill Series				
12			○ Fill Formatting Only				
13			○ Fill Without Formatting				
14							
15							

AutoFill Options button

FIGURE 20–12
AutoFill Options menu

Used with permission from Microsoft Corporation

12. Select the option **Fill Formatting Only**. The values are removed from the range B5:B8, but the cell format remains in the range of cells.

13. Enter the following values in cells B5:B8. As you enter the values, the calculations are performed, the cell format is applied, and the values in the F column are updated.

    450000

    310000

    350000

    275000

14. Save the changes, and then close the workbook.

Using Graphics to Represent Data

Obviously a worksheet can contain a great deal of information. The results of a worksheet are only accurate if correct data and formulas have been entered. If you are certain of the accuracy of the content of the worksheet, then the next questions are: What does the data in this worksheet tell me? What logical conclusions can I draw from it?

As you analyze worksheet data, you may notice in a column that the values are continually increasing. If this column is a chronological listing of your company's sales, you could conclude that there is a trend—that your company's sales are increasing each year. On the other hand, if this same column is not a chronological listing of sales, but rather a listing of sales by region, it is not logical to interpret a trend, but you can compare the data for each region.

To draw conclusions from the worksheet data, you can translate the data to a *chart*, which is a graphic representation of your worksheet data. Charts are an excellent means of conveying information, and they are extremely useful for summarizing, clarifying, or highlighting data. In a business, management at all levels must understand the data generated on a daily basis, but upper-level management relies on charts to look for trends and oddities.

▶ **VOCABULARY**
chart

2-3.1.2
2-3.2.10

When the values and their representation are correct, a chart can help you gain an understanding that would perhaps not be clear when looking at the worksheet. However, if a chart is not set up correctly, the representation can be confusing or misleading. The first step in creating a chart is to decide what type of chart you want to create. Excel provides several options for chart types. The chart type you select will depend on the data you want to represent. **Table 20–5** lists some of the Excel chart types and a description of the types of data you can illustrate with each chart.

TABLE 20–5   Chart types

CHART TYPE	DESCRIPTION
Column chart	Useful in showing changes over a period of time, or for making comparisons among individual items
Line chart	Illustrates trends in data at equal intervals
Pie chart	Compares the sizes of portions as they relate to a whole unit, and illustrates that the parts total 100 percent; effective for one data series, such as one column or row of data with one column or row of column and row headings
Bar chart	Helpful when you want to make comparisons among individual items
Area chart	Effective for emphasizing trends because it illustrates the magnitude of change over time
Scatter chart	Illustrates scientific data, and it specifically shows uneven intervals—or clusters—of data
Other charts	Stock, Surface, Doughnut, Bubble, and Radar

ABOVE AND BEYOND

With the exception of the pie and doughnut charts, all chart types have a horizontal and a vertical axis.

An attractive chart will grab attention and Excel provides many predesigned chart layouts and styles that make it easy for you to create professional-looking charts. But to convey meaning, the values represented in the charts must be correctly labeled. After you decide which chart type to create, the next step is to decide which chart options you want to use. To do this, you must first understand the elements in a chart. **Figure 20–13** identifies the chart elements. Take time to review and become familiar with the various parts. Customizing the table elements helps identify and clarify the chart contents.

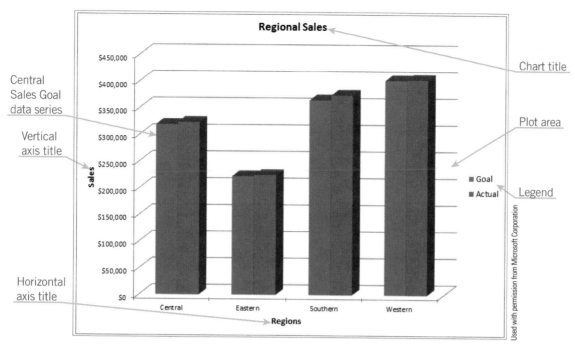

FIGURE 20–13   Chart elements

Creating a Chart

When creating a chart, you define specific data to be included in the analysis. As a result, you frequently need to select nonadjacent cells. To select nonadjacent cells, click the first cell, press and hold Ctrl, and then click the next cell.

There may be occasions when the data used to create the chart changes after the chart has been created. Fortunately, you do not need to create a new chart. When you edit the data in the worksheet, the chart is automatically updated to reflect the changes. And, if you decide the chart type is not effective, you can choose a new chart type without starting over.

ABOVE AND BEYOND

You can create an instant chart by selecting the data you want to chart and then pressing F11. A two-dimensional column chart is created. However, there are no data labels or chart title in this instant chart.

Step-by-Step 20.8

1. Open the file **News Data** from the drive and folder where your Data Files folder is stored. Save the News Data workbook as **Revised News Data 1**, followed by your initials.

2. Select the range **A5:A9**, and then press and hold **Ctrl** as you select the range **C5:C9**. Two ranges of data are selected.

3. Click the **Insert** tab. In the Charts group shown in **Figure 20–14**, click the **Column** button.

2-3.1.1
2-3.1.4
2-3.1.10
2-3.2.9
2-3.2.10

FIGURE 20–14
Charts group on the Insert tab

4. Under 3-D Column, click the first option **3-D Clustered Column**. The chart is inserted in a canvas on the active worksheet, similar to how a SmartArt object is inserted in a Word document. Also, the Ribbon adapts to show the Chart Tools Design tab.

5. In the Chart Layouts group shown in **Figure 20–15**, click the **Layout 3** chart layout. The chart changes to the new layout.

FIGURE 20–15
Chart Layouts group on the Chart Tools Design tab

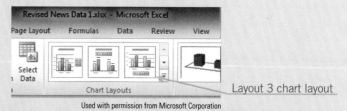

Used with permission from Microsoft Corporation

6. Click the **Chart Tools Layout** tab. In the Labels group shown in **Figure 20–16**, click the **Chart Title** button. Then click **Centered Overlay Title**. The text box, which is a placeholder for the chart title, is selected.

FIGURE 20–16
Labels group on the Chart Tools Layout tab

7. Click inside the text box, and then select all of the text in the text box. Type **Where People Get the News**. Click a blank area on the canvas to deselect the text box.

8. In the Labels group, click the **Axis Titles** button, and then point to **Primary Horizontal Axis Title**. In the submenu click **Title Below Axis**. A new text box is positioned at the bottom of the chart. Select the text in the text box, and type **Media**. Click a blank area on the canvas to deselect the text box.

9. You decide a pie chart will communicate the data more effectively. Click the **Chart Tools Design** tab, and in the Type group click the **Change Chart Type** button. The Change Chart Type dialog box shown in **Figure 20–17** opens.

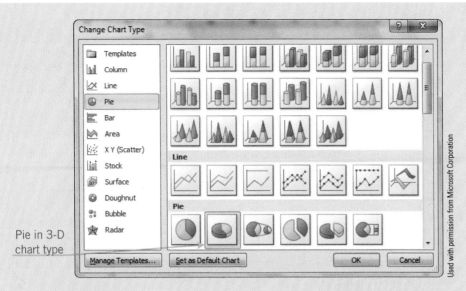

Pie in 3-D
chart type

FIGURE 20–17
Change Chart Type dialog box

10. In the left pane, click **Pie**. If necessary, scroll down to view the Pie chart designs. Under Pie, click the **Pie in 3-D** chart type, and then click **OK**.

11. Click the **Chart Tools Layout** tab. In the Labels group, click the **Legend** button, and then click **Show Legend at Left**.

12. Click the **Data Labels** button, and then click **Best Fit**.

13. You learn that your data for Television and Internet/online are reversed. Click cell **B5,** and type **924**. Click cell **B8**, type **887**, and press **Enter**. As you enter the new data, the values in cells C5 and C8 are updated and the chart is also updated.

14. Save the changes, and leave the workbook open for the next Step-by-Step.

Changing Chart Formats

Many of the parts of the chart such as the chart title and the axis titles are positioned on the chart in a text box. When you click the part of the chart you want to change, the object boundaries will appear, and then you can change the formats.

You can choose whether to keep the chart in the same worksheet as the data the chart is based on, or you can move the chart to a different worksheet. An *embedded chart* is a chart created on the same sheet as the data used in the chart. One advantage of embedding a chart on the same page as the data is that the data and the chart can be viewed at the same time. If the chart will not fit on the same sheet with the data, or if you want to create more than one chart from the same data, you will probably want to move the chart to a separate sheet.

▶ **VOCABULARY**
embedded chart

Step-by-Step 20.9

2-3.2.9

1. If necessary, open **Revised News Data 1** from your solution files. Save the Revised News Data 1 workbook as **Revised News Data 2**, followed by your initials.

2. Point to any white area above the legend area. When the mouse pointer changes to a four-headed arrow, click and drag the **chart** to reposition it on the worksheet. Align the lower-left corner of the canvas with the lower-left corner of cell E24.

3. Click anywhere in the chart to select it. Position the mouse pointer over the upper-right corner of the canvas. When the pointer changes to a two-headed arrow, drag the **corner** of the canvas upward and to the right to increase the size of the canvas. Stop when the canvas is approximately the width of columns E:M.

4. Click the **Chart Tools Format** tab. With the canvas selected, in the Shape Styles group shown in **Figure 20–18**, click the **More** button. Use Live Preview to explore the various styles. Click the **Subtle Effect – Blue, Accent 1** shape style (light blue background in the second column).

QUICK TIP

The chart is an object, just like a clip-art image or a photo. When the chart is selected, sizing handles are displayed on the canvas. You can resize the chart by dragging a sizing handle on the canvas. Be sure to drag a corner handle if you want to resize the chart proportionally.

FIGURE 20–18
Shape Styles group on the Chart Tools Format tab

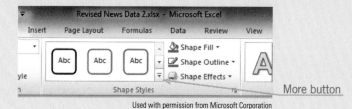

Used with permission from Microsoft Corporation

5. Click the **legend** object to select it, and then right-click to open the Mini toolbar. Change the font size to 12 point.

6. Click the **40%** label on the pie chart. All the labels on the chart are selected. Right-click one of the selected text boxes, and change the font size to 14 point.

QUICK TIP

To remove a chart element, such as the legend, select the element and then press Delete.

7. Click the **40%** label again, and only the 40% text box is selected. Change the font color to white. Format the 8%, 12%, and 38% labels white. (*Hint*: Use the Format Painter button on the Mini toolbar.) Leave the 1% label formatted in the dark font color.

8. Click the **Chart Tools Design** tab. In the Location group, shown in **Figure 20–19**, click the **Move Chart** button.

FIGURE 20–19
Location group on the Chart Tools Design tab

Used with permission from Microsoft Corporation

9. The Move Chart dialog box shown in **Figure 20–20** opens. The current setting shows the chart is placed as an object in Sheet1. Enable the option **New sheet**, and then click **OK**. A new worksheet is created with the tab name Chart1. The chart is moved to the new worksheet, and the chart fills the worksheet window.

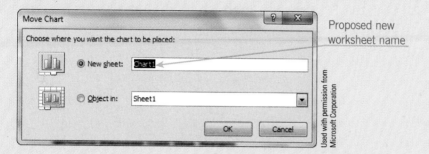

Proposed new worksheet name

Used with permission from Microsoft Corporation

FIGURE 20–20
Move Chart dialog box

10. Save the changes to the workbook, and leave the workbook open.

11. Launch **Microsoft Word 2010**, and open the file **Survey.docx** from the drive and folder where your Data Files folder is stored. Save the Survey document as **Revised Survey**, followed by your initials.

12. In the taskbar, click the **Revised News Data 2** workbook button, and, if necessary, make Chart1 the active worksheet. Right-click in the blank area under the legend, and in the shortcut menu click **Copy** to copy the chart to the Clipboard.

13. Click the **Revised Survey** document button on the taskbar. Position the insertion point at the end of the document. Right-click to display the shortcut menu. Under Paste Options, click the first option **Use Destination Theme & Embed Workbook**.

14. Save the changes to the Word document, and then close Word. Close the Excel workbook, and leave Excel open for the next Step-by-Step.

Using Sparklines to Represent Data

Another option for using graphics to represent data is to add a sparkline to the data. A *sparkline* is a tiny chart embedded in a cell. The sparkline provides a snapshot of data in a row or column, such as a trend or an increase or decrease in values. They are especially useful when you want to present and summarize data in a small amount of space.

You can insert a single sparkline for a set of data, or you can create multiple sparklines at the same time. After inserting a sparkline, you can use built-in formats to apply a color scheme, or you can customize the graphic by using commands to choose a color for high, low, first, and last values. When the data in the correlated cells changes, the sparklines are immediately updated.

▶ **VOCABULARY**
sparkline

Step-by-Step 20.10

2-3.2.9
2-3.2.10

1. Open the file **Gross Profits** from the drive and folder where your Data Files folder is stored. Save the Gross Profits workbook as **Revised Gross Profits**, followed by your initials.

2. Click cell **F3**. Click the **Insert** tab. In the Sparklines group shown in **Figure 20–21**, click the **Line** button.

FIGURE 20–21
Sparklines group on the Insert tab

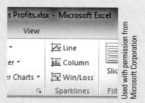

3. The Create Sparklines dialog box opens. Drag the mouse pointer over the worksheet cells to select the range **B3:E3**. A marquee appears around the selected cells, and the range is displayed in the Data Range text box in the dialog box. When your settings match those shown in **Figure 20–22**, click **OK**.

FIGURE 20–22
Selected range for sparkline

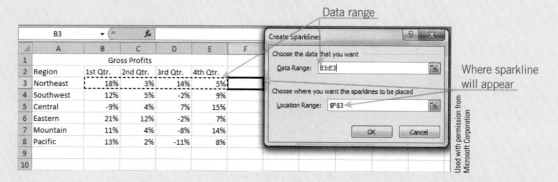

4. A tiny line graphic displays in cell F3. Drag the F3 fill handle and fill down to cell **F8**. The tiny graphics now display in each of the selected cells, as shown in **Figure 20–23**.

FIGURE 20–23
Line sparklines added to worksheet

	A	B	C	D	E	F	G
1		Gross Profits					
2	Region	1st Qtr.	2nd Qtr.	3rd Qtr.	4th Qtr.		
3	Northeast	18%	3%	14%	5%		
4	Southwest	12%	5%	-2%	9%		
5	Central	-9%	4%	7%	15%		
6	Eastern	21%	12%	-2%	7%		
7	Mountain	11%	4%	-8%	14%		
8	Pacific	13%	2%	-11%	8%		
9							
10							

5. Select the range **G3:G8**. Click the **Insert** tab. In the Sparklines group, click the **Column** button. The Create Sparklines dialog box opens. In the worksheet, select the range **B3:E8**. Click **OK**. Tiny column graphics are now displayed in column G.

6. Select the range **H3:H8**. Click the **Insert** tab. In the Sparklines group, click the **Win/Loss** button. In the worksheet, select the range **B3:E8**, and then click **OK**.

7. Deselect the cells. Compare your worksheet to **Figure 20–24**. Columns F, G, and H display the three different types of sparklines. The sparklines in column F show the trends, the sparklines in column G compare the values, and the sparklines in column H highlight the positive and negative values.

⊿	A	B	C	D	E	F	G	H	I
1		Gross Profits							
2	Region	1st Qtr.	2nd Qtr.	3rd Qtr.	4th Qtr.				
3	Northeast	18%	3%	14%	5%				
4	Southwest	12%	5%	-2%	9%				
5	Central	-9%	4%	7%	15%				
6	Eastern	21%	12%	-2%	7%				
7	Mountain	11%	4%	-8%	14%				
8	Pacific	13%	2%	-11%	8%				
9									
10									

Used with permission from Microsoft Corporation

FIGURE 20–24
Line, Column, and Win/Loss sparklines added to worksheet

8. Click cell **D8**. Type **12**. As you press **Enter**, watch the sparklines change in cells F8:H8.

9. Select the range **F3:F8**. Click the **Sparkline Tools Design** tab. In the Style group shown in **Figure 20–25**, click the **More** button to show all the color schemes. In the bottom row, select the last style, **Sparkline Style Colorful #6**. The markers are shown in black.

Used with permission from Microsoft Corporation

FIGURE 20–25
Style group on the Sparkline Tools Design tab

10. The range F3:F8 should still be selected. In the Style group, click the **Sparkline Color** button arrow to show the color grid. In the first row under Theme Colors, click the **Blue, Accent 1** color. Note the color change for the markers in column F.

ABOVE AND BEYOND

Because a sparkline is a graphic embedded in a cell, you can enter text in the same cell, and then the sparkline will be displayed as a background image in the cell.

FIGURE 20–26
Marker colors for high points and low points

11. The range F3:F8 should still be selected. In the Style group, click the **Marker Color** button, and then point to **High Point**. Under Standard Colors, click the **Green** color. Click the **Marker Color** button, and then point to **Low Point**. Under Standard Colors, click the **Red** color. Deselect the cells. As shown in **Figure 20–26**, the green high points and red low points in each graphic are easily identified.

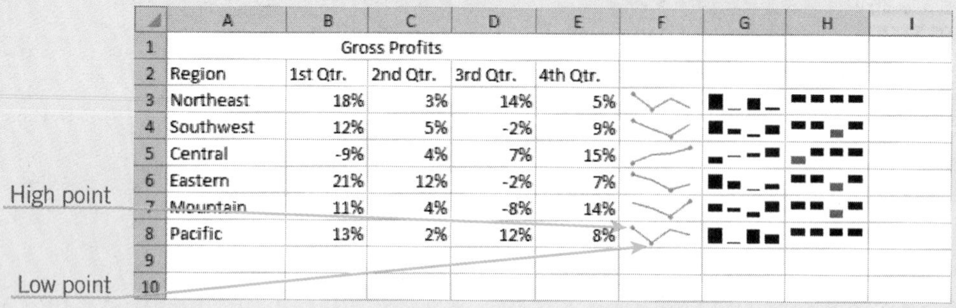

	A	B	C	D	E	F	G	H	I
1	Gross Profits								
2	Region	1st Qtr.	2nd Qtr.	3rd Qtr.	4th Qtr.				
3	Northeast	18%	3%	14%	5%				
4	Southwest	12%	5%	-2%	9%				
5	Central	-9%	4%	7%	15%				
6	Eastern	21%	12%	-2%	7%				
7	Mountain	11%	4%	-8%	14%				
8	Pacific	13%	2%	12%	8%				
9									
10									

High point
Low point

12. To remove the sparklines in column H, select the range **H3:H8**. Right-click the selected range, and in the shortcut menu point to **Sparklines**. In the submenu, click **Clear Selected Sparklines**.

13. To remove a group of sparklines, click cell **G3**. Right-click the selected cell, and in the shortcut menu point to **Sparklines**. In the submenu, click **Clear Selected Sparkline Groups**. All the sparklines in column G are removed.

14. Save the changes, and then close the workbook.

SUMMARY

In this lesson, you learned:

- One of the primary uses for Excel spreadsheets is to perform calculations. All formulas begin with the equal sign (=).

- If you do not want the cell reference to change when the formula is moved or copied to a new location, the cell reference must be formatted as an absolute cell reference.

- Functions are special formulas that do not require operators. Excel provides more than 300 built-in functions to help you perform mathematical, statistical, and other functions.

- The AutoSum feature enables you to quickly identify a range of cells and enter a formula. For a range of cells specified in the argument, the AVERAGE function finds the average, the SUM function totals the values, and the COUNT function shows the number of cells with numerical values.

- You can use the MIN and MAX functions to find the smallest or largest number in a range.

- Formulas can reference cells in multiple worksheets, and 3D references are often used to condense and total data from other worksheets.

- If Excel cannot perform a calculation, an error value and an Error Checking button will appear to alert you and help you fix the error. Then, you can edit the formula directly in the cell or in the formula bar.

- A chart shows the worksheet data visually and often helps the audience understand and interpret the information more clearly. To draw logical conclusions from the data and make a correct assessment, you must ensure that the data is accurate and that you know what the values represent.

- When the worksheet data is changed, the chart is automatically updated to reflect those changes. Chart types, formats, and options can be changed at any time, even after the chart has been created.

- Instead of using charts, you can use sparklines to provide a visual representation of the data.

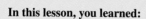 LESSON REVIEW

TRUE / FALSE

Circle T if the statement is true or F if the statement is false.

T F   **1.** All Excel formulas begin with the equal sign.

T F   **2.** When you edit the data in the worksheet, the chart is automatically updated to reflect the changes.

T F   **3.** The SUM function is a statistical function.

T F   **4.** In the order of evaluation, multiplication and division are performed before addition or subtraction.

T F   **5.** A formula must reference more than one cell.

MULTIPLE CHOICE

Select the best response for the following statements.

1. The result for the formula =24-(5+3)/2 is _____.

   A. 20   C. 8

   B. 9   D. 12

2. A function formula has _____.

   A. the equal sign   C. the argument

   B. the function name   D. all of the above

3. A _____ chart is helpful when you want to make comparisons among individual items.

   A. line   C. scatter

   B. pie   D. bar

4. Formulas containing more than one operator are called _____.

   A. operational formulas   C. function formulas

   B. complex formulas   D. evaluation formulas

5. A(n) _____ cell reference is adjusted when the formula is copied or moved to a new location.

   A. embedded   C. relative

   B. absolute   D. fixed

6. _____ functions describe large quantities of data.

   A. Logical   C. Statistical

   B. Mathematical   D. Mass

7. A(n) _____ is a number or cell reference in a formula.

   A. operator   C. function

   B. operand   D. operative

8. By default, when you create formulas, the cell references are formatted as _____ cell references.

   A. relative   C. mixed

   B. absolute   D. complex

9. To enter a cell reference into a formula, you can _____.

   A. type the cell reference in uppercase

   B. type the cell reference in lowercase

   C. click the cell

   D. all of the above

10. The _____ function is a statistical function that shows the number of occurrences of numerical data.

   A. COUNT   C. SUM

   B. AVERAGE   D. MAX

WRITTEN QUESTIONS

Write a brief answer to the following questions.

1. How do you create an absolute cell reference?

2. How can you change the sequence in the order of evaluation in a formula?

3. What does Garbage In, Garbage Out (GIGO) refer to?

4. What is the benefit of using cell references instead of cell values when creating a formula?

5. How do you select nonadjacent cells in a worksheet?

■ PROJECTS

PROJECT 20–1

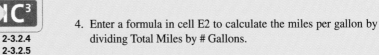

1. Open the file **MPG Report** from the drive and folder where your Data Files folder is stored. Save the MPG Report workbook as **Revised MPG Report**, followed by your initials.

    2-3.2.4
    2-3.2.5

2. Enter a formula in cell C2 that will subtract the Odometer Start value from the Odometer End value.

3. Copy the formula to the range C3:C11.

4. Enter a formula in cell E2 to calculate the miles per gallon by dividing Total Miles by # Gallons.

5. Copy the formula to the range E3:E11.

6. Enter a formula in cell E13 to calculate the average miles per gallon for the range E2:E11.

7. Save the changes, and then close the workbook.

PROJECT 20–2

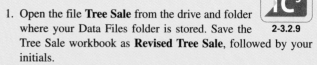

1. Open the file **Mileage Report** from the drive and folder where your Data Files folder is stored. Save the Mileage Report workbook as **Revised Mileage Report**, followed by your initials.

    2-3.2.3
    2-3.2.4
    2-3.2.5
    2-3.2.6
    2-3.2.7

2. In the April worksheet, in cell D3, enter a formula to calculate the number of miles driven by subtracting the Odometer Start values from the Odometer End values. Fill the formula down to cover all the days of travel.

3. In the April worksheet, in cell E3, enter a formula to calculate the cost by multiplying the daily miles by the cost per mile. Be sure to create an absolute reference for the cost per mile cell reference. Fill the formula down to cover all the days of travel in the worksheet.

4. Copy the formulas and the format in cells D3 and E3, and paste them to the same cells in the May and June worksheets, keeping the source formatting. Then fill the formulas down to cover all the days of travel in the May and June worksheets.

5. In the April worksheet, in cell D20, enter a function formula to total all the daily miles in the column. Fill the function formula to cell E20 to total all the expenses in that column. In cell E20 apply the Currency number format with two decimal places. Then copy the formulas, with the formats, to calculate the daily miles and expenses in Row 18 of the May worksheet and row 20 of the June worksheet. Adjust column widths as needed.

6. In the April worksheet, in cell C23, enter a function formula using the values in the Date column to count the number of days of travel. In cells C24, C25, and C26, enter function formulas using the values in the Daily Miles column to calculate the minimum, maximum, and average daily miles driven during the month.

7. Copy these function formulas to the same cells in the May and June worksheets to perform the same calculations and keep the same formatting. You will need to adjust the formula in the May sheet to fit the data so the total is not included.

8. You just learned that the cost per mile increased to $0.58 in June. Make this change in the June worksheet only.

9. Open the 2nd Qtr. worksheet, and enter cell references for the total miles and expenses from the April, May, and June worksheets. For example, the cell references for the April worksheet are D20 and E20.

10. In the 2nd Qtr. worksheet, calculate the total miles and the total expenses for the 3 months.

11. Save the changes, and then close the workbook.

PROJECT 20–3

1. Open the file **Tree Sale** from the drive and folder where your Data Files folder is stored. Save the Tree Sale workbook as **Revised Tree Sale**, followed by your initials.

    2-3.2.9

2. In the Eastland Store worksheet, select the range **A5:E12**, and create a chart that you think would be most effective for this data.

3. Add the chart title **Fall Tree Sale** above the chart.

4. Add titles for the horizontal axis and the vertical axis. Rotate the vertical axis title if desired. Change the font sizes for the axis labels to 12 pt.

5. Move the chart so it is positioned at the left side of the worksheet and below row 15.

6. In the Westland Store worksheet, create a chart as described in Steps 2 through 5 using the Westland Store data.

7. In the Eastland Store worksheet, copy the values in the range F6:F12 to the Clipboard. Switch to the Summary worksheet, click cell **B5**, and paste the copied values so the values are pasted with the source formatting.

8. In the Westland Store worksheet, copy the values in the range F6:F12 to the Clipboard. Switch to the Summary worksheet, click cell **C5**, and paste the copied values so the values are pasted with the source formatting.

9. In all three worksheets, add formulas to calculate the total revenues for all columns. Adjust column widths as necessary. In the Summary worksheet, use the Format Painter to apply the same font format to the new values.

10. In the Summary worksheet, select the range **A4:C11**, and create an appropriate chart. Add the chart title **Fall Tree Sale**, centered and overlayed on the chart. Add titles for the vertical axis and the horizontal axis.

11. Move the chart so it is positioned on a new worksheet titled **Total Sales**. Increase the font size for the chart title label to 24 point, and increase the font size for the axis labels to 16 point.

12. Save the changes, and then close the workbook.

PROJECT 20–4

1. Open the file **Demographics** from the drive and folder where your Data Files folder is stored. Save the Demographics workbook as **Revised Demographics**, followed by your initials. 2-3.2.9 2-3.2.10

2. Select the range **A2:B7**, and create a Stacked Horizontal Cylinder bar chart.

3. Change the chart title to **Centerville Population**.

4. Reposition the chart below the data on Sheet1, at the left side of the worksheet.

5. Change the 1990 population value to **71,436**. Change the 2000 population value to **72,818**.

6. Change the chart type to a Clustered Bar chart, and change the chart title to **Population Growth**. Apply the Style 35 chart style to add some color to the chart.

7. Click cell **F2**, and enter the column heading **Population Density**. Format the heading text to wrap in the cell, and adjust the width of the column so the word *Population* is displayed on one line.

8. Click cell **F3**, and enter a formula to calculate the population divided by the area. Decrease the number of decimal places to zero. Fill the formula down for the range F4:F7.

9. Select the cell range **A2:A7** and the range **F2:F7**, and create a Clustered Bar chart. Add the horizontal axis title **Population per Square Mile**, and apply the Style 35 chart style. Position the new chart below the Population Growth chart.

10. Select the ranges **A2:A7** and **D2:E7**, and create a Stacked Horizontal Cylinder bar chart. Move the chart so it is placed as an object in Sheet2. Align the chart in the upper-left corner of the worksheet.

11. On Sheet1, select the ranges **A2:B7**, and create a Line with Markers chart. Position the new chart to the right of the Population Growth chart.

12. Select the ranges **A2:A7** and **F2:F7**, and create a Line with Markers chart. Position the new chart next to the Population Density bar chart.

13. Create two new Line with Markers charts based on the Housing Units and Vehicle Registration data:

    a. Select the ranges **A2:A7** and **D2:D7**, and create a Line with Markers chart. Position the new chart as an object on Sheet2. Reposition the new Housing Units chart below the cylinder chart.

    b. On Sheet1, select the ranges **A2:A7** and **E2:E7**, and create a Line with Markers chart. Move the new chart as an object on Sheet2 and reposition it next to the Housing Units chart.

14. Save the changes, and close the workbook.

PROJECT 20–5

1. Open the file **Utility Bills** from the drive and folder where your Data Files folder is stored. Save the Utility Bills workbook as **Revised Utility Bills**, followed by your initials. 2-3.2.4 2-3.2.5 2-3.2.9 2-3.2.10

2. Use function formulas to calculate the following:

    a. In cell G2, calculate the total value for the range B2:F2. Then fill the formula in the cell range G3:G13.

    b. In cell B14, calculate the total value for the range B2:B13. Then fill the formula in the cell range C14:G14.

    c. In cell B16, calculate the minimum value for the range B2:B13. Then fill the formula in the cell range C16:G16.

    d. In cell B17, calculate the maximum value for the range B2:B13. Then fill the formula in the cell range C17:G17.

    e. In cell B18, calculate the average value for the range B2:B13. Then fill the formula in the cell range C18:G18.

3. In cell B20, enter an arithmetic formula to perform the following calculation: subtract the previous year average from the current year average, and then divide the results by the previous year average. Then fill the formula in the cell range C20:G20.

4. In cell H2, create a column sparkline to compare the five utility expenses in the range B2:F2. Then fill the formula in the cell range H3:H14. Change the color scheme as desired.

5. In cell B15, create a line sparkline to show the trend of the Electric expenses in the range B2:B13. Then fill the formula in the cell range C15:G15. Change the sparkline color and the marker colors for the high point and low point.

6. In the cell range B21:G21, create a Win/Loss sparkline to provide a visual aid of the positive and negative values in the range B20:G20.

7. Save the changes, and close the workbook.

TEAMWORK PROJECT

As you have learned in this lesson, functions can help you analyze data in a number of ways. Excel includes hundreds of functions to help you with financial, statistical, mathematical, and other problems. In this project, explore two functions of your choice with a partner to learn how they can be applied to specific data analysis situations. Make sure your functions are not covered in this lesson. Follow these steps:

1. In a blank Excel worksheet, open the Insert Function dialog box. Review the functions in each category to find two you are interested in exploring with your teammate. (Your functions should come from two different categories.)

2. Read the Excel Help files for the functions you have chosen to learn what kind of data the function can analyze and what kinds of

2-3.2.5
2-3.2.10

information you must supply as arguments for the functions. Consider where this type of data might occur, such as the type of job where you would encounter it.

3. Save the worksheet as **TP 20-1**, followed by your initials.

4. Construct the worksheet(s) containing data appropriate for each function, and then use the functions to calculate the data.

5. After you are sure you are using the function correctly, save the changes to the workbook.

6. Make a team presentation to share what you have learned about the functions you explored.

CRITICAL THINKING

CRITICAL THINKING 20–1

2-3.2.10

To complete this activity, you must first complete Project 20–4.

1. Open the file **Revised Demographics** from your solution files.

2. Create a new Word document, and save the document as **CT 20-1**, followed by your initials. Analyze the charts in the Revised Demographics workbook to answer the following questions:
   a. How does the Population Growth chart differ from the Population Density chart?
   b. What, if anything, can we learn from the charts comparing houses and vehicles?
   c. Compare the charts on Sheet2 that show the data for Housing Units and Vehicle Registration. Why does the comparison of the combined data look different from the data in the line charts?
   d. What other questions can be answered with this data?

3. Save the changes, and close the Word document. Close the Revised Demographics workbook without saving any changes.

CRITICAL THINKING 20–2

2-3.2.10

To complete this activity, you must first complete Project 20–5.

1. Open the file **Revised Utility Bills** from your solution files.

2. Create a new Word document, and save the document as **CT 20-2**, followed by your initials.

3. Using the sparklines in column H to analyze the data, identify the two most expensive utilities, and comment on the seasonality of the two.

4. Using the sparklines in row 15 to analyze the data, describe the trends for each of the utilities.

5. Save the changes, and close the Word document. Close the Revised Utility Bills workbook without saving any changes.

ONLINE DISCOVERY

There are many online Web sites available to help you find current gasoline prices.

1. Choose four locations around the country (the East coast, the West coast, the Gulf coast, and the Midwest).

2. Create a new workbook, and save the workbook as **OD 20-1**, followed by your initials.

3. Track the gas prices daily for all four locations for at least 7 to 10 days. Also, track the price of a barrel of oil for each of those days.

2-3.2.9

4. Create a chart to illustrate the data.

5. Save the changes to the workbook.

JOB SKILLS

In this lesson, you learned about using charts and sparklines to create graphics to represent data. Now that you are familiar with Excel and its features, consider how you can use Excel charts and/or sparklines on the job or for personal use to help you organize and maintain data.

1. Create a new Word document, and save the document as **JS 20-1**, followed by your initials.

2. List how you can use Excel charts and sparklines.

2-3.2.9
2-3.2.10

3. Save the changes, and close the document.

LESSON 21

Getting Started with PowerPoint Essentials

■ OBJECTIVES

Upon completion of this lesson, you should be able to:

- Identify the parts of the PowerPoint screen and navigate through a presentation.
- Change the slide view and magnification.
- Manage slides by adding, deleting, duplicating, and reordering them.
- Create a new presentation with effective planning.
- Apply a theme for consistent formatting and styles.
- Edit slide content by moving text and modifying placeholders.
- Work with a Slide Master to add universal elements for all slides in the presentation.
- Preview a presentation using Slide Show view.

■ WORDS TO KNOW

presentation

slide layout

Slide Master

slide pane

■ DATA FILES

To complete this lesson, you will need these data files:

Exchange Students.pptx

Logo.jpg

Search Tips.pptx

Three Rs.pptx

PowerPoint helps you create, edit, and manipulate professional-looking slides that you can use to facilitate meetings, supplement classroom learning, and share information using a wide variety of media including graphics, pictures, and audio and video clips. Creating a slide show may seem like an overwhelming task, but PowerPoint provides many features that make that task easy and fun.

2-4.1.12

▶ **VOCABULARY**

presentation

slide pane

Identifying the Parts of the PowerPoint Screen

In PowerPoint, the document file is called a ***presentation***. When you first launch PowerPoint, a new blank presentation file opens. As in other Office applications, you can quickly access the most recently opened presentations by clicking the File tab, which opens Backstage view. In Backstage view, you can search for additional files by using the Open command in Backstage view, and you also have access to the Save and Save As commands.

The PowerPoint application window in **Figure 21–1** shows many familiar parts, including the Ribbon, Quick Access Toolbar, title bar, sizing buttons, Close button, and status bar. Scroll bars are displayed when the presentation includes more than one slide. Two tabs are displayed in a pane on the left—the Slides tab and the Outline tab. The Slides tab shows a thumbnail for each slide in the presentation file. When active, the Outline tab shows the text on each slide, and it enables you to organize the content of the presentation. The ***slide pane*** is the area in the presentation window that contains the slide content, and the dotted borders in the slide pane identify placeholders where you can insert text and graphics on the slide. The Notes pane provides space for adding notes you can refer to while preparing for and while showing your presentation.

FIGURE 21–1   PowerPoint application window

Step-by-Step 21.1

1. Launch **Microsoft PowerPoint 2010**. A new presentation titled Presentation1 opens.

2. Compare your screen with Figure 21–1 to identify the various components of the PowerPoint presentation window and their names.

2-1.1.1
2-1.1.2
2-1.2.2
2-1.2.4

3. Move the mouse pointer around the application window. When you position the mouse pointer over the Slides tab and the Ribbon, the mouse pointer is displayed as an arrow. When you position the pointer within the slide pane, it still is displayed as an arrow, but when you position the pointer over a placeholder, the pointer changes to an I-beam, which indicates you can add text inside the placeholder.

4. If necessary, click the **Maximize** button ▣ to change the size of the window to fill the screen. If the Maximize button is not displayed in the upper-right corner of the screen, the application window is already maximized.

5. Click the **Minimize** button ▬ in the row of sizing buttons. The application window is minimized. Click the **Presentation1 – Microsoft PowerPoint** button in the taskbar to restore the application window.

6. Click the **Restore Down** button ▣, and the application window size is reduced. The Ribbon and the Slides tab adapt to the smaller size. You can drag the title bar to move the application window around on the screen. You can also point to the window border, and when the pointer changes to a double-headed arrow ⬌, you can drag the border to resize the window.

7. Click the **Maximize** button to restore the window to its full size.

8. Click the **File** tab, and then click **Open**. In the Open dialog box, navigate to the drive and folder where your Data Files folder is stored. Select the filename **Three Rs.pptx**, and then click **Open**.

9. Click the **File** tab, and then click **Save As**. In the Save As dialog box, navigate to the drive and folder where you save your solution files. In the File name box, type the new filename **Revised Three Rs 1**, followed by your initials, and then click **Save**.

10. Leave the presentation open for the next Step-by-Step.

Navigating Through a Presentation

You can move to a different slide in a presentation by using the keyboard, by clicking the thumbnail on the Slides tab, or by clicking the slide content on the Outline tab. You can also use the vertical scroll bar or the keyboard to navigate through slides in a presentation.

Step-by-Step 21.2

2-1.1.3

1. If necessary, open the file **Revised Three Rs 1** from your solution files. Compare your screen to **Figure 21–2**. Slide thumbnails are displayed on the Slides tab in a pane on the left, and the status bar shows Slide 1 of 8. A vertical scroll bar is displayed next to the thumbnails, and there is also a vertical scroll bar on the right side of the window.

FIGURE 21–2
Revised Three Rs 1
presentation

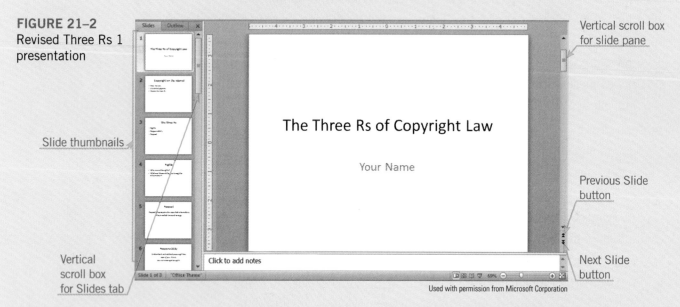

Used with permission from Microsoft Corporation

2. Press the **down arrow** key. The slide pane changes to show the second slide in the presentation. Notice that the second slide is now highlighted on the Slides tab.

3. Press the **Page Up** key to move to the previous slide, and then press the **Page Down** key to move to the next slide. The second slide is the active slide.

4. On the Slides tab, click the **slide 3** thumbnail. Again, the slide pane adapts, and the highlight shows the active slide.

5. Use the scroll bar on the Slides tab to scroll down and show the thumbnail for the last slide in the presentation. Then click the **slide 8** thumbnail.

6. Drag the **scroll box** up the vertical scroll bar on the right side of the presentation window. As you drag the box, a ScreenTip to the left of the scroll bar shows the title and number of the slide. When you see *Slide: 2 of 8 Copyright on the Internet*, as shown in **Figure 21–3**, release the mouse button. The second slide of the presentation is displayed in the slide pane, and the slide 2 thumbnail is highlighted on the Slides tab.

QUICK TIP

If your mouse includes a scroll wheel, you can use the wheel to navigate through the slides both forward and backward in Normal view.

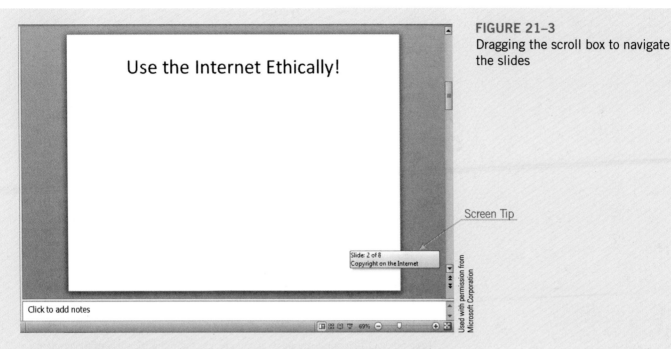

FIGURE 21–3
Dragging the scroll box to navigate the slides

7. At the bottom of the vertical scroll bar on the right side of the presentation window, click the **Next Slide** button three times. Each time you click the Next Slide button, you move to the next slide in the presentation. The fifth slide should be active.

8. At the bottom of the vertical scroll bar, click the **Previous Slide** button. Each time you click the Previous Slide button, you move to the previous slide in the presentation. The fourth slide should be active.

9. In the pane on the left, click the **Outline** tab. All of the text contained on each of the eight slides in the presentation is displayed in outline form as shown in **Figure 21–4**.

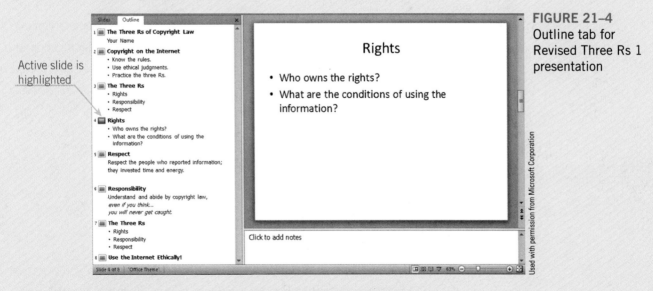

FIGURE 21–4
Outline tab for Revised Three Rs 1 presentation

10. On the Outline tab, click the slide 3 title, **The Three Rs**. The slide pane changes to show the content for the third slide.

11. Press **Ctrl+Home**. The first slide becomes the active slide. Press **Ctrl+End** to move to the last slide.

12. In the pane on the left, click the **Slides** tab to show the thumbnails again.

13. Leave the presentation open for the next Step-by-Step.

Changing the Slide View

PowerPoint offers five different ways to view your presentation. Normal view is the default view and the one you have used in PowerPoint so far. Slide Sorter view gives you an overall picture of your presentation and enables you to easily add and delete slides, copy slides, and rearrange the order of the slides. Reading view is especially useful when someone is viewing the presentation on their own computer because it has simple controls that make it easy to review the slides. In Notes Page view, you can edit your notes and see how the notes will look when printed. In Slide Show view, the current slide fills the whole screen. You use this view when you present the show to your audience. You will learn more about using Notes Page view and Slide Show view later in this lesson.

　　Like other Office applications, you can change the magnification of the content on the screen by using the Zoom button in the Zoom group on the View tab, or by using the zoom controls in the status bar at the bottom of the window. Before changing the zoom setting, you must click the Slides tab, the Outline tab, or the slide pane to indicate where you want to change the zoom level. You can use the Fit to Window command to automatically fit the slide pane in the available space in the application window.

Step-by-Step 21.3

2-1.1.5
2-1.1.6
2-4.1.3

1. If necessary, open the file **Revised Three Rs 1** from your solution files. Save the Revised Three Rs 1 presentation as **Revised Three Rs 2**, followed by your initials.

2. Scroll up on the Slides tab, and then click the **slide 3** thumbnail. Clicking inside the Slides tab indicates you want to change the magnification of the Slides tab. On the Ribbon, click the **View** tab, and in the Zoom group shown in **Figure 21–5**, click the **Zoom** button to show the zoom level options. In the Zoom dialog box, click to enable the **100%** option, and then click **OK**. The magnification of the Slides tab is increased.

FIGURE 21–5
Zoom group on the View tab

3. Click anywhere in the slide pane to indicate that is where you want to change the magnification. In the Zoom group, click the **Zoom** button. Change the zoom level to **33%**, and then click **OK**. The slide pane is reduced in size, and the Slides tab remains unchanged.

4. Click the **Outline** tab, and then click the slide 3 title, **The Three Rs**. Click the **Zoom** button, change the magnification to **50%**, and then click **OK**.

5. In the Zoom group, click the **Fit to Window** button. The slide pane is adjusted to fit within the available space.

6. Slide 3 on the Outline tab should already be selected. Click the **Zoom** button, change the zoom level to **33%**, and click **OK**. The size of the text on the Outline tab is reduced, but the width of the Outline tab remains unchanged.

7. Click the **Slides** tab. Click the **Zoom** button, change the zoom level to **50%**, and click **OK**. The width of the Slides tab is reduced, and the slide pane is adjusted to fit in the available space.

8. On the View tab, in the Presentation Views group shown in **Figure 21–6**, click the **Slide Sorter** button. The window changes to show small images (but bigger than thumbnails) of the slides in the presentation. All the slides are displayed in the window, as shown in **Figure 21–7**. (The layout on your screen may differ somewhat.) Note that the Slides tab and Outline tab are no longer displayed.

FIGURE 21–6
Presentation Views group on the View tab

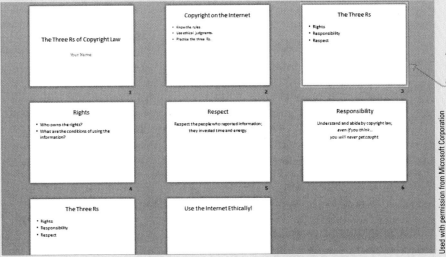

FIGURE 21–7
Slides shown in Slide Sorter view

Active slide is highlighted with an orange border

9. Click the **Zoom** button, change the zoom level to **50%**, and then click **OK**. The size of the slides is decreased, so more slides will fit in the window. When the presentation contains more slides than can fit in the window, a vertical scroll bar is displayed so you can scroll through all the slides. Click the **Fit to Window** button.

10. In the status bar at the lower-right corner of the window, click the **Reading** view button 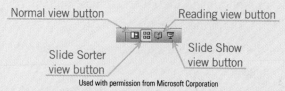 shown in **Figure 21–8**.

FIGURE 21–8
View buttons on status bar

Normal view button   Reading view button
Slide Sorter   Slide Show
view button   view button

Used with permission from Microsoft Corporation

QUICK TIP

In Reading view, you can press Page Up and Page Down to navigate through the slides.

11. To navigate through the slides, you can use the buttons on the status bar in the lower-right corner of the screen. See **Figure 21–9**. Click the **Next** button three times to review some of the slides, and then click the **Previous** button twice.

FIGURE 21–9
Buttons on the status bar in Reading view

Previous button   Next button
Menu button   Used with permission from Microsoft Corporation

12. On the status bar, click the **Menu** button  to display a menu of commonly used commands. In the menu, point to **Go to Slide**. In the submenu shown in **Figure 21–10**, click **1 The Three Rs of Copyright Law**. The first slide in the presentation is now displayed.

FIGURE 21–10
Menu and submenu in Reading view

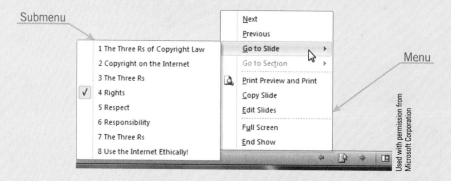

Submenu

1 The Three Rs of Copyright Law
2 Copyright on the Internet
3 The Three Rs
√ 4 Rights
5 Respect
6 Responsibility
7 The Three Rs
8 Use the Internet Ethically!

Next
Previous
Go to Slide
Go to Section
Print Preview and Print
Copy Slide
Edit Slides
Full Screen
End Show

Menu

Used with permission from Microsoft Corporation

13. Right-click anywhere in the slide to display the menu. At the bottom of the menu, click **End Show**. The presentation is displayed in the previous view, which in this case is Slide Sorter view. On the status bar in the lower-right corner of the screen, click the **Normal** view button 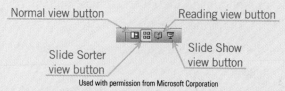 to return to the default view.

14. Save the changes, and leave the presentation open for the next Step-by-Step.

Managing Slides

As you prepare a presentation, it is common to add new slides, copy slides, and delete slides. It is also common to rearrange the sequence of the slides. You can easily manage the slides in Normal view and in Slide Sorter view.

You can use the Cut, Copy, and Paste commands to copy or move slides. The slide content, layouts, and formats are stored on the Clipboard. Remember that the Clipboard is a temporary storage place in the computer's memory. You can paste Clipboard items as many times as you want.

You can change the order of the slides by using drag-and-drop editing as well as by using the cut-and-paste method. It may be a little easier to use drag-and-drop editing in Slide Sorter view, where all the slides are arranged in rows in one screen, but you can also rearrange slides in the Slides tab and the Outline tab in Normal view.

Step-by-Step 21.4

1. If necessary, open the file **Revised Three Rs 2** from your solution files. Save the Revised Three Rs 2 presentation as **Revised Three Rs 3**, followed by your initials.

2. On the Slides tab, click the **slide 4** thumbnail. Click the **Home** tab. In the Slides group shown in **Figure 21–11**, click the **New Slide** button 🖼. (Do not click the arrow on the button.) A new blank slide is created and placed after slide 4. The placeholders for the new slide are the same as slide 4. Note the Slides tab is updated and shows the new blank slide, slide 5, as the active slide.

2-1.2.5
2-1.3.2
2-4.1.1
2-4.1.3
2-4.1.7

FIGURE 21–11
Slides group on the Home tab

3. Click the **New Slide** button, and then at the bottom of the menu click **Duplicate Selected Slides**. The active slide is duplicated, and a new blank slide is displayed after slide 5. The new slide 6 is the active slide.

4. In the Clipboard group, click the **Copy** button. The blank slide is copied to the Clipboard.

5. On the Slides tab, click between the slide 7 and 8 thumbnails. A flashing black horizontal line indicates the location of the insertion point. In the Clipboard group, click the **Paste** button. The blank slide is copied to the designated location, and the active slide is now the new blank slide, slide 8.

6. Click the **slide 6** thumbnail. Press **Delete**. The slide is removed from the presentation.

7. On the status bar, click the **Slide Sorter** view button 🔳. Click the **View** tab. In the Zoom group, click the **Zoom** button, change the zoom level to **66%**, and click **OK**. Note there are two blank slides, slides 5 and 7.

8. Click between slides 4 and 5 to position the insertion point between the two slides. The insertion point will appear as a flashing black vertical line between the two slides.

9. Click the **Home** tab, and in the Slides group click the **New Slide** button. A new blank slide is inserted between slides 4 and 5. There are now a total of 11 slides in the presentation, and slide 5 is active.

ABOVE AND BEYOND

You can select multiple slides and delete or copy and paste them. To select a series of slides, on the Slides tab click the first slide thumbnail in the series, press and hold Shift, and then click the last slide thumbnail in the series. All thumbnails between and including the two thumbnails you clicked are selected. To select noncontiguous slides, click the first slide thumbnail, press and hold Ctrl, and then click the remaining slide thumbnails you want to include in the selection.

10. Press and hold **Ctrl**, and click **slide 6** and **slide 8**. Three slides are highlighted. Press **Delete**. All three slides are removed, and now there are eight slides in the presentation.

11. Click **slide 6**. In the Clipboard group, click the **Cut** button to save the slide to the Clipboard. Then, click to the left of slide 4 to position the mouse pointer between slides 3 and 4. The flashing black vertical line should appear to the left of slide 4. Click the **Paste** button to move the slide to the new position.

12. Click **slide 6**, and drag it to position it between slides 3 and 4. When you see the black vertical line to the left of slide 4, release the mouse button, and the slides are once again rearranged.

13. In the status bar, click the **Normal** view button. The slides are still not in the correct order. Click the **Outline** tab. Point to the small slide icon for slide 5. When the pointer changes to a four-headed arrow ✛, click and all the text for the slide is selected. Point to the title, **Rights**, and then click and drag the selected text and position the mouse pointer above slide 4. When you see the black horizontal line above slide 4, release the mouse button, and the slides are rearranged.

14. Save the changes. Click the **File** tab, and then click **Close** to close the presentation. (If you click the Close button in the application window, the presentation and the application will both close.)

Creating a New Presentation

PowerPoint provides several options for creating a new presentation. You can create a new blank presentation and apply preformatted colors, styles, and layouts. PowerPoint provides several presentation templates that already contain formatted content that you can modify to customize the presentation for your needs. You can also open an existing presentation, save it with a new filename, and then add and delete slides and edit the existing slides.

When you create a presentation, it is important to keep in mind a few basic principles for effective design. PowerPoint offers so many templates and designs that it is tempting to use many different layouts and formats in your presentation. But if your presentation is too busy, the formatting can detract from your content. You want the design features you choose to emphasize your content, not overwhelm it. Following are a few design guidelines to keep in mind when you are creating a presentation.

- Do not overload a slide with too much content; include only essential information to keep your message clear and concise.
- Select only one or two fonts that are easy to read, and use the same fonts for the same features in all the slides in a presentation to create a consistent appearance.
- Use numbered lists to show the steps in a process or data that should be examined in order.
- Use bullets to present lists of information.

- Limit the number of special features, such as bullets, numbered items, or graphics, on a single slide.

- Use graphics or charts only to highlight relevant information. Do not use graphics just to decorate a slide.

- Tables and charts can illustrate numerical data or trends, but keep the charts simple and easy to read.

- Add elements such as a company name for consistency from slide to slide.

When you create a new blank presentation, the file opens with one blank slide with a proposed slide layout. *Slide layout* refers to the arrangement of placeholders on the slide. The placeholders provide placement guides for adding text or objects such as pictures, tables, or charts. You can choose from several different slide layouts. To modify the slide layout, you can resize the placeholders and move them to another position in the slide pane. If you do not use a placeholder, you can leave it empty, or you can delete it. An empty placeholder will not appear in Slide Show view or when the slide is printed.

To add text to a slide or to manipulate the text on a slide, the presentation must be shown in Normal view. You can add text in the placeholders in the slide pane, or you can add text on the Outline tab. When you fill a placeholder with several lines of text and keep entering text, PowerPoint reduces the font size as needed so all the text fits inside the text box. If there are not enough placeholders in the slide layout, you can add new text boxes.

As you enter text in a placeholder, PowerPoint automatically checks for misspelled words. However, you must also proofread all of your work because the spelling checker will not identify all spelling errors. The AutoCorrect feature is also available, and PowerPoint automatically corrects common spelling errors. For example, when you type *teh* it is automatically corrected to *the*.

The Notes pane provides a place for you to write speaker notes that you can use to provide reminders about information you want to emphasize. The notes are not displayed on the slide when the presentation is shown in Slide Show view. There is plenty of space available for notes, so you can even include the dialogue you want to use when you present the slide show to an audience.

2-4.1.12

▶ **VOCABULARY**
slide layout

Step-by-Step 21.5

1. If necessary, launch **PowerPoint**. Click the **File** tab, and then click **New**. In the right pane, click the **Create** button. A new presentation with one blank slide opens.

2. The slide pane shows a slide layout for a Title Slide with a title placeholder at the top and a subtitle placeholder below. In the title placeholder, click anywhere within the placeholder text **Click to add title**. The placeholder text disappears. Type **A New Country;**. Press **Enter**, and then type **A New Experience**.

3. In the subtitle placeholder, click anywhere within the placeholder text **Click to add subtitle**, and type your first and last name. Notice the font size and color are different. These are the default settings for the Title Slide layout.

2-1.2.1
2-1.3.5
2-4.1.2
2-4.1.3
2-4.1.9
2-4.1.12

4. In the Slides group, click the **New Slide** button arrow. The slide layout options shown in **Figure 21–12** are displayed.

FIGURE 21–12
Slide layout options

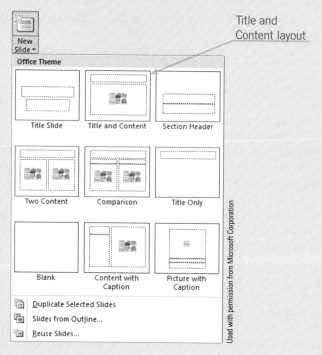

5. Click the **Title and Content** layout. A new slide is created with two place-holders, as shown in **Figure 21–13**.

FIGURE 21–13
Title and Content
layout

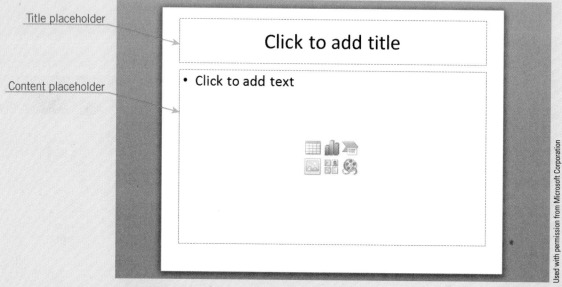

6. Click the title placeholder text **Click to add title**, and type **Open your door to teh future....** Note that PowerPoint automatically corrects the misspelled word *teh*.

7. Move the mouse point over the object buttons in the content placeholder to see the options. You use these buttons to enter tables, charts, graphics, and video clips, which you will learn about in Lesson 22.

8. Click the content placeholder text **Click to add text**, and type **An international education is important.**, and then press **Enter**. The line of text is formatted with a bullet. A dimmed bullet is displayed for the new blank paragraph, but it will not show in Slide Show view if you do not enter text on this line.

9. Type **Fluency in another language is valued.**, and then press **Enter**. The second paragraph of text is also formatted with a bullet.

10. In the Notes pane below the slide pane, click the notes placeholder text **Click to add notes**. Type **Ask how many in the audience can speak a foreign language.**, and press **Enter**. The note you entered is not displayed in the thumbnail on the Slides tab. Click the **Outline** tab, and you will see that the notes are not displayed in the slide outlines either. Click the **Slides** tab.

11. Click the **View** tab. In the Presentation Views group, click the **Notes Page** button. The slide pane changes to show an image of the slide with the Notes pane below. This view is better for entering and viewing a long note or editing text in an existing note.

12. In the Presentation Views group, click the **Normal** button. Click the **Home** tab. Click the **New Slide** button. A new slide 3 opens with the same slide layout as the previous slide. You only need to click the New Slide button arrow when you want to change the slide layout for the new slide.

13. In the title placeholder, type **Get Involved**. Then enter the following three lines of text in the content placeholder:

```
Become a volunteer.
Become an exchange student.
Become a host family.
```

14. Save the presentation as **International 1**, followed by your initials. Leave the presentation open for the next Step-by-Step.

Applying a Theme

You can easily give your presentation a professional look by applying a theme, which specifies a color scheme, fonts, and effects. Each theme has a specific look and feel. The theme you choose for your presentation should reflect the tone of the presentation topic. Moreover, the theme should not detract from the message you want to deliver.

To apply a theme, the presentation must be shown in Normal view. The theme is applied to all the slides, but the content of the slides does not change. You can apply a different theme at any time to change the look of your presentation. If you like a theme, but you do not like the colors used in the design, you can easily change the color scheme of the theme. PowerPoint offers several standard color schemes for each theme. You can apply a new color scheme to all the slides or apply it only to selected slides.

Step-by-Step 21.6

2-4.1.2
2-4.1.5
2-4.1.12

1. If necessary, open the file **International 1** from your solution files. Save the International 1 presentation as **International 2**, followed by your initials. Move to the first slide, and show the Slides tab.

2. Click the **Design** tab. In the Themes group shown in **Figure 21-14**, move the mouse pointer over several of the options to see the Live Preview of the themes. The theme names appear in ScreenTips.

FIGURE 21-14
Themes group on the Design tab

Used with permission from Microsoft Corporation

3. Click the **More** button to show all the theme options. In the third row, click the **Flow** theme. The theme is applied to all slides in the presentation, and the slide pane changes to show the updated font styles, alignments, and colors. A graphic (wavy line) also is displayed at the top of all the slides. You will also notice by looking at the thumbnails on the Slides tab that the first slide in the presentation has a background color, but the other two slides do not. That is because the first slide is formatted as the title slide.

4. In the Themes group, click the **Colors** button to show the built-in color options. Move the mouse pointer over some of the options to see the Live Preview. Scroll down and click the **Foundry** option.

5. In the Themes group, click the **Fonts** button to show the built-in font options. Use the scroll bar to move down through the list of fonts. Move the mouse pointer over some of the options to see the Live Preview. Click the **Apex** option. The new font style is applied to all the slides.

6. In the Themes group, click the **Effects** button to show the built-in effects. When you move the mouse pointer over the options to see the Live Preview, you will not see any changes. That is because the theme effects are sets of lines and fill effects, which apply to graphics such as AutoShapes, WordArt, and SmartArt. Click outside the list of options without making any changes.

7. You decide you would like the background color that appears on slide 1 to appear on all slides. In the Background group on the Design tab shown in **Figure 21–15**, click the **Background Styles** button.

FIGURE 21–15
Background group on the Design tab

8. The background options shown in **Figure 21–16** are displayed. The current background style for slide 1 is the highlighted option. Position the mouse pointer over the highlighted style, and a ScreenTip will appear showing *Style 7*. Click outside the background styles menu to close it without making changes.

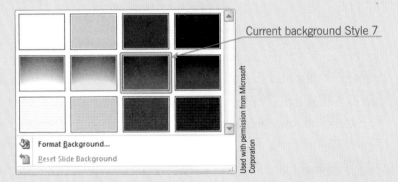

Current background Style 7

FIGURE 21–16
Background options

9. On the Slides tab, click the **slide 2** thumbnail. Click the **Background Styles** button, and then click the **Style 7** background style. The background is now applied to slides 2 and 3, and the Style 7 background will be applied to any slides you add to the presentation.

10. In the Background group, click the **Hide Background Graphics** check box. The graphic is removed from the top of the current active slide, but when you look at the thumbnails on the Slides tab, you can see the graphic is still on slides 1 and 3.

11. In the Background group, click the **dialog box launcher** to open the Format Background dialog box shown in **Figure 21–17**. At the bottom of the dialog box, click **Apply to All**. The thumbnails on the Slides tab now show that the graphic was removed from all slides in the presentation. Close the dialog box.

FIGURE 21–17
Format Background dialog box

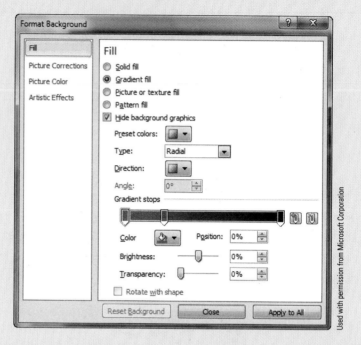

12. On the Quick Access Toolbar, click the **Undo** button twice to restore the graphic on all slides.

13. On the Slides tab, click the **slide 3** thumbnail. Click the **Home** tab, and then click the **New Slide** button to add a new slide with the same slide layout. The theme is applied to the new slide.

14. Save the changes, and leave the presentation open for the next Step-by-Step.

Editing Slides

As you work with a presentation, you will likely want to change the content of one or more of the slides. As you change the content of a slide, you may find you need to change the slide layout and the text formats. You also may want to add some universal elements to all the slides, such as a company name or logo. PowerPoint makes it easy for you to edit and manipulate the text and objects on a slide. If you accidentally delete contents, or if you change your mind, you can undo your edits. You can also redo an undo edit, and you can repeat previous actions.

When you add and edit text, the contents that are displayed on the Outline tab are automatically updated. You can also change the slide layout to accommodate the text you want to add. The content and formatting will remain intact; only the layout of the slide will change. You may find that if you select a layout that does not have placeholders for all the text and content in the original slide, elements of the slide may overlap. If so, you can move any placeholder and rearrange the elements of a slide.

When you use a theme, the format of the text on each of the slides is predetermined. There may be occasions, however, when you want to alter the text format. You may want to change the font style or point size. Changing the color of the text or changing the font style can add emphasis to the slide content, but be sure you choose the font styles carefully, because sometimes the font style can make it difficult to read text. Use Live Preview to see the formatting effects before you apply them.

Step-by-Step 21.7

1. If necessary, open the file **International 2** from your solution files. Save the International 2 presentation as **International 3**, followed by your initials.

2. Click the **slide 3** thumbnail on the Slides tab. Select all the text for the first bulleted item **Become a volunteer.**. Notice the boundaries of the placeholder, as indicated by the dashed line and the sizing handles, are selected. The placeholder is a text box.

3. Drag the selected text down and position the insertion point in front of the third bulleted item, then release the mouse button. The text *Become a volunteer.* is now the second bulleted item.

4. Click the **Outline** tab. Notice the text was updated on the Outline tab.

5. On the Outline tab, select all the text for the third bulleted item **Become a host family.**. Drag the selected text up and position the insertion point in front of the second item in the list. The sequence should now be *Become an exchange student.*, *Become a host family.*, and *Become a volunteer.*.

6. On the Outline tab, select the text **exchange student**. On the Mini toolbar, click the **Font Color** button arrow. Under Theme Colors, click the **Sky Blue, Accent 3** color. Although the new format is not displayed on the Outline tab, it is displayed in the slide pane. You are overriding the theme format.

7. On the Outline tab, select the text **host family.** On the Quick Access Toolbar, click the **Repeat** button. In the slide pane, select the text **volunteer**, and press **F4** to repeat the text color format edit.

8. In the slide pane, select the title **Get Involved**. On the Home tab, in the Drawing group (shown in **Figure 21–18**), click the **Quick Styles** button. Several styles that fit the theme colors are displayed. Move the mouse pointer over several styles to see the Live Preview. Then, in the second row, click the fourth style **Colored Fill – Sky Blue, Accent 3**. Deselect the text to see the effects of the new style.

2-1.3.3
2-4.1.2
2-4.1.4
2-4.1.12

FIGURE 21–18
Drawing group on the Home tab

9. If necessary, click anywhere in the bulleted list to show the placeholder boundaries. Point to the lower-right corner on the placeholder. When the pointer changes to a double-headed arrow, drag the **corner handle** up and to the left to resize the placeholder as shown in **Figure 21–19**. When you release the mouse button, the placeholder is significantly reduced in size and the font size changes so all the text still fits inside the placeholder.

FIGURE 21–19
Resizing a placeholder

Get Involved
• Become an exchange student.
• Become a host family.
• Become a volunteer.

Corner handle in new position

Used with permission from Microsoft Corporation

10. The placeholder should still be selected. Point to the lower-right corner and drag the **corner handle** down and to the right until the placeholder is approximately doubled in size. With the placeholder still selected, point to one of the placeholder borders. When the mouse pointer changes to a four-headed arrow, drag the **placeholder** and position it in the center of the slide.

11. Select all the text for the three bulleted items. In the Paragraph group on the Home tab, click the **Bullets** button arrow, and then click the **Star Bullets** option. The round bullets are changed to star bullets.

12. In the Slides group on the Home tab, click the **Layout** button. Note the layout options now also show the design for each slide layout, and the Picture with Caption layout does not include the graphic in the background. Click the **Two Content** layout. Now you can add text or an object, such as a picture, on the right side of the slide.

13. In the slide pane, select **Get Involved**, and use the Mini toolbar to apply the center alignment.

14. Click the **Slides** tab. Save the changes, and leave the presentation open for the next Step-by-Step.

Working with Slide Masters

A Slide Master is added to your presentation when you apply a theme. A *Slide Master* is the main slide that stores information about the theme and layouts of the presentation. The information can include formatting, bullets, backgrounds, placeholder positions, and even graphics (such as a company logo). The Slide Master ensures consistency on each slide. When you update one or more of the elements, such as the company logo, you can make a universal change and the edits will be reflected on all the slides in the presentation. You can view the Slide Master in Slide Master view.

The text on the Slide Master is only for styling. To include a company name in a footer on all slides, you need to create a footer in Normal view using the Header and Footer dialog box.

▶ **VOCABULARY**
Slide Master

Step-by-Step 21.8

1. If necessary, open the file **International 3** from your solution files. Save the International 3 presentation as **International 4**, followed by your initials.

2. Click the **slide 2** thumbnail on the Slides tab. Click the **View** tab. In the Master Views group, shown in **Figure 21–20**, click the **Slide Master** button. The Slide Master, similar to **Figure 21–21**, opens in the slide pane. The Ribbon adapts to show options for the Slide Master.

2-4.1.2
2-4.1.3
2-4.1.12

FIGURE 21–20
Master Views group on the View tab

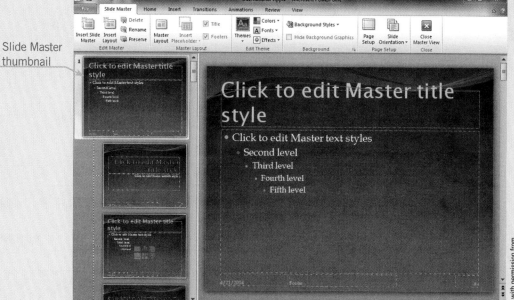

FIGURE 21–21
International 4 presentation in Slide Master view

Slide Master thumbnail

Used with permission from Microsoft Corporation

3. The Slides tab and the Outline tab are no longer visible. Also, there are several new thumbnails at the left. The first thumbnail is the Slide Master for the presentation, and the thumbnails below the Slide Master are the supporting default slide layouts that are associated with the Slide Master.

4. At the top of the left pane, click the **Slide Master** thumbnail, as shown in Figure 21–21. Click the **Insert** tab. In the Images group, shown in **Figure 21–22**, click the **Picture** button. Navigate to the drive and folder where your Data Files folder is stored. Click the filename **Logo.jpg**, and then click **Insert**. The graphic (showing the letters INTL for International) is inserted on the Slide Master that is displayed in the slide pane.

FIGURE 21–22
Images group on the Insert tab

5. The graphic is already selected, so sizing handles are displayed on the graphic borders, as shown in **Figure 21–23**. Position the mouse pointer on one of the borders. When the mouse pointer changes to a four-headed arrow, click and drag the **graphic** and position it in the lower-right corner of the Slide Master as shown.

FIGURE 21–23
Repositioning graphic in slide pane

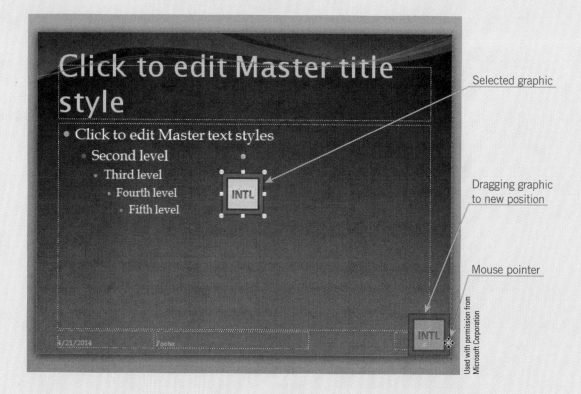

6. When you release the mouse button, the logo is repositioned on the slide. Note, too, that because the graphic was added to the Slide Master, the logo is displayed on all thumbnails in the left pane.

7. Click the **Slide Master** tab. In the Close group on the right side of the Slide Master tab, click the **Close Master View** button. The presentation is displayed in Normal view again.

8. Click the **Insert** tab. In the Text group shown in **Figure 21–24**, click the **Header & Footer** button. The Header and Footer dialog box shown in **Figure 21–25** opens.

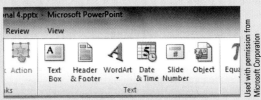

FIGURE 21–24
Text group on the Insert tab

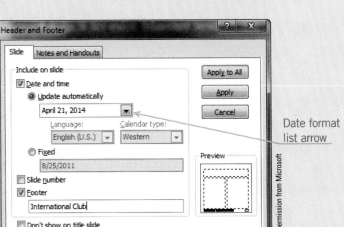

FIGURE 21–25
Header and Footer dialog box

9. Under Include on slide, click the **Date and time** check box, and if necessary click to enable the **Update automatically** option. Then click the **date format** list arrow, and select the Month DD, YYYY format. For example: April 21, 2014.

10. Click the **Footer** check box, and then in the text box type **International Club**. The settings should match those shown in Figure 21–25, with the current date shown in the date format box.

11. In the upper-right corner of the dialog box, click **Apply to All**. As you can see in the slide pane and in the thumbnails on the Slides tab, the footer with the date and club name have been added to all three slides.

12. Save the changes, and leave the presentation open for the next Step-by-Step.

Previewing and Showing a Presentation

Now that you have had some practice creating and editing presentation slides, you probably want to see what the slides look like in Slide Show view. As you view the presentation, to advance to the next slide you can click the left mouse button, press Enter, or press the spacebar. You can also use the arrow keys or the Page Up and Page Down keys to navigate forward or backward.

You can click the Slide Show button on the View tab, or you can click the Slide Show tab on the Ribbon for more options. In Slide Show view, when you move the mouse pointer around the lower-left corner of the screen, four buttons appear that help you navigate and add annotations to the slides while in Slide Show view.

If your computer is capable of supporting more than one monitor, and if you have access to two monitors, you can show the presentation in Presenter view. In Presenter view, the presentation is displayed on two monitors. One of the monitors can show the speaker notes in large clear type and with thumbnails of slides to preview text. The second monitor shows the presentation in Slide Show view for the audience.

If your presentation time is cut, you may need to skip some slides in your presentation. Instead of deleting the slides, you can create a custom slide show by selecting only those slides you want to include.

Step-by-Step 21.9

2-4.1.10
2-4.1.11

1. If necessary, open the file **International 4** from your solution files. Save the International 4 presentation as **International 5**, followed by your initials.

2. Click the **Slide Show** tab. In the Start Slide Show group shown in **Figure 21–26**, click the **From Beginning** button. The first slide fills the screen. Move the mouse pointer across the screen. You can use the arrow to point out parts of the slide during your presentation. To navigate forward and backward through the slides:

   a. Click the left mouse button to advance to the next slide. Slide 2 fills the screen.

   b. Press **Page Up** to move to the previous slide.

   c. Press the **down arrow** to advance to the next slide.

   d. Press **Enter** to advance to the next slide.

   e. Press the **spacebar** to advance to the next slide.

   f. Press the **up arrow** twice to move up two slides in the presentation.

> ### QUICK TIP
>
> If your mouse includes a scroll wheel, you can use the wheel to navigate through the slides both forward and backward in Slide Show view.

FIGURE 21–26
Start Slide Show group on the Slide Show tab

3. Position the mouse pointer in the lower-left corner of the screen. As you drag the pointer over the bottom edge of the screen (which happens to be over the date in the footer), four different semitransparent buttons will appear. Click the **Previous Slide** button ⬅ to move to the previous slide. Then move the mouse pointer in the same area but farther to the right, and when it appears, click the **Next Slide** button ➡ to move to the next slide.

4. Continue to move the mouse pointer around the date in the footer, and click the **Pen Options Tool** button ✏. In the menu, point to **Ink Color**, and then under Standard Colors select the **Yellow** color. (The mouse pointer is now a yellow dot.) Click the **Pen Options Tool** button again, and then click **Highlighter**. Then drag the mouse across the word *education*, just as you would highlight text on paper.

5. You can also use the pen tool to add annotations to the slides during a presentation. Click the **Pen Options Tool** button. In the menu, click **Pen**, and use the pen tool to underline the text *important* on the screen. The pen marks overlay the text and objects that are displayed on the slide.

6. Move the mouse pointer down to the lower-left corner, and click the **Menu** button 🗏. In the menu, point to **Screen**, and then in the submenu click **Show/Hide Ink Markup** to hide the highlighted text and the underline. The pen tool is toggled off.

7. Right-click anywhere on the screen. In the menu that opens, point to **Go to Slide**. The slide numbers with the slide titles are displayed in a submenu, and the active slide is checked. Click **3 Get Involved** to show that slide.

8. Press **B**, and the entire screen goes black. This option is helpful when you stop for a discussion or a break because you can stop the projection of the slide without exiting Slide Show view. Press **B** again to toggle the black screen off.

9. Press **Esc** to return to Normal view. When prompted to keep your ink annotations, click **Discard**. Note that if you choose to keep the ink annotations, the highlight and underline would be saved in the presentation file and would appear in Slide Show view.

QUICK TIP

You can also toggle off the Pen Options Tool by pressing Esc.

QUICK TIP

You can also toggle a white screen on and off by pressing W.

FIGURE 21–27
Define Custom Show dialog box
with selected slides

10. In the Start Slide Show group, click the **Custom Slide Show** button, and then click **Custom Shows**. The Custom Shows dialog box opens. Click **New**. A list of all the slides in the presentation is displayed in the Define Custom Show dialog box.

11. In the Slide show name text box, leave the proposed slide show name *Custom Show 1* as is. Under Slides in presentation, click **1. A New Country; A New Experience**. Press and hold **Ctrl** and then click **3. Get Involved**.

12. When your dialog box matches the one shown in **Figure 21–27**, click **Add**. The selected slides are copied to the pane on the right and will be included in the new custom show. Click **OK.** Close the Define Custom Show dialog box.

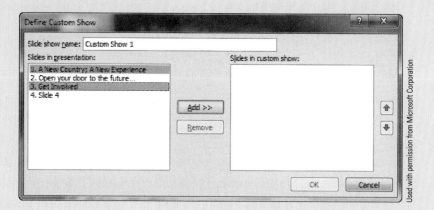

13. In the Start Slide Show group, click the **Custom Slide Show** button, and then click **Custom Show 1**. The custom slide show opens. Press **Page Down** twice to advance to the next slide and then to the end of the show. Then, press **Page Down** one more time to exit Slide Show view and return to Normal view.

14. Save the changes, and close the presentation.

TECHNOLOGY CAREERS

Career Communication Skills

Chances are that you have given some thought to the kind of career or job you want when you finish school. Are you interested in entering the corporate world, perhaps as an account manager in a marketing or advertising firm? Or maybe you have always wanted to teach in a classroom or train workers on the job. If you like science, you may be considering a career as a researcher for a large company or a university. In any of these careers, the individuals most likely to be promoted and succeed have something in common—they have good oral and written communication skills. The ability to make formal presentations is an increasingly important skill for many different occupations. In fact, communication skills can greatly enhance one's success in the classroom or on the job.

Many jobs require that an employee be able to organize, analyze, and communicate information. Moreover, employees are often called on to formally present information. For example, an account manager may use a presentation to pitch a new idea to a client. An instructor plans and presents material to other people every day. And a research scientist may be called on to report findings to colleagues, create a presentation on future projects for a grant application process, or even conduct a press conference to introduce a scientific breakthrough! The audience may be as small as one or two coworkers, or it may be a much larger group of people, and the presentation may be in person or on camera. In most cases, you will use some type of technology. To deliver an effective presentation, you must possess the technology skills and confidence to deliver an effective presentation.

SUMMARY

In this lesson, you learned:

- In addition to using the Slides and Outline tabs to move to a different slide, you can use the scroll bar, mouse, or keyboard to navigate through a presentation in Normal view.

- You work in either Normal view or Slide Sorter view as you create and edit your presentation. You use Slide Show view when you present the show to an audience.

- You can use the Cut, Copy, and Paste commands to delete, move, or copy slides in a presentation. You can also easily rearrange the order of slides using drag-and-drop editing.

- To create an effective presentation, the design features for layouts and formats should emphasize the content without overwhelming it. For example, use the same fonts for the same features in all slides for a consistent appearance, and limit the number of special features on a single slide.

- The slide theme automatically formats slides with color schemes, font styles, and effects. A theme ensures that all slides in a presentation have a consistent look. You can apply a theme at any time without affecting the underlying content of the slides.

- You can change the slide layout even when the slide contains content, and you can modify the slide layout by resizing and repositioning the placeholders.

- You can add elements such as a company logo to the Slide Master so the elements appear consistently on all slides. You can create a footer to display a company name or date on one or all slides in the presentation.

- In Slide Show view, the slides are displayed full screen, and you can move through the presentation using the mouse or keyboard.

- You can add annotations to slides and highlight text when showing slides in Slide Show view.

- So that only designated slides are displayed in Slide Show view, you can create a custom slide show.

◼ LESSON REVIEW

TRUE / FALSE

Circle T if the statement is true or F if the statement is false.

T   F   **1.**   In PowerPoint, the document file is called a presentation.

T   F   **2.**   You can apply a different theme at any time to change the look of your presentation.

T   F   **3.**   When you use a theme, the format of the text on each of the slides is predetermined.

T   F   **4.**   You can use the Cut, Copy, and Paste commands to copy or move slides.

T   F   **5.**   Presenter view is only available for computers that have access to two monitors.

T   F   **6.**   When you create a custom slide show, unselected slides are deleted.

T   F   **7.**   As you enter text in a placeholder, PowerPoint automatically checks for misspelled words and corrects common spelling errors.

T   F   **8.**   You can edit text on the Outline tab or in the slide pane.

T   F   **9.**   A blank placeholder will print and be displayed in Slide Show view.

T   F   **10.**   The Notes pane is displayed in all views.

MULTIPLE CHOICE

Select the best response for the following statements.

1. When planning slide content, use _____ to illustrate lists of information.

   A.   bulleted lists   C.   font styles and colors

   B.   annotations   D.   tables and charts

2. The _____ view enables you to easily rearrange the order of the slides.

   A.   Normal   C.   Slide Sorter

   B.   Slide Show   D.   Reading

3. To add text to a slide or to manipulate the text on a slide, you must display the slide in _____ view.

   A.   Normal   C.   Reading

   B.   Slide Sorter   D.   A or B

4. To navigate through slides in a presentation in Normal view, you can _____ .

   A.   click a thumbnail on the Slides tab

   B.   click the slide content on the Outline tab

   C.   use the vertical scroll bar or the keyboard

   D.   all of the above

5. To navigate forward and backward through slides in Slide Show view, you can click or press _____ .

   A.   the left mouse button

   B.   the Page Up or the Page Down key or the arrow keys

   C.   the spacebar or Enter

   D.   all of the above

WRITTEN QUESTIONS

Write a brief answer to the following questions.

1. What is the benefit of applying a theme?

2. What is the purpose of a Slide Master?

3. What is the purpose of the Notes pane?

4. Why is the font style important?

5. How can you add annotations to a slide?

■ PROJECTS

PROJECT 21–1

1. Create a new presentation file. Save the presentation as **Heroes**, followed by your initials.

2. On the first slide, using the Title Slide layout, enter the title **Recognition of Unsung Heroes**. Then enter the subtitle **For Acts of Conscience and Courage**.

3. Insert a new slide with the Title and Content layout. In the title placeholder enter the title **Definition of an Unsung Hero**. In the content placeholder enter **One who does great deeds,**. Press **Shift+Enter** and type **unrecognized and unacknowledged**.

4. In the slide pane, select the two bulleted items, and remove the bullets from the paragraphs. (*Hint*: In the Paragraphs group, click the Bullets button.)

5. Insert a new slide with the Two Content layout. In the title placeholder, enter **Characteristics of an Unsung Hero**. Then in the content placeholders, enter the following two lists. Keep the bullet formats.

```
Strength        Selflessness

Compassion      Dedication

Perseverance    Integrity
```

6. Show the Outline tab. On the Outline tab at the bottom of the first bulleted list in slide 3, position the insertion point at the end of the word *Perseverance*. Press **Enter**, and type **Humility**. Then add the word **Initiative** at the bottom of the second bulleted list.

7. Insert a new slide with the Title Only layout. In the Title placeholder enter **Applications for Nominations**. In the Notes pane, enter **Be sure to have copies of application forms available.**.

8. Apply an appropriate theme. If desired, modify font sizes to change how text wraps in the title placeholders.

9. Save the changes, and close the presentation.

Reference codes (Project 21–1):
2-1.2.1
2-1.2.5
2-4.1.1
2-4.1.2
2-4.1.3
2-4.1.4

PROJECT 21–2

1. Open the file **Exchange Students** from the drive and folder where your Data Files folder is stored. Save the Exchange Students presentation as **Revised Exchange Students**, followed by your initials.

2. Switch to Slide Sorter view, and make the following changes:

    a. Select slides 1, 2 and 5, and then delete the selected slides.

    b. Move slide 2 to the end of the presentation.

    c. Move slide 3 so it is positioned before slide 2.

3. Switch to Normal view. Select a thumbnail in the Slides tab, change the zoom setting for the Slides tab to **66%**, and, if necessary, fit the slide pane to the window.

4. Navigate to the first slide in the presentation. Insert a new slide with the Title Slide layout. Then reposition the new slide so it is the first slide in the presentation. In the title placeholder, enter **Exchange Students**. In the subtitle placeholder, enter **An International Education Opportunity**.

5. Resize the subtitle placeholder to decrease the width of the placeholder so the text wraps to four lines. Then reposition the subtitle placeholder to center it under the title on the slide.

6. Copy slide 6 and paste it after slide 1.

7. Apply a theme of your choice. Change the background style and/or the color scheme. Make any desired modifications, such as text alignment, text box placement, or font colors.

8. Save the changes to the presentation. Then preview each of the slides in the presentation in Reading view.

9. Switch to Slide Show view and navigate to slide 4. Toggle on the **Pen** option. Change the ink color to a color that will stand out in the slide design, and then use the pen to underline the word *Benefits*. Press **Esc** to toggle off the Pen tool.

10. Switch to Normal view. When prompted to keep the annotations, click **Keep**.

11. Save the changes, and close the presentation.

Reference codes (Project 21–2):
2-1.1.3
2-1.1.6
2-1.2.2
2-1.2.5
2-4.1.1
2-4.1.2
2-4.1.3
2-4.1.5
2-4.1.7

PROJECT 21-3

1. Open the file **Search Tips** from the drive and folder where your Data Files folder is stored. Save the Search Tips presentation as **Revised Search Tips**, followed by your initials.

2. Change the slide 2 layout to the Title Only layout. Then insert a new blank slide after slide 2, using the same layout.

3. On the new slide number 3 add the title **Then, choose a tool...**. Then, using the Slides tab, move the new slide 3 to become the fourth slide.

4. Apply a design of your choice. Change the color scheme and theme fonts as desired.

5. Add the footer **Internet Search Tips**. Apply the footer to all slides.

6. Preview each slide in the presentation in Slide Show view using the mouse button and the Page Down key, the Page Up key, and the down arrow and up arrow keys. Then use the menu to navigate to slide 7. Exit Slide Show view.

7. Create a custom slide show, using the default slide show name. Include only slides 1, 5, 6, 7, 8, and 9. Preview each of the slides in the custom slide show, and then exit Slide Show view.

8. Save the changes, and then close the presentation.

2-1.1.3
2-1.2.2
2-1.2.5
2-4.1.1
2-4.1.3
2-4.1.4
2-4.1.10
2-4.1.11
2-4.1.12

TEAMWORK PROJECT

One of the best uses of a PowerPoint presentation is to persuade an audience to adopt a particular point of view. Follow these steps:

2-4.1.12

1. As a class, brainstorm some issues of interest to the entire class (such as a proposal for a new community park or bike path). Or, your instructor may have a list of issues already prepared.

2. Form groups of two learners who have different opinions on one topic. Each learner will create a slide show that presents their position.

3. Gather information on the issue from surveys or research, and then create a presentation to support your own particular point of view. Save the presentation as **TP 21-1**, followed by your initials.

4. Organize the slide content to emphasize your points clearly. Select a theme and slide layouts that present your information effectively.

5. Each team member will then present their argument, and classmates will critique each presentation for design, content, and persuasiveness.

■ CRITICAL THINKING

CRITICAL THINKING 21-1

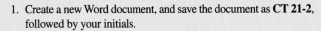

One of the files you worked with in this lesson, Three Rs, addressed the importance of knowing the rules of copyright law for the Internet. If a classmate copies pictures from Web pages and uses the pictures in a report for a class assignment, is the classmate violating copyright laws? Search the Internet for information about copyright laws, and then do the following:

2-4.1.12

1. Create a new Word document, and save the document as **CT 21-1**, followed by your initials.

2. Explain why you think the classmate has or has not broken any copyright rules. Use the information gathered from your Internet search to support your argument. Be sure to respect those who provided the information at the Web site and give them credit by citing your sources!

3. Save the changes to the document.

CRITICAL THINKING 21-2

The slide layout and design are essential for emphasizing the presentation content. Through your own experience, you can probably relate to viewing an ineffective slide show. To avoid making similar mistakes, consider the guidelines you should follow when creating your own presentations.

2-4.1.12

1. Create a new Word document, and save the document as **CT 21-2**, followed by your initials.

2. Describe at least three design elements that are essential for developing an effective presentation.

3. Save the changes, and close the document.

ONLINE DISCOVERY

To complete this activity, you will need permission to access files online and download a file.

In the Word lessons, you learned about using templates to create documents. PowerPoint provides access to several templates to help you create professional-looking presentations. Not only do these presentation templates include preformatted designs, but some of them also include content that you can use as a guide as you create your own content. Some of these templates are provided by PowerPoint users like yourself.

1. In PowerPoint, click the **File** tab, and then click **New**. In the center pane, under Office.com Templates, click the **PowerPoint presentations and slides** icon.

2. Choose a folder, such as *Academic presentations*, and double-click to open the folder. Scroll through the thumbnails and select one of the templates that you think might be useful, and then click the thumbnail. A larger image of the thumbnail appears in the right pane, and customer ratings are provided above the image, which will help you decide if you want to download the template.

2-1.1.9

3. If permitted, download one of the templates and review the slides.

4. Open a new Word document, and save the document as **OD 21-1**, followed by your initials. Write a brief paragraph about whether or not you think the template will be useful for future presentations, and explain why.

5. Save the changes, and close the document.

JOB SKILLS

1. In this lesson, you created several presentations. Choose one of your solution files (or another presentation file you have created), and review the content on each slide. If desired, add notes to the Notes pane to help you prepare for the presentation.

2. Practice using the keyboard and mouse to navigate through the files, and also practice using the highlighter and pen tools.

3. Deliver the presentation in Slide Show view to your classmates. If there is not enough time to deliver the presentation to the class, ask a partner to sit through the presentation.

2-4.1.12

LESSON 22

Enhancing Presentations with Multimedia Effects

■ OBJECTIVES

Upon completion of this lesson, you should be able to:

- Add clip art, shapes and drawn objects, SmartArt graphics, and pictures from files to a slide.

- Change the size and position of a graphic object, and add borders and shading to graphic objects on a slide.

- Create charts and tables using Excel and Word features.

- Create hyperlinks on slides to link to Web pages, e-mails, and other documents.

- Add slide transitions to control how the slides are introduced in a slide show.

- Animate objects on a slide to draw attention and add emphasis.

- Insert sound and video clips to add an extra dimension to a slide show.

- Prepare hard copies for handouts and speaker's notes, and distribute presentations via electronic copies.

■ WORDS TO KNOW

animation

emphasis effects

entrance effects

exit effects

motion paths

slide transitions

trigger

■ DATA FILES

To complete this lesson, you will need these data files:

Blue.jpg

Bucket.jpg

Community Report.pptx

Dogs.pptx

Kylie Video.wmv

Managing Time.pptx

Recycle Video.wmv

Resort.pptx

Taffy.jpg

Time Management.pptx

A good presentation holds your audience's attention without distracting them from understanding the information you are presenting. PowerPoint allows you to use colors, designs, graphics, links, sound, and video to illustrate your information effectively by emphasizing and clarifying your points.

Inserting and Editing Graphics

Graphics can help your audience remember your message. Graphics include shapes, clip art, photographs, WordArt, SmartArt graphics, tables, and charts. PowerPoint provides special content placeholders in slide layouts to make the task of adding graphics easy. But do not let your message get lost by overloading your slide show with the abundant special effects available. Use graphics only when they illustrate relevant points in a presentation.

Adding Clip Art to a Slide

When you insert a graphic in a placeholder, the graphic replaces the placeholder. You can insert clip art and photographs from the Clip Art task pane, and you can also insert a picture from a file, such as a digital photograph or a scanned image of a drawing.

When a graphic is selected, eight small squares and circles called sizing handles appear on the border of the graphic. When the graphic is selected, you can cut, copy, paste, delete, move, or resize it. To resize the graphic, drag a sizing handle and you will see the effect on the screen as you drag. To resize the graphic proportionally, drag a corner sizing handle.

Microsoft provides access to a gallery of clip art files at Office.com. If you do not have access to the Internet, you can access a few clip art files that are installed with your Office applications. Or, you may have access to other clip art resources.

Step-by-Step 22.1

2-1.3.7
2-4.1.2
2-4.1.12

1. Launch **Microsoft PowerPoint 2010**, and open the file **Time Management** from the drive and folder where your Data Files folder is stored. Save the Time Management presentation as **Revised Time Management 1**, followed by your initials.

2. Go to slide 2. It is a blank slide. The slide layout includes title and content placeholders. The content placeholder shows six different graphics buttons, as shown in **Figure 22–1**. Point to each of the graphics buttons to show the ScreenTips. You can insert a table, a chart, a SmartArt graphic, a picture from a file, a clip art image, and a media clip.

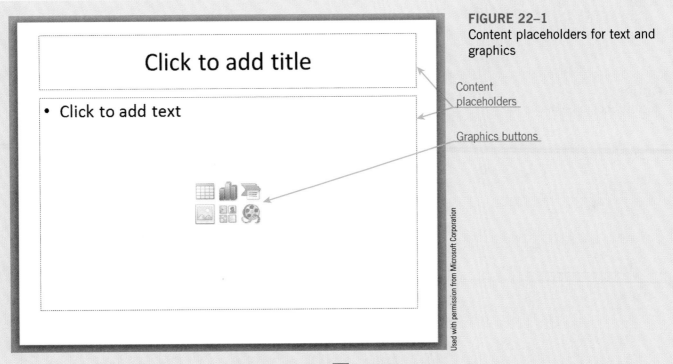

Used with permission from Microsoft Corporation

FIGURE 22–1
Content placeholders for text and graphics

Content placeholders

Graphics buttons

3. In the content placeholder, click the **Clip Art** button ▦. The Clip Art task pane, as shown in **Figure 22–2**, is displayed. Do not be concerned if there is text in the Search for text box in your task pane. If necessary, click to enable the **Include Office.com content** option.

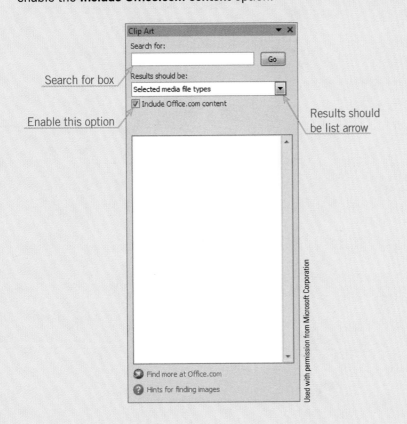

Search for box

Enable this option

Results should be list arrow

Used with permission from Microsoft Corporation

FIGURE 22–2
Clip Art task pane

4. Click the **Results should be** list arrow, and select the check box for the **Illustrations** media type, as shown in **Figure 22–3**. If necessary, click the other check boxes to deselect the other media type options.

FIGURE 22–3
Results should be menu

5. Click in the **Search for** text box. If necessary, select any existing text. Type **clock**, and then click **Go**. PowerPoint searches for all illustrations related to the word *clock*. If you have an Internet connection, several thumbnails will be displayed as shown in **Figure 22–4**, and you can scroll through the thumbnails. If you do not have an Internet connection, only one result will be displayed.

FIGURE 22–4
Illustrations related to the search text *clock*

Click the first thumbnail

6. Click the first thumbnail. The clip art replaces the content placeholder on the slide. Close the Clip Art task pane.

7. Eight sizing handles appear around the clip art, as shown in **Figure 22–5**. Point to the sizing handle in the upper-left corner. When the pointer changes to a double-headed arrow ⬉, drag the sizing handle up and to the left to make the clip art bigger so the clip art overlaps the title placeholder.

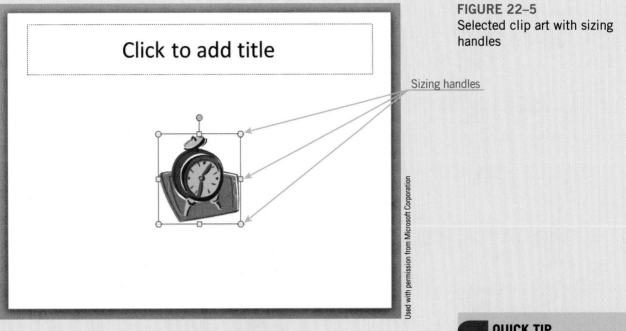

FIGURE 22–5
Selected clip art with sizing handles

Sizing handles

Used with permission from Microsoft Corporation

8. Point to the center of the clip art. The pointer will change to a four-headed arrow ✛. Drag the **clip art** to center it on the slide.

QUICK TIP

You can crop clip art after inserting it on a slide.

9. Go to slide 3. In the content placeholder on the left, click the **Clip Art** button. In the Clip Art task pane, change the Search for text to **search.** Click the **Results should be** list arrow. Deselect the **Illustrations** media type, and select the **Photographs** media type. Click **Go**. If you have an Internet connection, the results will be similar to those shown in **Figure 22–6.** (If you do not have Internet access, there will be no results; go to step 10.) Scroll through the results and click one of the photograph thumbnails to insert it in the content placeholder. Close the Clip Art task pane.

FIGURE 22–6
Photographs related to the search text *search*

Used with permission from Microsoft Corporation

10. In the content placeholder on the right, click above the graphics buttons, and type **Time lost is never found.**. The text is contained in a text box and formatted with a bullet. Click anywhere within the line of text. In the Paragraph group on the Home tab, click the **Bullets** button to remove the bullet format. Your slide should look similar to **Figure 22–7**.

FIGURE 22–7
Slide with graphic and text

11. You can resize and reposition this text box just as you would change a graphic. Point to the lower-middle sizing handle of the text box border, and then click and drag the **border** up towards the text, as shown in **Figure 22–8**, to reduce the size of the text box.

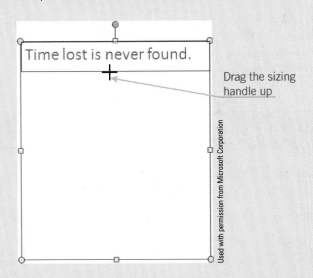

FIGURE 22–8
Adjusting the size of the text box

12. The text box should still be selected. Click the **Drawing Tools Format** tab, and in the Shape Styles group shown in **Figure 22–9**, click the **More** button to open the Shape Styles gallery. Click a color style that complements the photograph on the left, and then click outside the text box to see the results of the new style.

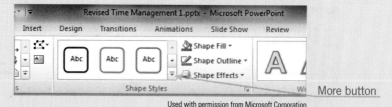

Used with permission from Microsoft Corporation

13. Go to slide 4. Click anywhere within the bulleted list to select the text box. Then, select all of the text in the text box. Click the **Home** tab, and in the Paragraph group, click the **Numbering** button. The bullets are converted to numbers.

14. Deselect the text. Save the changes, and leave the presentation open for the next Step-by-Step.

Adding WordArt, Shapes, and SmartArt Graphics to a Slide

You can also create WordArt objects and draw objects on a slide using the same shape tools that you learned to use in Word. SmartArt graphics enable you to convert text to a professional-looking visual element. As you already know, SmartArt graphics are easy to create, and you can even create them from existing text.

Step-by-Step 22.2

2-1.3.7
2-4.1.2

1. If necessary, open the file **Revised Time Management 1** from your solution files. Save the Revised Time Management 1 presentation as **Revised Time Management 2**, followed by your initials.

2. On slide 1, click anywhere within the title text box. The sizing handles on the border of the text box are white, and the border is displayed with broken lines. Point to the **text box** border, and when the pointer changes to a four-headed arrow, click to select the text box. When the text box is selected, the borders are solid lines and the sizing handles are blue.

3. Press **Delete** to remove the text box contents. Select the **text box** again, and then press **Delete** to remove the text box.

4. Click the **Insert** tab, and then in the Text group, click the **WordArt** button. In the fifth row, click the third option, **Fill – Red, Accent 2, Warm Matte Bevel**. A new placeholder text box is inserted on the slide. Type **Time Management**.

5. Point to one of the text box borders, and when the pointer changes to a four-headed arrow, drag the text box up to position it near the top of the slide.

6. Go to slide 3. On the **Home** tab in the Slides group, click the **New Slide** button arrow, and then select the **Title and Content** layout. In the new slide, click anywhere within the title placeholder text **Click to add title**, and type **Not enough time...**.

7. On the Home tab in the Drawing group, click the **Shapes** button (or the More button for shapes), and under Basic Shapes, click the **Smiley Face** shape tool. The mouse pointer changes to a crosshair ✛. Starting above and to the left of the graphics buttons, click and drag the mouse pointer diagonally down and to the right to create a smiley face object that covers all the graphics buttons. The object overlays the content placeholder.

8. The smiley face object should still be selected. In the Drawing group, click the **Shape Fill** button arrow, and under Standard Colors, click the **Yellow** color.

9. To change the smile to a frown, point to the **diamond** shape on the smile and click and drag the line upward, as shown in **Figure 22–10**.

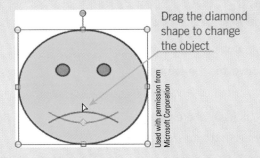

Drag the diamond shape to change the object

Used with permission from Microsoft Corporation

FIGURE 22–10
Changing the smile on the smiley face

10. Go to slide 5. Click anywhere within the numbered list to select the text box. In the Paragraph group on the Home tab, click the **Convert to SmartArt Graphic** button 🔳. Then click the first option, **Vertical Bullet List**. The contents in the text box are converted to a graphic.

11. Click the first row **Pay utilities due Thursday** to select the object. Click the **SmartArt Tools Format** tab. In the Shape Styles group, click the **Shape Fill** button arrow, and under Standard Colors, click the **Red** color.

12. Click the second row **Summary report due Friday** to select the object. On the Quick Access Toolbar, click the **Repeat** button to repeat the edit. Then click the **Undo** button to restore the second row to its original color.

13. Go to slide 3. Select the photograph. Click the **Picture Tools Format** tab. In the Picture Styles group shown in **Figure 22–11**, click the **Picture Border** button arrow. Under Theme Colors or Standard Colors, select a color that complements the photograph. Click the **Picture Border** button arrow again, point to **Weight**, and then click **3 pt**.

FIGURE 22–11
Picture Styles group on the
Picture Tools Format tab

14. Save the changes, and close the presentation.

Adding Tables, Text Boxes, Charts, and Pictures from Files to Slides

You can add tables and simple charts to illustrate numerical data or trends. The placeholders make it easy to create a table or chart on a slide using features in Word and Excel that you are already familiar with. To add new placeholders for text, you can insert additional text boxes. To further enhance a slide and add another type of visual element, you can insert from a file a photograph, drawing, or scanned image.

Step-by-Step 22.3

2-1.3.7
2-4.1.2

1. Open the file **Dogs** from the drive and folder where your Data Files folder is stored. Save the Dogs presentation as **Revised Dogs 1**, followed by your initials. If necessary, maximize the presentation window.

2. On slide 1, click anywhere within the placeholder text **Click to add subtitle**, then type your first and last name.

3. Go to slide 2. In the content placeholder, click the **Insert Table** button [icon]. The Insert Table dialog box opens. Change the settings to **4** columns and **6** rows.

4. Click **OK**. A table is inserted on the slide. Enter the table data shown in **Figure 22–12**.

Name	Gender	Age	Breed
Sebastian	Male	Young	Beagle
Marcy	Female	Baby	Saint Bernard
Snickers	Female	Adult	Brittany Spaniel
Marshall	Male	Young	Terrier
Max	Male	Young	Siberian Husky

FIGURE 22–12
Table data for slide 2

Used with permission from Microsoft Corporation

5. Click the **Insert** tab. In the Text group, click the **Text Box** button. The mouse pointer changes to a crosshair ↓. Drag the mouse pointer below the table to create a text box the width of the first two table columns.

6. The insertion point is positioned in the new text box. Type **This list changes daily.**. Click outside the text box to deselect it.

7. Go to slide 3. In the content placeholder, click the **Insert Chart** button ▥. The Insert Chart dialog box opens. The first option, Clustered Column, should already be selected. Click **OK**. An Excel workbook opens, and the screen is split to show both your PowerPoint presentation and an Excel worksheet. The worksheet contains sample data, and a sample chart is inserted on the PowerPoint slide, as shown in **Figure 22–13**.

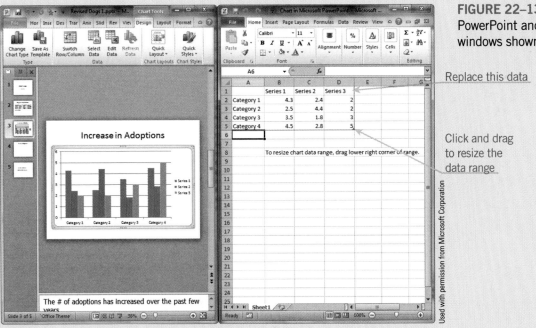

FIGURE 22–13
PowerPoint and Excel application windows shown side by side

Replace this data

Click and drag to resize the data range

Used with permission from Microsoft Corporation

8. In the Excel application window, point to the lower-right corner of the selected data range. When the pointer changes to a double-headed arrow, drag the **border** down to cell D6 to add one more row to the data range. The data range should now be A1:D6. In the worksheet, replace the sample data with the data shown in **Figure 22–14**. As you enter the data, the chart in the slide in the PowerPoint application window is updated.

FIGURE 22–14
Chart data for slide 3

◢	A	B	C	D	E
1		Baby	Young	Adult	
2	2009	45	38	37	
3	2010	52	45	39	
4	2011	61	59	47	
5	2012	79	66	64	
6	2013	86	71	72	
7					

Used with permission from Microsoft Corporation

QUICK TIP

You can also copy and paste tables and charts from Word and Excel documents.

9. In the Excel application window, click the **File** tab, and then click **Save As**. Navigate to the drive and folder where your solution files are saved. Save the worksheet as **Dog Data**, followed by your initials. Then close the Excel application. The PowerPoint application is still open, and the updated chart is shown on slide 3.

10. Go to slide 4. In the content placeholder on the left, click the **Insert Picture from File** button [icon]. The Insert Picture dialog box opens. Navigate to the drive and folder where your Data Files folder is stored. Click **Taffy.jpg**, and then at the bottom of the dialog box click **Insert**. The picture is inserted in the placeholder on the slide.

11. In the text placeholder above the picture, type **Taffy**. Select the new text. Using the Mini toolbar, change the font size to **36** point, and click the **Center** button [icon] to center-align the text.

12. In the content placeholder on the right, click the **Insert Picture from File** button. If necessary, navigate to the drive and folder where your Data Files folder is stored. Click the **Blue.jpg file**, and then click **Insert**. The pictures are positioned side by side on the slide.

13. In the text placeholder above the picture, type **Blue**. Select the new text. Using the Mini toolbar, change the font size to **36** point and center-align the text.

14. Save the changes, and leave the presentation open for the next Step-by-Step.

Creating Hyperlinks

In PowerPoint, you can create hyperlinks to slides in the same presentation, to slides in another presentation, or to an e-mail address, a Web page, or another file. You can create the hyperlink from text on a slide, and you can also create the hyperlink from a graphic object on a slide. Hyperlinks are only functional in Slide Show view, and you can customize the ScreenTip that appears when you position the mouse pointer over the hyperlink text or object while in Slide Show view.

Step-by-Step 22.4

1. If necessary, open the file **Revised Dogs 1** from your solution files. Save the Revised Dogs 1 presentation as **Revised Dogs 2**, followed by your initials.

2. Go to slide 5. Select the text **www.clintonadoptadog.org**. Click the **Insert** tab. In the Links group shown in **Figure 22–15**, click the **Hyperlink** button.

2-1.3.7
2-4.1.2
2-4.1.11

FIGURE 22–15
Links group on the Insert tab

3. The Insert Hyperlink dialog box, similar to the one shown in **Figure 22–16**, opens. The option to link to an existing file or Web page is already selected, and the selected text is displayed in the Text to display box at the top of the dialog box.

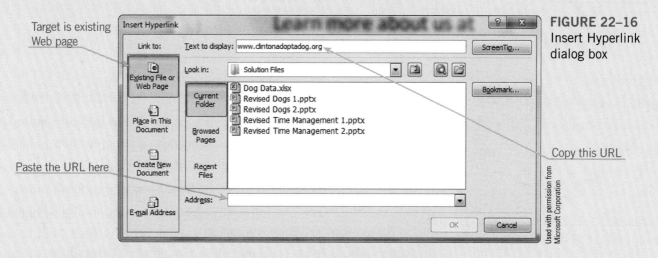

FIGURE 22–16
Insert Hyperlink dialog box

4. In the Text to display box, select the text **www.clintonadoptadog.org**. Press **Ctrl+C** to copy the selected text to the Clipboard. Click the **Address** box to place the insertion point in the text box. Press **Ctrl+V** to paste the URL copied from the Text to display box.

5. In the upper-right corner of the dialog box, click **ScreenTip**. The Set Hyperlink ScreenTip dialog box opens. In the ScreenTip text box, type **Visit our Web site**, and then click **OK** twice to close the dialog boxes. Deselect the text. The linked text is automatically formatted in a different color with an underline to designate the hyperlink.

6. Go to slide 3. Click anywhere in the chart to select it.

7. Click the **Hyperlink** button to open the Insert Hyperlink dialog box. If necessary, click the list arrow in the Look in box to navigate to the folder where you saved the Dog Data file. Click **Dog Data.xlsx**, and then click **OK**. A link to the Excel file is created, but unlike the linked text, no format appears to designate the hyperlink. The link will help you quickly access the worksheet if you need to update the data.

8. Go to slide 4. Click the picture on the left to select it, and then click the **Hyperlink** button. In the Insert Hyperlink dialog box, under Link to, click **Place in This Document**. A list of the slides with the slide titles is displayed, as shown in **Figure 22-17**.

FIGURE 22-17
Options for hyperlinks to place in this document

Click slide 2 as hyperlink target

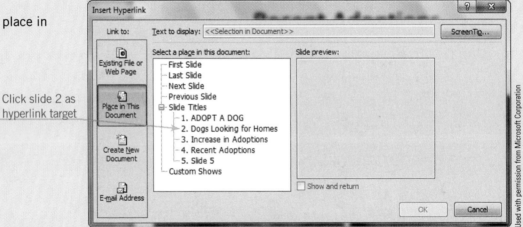

9. Click **2. Dogs Looking for Homes**. The selected slide is displayed in the Slide preview pane. Click **OK**. A link has been created to slide 2, but unlike linked text, no format appears to designate the hyperlink.

10. Go to slide 3. In the status bar, click the **Slide Show** view button to switch to Slide Show view so you can test the hyperlinks. Slide 3 is displayed in full screen view. Position the mouse pointer over the chart, and the pointer changes to a hand ⟨ᕁ⟩ indicating a hyperlink. A ScreenTip with the path for the linked file also appears.

11. Click anywhere in the chart and the linked worksheet opens in the Excel application window. Close Excel.

12. Press **Page Down** to move to the next slide. Position the mouse pointer over the picture on the left. When the pointer changes to a hand, click. Slide 2 is displayed.

13. Press **End** to move to the last slide in the presentation. Position the mouse pointer over the URL. The customized text *Visit our Web site* is displayed in the ScreenTip. (Do not click the hyperlink.)

14. Press **Esc** to return to Normal view in PowerPoint. Save the changes, and leave the presentation open for the next Step-by-Step.

Formatting Slide Transitions

Slide transitions are settings that control how a slide is introduced as you move from one slide to another in Slide Show view. For example, you can format the transition so the current slide fades to black before the next slide is displayed. Or you can choose to have the next slide automatically appear after a designated number of seconds. You can even choose a sound effect that plays as the transition occurs. When used effectively, the transitions you add between the slides add interest and help keep the attention of your audience focused on the presentation. You can apply the transition settings to a single slide or to all the slides in the presentation.

▶ **VOCABULARY**
slide transitions

Step-by-Step 22.5

1. If necessary, open the file **Revised Dogs 2** from your solution files. Save the Revised Dogs 2 presentation as **Revised Dogs 3**, followed by your initials.

2. Go to slide 3. Click the **Transitions** tab to display the transition options, shown in **Figure 22–18**.

2-4.1.6

Push transition   Default setting   Used with permission from Microsoft Corporation

FIGURE 22–18
Transitions tab

3. In the Transition to This Slide group, click the **Push** transition. You will see the Live Preview of the transition from slide 2 to slide 3. Click the **Wipe** transition. Then click the **Split** transition. The previews show different options for introducing the slide.

4. In the Transition to This Slide group, click the **More** button to display the Transitions gallery. The options are organized in three categories: Subtle, Exciting, and Dynamic Content. Under Exciting, in the second row, click the **Switch** transition and Live Preview shows the new transition.

5. Note that the Ribbon now displays options for the Exciting category. In the Transition to This Slide group, click the **Cube** transition.

6. In the Transition to This Slide group, click the **Effect Options** button, and then click **From Left**. A preview of the transition is shown.

7. In the Timing group, using the up arrow in the Duration box, change the setting to **02.00**. In the Preview group at the left, click the **Preview** button. Note that the transition is now slower.

8. In the Timing group, click the **Apply To All** button. The transition settings are applied to all slides in the presentation.

9. Go to slide 4. Because the Cube transition was applied to all slides, the Cube transition is selected on the Ribbon. In the Timing group, click the **Sound** list arrow to show a list of sound options. Point to the **Drum Roll** option. A preview of the sound occurs. Click the **Drum Roll** option. Because you did not click the Apply to All button, the sound will occur only with the transition for this slide.

10. In the Timing group, under Advance Slide, click to disable the default option **On Mouse Click**. Enable the option **After**, and then use the up arrow next to the After box to set the timer to **00:05.00**. In Slide Show view, the slide show will automatically advance to the next slide after 5 seconds.

11. Go to slide 1. On the status bar, click the **Slide Show** view button, and click the mouse to move through the slides to see the effects of the transitions. You do not need to click the mouse when the slide with the two dog pictures appears. The slide show automatically advances to the next slide after 5 seconds.

12. Press **Esc** to return to Normal view.

13. Save the changes, and close the presentation.

14. If time permits, reopen **Revised Dogs 3** from your solution files and explore other transitions and speed and sound options, then close the presentation without saving the changes.

Formatting Animations

animation

entrance effects

emphasis effects

exit effects

motion paths

trigger

When you add *animation*, you add special visual or sound effects to text or an object. Without animation, text and objects automatically appear all at once when a slide is opened in Slide Show view. However, when you format animations for the text boxes and graphics, you can control how and when the text and graphics appear on each slide.

Applying Animations

PowerPoint provides many built-in animations for four types of effects. *Entrance effects* control how the object enters onto the slide. *Emphasis effects* draw attention to an object that is already visible on the slide, and *exit effects* control how an object leaves the slide. *Motion paths* enable you to create a path for the object to follow on the slide, which you will practice in Step-by-Step 22.7. The animation options for each type of effect are organized in four categories: Basic, Subtle, Moderate, and Exciting.

By default, a mouse click is the *trigger*, the instruction that starts the animation segment.

Step-by-Step 22.6

1. Open the file **Revised Time Management 2** from your solution files. Save the Revised Time Management 2 presentation as **Revised Time Management 3**, followed by your initials.

2. Go to slide 2. Click the **clip art** object to select it, and then click the **Animations** tab. In the Animation group shown in **Figure 22–19**, point to the **Fly In** animation. A preview of the animation shows the illustration fly in from the bottom of the slide.

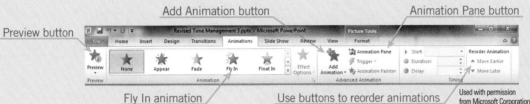

Preview button   Add Animation button   Animation Pane button   **FIGURE 22–19**
Animations tab

Fly In animation   Use buttons to reorder animations   Used with permission from Microsoft Corporation

3. In the Animation group, click the **More** button to show the Animation gallery. If necessary, use the scroll bar on the right to scroll down through the menu. The animations are organized in four categories: Entrance, Emphasis, Exit, and Motion Paths.

4. Under Entrance, click the **Wheel** animation. Live Preview shows how the animation appears in the slide pane, and the gallery closes. To see the animation again, in the Preview group at the far left side of the Animations tab, click the **Preview** button. Note that the numeral *1* appears to the left of the illustration, indicating the first animation format on that slide. Also note that the Play Animations icon [star icon] is displayed to the left of the slide 2 thumbnail in the Slides tab.

5. Go to slide 3. Click the **Time lost is never found** text placeholder to select it. In the Advanced Animation group, click the **Add Animation** button. The Animation gallery opens. Under Entrance, click the **Wipe** animation. Live Preview shows the animation, but you may not have seen the preview. In the Slides tab, next to the slide 3 thumbnail, click the **Play Animations** icon to see the text box background and then the text appear from the bottom to the top.

6. In the Animation group, click the **Effect Options** button, and then click **From Left**. In the Preview group, click the **Preview** button. The text box and text will now enter from the left and at a slower pace. In the Timing group, the Start box shows the setting On Click, which is the trigger. The animation will not occur until you click the mouse button in Slide Show view.

2-4.1.2

QUICK TIP

If you do not automatically see a preview of the animation, in the Preview group at the left side of the Animations tab, click the Preview button arrow, and then enable the AutoPreview option.

7. Go to slide 5. Click the slide title **Prioritize** to select the placeholder. In the Advanced Animation group, click the **Add Animation** button, and at the bottom of the menu, click **More Entrance Effects**. The Add Entrance Effect dialog box shown in **Figure 22–20** opens. Point to the title bar of the dialog box, and drag the box to the left to reposition it so you can see most of the content on the slide.

FIGURE 22–20
Add Entrance Effect dialog box

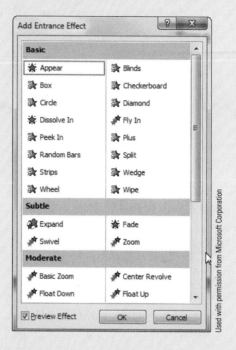

8. There are four categories for entrance effects: Basic, Subtle, Moderate, and Exciting. Use the scroll bar to move to the bottom of the list. Under Exciting, click **Float**. A preview of the animation occurs, but the animation is not applied. Under Exciting, click **Whip**, and then click **OK** to apply the animation. Click anywhere in the **SmartArt** object to select it. Click the **Add Animation** button, and then click **More Entrance Effects**. Note that some of the animation options in the Add Entrance Effect dialog box are dimmed, which means they cannot be applied to the selected object. Under Subtle, the option Expand is already selected. Click **OK**.

9. In the Advanced Animation group, click the **Animation Pane** button. The Animation Pane shown in **Figure 22–21** is displayed at the right. Note in the slide pane that the numeral *2* is displayed to the left of the SmartArt object. In the Animation Pane, click the **2 Content Place** list arrow, and then click **Start With Previous**. Now the numbers to the left of the text box and the SmartArt object on the slide are both the numeral *1*, indicating that both animations will occur at the same time.

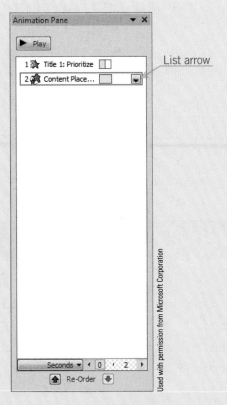

FIGURE 22–21
Animation Pane

10. In the Animation Pane, click the **Play** button to preview the two animations. On the Quick Access Toolbar, click **Undo** to restore the animation settings to two separate animations.

11. In the Animation group, click the **Effect Options** button. In the submenu, point to **One by One**. Live Preview shows the rows of the object introduced individually. Click **One by One**. The numerals *2* through *6* are now displayed to the left of the SmartArt object. In the Animation Pane, below the 2 Content Place box, click the **Expand** button ⟨⟩ to show the animations 3 through 6.

12. Click the **Add Animation** button, and under Exit, click the **Float Out** animation. In the Animation Pane, click the **7 Content Place** list arrow, and then click **Start After Previous**. This animation causes the rows to exit, one by one, after the last row of the SmartArt object appears. Because the option Start After Previous is enabled, the animation is now part of the previous animation, so the number 7 is removed from the animation title.

13. Go to slide 4. Click the **smiley face** object to select it. Click the **Add Animation** button. Under Emphasis, click the **Teeter** animation. Preview the animation.

14. Save the changes, and leave the presentation open for the next Step-by-Step.

Rearranging, Changing, and Customizing Animations

If you change your mind after applying animations, you can rearrange the order of animations, remove an animation, or change the existing animation. To change the animation effect, you must first remove the existing animation. If you apply a new animation effect without removing the existing animation, the new effect is added to the object. In other words, the object would have two animations, not one.

You can customize the animations by modifying the timing of the effects. For example, you can make text disappear very subtly by slowing down the duration of the animation, or you can make an object disappear with a much more dramatic exit by making it disappear quickly. You can also format delays before an animation is executed.

Step-by-Step 22.7

2-4.1.2

1. If necessary, open the file **Revised Time Management 3** from your solution files. Save the Revised Time Management 3 presentation as **Revised Time Management 4**, followed by your initials. If necessary, click the **Animations** tab, and then click the **Animation Pane** button to show the Animation Pane.

2. Go to slide 5. In the Animation Pane, click **1 Title 1: Prioritize**. In the Timing group, under Reorder Animation, click the **Move Later** button twice. The selected animation is now third in the sequence of animations. In the Timing group, click the **Move Earlier** button. The animations are renumbered both in the Animation Pane and in the slide pane.

3. Click and drag the **2 Title 1: Prioritize** animation to the bottom of the list. When a black line appears below the last animation in the list, as shown in **Figure 22–22**, release the mouse button. The title will now be the last object on the slide to be displayed.

FIGURE 22–22
Rearranging animation order in the Animation Pane

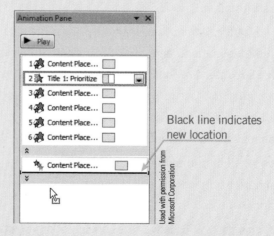

4. Go to slide 4. Click the **smiley face** object, and press **Ctrl+C** to copy it to the Clipboard. Deselect the object, click outside the placeholder, and then press **Ctrl+V** to paste the object on the slide. Drag the **diamond** on the mouth down to create a smile.

5. Note that two animations are displayed in the Animation Pane. The Teeter animation applied to the original object was also copied to the second smiley face object. In the Animation Pane, click the **2 Smiley Face** list arrow, and then click **Remove**.

6. In the slide pane, select the copied **smiley face** object. In the Animation group, click the **More** button. Under Entrance, click the **Fade** animation. In the Timing group, change the Duration setting to **1.00**, and change the Delay setting to **1.50**. When you click to trigger the animation, there will be a pause of 1.5 seconds before the animation begins, and then the animation will play over a 1-second time span.

7. Select the copied **smiley face** object, and reposition it so it is positioned exactly over the original smiley face object. (*Hint*: Use the arrow keys to move the object.) Preview the animation to see the frown turn into a smile.

8. Go to slide 1. Select the text in the subtitle placeholder (*Your Name*). Type **Racing the clock...**. Select the new text. Click the **Home** tab, and in the Font group, change the font color to **Red**.

9. Click anywhere inside the **subtitle** placeholder. Click the **Animations** tab. Click the **Add Animation** button. Scroll down and under Motion Paths, click the **Loops** animation.

10. Position the mouse pointer over the dotted line in the motion path. When the mouse pointer changes to a four-headed arrow, reposition the custom path in the lower-left corner of the slide. Press **Delete** to remove the selected motion path.

11. Close the Animation Pane. Click anywhere inside the **subtitle** placeholder. Click the **Add Animation** button. Scroll down and under Motion Paths, click the **Custom Path** animation. The mouse pointer changes to a crosshair.

12. Starting in the middle of the bottom of the slide pane, just below the subtitle placeholder, drag the mouse pointer on the slide pane to create a custom path similar to the one shown in **Figure 22–23**. Be sure to draw the path all the way off the slide and to the edge of the screen. Double-click to end the path. The custom path is automatically positioned to begin at the center of the selected placeholder.

> **ABOVE AND BEYOND**
>
> You can easily reposition motion paths on the slide by dragging and dropping the motion path.

FIGURE 22–23
Creating a custom motion path

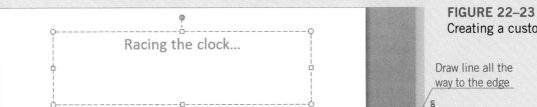

Draw line all the way to the edge

Used with permission from Microsoft Corporation

13. Save the changes. Switch to Slide Show view. Advance through the slides. Remember that many of the elements will not appear without the trigger of a mouse click. Also remember that after the last row appears in the SmartArt object on slide 5, the rows will automatically exit the slide without a trigger, but you will need to click to see the slide title animation.

14. At the end of the slide show, click the mouse button to exit Slide Show view and return to Normal view. Close the presentation.

Inserting Audio and Video Clips

Sound and video add an extra dimension to a presentation. You can use sound and video at any point in a presentation to add emphasis or set the mood for the audience. Animated graphics and sound clips are available in the Clip Art task pane. You can also use clips from other sources. To play a sound during a presentation, the sound clip must be in one of the following formats: .aiff, .au, .mid or .midi, .mp3, .wav, or .wma. To play a video during a presentation, the video must be in one of the following formats: .asf, .avi, .mpg, .mpeg, or .wmv.

Adding audio and video clips is similar to adding graphics. When you insert the video and sound files into the slide presentation, the files are either embedded and stored with the presentation, or the files are linked to the presentation. By default, .wav sound files under 100 kilobytes (KB) are embedded. All other media file types and .wav sound files that are 100 KB and over are linked and stored outside the presentation file. Movie files are always linked and stored outside the presentation file.

Step-by-Step 22.8

2-4.1.2

1. Open the file **Revised Dogs 3** from your solution files, and save the Revised Dogs 3 presentation as **Revised Dogs 4**, followed by your initials.

2. Click the **Home** tab. From slide 1, insert a new slide with the Title and Content layout. The new slide 2 is the current slide. In the content placeholder, click the **Insert Media Clip** button. The Insert Video dialog box opens. Navigate to the drive and folder where your Data Files folder is stored, and select **Kylie Video.wmv**. Then click **Insert** to link the video file to the presentation file.

3. Compare your screen to **Figure 22–24**. A graphic representing the video appears on the slide. Because the video object is selected, the Video Tools Format tab is displayed.

FIGURE 22–24
Video object positioned on a slide

Video object

Used with permission from Microsoft Corporation

4. Click the **Video Tools Playback** tab. In the Video Options group, click the **Start** list arrow, and then click **Automatically**. Click to enable the **Play Full Screen** and **Hide While Not Playing** options as shown in **Figure 22–25**.

Enabled options   Start list arrow

FIGURE 22–25
Video Options group on the Video Tools Playback tab

Used with permission from Microsoft Corporation

5. Switch to **Slide Show** view to view the video in full screen. Initially the screen will show a blank slide, and then the video will automatically play. When the video ends, press **Esc** to return to Normal view.

ABOVE AND BEYOND

If you want to trigger a video manually, use the default Start setting On Click and do not enable the Hide While Not Playing option. In Slide Show view, you will need to click the video object on the slide.

6. Go to slide 6. Click the **Insert** tab. In the Media group shown in **Figure 22–26**, click the **Audio** button arrow. Click **Clip Art Audio**. The Clip Art task pane opens. If necessary, click to enable the Include Office.com content option.

FIGURE 22–26
Media group on the Insert tab

7. In the Clip Art task pane, in the Search for box, type **dog**, and then click **Go**. If you have an Internet connection, thumbnails for several results will be displayed. (If you do not have an Internet connection, delete the text in the Search for box and click Go. Thumbnails for two results will be displayed, but the results are not related to dog sounds.)

8. Click the **Husky Dog Bark** thumbnail. (If you do not have an Internet connection, click the Claps Cheers thumbnail.) An audio symbol and a media bar are inserted in the center of the slide. Select the **audio symbol**, and drag it and the media bar to the lower-right corner of the slide as shown in **Figure 22–27**. Click the **Play** button ▶ to preview the audio clip.

FIGURE 22–27
Audio symbol and media bar

Used with permission from Microsoft Corporation

9. Close the Clip Art task pane. Click the **Audio Tools Playback** tab. In the Audio Options group shown in **Figure 22–28**, click the **Start** list arrow, and then click **Automatically**. Enable the **Hide During Show** and **Loop until Stopped** options. When the slide is active in Slide Show view, the audio clip will play automatically, and the clip will continue to play until you click the mouse button.

FIGURE 22–28
Audio Options group on the Audio Tools Playback tab

10. Save the changes.

11. Go to slide 1. Switch to **Slide Show** view. Click the mouse button to advance to slide 2. When the video stops playing, a blank slide is displayed. Click to advance to slide 3, and then click again to advance to slide 4.

12. To advance to slide 5, press **Page Down**. (If you accidentally click the chart, the Excel spreadsheet opens.) When slide 5 (Recent Adoptions) appears, you do not need to click to advance to the next slide. After five seconds, the slide show advances to the last slide, and the barking audio automatically plays, and repeatedly plays.

13. Click the mouse button to exit the slide. The audio clip stops, and you are at the end of the slide show. Click to exit Slide Show view and return to Normal view.

14. Leave the presentation open for the next Step-by-Step.

Distributing Presentations

PowerPoint offers several options for distributing your presentation. Obviously, the primary way to distribute the presentation is to project the slide show before an audience. In addition, you can provide hard copies of slides, handouts, and notes, and you can also distribute electronic copies (soft copies) of the presentation. If you are unable to make your presentation in person, you can instead share the presentation via e-mail, Web pages, or over networks.

Printing Handouts and Speaker Notes

You can print individual slides, handouts, the presentation outline, and speaker notes. You can also prepare handouts by formatting the slides in the various page layouts available in Word documents.

Step-by-Step 22.9

2-4.1.8
2-4.1.9

1. If necessary, open the file **Revised Dogs 4** from your solution files.

2. Click the **File** tab, and then click **Print** to open the Print options in Backstage view, as shown in **Figure 22–29**. Your printer will differ.

FIGURE 22–29
Print options in
Backstage view

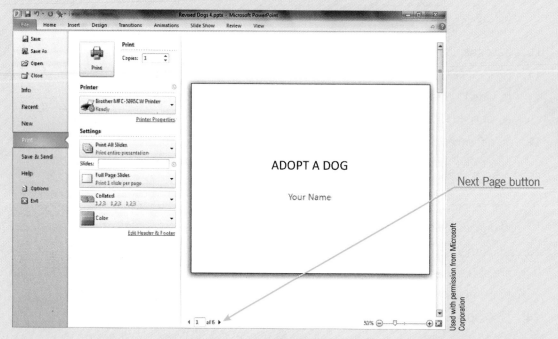

ADOPT A DOG

Your Name

Next Page button

Used with permission from Microsoft Corporation

3. In the middle pane, under Settings, the Print All Slides option is already selected, and a preview of the first slide as it will print appears in the right pane. At the bottom of the right pane, click the **Next Page** button ▶ to advance to the preview of slide 2. Note in the preview that each slide is on a separate page. If you were to print the slides, each slide would fill the page and would be printed in full color in landscape orientation.

4. In the middle pane, under Settings, click **Print All Slides**, and then click **Custom Range**. The insertion point is positioned in the Slides box. Type **1-3,6**. This custom range includes slides 1, 2, 3, and 6.

5. Under Settings, click **Full Page Slides**. Under Handouts, click the **6 Slides Horizontal** layout. Although you chose a layout for six slides, only four slides are displayed in the preview pane because you only identified four slides in the custom range. If you were to print the handouts, the page would be printed in full color in portrait orientation.

6. Under Settings, click **6 Slides Horizontal**. Under Handouts, click the **3 Slides** layout. The preview changes and now includes lines for notes next to each of the printed slides.

7. Under Settings, click **Custom Range,** and then click **Print All Slides**. Then click **3 Slides,** and under Print Layout, click the **Notes Pages** layout. At the bottom of the right pane, click the **Next Page** button to

advance to the preview of slides 3, 4, and 5. An image of each slide is displayed on a page by itself, and the notes from the Notes pane are displayed below the image. As you can see, there is plenty of white space on the page to add written notes. If you were to print the notes pages, each page would be printed in full color in portrait orientation.

8. Under Settings, click **Notes Pages,** and then, under Print Layout, click the **Outline** layout. A preview showing a list of all six slides is displayed in the preview pane. If the slide contains text in placeholders, that text is displayed in the outline. However, when you add a text box to a slide as you did for slide 3 in this presentation, the text box text is not displayed in the outline.

9. In the left pane, click **Save & Send**. In the middle pane, under File Types, click **Create Handouts**. In the right pane, click the **Create Handouts** button. The Send to Microsoft Word dialog box opens, displaying several options for page layouts.

10. In the Send to Microsoft Word dialog box, enable the option **Blank lines next to slides**, and then click **OK**. A new Word document is created and opened in the Word application. In the taskbar at the bottom of the screen, click the **Word** button.

11. Images of slides 1, 2, and 3 are positioned on the page with blank lines on the right side of each slide. Save the document as **Dogs Handouts**, followed by your initials. Close the Word document and the Word application.

12. Leave the presentation open for the next Step-by-Step.

Preparing Presentations for Distribution

When distributing electronic copies of the presentation, you can attach the file as an attachment to an e-mail message. Before sharing the presentation, you may want to control what others can see in the file. For example, you may not want them to see the author of the presentation or the date the presentation was created. Information like this can easily be removed from the file.

In Word, you learned how to save documents in PDF and XPS formats. You can also save presentations in these formats. Readers can see the slides, but they cannot edit the slides or use them in a slide show.

It is also common for presentations to be published on Web pages. Instructors of online courses often make course information available in this format. If you have a Windows Live account, you can quickly save the presentation in a Web format. Another way to distribute a presentation is to publish the presentation to a document management server or to a document workspace. Of course, you must be connected to a network or the Internet, and you must have sufficient bandwidth for transferring the electronic files. You must have authorization to publish to or access files from a document workspace or document management server. Accessing files in a document management server or creating a new document workspace is beyond the scope of this lesson.

QUICK TIP

A computer must be properly configured to output or receive and open PDF and XPS documents. Microsoft provides a free add-in that you can download so you can use the PDF and XPS formats.

Step-by-Step 22.10

2-4.1.8
2-4.1.9

1. If necessary, open the file **Revised Dogs 4** from your solution files. Save the Revised Dogs 4 presentation as **Revised Dogs 5**, followed by your initials.

2. Click the **File** tab. In the left pane, Info is already selected. In the middle pane, click the **Check for Issues** button, and then click **Inspect Document**. The Document Inspector dialog box opens.

3. Make sure all options are enabled, and then at the bottom of the dialog box, click **Inspect**.

4. The results are displayed in the Document Inspector dialog box. An exclamation point appears next to Document Properties and Personal Information and also next to Presentation Notes. Click both **Remove All** buttons in the dialog box to remove this information from the file.

5. The dialog box adapts to update the status. Click **Reinspect**, and then click **Inspect** to check one more time. Close the dialog box. Save the changes to the document.

6. Click the **File** tab, and then click **Save & Send**. In the middle pane, under Save & Send, the option Send Using E-mail is already selected. In the right pane, click the **Send as PDF** button. A new message window is opened in Outlook, and a PDF version of the document is already attached to the message. The presentation file format was converted to PDF, but the PDF file has not been saved on your system.

7. Close the Outlook application without saving any changes.

8. Click the **File** tab, and then click **Save & Send**. In the middle pane, under File Types, click **Create PDF/XPS Document**. In the right pane, click the **Create PDF/XPS** button. The Publish as PDF or XPS dialog box opens. Navigate to the folder where you save your solution files. If necessary, change the Save as type box setting to **PDF (*.pdf)**. Click **Publish**. The presentation opens in Adobe Reader.

9. Scroll through and preview the slides in PDF format, and then close the Adobe Reader application.

10. Click the **File** tab, and then click **Save & Send**. In the middle pane, under Save & Send, click **Save to Web**. In the right pane, there is a Sign-In button which allows you to sign in to Windows Live ID. Do not sign in. Instead, in the left pane, click **Close**.

ETHICS IN TECHNOLOGY

Respecting Intellectual Property

The term *intellectual property* is used to refer to information, material, or processes that were created by and belong to a person or corporation. Computers make it very easy to copy and disseminate art, documents, inventions, and music, and this has created many legal concerns about the rights of a creator.

Often people think that any information available on the Internet is in the public domain and free for the taking. This is not always the case. There are protections for intellectual property, including copyright for literary works, art, and music; patents for inventions and procedures; trademarks for company and product logos; and trade secrets, which include recipes, codes, and manufacturing processes. Be careful not to use protected material in your own work without securing permission from the person who owns the material. And when referencing this information in classroom assignments, give credit to those who own the material by citing sources in the slide show and in your presentation handouts.

SUMMARY

In this lesson, you learned:

- Graphics help to clarify the message of your presentation. Graphics can make your audience remember your message, and PowerPoint makes it easy for you to add graphics to a slide.

- You can create WordArt, drawn objects, and SmartArt graphics to add visual effects to slides.

- You can easily reposition and resize graphic objects on slides, and you can also format the objects with borders and shading.

- Placeholders make it easy to create a table or chart to illustrate numerical data or trends.

- You can add hyperlinks to text and graphics so you can link slides to other slides, other documents, or Web pages.

- The slide transition affects how each new slide appears. You can apply transition settings to a single slide or to all the slides in the presentation.

- PowerPoint provides special effects that can add emphasis, animation, or sound to the text and graphics, or that can enhance how a slide opens or closes.

- You can easily insert sound and video clips on slides and format the clips to play automatically.

- PowerPoint provides several options for printing a presentation, including slides, handouts, notes pages, and an outline of the slide show content.

LESSON REVIEW

TRUE / FALSE

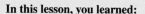

Circle T if the statement is true or F if the statement is false.

T   F   **1.**   You can create hyperlinks from text or a graphic object on a slide.

T   F   **2.**   You can choose a sound effect that plays as a transition occurs.

T   F   **3.**   Applying animations enables you to control how and when the text or graphics appear on each slide.

T   F   **4.**   By default, all media type files are embedded in the presentation file.

T   F   **5.**   When you insert a graphic in a placeholder, the placeholder is still visible.

MULTIPLE CHOICE

Select the best response for each of the following statements.

1. To add a graphic to a slide, insert _____ .

    A.   clip art and photographs from the Clip Art task pane

    B.   a picture from a file

    C.   a table or chart

    D.   any of the above

2. Animation effects are organized in four categories: Basic, Subtle, Moderate, and _____ .

    A.   Exciting   C.   Extreme

    B.   Intense   D.   Excessive

3. The print options for a presentation include _____ .

    A.   slides, handouts, and notes pages   C.   slides, handouts, speaker notes, and an outline

    B.   slides and notes pages   D.   handouts and notes pages

4. Sound effects can be applied to _____ .

    A.   objects   C.   text

    B.   slide transitions   D.   all of the above

5. _____ control how the object enters onto the slide.

    A.   Emphasis effects   C.   Slide transitions

    B.   Entrance effects   D.   all of the above

6. _____ control how an object leaves the slide.

    A.   Slide transitions   C.   Exit effects

    B.   Motion paths   D.   Motion paths

7. _____ draw attention to an object that is already visible on the slide.

    A.   Entrance effects   C.   Exit effects

    B.   Emphasis effects   D.   all of the above

8. A(n) _____ starts a sound effect or animation segment on a slide.

    A.   entrance effect   C.   slide transition

    B.   exit effect   D.   trigger

9. To share a presentation, you can _____ .

    A.   share the presentation via e-mail, Web pages, or over networks

    B.   print hard copies of slides, handouts, and notes

    C.   distribute electronic copies

    D.   all of the above

10. Before sharing a presentation, you can control the personal information users can see by _____ the file.

    A.   inspecting   C.   encrypting

    B.   protecting   D.   publishing

FILL IN THE BLANK

Complete the following sentences by writing the correct word or words in the blanks provided.

1. _____ are settings that determine how a slide is introduced in Slide Show view.

2. To resize a graphic proportionally, drag a(n) _____ sizing handle.

3. _____ are settings that control how a slide is introduced as you move from one slide to another in Slide Show view.

4. To add special visual or sound effects to text or an object on a slide, you must apply a(n) _____ .

5. _____ enable you to create a path for the object to follow on the slide.

■ PROJECTS

PROJECT 22–1

1. Open the file **Resort** from the drive and folder where your Data Files folder is stored. Save the Resort presentation as **Revised Resort**, followed by your initials.

2. Review the slide content, and apply an appropriate theme or background. Modify the color and/or font styles if desired.

3. Go to slide 2. Select the bulleted list, and convert the text to a SmartArt graphic using a List layout and design of your choice. Modify the colors if desired.

4. Go to slide 3. Insert clip art (an illustration or a photograph) that helps describe hiking or biking. (If you do not have an Internet connection, search for the keyword *nature* and choose an image.) Close the Clip Art task pane. Resize the graphic as necessary.

5. Go to slide 4. Insert clip art that helps describe the wildlife viewing. (If you do not have an Internet connection, search for the keyword *nature* and choose an image.) Close the Clip Art task pane. Resize and reposition the graphic as necessary.

6. Format a border for the graphics on slides 3 and 4, using border colors and weights that complement the graphics.

7. On slide 5, insert a 2 × 6 table, and add the data below. Resize and reposition the table as needed so it fits in the center of the slide, and, if desired, change the table style and colors.

Activity	Regulation
Fishing/crabbing	Permitted in designated areas
Hiking/biking	Trails open year round
Boats	Permitted from May 1 to October 1
Camping	Permitted from May 1 to October 1
Open fires	Prohibited except by permit

2-4.1.2
2-4.1.6
2-4.1.10
2-4.1.11

8. Go to slide 6. Remove the bullet format from the last line of text. Center the text for the URL, and then create a hyperlink to the URL.

9. Apply an appropriate slide transition to all the slides. Include sound effects if desired.

10. Preview the slide show, and make any necessary changes. Save the changes to the presentation.

11. Save the presentation in PDF format, using the same filename. Close the Adobe Reader application.

12. If time permits, practice giving the presentation in front of a group of classmates.

13. Close the presentation.

PROJECT 22–2

2-4.1.2
2-4.1.6
2-4.1.9

1. Open the file **Managing Time** from the drive and folder where your Data Files folder is stored. Save the Managing Time presentation as **Revised Managing Time**, followed by your initials.

2. Review the slide content, and apply an appropriate theme or background. Modify the color and/or font styles if desired. If necessary, reposition the text placeholders.

3. Go to slide 2. If you have access to the Internet, search the Clip Art task pane for videos that help describe "racing the clock." The video clip art is already formatted to play automatically. Resize and position the video object so it is an appropriate size and positioned in the center of the slide.

4. Go to slide 3. Insert a new slide with the Two Content layout. Add the title **Organize**. Then insert clip art (an illustration or a photograph) in the content placeholder on the left to illustrate a messy or cluttered desk, or an individual overwhelmed with work. Then insert clip art in the content placeholder on the right to illustrate organized documents, such as a file drawer or file cabinet. If you use a photograph on the left, then use a photograph on the right. Apply borders if desired. Resize the images as needed so they are approximately the same size, and position the objects side by side on the slide.

5. Add custom animation effects so the cluttered desk image appears first triggered by a click, and then the filing cabinet appears on the right triggered by a click. The cluttered desk should go away as the file cabinet appears. If desired, change the duration and delay settings for the animations.

6. Insert a new slide after slide 4, using the Comparison layout. Type the title **Plan Ahead**. In the subheading placeholder on the left, type **Daily/Weekly Planner**. In the subheading placeholder on the right, type **Monthly Planner**.

7. Insert appropriate clip art (illustration or photograph) below each subheading to illustrate using planners and calendars. If you use an illustration on the left, then use an illustration on the right. Resize and reposition the graphics as needed, and apply borders to the images if desired.

8. Insert a new slide after slide 5 with the Title and Content layout. Type the title **The clock is ticking…**.

9. Search the clip art gallery, and insert a video clip of a clock. Resize and position the clip as needed. From the clip art gallery, insert an audio clip of a clock ticking. Reposition the audio symbol in the lower-right corner of the slide. Format the audio clip to play automatically, hide the audio symbol during the show, and loop the audio clip until stopped.

10. Apply slide transitions with sound effects, if desired. Preview the presentation in Slide Show view.

11. Save the presentation.

12. Inspect the document, and remove the document properties, personal information, and the presentation notes. Save the changes and close the presentation.

PROJECT 22–3

2-4.1.2
2-4.1.6

1. Open the file **Community Report** from the drive and folder where your Data Files folder is stored. Save the Community Report presentation as **Revised Community Report**, followed by your initials.

2. Review the slide content, and apply an appropriate theme or background. Modify the color and/or font styles if desired. If necessary, reposition the text placeholders.

3. On slide 1, type your first and last name in the subtitle placeholder.

4. Go to slide 2. In the placeholder, create a Pie in 3-D chart by adding the data below in the Excel spreadsheet. Save the workbook as **Waste Info**, followed by your initials, and then close the Excel application.

	% of Waste
Residential	48.9
Commercial	36.7
Construction	8.9
Yard	5.5

5. Go to slide 3. In the placeholder on the right, insert the picture file **Bucket.jpg** from your Data Files folder.

6. Go to slide 6. In the placeholder, insert a 5 × 5 table, and enter the data below in the Word table. Adjust the table size and formats as needed.

	1995	2000	2005	2010
Aluminum	18%	21%	29%	37%
Glass	12%	14%	19%	23%
Paper	22%	39%	44%	49%
Plastics	3%	5%	6%	7%

7. Go to slide 7. Insert a new slide with the Title and Content layout. On the new slide 8, in the content placeholder, insert the media clip **Recycle Video.wmv** from your Data Files folder. Format the video to play automatically. Hide the image during the show, and enable the settings so the movie fills the screen when playing.

8. Go to slide 7, and format a transition so the slide show advances automatically after 2 seconds.

9. Go to slide 3. Click anywhere within the bulleted list. Apply the Wipe animation, and format the bulleted items to enter the slide from the left. By default, the bulleted items will appear one paragraph at a time. Change the duration setting to 01.50. Go to slides 4 and 5, and apply the same settings for the bulleted lists on those slides.

10. Go to slide 3, and apply an animation to the picture so the picture fades in. Change the duration setting to 03.00.

11. Go to slide 1, and view the slide show. After the Make a Difference slide appears, you should not have to click. The next slide appears automatically, and the video starts. Exit Slide Show view and return to Normal view.

12. Save the changes, and close the presentation.

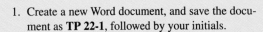
 TEAMWORK PROJECT

PowerPoint provides many features that empower you to be creative and show your preferences of styles. Choose a partner, and review your solution files for Projects 22–1, –2, and –3 in this lesson with each other. Explain to your partner why you chose the themes, colors, graphics, slide transitions, and sound effects for each presentation. Ask your partner to provide constructive feedback regarding whether or not he or she thinks your choices were effective.

1. Create a new Word document, and save the document as **TP 22-1**, followed by your initials. 2-4.1.12

2. Write a brief summary of the feedback you received from your partner about your choice of designs and effects.

3. Save the changes, and close the document.

■ CRITICAL THINKING

CRITICAL THINKING 22–1

You have prepared a presentation with 32 slides. Most of the slides include a title and a picture or a graphic, and only a few of the slides included bulleted lists with text. You added comments in the Notes pane as reminders for the key points related to each slide. You will be presenting the slide show in a few days. Consider all the printing options, and then choose which option would be most useful to you when showing the slide show in front of an audience.

2-4.1.8
2-4.1.9

1. Create a new Word document, and save the document as **CT 22-1**, followed by your initials.

2. Write a few sentences explaining which print option you would use and why.

3. Save the changes, and close the document.

CRITICAL THINKING 22–2

Explore the photo album templates available in PowerPoint by clicking **File** and then clicking **New**. Under Available Templates and Themes, click **Sample templates**. You will see the Classic Photo Album, Contemporary Photo Album, and Urban Photo Album templates. If you have access to the Internet, explore more photo album templates at Office.com. Review the features provided in the templates, such as backgrounds, themes, layouts, captions, and frames.

2-4.1.12

1. Create a new Word document, and save the document as **CT 22-2**, followed by your initials.

2. Describe the features in the templates that help you easily create a professional photo album.

3. Save the changes to the Word document.

■ ONLINE DISCOVERY

Microsoft provides thousands of free clip art—images, photographs, and movie and sound clips—at Microsoft Office Online. Choose a topic that interests you, such as basketball or mountain climbing. Explore the free clip art and media at www.microsoft.com to see what is available for that topic. Then search the Internet for other Web sites that offer free clip art, free photographs, and free sound and video clips. Explore and evaluate three to five Web sites.

1. Create a new Word document, and save the document as **OD 22-1**, followed by your initials.

2. Write a few sentences about each site explaining whether you believe that the site is credible and if the media is truly free and in the public domain. Also comment on whether the site offers quality images and media. 2-4.1.2

3. Save the changes to the document.

■ JOB SKILLS

You have been chosen to lead a group project for a fundraiser. You decide the best way to prepare for the first meeting is to create a presentation with the meeting agenda.

1. Create a new presentation, and save it as **JS 22-1**, followed by your initials. Develop at least five slides with an agenda to cover the following topics:

   a. Introduce group members.

   b. Set fund-raising goal to raise $1,000.

   c. Brainstorm ideas.

   d. Assign tasks.

   e. Schedule next meeting.

2. Apply an appropriate design and format the slides as desired. Save the changes and close the presentation.

3. Create a new Word document, and save the document as **JS 22-1**, followed by your initials.

2-4.1.8
2-4.1.12

4. Write a brief summary explaining how you plan to distribute the meeting agenda prior to the meeting.

5. Save the changes, and close the Word document.

LESSON 23

Getting Started with Access Essentials

■ OBJECTIVES

Upon completion of this lesson, you should be able to:

- Identify the parts of the Access screen.
- Identify and navigate objects in a database.
- Create a database, then create a new table and enter records in Datasheet view.
- Change the column width in a table in Datasheet view.
- Add and delete fields in Design view.
- Change field data types and field properties.
- Add and edit records in a table in Datasheet view.
- Delete and copy records and fields in Datasheet view.

■ WORDS TO KNOW

data type

database

datasheet

entry

field

field name

field properties

primary key

record

relational database

■ DATA FILES

To complete this lesson, you will need these data files:

Classic Books.accdb

Community Club.accdb

Films.accdb

A *database* is a collection of related information. Databases can contain all types of data—from an address list to schedules for a soccer tournament. Access is the Microsoft Office database program that enables you to organize, retrieve, and analyze data in many ways.

You might wonder what the difference is between an Excel spreadsheet and an Access database. Actually, there are many similarities in both applications. Like spreadsheets, databases are composed of rows and columns. While both applications enable you to organize, sort, and calculate the data, Access offers much more comprehensive functions for manipulating data. Access is a relational database management system. In a *relational database*, information is organized into separate subject-based tables, and the relationship of the data in one or more tables is used to bring the data together. For example, a relational database can be used to track the customers, orders, and inventory for a retail business. One table stores information about the customers, one table stores information about the customers' orders, and yet another table stores product information. In Access, the information in the tables can be used to generate invoices based on customer orders. The invoices contain contact information from the customer table, as well as product details from the products table. If the business is planning to send out notices of a sale on a certain product brand, Access can quickly use the information in the orders table and the customers table to generate mailing labels for all those customers who have purchased products of that brand in the past.

Furthermore, in Access you can import or link data from other Access databases, Excel, Outlook, and many other data sources. And, Access data can be exported to many other data formats for use in other applications. Access is a powerful program that offers many features, most of which are beyond the scope of this course. The Access lessons in this module will introduce you to some of the basic features for viewing, entering, editing, querying, and reporting data.

Identifying the Parts of the Access Screen

The Access screen is similar to other Office 2010 applications, with the title bar, Ribbon, Quick Access Toolbar, application window sizing buttons, Close button, and status bar. You can open only one database at a time in an Access window. To open a new database in the application window, you will need to close the current database. If you would like to work with multiple databases at the same time, you can launch Access multiple times and then open a different database in each application window.

Unlike Word and Excel, Access does not have a standard document view. An Access database is composed of objects of several different types. The Access document window changes based on the object you are working with. **Table 23–1** describes four basic objects (tables, forms, reports, and queries) that you will work with in this lesson and in Lesson 24. These objects help you organize and report the information that is stored in the database.

TABLE 23–1   Basic database objects

OBJECT	PURPOSE
Table	Stores data in columns and rows; all data is stored in a table
Form	Makes it easy for you to view, enter, and edit data in a table
Report	Organizes data in a specific layout
Query	Finds and shows data that meet a specified criteria

The objects are organized into categories in the Navigation Pane so you can quickly find and access the objects. The Navigation Pane can be collapsed to allow more space for the object.

Step-by-Step 23.1

1. Launch **Microsoft Access 2010**. Backstage view, shown in **Figure 23–1**, opens. Do not be concerned that the files listed in the left pane are different. Up to 17 most recently accessed files can be displayed in this list.

Open command

Most recently accessed files

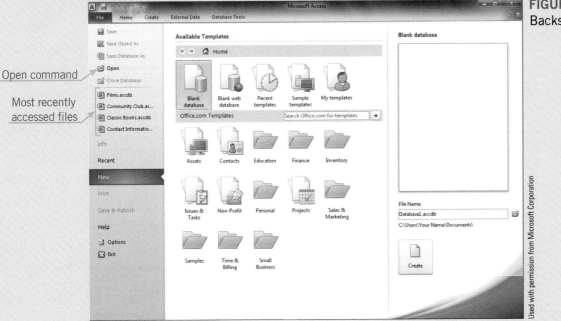

FIGURE 23–1
Backstage view

Used with permission from Microsoft Corporation

2. In the left pane, click **Open**. In the Open dialog box, navigate to the drive and folder where your Data Files folder is stored. Select the filename **Community Club**, and then click **Open**. The Community Club : Database (Access 2007) window, similar to that shown in **Figure 23–2**, is displayed. If a yellow Security Warning message pane appears below the Ribbon, click **Enable Content**.

FIGURE 23–2
Community Club :
Database (Access 2007)
window

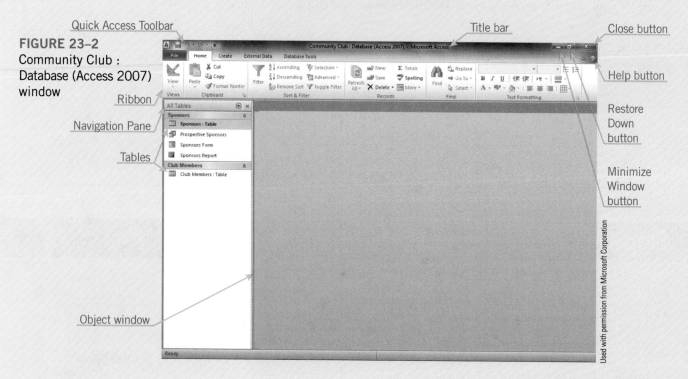

Quick Access Toolbar

Ribbon

Navigation Pane

Tables

Object window

Title bar

Close button

Help button

Restore
Down
button

Minimize
Window
button

Used with permission from Microsoft Corporation

3. Compare your screen with the figure, and identify the parts of the Access window to familiarize yourself with the application. There are two tables in this database: Sponsors and Club Members.

4. Click the **File** tab. In the left pane, click **Save Database As** to open the Save As dialog box. The current filename with a *1* at the end is already displayed and is selected in the File name box. Navigate to your solution folder, type **Updated Community Club**, followed by your initials, and then click **Save**. If a yellow Security Warning message pane appears below the Ribbon, click **Enable Content**.

5. In the Navigation Pane, under Sponsors, double-click **Sponsors : Table** to open the Sponsors table. The table shown in **Figure 23–3** opens in the object window.

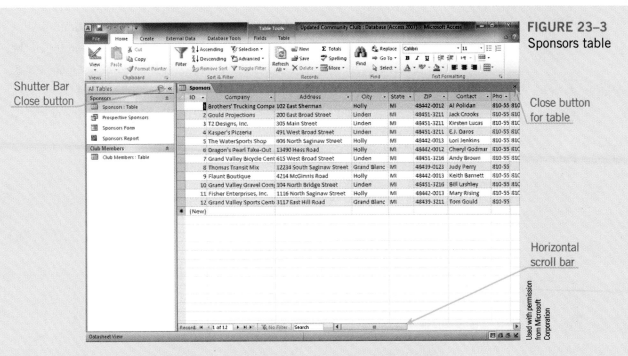

FIGURE 23-3
Sponsors table

6. To allow more space to show the table contents, in the Navigation Pane, click the **Shutter Bar Close** button. The Navigation Pane collapses, as shown in **Figure 23–4**, and you can see more of the table columns. Drag the scroll box on the horizontal scroll bar (at the bottom of the screen) to view the columns to the right. This table provides data about companies that currently provide sponsorship for a club as well as companies that could potentially become sponsors.

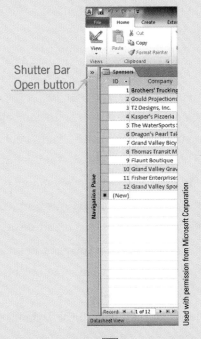

FIGURE 23-4
Collapsed Navigation Pane

7. Click the **Shutter Bar Open** button to expand the Navigation Pane and show the objects in the database.

8. In the Navigation Pane, under Club Members, double-click **Club Members : Table**, and the Club Members table opens on top of the Sponsors table and becomes the active table, as shown in **Figure 23–5**. The table icon is also displayed on the new object tab. In the Object window, click the **Sponsors** object tab to show the Sponsors table.

FIGURE 23–5
Club Members table

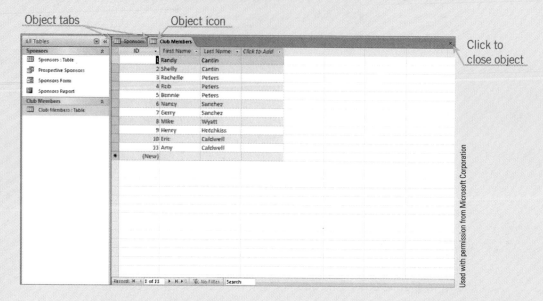

Used with permission from Microsoft Corporation

9. At the upper-right corner of the object window, click the **Close** button for the table. The Sponsors table closes, but the Club Members table is still open.

10. In the Navigation Pane, under Sponsors, double-click **Sponsors Form**. On top of the Club Members table object, a form object is displayed in Form view, which makes it easy for you to enter data. All data entered in the form is saved in the Sponsors table.

11. In the Navigation Pane, under Sponsors, double-click **Prospective Sponsors**, and a query object opens on top of the Sponsors Form object. Note the Query icon is displayed on the object tab. This query object finds and shows only the companies that are considered to be prospective sponsors. The information comes from the Sponsors table.

12. In the Navigation Pane, under Sponsors, double-click **Sponsors Report**. A report object opens on top of the query object and shows the data contained in the Sponsors table in a report design.

13. In the object window, click the **Sponsors Form** object tab. Then click the **Prospective Sponsors** object tab. Four objects are open, but you can only work with one object at a time.

14. Click the **File** tab, and then click **Close Database**. The objects and the database are closed, and the application window displays Backstage view. Leave Access open.

Creating a New Database

You can create a new database file using a blank database template or by using templates that are predefined with objects already created. In this lesson you will learn to create tables, and in Lesson 24 you will learn to create reports, forms, and queries. Then when you open a predesigned database template, you will be familiar with all the elements of each type of object, and you will be able to modify and customize the objects as needed.

Saving a Database File and Creating a Table in Datasheet View

When you create a new database, the first step is to create a table. A table, often referred to as a *datasheet*, is the primary object in the database. Each of the objects and everything you do in a database relies on the data stored in the tables. Therefore, at least one table must be created before any additional objects can be created. You can create as many tables as you need to store the information.

A database table contains fields and records. A *field* is a single piece of database information, such as a first name, a last name, or a telephone number. Fields are displayed as columns, and each column has a *field name*, which is a label that helps identify the field. When you create a new field, you can choose a *data type*, which determines the type of data the field can store, such as text or numbers. A *record* is a group of related fields in a database, such as all the contact information for an individual, including first and last name, address, postal code, telephone number, and so forth. When you create a table in Access, the default setting creates a primary key for each record, which uniquely identifies each record in the table. The *primary key* is useful in sorting records, and it prevents duplicate entries. For example, you may have a student ID number, and no other student has exactly the same number as you.

By default, a table opens in Datasheet view, and the table data is shown in a row-and-column format. In this view, the table looks much like a spreadsheet. The intersection of a row and a column is called a cell, just as in an Excel worksheet. Field names are used for column headings, and each row in the table contains one single record of the entire database.

> **VOCABULARY**
> datasheet
> field
> field name
> data type
> record
> primary key

Step-by-Step 23.2

1. If necessary, launch **Access**. The application window should display Backstage view.

2. In the right pane, in the File Name box shown in **Figure 23–6**, replace the default filename with **Customers 1**, followed by your initials.

New filename

New path

Browse button

3. To the right of the File Name box, click the **Browse** button. The File New Database dialog box opens. Navigate to the drive and folder where you save your solution files. Click **OK**. The new path is displayed under the File Name box as shown in Figure 23–6.

4. Click the **Create** button. A new database window like the one shown in **Figure 23–7** opens.

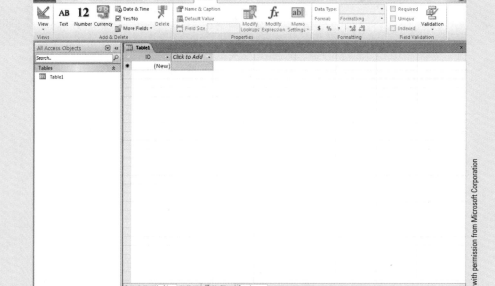

5. In the second column of the table, click the **Click to Add** column heading to display the menu for data types. Click **Text**. When the column heading is replaced with the default field name *Field1*, type **Last Name** and press **Enter**. The new field name appears in the column heading, the insertion point moves to the first cell in the third column, and the menu of data types is displayed.

6. In the menu, click **Text**. Then type **Address**, and press **Enter**. The insertion point moves to the first cell in the fourth column, and the menu with data types is displayed.

7. Continue using the same procedure to enter the following additional field names. The Postal Code field should also be assigned the Text data type instead of the Number data type because the postal codes will include a hyphen, which is not considered a number.

```
City
State/Province
Postal Code
Country/Region
```

8. On the Quick Access Toolbar, click the **Save** button. Because the table has not been assigned a name, the Save As dialog box opens. In the Table Name text box, type **Contact Information**, and then click **OK**. The new table name appears in the Navigation Pane.

9. To create a second table in the database, on the Ribbon, click the **Create** tab. In the Tables group shown in **Figure 23–8**, click the **Table** button. A new table is displayed in the object window on top of the Contact Information table, and the Navigation Pane also shows the new table, which is currently labeled *Table1*.

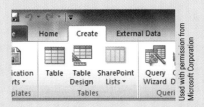

FIGURE 23–8
Tables group on the Create tab

10. The Ribbon adapts and now shows the Table Tools Fields tab. In the Add & Delete group shown in **Figure 23–9**, click the **More Fields** button.

FIGURE 23–9
Add & Delete group on the Table Tools Fields tab

11. The menu shown in **Figure 23–10** opens to show a list of built-in fields. Scroll down to the bottom of the menu. Under Quick Start, click **Name**. The field name *Last Name* is now displayed at the top of the second column, and the field name *First Name* is now displayed at the top of the third column.

FIGURE 23–10
Menu of built-in fields

Used with permission from Microsoft Corporation

12. In the Add & Delete group, click the **Text** button. A new text field is added at the top of the fourth column. Type **Item** to replace the default field name *Field1*. Click the **Text** button again, and type **Description**. Click the **Text** button once more, type **Purchase Price**, and press **Enter**. The new table now has six column headings, including the ID column.

13. On the Quick Access Toolbar, click the **Save** button. In the Table Name box, type **Orders**, and then click **OK**. The database now has two tables, and both tables are open. In the upper-right corner of the Orders table, click the **Close** button. Then in the upper-right corner of the Contact Information table, click the **Close** button.

14. Leave the database open for the next Step-by-Step.

Entering Records in Datasheet View

When you enter data into a cell, you are making an *entry*. To move from one cell to another, you can use the mouse to click in a cell. You can also use the keyboard to navigate in a table. **Table 23–2** describes the keys you can use to move around in a table in Datasheet view.

▶ **VOCABULARY**
entry

TABLE 23–2   Keys for navigating in Datasheet view

KEY	DESCRIPTION
Enter, Tab, or right arrow	Moves the insertion point to the next field
Left arrow or Shift+Tab	Moves the insertion point to the previous field
Home	Moves the insertion point to the first field in the current record
End	Moves the insertion point to the last field in the current record
Up arrow	Moves the insertion point up one record and stays in the same field
Down arrow	Moves the insertion point down one record and stays in the same field
Page Up	Moves the insertion point up one screen
Page Down	Moves the insertion point down one screen

Step-by-Step 23.3

1. If necessary, open the **Customers 1** database from your solution files. Save the Customers 1 database as **Customers 2**, followed by your initials. If a Security Warning message pane appears below the Ribbon, click **Enable Content**.

2. In the Navigation Pane, under Tables, double-click **Contact Information** to open the table.

3. To enter the first record, press **Tab** to move to the cell under the field name *Last Name*, and type **McGuirk**. Note that as you create the entry in the Last Name field, Access automatically assigns the primary key *1* in the ID field.

4. Press **Tab** to move to the next field, and complete the record by entering the following information in the respective fields:

Address:	**610 Brae Burn**
City:	**Mansfield**
State/Province:	**OH**
Postal Code:	**44907-1112**
Country/Region:	**USA**

5. Press **Tab** twice to move to the Last Name field in the next row. Enter the following data for two more records:

Last Name:	**Bain**
Address:	**117 Yorkshire Road**
City:	**Lexington**
State/Province:	**OH**
Postal Code:	**44904-3455**
Country/Region:	**USA**

Last Name:	**Smith**
Address:	**4645 Rule Road**
City:	**Bellville**
State/Province:	**OH**
Postal Code:	**44813-3231**
Country/Region:	**USA**

6. On the Quick Access Toolbar, click the **Save** button. All the changes to the database are now saved. Close the table.

7. Leave the database open for the next Step-by-Step.

Modifying a Database Table in Design View

The default column widths are often too wide or too narrow for the data in the table. This is the case with your database. The Address field is not wide enough to show all the text in the street address, and the ID field has extra white space. You can adjust the column widths in a database table just as you adjust the column widths in an Excel spreadsheet.

Adding and Deleting Fields

Often, after you create a table and enter data, you decide you want to add or delete fields. You can add fields in either Datasheet view or Design view. However, Design view provides features that make the task easier. Design view shows details about the structure of the object, including the data type and the field properties. *Field properties* define the characteristics and behavior of a field, such as the number of characters allowed.

▶ **VOCABULARY**
field properties

Step-by-Step 23.4

1. If necessary, open the **Customers 2** database from your solution files. Save the Customers 2 database as **Customers 3**, followed by your initials. If you see a Security Warning message panel, click **Enable Content**. Open the **Contact Information** table.

2. Point to the right border of the cell containing the field name (column heading) *Address*. When the pointer changes to a column border resize pointer ↔, click and then drag the **column border** to the right until the column is wide enough to show the complete entry for all records.

3. Point to the **ID** field name column heading. When the column border resize pointer appears, double-click and the width of the ID column is automatically adjusted for the contents in the column.

4. Position the mouse pointer over the field name *Address*. When the pointer changes to a down arrow ↓, click and drag the pointer to the right to the column heading *Country/Region*. Five columns are now selected. Position the mouse pointer over the right border for the column heading *Country/Region*. When the mouse pointer changes to a column border resize pointer, double-click. The widths for all the selected columns are automatically adjusted for the contents in each column.

5. Click the first cell in the first data row of the table, **1**. On the Home tab, in the Views group, click the **View** button arrow, and then click **Design View**.

> **QUICK TIP**
>
> The upper portion of the button always shows the icon for an alternative view, which you can click to switch to that view. For example, when you are in Design view, the upper portion of the View button shows the icon for Datasheet view. Clicking the upper portion toggles your view to Datasheet view.

6. The table is displayed in Design view, as shown in **Figure 23–11**. The Ribbon adapts to show the Table Tools Design tab. In the Tools group, the Primary Key button is highlighted, indicating that the Primary Key field is selected. In the table, the field names are displayed in the first column, and the data type for each field is displayed in the second column. Field properties for the active field are displayed in a pane at the bottom of the window.

FIGURE 23–11
Contact Information
table in Design view

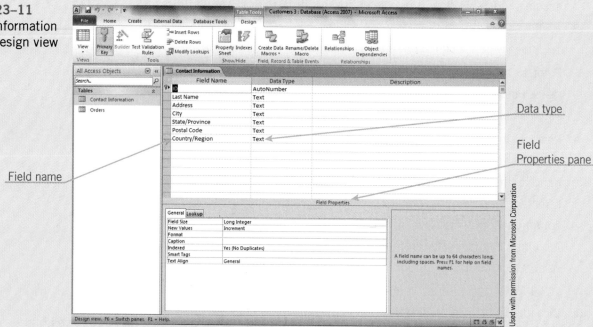

7. Position the mouse pointer to the left of the *Country/Region* field name. When a right-pointing arrow ➡ appears, as shown in **Figure 23–12**, click to select the entire row.

FIGURE 23–12
Selecting a row

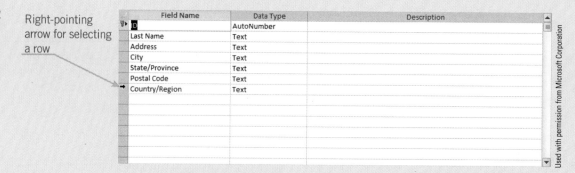

8. On the Table Tools Design tab, in the Tools group, click the **Insert Rows** button. Click the blank cell directly below the field name *Postal Code*. Type **Email**, and press **Enter**. The new field is entered, and the Data Type cell to the right is active and shows the default data type, Text.

9. Edit the field name *Email* so it reads **E-mail**.

10. Click the blank cell directly below the field name *Country/Region*. Type **Birth Date**, and press **Enter**. The new field is entered, and the Data Type cell to the right is active and shows the default data type, Text.

11. Select the row for the field name *Last Name*, and click the **Insert Rows** button. In the blank cell above the field name *Last Name*, type **First Name**, and then press **Enter**.

12. Select the row containing the *Country/Region* field. In the Tools group on the Table Tools Design tab, click the **Delete Rows** button. When prompted to permanently delete the selected field and all the data in the field, click **Yes**. The field and all the data entered in the field are removed from the table.

13. Save the changes to the table, and then close the table.

14. Leave the database open for the next Step-by-Step.

Changing Field Data Type and Field Properties

As you saw in the previous Step-by-Step, the default data type for a field is Text. In Design view, you can specify the data type for each field. For example, you can specify Text, Number, Currency, and even Yes/No. Text is appropriate for most of the fields in the Contact Information table. However, for some fields, such as the Birth Date field, you may want to specify a Date/Time data type instead of Text.

When you choose a data type, you can also change the field properties. The field properties available depend on the data type selected. For example, the default Field Size property for the Text data type is 255 characters, but you can specify that the field allow up to only 50 characters. Most data types include a Format property. The Format property specifies how you want Access to show numbers, dates, times, and text.

Step-by-Step 23.5

1. If necessary, open the **Customers 3** database from your solution files. Save the Customers 3 database as **Customers 4**, followed by your initials. If you see a Security Warning message panel, click **Enable Content**. Open the **Contact Information** table.

2. On the Home tab, in the Views group, click the **View** button arrow, and then click **Design View**.

3. In the Birth Date row, click the **Text** data type cell for the field. When the list arrow appears at the right side of the cell, click it to open the list of data type options. Click **Date/Time** to change the data type. The Field Properties pane changes to show the values for the Date/Time data type.

4. In the Field Properties pane, in the first row, click the **Format** property box, the cell to the right of *Format*. When the Format property list arrow is displayed in the empty cell, click it to open the list of Format property options shown in **Figure 23–13**. In the list of options, click **Short Date**.

FIGURE 23–13
Date/Time field format property options

Selected data type

Click here

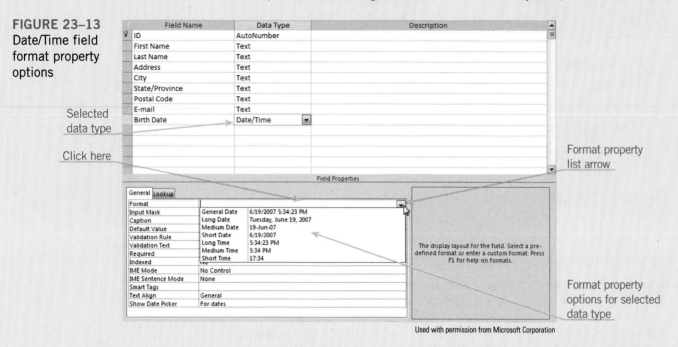

Format property list arrow

Format property options for selected data type

Used with permission from Microsoft Corporation

5. In the State/Province row, click the **Text** data type cell for the field. In the Field Properties pane below, click the **Field Size** property box. The field size is currently set at 255. Change the field size to 2. This requires that the user use two-letter state abbreviations when entering the state name in the table.

6. Click the **View** button to toggle to Datasheet view. You must save changes to objects before you switch views, so when prompted to save the table, click **Yes**. When prompted that some data may be lost, click **Yes** to continue.

7. Click the **Shutter Bar Close** button to collapse the Navigation Pane.

8. Enter the following data in the First Name, E-mail, and Birth Date fields. As you enter the birth date data, Access automatically formats the date using the short date format you specified in the field properties.

ID	First Name	E-mail	Birth Date
1	Jaimey	jmcguirk@nets.xyz	March 13, 1982
2	Jesse	jbain@lfsc.xyz	June 18, 1984
3	Matt	msmith@qry.xyz	April 11, 1983

9. Enter the following new record. Remember that as you enter the state name, Access will not permit you to enter more than two characters. You must enter the two-letter state abbreviation for Ohio.

First Name:	**Kelsey**
Last Name:	**Erwin**
Address:	**2038 Leiter Road**
City:	**Lucas**
State/Province:	**Ohio**
Postal Code:	**44843-3197**
E-mail:	**kerwin@csfa.xyz**
Birth Date:	**October 6, 1983**

10. Select the **E-mail** and **Birth Date** columns and automatically adjust the column widths. Click one of the entries in the table to deselect the columns.

11. Click the **Shutter Bar Open** button to expand the Navigation Pane.

12. Save the changes to the table, and then close the table.

13. Click the **File** tab, and then click **Close Database**.

Adding and Editing Database Records

It is common for data to change after you have entered it into your database. For example, people move, so you have to change their addresses and probably their phone numbers. Access provides several navigation features that make it easy for you to move around in a table to make necessary edits. These features are especially useful when you are working in large databases.

If you make a mistake adding or editing data in a record, you can choose the Undo command to reverse your last action. As soon as you begin editing another record, however, the Undo command is no longer available. That is because Access constantly saves the changes. As you experienced in the previous Step-by-Step, when you make changes in Design view and then switch to Datasheet view without first saving the object, Access prompts you to save the changes. However, when you work in Datasheet view, the changes are saved as they are made. When you switch from Datasheet view to a different view, or when you close the database, you are not prompted to save the changes because they were already saved.

Step-by-Step 23.6

1. Open the database **Classic Books** from the drive and folder where your Data Files folder is stored. Save the Classic Books database as **Revised Classic Books 1**, followed by your initials. If you see a Security Warning message panel, click **Enable Content**.

2. Open the **Classics** table. An orange highlight indicates that the first cell in the table (ID number *1*) is the active cell.

3. In the Navigation bar, shown at the bottom of the table in **Figure 23-14**, click the **Next record** navigation button ▶. The highlight moves to the ID number 2 in the second row in the table.

FIGURE 23-14
Navigation bar

4. In the Navigation bar, click the **Previous record** navigation button ◀ to move back to ID number 1. The highlight moves to a new row, and the active cell is still in the ID field.

5. In the middle of the navigation buttons, in the Current Record number box, select the number **1**, and type **23**. Press **Enter**. The highlight moves to the cell in the ID field with the ID number 23.

6. Click the ID field entry **23**. Press **Tab** twice to move the insertion point to the Author First field in the same row. The entry in that cell is selected. Type **John** to change the entry. Note that a pencil (an Edit Record icon) ✎ appears at the left edge of the row, indicating the record is being edited.

7. Click the **Next record** navigation button. The highlight moves to the next row in the Author First field, and the entry in that cell is selected. The pencil is no longer displayed to the left of row 23 because when you clicked the Next record navigation button, the edit was completed. When you navigate out of the row, the entry is updated.

8. Click the **First record** navigation button ◀◀. The insertion point moves to the Author First field in the first row in the table.

9. Click the **Last record** navigation button ▶▶. The insertion point moves to the Author First field in the last row in the table.

10. Click the **Previous record** navigation button two times to move up two rows. Press **Tab** two times to move to the Cover field in the same row. Type **Paperback** to replace the entry. Press **Tab** to move to the # Pages field.

11. The last change was not necessary, and because you have not navigated out of the row, the changes have not been updated and you can undo the edit. On the Quick Access Toolbar, click the **Undo** button. The action is reversed, and the cell shows *Hardcover*.

12. Save the changes to the table, and then close the table. Leave the table and the database open for the next Step-by-Step.

Deleting and Copying Records and Fields in Datasheet View

Deleting records is similar to deleting rows in an Excel spreadsheet. To delete a record, you must first select the record. You can delete multiple records at the same time by selecting more than one row. After a record is selected, you can press the Delete key to remove the data. Take care, though. Once you have deleted a record, you cannot use the Undo command to restore it.

Selected data can also be copied or moved from one location in an Access table to a new location within the same table or to a different table. The Cut, Copy, and Paste commands you have used in other Office applications are also available in Access. Access stores cut or copied text in the Clipboard.

To remove a table field and all the data for the field, you delete the column, similar to how you delete a column in Excel. To change the sequence of the fields in the table, you can rearrange the sequence of the columns.

Step-by-Step 23.7

1. If necessary, open the **Revised Classic Books 1** database from your solution files. Save the Revised Classic Books 1 database as **Revised Classic Books 2**, followed by your initials. If you see a Security Warning message panel, click **Enable Content**.

2. Open the **Classics** table. Collapse the Navigation Pane. In the group of navigation buttons at the bottom of the table, click the **New (blank) record** button. The first empty cell in the ID field is highlighted.

3. Press **Tab** to move to the Title field. Access automatically inserts an ID number for the primary key when you begin to enter data. Enter the following data for the new record. Press **Enter** after you enter the price.

Title:	`Crime and Punishment`
Author First:	`Fyodor`
Author Last:	`Dostoyevsky`
Cover:	`Hardcover`
Pages:	`499`
Publisher:	`HarperCollins Publishers, Inc.`
Price:	`16.99`

4. Point to the left of the record with the ID field 26 (Lord Jim). When the pointer changes to a right-pointing arrow, click to select the entire row.

5. Press **Delete**. When prompted to confirm the deletion of the record, click **Yes**. The record is deleted from the table. Note that the ID numbers for the records below the deleted row do not change.

6. Point to the left of the ID field 27 (Emma). When the pointer changes to a right-pointing arrow, click to select the entire row.

7. In the Clipboard group, click the **Copy** button, point to the left of the ID field in the empty row (New) at the bottom of the table. When the pointer changes to a right-pointing arrow, click to select the entire row.

8. In the Clipboard group, click the **Paste** button to paste a copy of record 27 in the new row. Change the title to **Northanger Abbey**, the number of pages to **230**, and the publisher to **Modern Classics Library**. Press **Enter**.

9. If necessary, drag the horizontal scroll box to the left to show the ID column. In the record 30 row (The Hunchback of Notre-Dame), double-click the Cover field entry **Paperback**, and then press **Ctrl+C** to copy the entry.

10. In the new Northanger Abbey record row, double-click the Cover field entry **Hardcover**, and then press **Ctrl+V** to replace the entry with the data on the Clipboard (*Paperback*).

11. Position the mouse pointer over the field name *# Pages*. When the pointer changes to a down-pointing arrow, click to select the entire column.

12. Click the **Table Tools Fields** tab. In the Add & Delete group, click the **Delete** button. When prompted to permanently delete the fields and data, click **Yes**.

13. Select the **Publisher** column. Click and drag the **column heading** to the left. When the black vertical border shown in **Figure 23–15** appears to the left of the Cover column, release the mouse button. The Publisher column is repositioned and now appears before the Cover column.

FIGURE 23–15
Repositioning a table column

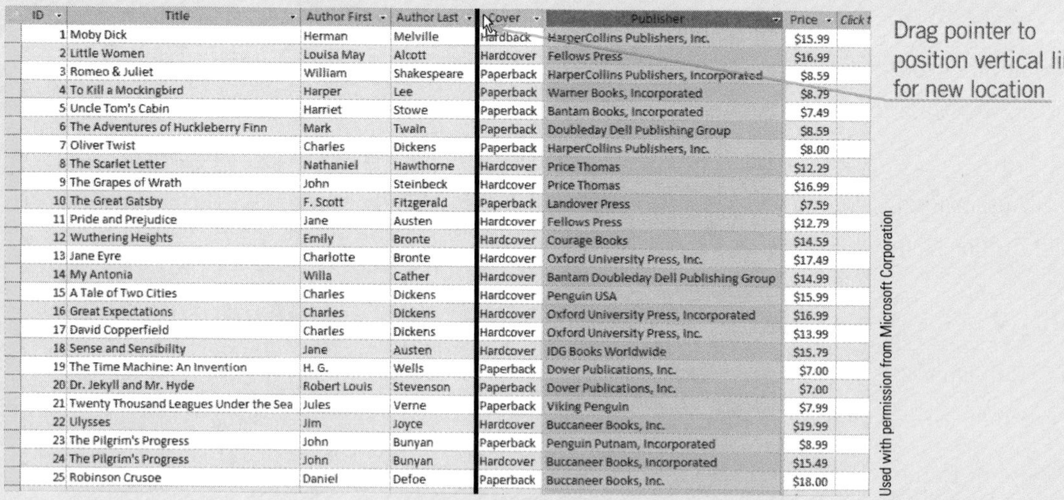

Drag pointer to position vertical line for new location

14. Save the changes to the table, and then close the database.

TECHNOLOGY CAREERS

Database Security

Protecting data is more important than ever, and securing database systems is taken very seriously as networks are progressively opened to wider access, especially access to the Internet. Hackers are not just attacking large corporations to steal information such as credit card numbers. They are also attacking smaller organizations and accessing sensitive data such as financial transactions, medical records, and Social Security numbers.

To protect against such compromises, companies of all sizes depend upon several levels of security controls to protect the network, host, and applications used to store data. Specialists in implementing security measures are needed for the software development process as well as on an ongoing basis to anticipate and safeguard against threats.

SUMMARY

In this lesson, you learned:

- Many parts of the Access screen are similar to other Office 2010 applications. However, Access also has different views to perform tasks unique to Access.

- The first step in creating a new database is to create a table. Tables are the primary objects in a database. A database can have multiple tables. All other objects are based on data stored in tables.

- You can automatically adjust table column widths in Datasheet view similar to how you adjust column widths in Excel.

- A table can be modified after it is created, and you can add or delete fields in the table even after records have been entered. You can modify a table in Datasheet view or in Design view.

- You can easily switch between Design view and Datasheet view, but you must save changes and close a table before switching views.

- In Design view, you can specify the data type and properties for each field. The field properties control the characteristics

- and behavior of a database field, such as the maximum number of characters.

- If you make a mistake adding or editing data in a record, you can choose the Undo command to reverse your last action, but only if the changes have not yet been updated. Once you navigate to another record, the Undo command is no longer available.

- Deleting records is similar to deleting rows in Excel. Once you have deleted a record, you cannot use the Undo command to restore it.

- Selected data can be copied or moved from one location to another in an Access table, or to another table, using the Cut, Copy, and Paste commands.

- To change the sequence of fields in a table, you rearrange the sequence of columns.

◼ LESSON REVIEW

TRUE / FALSE

Circle T if the statement is true or F if the statement is false.

T   F   **1.**   A database is a collection of related information.

T   F   **2.**   You can open only one database at a time in an Access application window.

T   F   **3.**   In Access, you can import or link data from other Access databases, Excel, Outlook, and many other data sources.

T   F   **4.**   By default, a table opens in Design view.

T   F   **5.**   You can drag a column border to adjust column widths in a database table.

MULTIPLE CHOICE

Select the best response for each of the following statements.

1. _____ view shows the table data in a row-and-column format.

   A. Datasheet   C. Table

   B. Design   D. Normal

2. A _____ is a single piece of information in a database, such as a first name, a last name, or a telephone number.

   A. record   C. column

   B. row   D. field

3. The _____ uniquely identifies each record in a table.

   A. field name   C. entry number

   B. primary key   D. none of the above

4. A database table contains _____.

   A. fields   C. primary key

   B. records   D. A and B

5. The _____ specifies how you want Access to show numbers, dates, times, and text.

   A. data type   C. field type

   B. format property   D. field property

FILL IN THE BLANK

Complete the following sentences by writing the correct word or words in the blanks provided.

1. A(n) _____ is a group of related fields, such as all the personal information about an employee.

2. A(n) _____ is a label that helps to identify the field.

3. When you enter data into a cell, you are making a(n) _____.

4. The _____ object organizes data in a specific layout.

5. The _____ object finds and shows data that meet specified criteria.

WRITTEN QUESTIONS

Write a brief answer to the following questions.

1. What are the similarities and differences of Excel spreadsheets and Access databases?

2. What is a relational database management system?

3. What is the primary object in a database, and why?

4. What is the purpose of the primary key?

5. What are the advantages to switching to Design view before adding and deleting fields?

■ PROJECTS

PROJECT 23–1

1. Open the **Films** database from the drive and folder where your Data Files folder is stored. Save the Films database as **Revised Films 1**, followed by your initials. If necessary, enable the content. This database stores membership information and the current video collection of the Oak Creek Film Society (OCFS), a club for lovers of classic films. This database contains two tables: Collection and Members.

2. Open the **Collection** table to see the films the OCFS has collected so far, and then close the table. Open the **Members** table to preview the members of the club, and then close the table.

3. Create a new table for the database to store information on special events that the OCFS sponsors. Add the following fields to the new table in this order: **Title**, **Location**, **Start Time**, **End Time**, and **Description**. Use the **Text** data type for all the fields.

4. Save the table with the name **Events**.

5. In Datasheet view, enter the following data:

Title	Location	Start Time	End Time	Event Description
Holiday Classics	Odeon Theatre	12/15/ 2014	12/16/ 2014	Christmas theme
Horror Classics	Odeon Theatre	1/17/ 2015	1/19/ 2015	Horror theme
Hitchcock Classics	Odeon Theatre	2/23/ 2015	2/24/ 2015	Suspense theme

6. Automatically adjust the column widths for the first eight columns so complete entries are shown in all columns.

7. Save the changes to the table, and close the table. Leave the database open for the next Project.

PROJECT 23–2

1. If necessary, open the **Revised Films 1** database from your solution files. Save the Revised Films 1 database as **Revised Films 2**, followed by your initials. If necessary, enable the content.

2. Open the **Events** table. Switch to Design view. Change the field name *Title* to **Event**. Edit the two field names *Start Time* and *End Time* to read as **Start Date** and **End Date**.

3. Delete the Description field and all contents.

4. Insert a new field following the End Date field named **Start Time**. Change the data type to **Date/Time**. Set the Format property for the new field to **Medium Time**.

5. Insert a new field above the Start Date field, and name the new field **Films** using the default Text data type. Change the Field Size property for the new field to **200**.

6. Switch to Datasheet view. Insert the following data in the new fields:

Event	Films	Start Time
Holiday Classics	A Christmas Story, A Christmas Carol	7:30 pm
Horror Classics	Dracula, Frankenstein	7:45 pm
Hitchcock Classics	The Birds, Vertigo	7:30 pm

7. Insert the following new record.

Event:	Spoofing the Classics
Location:	Odeon Theatre
Films:	The Pink Panther, Young Frankenstein, Dr. Strangelove
Start Date:	3/15/2015
End Date:	3/17/2015
Start Time:	4:15 pm

8. Adjust the column widths to show all entries in the fields.

9. Save the changes to the table, and then close the table. Leave the database open for the next Project.

PROJECT 23–3

1. If necessary, open the **Revised Films 2** database from your solution files. Save the Revised Films 2 database as **Revised Films 3**, followed by your initials. If necessary, enable the content.

2. Open the **Collection** table. Adjust the width of the columns to show the complete entry for all records.

3. Collapse the Navigation Pane.

4. Go to record 24 (The Haunting). In the Title field, change the title to **The Haunting of Hill House**. Press **Enter**.

5. Your original title was correct. Undo the edit to restore the original title *The Haunting*.

6. Add two new films that were acquired for recent events. Enter the data below.

   ```
   Title:      Vertigo
   Year:       1958
   Length:     128 m
   MPAA:       NR
   Color/BW:   Color
   Director:   Hitchcock
   Category:   Suspense
   Actor:      James Stewart
   Actress:    Kim Novak
   ```

   ```
   Title:      Dr. Strangelove
   Year:       1964
   Length:     93 m
   MPAA:       NR
   Color/BW:   BW
   Director:   Kubrick
   Category:   Comedy
   Actor:      Peter Sellers, George C. Scott
   ```

7. Copy record **29** (Star Wars), and paste it in a new record. Change the title to **The Empire Strikes Back**, the year to **1980**, the length to **124 m**, and the director to **Kershner**. In the Actor field, replace Alec Guinness with **Billy Dee Williams**. Replace the existing entry in the Award field with **Sound**.

8. You have discovered that the 1969 version of Hamlet (record 14) is damaged. Delete this record from the table.

9. Expand the Navigation Pane.

10. Save the changes to the table, close the table, and then close the database.

 TEAMWORK PROJECT

Databases are ideal for storing statistics such as those of sports teams. With a partner, create a database to record statistics for a sports team. Follow these steps:

1. With your teammate, choose a sports team for further study.

2. Determine the categories of statistics you need to gather for your database, such as players' names, number of games completed in the current season, scores, and individual or team statistics for each game. Divide up the categories so you share the responsibility for gathering the data.

3. Create a database table with appropriate field names and data types to store the data you collect. Save the database as **TP 23-1**, followed by your initials.

4. Enter the collected data, and save the changes to the table.

CRITICAL THINKING

CRITICAL THINKING 23–1

Open an Access table in Datasheet view, and then open an Excel worksheet on the same computer. Restore down both application windows, and position the windows side by side. If possible, look at two applications on computer screens, side by side. Compare the two application windows.

1. Create a new Word document, and save the document as **CT 23-1**, followed by your initials.

2. Create two lists—one to describe at least three similarities and one to describe at least three differences in the applications.

3. Save the changes, and close the Word document.

CRITICAL THINKING 23–2

A good database design is essential for entering data efficiently, consistently, and accurately.

1. Create a new Word document, and save the document as **CT 23-2**, followed by your initials.

2. Write a brief paragraph describing how design elements such as the arrangement of fields, field names, and data types can make it easier to enter data and to ensure consistency for the data entered.

3. Save the changes, and close the Word document.

 # ONLINE DISCOVERY

Contact information generally includes postal codes. If you mail a letter or a package without a postal code, the item must be manually sorted at the post office, and the delivery of the item can be delayed by several days. Furthermore, if the data for the postal code is incorrect, mailed documents and packages may be returned as undeliverable. So, how can you find a postal code or verify that the postal code you have in your record is correct? The United States Postal Service provides an online zip code lookup feature. You can search for zip codes by address, city, or company. You can also search for a list of all the zip codes within a city. The search results can verify a correct address and zip code, and the proper standard postal format for the address is also provided.

1. Create a new Word document, and save the document as **OD 23-1**, followed by your initials.

2. Open your Web browser, and go to **www.usps.com**.

3. Navigate to the Look Up a ZIP Code feature, and find the zip code for the following address, and then enter the address with the correct zip code in the Word document.

   `892 Hickory Drive`
   `Marysville, OH`

4. Verify the zip code for the following company address. In the Word document, enter the address with the correct zip code in the standardized format.

   `Cengage Learning`
   `20 Channel Center Street`
   `Boston, MA 02300-3401`

5. Save the changes, and close the Word document and the Web browser.

JOB SKILLS

Job skills are critical for success in the workplace. To prepare for the work environment and move forward in your career, you must identify and assess the skills you have, and then set goals for further developing your personal values. Developing and maintaining job skills is an ongoing process.

1. Create a new Word document, and save the document as **JS 23-1**, followed by your initials.

2. Create a list of the skills and personal values you currently possess, and then create a second list of the skills you need to learn or further develop. The skills provided below can be used as a

guide to get you started, but you can also discuss this topic with classmates and include skills and values not included here:

- Communication skills (listening, oral, and written)
- Critical thinking and problem-solving skills
- Computer or technical literacy skills
- Teamwork and collaboration skills
- Leadership skills
- Time management skills

3. Save the changes, and close the Word document.

LESSON 24

Managing and Reporting Database Information

■ OBJECTIVES

Upon completion of this lesson, you should be able to:

- Create a form using the Form button and using the Form Wizard.
- Enter and edit data in a form.
- Sort table data in Datasheet view.
- Find and replace table data in Datasheet view.
- Create a query using the Query Wizard.
- Create a report using the Report Wizard.
- Preview and print a report.
- Create mailing labels using the Label Wizard.

■ WORDS TO KNOW

form

query

report

■ DATA FILES

To complete this lesson, you will need these data files:

Book Club.accdb

Grand Oaks Construction.accdb

RCC Data.accdb

As the amount of data in a database increases, it becomes more difficult to manage records and find information. Access has several useful features that help you work with larger databases. These features help you enter the data, order the data, find the data, and summarize and report the data.

Creating a Form

▶ VOCABULARY
form

In the previous lesson, you entered data in an Access table. You can create a *form*, a database object that provides a more convenient way to enter and edit data. A well-designed form can also make the process of entering data more efficient and more accurate. When you create a form, you add a new object to the database. Access offers two features that make the process quick and easy: the Form button and the Form Wizard.

Creating a Form Using the Form Button

You can create a form with a single click using the Form button. All the fields from the table or query are included on the form, and the form is predesigned. You can apply built-in designs, and if desired, you can modify the form layout and design using either Layout view or Design view.

Step-by-Step 24.1

QUICK TIP

Note that the Book Club database is similar to, but not exactly the same as, the database file Classic Books that you worked with in the previous lesson.

1. Open the database **Book Club** from the drive and folder where your Data Files folder is stored. Save the Book Club database as **Updated Book Club 1**, followed by your initials. (Throughout this lesson, if you see a yellow Security Warning message panel, click **Enable Content**.)

2. In the Navigation Pane, double-click **Book List : Table** to open the table. Look at the data stored in the table, and then close the table. Double-click **Officers : Table** to open the table and review the data. Then close the table.

3. In the Navigation Pane, click **Book List : Table** to select it. (You select the table because you want to base the form on the table.) On the Ribbon, click the **Create** tab. In the Forms group shown in **Figure 24–1**, click the **Form** button.

FIGURE 24–1
Forms group on the Create tab

4. The form shown in **Figure 24–2** is displayed. The form appears in Layout view, and the Ribbon shows the Form Layout Tools Design tab. Labels identify all the fields included in the table, and the fields appear in the same sequence they appear in the table. Text boxes in the form show the field data for the first record in the Book List table.

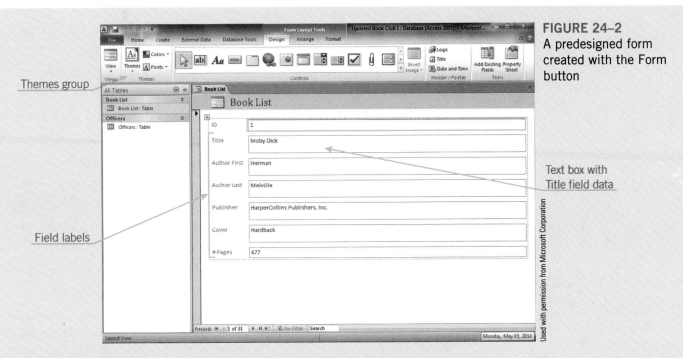

FIGURE 24-2
A predesigned form created with the Form button

Text box with Title field data

Field labels

Themes group

5. In the Themes group, click the **Themes** button. A gallery of several prede-signed formats appears. Under Built-In, click the **Civic** style (the first option in the third row). You will notice changes in the colors and font styles. This theme applies only to the form; the table style remains unchanged.

6. In the Object window, click the text box for the Title field to select the text box. Click the **Form Layout Tools Format** tab. In the Font group shown in **Figure 24-3**, click the **Font Color** button arrow [A ▾]. In the menu, in the first row of colors under Theme Colors, click the **Red, Accent 1** color. As you enter the title for each record, the text appears in red, but only on the form. The formats applied to the font have no effect on the data stored in the Book List table.

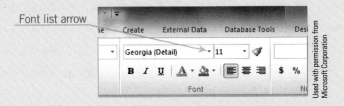

Font list arrow

FIGURE 24-3
Font group on the Form Layout Tools Format tab

7. Click the **Author First** text box. Click the **Font Color** button arrow. In the first row of colors under Theme Colors, click the **Blue-Gray, Text 2** color.

8. The Author First text box should still be selected. In the Font group, click the **Font** list arrow, and in the list of font styles, click **Arial**. Click the **Font Size** list arrow, and then click **12**.

9. The Author First text box is still selected. In the Font group, double-click the **Format Painter** button ☑. Then, click the text boxes for the Title, Author Last, Publisher, Cover, and # Pages fields to apply the new font formats to those text boxes.

10. Click the **Format Painter** button (or press Esc) to toggle off the Format Painter mode.

11. On the Quick Access Toolbar, click the **Save** button. The Save As dialog box appears. In the Form Name text box, type **Book Form**, and then click **OK**. The new form appears in the Navigation Pane under the Book List table.

12. Close the form, and then close the database.

Creating a Form Using the Form Wizard

You may not always want to include all the database fields on the form. To illustrate, consider the following scenario. You are working with a vendor database that includes contact information as well as data about past purchases, billings, and payments. You want to create a form to add new vendors to the database. You want the form to include only the fields related to contact information. The Form Wizard makes it easy to create a form with your preferences because it prompts you to select the fields and the form layout for the new form.

When you work with a form, you have three options for viewing the object. Form view is used for adding, editing, and viewing data. Layout view enables you to make changes to the font styles and colors and predesigned themes. In this view, data appears, so you can see how the changes you make will look when you open the form in Form view. Design view provides a detailed view of the structure of the form, and you can use this view to change the properties and add new fields.

Step-by-Step 24.2

1. Open the database **Grand Oaks Construction** from the drive and folder where your Data Files folder is stored. Save the Grand Oaks Construction database as **Updated Grand Oaks Construction 1**, followed by your initials.

2. Open the **Vendors** table. Scroll through the table to view the data stored in the table. Leave the table open.

3. Click the **Create** tab. In the Forms group, click the **Form Wizard** button. The Form Wizard dialog box shown in **Figure 24–4** opens. Under Table/Queries, Table: Vendors is already selected. This indicates that the form will be based on the Vendors table. Also note that under Available Fields all the fields that are available in the Vendors table are listed.

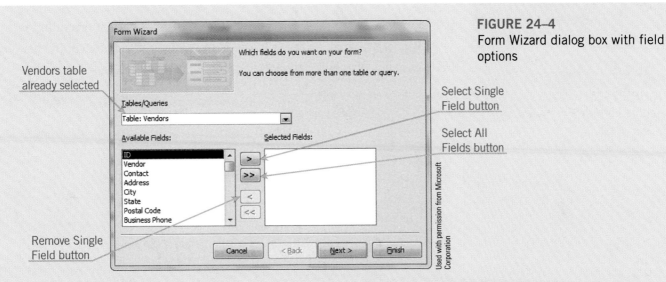

Used with permission from Microsoft Corporation

FIGURE 24-4
Form Wizard dialog box with field options

Vendors table already selected

Select Single Field button

Select All Fields button

Remove Single Field button

4. You need to identify the fields you want to appear on the form. Click the **Select All Fields** button. All of the field names are moved to the Selected Fields list. All the fields in the table will be included in the form.

5. You decide you do not want the Account Balance and the Last Purchase fields to appear on the form. In the Selected Fields list, click **Account Balance** to select the field name. Then click the **Remove Single Field** button to remove the field from the list.

6. In the Selected Fields list, the field name *Last Purchase* is already selected. Click the **Remove Single Field** button to remove that field from the list.

7. Click **Next** to advance to the next step in the wizard. The new Form Wizard dialog box prompts you to select a layout for the form. Select each of the four layout options to see a preview of each layout. Then select the **Columnar** layout option, and click **Next** to advance to the final step in the wizard.

8. The Form Wizard dialog box prompts you to create a name for the form. A proposed title appears in the text box. Edit the proposed form name so it is **Vendors Form**.

9. The option to open the form to view or enter information is already enabled. Note that you can choose to modify the form's design. Click **Finish**. The new form is displayed in Form view.

QUICK TIP

When you enable the Modify the form's design option, the new form opens in Design view.

10. Compare your screen to **Figure 24–5**. Data from the first record in the Vendors table is displayed in the form text boxes. Notice, too, the new form object appears in the Navigation Pane under the Vendors table.

FIGURE 24–5
Vendors Form in Form view

New form added
to list of objects

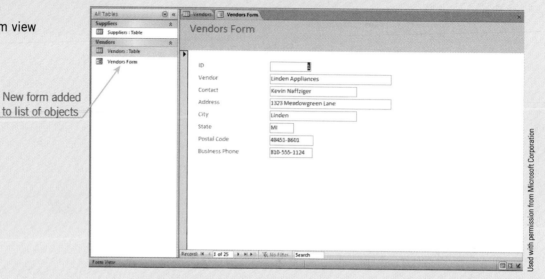

11. Click the **Home** tab. In the View group, click the **View** button arrow, and then click **Layout View**. The Layout of the form does not change, but the Ribbon tabs do adapt so you can change the formats.

12. Click the **View** button arrow, and then click **Design View**. In this view you can add fields and change the property settings.

13. Click the upper portion of the **View** button to toggle back to Form view.

14. Close the form and the table. Leave the database open for the next Step-by-Step.

Entering and Editing Data in a Form

Entering data in a form is similar to entering data in a table in Datasheet view. You can use Tab and the arrow keys to move the insertion point among the fields. Furthermore, the same navigation buttons are available at the bottom of the form. When you enter or edit a record in Form view, Access automatically updates the records in the table.

Step-by-Step 24.3

1. If necessary, open the **Updated Grand Oaks Construction 1** database from your solution files. Save the Updated Grand Oaks Construction 1 database as **Updated Grand Oaks Construction 2**, followed by your initials.

2. Open the **Vendors** table, and then open the **Vendors Form** object. In the Navigation bar at the bottom of the form, click the **New (blank) record** button ![icon]. A new record appears with labels, but no data appears in the text boxes.

3. Press **Tab** to position the insertion point in the text box for the Vendor field. Access will assign an ID number when you begin to enter data. Type **Roy's Refrigerator Repair**. Note that the Edit Record icon 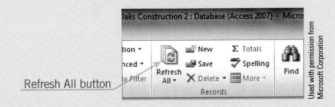 is displayed at the upper-left corner of the form, indicating that you are editing the record.

4. Press **Tab**, and type **Roy Fowler**.

5. Press **Tab**, and enter the following information into the form:

   Address: `2531 Owen Road`

   City: `Fenton`

   State/Province: `MI`

   Postal Code: `48430-2082`

   Business Phone: `810-555-6609`

6. Press **Tab** (or Enter). A new blank form opens.

7. In the Navigation bar at the bottom of the form, select **27 of 27** (or triple-click) in the Record Number box. Type **8**, and press **Enter**. A form containing the data record #8 is displayed.

8. The business phone number has changed. Click the text box for the Business Phone field, and edit the phone number so it is **810-555-9938**. Press **Enter**. The revised data is saved.

9. Click the **Vendors** object tab to view the Vendors table. Scroll to the bottom of the table. Notice the table has not yet been updated, and the new record does not appear. On the Home tab, in the Records group, shown in **Figure 24-6**, click the **Refresh All** button. The table is updated. Scroll down to view the new record at the bottom of the table.

FIGURE 24-6
Records group on the Home tab

10. Navigate to record 8. Scroll to the right to view the Business Phone field. The phone number has been updated and now shows *810-555-9938*.

11. Save the changes, and close the table. Close the form, and leave the database open for the next Step-by-Step.

Sorting Table Data in Datasheet View

Databases typically contain numerous records. Organizing records in a specific order can help you access the data more quickly. You can sort text and numbers in either ascending or descending order. As you may recall, ascending order sorts alphabetically from *A* to *Z* and numerically from the lowest to the highest number. Descending order sorts alphabetically from *Z* to *A* and numerically from the highest to the lowest number.

If you change your mind after sorting the table data, you can use the Undo command to undo the action. You can also easily restore the table to its original arrangement.

Step-by-Step 24.4

1. If necessary, open the **Updated Grand Oaks Construction 2** database from your solution files. Save the Updated Grand Oaks Construction 2 database as **Updated Grand Oaks Construction 3**, followed by your initials.

2. Open the **Vendors** table. Click any record in the City column. On the Home tab, in the Sort & Filter group shown in **Figure 24–7**, click the **Ascending** button. The records in the table are rearranged and placed in alphabetical order from *A* to *Z* by city. A vertical arrow appears in the column label indicating the data is sorted.

FIGURE 24–7
Sort & Filter group on the Home tab

3. Scroll to the right, and click any record in the Account Balance column. In the Sort & Filter group, click the **Descending** button. The records are rearranged and placed in numerical order with the largest account balance listed first.

4. If necessary, scroll further to the right, and click any record in the Last Purchase column. Click the **Descending** button. The records are rearranged in numerical order with the most recent purchase listed first.

5. You change your mind about the sort order. On the Quick Access Toolbar, click the **Undo** button. The records are restored to the arrangement prior to the last sort.

6. Scroll back to the left, and click any record in the Vendor column. Click the **Ascending** button. The records are rearranged and placed in alphabetical order from *A* to *Z*.

7. In the Sort & Filter group, click the **Remove Sort** button . All sorts are cleared, and the records are restored to the original order.

8. Save the changes, and close the Vendors table, and then close the database.

Finding and Replacing Table Data

Sometimes, records contain common data, and that data needs to be updated. In a small database, you can locate specific data by scrolling through the records. However, if the database is quite large, finding a particular record or value can be tedious and time consuming. Whether the database has a few records, hundreds of records, or even thousands of records, using the Find and Replace commands simplifies this task.

Finding Data

For example, assume you want to see if there are any books about Huckleberry Finn included in the Book Club database that you worked with in Step-by-Step 24.1. You could sort the records in the Book List table in alphabetical order by title and then scroll down through the list to look for the title. However, if the database had hundreds or thousands of records, scrolling through the records to find the title could take a lot of time. The Find command provides a quick and easy way for you to locate specific records or find certain values within fields. You can search for data within a specific field, or you can search the entire table.

Step-by-Step 24.5

1. Open the **Updated Book Club 1** database from your solution files. Open the **Book List** table.

2. Position the insertion point in the first row in the Title column. Be careful, though, not to select any text in the cell.

3. On the Home tab, in the Find group shown in **Figure 24–8**, click the **Find** button.

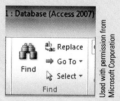

Used with permission from Microsoft Corporation

FIGURE 24–8
Find group on the Home tab

4. The Find and Replace dialog box shown in **Figure 24-9** opens. With the insertion point already positioned in the Find What text box, type **Huckleberry Finn**. If there is already text in the box, it will be replaced when you enter the new search text.

FIGURE 24-9
Find tab in Find and Replace dialog box

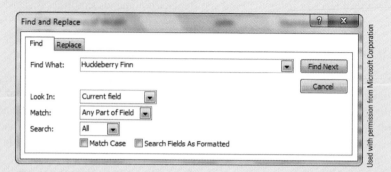

5. Compare your screen to Figure 24-9. Change the options, if necessary, to match the following:

   a. The setting in the Look In box already displays *Current field*. This option is correct as is. It tells Access to look for all occurrences in the field where the insertion point is positioned. (To search the entire table, you would click the list arrow and select Current document.)

   b. Click the **Match** box list arrow, and select **Any Part of Field**. Access will locate any book title that has the words *Huckleberry* and *Finn* in it.

   c. If necessary, select All in the Search box.

   d. The Match Case and the Search Fields As Formatted options should not be selected. If they are selected, click the option once to uncheck the box and disable the option. When these options are turned off, Access ignores capitalization and data formats when searching for matching text.

6. When the settings in your dialog box match those in the Figure 24-9, click **Find Next**. The first occurrence of the search text is highlighted in the Title column for record #6.

7. Click **Find Next** again. A message is displayed indicating that there are no more occurrences of the search text. Click **OK** in the message box to close the message. Leave the Find and Replace dialog box open.

8. In the Find and Replace dialog box, the text in the Find What box is already selected. Type **Dickens**. Then click the **Look In** box list arrow, and select **Current document**. Click **Find Next**. The first occurrence of the search text is selected in the Author Last column for record #7.

9. Click **Find Next**. The second occurrence of the search text is selected in the Author Last column for record #15.

10. Continue to click **Find Next** to see all remaining occurrences of the search text (two more records). When the message appears indicating there are no more occurrences of the search text, click **OK**. Then close the Find and Replace dialog box.

11. Press **Shift+F4**. Even though the Find and Replace dialog box is closed, the keyboard shortcut used the search criteria from the previous search and located the first occurrence in record #7.

12. Press **Ctrl+F** to open the Find and Replace dialog box. The previous search text is already highlighted in the Find What box. Type **Bronte**. Click the **Search** box list arrow, and then click **Up**. Click **Find Next**. Because there are no occurrences of *Bronte* above record #7, a message appears indicating the search item was not found. Click **OK**.

13. Click the **Search** box list arrow, and then click **Down**. Click **Find Next**. The first occurrence of *Bronte* moving downward in the table is selected (record #12). Close the dialog box.

14. Close the Book List table, and leave the database open for the next Step-by-Step.

Using the Replace Command

The Replace command locates the search text and replaces it with new text that you specify. For example, in the Classics field in the Book Club database, there is no consistency in the spelling of the word *Incorporated*. Sometimes it is spelled out completely, and sometimes it is abbreviated as *Inc.*. You can search for all the occurrences when the word is abbreviated and then automatically replace those abbreviations with the complete spelling.

When you use the Replace command, you can choose to view and confirm each replacement individually or you can choose to replace all occurrences of the search text with a single click. You should use the Replace All option only when you are confident about making all the replacements without reviewing them first.

Step-by-Step 24.6

1. If necessary, open the **Updated Book Club 1** database from your solution files. Save the Updated Book Club 1 database as **Updated Book Club 2**, followed by your initials.

2. Open the **Book List** table. Position the insertion point at the beginning of the text in the first record in the Publisher column. Be careful not to select the contents in the cell.

3. In the Find group, click the **Replace** button to open the Find and Replace dialog box. The Find What box still contains the text from your last search. Type **Inc.** to replace the old search text. In the Replace With text box, type **Incorporated**.

4. Compare your screen to **Figure 24–10**, and make any necessary changes to the settings. The Look In box should show *Current field*, the Search box should show *All*, and the Search Fields As Formatted option should be enabled.

FIGURE 24–10
Replace tab in Find and Replace dialog box

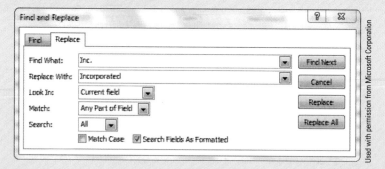

5. When your settings match those shown in Figure 24–10, click **Find Next**. The first occurrence of the search text *Inc.*, which is in record #1, is highlighted.

6. In the dialog box, click **Replace**. The next occurrence of *Inc.* (record #3) is highlighted. If necessary, click and drag the dialog box title bar to reposition the dialog box on the screen so you can see the data in the table for record #1. In the record #1 entry, *Inc.* was replaced with *Incorporated*, and the other text in the publisher name was not changed.

7. You change your mind. On the Quick Access Toolbar, click the **Undo** button. You can use the Undo command to reverse the action; however, you must choose the Undo command before editing another record.

8. Position the insertion point in any one of the records in the Publisher column. Be careful not to select the contents. In the Find and Replace dialog box, click the **Replace All** button. When prompted to continue, click **Yes**. Throughout the Publisher column, all occurrences of *Inc.* are replaced with *Incorporated*.

9. Close the dialog box. Scroll up and down to view all the entries in the column. Note that there are no more instances of *Inc.* as an abbreviation.

10. Save the changes, and close the table. Leave the database open for the next Step-by-Step.

Creating a Query

Although the Find command provides an easy way to find data, you only see the search results for one record at a time. You may need to locate multiple records, all containing the same values. If you have a large database, and several records contain the value you are searching for, this is another task that can be tedious. In this case, you can create a *query*, a database object that enables you to locate multiple records matching specified criteria. Remember, you learned in Lesson 23 that a query is one of the types of database objects that appears in the Navigation Pane. The query

▶ **VOCABULARY**
query

provides a way for you to ask a question about the information stored in one or more database tables. Access searches for and retrieves data from the table or tables to answer your question.

To illustrate the benefits of using a query, consider the following example. Suppose you just read a book by Charles Dickens. You really enjoyed the book and you would like to read another book authored by him. You could locate the books by Charles Dickens one at a time in the Book Club database by using the Find command. But a query makes your search easier, and it also creates a list of the titles for you.

When you create a query, you must identify all the fields you want to retrieve and show information for. For example, you might want to retrieve records and show only the title and the author name. The order in which you select the fields will be the order in which the information appears in the query results. The easiest way to create a query is to use the Query Wizard, which guides you through most of the process.

Step-by-Step 24.7

1. If necessary, open the **Updated Book Club 2** database from your solution files. Save the Updated Book Club 2 database as **Updated Book Club 3**, followed by your initials. Note there are currently no query objects for this database.

2. In the Navigation Pane, click **Book List : Table** to select the object. Click the **Create** tab. In the Queries group shown in **Figure 24–11**, click the **Query Wizard** button.

FIGURE 24–11
Queries group on the Create tab

3. The New Query dialog box shown in **Figure 24–12** opens. In the right pane, the Simple Query Wizard option is already selected, and a description of the query is displayed under the image in the left pane. To become familiar with the different types of queries, click each of the options in the right pane, and read the description of each query in the left pane.

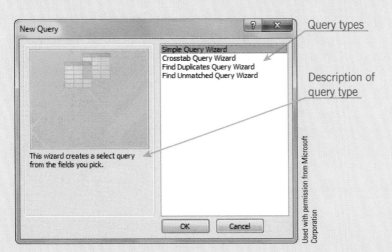

Query types

Description of query type

FIGURE 24–12
New Query dialog box with type options

4. In the right pane of the dialog box, click **Simple Query Wizard**, and then click **OK**. The Simple Query Wizard dialog box shown in **Figure 24–13** opens. Because you selected the Book List table in the Navigation Pane before you started the wizard, *Table: Book List* already is displayed under Tables/Queries.

FIGURE 24–13
Simple Query Wizard with
field options

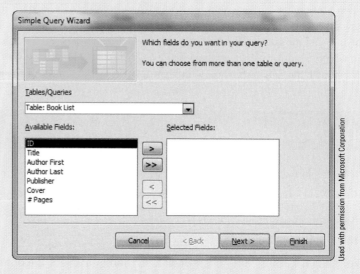

5. Under Available Fields, select **Author Last**, and then click the **Select Single Field** button 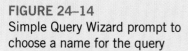. Under Available Fields, select **Title**, and click the **Select Single Field** button. Author Last and Title will be the fields included in the query, in that sequence. Click **Next** to advance to the next step in the wizard.

6. The next step in the wizard, shown in **Figure 24–14**, prompts you to choose a name for the query. In the text box at the top of the dialog box, select the default name **Book List Query**, and type **Dickens Query**. If necessary, enable the option to open the query to view the information.

FIGURE 24–14
Simple Query Wizard prompt to
choose a name for the query

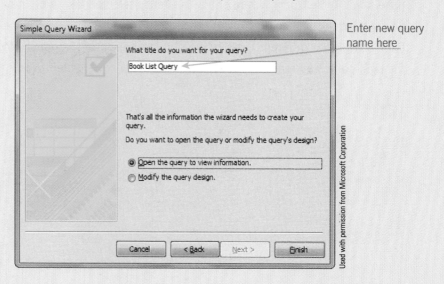

7. Click **Finish**. The query object is opened in Datasheet view. All entries for the Author Last and Title fields are displayed. The Dickens Query object is displayed in the Navigation Pane under the Book List table. The Query icon 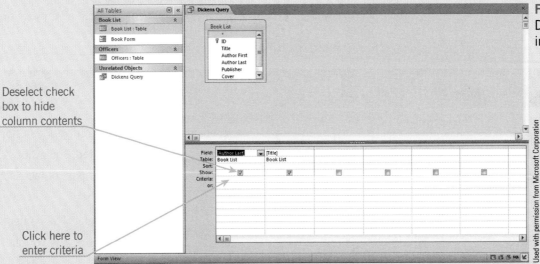 next to the object name identifies the object type.

8. You want to show only entries for the author last name *Dickens*, so you still need to adjust the query. Click the **Home** tab. In the View group, click the **View** button arrow, and then select **Design View**. As shown in **Figure 24–15**, the two fields included in the Dickens query appear at the bottom of the object window.

Deselect check box to hide column contents

Click here to enter criteria

FIGURE 24–15
Dickens Query shown in Design view

Used with permission from Microsoft Corporation

9. In the first column next to Criteria, click the cell. Type **"Dickens"**, and then press **Enter**. This specifies that only records written by authors with the last name *Dickens* are included in the query.

10. In the Author Last column, click the **check box** to disable the option to show the field data. The data in this field will be used to retrieve records with *Dickens* as the author, but the data from this column will not show in the query results.

11. On the Quick Access Toolbar, click the **Save** button to save the changes to the query object. Then click the **View** button, and switch back to Datasheet view. Now the query shows only the title for the four records containing *Dickens* in the Author Last field. Although data was retrieved from two fields, only the data from the Title field appears in the query. Close the query.

12. Leave the database open for the next Step-by-Step.

Creating and Printing a Report

▶ **VOCABULARY**
report

You can print a database in Datasheet view, but when you do, all of the data contained in the database is printed. This can waste a lot of paper if the database is large or if you need only certain information from the database. A *report* is a database object that allows you to organize, summarize, and print all or a portion of the data in a database. You can create a report based on a table or a query.

Although you can prepare a report manually, the Report Wizard provides an easy and fast way to create a report. The wizard prompts you to specify the data you want to include in the report and how you want to format that data. One of the format options you apply in the report is page orientation. Remember, you learned in earlier lessons that the orientation determines how the report will be printed on the page. Landscape orientation formats the report with the long edge of the page at the top; portrait orientation formats the report with the short edge of the page at the top.

You can preview a report to see what the page(s) look like before you send the data to the printer.

Step-by-Step 24.8

1. If necessary, open the **Updated Book Club 3** database from your solution files. Save the Updated Book Club 3 database as **Updated Book Club 4**, followed by your initials. Note there are currently no report objects for this database.

2. In the Navigation Pane, click **Book List : Table** to select the object. Click the **Create** tab. In the Reports group shown in **Figure 24–16**, click the **Report Wizard** button.

FIGURE 24–16
Reports group on the Create tab

3. The Report Wizard dialog box shown in **Figure 24–17** opens. In the text box under Tables/Queries, *Table: Book List* is displayed because you identified the table before starting the wizard.

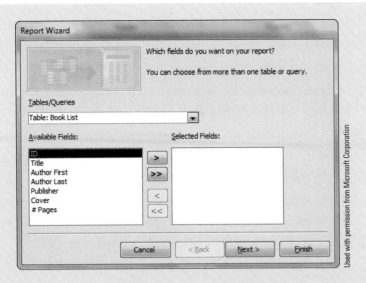

FIGURE 24–17
Report Wizard dialog box with
field options

4. Choose the field names from the Available Fields list, and arrange them in the order you want them to appear in the report:

   a. Click **Author First**, then click the **Select Single Field** button to move the field name to the Selected Fields list.

   b. *Author Last* is already selected. Click the **Select Single Field** button.

   c. Click **Title**, and then click the **Select Single Field** button.

   d. *Publisher* is already selected. Click the **Select Single Field** button.

5. Four fields to be included on the report are displayed in the Selected Fields list. Click **Next** to advance to the next step in the wizard. The options for grouping the fields are not necessary for this report. Click **Next** to move on to the next step.

6. Options for the sort order of the records are displayed, as shown in **Figure 24–18**. In the first box, click the **list arrow**, and then click **Author Last**.

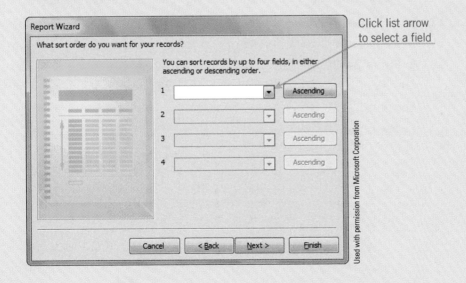

Click list arrow
to select a field

FIGURE 24–18
Report Wizard dialog box with
sort options

7. Next to the first box, click **Ascending**. The option toggles to *Descending*. Click **Descending** to toggle back to the default *Ascending* setting.

8. Click the **list arrow** in the second box, and then click **Title**. If there are two or more books by the same author, the titles will be ordered first by the author last name, then by the book title, in ascending order. Click **Next** to move to the next step in the wizard.

9. Options for layout and orientation appear. If it is not already enabled, click the **Tabular layout** option. Then click the **Landscape** orientation option to enable it. If necessary, enable the **Adjust the field width so all fields fit on a page** option. When your settings match those shown in **Figure 24–19**, click **Next** to move on to the last step.

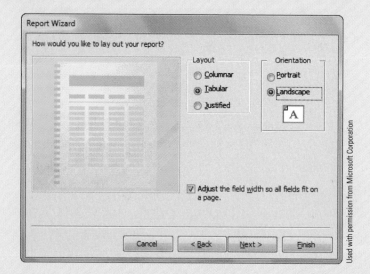

10. The new dialog box prompts you to enter a title for the report. The current title is *Book List*, because that is the name of the table. Change the title to **Classic Books**. If necessary, enable the option to preview the report.

11. Click **Finish**. A preview of the report opens in Print Preview, and the Ribbon adapts to show the Print Preview tab. In the Zoom group, shown in **Figure 24–20**, click the **Zoom** button arrow, and then click **50%**. The preview of the report is reduced so you can see how the entire page will be printed.

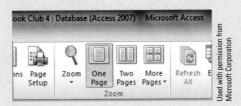

Used with permission from Microsoft Corporation

FIGURE 24–20
Zoom group on the Print Preview tab

12. If you were printing the report, you would click the Print button in the Print group on the left side of the Print Preview tab. On the right side of the Print Preview tab, click the **Close Print Preview** button. The report is now displayed in Design view. On the Home tab, click the **View** button arrow, and then click **Layout View**. Then click the upper half of the **View** button to show Report view.

13. Close the Report. The Classic Books report object appears in the Navigation Pane. The Report icon ▦ next to the object name identifies the object type.

14. Close the database, but leave Access open for the next Step-by-Step.

> **ABOVE AND BEYOND**
>
> To change the appearance of the report, switch to Design view and then apply a different theme and/or colors and fonts.

Creating Mailing Labels

Because databases often contain data regarding names and addresses, it is common to create mailing labels based on the database information. For example, you can quickly create labels for the vendors or suppliers in the Grand Oaks Construction database. Access provides a wizard to use a report format to create the labels. When you use the Label Wizard, you can customize the layout of the fields that controls how the data appears on the label.

The Label Wizard includes a step to sort the database records. For bulk mail rates, the mail must be sorted by postal code, so sorting the labels before printing saves a lot of time.

TECHNOLOGY CAREERS

Data Entry Keyers

The amount of information that businesses maintain continues to grow, and this information needs to be entered into a database. If you are a fast and accurate keyboarder, have a good eye for detail, and enjoy working at the computer all day, a data entry job might be the right career choice for you. In addition to entering data, data entry keyers verify the accuracy of the data they enter. They proofread entries, perform accuracy tests, correct errors, and compile and sort data. Accuracy is emphasized; inaccurate data means inaccurate records, and errors can cost the business a lot of money.

Data entry keyers are employed in every sector of the economy. Primary employers include data processing firms; accounting, auditing, and bookkeeping firms; banks and credit unions; and state and local governments. Typical job titles include billing clerk, accounting clerk, production clerk, data entry operator, and key data operator. Many data entry keyers work regular workdays, but they can work from remote locations with flexible hours as well. A data entry job can help you get your foot in the door with an employer, and then you can work your way up to a better paying job with more responsibilities.

Step-by-Step 24.9

1. Open the **Updated Grand Oaks Construction 3** database from your solution files. Save the Updated Grand Oaks Construction 3 database as **Updated Grand Oaks Construction 4**, followed by your initials.

2. In the Navigation Pane, select the **Vendors : Table**. (The wizard will not prompt you to choose a table, so you must make sure the correct table is selected.) Click the **Create** tab. In the Reports group, click the **Labels** button. The Label Wizard dialog box shown in **Figure 24–21** opens.

FIGURE 24–21
Label Wizard dialog box with label type options

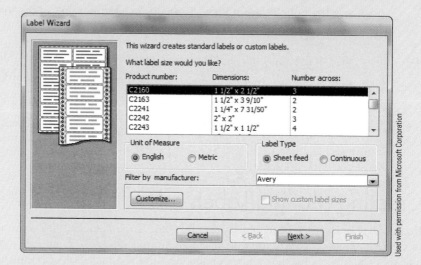

Used with permission from Microsoft Corporation

3. If necessary, under Product number, scroll to the top of the list and click **C2160** to specify the label size. (Product numbers appear on the label packaging.) If necessary, under Label Type, enable the **Sheet feed** option. Also, if necessary, in the Filter by manufacturer list box select **Avery**. When your settings match those shown in Figure 24–21, click **Next** to advance to the next step in the wizard.

4. The next step in the wizard, shown in **Figure 24–22**, describes the font formats on the mailing label. If necessary, change the font name to **Arial**, the font weight to **Light**, and the font size to **10**. The preview in the dialog box reflects the font changes as you apply them. When your settings match those shown in Figure 24–22, click **Next** to move to the next step in the wizard.

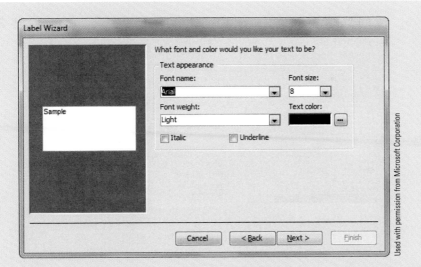

FIGURE 24–22
Label Wizard dialog box with font options

5. In this step you choose the fields and arrange them on a prototype label. Select and arrange the fields as follows:

   a. Under Available fields, click **Vendor**. Click the **Select Single Field** button. The field is moved to the Prototype label list, and brackets are inserted before and after the field name.

   b. Press **Enter**. With the insertion point still positioned in the Prototype label box, type **ATTN**, and then press the **spacebar**.

   c. Under Available fields, the field name *Contact* is already selected. Click the **Select Single Field** button. The Contact field is inserted at the location of the insertion point. Press **Enter**.

   d. Under Available fields, the field name *Address* is already selected. Click the **Select Single Field** button, and press **Enter**.

   e. Under Available fields, the field name *City* is already selected. Click the **Select Single Field** button. Press the **spacebar**, and then click the **Select Single Field** button to insert the State field. Press the **spacebar**, and then click the **Select Single Field** button to insert the Postal Code field. The City, State, and Postal Code fields are all moved to the Prototype label list and will appear on the same line of text.

> **QUICK TIP**
>
> Instead of clicking the Select Single Field button, you can double-click a field name to move it to the Prototype label.

6. When your prototype label looks like the one shown in **Figure 24–23**, click **Next**.

Used with permission from Microsoft Corporation

FIGURE 24–23
Label Wizard dialog box with
Prototype label layout

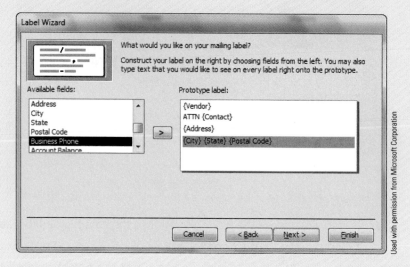

7. The next step in the wizard is to sort the labels. In the Available fields list, click **Postal Code**, and then click the **Select Single Field** button. The field name is moved to the Sort by list. Click **Next**.

8. The last step in the wizard is to name the report. The proposed name *Labels Vendors* is good, so no changes are necessary. If necessary, enable the **See the labels as they will look printed** option. Click **Finish**. The report opens in Print Preview. If you were printing the labels, you would put the label sheets in your printer and then click the Print button on the Print Preview tab.

9. On the right side of the Print Preview tab, click the **Close Print Preview** button. The report is displayed in Design view.

10. Click the **View** button arrow, and then click **Report View**. The labels appear in a single column. Click the **View** button arrow again, and then click **Layout View**. Click the **View** button arrow again, and then click **Print Preview**. The information appears as it will print only when you display the report in Print Preview.

11. Close the report. The Labels Vendors object appears in the Navigation Pane, and the report icon indicates that the object is a report.

12. Close the database.

SUMMARY

In this lesson, you learned:

- You can create a form object using the Form button or the Form Wizard. The Form Wizard helps you create a customized layout for entering data.

- Entering and editing data in a form is similar to entering data in a table in Datasheet view. You use the same navigation buttons to move from one record to another.

- You can sort records in Datasheet view in either ascending or descending order.

- The Find command can save you time looking for records and specific values in a table.

- The Replace command can save you time finding and replacing specific text. You can choose to replace text in individual occurrences or all at once.

- You can create a query to find field data for records that match specified criteria. You can use the Query Wizard to create the query, and then you can identify criteria to retrieve specific data.

- A report allows you to organize, summarize, and print all or a portion of the data in a database. You can choose the Report Wizard to guide you through the process in creating a report.

- After creating a report using the Report Wizard, you can review the report in Print Preview before sending it to the printer.

- When you want to create mailing labels, you create a report object using the Label Wizard.

■ LESSON REVIEW

TRUE / FALSE

Circle T if the statement is true or F if the statement is false.

T   F   **1.**   When you work with a form, you have three options for viewing the object.

T   F   **2.**   You can create a report based on a table or a query.

T   F   **3.**   After entering or editing a record in Form view, you must manually update the records in the table.

T   F   **4.**   Ascending order sorts alphabetically from *A* to *Z* and numerically from the lowest to the highest number.

T   F   **5.**   Once you sort table data, you cannot undo the action, nor can you restore the table to its original arrangement.

T   F   **6.**   When you use the Replace command, you must view and confirm each replacement individually.

T   F   **7.**   When you create a query, the order in which you select the fields will be the order in which the information appears in the query results.

T   F   **8.**   When you create a report, you can choose the order the information appears in.

T   F   **9.**   Landscape orientation formats the report with the short edge of the page at the top.

T   F   **10.**   When you use the Label Wizard to create mailing labels, you cannot control how the data appears on the label.

MULTIPLE CHOICE

Select the best response for each of the following statements.

1. A _____ can make the process of entering data more efficient and more accurate.

    A. query   C. wizard

    B. form   D. report

2. When you create mailing labels, you create a new _____ .

    A. query   C. table

    B. report   D. form

3. _____ view enables you to make changes to the form's design.

    A. Layout   C. Datasheet

    B. Form   D. A or B

4. A _____ enables you to locate all records that match certain criteria.

    A. report   C. form

    B. sort   D. query

5. When searching for a record, you can search for data contained in _____ .

    A. a specific field   C. all the tables in the database

    B. the entire table   D. A and B

FILL IN THE BLANK

Complete the following sentences by writing the correct word or words in the blanks provided.

1. In _____ view, you can change the properties and add new fields to a form.

2. When you work with a form, _____ view is used for adding, editing, and viewing data.

3. In _____ view, you can see how the changes you make will look when you enter data in the form.

4. To arrange data with the most recent date at the top of the list, sort the data in _____ order.

5. To locate search text and replace it with new text, use the _____ command.

WRITTEN QUESTIONS

Write a brief answer to the following questions.

1. What are the advantages of using the Form button to create a form?

2. What are the advantages of using the Form Wizard, instead of the Form button, to create a form?

3. Explain when you would use the Replace All option in the Find and Replace dialog box.

4. Why would you create a query when you can use the Find command to locate data?

5. What are the advantages of creating a report before printing data?

■ PROJECTS

PROJECT 24–1

In this project and the next two, you will work with a database containing information about the River Cleanup Crew, a volunteer program that coordinates annual events to clean up and remove trash from the local rivers, creeks, and streams.

1. Open the database **RCC Data** from the drive and folder where your Data Files folder is stored. Save the RCC Data database as **Updated RCC Data 1**, followed by your initials.

2. Use the Form Wizard to create a form based on the Volunteers table:

   a. Include all the fields, in the same sequence, except # Hours.

   b. Apply the Columnar layout.

   c. Name the form **Volunteer Form**. Preview the form in Print Preview.

3. Switch to Layout view, and apply the Hardcover theme. Save the changes to the form design.

4. Switch to Form view, and use the new form to add the following two new records to the Volunteers table:

First Name:	Justin
Last Name:	Kennedy
Address:	4513 Cove Trail
City:	Anderson
State:	SC
Postal Code:	29621-2134
Phone:	864-555-4911
Birth Date:	6/11/1999
River:	Savannah
Join Date:	5/1/2014

First Name:	Jessica
Last Name:	Jones
Address:	506 Heritage Drive
City:	Anderson
State:	SC
Postal Code:	29621-1666
Phone:	864-555-1985
Birth Date:	4/18/1989
River:	Savannah
Join Date:	5/1/2014

5. Navigate to record #10. Edit the phone number to **864-555-5015**.

6. Gary Phillips has moved. Find his record (search for the last name), and change the street address to **2116 Woodside Avenue, Anderson, SC 29625-2810**. His new phone number is **864-555-9655**.

7. Several of the area codes in the Phone field are incorrect. The numbers have been transposed. Search the Phone field for all occurrences of *846*, and replace all occurrences with **864**.

8. Sort the table data in ascending order based on the Last Name field.

9. Save the changes to the table, and then close the table. Close the form. Leave the database open for the next Project.

PROJECT 24–2

1. If necessary, open the database **Updated RCC Data 1** from your solution files. Save the Updated RCC Data 1 database as **Updated RCC Data 2**, followed by your initials.

2. You would like to contact the volunteers who clean up the Saluda River. Use the Query Wizard to create a simple query based on the Volunteers table:

   a. Include the Last Name, First Name, Phone, and River fields, in that order.

   b. Save the query as **Saluda Volunteers**.

3. The criteria for the query is for those who clean the Saluda River. Specify the criteria **"Saluda"** in the River field. The River field does not need to show in the query.

4. Save and close the query, and, if necessary, close the Volunteers table.

5. You would like to print a list of the names and phone numbers of all sponsors. Use the Report Wizard to create the report based on the Sponsors table:

   a. Include the Name and Phone fields, in that order.

   b. Do not group the report.

   c. Sort the report by Name in ascending order.

   d. Choose the Columnar layout and Portrait orientation.

   e. Name the report **Sponsors Phone List**, and preview the report.

6. Close Print Preview, and then close the report.

7. For an upcoming recognition event, you want to prepare a list of all the volunteers and the number of hours they have devoted to the organization. Use the Report Wizard to create the report based on the Volunteers table:

   a. Include the # Hours, First Name, and Last Name fields from the Volunteers table, in that order.

   b. Do not add any grouping levels.

   c. Sort the report by the # Hours field, in descending order.

   d. Choose the Columnar layout and Portrait orientation.

   e. Name the report **Volunteer Hours**, and preview the report.

8. Close the report. Leave the database open.

PROJECT 24–3

1. If necessary, open the database **Updated RCC Data 2** from your solution files. Save the Updated RCC Data 2 database as **Updated RCC Data 3**, followed by your initials.

2. To mail the quarterly newsletter to the volunteers, create mailing labels based on the Volunteers table. Launch the Label Wizard, and use the following label and font settings:

Product number:	**8371**
Unit of Measure:	**English**
Label Type:	**Sheet feed**
Manufacturer:	**Avery**

3. Set the text settings as follows:

Font name:	**Cambria**
Font size:	**11**
Font weight:	**Light**
Text color:	**Black**

4. In the prototype label:

   a. Enter the First Name and Last Name fields on the first line, separated by a space.

   b. Insert the Address field on the second line.

   c. Insert the City, State, and Postal Code fields on the third line. Enter a blank space after the City and State fields, and do not use any punctuation between the city and state fields.

5. Sort the labels by the Postal Code field.

6. Name the report **Volunteers Mailing Labels**, and preview the report.

7. Close the report, and then close the database.

TEAMWORK PROJECT

Create a roster for your computer class or workgroup to record the names, addresses, phone numbers, e-mail addresses, and other information about your classmates or coworkers. Follow these steps:

1. With a teammate, determine what information you want to gather and organize. Divide the names of your classmates or coworkers so each of you will gather information for half the group.

2. After you have gathered the information, create a new database and a table with the fields you identified in Step 1. Save the document as **TP 24-1**, followed by your initials.

3. Then create a form to make data entry easier. Select the options you think will present the information you have collected in the best way, and give your form a relevant title. Enter the information into the form.

4. Save the changes to the database.

CRITICAL THINKING

CRITICAL THINKING 24–1

In Projects 24–1, 24–2, and 24–3, you worked with a database for a community volunteer program. The program manager wants to recognize the youth volunteers. How can the Volunteers table data be arranged so the program manager can easily identify those volunteers who are under 18 years old?

1. Create a new Word document, and save the document as **CT 24-1**, followed by your initials.

2. Write two or three sentences explaining how you would manipulate the table data to help the manager.

3. Save the changes to the document.

CRITICAL THINKING 24–2

As you know, databases are not just for storing data. Databases are also used as tools for analyzing and organizing data. To ensure that the database meets your needs, a lot of thought must go into the planning before the database is created.

1. Create a new Word document, and save the document as **CT 24-2**, followed by your initials.

2. Create a list of steps you would follow in planning a database.

3. Save the changes to the document.

ONLINE DISCOVERY

When mailing a letter to another country, how can you be sure you have addressed the envelope or package correctly? Go to **www.usps.com**, and then search for information regarding addressing international mail. Also search online for this information on the destination country's postal services.

1. Create a new Word document, and save the document as **OD 24-1**, followed by your initials.

2. Using the information you find online, edit the following information to show the address data in the correct format required for delivery of a letter in the destination country. Cite the URLs for the Web pages where you find the supporting information.

```
First and Last Name

36 Silvergrove Court N.W.

Calgary, Alberta

Canada

T3B5A3
```

```
First and Last Name

P.O. Box 30009

Wonderbooj Poort

0033 South Africa
```

```
First and Last Name

38 Upland Drive

Brookmans Park

Hatfield, Hertfordshire

AL9 6PT

England
```

```
First and Last Name

Blk 35 Mandalay Road

# 15 Mandalay Towers

Singapore 308215
```

3. Save the changes to the document.

JOB SKILLS

Use the Internet to research job prospects for data entry keyers. Explore the education and skills required, the job outlook, the average salary, and related occupations.

1. Create a new Word document, and save the document as **JS 24-1**, followed by your initials.

2. Write a brief summary of the information you gathered.

3. Save the changes, and close the Word document.

MODULE 2 REVIEW

Key Applications

■ UNIT REVIEW

■ DATA FILES

To complete this review, you will need these data files:

Bird.jpg

Elephant.jpg

Giraffe.jpg

Rail Trail.pptx

Safari.docx

Scenic Trail.docx

Species.accdb

Survey.xlsx

The Climb.pptx

Travel Data.xlsx

Travel Notes.docx

Volunteers.accdb

■ REVIEW QUESTIONS

TRUE / FALSE

Circle T if the statement is true or F if the statement is false.

T   F   **1.**   When text is too wide to fit in a cell, by default Excel automatically wraps the text in the cell.

T   F   **2.**   The Undo command is always available in Access.

T   F   **3.**   Excel provides function formulas to perform both mathematical and statistical functions.

T   F   **4.**   Format Painter will copy and apply font and paragraph formats.

T   F   **5.**   By default, Excel automatically fits number values in a cell.

T   F   **6.**   When you apply a style, you apply multiple formats in one simple step.

T   F   **7.**   Landscape orientation is the default setting for Word, Excel, and Access.

T   F   **8.**   In PowerPoint, you can edit slide contents in Normal view and in Outline view.

T   F   **9.**   In Excel, the COUNT function shows the sum of the numerical values in the argument range.

T   F **10.**   In PowerPoint, text boxes enable you to position text anywhere on a slide, even outside a placeholder.

T   F **11.**   You can automatically adjust column widths in Word tables, Excel worksheets, and Access datasheets.

T   F **12.**   You can change the order of PowerPoint slides in Slide Sorter view by dragging and dropping the slide thumbnails.

T   F **13.**   When you create a form, query, or a report, you add a new object to an Access database.

T   F **14.**   The Replace command is useful when you need to find or reformat multiple occurrences of the same text.

T   F **15.**   When sharing a Word document, saving the document as a read-only document is the most secure option for restricting others from editing the document.

MULTIPLE CHOICE

Select the best response for each of the following statements.

1. A(n) _____ is a number or cell reference in an Excel formula.

   A.   argument

   B.   operator

   C.   operand

   D.   function

2. _____ are settings that determine how a slide is introduced as you move from one PowerPoint slide to another in Slide Show view.

   A.   Triggers

   B.   Entrance effects

   C.   Slide transitions

   D.   Motion paths

3. The _____ serves as the primary interface between the user and the application.

   A.   status bar

   B.   taskbar

   C.   document window

   D.   application window

4. When a Word paragraph is formatted with a _____, the first line of text is indented, and all other lines of the paragraph are aligned at the left margin.

   A.   first line indent

   B.   hanging indent

   C.   right indent

   D.   none of the above

5. In an Excel worksheet, you can edit a formula cell by _____.

   A.   selecting the cell, pressing F2, and then editing the formula in the cell or in the formula bar

   B.   double-clicking the cell and then editing the formula in the cell

   C.   selecting the cell and then editing the formula in the formula bar

   D.   all of the above

6. When working in _____ mode in Word, the existing text shifts to the right to make room for the new text.

   A.   Edit

   B.   Insert

   C.   Overtype

   D.   none of the above

7. To prevent users from seeing personal data related to a file, _____.

   A.   inspect the document and remove hidden text

   B.   inspect the document and remove metadata

   C.   save the document as a read-only document

   D.   restrict access

8. The _____ is a unique identifier of each record in an Access table.

   A.   field name

   B.   field property

   C.   field data type

   D.   primary key

9. A _____ is a database object that enables you to locate multiple records matching specified criteria in an Access database.

   A.   form

   B.   report

   C.   query

   D.   table

10. When sorting data, _____ rearranges the numbers from the highest value to the lowest value.

   A.   ascending order

   B.   descending order

   C.   reverse order

   D.   MAX order

11. To combine two or more worksheet cells into a single cell, _____ the cells.

   A.   split

   B.   merge

   C.   join

   D.   expand

12. To protect the content from change as well as preserve the visual appearance and layout of each page, save a Word document in a(n) _____ format.

   A. read-only compatible

   B. compatible

   C. PDF or XPS

   D. encrypted

13. To make it easy to add and delete multiple slides and rearrange the order of PowerPoint slides, switch to _____ view.

   A. Normal

   B. Slide Sorter

   C. Layout

   D. Notes Page

14. A _____ chart is useful for illustrating trends in data at equal intervals.

   A. line

   B. pie

   C. column

   D. bar

15. You can create links in PowerPoint presentations to _____ .

   A. slides in the same presentation

   B. slides in another presentation

   C. an e-mail address or a Web page

   D. all of the above

FILL IN THE BLANK

Complete the following sentences by writing the correct word or words in the blanks provided.

1. In a formula, a(n) _____ is a symbol that indicates the mathematical operation to perform.

2. A(n) _____ is descriptive text that is displayed when you position the mouse pointer over a command or control in the application window.

3. A(n) _____ is a printed copy of a document.

4. A(n) _____ is a graphic representation of worksheet or table data.

5. The _____ feature enables you to cut off portions of a graphic that you do not want to show.

6. A(n) _____ is three or four characters automatically added to the filename when the document is saved.

7. A(n) _____ contains column headings or field names in a data source, such as a table or spreadsheet.

8. _____ are built-in document parts that are already designed and formatted.

9. _____ is the revision marks and comments that appear in a document.

10. When you _____ a row or a column, the locked area is visible as you scroll through the worksheet.

11. A cell reference that contains both relative and absolute references is called a(n) _____ cell reference.

12. A(n) _____ is information and/or graphics that is printed in the bottom margin of each page.

13. The _____ is a horizontal bar that is displayed at the bottom of the desktop, and it displays the Start button and minimized window buttons.

14. _____ effects are settings used to control how an object leaves a slide in a PowerPoint presentation.

15. The _____ is a Word feature that enables you to quickly find alternative words or synonyms for a word in your document.

PROJECTS

PROJECT 2-1

1. Launch **Word**, and open the **Safari.docx** file from the drive and folder where your Data Files folder is stored. Save the Safari document as **Revised Safari**, followed by your initials. The document is a promotional flyer for visitors at the Madikwe Game Reserve, and the document will be printed using a duplex printing setting.

2. Change the page layout settings so that all margins are ½".

3. Several words are misspelled, and there are a few grammatical errors. Locate these errors, and make the necessary corrections. All occurrences of *Madikwe* are spelled correctly.

4. Find the first occurrence of *Big Five*. Change *Five* to **5**, and then add the following sentence immediately after that sentence.

   `The Big 5 are the lion, elephant, rhino, buffalo, and leopard, which are all considered to be the most dangerous animals to hunt.`

5. Search from the beginning of the document and find the phrase *constantly train*. This text appears twice in this article, so change this first occurrence so it is not used repetitively. Use the Thesaurus feature to find and replace the word *constantly* with a synonym.

6. Under the subheading *Wildlife and Ecosystem*, select all the italicized text and apply a bullet format. Then, indent all paragraphs in the document, excluding the subheadings and the bulleted list, with a .25" first line indent.

7. If necessary, display nonprinting characters. Position the insertion point in front of the paragraph marker under the subheading *Safari Options*, and then create a 2×5 table, and enter the following data in the table. Use the AutoFit feature so the column widths fit the content, and apply a table style.

Safari Name	Description
Bush Walk	A guided walking tour; approximately 3 miles; 1 day
The Expedition	Combines hiking and camping for those who want to get close to nature; 3 days, 2 nights
Photo Workshop	Photography instruction in prime wildlife locations; overnight stay in thatch roof guesthouses; 4 days, 3 nights
Classic Experience	Morning, afternoon, and evening game drives in safari vehicle; lodge suites are ideal for families with children; 3 days, 2 nights

8. In the article with the subheading *History*, format the two paragraphs in two columns, using the right preset with a line between the columns. In the article with the subheading *Excellent Bird Watching and Wildlife Viewing*, format the three paragraphs of text in two columns of equal width. Apply justified alignment to all paragraphs under both subheadings.

9. In the *Excellent Bird Watching and Wildlife Viewing* article, insert the **Bird.jpg** picture file from the drive and folder where your Data Files folder is stored. Resize the picture so it is approximately 1.3" wide by 1.5" high. Position the picture at the left side of the first paragraph. Apply square text wrapping.

10. In the same article, insert the **Elephant.jpg** picture file from the drive and folder where your Data Files folder is stored. Resize the picture so it is approximately 2.5" wide by 2" high. Position the picture in the second column below the last paragraph in the article. Apply top and bottom text wrapping. If necessary, reduce the size of the pictures so the two articles fit on the first page of the document. The subheading *Safari Options* should be displayed at the top of page 2.

11. Position the insertion point at the end of the document, and insert the **Giraffe.jpg** picture file from the drive and folder where your Data Files folder is stored. Resize the picture so it is approximately 4" wide by 3" high. Position the picture on the right side of the bulleted list, aligned with the right margin, using Tight text wrapping. Add a black, 1½-point border to each of the three pictures.

12. Select the first subheading **History**. Change the font to Cambria, 16 point. Add a double-line border above and below the paragraph, using a color that complements the colors in the pictures. Choose an appropriate border width. Then add appropriate shading for the paragraph. Center the text. Use the Format Painter to copy the paragraph formats to the three other subheadings.

13. Preview the document in Backstage view. Insert a manual page break, and make adjustments to the margins and the picture sizes as needed so the entire document fits on two pages, with two articles on each page. If necessary, change the table style colors to complement the heading formats.

14. Save the changes. Then save the document in PDF format as **Revised Safari**. Close the PDF file and the Word document.

PROJECT 2–2

1. Launch **Excel**, and open the **Travel Data.xlsx** file from the drive and folder where your Data Files folder is stored. Save the Travel Data workbook as **Updated Travel Data**, followed by your initials.

2. Rename the Sheet1 tab **Expenses**. Rename the Sheet2 tab **Hours**.

3. In the Expenses worksheet, insert a new column to the left of the Fuel column. Add the heading **Ent.** at the top of the new column. *Ent.* is an abbreviation for *Entertainment*, which refers to expenses incurred for entertaining clients, such as taking them to dinner.

4. Click cell **F1**, and enter the heading **Total**. Insert a new row at the top of the worksheet. Select the range **A1:F1**, and merge and center the cells. Enter the heading **Monthly Expense Report**. Select the first two rows, and apply the bold format.

5. Click cell **A14**, and fill down the cell contents through cell **A32** so all the dates in the month of June are displayed.

6. If necessary, launch **Word**. In Word, open **Travel Notes.docx** from the drive and folder where your Data Files folder is stored. This document simulates handwritten notes for incurred expenses. Enter this new data in the Expenses worksheet. (*Hint*: If you have a large monitor, you can display the Excel and Word application windows side by side.) Close the Word document.

7. Select the range **A3:A32**, and then apply the Short Date format (*6/1/2014*). Select the range **B3:F34**, and apply the Currency number format.

8. Click cell **F3**, and enter a formula to calculate the sum of the values in the range B3:E3. Then, fill the formula down to cell F34. Many adjacent cells are empty, so do not be concerned if the error flag appears with the results.

9. Click cell **A34**. Enter **Total**, and format the text bold. Click cell **B34**, and enter a formula to calculate the sum of the values in the range B3:B32. Then, fill the formula to the right for the range C34:E34. Use the AutoFit feature to make the column widths fit the cell contents.

10. Switch to the Hours worksheet. Delete column B. Then, select the range **B2:B36**, and increase the number of decimal places to **2**.

11. Enter some formulas to calculate the data recorded for the month:

    a. Click cell **A32**, and enter **Total days worked**. Click cell **B32**, and enter a formula to count the number of cells in the column that contain numbers in the range B2:B31.

    b. Click cell **A33**, and enter **Total hours worked**. Click cell **B33**, and enter a formula to calculate the total number of hours worked for the range B2:B31.

    c. Click cell **A34**, and enter **Fewest hours worked**. Click cell **B34**, and enter a formula to calculate the fewest hours worked in one day in the range B2:B31.

    d. Click cell **A35**, and enter **Most hours worked**. Click cell **B35**, and enter a formula to calculate the most hours worked in one day in the range B2:B31.

    e. Click cell **A36**, and enter **Average daily hours worked for 21 days**. Format the text to wrap in the cell. Click cell **B36**, and enter a formula to calculate the average daily hours for the 21 working days. (*Hint*: You cannot use the AVERAGE function to perform this calculation; you must create your own formula.)

12. Use the AutoFit feature to make the column widths fit the contents.

13. Save the changes, and close the workbook.

PROJECT 2–3

1. Launch **PowerPoint**, and open **The Climb.pptx** file from the drive and folder where your Data Files folder is stored. Save the The Climb presentation as **The Everest Climb**, followed by your initials.

2. Delete the fourth slide. Then move slide 6 to follow slide 3.

3. Add a new slide with the Title and Content layout after slide 3. Enter the title **Risky Business**. In the lower placeholder text box, enter **1 out of 10**. Increase the lower placeholder text font size to 96 point. Remove the bullet format, and center the text.

4. Go to slide 5. Change the title *Risky Business* to **What happens?**.

5. Go to slide 2. Insert clip art or a photograph of mountains. Resize the picture to fill the slide. Send the picture to the back so the title *29,035 feet high* appears at the top of the photograph. If necessary, change the font color to white or a light color so you can easily read the title.

6. Go to slide 3. Change the slide layout to Two Content. Position the bulleted list on either the left or right side of the slide. On the other side of the slide, insert clip art (an illustration or photograph) that helps describe the words in the bulleted list. For example, insert an image of a calendar or the number 6. Resize the image as needed.

7. Go to slides 5 and 6. Insert clip art (illustrations or photographs) that help to describe the text in the bulleted list, such as blowing snow, a thermometer, or a mountain climber on the side of the mountain. Remember, you can remove picture backgrounds and format pictures with styles and special effects.

8. Go to slide 7. Edit the 2001 record so it reads **2010: Youngest climber: Age 13, Jordan Romero**, and switch the order of the records so they are in chronological order. Convert the bulleted items to a SmartArt graphic. If necessary, decrease the font size so each item fits on one line. If time permits, research the Internet and see if any of the other records need to be updated.

9. Apply a design or custom background to all the slides. If you choose to apply a theme, make any necessary adjustments if the slide titles are not positioned correctly relative to inserted pictures.

10. Format custom animations for the objects and text boxes on each slide. Be sure to set the trigger and speed for each animation.

11. Format a slide transition for one or more slides. Be sure to set the transition speed.

12. Preview the slide show, and make any necessary changes so the content flows smoothly. Make sure the animations and transitions are effective.

13. Go to slide 6. In the Notes pane, enter **There is a short window of time in the spring to climb the mountain.**.

14. Save the changes, and close the presentation.

PROJECT 2–4

1. Launch **Access**, and open the **Species.accdb** file from the drive and folder where your Data Files folder is stored. Save the Species database as **Updated Species**, followed by your initials.

2. Open the **Species table**. Adjust the widths of all the columns so you can see the complete entry in every field column.

3. Show the Species table in Design view, and rearrange the field names so the Common Name field appears in the list before the Group field name. Save the changes, and close the Species table.

4. Create a form for all the fields in the Species table, in the same order they appear in the table. Name the form **Species Form**.

5. Use the form to enter the following two new records, and then close the form.

Common Name:	Mandarin duck
Group:	Birds
Species Name:	Aix galericulata
Order:	Angeriformes
Family:	Anatidae
Habitat:	Eastern Asia

Common Name:	Grant's zebra
Group:	Mammals
Species Name:	Equus burchelli
Order:	Perissofactyla
Family:	Equidae
Habitat:	Southeastern Africa

6. Go to record 22, *Arctic wolf*. In the Species Name field, change the entry to **Canis lupus tundranum**. Close the form.

7. Open the **Species** table. In the Order field, search for all occurrences of *Arteodactyly*, and replace all occurrences in the current field with **Artiodactyla**.

8. Use the Query wizard to create a simple query based on the Species table:

   a. Include the Common Name, Group, Species Name, and Habitat fields, in that order.

   b. Name the query **Mammals**.

   c. In the Group field, add the criteria **"Mammals"** in the Group field.

   d. All fields except Group should show in the query.

9. Use the Report Wizard to create a report:

    a. Include the Common Name, Group, Habitat, Family, Species Name, and Order fields, in that order.

    b. Do not group the report.

    c. Sort the report by the Common Name field in ascending order.

    d. Choose the Tabular layout with landscape orientation.

    e. Name the report **Species Report**.

10. Close the report and the table, and then close the database.

■ INTEGRATED PROJECT

You volunteer at the local Rails-to-Trails organization, which converts old, unused railroad beds into trails for public use. These trails can be used for a variety of activities including walking, jogging or running, biking, and in-line skating. The organization has asked you to help communicate information about rail trails in your area. You want to prepare an announcement to distribute throughout the community, and create a slide show to present information about the organization at a community meeting next week.

JOB 2–1

You decide to begin by organizing some data in an Excel spreadsheet.

1. If necessary, launch **Excel**. Open the **Survey.xlsx** file from the drive and folder where your Data Files folder is stored. Save the Survey worksheet as **Revised Survey**, followed by your initials.

2. Click cell **C4**. Enter a formula to calculate the percentage of positive responses. (*Hint*: Divide the number of positive responses by the total surveyed. In the equation, the value for the total surveyed needs to be an absolute reference.)

3. Apply the Percent Style number format to cell C4. Then, fill the formula down through cell C8.

4. Copy the formula in cell C4 to the Clipboard, and then paste the formula in cells E4 and G4. Then, fill the formula down in both of those columns, and apply the Percent Style number format as necessary.

5. Hide columns B, D, and F. Then select rows 3 and 4. Create a 3-D pie chart. If necessary, add a legend and data labels. Format data labels for Best Fit. If necessary, change the color, and increase the font size for the legend and the labels to 14 point so the text can be read easily. Apply the bold format to the labels. In the chart title, change *crime rate* to **Crime Rate**.

6. Position the chart below the data.

7. Select rows 3 and 5, and create a second 3-D pie chart, using the same settings described in Step 5. In the chart title, change *home value* to **Home Value**. Move the chart to Sheet2.

8. Save the changes to the workbook, and leave the workbook open for the next Job.

JOB 2–2

A new section of a popular rail trail is about to open, so the timing is perfect to provide general information to community residents about rail trails. You already created a draft of an announcement, and you asked another member of the organization to review it and provide feedback.

1. If necessary, launch **Word**. Open the **Scenic Trail.docx** file from the drive and folder where your Data Files folder is stored. Save the Scenic Trail document as **Revised Scenic Trail**, followed by your initials.

2. Navigate through the revisions and comments, and review the markup. Accept all the revisions and delete the comments. Toggle off Track Changes. Scroll down through the document, and correct any errors in spacing and punctuation.

3. Select the title at the top of the document. Apply the bold format, and change the font size to 14 point.

4. Select the third paragraph in the body of the document beginning *Rail trails such as* and move the paragraph so it follows the introductory paragraph.

5. Find every occurrence of *rail-trail*, and replace the hyphen with a blank space. Find the occurrence of *14,000*, and change it to **15,000**.

6. If necessary, open the **Survey.xlsx** workbook from your solution files. Select the chart on Sheet2 (Impact on Home Value), and copy it to the Clipboard. Switch back to the Revised Scenic Trail document. Position the insertion point at the beginning of the last paragraph of text (beginning *Not only are rail trails*). Paste the chart into the Word document.

7. Format the chart for square text wrapping. Change the zoom setting so you can see the entire page. Position the chart in the lower-right corner of the page. Make sure the entire document fits on one page. Resize the chart if necessary.

8. Save the changes to the Word document. Leave the document and the workbook open for the next Job.

JOB 2–3

The next step is to prepare the slide show for next week's community meeting.

1. If necessary, launch **PowerPoint**. Open the **Rail Trail.pptx** file from the drive and folder where your Data Files folder is stored. Save the Rail Trail presentation as **Revised Rail Trail**, followed by your initials.

2. Instead of adding words to the presentation, add visuals to deliver the message. Tips in the Notes pane for each slide will help you choose appropriate clip art and photographs.

3. After you insert the images on the slides, replace the tips in the Notes pane with points you want to emphasize during the presentation. Refer to the **Revised Scenic Trail.docx** document and use it as a guide.

4. Insert a new slide after slide 5 with the blank layout. Into the new slide, copy and paste the Impact on Home Value chart from the Revised Survey workbook in your solution files. Resize the chart to fill the slide. If necessary, enlarge the chart title, legend text, and label text.

5. Select the image on slide 7, and create a hyperlink to slide 3 in the same presentation. (When you click the image in Slide Show view, slide 3 will open and you can use this slide for the closing comments in the presentation. Then to exit the presentation instead of advancing to slide 4, press Esc.)

6. Add a design or a custom background to all the slides. Remove backgrounds to images, apply borders and effects to images, and resize and reposition images as needed.

7. Add custom animations and/or sounds for the clip art and photographs to appear on the slide. If desired, also format one or more slide transitions.

8. Preview the slide show, and make any necessary edits to the triggers and timing for the animations and transitions.

9. Save the changes to the presentation, and close the presentation, the Word document, and the Excel workbook.

JOB 2–4

The final step is to prepare mailing labels so you can mail copies of the announcement to other volunteers in the organization who will then assist in distributing the copies of the announcement throughout the community.

1. If necessary, launch **Access**. Open the **Volunteers.accdb** file from the drive and folder where your Data Files folder is stored. Save the Volunteers database as **Updated Volunteers**, followed by your initials.

2. Use the Label Wizard to create mailing labels based on the Volunteers table:

   a. Create labels for the Avery C2160 label type.

   b. Change the font to Comic Sans MS, 12 point, Normal weight.

   c. Add the fields to the prototype label for the appropriate mailing format.

   d. There is no need to sort the records.

   e. Name the report **Volunteer Mailing Labels**.

3. Review the labels in Print Preview to make sure they look correct, and make any necessary changes.

4. Close the database, and then close all open applications.

Estimated Time for Module: 9 hours

MODULE 3

LIVING ONLINE

LIVING ONLINE

 LESSON 25
Network Fundamentals

 LESSON 26
Communication Services

 LESSON 27
Communications and Collaboration

 LESSON 28
Using the Internet and the World Wide Web

 LESSON 29
Web Content

 LESSON 30
Technology and Society

 LESSON 31
Computer Safety and Ethics

LESSON 25

Network Fundamentals

■ OBJECTIVES

Upon completion of this domain, you should be able to:

- Describe a network.
- Identify the benefits of a network.
- Evaluate the risks of network computing.
- Identify client/server networks.
- Identify network types.
- Understand network communications.
- Resolve network security issues.

■ DATA FILES

You do not need data files to complete this lesson.

■ WORDS TO KNOW

biometric security measure

cable modem

client

client/server network

communications channels

digital subscriber line (DSL)

extranet

firewall

hacker

hub

Internet

intranet

local area network (LAN)

modem

node

peer-to-peer (P2P) network

proxy server

Public Switched Telephone Network (PSTN)

router

server

server operating system

T-1 line

wide area network (WAN)

WiMAX

wireless Internet service provider (WISP)

wireless LAN (WLAN)

As companies grow and purchase more computers, they often find it advantageous to connect those computers through a network, a group of two or more computers linked together. This setup allows users to share software and hardware such as printers, scanners, and other devices. In addition to using a local network, organizations use more far-reaching networks to connect to employees, suppliers, and customers nationally and even internationally. The locations can be in the same city or in different locations all over the world.

3-1.1.1

Introducing Networks

When most people think of networks, they envision something fairly complicated. However, at the lowest level, networks are not that complex. In fact, a network is simply a group of two or more computers linked together. As the size of a network increases and more devices are added, installing devices and managing the network becomes more technical. Even so, networking concepts and terminology basically remain the same regardless of size or type.

Different types of networks transfer different types of data. For instance, over a computer network, you can transfer text, images, video, and audio files. A telephone network is similar in makeup to a computer network, though it transfers voice data. The *Public Switched Telephone Network (PSTN)* supports telephone service and is the world's collection of interconnected commercial and government-owned voice-oriented systems. Digital, mobile, and standard telephones are supported through this network. **Figure 25–1a** and **Figure 25–1b** show the similarities between a home network and the telephone network.

▶ **VOCABULARY**
Public Switched Telephone Network (PSTN)

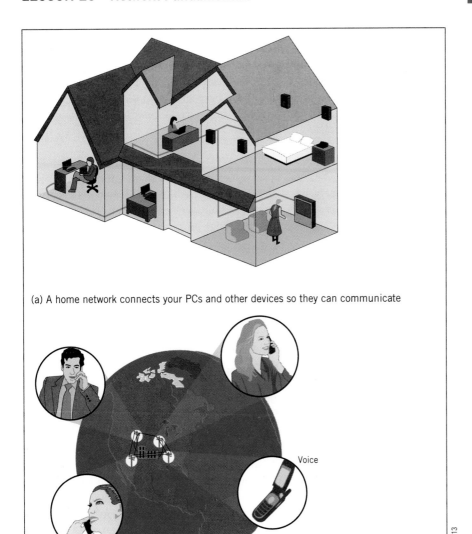

(a) A home network connects your PCs and other devices so they can communicate

Voice

(b) The telephone network functions much like your home network except on a larger scale

FIGURE 25–1   Home and telephone networks

3-1.1.2

Identifying the Benefits of a Network

To identify the benefits of a network, you might think first about the biggest network of all—the Internet. Consider some of the many changes that have occurred in our society in the last few years because of the Internet. One profound change is electronic mail. A network provides instant communication, and e-mail messages are delivered almost immediately. Other network benefits include the following:

- *Information sharing*: Authorized users can access computers on the network to share information, data, and other resources. People share information through special group projects, news groups, databases, blogs, FTP, Internet telephony, instant messaging, social media, and so on. Users around the world can connect to each other to access, share, and exchange information. See **Figure 25–2**.

- *Collaborative environment*: A shared environment enables users to exchange files and collaborate on group projects by combining the power and capabilities of diverse equipment and software, thus increasing personal productivity.

- *Hardware sharing*: It is not necessary to purchase a printer or a scanner or other frequently used peripherals for each computer. Instead, one device connected to a network can serve the needs of many users.

- *Software sharing*: Instead of purchasing and installing software on every computer, it can be installed on the server. All of the users can then access the program from this one central location. Software sharing saves money because companies can purchase a site license for their users. This practice is less expensive than purchasing individual software packages, and updating software on the server is much easier and more efficient than updating it on individual computers.

- *Enhanced communications*: Electronic mail, text messages, social media, and other electronic communication have changed the way the world interacts. One advantage is the almost instantaneous delivery of e-mail. The cost for e-mail does not depend on the size of the message or the distance the message has to travel.

FIGURE 25–2   Information sharing

Evaluating the Risks of Networked Computing

3-1.1.3

As with any technology, you should consider the disadvantages of using a network along with the benefits. For instance, data insecurity and the vulnerability to unauthorized access are primary weaknesses of many networks. The security of a computer network is challenged every day by equipment malfunctions, system failures, computer hackers, and virus attacks.

Equipment malfunctions and system failures are caused by a number of factors, including natural disasters such as floods or storms, fires, and electrical disturbances such as brownouts or blackouts. Server malfunctions or failures mean users temporarily lose access to network resources, such as printers, drives, and information.

Computer hackers and viruses present a great risk to networked environments. *Hackers* are people who break into computer systems to steal services and information, such as credit card numbers, passwords, personal data, and even national security information. Hackers can also delete data. Other people threaten networks and data by creating viruses and other types of malicious software, which are particularly dangerous to networked computers because these programs usually are designed to sabotage shared files (see **Figure 25–3**).

▶ **VOCABULARY**
hacker

FIGURE 25–3   Computer criminal

The following are some other disadvantages of networks:

- *Individual loss of autonomy*: Networks can play a part in taking away an individual's autonomy by controlling which software programs are accessible, and keeping a record of how the computer is used and what sites are accessed, for example.

- *Malicious code*: Compared to standalone computers, networks are more vulnerable to viruses, worms, Trojan horses, e-mail bombs, and spyware.

- *Network faults*: Network equipment problems can result in loss of data and resources.

- *Setup and management costs*: Setting up a network requires an investment in hardware and software; ongoing maintenance and management of the network requires the care and attention of at least one IT professional.

- *Lack of privacy*: For example, e-mail is not necessarily private. Messages travel through a number of systems and networks and provide opportunities for others to intercept or read the messages (see **Figure 25–4**). Junk e-mail also can become a problem. On the other hand, a standalone system is not vulnerable to many of these risks because it does not share connections with other computers.

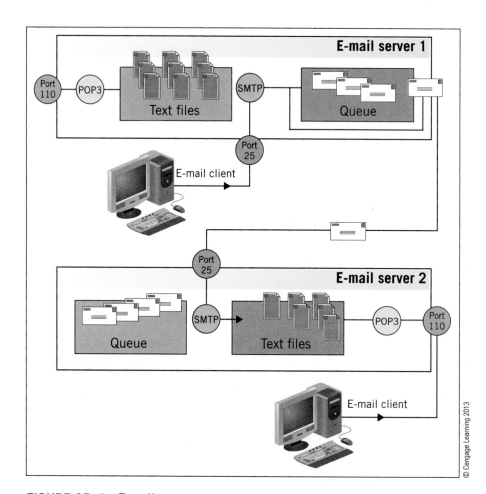

FIGURE 25–4   E-mail system

ETHICS IN TECHNOLOGY

Hackers

Computer security violations are one of the biggest problems experienced on computer networks. People who break into computer systems are called hackers. The reasons they break in are many and varied. Common types of violations follow:

- *Theft of services*: Many password-protected services charge a fee for usage. A hacker finds a way to bypass the password and uses the service without paying for it.

- *Theft of information*: A hacker might break into a system to steal credit card numbers, test data, or even national security data.

- *Unfair competition or vengeance*: Hackers might access an organization's system to destroy files as a form of revenge for real or imagined grievances. They also might steal information to sell to opposing groups or to use to compete with the organization.

- *Thrill*: Some hackers break into sites for the challenge. The thrill is in breaking the code or feeling superior to the security system.

Identifying Client/Server Networks

The term *client/server network* describes a network design model. Most common network functions such as database access, e-mail exchange, and Internet access are based on this model. In most instances, the *client* is a software program such as Internet Explorer. The *server* is hardware (a computer) and can be one of many types of servers, such as a mail server, a database server, an FTP server, an application server, a Web server, and so on. When you access the Internet using a browser, the browser is the client you use to access any available server in the world. This access enables the server and client to share files and other resources such as printers and external storage devices. In general, a server provides a service, such as Web access, to one or many clients.

For network administrators, selecting a server can be a simple or a complicated task, depending on the network size, the amount of storage needed, the number of users, and so on. Similar to a desktop computer, a network server requires an operating system.

Server operating systems are high-end programs designed to provide network control and include special functions for connecting computers and other devices into a network. Three of the more popular server operating systems are Microsoft Windows, Mac OS X, and UNIX/Linux. The selection of an operating system is determined by how the server will be accessed, security issues, whether the server will host a database, whether forms will be processed, whether programs such as Microsoft Expression Web or Adobe Dreamweaver will be used, and other individual factors. Client access to the server can be through desktop or notebook computers, handheld devices, game systems, and other similar electronic devices.

3-1.1.4

▶ **VOCABULARY**

client/server network

client

server

server operating system

local area networks (LAN)

wide area networks (WAN)

Identifying Network Types

3-1.1.5

Networks can be categorized by size as *local area networks (LANs)* or *wide area networks (WANs)*. They can also be classified by type, which includes client/server, peer-to-peer, intranet, extranet, and the Internet.

Local Area Networks

Most LANs connect personal computers, workstations, and other devices such as printers and scanners in a limited geographical area, such as an office building, school, or home. Each device on the network is called a *node*, and each node generally shares resources such as a printer, programs, and other hardware. A *wireless LAN (WLAN)* is a variation of the LAN that uses few if any physical wires to connect devices. To communicate on a WLAN, the computer and other devices that access the network must each contain a wireless device such as a network card, flash card, PC card, USB network adapter, or other type of built-in wireless capability or a wireless network card (see **Figure 25–5**).

VOCABULARY

node

wireless LAN (WLAN)

router

communications channels

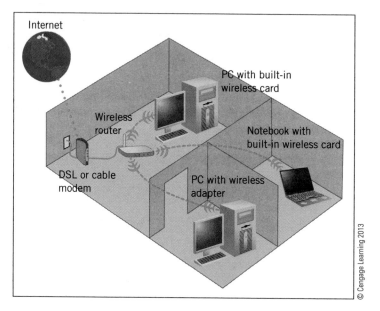

FIGURE 25–5   Wireless LAN

Wide Area Networks (WAN)

A WAN covers a large geographical area and can contain communication links across metropolitan, regional, or national boundaries. The communications area might be as large as a state, country, or even the world. The largest WAN is the Internet. Most WANs consist of two or more LANs and are connected by *routers*, which direct traffic on the Internet or on multiple connected networks. *Communications channels* can include telephone systems, fiber optics, satellites, microwaves, or any combination of these.

Other Types of Networks

The design of a network, including how it is set up physically, is called its architecture. The two broad categories of network architecture are client/server and peer-to-peer.

- *Client/server network*: In this type of architecture, one or more computers on the network acts as a server. The server manages network resources. Depending on the size of the network, several servers might be connected. For example, a print server manages the printing and a database server manages a large database. In most instances, a server is a high-speed computer with considerable storage space. The network operating system software and network versions of software applications are stored on the server. All of the other computers on the network are called clients. They share the server resources and other peripherals such as hubs, firewalls, and routers. A *hub* is a small, simple, inexpensive device that joins multiple computers together. Users access the server by entering a user name and password. See **Figure 25–6**. Some networks use a switch, which performs the same tasks as a hub and is much faster.

▶ **VOCABULARY**
hub

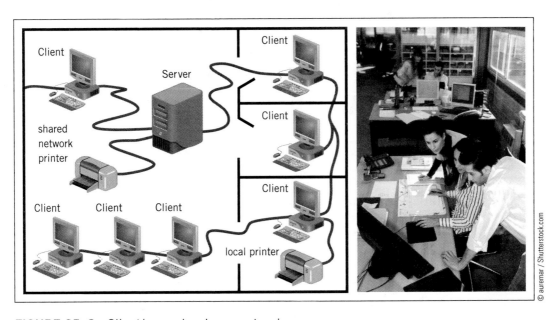

FIGURE 25–6   Client/server local area network

▶ **VOCABULARY**
peer-to-peer (P2P) network

intranet

extranet

Internet

■ *Peer-to-peer network*: In a ***peer-to-peer (P2P) network***, all the computers are equal. No computer is designated as the server. People on the network each determine what files on their computer they share with others on the network. This type of network is much easier to set up and manage. Many small offices use P2P networks. Some types of P2P networks allow you to download different parts of files simultaneously from several computers at the same time. Using this format, you can potentially get much faster downloads and get larger files more quickly. See **Figure 25–7**.

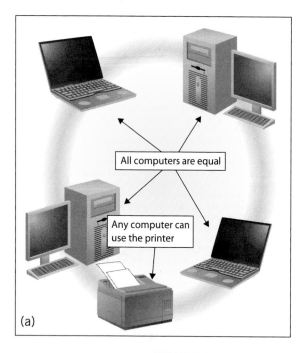
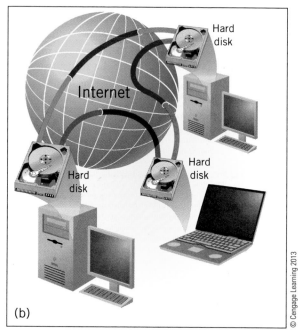

© Cengage Learning 2013

FIGURE 25–7   (a) Peer-to-peer network using a printer resource (b) Internet peer-to-peer network

■ **ABOVE AND BEYOND**

In discussions about networks, you might hear someone mention bridges, which are also a type of communications device. A bridge is a special computer that connects one LAN to another LAN. For the most part, however, bridges are rarely used in modern networks.

Networks are also classified by the type of technology they use to share information. Most networks use the Internet Protocol (IP) technology to share data and resources. The following types of networks use IP technology:

■ *Intranet*: An ***intranet*** is designed for the exclusive use of people within an organization. Many businesses have implemented intranets. Documents such as handbooks and employee manuals, newsletters, employment forms, and other relevant company documents are the types of files stored on an intranet server.

■ *Extranet*: An ***extranet*** is similar to an intranet, but it allows specific users outside of the organization to access internal information systems. Like the Internet, intranets and extranets use and support Web technologies, such as hyperlinks and Web pages coded in hypertext markup language (HTML).

■ *Internet*: The ***Internet*** is a worldwide system composed of thousands of smaller networks. This global network allows computers worldwide to connect and exchange information. The Web and electronic mail are two of the more popular components of the Internet.

In Step-by-Step 25.1, you research home wireless networks.

Step-by-Step 25.1

1. Click the **Start** button on the taskbar, and then click **Help and Support**.

2. Search for Help topics on networking.

3. Select the **Setting up a wireless network** topic.

4. Read the topic and then use your word-processing program to answer the following questions:

   ■ What equipment do you need to set up a wireless network?

   ■ Where should you position a wireless router?

   ■ What two tasks should you perform to secure the wireless network?

   ■ How do you add a computer to the network?

   ■ How can you share files on a Windows 7 network?

5. Save your file as **networking** and submit it to your instructor.

Understanding Network Communications

Most networks consist of a network server and computer clients. In addition, networks use two other categories of hardware: communications devices and devices that connect the network cabling and amplify the signal.

IC³

3-1.1.6

Communication Hardware

Communication hardware devices help to transmit and receive data. When we think about communication hardware, the first thing that generally comes to mind is the desktop computer and router. However, other types of computers and devices send and receive data. Some examples are mainframe computers, minicomputers, and large computers such as supercomputers; handheld and laptop computers; and even fax machines and digital cameras. All of these devices require some type of transmitting hardware device. Examples of communication hardware follow:

■ *Modem*: The word **modem** is an acronym for *mo*dulate-*dem*odulate, which means to convert analog signals to digital and vice versa. This device enables a computer to transmit data over telephone lines. Computer information is stored digitally (in binary code of 0s and 1s), whereas information sent over telephone lines or other media generally is transmitted in the form of analog waves. Both the sending and receiving users must have a modem. The speed at which modems can transmit data has increased dramatically in the past few decades. The first modems introduced in the 1960s could send data at a rate of about 300 bits per second (bps). By the early 1990s, the speed of data transmission via modem had increased to 9600 bps, with the standard modem speed of 56 Kbps (kilobits per second) reached by the middle of the decade. Special modems can transmit data as fast as 8 Mbps (megabits per second) over telephone lines.

▶ **VOCABULARY**
modem

> VOCABULARY

cable modem

digital subscriber line (DSL)

T-1 line

- *Cable modem*: A ***cable modem*** uses coaxial cable to send and receive data. This is the same type of cable used for cable TV. The bandwidth, which determines the amount of data that can be sent at one time, is much greater with a cable modem than with the older technology of a dial-up modem. For this reason, cable modems are used to deliver broadband Internet access, which is a high data rate connection to the Internet. Cable modems allow as many as 1,000 users to transmit data on one 6-MHz (megahertz) channel and can transmit data at speeds of 30 to 40 Mbps. A cable modem can be connected directly to your computer, enabling you to connect to the Internet, or it can be connected to a router so that your computer has wireless access to the Internet. See **Figure 25–8**.

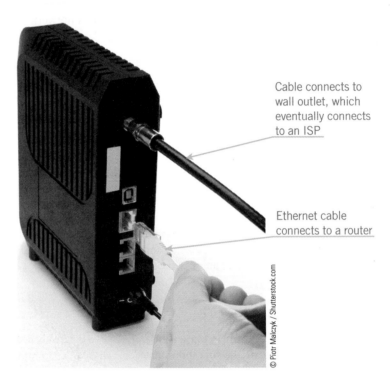

FIGURE 25–8   Cable modem

- *Digital subscriber line*: A ***digital subscriber line (DSL)*** is an Internet connection technology that provides for the transfer of information to a computer at a high-speed bandwidth over ordinary copper telephone lines. A DSL can carry both data and voice. The data part of the line is a dedicated connection to the Internet. High bit-rate DSL (HDSL) was the first DSL technology to use twisted-pair cables. Very-high bit-rate DSL (VDSL) can support HDTV, telephone services, and Internet access over a single connection. Like cable modems, DSL modems are widely used to provide broadband Internet access.

- *T-1 line*: A ***T-1 line*** is a type of fiber-optic telephone line that can transmit up to 1.544 megabits per second or can be used to transmit 25 digitized voice channels. T-1 lines can be used for data transfer on a network or to provide phone service for a commercial building.

■ *Wireless*: ***Wireless Internet service providers (WISPs)*** provide connection speeds more than 30 times faster than dial-up connections—from 384 Kbps to 2.0 Mbps. ***WiMAX*** (Worldwide Interoperability for Microwave Access) is a wireless technology that can deliver maximum speeds of up to 1 Gbps to your cell phone, home computer, or car. WiMAX is an alternative to cable and DSL, especially for users in areas that cable and DSL service providers do not serve. It is also used to connect mobile computer users to the Internet across cities and countries. You can use a WiMAX USB modem to connect to a WiMAX network. See **Figure 25–9**.

▶ **VOCABULARY**

wireless Internet service provider (WISP)

WiMAX

© cheyennezj / Shutterstock.com

FIGURE 25–9 USB modem for connecting to a WiMAX network

As indicated earlier, connecting to the Internet requires special devices—typically a cable or DSL modem linked to a computer using an Ethernet cable, a type of cable designed to connect devices on a network. To connect devices such as personal computers, cell phones, and game systems wirelessly to the Internet, the following components are needed:

■ A notebook computer or other type of device such as a computer game system, an iPhone or other smart phone, or similar device

■ An internal wireless adapter or a USB port for connecting an external adapter; the adapter must be compatible with the wireless provider's protocols

■ A high-speed, wireless Internet access plan from a provider

■ "Sniffer" software, used to locate hot spots; usually built into the device

Communication standards enable all of these different devices to communicate with each other.

ABOVE AND BEYOND

Broadband is high-speed Internet access; most Internet users in the United States have broadband access.

3-1.1.7

Resolving Network Security Issues

Establishing and maintaining computer security is necessary to keep hardware, software, and data safe from harm or destruction. Some risks to computers are natural causes, some are accidents, and others are intentional. It is not always evident that some type of computer crime or intrusion has occurred. Therefore, safeguards for each type of risk should be put into place. It is the responsibility of a company or an individual to protect its data.

The best way to protect data is to effectively control access to it. Generally, this protection is the responsibility of the network administrators and security personnel. If unauthorized persons gain access to data, they may obtain valuable information or trade secrets. Perhaps worse, they might change data outright so that no one can use it.

The most common form of restricting access to data is the use of passwords, which are similar to combinations you need to remove a lock, as shown in **Figure 25–10**. Users may need a password to log on to a computer system or to specific parts of it. Companies often establish password-protected locations on hard drives and networks so that designated people have access to certain areas but not to others.

© zimmytws / Shutterstock.com

FIGURE 25–10   Password-protected computer

To maintain secure passwords, you should change them frequently so that people who no longer need access are locked out. Tips for creating secure passwords include using a mixture of upper- and lowercase letters, using numbers as well as letters, and adding special characters such as & or % to the password. The challenge is to create passwords that are easy for you to remember but difficult for anyone else to decipher, because you should never write down a password or share it with anyone else (see **Figure 25–11**). The challenge is to create passwords that are easy for you to remember, but difficult for anyone else to decipher. You should never share or write down a password. More password protection is broken by people who gain access through a shared password or lost "cheat sheet" than by anyone guessing your "secret code."

Bullets are shown instead of text to keep the password private

FIGURE 25-11   Passwords protect data against unauthorized use

All users should maintain password security to keep out unauthorized users, hackers, and other computer criminals. Never reveal a password to anyone without authorization. Inform the appropriate people if you discover that an unauthorized user knows or can access passwords. Avoid using the same or similar passwords for other applications or Internet accounts.

Other security measures include the following:

- Electronic identification cards are used to gain access to certain areas within a building or department.

- *Firewalls*, which consist of special hardware and software, protect an internal network from external networks. A firewall gives users inside an organization the ability to access computers outside of their organization but keeps unauthorized users from accessing the organization's computers.

- Antivirus software is used to protect data on your computer. It always should be running on a computer to protect data and programs from corruption or destruction.

- A *proxy server* acts like a switchboard through a firewall. The server is an intermediary between a user and the Internet, ensuring security, administrative control, and caching service. A cache (pronounced *cash*) is a place to store something temporarily.

▶ **VOCABULARY**
firewall

proxy server

biometric security measure

Planning for Security

Companies must plan for security before it is needed rather than handle breaches in security as they occur. For example, any company that deals with sensitive information or needs to protect its data should consider the following guidelines:

- Institute a selective hiring process that includes careful screening of potential employees. Do not keep employees on staff that refuse to follow security rules. This measure can prevent internal theft or sabotage.

- Regularly back up data and store it off site.

- Employ *biometric security measures*, which examine a fingerprint, a voice pattern, or the iris or retina of the eye. These must match the entry that was originally stored in the system for an employee to gain access to a secure area. This method of security is usually applied when high-level security is required.

Wireless Security

Wireless networking (Wi-Fi) is now so common that you can access the Internet just about anywhere at any time. Most laptop computers are sold with wireless cards installed. Wireless networking, however, has many security issues, and hackers have found it easy to access wireless networks. For example, one way to access a wireless network is through accidental association, when the user turns on the computer and the computer automatically connects to a wireless access point (see **Figure 25–12**). In Step-by-Step 25.2, you research wireless network security.

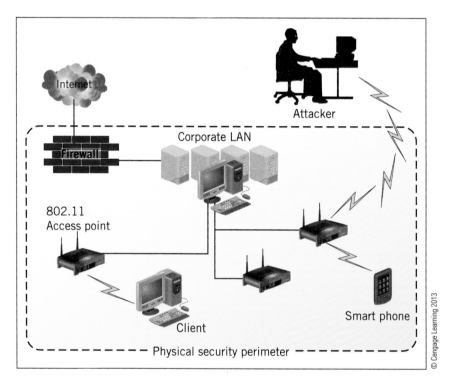

FIGURE 25–12   Securing wireless networks

Step-by-Step 25.2

1. Click the **Start** button ⊕ on the taskbar, and then click **Help and Support**.

2. Search for Help topics on wireless networks, and then click a link such as the **Why can't I connect to a network?** link.

3. Read the information and then use your word-processing program to summarize what you learned.

4. Define the terms *Internet Connectivity Evaluation tool* and *Windows Compatibility Center*.

5. Submit your word-processing document to your instructor.

TECHNOLOGY CAREERS

Building Communities with Computers

Computer modeling is a term that describes the use of computers to create a mathematical model of a real-life system or process and then test it under different conditions. If you have played the computer game SimCity, you already have some experience with computer modeling. When you play the game, create a city, and then change certain data, such as the population or the location of a utility system, you can see how those changes affect the city overall. The future is still bright for computer gaming and simulation. If you are looking for a career that stays on top of the latest technical innovations, consider one in computer simulation.

SUMMARY

In this lesson, you learned:

- A network is a group of two or more computers linked together.

- A telephone network is similar in makeup to a computer network. The Public Switched Telephone Network (PSTN) supports telephone service, and it is the world's largest collection of interconnected commercial and government-owned voice-oriented systems.

- You can use a network for information sharing, hardware sharing, software sharing, and as a collaborative environment.

- Networks are categorized according to size as local area networks (LANs) and wide area networks (WANs).

- LANs connect personal computers, workstations, and other devices such as printers and scanners in a limited geographical area, such as an office building, a school, or a home.

- A WAN is made up of several connected local area networks.

- In a client/server network, one or more computers on the network acts as a server. The server manages network resources. In a peer-to-peer (P2P) network, all of the computers are equal. No computer is designated as the server. People on the network each determine what files on their computer they share with others on the network.

- Data insecurity is a risk with many networks. Some risks to computers are natural causes, some are accidents, and others are intentional.

- The best way to protect data is to effectively control the access to it. Generally, this protection is the responsibility of the network administrators and security personnel. If unauthorized persons gain access to data, they may obtain valuable information or trade secrets. Hackers are people who break into computer systems to steal services and information.

- Transmission media can be either physical or wireless.

- A modem is a type of communications device. A hub is a device that controls the incoming and forwarding of data. A router directs traffic on the Internet or on multiple connected networks.

■ LESSON REVIEW

TRUE / FALSE

Circle T if the statement is true or F if the statement is false.

T   F   **1.**   The biggest network is the Internet.

T   F   **2.**   E-mail always is private.

T   F   **3.**   A WAN covers a large geographical area.

T   F   **4.**   The best way to protect data is to effectively control access to it.

T   F   **5.**   Networks are classified according to speed.

MULTIPLE CHOICE

Select the best response for the following statements:

1. A telephone network is similar in makeup to a _____ network.

    A. computer network   C. tiny area network

    B. local area network   D. metropolitan area network

2. A _____ server acts as an intermediary between a user and the Internet.

    A. high-level   C. connected-level

    B. proxy   D. biometric

3. The two broad categories of network architecture are _____ and peer to peer.

    A. intranet/extranet   C. client/server

    B. DSL   D. proxy/server

4. A(n) _____ can carry both data and voice.

    A. SLD   C. WAN

    B. bridge   D. DSL

5. A _____ is a variation of the LAN that uses no physical wires.

    A. WLAN   C. P2P

    B. PSTN   D. WiMAX

FILL IN THE BLANK

Complete the following sentences by writing the correct word or words in the blanks provided:

1. _____, which consist of special hardware and software, protect internal networks from external networks.

2. A(n) _____ converts analog signals to digital and vice versa.

3. A(n) _____ _____ is a type of fiber-optic telephone line.

4. The _____ is a worldwide system composed of thousands of smaller networks.

5. In a client/server network, the _____ manages network resources.

■ PROJECTS

PROJECT 25–1

As indicated in this lesson, the best way to protect data is to control access to the data.

3-1.1.1
3-1.1.3
3-1.1.7

1. Obtain a copy of the student use policy from your school. If one is not available, then locate a student use policy online from a school similar to yours.

2. After reading the policy carefully, rewrite it to include any additional guidelines and rules you believe should be included.

3. Explain why you selected these additional guidelines and rules and how they would benefit your educational environment.

4. Submit the document to your instructor as requested.

PROJECT 25–2

You want to set up a network in your home with the following elements:

3-1.1.5
3-1.1.6

■ DSL, cable, or satellite Internet connection

■ Desktop PC and two laptop computers that share the same Internet connection

■ A printer and wireless router

■ No additional charges from your Internet service provider

1. Use the Internet to research how to set up the home network according to this description.

2. Describe the network in a one- or two-page document.

3. Submit the document to your instructor as requested.

PROJECT 25–3

In recent times, schools have been criticized concerning the use of computers, especially in education at the primary and high school levels. Respond to the following questions:

3-1.1.2
3-1.1.3

1. Do you believe that computers should be used in elementary and high schools? Explain why or why not.

2. Should students have access to the Internet? Why or why not?

3. List at least two other options supporting computer access and two other options against computer access.

■ TEAMWORK PROJECT

You work at a local retail store that sells building supplies. Your supervisor at work is interested in learning about computers and various networking options as well as other technology solutions. In particular, she would like to know the best solutions for the store's environment. Assume that the hardware store has 14 employees and is part of a national chain. Develop a plan that you think would best serve the needs of your store for employee payroll, a directory and location of all store items, and a weekly review that would provide a list of what was sold and what needed to be replaced. Submit your final document to your instructor.

3-1.1.1
3-1.1.4

■ CRITICAL THINKING

Use the Internet and other resources to identify early security measures that were used to protect computers and computer data. Describe how these measures counteracted the intrusions made. Then, visit the Web sites of some companies that make computer security devices such as *www.computersecurity.com/individual.htm*. Compare these early security measures to today's current needs and practices. Write a report of your findings.

3-1.1.3
3-1.1.7

ONLINE DISCOVERY

Smart phones and notebook computers each use Wi-Fi to connect to the Internet. Use the Web to research the similarities and differences between Wi-Fi networks that smart phones use and those that notebook computers use. Organize your findings into a one-page document and submit it to your instructor.

3-1.1.5
3-1.1.6

JOB SKILLS

Netiquette—a word made from combining network and etiquette—refers to conventions to follow when using networks, including network services such as e-mail, blogs, and forums. Because so much workplace communication occurs on a network, knowing the rules of netiquette helps you set and maintain a professional reputation at work. Use the Internet to research the current rules of netiquette, and then list at least five rules in a document. Submit the document to your instructor.

LESSON 26

Communication Services

■ OBJECTIVES

Upon completion of this domain, you should be able to:

- Categorize electronic communication.
- Identify users of electronic communication.
- Identify components of electronic communication.
- Manage e-mail with Microsoft Outlook.
- Send and receive e-mail.
- Save a message.

■ DATA FILES

You do not need data files to complete this lesson.

■ WORDS TO KNOW

Address Book

archiving

attachment

Contact Group

e-mail address

electronic mail (e-mail)

instant messaging

packet

save a message

signature

spam

text messaging

user agent

Windows Live Mail

The Internet, electronic mail (e-mail), and other forms of electronic communications provide new ways to communicate. Using e-mail, you can combine numerous media—text, graphics, sound, video—into a single message, and then quickly exchange information in dynamic, two-way communications. Using the Internet, you can quickly transmit information to and receive information from individuals and workgroups around the world.

3-2.1.1

Categorizing Electronic Communication

As a worldwide electronic communications system, the Internet provides many communication services, which can be organized into the following categories:

▶ **VOCABULARY**

electronic mail (e-mail)

instant messaging

text messaging

- *Electronic mail*: **Electronic mail**, or **e-mail**, is similar to regular mail. You have a message, an address, and a carrier that figures out how to transfer the message from one location to another. You can send e-mail to other people on a network at an organization, or you can use an Internet service provider to send e-mail to any computer in the world.

- *Instant messaging (IM)*: You use **instant messaging** services to send messages in real time. In other words, you can send and receive messages while you and someone else are both connected to the Internet.

- *Text messaging*: Instead of using a computer, with **text messaging** you use a cell phone or other mobile device to send and receive written messages.

- *Voice over IP (VoIP)*: Sometimes called audio over IP, you use this service to make phone calls with an Internet connection instead of a regular telephone line. Your voice is converted into a digital signal that travels over the Internet. With VoIP, you can make a call directly from a computer, a special VoIP phone, or a traditional phone connected to a special adapter.

- *Online conferencing*: Also referred to as video conferencing, you can conduct a conference with yourself and one or more other participants at different sites by using computer networks to transmit audio and video data.

- *Chat rooms*: Chat rooms are Web sites that allow real-time communication so you can exchange messages with others through the computer. You use the keyboard to type text, which is displayed on the other person's monitor.

- *Social networking sites*: These Web sites provide a way to build online communities of people who share common interests or activities.

- *Blog postings/comments*: A blog (short for Web log) is a type of personal journal created by one person or by a group; entries are published in reverse chronological order.

- *Message boards and newsgroups*: Both of these services provide bulletin board systems that serve as discussion sites; users can post messages asking for assistance.

3-2.1.2

Identifying Users of Electronic Communication

Millions of people use the Internet, and each is required to have unique identification in the form of an e-mail address, sign-in or logon credentials, and password in the same way that each person has a unique phone number. Your e-mail address is used not only to send and receive e-mails but also for a variety of other options. For example, you can use your e-mail address to fill out a form to subscribe to a Web site, set up your checking account, order a book from Amazon.com, exchange instant messages, and so on. Other services that require a unique logon are blogs, social networks, and video conferencing services.

Identifying Components of Electronic Communication

3-2.1.3

Electronic communication is the technology that enables computers to communicate with each other and other devices. It is the transmission of text, numbers, voice, and video from one computer or device to another. Electronic communication has changed the way the world does business and the way we live our lives.

When computers were developed in the 1950s, they did not communicate with each other. This all changed in 1969. ARPANET was established and served as a testing ground for new networking technologies. ARPANET was a large wide area network created by the United States Defense Advanced Research Project Agency (ARPA).

Today's electronic communication requires the following components:

- *Software*: Software applications (***user agents***) installed on the local PC, network, or Web, such as e-mail, text message, and instant messaging programs

- *Sender*: The computer sending the message (server)

- *Receiver*: The computer receiving the message (server)

- *Channel*: The media that carries or transports the message: telephone wire, coaxial cable, radio signal, microwave signal, or fiber-optic cable

- *Communication*: The information transferred between user agents

- *Protocols*: The rules that govern the transfer of data and ensure that information created by one system can be interpreted and read by another

Electronic communication technology has made it possible to communicate around the globe using tools such as the Internet, electronic mail (e-mail), social media, e-commerce, and electronic banking. See **Figure 26–1**.

▶ **VOCABULARY**
user agents

© Toria / Shutterstock.com

FIGURE 26–1   Electronic communication

3-2.2.1

Interpreting E-Mail Addresses

When you send postal mail to someone, you must know the address of that person. The same thing is true for e-mail. For instance, David Edward's e-mail address could be *dedwards@gmail.com*. Each user on the Internet must have a unique e-mail address.

An *e-mail address* consists of three parts:

- The user name of the individual
- The @ symbol
- The user's domain name

David Edward's e-mail address *dedwards@gmail.com* ends with the domain code .com. The first set of domain codes were defined in October 1984 and are used on the Internet's Domain Name System (DNS). This set of codes included the following:

- .com (commercial)
- .edu (education)
- .gov (government)
- .mil (military)
- .org (organizations)

Currently, a limited range of 21 top-level domains are available. These include specialty domain names such as .cat, .jobs, .mobi, .post, .tel, .info, and .travel.

3-2.2.2

Parts of an E-Mail Message

When you compose an e-mail message, it should contain four main components. First, enter the address of one or more people to whom you are sending the message. Be sure to include a subject line, which should grab the recipient's attention or fully but briefly describe the purpose of the message. Many people scan the subject lines of their messages before opening them, so your subject lines should be meaningful and accurate. Next, include the body of the message, which should be clear, concise, and free from spelling errors. Any attachments should be noted in the body of the message.

3-2.2.3

E-Mail Options

E-mail programs typically include the following options when responding to a message:

- *Reply to Sender*: One way to reply to an e-mail message is to click the Reply button, type your reply message, and then send the message. With this type of reply, the original message is included along with your reply message, so it is appropriate when you are answering a question or responding to specifics in the original message. When you reply to an e-mail message, the recipient normally sees *RE:* preceding the text in the subject line to indicate that it is a reply message.
- *Reply All*: If more than one person is listed on the To or From line of the e-mail message, you can click the Reply All button instead of Reply. You then follow the same steps as when replying, except your message is sent to everyone who received the original message.

■ *Forward*: This option is similar to replying to a message; however, when you forward a message, you send it to people other than those who sent the original message. Forwarding a message helps cut down on the time you spend creating messages from scratch. It is also a quick way to share information with a number of people. When you forward a message, a recipient normally sees *FW*: preceding the text in the subject line to identify it as a message that is being forwarded.

■ *Courtesy copy (Cc)* and *blind copy (Bcc)*: To send a copy of an e-mail to another person, type his or her e-mail address into the Cc text box, or click the Cc button and then select the person's name. To send a blind copy to someone, type the e-mail address in the Bcc text box, or click the Bcc button and then select the person's name. The recipient of the Bcc is not visible to the other people receiving the message.

Unless a technical problem occurs, e-mail travels much faster than regular mail (sometimes referred to as "snail mail"). When you send someone an e-mail message, it is broken down into small chunks called *packets*. These packets travel independently from server to server. You might think of each packet as a separate page within a letter. When the packets reach their final destination, they are recombined into their original format. This process enables the message to travel much faster than if it were sent in one file. In fact, some messages can travel thousands of miles in less than a minute.

▶ **VOCABULARY**
packets
Windows Live Mail

Accessing E-Mail

Since e-mail has become a widespread way of communicating in our business and personal lives, the methods used to access e-mail have multiplied. Many Web sites and Internet service providers offer e-mail as part of a monthly fee or even at no charge. Google Gmail and Microsoft Hotmail are examples of Web-based e-mail services. After you set up an e-mail account with a service, you access your account using the company's Web site and entering your account name (usually your e-mail address) and a password. The Web site often directs you to a built-in e-mail program where you can read and send messages and manage your electronic communication.

Wireless communication also has expanded the ways e-mail can be transmitted and retrieved. Many people have cell phones or handheld computers that can send and receive e-mail almost anywhere.

Managing E-Mail with Microsoft Outlook

3-2.2.7

Microsoft Outlook is an Office application you can use to manage e-mail. Outlook is a versatile application that you can use to organize appointments, tasks and to-do lists, addresses, and e-mail. The e-mail features of Outlook are very similar to the features of *Windows Live Mail* (another e-mail program provided free of charge from the Windows Live Web site), so after you practice using Outlook in the exercises in this lesson, you will find that you can also use Windows Live Mail.

When you start Outlook, a window similar to the one shown in **Figure 26–2** is displayed. The default opening window is the Outlook Today window, which gives you an overview of the calendar, tasks, and mail features of the program. Figure 26–2 shows the Outlook Inbox, which displays the messages you receive.

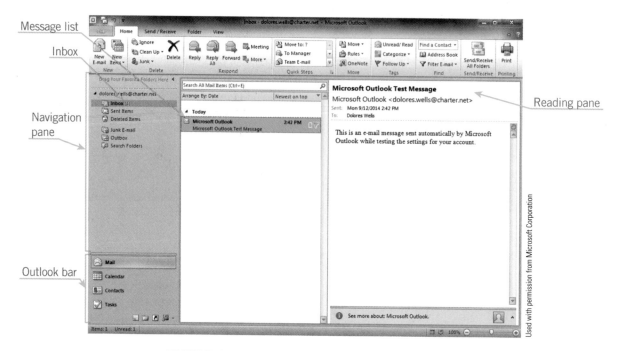

FIGURE 26–2   Outlook window

Mail management is handled primarily through the Inbox. The Inbox contains a number of elements. Using the Inbox, you can organize your mail by creating mail folders for various topics, special projects, and individuals. The folders can be divided into favorites and general mail folders. The Inbox contains a list of your messages. The messages can be arranged by date with the newest on top or the oldest on top. When a message first arrives in the Inbox, it is displayed in bold type. Once the message is read, it is no longer bolded.

The current task selected in the Outlook bar at the lower-left of the window is Mail. When Mail is selected, the left pane, also called the Navigation pane, lists a number of standard folders, including Inbox, Deleted Items, Sent Items, Junk E-mail, and Outbox. When you select a folder in the Navigation pane, such as Inbox, its contents appear in the message list, as shown in Figure 26–2. Click an item in the folder to see the full text in the Reading pane, the large pane at the right of the Outlook window.

You can manage the folders in the Navigation pane in the following ways:

- To create a new folder in the Navigation pane, click the Folder tab on the Ribbon, and then click the New Folder button in the New group.

- To delete a folder, right-click the folder name in the Navigation pane, and then click Delete Folder on the shortcut menu.

- To select and move or copy an e-mail message or other item from one folder to another, click the folder name containing the item you want to copy. This selects the folder and displays the folder contents in the Inbox. Drag the message or other item you want to move to the new folder. To copy and paste an item, select the item, click the Home tab on the Ribbon, click the Move button in the Move group, and then click Copy to Folder to open the Copy Items dialog box. In this dialog box, select the location for the item, and then click the OK button.

■   To delete an e-mail message, select the message you want to delete, and then click the Delete button in the Delete group on the Home tab. Deleted items are stored in the Deleted Items Mail folder. To undelete an item, click the Deleted Items folder and select the item you want to undelete. To permanently delete a message or to delete the contents of the Deleted Items folder, select the items you want to delete, right-click the items, and then select Delete.

■   To search for a message, select the folder you want to search, and then click in the Search All Mail Items text box (also called the Instant Search box). Type text contained in any part of the message. Items that contain the text that you typed appear with the search text highlighted.

■   To sort mail, click the Newest on top or Oldest on top column heading button to organize messages by date. You can also click the View tab, and then click the Arrange By button in the Arrangement group to select a sort option.

Archiving is the process of backing up your e-mail messages. After you install Outlook, AutoArchive automatically runs every 14 days and saves the backup file with a .pst extension. You can change how often AutoArchive runs by clicking the Folder tab, and then clicking the AutoArchive Settings button in the Properties group to open the AutoArchive tab of the Inbox Properties dialog box. When you make regular backups of your computer, be sure to back up the archive file with the .pst extension. If your hard disk fails (and they all eventually do), you will lose your messages and attachments such as pictures and videos unless you have a backup copy of the .pst file.

▶ **VOCABULARY**
archiving

Outlook can synchronize with other devices such as another computer, a cell phone, or other handheld devices. To use this service generally requires that you download and install updates for the particular device that you want to use.

Although you do not apply all of Outlook's options in this lesson, you can take a short tour of Outlook in the following Step-by-Step exercise by opening several Outlook folders. You can customize most Outlook folders to display information in a number of ways. When you open a folder, you see the view that was used the last time that folder was opened. The following steps assume that you already have an e-mail account set up in Outlook.

Step-by-Step 26.1

1.   Click the **Start** button 🍀 on the taskbar, point to *All Programs*, click **Microsoft Office**, and then click **Microsoft Outlook 2010**.

     (If your computer is on a network, you might be prompted to enter your profile name and a password when launching Outlook. If a dialog box appears asking you to make Outlook your default program for e-mail, calendar, and contacts, click **No**.)

2.   Click **Calendar** in the Outlook bar. You use this feature to set up appointments and meetings. If no one has entered any meetings in Outlook yet, this folder will be empty.

3.   Click **Contacts** in the Outlook bar. This feature stores information about personal and business contacts. If no one has entered any contacts in Outlook yet, this folder will be empty. (Additional information on using the Address Book is provided later in this lesson.)

4. Click **Tasks** in the Outlook bar. A grid used to organize information about tasks you want to accomplish is displayed in the Reading pane. If no one has entered any tasks in Outlook, this folder will be empty.

5. Click **Mail** in the Outlook bar and then click the **Deleted Items** folder for your account. The contents of the Deleted Items folder appear in the message list. When you delete items from other mail folders, the items are stored in this folder until you delete them permanently. If no one has deleted any items in Outlook, this folder will be empty.

6. Click the **Inbox** folder in the Navigation pane. Any messages waiting for you are displayed in the message list, with a closed envelope icon next to items that have not yet been read. The first time you start Outlook, you receive a message in the Inbox folder from Microsoft, similar to the one shown in Figure 26–2. **Figure 26–3** shows the Inbox with two messages, the message list, and the Reading pane, which displays an e-mail message that contains an image and text.

FIGURE 26–3
Messages in the Inbox window

Open envelope icon indicates message has been read

Selected message appears in the Reading pane

Message header of selected e-mail

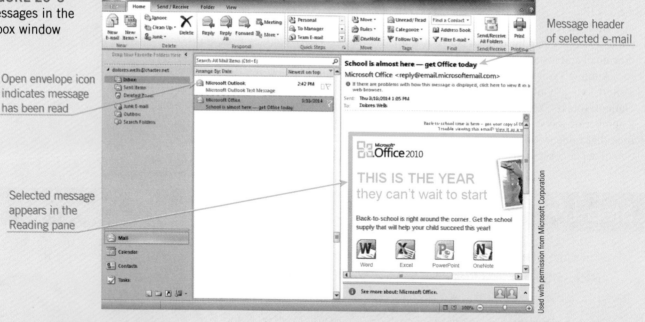

Used with permission from Microsoft Corporation

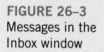
7. Click the **Outbox** folder. This folder is used to hold completed messages that have not yet been sent. If this folder contains messages, notice the icon—it looks like a small addressed and stamped envelope—that indicates the message is ready to send.

8. Leave this folder open for the next Step-by-Step exercise.

Sending and Receiving E-Mail

3-2.2.4
3-2.2.5
3-2.2.6

If your computer is set up to handle e-mail, you can use the Inbox folder in Outlook to send and receive e-mail messages. An advantage to using Outlook as your e-mail application is that as you create messages, you have easy access to the other Outlook features. You can quickly address the message to someone in your contacts list, check your calendar to make sure you are available for a meeting, or add a task to your task list when a message requests further action. In addition to sending a message, you can include attachments such as pictures or documents.

Receiving E-Mail

When you open Outlook, it sends a request to your mail server to check if you have any messages waiting. If you do, Outlook receives them and displays them in the Inbox folder. The message list displays message headers for any new messages. The message header tells you who sent the message, the subject of the message, and the date and time your server received it. The Reading pane of the Outlook window displays the actual text of the message. If you have a number of messages, you can read each one by clicking its message header to display the message text in the Reading pane.

    If you are already working in Outlook, you can check your e-mail at any time. Open the Inbox folder and click the Send/Receive All Folders button in the Send/Receive group on the Home tab. If you do not need to keep the messages after reading them, you can delete the messages by selecting each message header and clicking the Delete button in the Delete group on the Home tab.

E-Mail Features

3-2.2.8

Sending e-mail is as easy as clicking a few buttons and typing your message. The Outlook *Address Book* stores names, e-mail addresses, phone numbers, and other contact information so you can easily access it while you are sending and receiving e-mail messages. Some of the tasks you can perform in the Address Book follow:

▶ **VOCABULARY**
Address Book
Contact Group

- To add new data to the Address Book, click the Address Book button in the Find group on the Home tab to display the Address Book: Contacts window and then type the contact information, or copy and paste an address from an e-mail message that you received.

- To modify an e-mail address, display the Address Book: Contacts window, double-click the address, and then make the modifications.

- To delete an e-mail address, display the Address Book: Contacts window, click the address you want to delete, click File, and then click Delete.

    You can also use a *Contact Group* to send the same e-mail message to a group. To create a Contact Group, click Contacts in the Outlook Bar, and then click the New Contact Group button in the New group on the Home tab to open the Contact Group window. (Depending on your screen resolution, you might need to click the New button in the New group, point to More Items, and then click Contact Group.) In the Name box, type the name of your Contact Group, click the Add Members button in the Members group, and then click From Outlook Contacts, From Address Book, or New Email Contact.

3-2.2.4

Sending E-Mail

To send a message, you enter an e-mail address in the To text box of a Message window either by typing the address or by inserting an address stored in your Address Book. The Address Book generally contains a list of e-mail addresses of people or groups with whom you frequently correspond. You can also enter e-mail addresses in the Cc text box if you are sending copies of the message to other recipients. See **Figure 26–4**.

From button
is optional

To button

Cc button

Subject text box

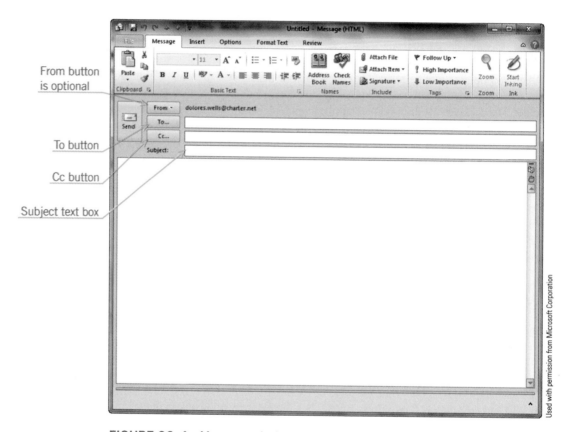

Used with permission from Microsoft Corporation

FIGURE 26–4   Message window

Recall that you can add another field labeled Bcc to enter e-mail addresses for recipients who are to be "blind" copied, meaning the primary addressee does not see that others are copied on the message. You can also add a From field to add your own name. To add these fields, click the Options tab in the Message window, and then click the Bcc or From button in the Show Fields group.

It is good e-mail etiquette to include a subject for your mail message. The subject should be brief, yet descriptive enough to tell the recipient what the message is about. After providing a subject, enter the text of your message. Next, click the Send button to send the e-mail message.

In the following Step-by-Step exercise, you practice creating an e-mail message that you send to yourself or to someone else in your class. If necessary, check with your instructor regarding the e-mail address (or addresses) to be used for the exercises in this lesson.

ABOVE AND BEYOND

The Cc in the e-mail window is the abbreviation for *carbon copy*. This originated with the old-fashioned typewriter. To send someone a copy of a letter or to create a file copy, a typist used a sheet of carbon paper between each sheet of paper.

Step-by-Step 26.2

1. In Microsoft Outlook, click the **Mail** button in the Outlook bar, if necessary, and then click the **New E-mail** button in the New group. The Untitled - Message window is displayed.

2. If necessary, click the **To** box. Type your e-mail address (or the e-mail address of the person to whom you are sending the message). If you do not know what e-mail address you should use, check with your instructor.

3. Click the **Subject** box and type **New Zealand trip**.

4. Click in the message area. The title of the window changes to *New Zealand trip*.

5. Type the following message:

   I am looking forward to the New Zealand trip next month. We will visit the following cities: Auckland, Christchurch, Wellington, and Taranga. As you know, Queenstown is the capital of New Zealand, but Auckland is the largest city with a population of over one million. You can find additional information at www.newzealand.com.

6. Press **Enter** two times, type your name, and then press **Enter**. Your screen should look similar to **Figure 26–5**.

7. Click the **Send** button to send the message. Leave Outlook open for the next Step-by-Step exercise.

> **ABOVE AND BEYOND**
>
> After you send a message, Outlook closes the Message window and temporarily stores the message in the Outbox folder. After the message is sent, Outlook moves the message to the Sent Items folder.

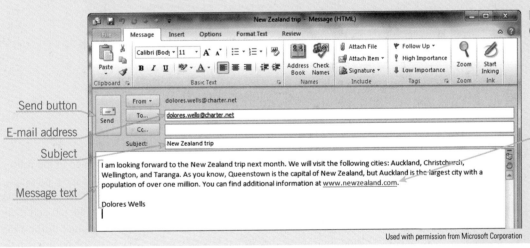

Send button
E-mail address
Subject
Message text

Web site address is underlined automatically

FIGURE 26–5
Completed message

Used with permission from Microsoft Corporation

Receiving and Opening E-Mail Messages

Now that you have sent a message to yourself (or someone in your class has sent you a message), you should receive it in the Inbox. You can click the Send/Receive All Folders button in the Send/Receive group on the Home tab to check for messages. In the following Step-by-Step exercise, you check for messages and then open the message sent in the previous exercise.

> **QUICK TIP**
>
> In Step-by-Step 26.2, you included a link to a Web site in the message text. Links to Web sites and e-mail addresses are ways you can add information to a message without making the message text too long.

Step-by-Step 26.3

1. Click the **Send/Receive All Folders** button in the Send/Receive group on the Home tab. The message appears in the Inbox where the message header is displayed, as shown in **Figure 26–6**.

FIGURE 26–6
Receiving a message

Number of unread messages

Closed envelope icon indicates message has not been read

Send/Receive All Folders button

Message header of new e-mail message

2. Click the message header in the message list. The message is displayed in the Reading pane, as shown in **Figure 26–7**. Leave Outlook open for the next Step-by-Step exercise.

FIGURE 26–7
Displaying a message

Reply button

Reply All button

Message header selected

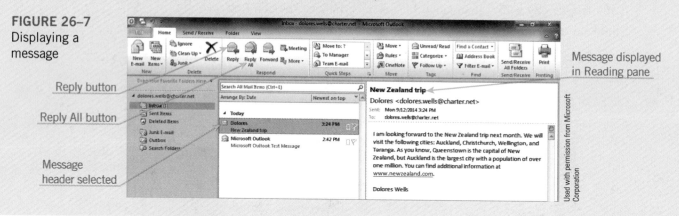

Message displayed in Reading pane

3-2.2.7

Saving a Message

When you receive a message, Outlook automatically saves the message in the Inbox or another designated folder until you delete the message. You can save a message, however, as a draft, a file in another format such as a text file, an HTML document, or a template. To save a message in one of these formats, click the File tab and then click Save As. When the Save As dialog box is displayed, type a name in the File name text box, and then select the format by clicking the Save as type button. Click the Save button to save the file.

E-mail messages require file management skills similar to any other references (electronic or hard copy) you want to keep and manage. Most people reply to messages they receive and save important messages for future reference. On the other hand, you might want to delete unneeded messages and spam. *Spam* is unsolicited e-mail, essentially electronic junk mail. In many instances, spam is used to advertise products and services. Other spam messages might contain phony offers.

▶ **VOCABULARY**
spam

Replying to a Message

When replying to a message, first select the message. Click the Reply or Reply All button in the Respond group on the Home tab, type your response, and then click the Send button. The original message is included along with your reply message. Suppose, for example, you received an e-mail from a friend and the friend used the Cc text box to send a copy of the message to several other people. To reply to the friend, click the Reply button. To reply to the friend and send a copy of the message to the others listed in the Cc text box, use the Reply All button. Using the Reply or Reply All option is appropriate when you are answering a question or responding to specifics in the original message.

When you click the Reply or Reply All button, a Message window is displayed. This window is similar to the window that was displayed when you created a new message. Recall that when you use this format to reply to an e-mail message, the recipient(s) normally sees RE: preceding the text in the subject line to indicate that it is a reply message.

3-2.2.4

Formatting a Message

The formatting tools on the Message window Ribbon provide many of the same features as those in your word-processing program and other similar software. You can change the font type, font size, and text color of an e-mail message. You can also add bold, italic, and underline styles to text as well as center it and add bullets.

3-2.2.4

Attaching a File to an E-Mail Message

Attachments are documents, images, figures, and other files that you can attach to your e-mail messages. To attach a file to a message, click the Attach File button in the Include group on the Message window Ribbon, locate the file or document you want to attach in the Insert File dialog box, and then click the Insert button.

In the following Step-by-Step exercise, you reply to a message. You change the font and text color, attach a file, and then send the message. Use a file you created in one of the other lessons in this course or as directed by your instructor for the attachment. Outlook should be open and a message should be displayed in the Reading pane.

3-2.2.5
3-2.2.6

▶ **VOCABULARY**
attachments

Step-by-Step 26.4

1. Click the **Inbox** folder in the Navigation pane, if necessary, and then double-click the **New Zealand trip** message to open it. Click the **Reply** button in the Respond group on the Message tab. The message window is displayed, similar to that shown in **Figure 26–8**. The e-mail address is displayed automatically in the To box, and the insertion point is blinking in the message area.

FIGURE 26–8
Replying to a message

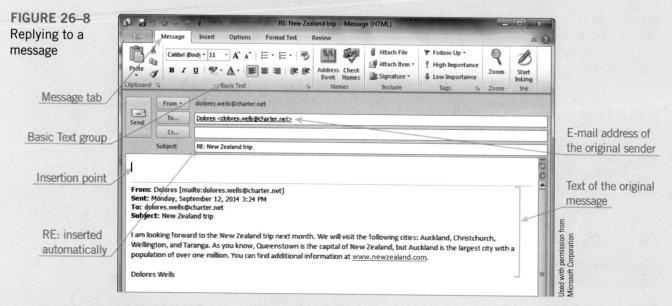

Message tab

Basic Text group

Insertion point

RE: inserted automatically

E-mail address of the original sender

Text of the original message

Used with permission from Microsoft Corporation

2. Type the following:

   Dolores (or substitute the name of your recipient), and then press **Enter** two times.

   Good to hear from you. I also am preparing for the trip and look forward to seeing you. I have attached some information for you.

   Press **Enter** two times, type your name, and then press **Enter** again.

3. Select the text of your message. Use the buttons in the Basic Text group on the Message tab to change the font to a style of your choice and the font size to **12**. Change the color to one of your choice. Format all of the text in bold.

4. Point to the *Attach File* button in the Include group to display the ScreenTip, as shown in **Figure 26–9**. The Insert File dialog box is displayed.

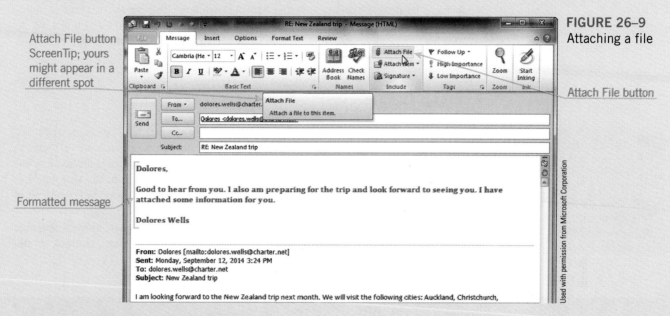

Attach File button ScreenTip; yours might appear in a different spot

Formatted message

FIGURE 26–9
Attaching a file

Attach File button

Used with permission from Microsoft Corporation

5. Click the **Attach File** button to display the Insert File dialog box. Locate and select a file that you want to attach, and then click the **Insert** button. The file is attached, as shown in **Figure 26–10**.

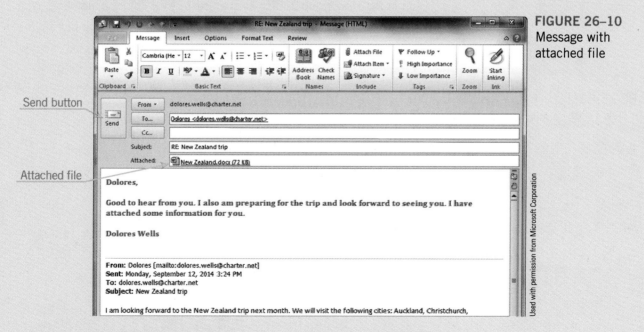

Send button

Attached file

FIGURE 26–10
Message with attached file

Used with permission from Microsoft Corporation

6. Click the **Send** button to send the message. Leave Outlook open for the next Step-by-Step exercise.

3-2.2.6

Managing Attachments

When you receive an attachment, you can read it in a few ways. You can preview its contents without opening the attachment by clicking the attachment in the Message window to display the contents in the Reading pane. You can also open the attachment by double-clicking it in the Message window. To save an attachment, right-click it, click Save As on the shortcut menu, select a location, and then click Save. To remove an attachment, right-click the attachment, and then click Remove Attachment on the shortcut menu.

Message Icons

Icons in the message headers in the message list offer clues about each message. For example, an icon that looks like the back of a sealed envelope indicates a message that has been received but not read; an exclamation point icon means the sender considers it an urgent or high-priority message; a paper clip icon indicates that the message has an attached file. You can also manually mark a message as read or unread or add a flag icon as a reminder to follow up on the message.

In the following Step-by-Step exercise, you create a folder, move a message from one folder to another, forward a message, and print a message. Outlook should be open and the Inbox displayed.

> **ABOVE AND BEYOND**
>
> When Outlook is open, you can check your e-mail at any time by clicking the Send/Receive All Folders button in the Send/Receive group on the Home tab.

Step-by-Step 26.5

1. Click the **Folder** tab on the Ribbon, and then click the **New Folder** button in the New group to display the Create New Folder dialog box. Type **New Zealand** in the Name text box. If necessary, click **Inbox** in the Select where to place the folder box. The dialog box should look similar to that shown in **Figure 26–11**.

FIGURE 26–11
Create New Folder dialog box

2. Click the **OK** button. The folder is displayed as a subfolder in the Inbox folder, as shown in **Figure 26–12**.

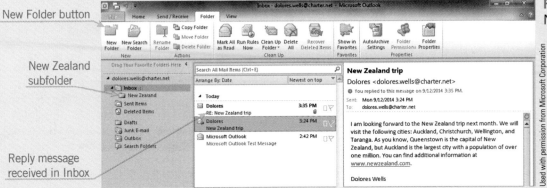

New Folder button

New Zealand subfolder

Reply message received in Inbox

FIGURE 26–12
New folder created

3. You should have two messages in your Inbox regarding the New Zealand trip. (If you do not, click the **Send/Receive All Folders** button in the Send/Receive group.) Click the first **New Zealand trip** message; hold down the **Ctrl** key and click the second **New Zealand trip** message to select both messages. (If you are creating other messages or do not have two New Zealand trip messages, select any other two messages.)

4. Right-click the selected messages, point to *Move* on the shortcut menu, and then click **New Zealand**. The messages are moved to the New Zealand folder.

5. Click the **New Zealand** folder to display the two messages, as shown in **Figure 26–13**.

New Zealand subfolder selected

Two messages in New Zealand subfolder

FIGURE 26–13
Messages moved to a new folder

6. Right-click the first message, and then click **Forward** on the shortcut menu. The message is displayed with *FW*: indicated in the Subject box.

7. Type your e-mail address (or a classmate's e-mail address) in the To box. Type your instructor's e-mail address (or an e-mail address to another classmate) in the Cc box. See **Figure 26–14**.

FIGURE 26–14
Message to forward

E-mail addresses
entered

FW: inserted
automatically

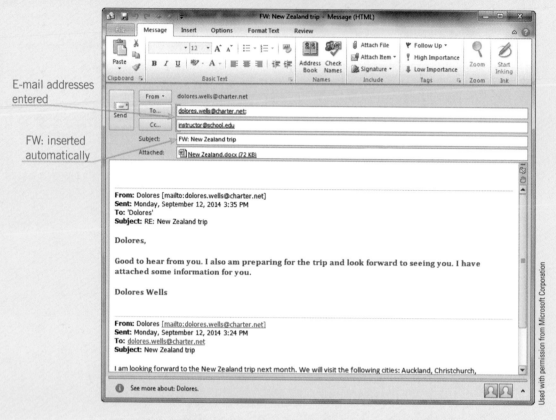

Used with permission from Microsoft Corporation

8. Click the **Send** button.
9. After you receive the forwarded message, right-click the message, and then click **Quick Print** on the shortcut menu to print a copy of the message.
10. Close Outlook.

QUICK TIP

As you begin typing an e-mail address you've used before, Outlook suggests one or more e-mail addresses that begin with the same characters. This feature is called AutoComplete. You can click a suggested e-mail address to insert it in the text box.

Most e-mail programs come with a variety of features and options that make it easy to send a copy to multiple recipients, generate an automatic reply, block messages from specific senders, and customize the look and feel of your messages.

Copying to Multiple Recipients

As previously indicated, you can insert more than one address in the To, Cc, and Bcc boxes. The message goes to all the addressees at the same time. If you are sending or copying an e-mail to more than one person, each e-mail address should be separated by a semicolon.

Mail Configuration Options

3-2.2.9

You can configure e-mail programs such as Outlook to deal automatically with e-mail messages you receive. The automatic controls you can set in Outlook include the following:

- *Automatic "out of the office" response*: Automatically reply to all received e-mail messages when you are unable to reply to messages yourself. This feature requires special e-mail servers and might not be available on your system.

- *Forwarding command*: Automatically redirect your mail to another e-mail address; this feature also requires special e-mail servers.

- *Redirect messages to your mobile phone*: Automatically redirect your mail to your mobile phone; you access this feature by clicking the File tab and then clicking the Options button. Click Mobile to display the option.

- *Block Senders List*: Prevent messages from designated addresses from being placed in your Inbox; this is particularly useful to block unwanted advertisements that often are sent repeatedly to the same e-mail address.

- *Safe Senders/Safe Recipients List*: Similar to the Block Senders list, selecting this option indicates to Outlook to accept all e-mails from the sender names contained in the list. A similar feature is the Safe Senders Domain List, which contains a list of all safe domains (*@msn.com*, for example) that you want to accept.

You access the Block Senders and Safe Senders lists by clicking the Junk button in the Delete group on the Home tab, and then clicking Junk E-mail Options. In the Junk E-mail Options dialog box, click the Safe Senders, Safe Recipients, or Blocked Senders tab. Type the e-mail address and then click the Add button.

A *signature* consists of text or pictures that you create so Outlook can add it to the end of any outgoing messages. You can create unique signatures for different addresses (see **Figure 26–15**). For instance, you might want a signature for friends and family and another signature for business purposes.

VOCABULARY
signature

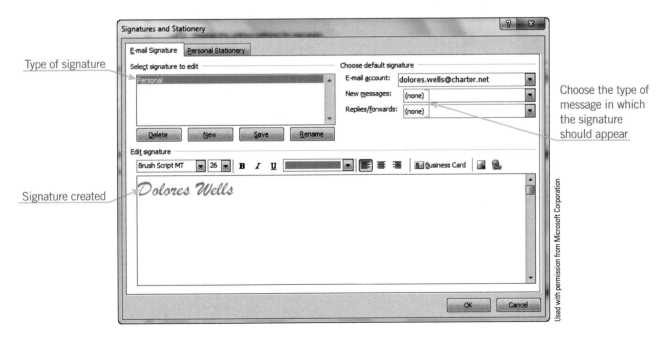

FIGURE 26–15   Creating a signature

ETHICS IN TECHNOLOGY

E-Mail/E-Aches

Although e-mail is a popular service of the Internet, its widespread use has created several problems. One time-consuming problem that e-mail causes is the overflow of e-mail messages many users find in their Inboxes. Similar to telemarketers using your phone number, online marketers and other groups can locate your e-mail address and use it to send you many unwanted e-mail messages.

E-mail communications can also lead to confusion and misinterpretation. Receivers are often guilty of not thoroughly reading an e-mail message before they reply, or they might not use the Reply All option correctly. Pay close attention to whom you are sending your messages and replies. You do not want to reply automatically to all recipients if the content of the message is not relevant to everyone.

SUMMARY

In this lesson, you learned:

- Electronic communication includes e-mail, instant messages, text messages, VoIP phone calls, online conferences, chat rooms, blogs, and social networks.

- The components of electronic communication include software, a sender, a receiver, a channel, communication content, and protocols.

- Wireless communication makes it possible to send and receive e-mail using a handheld computer or cell phone with e-mail capabilities.

- E-mail addresses consist of three parts: the user name, the @ symbol, and the domain name.

- Microsoft Outlook includes features to manage appointments, tasks, and e-mail. The Outlook bar displays shortcuts that give you quick access to each of the Outlook folders.

- Electronic mail is similar to regular mail because it requires an address, a message, and a carrier to get it from the sender to the receiver.

- You can access e-mail on a computer using a program such as Microsoft Outlook, or you can send and receive e-mail messages using a Web site with a built-in e-mail program, such as Gmail or Hotmail.

- An e-mail message header includes the address of the recipient, the subject of the message, and information about to whom the message is sent as a copy.

- You can use the Inbox folder in Outlook to send and receive e-mail messages.

- An attachment is a file that is sent with an e-mail message and that can be opened by the recipient.

- You can reply to an e-mail message, forward a message to a new recipient, delete a message, or save a message.

- Spam, or junk e-mail, consists of unsolicited messages that take up space in your Inbox unnecessarily.

- E-mail messages are organized in folders of incoming messages, sent messages, deleted messages, and junk e-mail. You can also create additional folders to organize your own e-mail.

- Special e-mail features let you add an automatic signature to messages, block messages from certain addresses, create personalized stationery for your messages, set up an automatic response, or forward your messages to another address.

■ LESSON REVIEW

TRUE / FALSE

Circle T if the statement is true or F if the statement is false.

T   F   **1.**   With Internet access, you can send e-mail to any computer in the world.

T   F   **2.**   An e-mail message header tells you the page number of the message.

T   F   **3.**   Each user on the Internet must have a unique e-mail address.

T   F   **4.**   The Cc feature is used only on old-fashioned typewriters, not in e-mail software.

T   F   **5.**   The Reading pane of the Outlook window displays the text of the selected message.

MULTIPLE CHOICE

Select the best response for the following statements:

1. In contemporary electronic communication, software applications installed on the local PC are also called _____.

   A.   attachments   C.   user agents

   B.   user names   D.   packets

2. An e-mail address consists of three parts: the user name, the @ symbol, and the user's _____.

   A.   domain name   C.   channel

   B.   protocol   D.   contact group

3. _____ is the process of backing up your e-mail messages.

   A.   Attaching   C.   Forwarding

   B.   Archiving   D.   Blocking

4. A(n) _____ icon in the message header indicates that the message has an attached file.

   A.   envelope   C.   exclamation point

   B.   paper clip   D.   folder

5. The Outlook _____ stores names, e-mail addresses, phone numbers, and other contact information.

   A.   Contact Group   C.   Address Book

   B.   Inbox folder   D.   Junk E-mail folder

FILL IN THE BLANK

Complete the following sentences by writing the correct word or words in the blanks provided:

1. If you are sending or copying an e-mail to more than one person, each e-mail address should be separated by a(n) _____.

2. _____ is unsolicited e-mail, essentially electronic junk mail.

3. You should include a(n) _____ for an e-mail message that is brief, yet descriptive enough to tell the recipient what the message is about.

4. You can use an Outlook _____ _____ to send the same message to a group.

5. The user name in the e-mail address dedwards@gmail.com is _____.

PROJECTS

PROJECT 26–1

The To-Do bar appears by default to the right of the Reading pane in the Outlook window. Click the Microsoft Outlook Help button (a question mark) on the title bar and use the Internet to answer the following questions:

1. What is the purpose of the To-Do bar?

2. By default, the To-Do bar contains four parts. What are these four parts of the To-Do bar?

3. How do you add an appointment to the To-Do bar?

PROJECT 26–2

3-2.2.5
3-2.2.9

To compare the signature features of Microsoft Outlook and Windows Live Mail, complete the following:

1. Research how to create and use signatures in Windows Live Mail by visiting the Windows Live Mail Help Center at *http://explore. live.com/windows-live-mail-create-signature*.

2. Learn how to perform the following tasks in Windows Live Mail:
   - Add a signature
   - Automatically include a signature in all of your messages
   - Use a signature only on specific messages

3. In a word-processing document, describe how to perform each of these tasks in Windows Live Mail. Indicate whether you perform the task in basically the same way in Microsoft Outlook or in a different way. If the task is different in Microsoft Outlook, explain how.

PROJECT 26–3

3-2.2.4
3-2.2.5

Microsoft provides learning resources on its Office Web site. Learn more about Outlook by completing the following:

1. Access the Office Web site at *http://office.microsoft.com/en-us*.

2. Scroll down, if necessary, to the Learning Resources section, and then click the Outlook link.

3. Click a learning resource, complete the tutorial or read the topic, and then write a report listing three new pieces of information you learned from the resource.

TEAMWORK PROJECT

3-2.2.9

People who use e-mail for frequent communication are often annoyed by unsolicited e-mail called spam. Spam can be obnoxious, offensive, and a waste of your time. Some countries have laws against spam. Your ISP might try to block spam before it reaches your mailbox. However, you still might be inconvenienced by junk e-mail. Working with a partner, research spam to learn more about the most common form of spam, other types of spam, and why spam can be harmful. Also learn how to protect yourself from spam. Prepare a report on your findings. At the end of your report, answer the following questions: Is spam ever useful? Should there be laws to restrict spam? Do you think you can block all spam from reaching your Inbox?

■ CRITICAL THINKING

Even with the popularity of social networks, e-mail activity continues to be nearly universal among computer users, even those using mobile devices. In fact, e-mail is the top activity on mobile devices. Considering tablets and smart phones, what modifications would you suggest to the developers of a future version of Microsoft Outlook? Why would these modifications be appropriate for mobile devices?

ONLINE DISCOVERY

A variety of e-mail programs work with Windows 7 and provide an alternative to Microsoft Outlook. Access the *Make Use of* Web site at *www.makeuseof.com/tag/free-email-clients-windows-7*, and read and review the free e-mail programs for Windows 7 that are discussed on this Web site. Select one program that has the best features for you. Then use your word-processing program to describe how and why you selected this program.

3-2.2.4
3-2.2.5

JOB SKILLS

In the Job Skills exercise for Lesson 25, you researched netiquette in general. (Netiquette refers to conventions to follow when using networks, including network services such as e-mail, blogs, and forums.) Use the Internet to research the current rules of e-mail netiquette in particular, and then list at least five rules in a word-processing document. These rules should be different from the ones submitted for Lesson 25. Submit the document to your instructor.

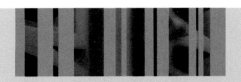

LESSON 27

Communications and Collaboration

■ OBJECTIVES

Upon completion of this domain, you should be able to:

- Explore communication methods.
- Identify the advantages of electronic communication.
- Solve electronic communication problems.
- Protect against viruses and other security risks.
- Engage in professional and effective communications.
- Use other e-mail options.
- Follow guidelines for electronic communication.

■ DATA FILES

You do not need data files to complete this lesson.

■ WORDS TO KNOW

filtering

fraud

hoax

logic bomb

netiquette

phishing

pyramid scheme

RDF Summary

spam

tagging

teleconferencing

time bomb

Trojan horse

urban legend

virus

worm

In Lesson 26, you learned about e-mail. In this lesson, you expand your knowledge of e-mail and learn about other electronic communication methods, the appropriate use of each method, and the advantages and disadvantages associated with them.

3-2.3.1

Exploring Communication Methods

When you work with computers to communicate, you can use a variety of electronic communication methods. In most instances, people with whom you are corresponding and the topic of the correspondence determine which communication method to select. Electronic mail (e-mail), which was discussed in detail in Lesson 26, is best used in the following situations:

- When the correspondence might require a paper trail
- When the correspondence covers multiple points
- When the correspondence needs to be accessed frequently

Instant messaging (or texting), also introduced in Lesson 26, is best used when correspondence needs to be accessed in real time. Each person can send and receive messages from a computer, cell phone, or other mobile device (see **Figure 27–1**).

FIGURE 27–1 Text messaging

Teleconferencing uses a telecommunications system to serve groups, permitting the live exchange and sharing of information between two or more people. Generally the communication medium is a telephone line. This communication method has expanded into video conferencing, which adds two-way video transmissions to the two-way audio of phone calls, and Web conferencing, which allows groups of people to communicate with each other online.

Syndication (Really Simple Syndication, or RSS), also known as Rich Site Summary and *RDF Summary*, are formats originally developed to syndicate news articles electronically. This communication method is now widely used to share the contents of blogs.

In some instances, a combination of the preceding communication methods may be used, especially for group collaboration. For example, a group of people who live in different parts of the country may be enrolled in an online class. This group can use e-mail, instant messaging, and teleconferencing to communicate about a class project. They could also use a blog to post project updates and social networks to keep in touch with each other.

Identifying the Advantages of Electronic Communication

3-2.3.2

Electronic communication offers many advantages over other types of communication. The communication is not restricted to a specific place and time, allowing people to communicate from remote locations using computers and cell phones. When you communicate electronically, you can use text and graphics, making it easy to forward and route messages. You can also use more than one type of correspondence, including one to one, one to many, and many to many. In one-to-one communication, one sender communicates with one receiver. E-mail is an example of one-to-one communication. One-to-many communication involves a sender communicating with many receivers. An e-mail message sent from one person to a group is an example of one-to-many communication, as is posting files on an FTP site and using Telnet. Many-to-many communication such as file sharing, blogs, wikis, and tagging enable people to both contribute and receive information. *Tagging* is used in blogs and other informational sites to simplify the search process. In a many-to-many example, a group might use a discussion board where everyone can post information and read all of the postings.

Using collaborative communication tools, you can engage in all three types of correspondence. Collaborative software allows you to use live voice, full-motion video, and interactive desktop sharing between yourself and one other person or an unlimited number of people (see **Figure 27–2**).

FIGURE 27–2   Collaborative communication

Electronic communication also fosters community building by connecting members of a group who share the same general interest. The community could be connected by a social media site, blog, mailing list, message board, or other type of electronic communication, which allows them to exchange information and organize their efforts to meet a goal.

Another advantage is online document sharing, which allows users to create and edit documents online while collaborating in real time with other users. Google Docs is an example of online document sharing.

Other advantages of electronic communication follow:

- Speed is almost instantaneous, which means increased accessibility and enhanced interaction.

- Cost is minimal or even free in some instances. E-mail, for example, is a service that is part of most networked computers. Price remains the same whether you send and receive a hundred messages or a thousand messages. Based on the device that is being used, instant messaging is a free service or has a minimal fee. Teleconferencing, on the other hand, generally involves a fee for the host. However, using this service can eliminate travel expenses for people who would otherwise need to meet in person.

- Access is available from various devices such as computers and cell telephones.

- Forwarding and routing of messages can be accomplished in an instant. Using e-mail software, you can click the message, select the address of the individual to whom it is to be forwarded, and then click the Forward button.

Routing is the process of selecting paths in a network along which to send network traffic. It can be an automatic or an individual process. For example, a network administrator might receive a message that a server is going to be offline for a specific time. The administrator can then route this message to everyone who would be affected.

Like many companies, Microsoft hosts blogs to communicate with customers. In the following Step-by-Step exercise, you visit a Microsoft blog for Windows users.

Step-by-Step 27.1

1. Click the **Internet Explorer** button 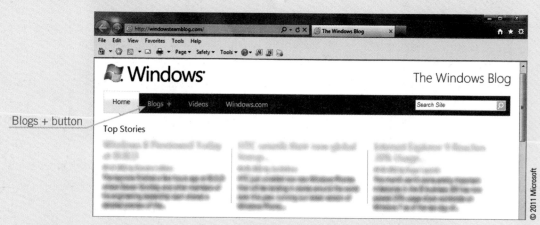 on the taskbar (or start Internet Explorer the way you usually do).

2. In the Address bar, type **http://windowsteamblog.com** and then press **Enter** to display the home page for Windows blogs (see **Figure 27–3**). Blogs change regularly, so the content displayed on your screen will differ from the figures.

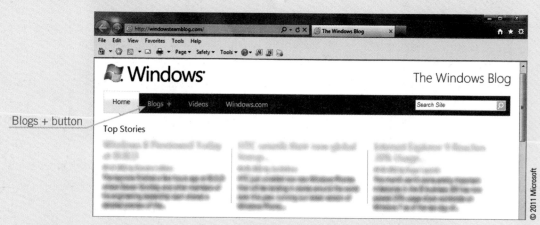

FIGURE 27–3
Windows blogs home page

3. Point to the *Blogs +* button, and then click **Blogging Windows** to display the most recent post for the Blogging Windows blog (see **Figure 27–4**).

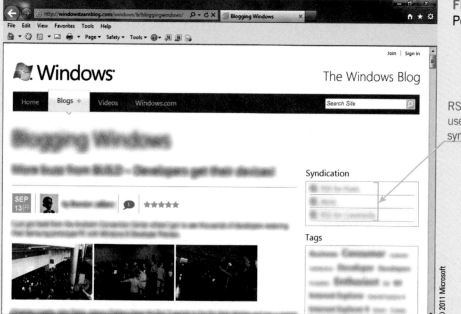

FIGURE 27–4
Post for the Blogging Windows blog

4. Scroll down to find a post that interests you. Use your word-processing program to write a summary of the post.

5. Return to the top of the page and then click the **Videos** button to display a showcase of Windows videos (see **Figure 27–5**).

FIGURE 27–5
Showcase of
Windows videos

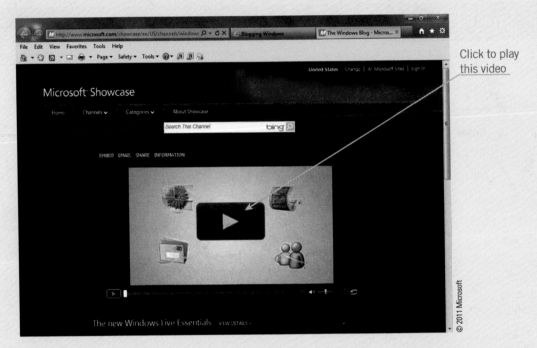

Click to play
this video

© 2011 Microsoft

6. Watch a video of your choice, and then return to your word-processing document. Add a summary of the video you watched. Save your document as **Windows_blog** and submit it to your instructor.

7. Close the Internet Explorer window.

3-2.3.3

Solving Electronic Communication Problems

Similar to other electronic technologies, electronic communication is not without problems. Windows 7, however, contains troubleshooting tools to help you identify and resolve computer communication problems.

Lost Internet Connection

Most electronic communication involves being connected to the Internet. You can then exchange e-mail messages, use Web conferencing software, or visit a collaboration Web site. Losing your Internet connection can be frustrating, especially if you are in the middle of an online conference or uploading important data for others to use. Depending on the problem, you may need to contact your ISP. However, you may be able to repair the problem with the Internet Connections troubleshooter. The following Step-by-Step exercise illustrates how to use this tool.

Step-by-Step 27.2

1. Click the **Start** button 🔵 on the taskbar, and then click **Control Panel** to display the Control Panel Home window.

2. Click **Network and Internet** to display the Network and Internet window (see **Figure 27–6**).

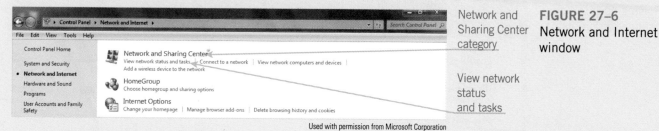

Network and Sharing Center category

View network status and tasks

FIGURE 27–6
Network and Internet window

Used with permission from Microsoft Corporation

3. Click **View network status and tasks** to display the Network and Sharing Center window (see **Figure 27–7**).

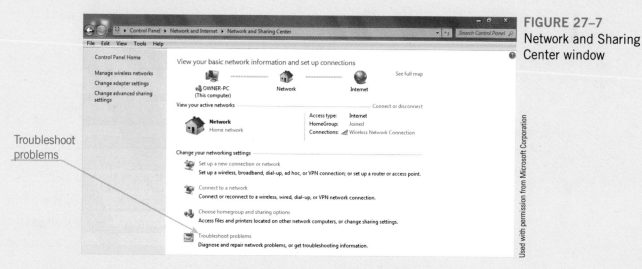

Troubleshoot problems

FIGURE 27–7
Network and Sharing Center window

Used with permission from Microsoft Corporation

4. In the Change your networking settings section, click **Troubleshoot problems** to display a list of network troubleshooters.

5. Click **Internet Connections** to open the Internet Connections dialog box.

6. Click the **Next** button to start the troubleshooter. When the Internet Connections dialog box opens, click **Troubleshoot my connection to the Internet**. Windows scans your network devices and software. If it finds a problem, it tries to correct it. In any case, Windows reports the results of the scan, as shown in **Figure 27–8**. Your results will differ.

FIGURE 27–8
Solving an Internet connection problem

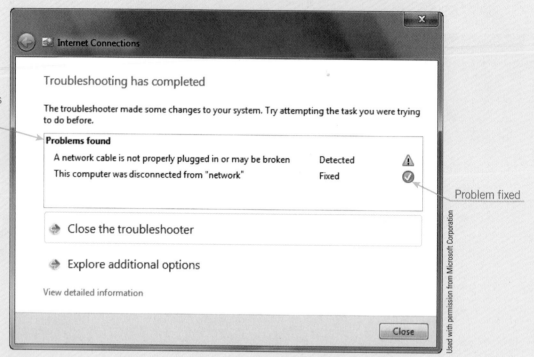

Two problems found

Problem fixed

Used with permission from Microsoft Corporation

7. Click the **Close** button or the **Cancel** button to close the window.
8. Use your word-processing program to write a summary of why you think the Internet Connections troubleshooter is important. Provide an example of when and how you would use this tool. Submit your assignment to your instructor.
9. Close the Network and Internet window.

E-Mail Software Problems

A failure in e-mail software to send or receive messages can result from various problems. Your service provider's connection could be down. If your connection to the Internet is still available, then checking your service provider's Web site could provide answers to your problem. Make sure your computer is connected to the Internet to isolate the problem to your e-mail service or software. Often, waiting a few minutes and then trying to send or receive messages results in success.

QUICK TIP

You can send an open Microsoft Office document without closing the file. Click the File tab, click Save & Send, and then click Send Using E-mail to send the document. You might perform this shortcut during a conference call to share an open document with participants.

Problems with Downloading and Viewing E-Mail Attachments

If you are unable to download or view an e-mail attachment, the size of the attachment might be the problem. Some e-mail programs limit attachment size and the number of attached files. If the message or attachment appears to contain harmful software (also known as malware), your antivirus software or e-mail program could be blocking the message. A third issue could relate to the sender and the type of e-mail—advertising, pornographic materials, or other unrecognizable documents, which also may be blocked by your e-mail program.

Windows Help provides suggestions on why you cannot view an attachment. In Step-by-Step 27.3, you access and review this Help information.

Step-by-Step 27.3

1. Click the **Start** button ⊕ on the taskbar, and then click **Help and Support** to display the Windows Help and Support window.

2. In the Search box, type **e-mail attachments** and then click the **Search** button to display a list of Help topics related to the search text (see **Figure 27–9**).

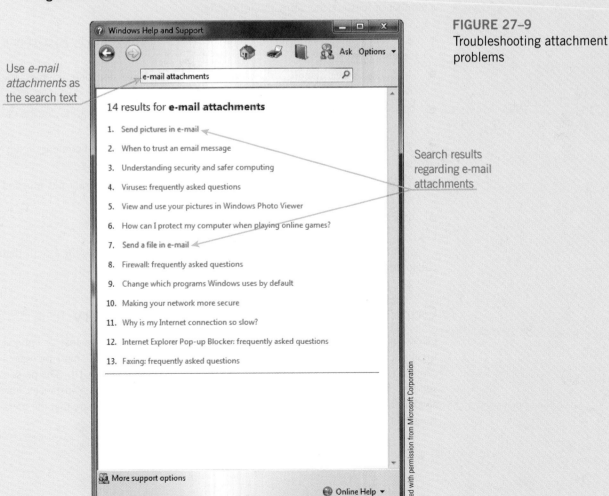

Use *e-mail attachments* as the search text

Search results regarding e-mail attachments

FIGURE 27–9
Troubleshooting attachment problems

Used with permission from Microsoft Corporation

3. Review the list of results. Two of the topics are directly related to e-mail attachments. Click the **Send pictures in e-mail** link and then read the topic, focusing in particular on the troubleshooting notes at the end of the topic.

4. Click the **Back** button ⬅ to return to the search results. Click the **Send a file in e-mail** link and then read the topic, focusing again on the troubleshooting notes at the end of the topic.

5. Use your word-processing program to explain what you should do before sending pictures as e-mail attachments. Also explain what types of files some e-mail programs block and what you can do if you have trouble sending these files.

6. Close the Windows Help and Support window.

7. Submit your word-processing document to your instructor.

Delivery Failure

E-mail delivery failure refers to a returned or "bounced" e-mail. This can happen for a number of reasons, including the following:

- The e-mail address was mistyped or is otherwise unrecognized by a server processing the message.

- An e-mail server handling the message is busy and does not route the message within a specified amount of time.

- The e-mail attachment may contain malware. The receiving program detects the problem and will not accept the message.

- The receiver has a spam-filtering program. Based on the e-mail content or subject, the program may identify the message as spam.

- The sender is known and the person to whom the message is sent has blocked the sender.

- The recipient's mailbox is full.

Some e-mail programs return delivery failure (bounce) notices for e-mail that cannot be delivered. Others do not provide this service.

Garbled Messages/No Guaranteed Delivery

Occasionally, e-mail and other transmissions over the Internet are lost or spliced together. This occurs most often when Internet traffic is heavy. E-mail messages sent in rich text format (RTF) are garbled frequently (see **Figure 27–10**). The person sending the message should change the format to HTML. In some instances, the sender does not receive a notification of delivery failure and is unaware that the message was not delivered properly.

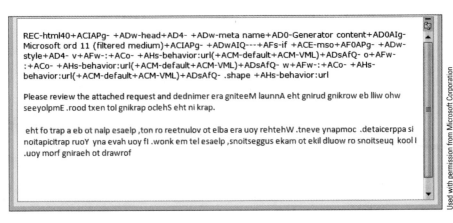

FIGURE 27–10 Garbled message

Lost Formatting

Microsoft Outlook and other e-mail programs provide at least two formatting options: HTML (Hypertext Markup Language) and Plain Text. Many programs also provide RTF formatting. HTML provides formatting options such as multiple fonts, bold text, colored headings, graphics, and links to Web sites. To use HTML when creating a message in Microsoft Outlook, click the Format Text tab in a New Message window, and then click the HTML button in the Format group. To format a message as plain text, click the Plain Text button in the Format group. Keep in mind that not all e-mail programs support HTML-formatted messages. If the recipient's e-mail program does not support HTML, the message is displayed as plain text with an HTML file attached.

Lack of a Paper Trail

A paper trail is a written record, history, or collection of evidence created by a person or organization in the course of activities. Paper trails have been used in legal cases as evidence, for example. E-mail and other electronically stored information provide a paper or electronic trail similar to that of traditional mail and other written documents. Other types of electronic communication such as instant messaging, teleconferencing, and online conferences might not provide a paper trail. When communication needs to be documented, electronic communication that does not produce a paper or electronic trail could create problems.

Hasty Responses

At one time or another, everyone has sent an e-mail that they wanted to take back. For instance, if you receive an e-mail message that makes you angry, your immediate response may be to send a quick reply. This action could accelerate the conflict instead of resolving it. To avoid sending a message you later may regret, consider the following options:

- Discuss your response with someone else.
- Write your message, but do not include the e-mail address in the To line. This will prevent an accidental sending of the message.
- Save your message overnight as a draft and then reevaluate your response the next day.

Professional and Informal Communication

With the advent of online communication formats, the boundary between professional and informal communication has blurred. Computer technology has provided the tools to make composing messages easier and faster. The fast-paced media used for electronic communication demand a writing style that is clear and concise without sacrificing speed. This often results in informal messages that include abbreviations and conversational language. When writing professional communications, however, you should be more formal, taking time to compose sentences and paragraphs.

Volume of E-Mail Replies

▶ **VOCABULARY**

netiquette

spam

Communications *netiquette*, a combination of the words net and etiquette, refers to good manners and proper behaviors when communicating through electronic media. Because most e-mail users report that their biggest problem is not spam but too much e-mail, keep the following netiquette guidelines in mind when replying to an e-mail message:

- *Reply to senders*: You have received an e-mail message and now you want to send a reply to the user. Click the Reply button, type your message, and then click the Send button. Verify, however, that your reply is necessary; do not send responses that do not apply to the original message.

- *Use Reply All only when necessary*: Reply All is another e-mail option. If you receive a message that also was sent to or copied to other recipients, for example, clicking the Reply All button sends your reply message to the sender and the other recipients. If the reply message does not apply to the other recipients, use Reply rather than Reply All to reduce the volume of e-mail replies.

- *Use Cc and Bcc sparingly*: Two other options are Cc and Bcc. Both options send copies of the message to other recipients. Use the Cc option only if someone needs to know about the information in the e-mail but does not need to respond. Use the Bcc for the same reason with someone whose address should not appear in the delivered e-mail message.

Junk Mail (Spam)

Just as you might receive unsolicited advertisements, flyers, and catalogs in your regular mail, you most likely receive junk e-mail, also called *spam*, in your e-mail inbox. This type of message might include advertisements, fraudulent schemes, pornography, or other illegitimate offers. This method of advertising is very inexpensive, and it is not uncommon for most people to receive numerous spam messages.
To help prevent spam:

- Use caution in giving out your e-mail address. Do not publish it online, on a Web site, in newsgroups, or in other public areas on the Internet.

- Check a Web site's privacy statement before you provide your e-mail address. Verify that it does not permit the sharing of your e-mail address with other companies.

- Never reply to a junk e-mail message. Once you reply, the sender will know that your e-mail address is valid. More than likely, you will receive even more junk e-mail, and the sender may also sell your e-mail address to others.

- Microsoft Outlook includes a junk e-mail filter that is turned on by default. The protection level is set to low and identifies only the more obvious junk e-mail messages. The program analyzes the content of your messages and moves suspicious messages to a special junk e-mail folder. You can then view and delete them. If a junk e-mail message is received in your inbox, you can specify that future messages from the sender are moved automatically to the junk e-mail folder.

In the following Step-by-Step exercise, you examine junk e-mail options in Microsoft Outlook.

Step-by-Step 27.4

1. Click the **Start** button 🔵 on the taskbar, point to *All Programs*, click **Microsoft Office**, and then click **Microsoft Outlook 2010**.

2. Click the **Junk** button in the Delete group on the Home tab, and then click **Junk E-mail Options** to display the Junk E-mail Options dialog box, shown in **Figure 27–11**.

Review the options on these tabs

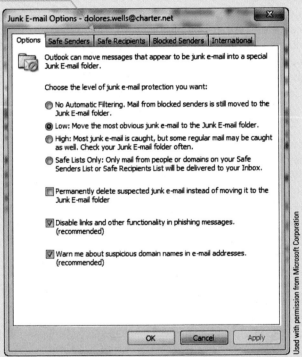

FIGURE 27–11
Junk E-mail Options dialog box

3. Review the settings on the Options tab, and then click the **Safe Senders**, **Safe Recipients**, and **Blocked Senders** tabs.

4. Use your word-processing program and write a summary of the information contained on each of the four tabs (Options, Safe Senders, Safe Recipients, and Blocked Senders). Submit the summary document to your instructor.

5. Close all open windows.

Fraud, Hoaxes, and Other False Information

Electronic *fraud*, such as e-mail fraud, is a computer crime that involves the manipulation of a computer or computer data to dishonestly obtain money, property, information, or other things of value, or to cause loss. The U.S. Secret Service reports that hundreds of millions of dollars are lost annually due to fraudulent activities.

E-Mail Fraud

E-mail messages are often used for fraudulent activities. Beware of messages you receive from e-mail addresses or senders you do not recognize. In many instances, the messages are well-written and appear to be legitimate. Typically, the messages request money for one reason or another. Unless you know the reason to be true, do not send a response to a message that requests money or personal information. Common fraudulent types of messages include *phishing*, which are personal information scams. This type of message appears to come from a legitimate source, such as your bank. The message asks that you update or verify your personal information. However, the information is used to commit identity theft. If you click a link in a phishing e-mail message, you are directed to a spoofed site, one that disguises its URL so it looks like you are visiting a legitimate Web site. Being misdirected to a fake site is called spoofing. *Pyramid schemes* are an illicit business model where profits are based on the investor's ability to recruit other people who are enrolled to make payments to their recruiters. Generally, neither a product nor a service is delivered.

Hoaxes

A *hoax* is an attempt to deceive an audience into believing that something false is real. Sometimes a hoax takes the form of a practical joke with a humorous intent; other times, it is an attempt to defraud and mislead. Many e-mail hoaxes appear to be warnings about potential viruses, a type of malware, but actually contain a virus themselves.

Perhaps one of the most well-known media hoaxes—one that many consider the single greatest of all time—occurred on Halloween eve in 1938. Orson Welles shocked the nation with his Mercury Theater radio broadcast titled "The War of the Worlds." Despite repeated announcements before and during the program, many listeners believed that invaders from Mars were attacking the world.

It is not always easy to spot an e-mail or chain letter containing a virus, but looking for some of the following hallmarks helps detect possible harmful files:

- The e-mail is a warning message about a virus.
- The message might be very wordy, contain all capital letters, or include dozens of exclamation marks.
- The message urges you to share information with everyone you know.
- The message appears credible because it describes the virus in technical terms.
- The message comes with an attachment, and you do not know who it is from.

If you identify any of these characteristics, it is wise to delete the e-mail immediately. Also, use antivirus software to scan e-mail messages, and keep the software updated.

In the twenty-first century, hoaxes, along with urban legends, myths, and chain letters, grow and flourish through the Internet. *Urban legends* are stories that at one time could have been partially true but have grown from constant retelling into a mythical yarn. Much of this false information is harmless; however, many urban legends are passed along in electronic chain letters, which can have viruses attached to the message. The Web site *liutilities.com* provides articles on computer topics, including virus myths and hoaxes. You visit this site in Step-by-Step 27.5.

▶ **VOCABULARY**

fraud

phishing

pyramid scheme

hoax

urban legend

ABOVE AND BEYOND

The first known computer crime, electronic embezzlement, was committed in 1958.

Step-by-Step 27.5

1. Click the **Internet Explorer** button  on the taskbar (or start Internet Explorer the way you usually do).

2. Type **www.liutilities.com/articles/computer-virus-myths-hoaxes** in the Address text box, and then press **Enter** to display the liutilities.com Web site, shown in **Figure 27–12**.

FIGURE 27–12
Computer virus myths and hoaxes article

© Uniblue Systems Limited 2010

3. Review the article, and then follow your instructor's directions to either print a copy or write a paragraph summarizing the six myths described on this Web page.

4. Close Internet Explorer.

Protecting Against Viruses and Other Security Risks

In an information-driven world, people and organizations must manage and protect against risks such as viruses, which are spread through electronic communications.

Viruses

A *virus* is a program that has been written, usually by a hacker, to corrupt data on a computer. The virus is attached to a file such as a program file, a document, or an e-mail message, and spreads from one file to another when the program is executed.

▶ **VOCABULARY**
virus

A virus can cause major damage to a computer's data or it can do something as minor as display messages on your screen. Descriptions of different types of viruses follow:

- A **worm** makes many copies of itself, consuming system resources so that the computer slows down or actually halts tasks. Worms don't have to attach themselves to other files.

- A **time bomb** is a virus that does not cause its damage until a certain date or until the system has been launched a certain number of times.

- A **logic bomb** is a virus triggered by the appearance or disappearance of specified data.

- A **Trojan horse** is a virus that does something different from what it is expected to do. It may look like it is performing one task while it is actually performing an opposite task (usually something disastrous).

To protect your computer against virus damage, try the following methods:

- Use antivirus software. This software should always be running on your computer and should be updated regularly.

- Be careful when opening e-mail attachments. It is a good idea to save attached files to disk before opening them so you can scan them.

- Do not access files copied from USB drives or other media, or those that are downloaded from the Internet without scanning them first.

You can prevent a virus from infecting your computer and spreading to other computers by diligently scanning files that you did not create to make sure they are clean. Many programs have a built-in virus scan feature that is activated when a new file is opened; in other cases, you can use an antivirus program to scan a file before opening it. **Figure 27–13** shows how a virus can spread.

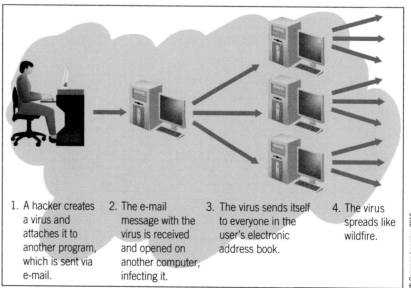

1. A hacker creates a virus and attaches it to another program, which is sent via e-mail.

2. The e-mail message with the virus is received and opened on another computer, infecting it.

3. The virus sends itself to everyone in the user's electronic address book.

4. The virus spreads like wildfire.

© Cengage Learning 2013

FIGURE 27–13   How a virus can spread

General Security Risks

Computer security can keep hardware, software, and data safe from harm or destruction. Some risks to computers are natural causes, some are accidents, and some are intentional. You cannot always detect that your computer is the object of a crime or intrusion. You should therefore install and use safeguards for each type of risk. It is your responsibility to protect your data.

The best way to protect data is to effectively control access to it. If unauthorized people gain access to data, they may obtain valuable information. Companies often establish password-protected locations on hard drives and networks so that designated users can use certain files but not others. Web sites also require passwords to access accounts or make transactions. For your personal computer, you can set a password to log on to the computer or to specific parts of it. To maintain secure passwords, you should change them frequently. This ensures that people who no longer need access cannot log on.

Other security measures include using the following:

- Electronic identification cards that provide access to designated areas within a building or department. See **Figure 27–14**.

> **QUICK TIP**
>
> You can create secure passwords that are easy for you alone to remember. String together the first letter of a line from a song or poem, for example, to create a password such as IlmhiSF!, so you only need to remember "I left my heart in San Francisco." Add a punctuation mark at the end. A password like this is difficult for someone to guess.

© Bork / Shutterstock.com

FIGURE 27–14 Using an electronic identification card

- A firewall, which is an integrated security system that prevents unauthorized electronic access to a network computer system while permitting outward communication.
- Antivirus software to protect data on your computer.

Organizations must plan for security before they need it rather than handling breaches in security as they occur. For example, any company that handles sensitive information or needs to protect its data should take the following precautions:

- Institute a selective hiring process that includes careful screening of potential employees. Do not keep employees on who refuse to follow security rules. This measure will prevent internal theft or sabotage.
- Regularly back up data and store it offsite.

■ Employ biometric security measures, which examine a fingerprint, handprint, voice pattern, or the iris or retina of the eye, as shown in **Figure 27–15**. These images must match the entry that was originally stored in the system for an employee to gain access to a secure area. This method of security is usually employed when high-level security is required.

FIGURE 27–15   Biometric security measures

WARNING

One type of e-mail scam to watch out for involves messages that appear to be from legitimate companies, but ask you to provide a Social Security number or account number to verify your account. Most companies assure customers that they would never ask for sensitive information in an e-mail, so it is best to be suspicious of any solicitation for private information via e-mail.

Another common security concern on the Internet is credit card information. Effective encryption technologies help keep credit card numbers secure, but you can add security by following simple precautions. For example, purchase from Web sites that you know are reputable and trustworthy. Read and understand the company's privacy and consumer-protection policy before you buy. Verify that any credit card information is transmitted in a secured, encrypted mode.

Engaging in Professional and Effective Communications

3-2.3.4

Electronic communications, as previously discussed, are available in a variety of formats—e-mail, instant messaging, teleconferencing, social networks, and so on. The level of formality and informality is based on the type of communication.

Statistics indicate that e-mail is the most popular of all Internet activities and that more than 90 percent of adult Internet users send or read e-mail. When used in the workplace for business communications, certain rules of etiquette and formality should be applied similar to those used in other business communications. The following list discusses elements of professionalism as applied to electronic communications:

■ The content, tone, and format of the message should be appropriate for its audience. Writing for a business or professional audience is different from writing for a personal or social audience. When composing a business message, assume that your audience has limited time and most likely will skim the contents to find the main idea. The content should be clear and the message should not contain spelling or other errors.

- Personal and social messages can be less formal. They should, however, be checked for spelling and punctuation errors. The purpose should be clearly stated. Avoid using sarcasm or too much humor unless the message is to someone you know very well.

- Select a communication method that suits the purpose of the message. For example, is the purpose of a message to invite someone to dinner or to submit a proposal? As with knowing the audience, knowing the purpose helps you craft the content, tone, and format. Instant messaging should be short and to the point. An e-mail message can contain more information.

- Respond to messages quickly. The type of message often dictates response time. For example, if a customer needs immediate assistance or has a complaint, you should reply within 30 minutes to 2–3 hours. If a student needs assistance on how to upload an assignment for his online class, the response time should be within 5–10 hours. Other nonemergency responses should be made within 24 hours.

- Messages should be concise and to the point. Ideally, the recipient should not have to scroll past one page to read the message. If the message is longer than that, consider moving the message content into a document and attaching it to the message.

- Include one subject per e-mail message. The subject line should describe the message content using short, direct text.

- The purpose of the message and its recipients should determine the level of formality. Adding elements such as emoticons, abbreviations, jokes, and other informal elements are appropriate for some audiences but not others. Business correspondence, for example, should be more formal than social correspondence. Even social correspondence can range from formal to informal.

- Repeating information and including material from previous e-mail messages is another consideration. Verify that you are not duplicating something that was sent previously. Also check that the recipient was not previously sent a copy of any attachments that you are adding.

> **QUICK TIP**
>
> Another often-used rule of netiquette is to not use all uppercase letters in a message. This is considered the equivalent of shouting.

Using Other E-Mail Options

In addition to the e-mail options discussed previously, other alternatives are available. The ability to send and receive e-mail attachments and other supplemental information is of great benefit and often a timesaver, though it does introduce a security risk.

3-2.3.5

- Recall that an attachment is a file that is sent along with an e-mail message. More than one file can be attached to the same message, and the files do not need to be of the same type. When recipients receive the message, they can open or save the attached file.

- Most e-mail services have a limit on the size of the message, including attachments. The size, based on the server settings, can be anywhere from 30 MB up to 2 GB or more. Some services, however, now support delivery of files of unlimited size.

- Some e-mail services set security on certain types of files, such as executable programs (.exe extensions), so they are rejected. In other instances, company security policies for e-mail might reject all attachments.

> **QUICK TIP**
>
> Most e-mail programs let you assign a priority to a message, such as high or low. For example, when you are creating a message in Microsoft Outlook, you can click the High Importance button or the Low Importance button to indicate the message priority to your recipients. High priority messages appear in the Inbox with a red exclamation mark.

- When creating an e-mail, you can add a hyperlink to the message rather than attaching a file. With this format, the recipient can click the link rather than opening an attachment. There are two ways to add hyperlinks to an e-mail message. One way is to type the Web site address. Most e-mail programs recognize the text as a Web site address and convert it to a hyperlink. The second method is to attach the Web site address to a word or a phrase in the message. This makes the word or phrase the hyperlinked text. You can embed hyperlinks only in e-mail messages created in the HTML format. The recipient of the message must also use a program that can display hyperlinks.

- Some e-mail readers cannot display embedded graphics or animation. Generally, this happens if the e-mail program reader is set to text only.

- Viruses and other similar threats can be delivered as e-mail attachments. Protecting a system requires a number of security tools. Nearly all e-mail programs provide security settings, phishing filters, and anti-spam tools. Other protective tools and procedures include firewalls, encryption, antivirus tools, spam filters, and user education (see **Figure 27–16**).

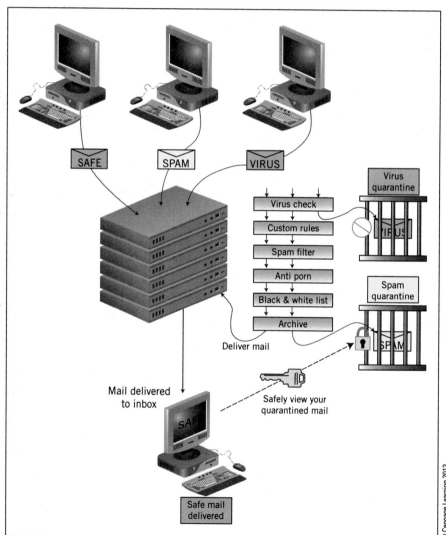

© Cengage Learning 2013

FIGURE 27–16　Controlling viruses and spam

Controlling Unsolicited E-Mail

3-2.3.6

E-mail filtering allows you to define rules to manage incoming e-mail. Filters automatically sort your incoming messages according to the rules you set up. You can filter your incoming e-mail messages to do the following:

- Sort incoming messages into folders
- Automatically tag messages
- Forward messages
- Discard messages

For example, you could define a filter rule to identify mail coming from your immediate supervisor and move it to a folder called "From My Boss" or to automatically move messages from a specific address to the Deleted Items folder.

Filtering Mail by Mail Servers

E-mail spam, or junk mail, was discussed earlier in this lesson. Spam has plagued users since the beginning of the Internet. Spam is an inexpensive way for people to market products and services, but a recent study by Nucleus Research, Inc., estimates that spam costs U.S. businesses more than $71 billion per year in lost productivity.

Although some spam still will get through, you can use a number of techniques to reduce the amount that finds its way to your inbox. In the past few years, the amount of spam received by most users has decreased because of *filtering*, which processes some e-mail but not others. E-mail servers are the computers that send and receive e-mail. They are usually set up to catch obvious spam and remove it before it is transferred to users. See **Figure 27–17**. Administrators can also define rules on the e-mail server to filter e-mail that might contain viruses or offensive language, for example.

VOCABULARY
filtering

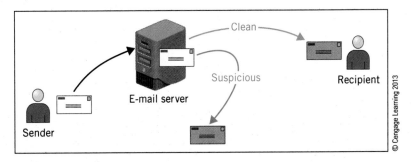

FIGURE 27–17   Filtering e-mail

Another preventive measure is to avoid posting your e-mail address in a public place. Marketers use database matching to obtain e-mail addresses. For example, the marketer has a database that contains names, addresses, and telephone numbers. They pay to have their database matched against another database that contains e-mail addresses to gather entries that include names, address, phone numbers, and e-mail addresses.

3-2.3.7

Following Guidelines for Electronic Communication

Most companies, institutions, government agencies, and other businesses and groups have guidelines for the use of electronic communications. The following is a checklist of guidelines, as discussed throughout this lesson:

- Check all incoming e-mail messages and attachments for viruses. It is critical that you use an antivirus program and update it on a regular basis.
- Review e-mail, instant messages, and other electronic communications prior to sending to make sure your communication is appropriate for its audience.
- Review and apply the rules of netiquette, company or school policies, cultural issues, and other guidelines.
- Verify that your e-mail program includes a feature that encrypts messages. Encrypting an e-mail message requires that you obtain a digital signature from a commercial digital ID group such as GlobalSign or VeriSign.
- Back up and archive correspondence on a regular basis.
- Understand the sensitive nature of data and of the rules related to sending data electronically.
- Be aware that electronic communications can leave an "electronic trail." Messages left on public sites such as blogs, message boards, or posts to social networking sites can be publicly and even permanently accessible.
- When using computers at schools or other organizations for electronic communications, follow the organization's guidelines for electronic communications.

ETHICS IN TECHNOLOGY

Physical Security

E-mail and attachments often contain information valuable to people and organizations, such as records of decisions, internal documents, and upcoming plans. Users should take steps to protect this information, including securing computer hardware and other equipment. It is generally fairly easy for an unauthorized person to access systems by removing them from a valid user's desk.

Computers and their devices should be kept in a secure place. Only a limited number of people should have access. A list of authorized users should be kept up to date. Some organizations have security guards or equipment to monitor computer rooms and control entry.

Remember that limited access means less opportunity for computer equipment or data to be stolen. Alternative methods for getting into a computer room should not be available. This includes hidden spare keys in an unsecured place.

Some organizations have taken computer safety a step further by securing equipment physically to desks and tables. This might seem like overkill, but it does help them protect their investment and their data.

SUMMARY

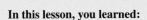

In this lesson, you learned:

- Teleconferencing uses a telecommunications system to serve groups, permitting the live exchange and sharing of information between two or more people.

- Syndication (Really Simple Syndication or RSS), also known as Rich Site Summary and RDF Summary, are formats originally developed to facilitate the syndication of news articles.

- Electronic communication offers many advantages over other types of communication. For example, the communication is not restricted to a specific place and time. Secondly, in most instances, it uses text and graphics rather than voice. These tools also provide for different types of correspondence such as one to one, one to many, or many to many.

- Typical communication problems include failing to connect to the Internet or to your e-mail server. Being unable to download or view an e-mail attachment could be due to the size of the attachment, a virus in the message, the sender, or the type of e-mail.

- Communications netiquette, a combination of the words *net* and *etiquette*, refers to good manners and proper behaviors when communicating through electronic media.

- Fraud is a computer crime that involves manipulating a computer or computer data to dishonestly obtain money, property, or other things of value or to cause loss.

- A virus is a program that has been written, usually by a hacker, to corrupt data on a computer. The virus is attached to a file and then spreads from one file to another once the program is started.

- Computer security can keep hardware, software, and data safe from harm or destruction. The best way to protect data is to effectively control access to it.

■ LESSON REVIEW

TRUE / FALSE

Circle T if the statement is true or F if the statement is false.

T   F   **1.**   Electronic communication offers many advantages over other types of communication.

T   F   **2.**   If you cannot download or view an e-mail attachment, the size of the attachment could be the problem.

T   F   **3.**   Personal and social messages should be formal.

T   F   **4.**   A time bomb is a virus that does not cause any damage.

T   F   **5.**   A hoax is an attempt to deceive an audience into believing that something false is real.

MULTIPLE CHOICE

Select the best response for the following statements:

1. It is not always easy to spot an e-mail or chain letter containing a(n) _____.

   A. virus   C. instant message

   B. picture   D. paragraph of text

2. Phishing is a type of e-mail _____.

   A. listing   C. fraud

   B. controller   D. hardware

3. Most companies, institutions, government agencies, and other businesses and groups have guidelines for the use of electronic _____.

   A. worms   C. communications

   B. filtering   D. policies

4. Viruses and other similar threats can be delivered as e-mail _____.

   A. attachments   C. servers

   B. spam   D. hyperlinks

5. A(n) _____ can corrupt data.

   A. RDF Summary   C. attachment

   B. urban legend   D. virus

FILL IN THE BLANK

Complete the following sentences by writing the correct word or words in the blanks provided:

1. _____ refers to good manners and proper behaviors when communicating through electronic media.

2. E-mail delivery _____ refers to a returned or "bounced" e-mail.

3. For e-mail messages, the _____ format provides formatting options such as multiple fonts, text, colored headings, graphics, and links to Web sites.

4. An e-mail message sent from one person to a group is an example of one-to-_____ communication.

5. _____ uses a telecommunications system to serve groups.

■ PROJECTS

PROJECT 27–1

3-2.3.7

Wikipedia.org describes e-mail filtering as the "processing of e-mail to organize it according to specified criteria." Access the Web page at *http://en.wikipedia.org/wiki/E-mail_filtering* and review the information. Then use your word-processing program to provide an overview of this article. As part of the overview, explain why people use e-mail filtering (motivation), how they use e-mail filtering (methods), and how they can configure it (customization).

PROJECT 27–2

3-2.3.7

Using the Internet or other resources, research the history of instant messaging. Then answer the following questions:

1. In what year did instant messaging become popular?
2. What is a chat room and how does it work?
3. What is ICQ as related to instant messaging?
4. When did AOL adopt instant messaging?
5. How does instant messaging software know when one of your contacts is online?
6. Name three popular instant messaging providers.
7. Is instant messaging a secure technology?

PROJECT 27–3

3-2.3.3
3-2.3.6

Junk mail, also known as spam, has continued to grow. The Federal Trade Commission's Web site, located at *www.ftc.gov/bcp/edu/pubs/consumer/alerts/alt063.shtm*, contains information on how to opt out of receiving unsolicited mail. Access this Web page and review the information it contains. Then describe the process you would use to opt out of receiving unsolicited e-mail. Describe what process someone could use if they did not have Internet access.

■ TEAMWORK PROJECT

3-2.3.3
3-2.3.6

Some countries have laws against spam. Your Internet service provider may try to block spam before it reaches your mailbox. However, you may still be inconvenienced by junk e-mail.

Working with a partner, research spam to learn more about what it is used for, how marketers get addresses, how effective spam is, and ways you can stop spam. You and your teammate should each select one of the two positions—pro spam (how effective it is and what it is meant to do) or against spam (it is a nuisance or problem that you want to stop before it reaches your e-mail inbox). Write a brief summary of your findings and compare them with your partner. At the end of your report, answer the following questions with your partner: Is spam ever useful? Should there be laws to restrict spam? Do you think you can block all spam from reaching your inbox?

■ CRITICAL THINKING

Several free e-mail services are available online. The Web site located at *http://email.about.com/od/freee-mailreviews/tp/free_e-mail.htm* provides an overview of the top 16 free e-mail services. Access this site and use your word-processing program to answer the following:

1. How many services are listed? (Hint: The Web site information is contained on two pages; don't forget to the click the Next link.)

2. Assume you are looking for a free e-mail service. Answer the following questions:
   - Which service would you select? Why?
   - Which service would be your second choice? Why?
   - Which services use the Google approach to e-mail?
   - Which services offer POP or IMAP access, and which allow you to download messages to any e-mail program?

   Select three of the services that you consider less popular. Review each of the three services you selected and list the pros and cons for each service.

ONLINE DISCOVERY

Google Docs is a Web site where you can create and share your work online. Complete the following:

1. In a Web browser, visit the Google home page at *www.google.com*.

2. Click the more link in the bar at the top of the Web page, and then click Documents.

3. Read the description of Google Docs, and then create an account and sign in. If you already have an account, sign in.

4. Create a Google document that explains what you can do with Google Docs. Enter your name in the document, and then save the document.

5. Click the Share button on the Google Docs toolbar to open the Sharing settings dialog box. Click the Add people text box, and then enter the e-mail address of your instructor.

3-2.3.2

6. Click the Paste the item itself into the e-mail check box, make sure the Notify people via email box is checked, and then click the Share & save button.

7. Click the Done button, and then close the browser.

JOB SKILLS

Many work projects in all fields involve collaborating with others. Even if you work in the same location, this collaboration often uses a form of electronic communication. On your own or working with a partner, brainstorm the types of skills and abilities someone needs to collaborate effectively. Select the top three skills and list them in a word-processing document. Briefly describe each skill.

LESSON 28

Using the Internet and the World Wide Web

■ OBJECTIVES

Upon completion of this lesson, you should be able to:

- Explore the Internet and the Web.
- Define Internet terminology.
- Connect to the Internet.
- Understand browser basics.
- Select Web browser settings.
- Identify browser issues.

■ DATA FILES

You do not need data files to complete this lesson.

■ WORDS TO KNOW

ActiveX

cookie

digital certificate

domain

File Transfer Protocol (FTP)

geographic imaging

home page

Hypertext Markup Language (HTML)

Hypertext Transfer Protocol (HTTP)

Internet Protocol (IP) address

Internet service provider (ISP)

podcast

portal

Secure Sockets Layer (SSL)

social networking site

Uniform Resource Locator (URL)

Web 2.0

Web app

Web cache

wiki

Each day millions of people explore the Internet and its popular service, the World Wide Web, or Web for short. People use the Internet to research information, shop for goods and services, go to school, communicate with family and friends, read the daily newspaper, and make airplane and hotel reservations, for example. They use the Internet at work, at home, and while traveling. Anyone with access to the Internet can connect to and communicate with anyone else in the world who also has Internet access.

3-3.1.1

Exploring the Internet and the Web

The Internet is made up of many services. Popular services include e-mail, instant messaging, newsgroups and bulletin boards, online conferencing, and Voice over Internet Protocol (VoIP). Its most popular service is the Web.

Many people use the terms Web and Internet interchangeably. In reality, they are two different things. The Web is part of the Internet. The Internet can exist without the Web, but the Web cannot exist without the Internet. The Web actually began in 1990, when Dr. Tim Berners-Lee, currently the director of the World Wide Web Consortium (W3C), wrote a small computer program for his own use. This program, called *Hypertext Transfer Protocol (HTTP)*, became the language computers use to transmit hypertext documents over the Internet. Dr. Berners-Lee next designed a scheme to give documents addresses on the Internet, and then developed a text-based program called *Hypertext Markup Language (HTML)* that creates hyperlinked documents. Clicking linked text or images in a hyperlinked document transfers you from one Web page to another or to another part of the same Web page. Dr. Berners-Lee's contributions laid the foundation, but they were not the catalyst that made the Web what it is today.

In 1993, the number of people using the Web increased significantly. This increase occurred when Marc Andreessen, working for the National Center for Supercomputing Applications at the University of Illinois, released Mosaic, the first graphical browser. See **Figure 28–1**.

VOCABULARY

Hypertext Transfer Protocol (HTTP)

Hypertext Markup Language (HTML)

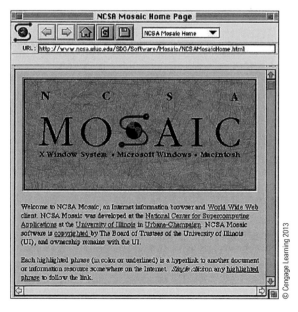

FIGURE 28–1   Mosaic Web page

In 1994, Marc Andreessen cofounded Netscape Communications. With the introduction of Mosaic and the Web browsers that followed, the Web became a communications tool for a much wider audience.

In 2004, the phrase *Web 2.0* was coined. Also called the participatory Web, this term has several definitions, although the most popular one refers to Web sites where users can modify the content. Web 2.0 includes a new generation of Web-based services such as blogs, social networking sites, wikis, and software built into the site. Because of these enhancements, the Web is one of the most widely used services on the Internet.

Defining Internet Terminology

The Internet and the Web have their own terminology. This section introduces Internet-related vocabulary in alphabetical order and provides definitions.

ActiveX is a programming interface developed by Microsoft for Windows. This set of rules controls Windows programs that are downloaded from the Internet and then run in a browser.

As you become an experienced Internet user, you may find that you want to change how your browser handles cookies. Windows Help defines a *cookie* as "A small text file that Web sites put on your computer to store information about you and your preferences." Web sites store cookies on your computer so that when you return to a site, it displays any preferences or other customized settings you selected, such as sign-in information or items stored in a shopping cart. However, some unscrupulous Web sites use cookies to track your Web habits, which many consider an invasion of privacy. You need to balance the ease of use provided by cookies with security concerns and the amount of storage space available on your computer. For the most part, the default settings for cookies and stored pages are appropriate for most Internet users. In Step-by-Step 28.1, you use the Windows online Help to find out more about cookies.

▶ **VOCABULARY**
Web 2.0
ActiveX
cookie

ABOVE AND BEYOND

Currently, the most popular Web browser is Internet Explorer. Other browsers include Firefox, Chrome, Opera, and Safari.

3-3.1.2

Step-by-Step 28.1

1. Click the **Start** button ⊕ on the taskbar, click **Help and Support**, type **cookies** in the Search text box, and then press the **Enter** button to display a list of Best 30 results for cookies (see **Figure 28–2**).

cookies entered in the Search text box

FIGURE 28–2
Search results for cookies

Cookies: frequently asked questions link

Used with permission from Microsoft Corporation

2. Click the **Cookies: frequently asked questions** link, and then click each question to read the answers (see **Figure 28–3**). Two of the links have been clicked in Figure 28–3.

FIGURE 28–3
Cookies: frequently asked questions Help page

Click a question to display the answer

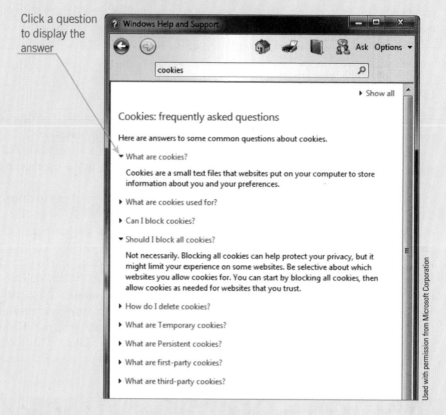

3. Use your word-processing program to write a brief explanation of what you learned from each of the answers. Save the document as **ic3-28**. Keep the document open for the next Step-by-Step exercise.

4. Close the Windows Help and Support window.

A *digital certificate* is an electronic document similar to an ID card. This digitally signed statement verifies the identity of a person or company and confirms that they own a public key. Also referred to as digital IDs, digital certificates are issued by third parties known as certification authorities (CAs). The certificate is designed to prevent fraud or other illegal activities and is validated by the CA. A typical digital certificate includes a serial number, issuer, private key, public key, signature algorithm, subject, thumbprint algorithm, thumbprint, valid from and valid to dates (see **Figure 28–4**).

▶ VOCABULARY

digital certificate

domain

File Transfer Protocol (FTP)

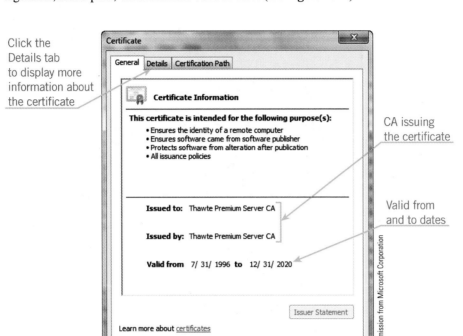

Click the Details tab to display more information about the certificate

CA issuing the certificate

Valid from and to dates

Used with permission from Microsoft Corporation

FIGURE 28–4   Digital certificate

A *domain* identifies a computer or Web site on the Internet. The domain name system (DNS) converts domain names to IP addresses. Examples of top-level domain names are .com, .edu, .org, .gov, and .net.

When data is sent over the Internet, it is sent in packets. Along the way, these packets can be intercepted. Encryption is the process of converting text into an unrecognizable format when it is sent. The data is converted to plain text (called decryption) when it reaches its destination. This process is used for sensitive online transactions, such as credit card purchases.

You use *File Transfer Protocol (FTP)* to transfer files between computers. You can upload (send) files from one computer to a server and retrieve (download) files from a server to a computer.

A *home page* is the first page that appears in the browser when you visit a Web site. The Cengage Learning home page is shown in **Figure 28–5**. (The home page also refers to the first page that is displayed when you start your browser.)

FIGURE 28–5   Cengage Learning home page

As mentioned earlier, HTML is the programming language used to create Web pages. The code is written using a text editor such as Windows Notepad or by using a program such as Adobe Dreamweaver. HTTP/HTTPS is the underlying protocol for the Web. This protocol defines how messages are formatted across the Internet. An HTTP client program is required at one end, and an HTTP server program is required on the other end. (Recall that a client is a type of computer program that makes a service request from a server.) For example, when you enter a Web site address in your browser, you send an HTTP command to the Web server to tell it to locate and transmit the requested Web page.

An *Internet service provider (ISP)* is an organization or company that provides connectivity to the Internet through a telecommunications line or wireless system.

An *Internet Protocol (IP) address* is a numerical addressing system that uniquely identifies computers and networks linked to the Internet. IP addresses consist of four sets of numbers separated by periods. Every client and server must have a unique IP address. A DNS server translates the IP address into a domain name such as *networksolutions.com*.

A *podcast* is a method of publishing files (primarily audio) to the Internet that can be streamed or downloaded for playback on a computer or a personal digital audio player. In other words, podcasts are downloadable audio broadcasts.

Recall that Really Simple Syndication (RSS), also known as Rich Site Summary and RDF Summary, is a format originally developed to syndicate news articles online. This communication method now is used widely to share the contents of blogs.

Secure Sockets Layer (SSL) is a protocol for managing the security of message transmissions on the Internet.

A *Uniform Resource Locator (URL)* is the address of a Web page, FTP site, audio stream, or other Internet resource.

A Web browser is a software program you use to view and retrieve documents from the Web and to display the documents in a readable format. The browser is the interface between the user and the Internet. The browser sends a message to a Web server to retrieve a requested Web page. The browser then renders the HTML code to display the page.

A *Web cache* is a temporary storage area on your computer for collecting data. Once the data is stored in the cache, a Web site can quickly access the stored copy rather than downloading the data again.

A Web site is a collection of related HTML-formatted Web pages located on the Web. All pages within the site are accessible from the Web site address. The pages within the Web site can contain text, images, and multimedia elements such as audio, video, and animation files.

A *wiki* is a collaborative Web site that people can use to add, edit, remove, and organize Web page content. **Figure 28–6** shows the *Wikipedia.com* Web site, a popular online wiki.

▶ VOCABULARY
Web cache
wiki

FIGURE 28–6   Wikipedia Web site

XML is the acronym for Extensible Markup Language, which is a flexible text format for creating structured computer documents. For example, programs, such as Microsoft Office, save files in a particular format. Generally, the file must be opened by the same program. However, leading software makers have introduced a new method of saving files: XML. This method saves the document as a simple text file, along with information on how the program interprets the text. Programs such as Microsoft Office, OpenOffice, and WordPerfect Office create their own versions for different operating systems such as Windows, Apple Macintosh, and Linux/UNIX. Recent versions of these programs provide the option to save in XML format, thus enabling easier file exchange.

◗ ABOVE AND BEYOND

Besides being a popular wiki, Wikipedia is one of the most visited sites on the Web. Wikipedia is managed by the Wikimedia Foundation, a nonprofit organization that sponsors other wikis, including Wiktionary (an online dictionary), Wikiquote (a free collection of quotations), and Wikibooks (a collection of open-content educational textbooks).

3-3.1.3

Understanding Web Page Elements

A Web page can be a simple text document or it can contain a variety of the following elements:

- Web site addresses that link to other Web sites
- Text, video, or other media
- Hyperlinked text and graphics
- Interactive objects such as buttons, text boxes, option buttons, check boxes, menus, and lists
- Images such as photos, pictures, maps, and drawings

Figure 28–7 shows a Web page that contains most of these items.

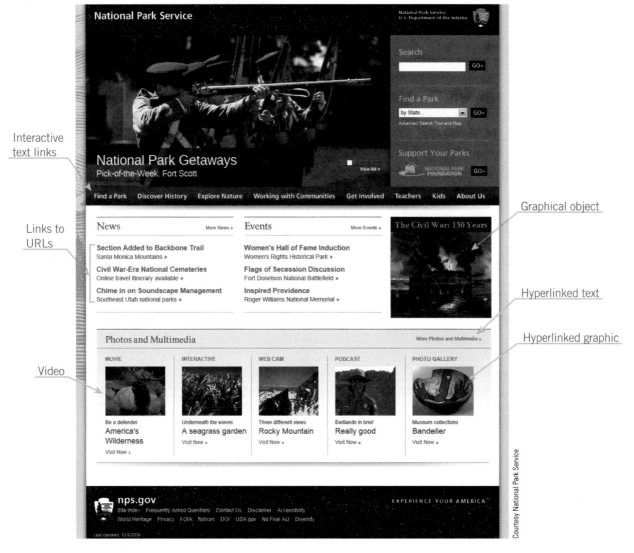

FIGURE 28–7   *nps.gov* Web page

Web sites can be organized into categories, each with a different purpose. The following list provides an overview of the types of Web sites available:

■ *Commercial*: Also known as an e-commerce site, a commercial site sells or promotes products or services. Almost every business today has a commercial Web site. Many of these Web sites also provide options to purchase products or services online (see **Figure 28–8a**).

■ *Academic*: Most educational facilities, elementary to university and public to private, have a Web site. Most higher education Web sites provide online registration, online courses, and other options. Many research facilities and both private and public companies also provide online training for their employees (see **Figure 28–8b**).

■ *Organizational*: Examples include Web sites of nonprofit organizations such zoos and advocacy groups such as wildlife and clean air supporters (see **Figure 28–8c**).

■ *Governmental*: Most local, state, regional, and national governments have a Web site or numerous Web sites. For instance, a medium-sized city could have a number of Web sites for employment, news of the day, parks and recreation, local services, utilities, visitors guide, citizens guide, customer service, and other public announcement sites (see **Figure 28–8d**).

■ *International*: Internet marketing of a product or service sometimes requires that Web sites be hosted in other countries because each country has unique search engines, which use different mathematical algorithms. Web page text also needs to be translated into the language of the country. Values and customs vary, so an effective Web site in one country may not work in other countries. Finally, local agencies most likely have a better understanding of the population and search engine optimization related to that population (see **Figure 28–8e**).

■ *Search sites*: A search engine is a software program used for online searching. Hundreds of search engines have been developed to find information on the Internet (see **Figure 28–8f**). Each search engine may work a little differently, but most share some common search features. For example, all search engines support keyword searches. Although keyword searches may not always be the most effective way to search, this is the search method most people use. Some search engines support an additional enhancement called concept-based searching. The search engine tries to determine what you mean and returns hits that relate to the keywords. Hits are the Web sites that contain text matching on your keywords. For example, if you search for "video games," the search engine might also return hits on sites that contain Nintendo and PlayStation. One of the best-known search engines using concept-based searching is Excite. Its search engine uses intelligent concept extraction (ICE) to learn about word relationships.

Another feature supported by some search engines is stemming. When you search for a word, the search engine also includes other "stems" of the word. For example, when you enter the search word *play*, you may also get back results for plays, playing, and player. The dogpile Web site, displayed in Figure 28-8f, is a metasearch engine that returns results from other search engines such as Google, Bing, Ask, Yahoo, About, and several others.

■ *Secure sites*: Some Web sites, such as those used for financial transactions or e-commerce, are more secure than sites that simply provide information. Most secure Web sites require you to log on using an account or user name and a password. You might see a message indicating that you are now entering (or leaving) a secure Web site, and you often see a padlock icon or another indicator in the status bar of a Web page to indicate that the information is secure. In Internet Explorer 7 and later, the Address bar turns green when you display secure Web sites. Occasionally, messages appear questioning the security of a site you are entering. Read the information in the message carefully before deciding whether to provide sensitive or private information on such a site. The secure Web site for a federal credit union is featured in **Figure 28-8g**.

You might also be required to provide a password for a Web site that limits access to members or subscribers. For example, if you access a university's Web site, you can browse and link to many parts of the site, but you might need a password to access a professor's class-specific Web site or your student account. Or, you might be able to read the current online edition of a newspaper, but if you want to search the paper's archives, you need to provide a password to show that you are a subscriber.

Recall that HTTP is a protocol for sending data back and forth between Web servers and clients. You often see this abbreviated in the browser window as http:// and https://. The letter s in this case stands for secure. You should never enter personal information, such as your credit card number, in an http:// Web site. You should always verify that the Web address begins with https://.

▶ **VOCABULARY**

Web app

portal

social networking site

geographic imaging

■ *Online applications*: Also known as **Web apps**, these sites host programs you can access with your Web browser. When using a Web app, the browser functions as a client. You interact with the software through your browser. Some programs allow you to store data on your local computer while others store your data and information on their servers. Some Web sites provide the service free of charge, and others charge a fee. For instance, TurboTax Online is a free service. However, if you choose to file online or to print a copy of your tax return, a minimum fee is charged. Google Docs and Microsoft Office Web Apps are other examples of this type of software. Both let you create documents online, edit from anywhere, and share your documents in real time for no charge (see **Figure 28–8h**).

■ *Portal*: A **portal** is a Web site that features useful content but also contains links to other sites. You can use a portal as your home page. For example, *besthistorysites.net*, shown in **Figure 28–8i**, is a portal that includes links to Web sites about history and research, for example.

■ *Weblog*: A Weblog, or blog, is a Web site designed as an online journal. These sites generally are maintained by one person or a small group and are similar to a diary. Postings generally are about personal experiences, hobbies, school, work, and opinion. Some companies also sponsor blogs. The blog in **Figure 28–8j** provides advice about saving and investing your money.

■ *Social networking*: A **social networking site** is an online community that provides interaction for groups of people who share a similar interest or activity. Users can post online profiles, pictures, video, music, and other information. There are dozens of social networking sites, but some of the more popular include Facebook, LinkedIn, Twitter, and Digg (see **Figure 28–8k**).

■ *Geographic imaging*: Mapping and **geographic imaging** Web sites use technology to change imagery of the Earth's surface into valuable information. This information is used by geographical information systems (GIS) to capture, store, analyze, and manage images. Google Earth is one example of this type of site. **Figure 28–8l** shows earthquake imaging data from the U.S. Geological Survey.

(a) Commercial   © 1996-2011, Amazon.com, Inc.

(b) Academic   © 2011 University of South Florida

(c) Organizational   © 2011 Tampa's Lowry Park Zoo.

(d) Governmental   Courtesy of USA.gov

(e) International   © Iberia

(f) Search site   © 2011 InfoSpace, Inc.

(g) Secure site   © 2011 Andera

(h) Online application   © 2011 Microsoft

(i) Portal   © 2008 EdTechTeacher Inc

(j) Weblog   © 1999-2011 by GetRichSlowly.org

(k) Social networking   © 2011 foursquare.com

(l) Geographic imaging   © 1995–2011 Esri.

FIGURE 28–8   Types of Web sites

3-3.1.5

Connecting to the Internet

Before you can access the Internet, you must connect to it. If you connect to the Internet from an office or academic setting, you probably are connecting through a local area network (LAN). You connect to the Internet using a network interface card (NIC), which is a special card inside your computer that allows the computer to be networked. A direct connection is made from the LAN to a high-speed connection line leased from the local telephone company.

Home users connect to the Internet using a dedicated high-speed digital telephone line ("dedicated" means it is always available for Internet access), a cable modem, or a wireless connection. Dial-up modems linked to telephone lines are becoming less common.

Connecting to the Internet is fairly simple and typically involves the following steps:

1. Locate an ISP or an online service. Of the thousands of ISPs, many are small local companies. Their service is primarily to provide a connection to the Internet. Other providers are large national and international companies, such as Verizon, AT&T, Comcast, and MSN. Generally, a local ISP is less expensive, but many people use the more expensive national services if they offer additional speed.

2. After you find an ISP, you must install some type of telecommunications software. This software enables your computer to connect to another computer. Your ISP or online service company provides this software, or you might be able to use software already installed on your computer. Most new computers are set up for a wireless connection.

3. You need a Web browser to visit Web sites. Most computers purchased today come with a browser already installed.

After you contract with an ISP and install telecommunications software and a browser, you are ready to connect to the Internet. This is the easy part. You may have to give instructions to your computer to dial a local telephone number if you are using a dial-up modem, but if you have a high-speed dedicated phone line, a cable connection, or a wireless service, you just start your browser. This connects you to your ISP's computer, which in turn connects you to the Internet. You are then online with the world. **Figure 28–9** shows a program that searches for available public wireless hookups, called hotspots. You can use hotspots to connect to the Internet when you cannot use your ISP, such as when you are traveling.

Hotspot detected at an airport

FIGURE 28–9 Searching for a hotspot

Different types of Internet connections provide a range of options. Be prepared to balance the features you want, such as connection speed and reliability, with the cost and availability of the options. For example, broadband connections can transmit multiple channels of information over a single link, so they can carry video, voice, and computer data simultaneously. Cable modems, digital subscriber lines (DSL), and T-1 lines offer high bandwidth, as opposed to a dial-up telephone modem, which has only a single bandwidth that can transmit voice or data, but not at the same time. Broadband cable connections allow home computer users to enjoy the benefits of faster connection speed and multiple channels to transmit data.

Understanding Browser Basics

Recall that a browser is a software program you use to retrieve documents from the Web and to display them in a readable format. The Web is the graphical portion of the Internet. The browser functions as an interface between you and the Internet. Using a browser, you can display both text and images. Browsers also support multimedia information, including sound and video.

To connect to the Internet, the browser sends a message to the Web server to retrieve your requested Web page. The browser then renders the HTML code to display the page. (Recall that HTML is the language used to create documents for the Web.) You navigate through the Web by clicking hyperlinked words and images.

Parts of the Browser Window

This lesson uses Microsoft Internet Explorer 9.0 as the browser. You should understand the parts of the browser window to use a browser effectively. **Figure 28–10** displays parts of the browser window. **Table 28–1** defines each part.

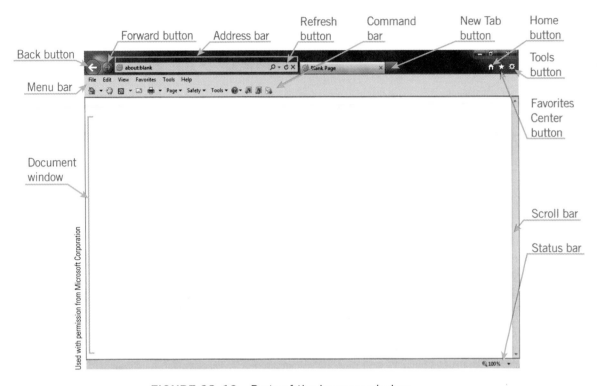

FIGURE 28–10   Parts of the browser window

TABLE 28–1   Parts of the Internet Explorer window

COMPONENT	DEFINITION
Address bar	Displays the URL or address of the active Web page; also is where you type the location for the Web page you want to visit
Back button	Displays the page you viewed before navigating to the Web page currently displayed in the browser window
Command bar	Provides a collection of buttons for selecting common commands
Document window	Displays the active Web page
Favorites Center button	Opens the Favorites Center, which lists Web pages designated as your favorites
Forward button	Displays the next page in a series of pages you previously viewed; this button is not active until the Back button has been clicked at least once
Home button	Displays the Web page designated as your home page
Menu bar	Lists menu names if you select the option to display the menu bar
New Tab button	Lets you open an additional Web page in the same browser window without closing the active page
Refresh button	Refreshes or reloads the active Web page
Scroll bar	Lets you scroll the Web page vertically, if necessary; if displayed, the horizontal scroll bar lets you scroll the Web page horizontally
Status bar	Shows status information, such as the current zoom level and the progress of Web page transactions
Tools button	Displays a menu of often-used commands

Navigating the Web

This lesson assumes that you have an Internet connection, such as a direct connection through school or a broadband connection at home. If you have a direct high-speed connection or a wireless connection, you start your Web browser to display your home page. In Windows 7, you can click the Internet Explorer icon on the task bar. If you are using a different browser, you might be able to double-click the browser icon located on your computer's desktop. If the icon is not available, open the browser from the Start menu. If you have a dial-up modem, first start your browser and then dial the Internet connection.

Your browser was installed with a default home page. The Address bar located near the top of the browser window contains the URL of the current page. The URL tells the browser where to locate the page on the Internet. If you want to visit a specific Web site, you need to know the address, which you enter in the Address bar. After you type the URL, press Enter to go to the Web site. In Step-by-Step 28.2, you visit the National Parks Service Web site and navigate through various options. Then you click the New Tab button to open another site.

> **QUICK TIP**
>
> To change the default home page, visit the Web page you want to use as your home page. Click Tools on the Internet Explorer menu bar and then click Options. On the General tab of the Internet Options dialog box, click the Use default button.

Step-by-Step 28.2

1. Start your Web browser the way you usually do. The first page you see is your home page.

2. In the Address bar, type **www.nps.gov** and then press **Enter** to access the National Park Service Web page (see **Figure 28–11**). The page that appears in your browser might be different from the one shown in Figure 28–11.

FIGURE 28–11
National Park
Service Web page

Web site address
entered in the
Address bar

Links bar

Scroll to display
the Photos and
Multimedia section

Find a Park box

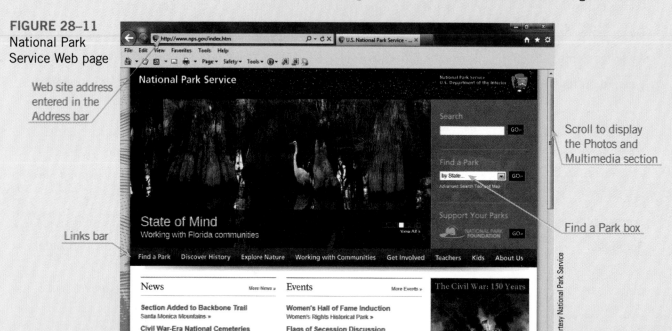

Courtesy National Park Service

3. You can navigate through the pages of the site using a number of navigation tools:

   a. In the Links bar below the main picture, click a link of your choice and review the information on the page. Then use your word-processing program to list the main points described on that page in your ic3-28 document.

   b. Click the browser's **Back** button ⬅ to return to the *nps.gov* home page.

   c. Scroll down to the Photos and Multimedia section. Click each item and then review the content.

   d. In your word-processing document, write a short overview of the content that you reviewed.

   e. Click the **Find a Park** box in the upper-right part of the page, and then click the name of your state. Select a link on the page, and then read the information. Click the **Back** button ⬅ as many times as necessary to return to the *nps.gov* home page.

   f. Below the Links bar are lists of news and events links. Click one of the links (your choice) and then scroll to view the entire page.

4. Press the **Print Screen** key to copy an image of the Web page to the Windows Clipboard. Paste the image into your ic3-28 document.

5. Click below the image, press **Enter**, and then add your name and the current date to the document. Create a list describing the article and features on the page you selected.

6. Save the document. Keep the document and the Web browser open for the next Step-by-Step exercise.

Refreshing or Reloading a Web Page

Cache memory is high-speed RAM that serves as a temporary storage area for data you access frequently. When you visit a Web page, a copy of the contents of the Web page is stored in your cache. If you access a Web page that contains updated information, such as a daily newspaper, most likely you will need to refresh or reload the information. Internet Explorer provides the following three options for reloading your browser:

- Click the Refresh button on the Address bar.
- Select View on the menu bar and then click Refresh.
- Press the F5 key.

3-3.1.6

QUICK TIP

Clear the cache regularly so you do not slow down the loading, displaying, and exiting of Web pages. To do so, click Safety on the Command bar and then click Delete Browsing History. This deletes temporary files, browsing history, cookies, saved form information, and saved passwords but not your list of Favorites or subscribed feeds.

Recent History

Your browser tracks the sites you have visited for a specified period of time. The default setting in Internet Explorer, for example, is to keep track of sites visited for approximately three weeks. You can view a list of recently visited Web sites by clicking the Favorites button and then clicking the History tab. You can display the list of visited Web sites using the following View options: By Date, By Site, By Most Visited, and By Order Visited Today. A Search History option is also available. In **Figure 28–12**, View by Date is selected.

3-3.1.7

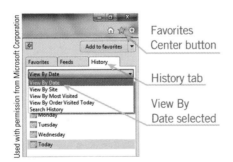

FIGURE 28–12   Displaying a recent history of visited Web sites

In Step-by-Step 28.3, you learn how to clear the History list, reload a Web page, and then display the history of recently visited Web sites.

Step-by-Step 28.3

1. In your browser, click the **Home** button 🏠 to return to your home page.
2. Click the **Refresh** button 🔁 to make sure the most recent version of the page is loaded. Do you notice any changes to the page after it has reloaded?
3. Click **Safety** on the Command bar, and then click **Delete browsing history** to display the Delete Browsing History dialog box (see **Figure 28–13**).

FIGURE 28–13
Delete Browsing History
dialog box

Select a check
box to delete
part of your
browsing history

About deleting
browsing
history link

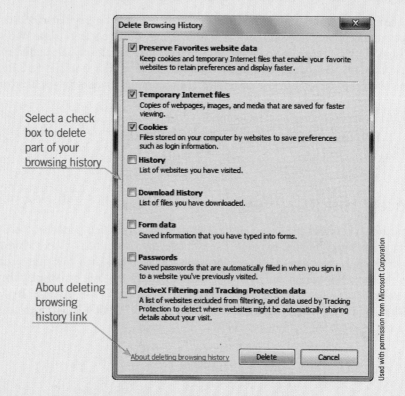

4. The Delete Browsing History dialog box provides check boxes you select to delete temporary Internet files, cookies, history, form data, and passwords. Click the **About deleting browsing history** link, and then read the Help topic to learn about deleting browsing history.
5. Close the Windows Help and Support window and the Delete Browsing History dialog box.
6. If necessary, open your **ic3-28** document. Write a paragraph explaining what you learned about deleting browsing history. Save your document. Keep the document and your Web browser open for the next exercise.

Finding Text on a Web Page

When searching for information on the Internet, the most widely used tool is a search engine. Because large Web sites contain many pages and links, they often provide a search tool specific to the site. You can also use the Find bar to find text on a Web page. Complete Step-by-Step 28.4 to use the Find bar.

3-3.1.8

Step-by-Step 28.4

1. Return to the home page of the National Park Service Web site using any technique you learned in this lesson. For example, click the **Back** ⬅ button or use the History list. Scroll down, if necessary, to display the nps.gov section.

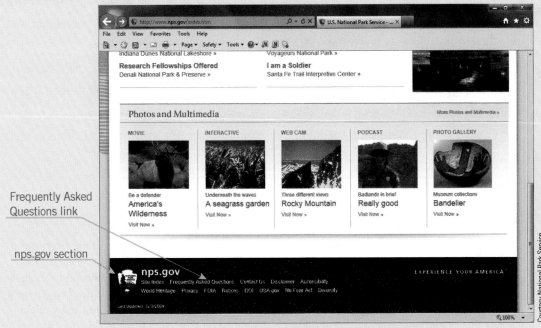

FIGURE 28–14
Home page of the National Park Service Web site

Frequently Asked Questions link

nps.gov section

Courtesy National Park Service

2. Press and hold the **Ctrl** key, and then click the **Frequently Asked Questions** link to open the Frequently Asked Questions page on a new tab (see **Figure 28–15**).

FIGURE 28–15
Frequently Asked Questions page

My Page link

Courtesy National Park Service

3. Scroll the page and view its contents. Press **Ctrl+F** to display the Find bar below the Command bar (see **Figure 28–16**).

FIGURE 28–16
Displaying the
Find bar

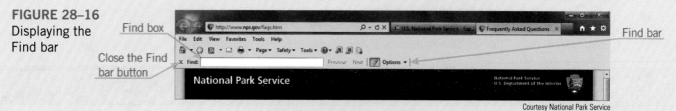

Courtesy National Park Service

4. In the Find box, type **recreation**, and then press **Enter** to find the first instance of *recreation*. Click the **Next** button repeatedly to find all instances of *recreation* on the page.

5. Click the **Close the Find bar** button X to close the Find bar, and then return to the home page of the National Park Service Web site (see **Figure 28–14**).

6. Scroll to the top of the page. In the Search box, type **recreation** and then press **Enter**. Review the first page of search results.

7. If necessary, open your **ic3-28** document. Write a paragraph describing the difference between using the Find box and using the Search box. Save your document.

8. Keep your document and Web browser open for the next Step-by-Step exercise.

3-3.1.9

Organizing and Managing Favorites

Internet Explorer and other browsers provide a tool that makes it easy for you to return to a particular Web site or to easily access a Web site that you visit frequently. Internet Explorer refers to these links as favorites. Other browsers refer to these as bookmarks. The Favorites list contains the addresses (URLs) of designated sites. When you add a Web site to your Favorites list, you can access the site by clicking the site name. In Step-by-Step 28.5, you add a Web page to your Favorites list.

Step-by-Step 28.5

1. Return to the *nps.gov* Web page. (If necessary, type **www.nps.gov** in the Address bar, and then press **Enter**.)

2. If the menu bar is not displayed, click **Tools** on the Command bar, point to *Toolbars*, and then click **Menu bar**. Click **Favorites** on the menu bar to display the Favorites list, as shown in **Figure 28–17**. Your Favorites list is most likely different from the one shown in Figure 28–17.

FIGURE 28–17
Favorites list

Add to favorites command

Favorites list

3. Click the **Add to favorites** command to display the Add a Favorite dialog box. In the Name text box, replace the Web site name with **NPS home page** (see **Figure 28–18**). This favorite name will appear in the Favorites list.

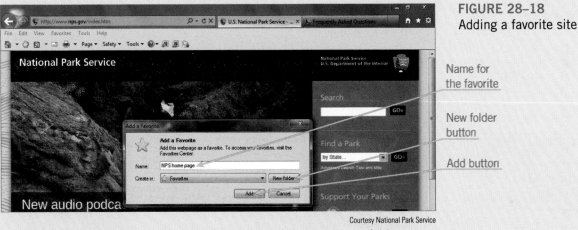

FIGURE 28–18
Adding a favorite site

Name for the favorite

New folder button

Add button

Courtesy National Park Service

4. Click the **New folder** button, and then type **environment** as the folder name.

5. Click the **Create** button to create the folder. In the Add a Favorite dialog box, make sure the Create in button displays *environment* as the location for creating the favorite, and then press the **Print Screen** key to copy an image of your desktop to the Windows Clipboard. Paste the image into your ic3-28 document, and then save the document.

6. In the Add a Favorite dialog box, click the **Add** button to add the environment folder and the *nps.gov* Web page to the Favorites list.

7. Click the **Close Tab** button ⊠ on the Frequently Asked Questions page tab to close the Web page.

8. Keep your ic3-28 document and Web browser open for the next Step-by-Step exercise.

After you add a Web site as a favorite or bookmarked site, you can access a site, move a favorite or bookmarked site between folders, and share favorite or book-marked sites with other users. To access a favorite site:

1. Open Internet Explorer, click the Favorites Center button, and then click the Favorites tab, if necessary.

2. If the site is not stored in a folder, click the site name to access the site. If the site is stored in a folder, click the folder name and then click the site name.

To move favorite or bookmarked sites between folders:

1. Open Internet Explorer, and then click the Favorites Center button.

2. Click the Add to favorites button arrow, and then click Import and export to display the Import/Export Settings Wizard.

3. Click the Export to a file option button, and then click the Next button.

4. If necessary, click the Favorites box to insert a check mark. Click the Next button.

5. Select the favorites folder (or all folders) that you want to export, and then click the Next button.

6. Enter or select the location for the exported favorites, and then click the Export button.

Internet Explorer creates a file titled bookmark.htm in the folder you specified and then exports your favorites into this folder. To export favorites or bookmarked sites to share with other users, first export your favorite or bookmarked sites into a separate folder as described earlier. Then select one of the following options:

- Option 1: Compress the folder and send it as an e-mail attachment.
- Option 2: If you use the Google toolbar, look for an option to export the favorite or bookmarked sites.

QUICK TIP

If you have a Gmail account, it includes a personalized Google Bookmarks service.

3-3.1.11

Downloading a File from a Web Site

You can download a file such as a program, graphic, or document from a Web page. Note that you should download files only from reliable sources, but there are many of these on the Web, including shareware and freeware sites. These sites offer useful computer programs and games that you can download for a small fee or at no cost. In other instances, you may need to download a patch or an update from a software manufacturer for a program installed on your computer, or you may want to download clip art, an informational file, or an audio or video clip. Most sites that have files to download provide an interface that makes the process of downloading simple. In the next Step-by-Step exercise, you download clip art.

Step-by-Step 28.6

1. In your browser, type **microsoft clip art** in the Address box and then press **Enter**. A list of search results is displayed.

2. One of the links in the search results list is to the Office online clip art collection, located at *office.microsoft.com/en-us/images*. The link is identified as *Images - Clip Art, Photos, Sounds, & Animations - Office.com*, or something similar.

3. Click the link to the Office online clip art collection to open the Office online clip art gallery. See **Figure 28–19**. The featured galleries change frequently, so the one displayed in your browser will probably differ from the one shown in Figure 28–19.

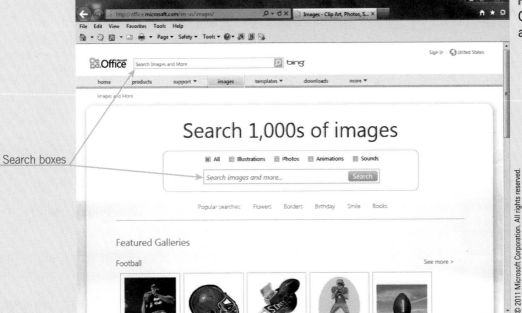

Search boxes

FIGURE 28–19
Office online clip art gallery

4. In a Search box, type **technology** and then press **Enter**.

5. When the results appear, point to a clip art image of a computer or a computer-related item to display a selection box with options for working with the image (see **Figure 28–20**).

Options appear
when you point
to an image

download link

6. Click the **download** link in the selection box. A message appears at the bottom of the Internet Explorer window, asking if you want to open or save the image file.

7. Click the **Save** button to save the image as a downloaded file.

8. To open the downloaded image file, click **Tools** on the menu bar, and then click **View downloads**. The image file appears in the list of downloaded files in the View Downloads window.

9. Click the **Open** button to open the file. Press the **Print Screen** key to copy an image of your desktop to the Windows Clipboard.

10. Open the **ic3-28** document and then paste the image at the end of the document. Save the document.

11. Close the program displaying the image, such as Windows Photo Viewer, and then click the **Close** button to close the View Downloads window.

12. Keep the ic3-28 document and your Web browser open for the next Step-by-Step exercise.

3-3.1.10
3-3.1.12

Copying and Printing Information from a Web Page

You can copy and save specific elements of a Web page to disk and use them in a new document or file. For example, you might want to save a photographic image to disk or copy a paragraph of text you want to quote in a report. You can then open these in other programs or paste them into new files, such as a word-processing document, where you can edit and manipulate them as desired.

You can also print a copy of a Web page directly from your browser. Most browsers provide previewing and page setup options that enable you to control how the Web page prints. Make sure your instructor has given you permission to print a Web page before completing the following exercise.

In Step-by-Step 28.7, you copy text and an image from a Web site to a Word document and then print information from a Web site.

Step-by-Step 28.7

1. Return to the NPS Home page you accessed earlier. (*Hint:* Use the Favorites list to return to the page.)

2. Click the **Explore Nature** link in the Links bar to display the Explore Nature page. Select a paragraph of text, right-click the selected text, and then click **Copy** on the shortcut menu to copy the text.

3. Switch to Word, and then paste the text into a new blank document.

4. Save the document with a name of your choice in the location where you save your assignments.

5. Return to your browser. Right-click a graphic image of your choice to display a shortcut menu (see **Figure 28–21**), and then click **Save picture as**. Save the picture with its default filename in the location where you save your assignments.

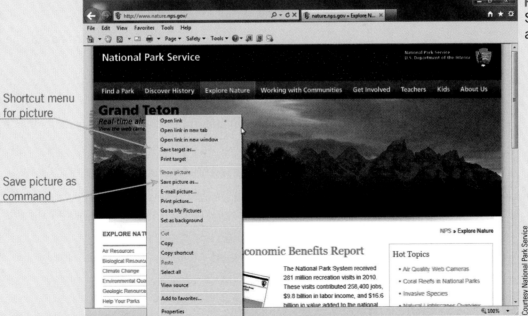

Shortcut menu for picture

Save picture as command

FIGURE 28–21
Saving a picture from a Web page

6. In Word, click the **Insert** tab and then click the Picture button in the Illustrations group to insert the picture in the same document in which you saved the text in Step 4.

7. Save the document, then close it and return to your browser.

8. Click **File** on the browser's menu bar, and then click **Print preview** to preview the Web page (see **Figure 28–22**). Your image will differ.

FIGURE 28–22
Displaying a Web page in Print Preview

Print Document button

Page Setup button

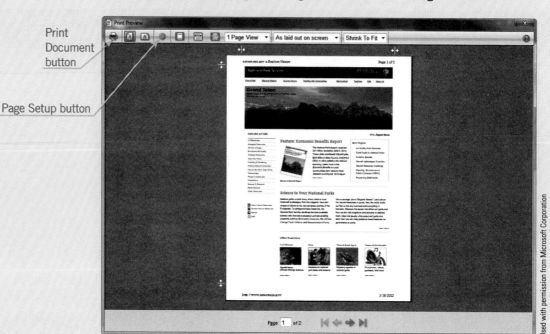

9. To print the Web page:
   a. Click the **Page Setup** button on the Print Preview toolbar to open the Page Setup dialog box.
   b. Change the top margin to **0.5** inches and then click **OK** to close the Page Setup dialog box.
   c. Click the **Print Document** button on the Print Preview toolbar to open the Print dialog box.
   d. Click the **Current Page** option button in the Page Range section.
   e. Click the **Print** button to print your document.

10. You return to the browser window. Leave the browser open for the next Step-by-Step exercise.

3-3.1.13

Selecting Web Browser Settings

As you become an experienced Internet user, you may find that you want to change your browser's security settings. In Step-by-Step 28.8, you review these security options.

Step-by-Step 28.8

1. In Internet Explorer, click **Tools** on the Command bar, click **Internet options** to open the Internet Options dialog box, and then click the **Security** tab. See **Figure 28–23**.

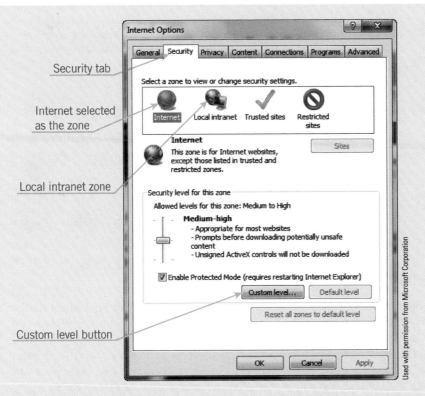

FIGURE 28–23
Security tab in the Internet
Options dialog box

2. Internet should be selected as the zone. Click **Local intranet** and review those settings. Then review the settings for Trusted sites and for Restricted sites.

3. Click the **Internet** zone icon and then click the **Custom level** button to display security settings for the Internet zone. Use the scroll bar to view the various options (see **Figure 28–24**).

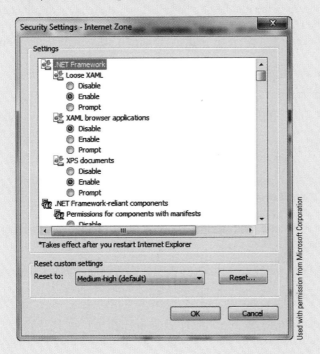

FIGURE 28–24
Security Settings - Internet Zone
dialog box

4. Click the **Cancel** button to return to the Internet Options dialog box.

5. Click the other three zones, click the **Custom level** button, review the settings for each zone, and then click the **Cancel** button to return to the Internet Options dialog box.

6. Click the **Cancel** button to close the Internet Options dialog box.

7. Open the **ic3-28** document, and then write a paragraph describing each of the four zones listed in the Internet Options dialog box. Save your document, and then close your ic3-28 file and submit it to your instructor as requested.

3-3.1.14

Identifying Browser Issues

The Internet and browsers are not without their problems. Web sites might not be displayed, a page is slow to load or the text is garbled, or pop-up ads distract you from or block the content on the page.

When you enter a Web site address and receive a "Page not found" message, the Web site might display a "404 error," which you receive because a) the page was moved, b) an old index is still maintained in a search engine, or c) you made a typing error when entering the Web site address. In some instances, the Web site is temporarily unavailable because the server is offline or the site is being updated.

A Web page may load slowly because of heavy server traffic or the page may contain a large number of images. A garbled or offset page could result from a number of issues, such as the rendering technique used by the browser. If you are using a recent browser, such as Internet Explorer 9, you can use the Compatibility View command to try to display the Web page using older settings.

Pop-up ads are another annoyance. Advertisers place these ads on Web sites and they pop up in the middle of a page that you are reading to call attention to their content. Internet Explorer contains a pop-up blocker that limits most pop-ups. The pop-up blocker is turned on by default. To turn it off, complete the following steps:

1. Open Internet Explorer, click Tools on the menu bar, and then point to Pop-up Blocker.

2. Click Turn off Pop-up Blocker. If a confirmation window is displayed asking if you are sure you want to turn off the blocker, click the Yes button to turn off the blocker or click the No button to cancel the request.

You can also change the settings to allow specific sites to display pop-ups. The following steps show how to select specific sites:

1. Open Internet Explorer, click Tools on the menu bar, and then point to Pop-up Blocker.

2. Click Pop-up Blocker Settings to display the Pop-up Blocker Settings dialog box.

3. Select the address of a site to allow pop-ups and then click the Add button.

4. You can also set the Blocking level from High to Low: High blocks all pop-ups, Medium blocks most automatic pop-ups, and Low allows pop-ups from secure sites (see **Figure 28–25**).

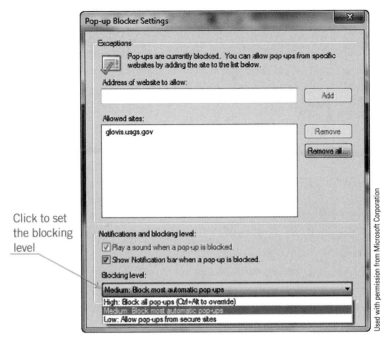

Click to set
the blocking
level

Used with permission from Microsoft Corporation

FIGURE 28–25 Pop-up Blocker Settings dialog box

WORKPLACE READINESS

Digital Literacy

To succeed in today's workplace, you need digital literacy, the ability to find, organize, understand, and analyze information using digital technology, including computing devices and the Internet. If you have digital literacy, you can communicate, collaborate, and work effectively, especially using online tools.

To find a job or select a career, you can take advantage of Web sites that provide information about job openings. Most of these sites also offer articles and videos about developing job-seeking and career-building skills, such as preparing for an interview, working with colleagues on a team, and solving typical workplace problems.

After you find a job, you may be required to have at least a basic knowledge of computers and the Internet; some careers demand more advanced knowledge or mastery. To be promoted in white collar or blue collar jobs, you often need to be proficient using portable devices such as smart phones and tablets. Digitally literate employees are also proficient in text messaging, blogging, creating a Web page, participating in social networking sites, creating and sharing podcasts, conducting and analyzing online searches, and using online collaboration tools.

SUMMARY

In this lesson, you learned:

- The Internet and the Web have their own terminology. You should be familiar with terms such as ActiveX, cookies, digital certificate, and domain.

- A Web page can be solely a text document or it can be made up of elements such as Web site addresses that link to other Web sites; audio, video, graphics, or other media; hyperlinked text and hyperlinked graphics; and interactive objects such as buttons, text boxes, option buttons, check boxes, menus, and lists.

- Select an Internet connection to balance the features you want, such as connection speed and reliability, with the cost and availability of the different options. For example, broadband connections allow multiple channels of information to be transmitted over a single link so more than one channel of video, voice, and computer data can be carried simultaneously.

- Parts of the Internet Explorer browser window include the Address bar, document tabs, status bar, and Command bar.

- A browser displays a home page when it starts. You use the Address bar to verify the address of the current page and enter addresses to visit other pages. A Web address is called the Uniform Resource Locator (URL), which uniquely identifies each Web page and tells the browser where to locate the page.

- Internet Explorer and other browsers provide a favorite or bookmarked sites list to make it easy for you to return to a particular Web site you visit frequently. Internet Explorer provides a Favorites Center that lists and organizes the Web pages in your Favorites list.

- Web sites used for financial transactions or e-commerce usually use encrypted communication to make them more secure than sites that simply provide information. Some Web sites also require you to log on using an account or user name and a password.

- Problems associated with using the Web include not being able to display Web sites, navigating to pages that are slow to load or contain garbled text, or finding pop-up ads distract you from or block the content on the page.

■ LESSON REVIEW

TRUE / FALSE

Circle T if the statement is true or F if the statement is false.

T   F   **1.**   You can print a copy of a Web page directly from your browser.

T   F   **2.**   Online Web applications are known as Web apps.

T   F   **3.**   It is safe to download any document from the Web.

T   F   **4.**   A browser displays the last page viewed when it starts.

T   F   **5.**   Internet Explorer is considered a Web browser.

MULTIPLE CHOICE

Select the best response for the following statements:

1. A _____ _____ can be a simple text document, or it can contain hyperlinked text and graphics along with other elements.

    A.   Web cache   C.   Web site

    B.   Web page   D.   client page

2. Web sites used for financial transactions generally use _____ communications.

    A.   accessible   C.   encrypted

    B.   personal   D.   graphical

3. A Web page may load slowly because of _____.

    A.   heavy service traffic   C.   domain overload

    B.   bookmarked sites   D.   missing Command bar

4. Which of the following is *not* a reason you might receive a "Page not found" or "404 error"?

   A. You made a typing error when entering the Web site address.

   C. The page was moved.

   B. The browser uses "fit-to-width" rendering.

   D. The site contains pop-up ads.

5. The first graphical browser was named _____.

   A. Mosaic

   C. Internet Explorer

   B. Netscape

   D. Wiki

FILL IN THE BLANK

Complete the following sentences by writing the correct word or words in the blanks provided:

1. Web sites store _____ on your computer so that when you return to a site, it displays any preferences or other customized settings you selected.

2. A(n) _____ identifies a computer or Web site on the Internet.

3. When data is stored in a(n) _____ _____, a Web site can quickly access the stored copy rather than downloading the data again.

4. In Internet Explorer, the _____ _____ button lets you open an additional Web page in the same browser window without closing the active page.

5. The protocol used for secure Web sites is _____.

■ PROJECTS

PROJECT 28–1

3-3.1.2

A digital certificate was briefly discussed in this lesson. Use your Web browser and search for information referring to a digital certificate. Then write a paragraph or two describing the function of a digital certificate and how it is used. Answer the following questions:

1. To what is a digital certificate attached and why?

2. What is the most common use of a digital certificate?

3. Which companies provide digital certificates?

4. What types of files are public keys and private keys?

5. What is the most widely used standard for digital certificates?

PROJECT 28–2

3-3.1.1

Domains and the domain name system (DNS) are discussed briefly in this lesson. Using the Internet and other resources, prepare a short report that includes the following information:

- Purpose of a domain name

- Definition of DNS

- Purpose of DNS

- How DNS makes it possible to assign domain names to groups of Internet resources

PROJECT 28–3

Several countries, including the United States, have proposed a taxing plan for the Internet. Complete the following:

1. Research the proposal for taxing Internet usage online. What are Internet taxes and how are they charged?

2. Prepare a one-page report discussing this topic. Answer questions such as the following:

   - Do you think Internet usage will eventually be taxed? Why or why not?

   - Do you think Internet usage should be taxed? Explain your answer.

   - Discuss the pros and cons of taxing the Internet.

◤ TEAMWORK PROJECT

3-3.1.5
3-3.1.6
3-3.1.7

This lesson describes several features of Web browsers such as Internet Explorer. Work with a partner to determine which of these features each of you would most likely use and why you would use it.

1. Make a list that includes all the browser features that were mentioned in this lesson, and make two columns, one for each member of your team.

2. Use a ranking scale of 1 to 5 (1 means you would probably never use this feature and 5 means that you would definitely use it) to rank how important you and your partner think each feature is.

3. Work together to prepare a report that explains your rankings and why you ranked each feature as you did.

■ CRITICAL THINKING

Wikis are quickly becoming a popular way to share information on the Internet. Use your favorite search engine to find out more about wikis, including the following information:

- Definition of "wiki"
- Why wikis are useful

- How businesses use wikis
- Characteristics of wikis
- Security concerns
- Examples (4–5) of wikis

3-3.1.4

■ ONLINE DISCOVERY

Google is more than a search engine. It provides services and Web apps in categories such as Mobile, Media, Geo, Home & Office, and Social. Visit the Google Products page by opening the Google home page in your browser (*www.google.com*), clicking the More button on the bar at the top of the page, and then clicking Even more. Select one tool or Web app that you have not used before. Research the following information about the Google tool you selected:

- Purpose of the tool
- Examples of how people use the tool
- Steps you perform to complete a typical task

■ JOB SKILLS

As mentioned in the Workplace Readiness sidebar, career Web sites such as *careerbuilder.com* and *monster.com* provide articles, videos, advice, and other resources to prepare for a job search, develop a career, change careers, and other topics. Visit a career Web site in the following list, and then search for an article that discusses using the Internet and the Web in a job search or on the job. List at least four ideas, tips, or steps mentioned in the article.

- *www.onestopcoach.org*
- *www.rileyguide.com/prepare.html*
- *www.job-hunt.org*
- *www.careerbuilder.com*

LESSON 29

Web Content

■ OBJECTIVES

Upon completion of this lesson, you should be able to:

- Understand Internet content.
- Search for information on the Web.
- Use a search engine.
- Evaluate the quality of Internet information.
- Identify how to evaluate the quality of information.
- Observe intellectual property laws.

■ DATA FILES

You do not need data files to complete this lesson.

■ WORDS TO KNOW

blog

Boolean logic

copyright

directory

feed

index

keyword

libel

link list

math symbol

news feed

phrase searching

plagiarism

podcatcher

public domain

related search

search engine

shared bookmark

trademark

wiki

wildcard character

As the use of online technology continues to grow, you should understand how to find and evaluate content on the Web. This lesson explores how to develop, locate, and use information available in Web sites.

3-3.2.1

Understanding Internet Content

You typically create content for the Internet by publishing it on a Web page and providing links for navigation. As the author, you control the content of the Web page and access to it. Viewers visit your site and interact with the information you provide. With the advent of Web 2.0, you can allow other types of interaction. Recall from the discussion of Web 2.0 in Lesson 28 that a new generation of Web software makes Web design and development options available, accessible, and easy to use. For example, you can now invite Web page viewers to contribute information to a site or exchange information, messages, and files with other viewers. You can create online content on the following types of sites:

- Web pages and Web sites are created by schools, governments, institutions, companies, nonprofit agencies, individuals, and others. Examples of Web site types include personal, entertainment, e-commerce, special causes, political, and government services. Lesson 28 contains an extensive overview of the various types of Web sites.

▶ **VOCABULARY**

blog

- A *blog* generally is managed by one person or a small group. The authors post commentary, journal entries, video, graphics, and other content and invite viewers to read and comment on the entries, which are usually displayed in reverse-chronological order. **Figure 29–1** shows an example of a blog for the Society of Professional Journalists.

Entries are posted in reverse-chronological order

FIGURE 29–1   Society of Professional Journalists blog

■ A *wiki* is a collaborative Web site that can be edited by anyone with access. ("Wiki" means quick in Hawaiian.) **Figure 29–2** shows an example of a wiki that focuses on quotations.

▶ **VOCABULARY**
wiki

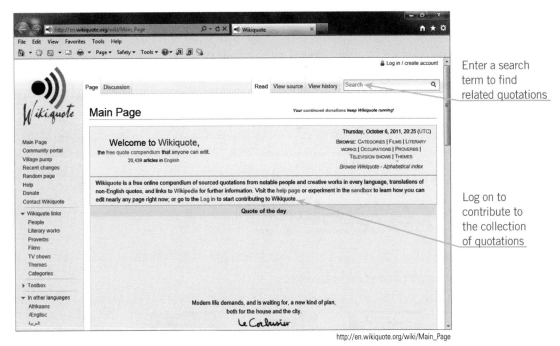

http://en.wikiquote.org/wiki/Main_Page

FIGURE 29–2 Wikiquote

■ Social networking sites, such as Facebook, MySpace, Bebo, Twitter, LinkedIn, hi5, Orkut, and others attract millions of users. These sites basically are groups of people who share similar interests or activities. The sites provide ways for users to interact such as through instant messages and e-mail. **Figure 29–3** shows the home page for the MySpace social networking site.

FIGURE 29–3 MySpace social networking site

- A podcast is a collection of multimedia files, usually audio or video files, that can be downloaded from the Internet to a mobile device or personal computer. You can download the files manually one at a time or automatically through a subscription using Really Simple Syndication (RSS). To subscribe to a podcast, you use a software program called a *podcatcher*. This program checks a *feed* for new content on a regular basis. When the podcatcher finds a new podcast, it downloads the podcast to your specified device. For example, you can download podcasts from the Apple iTunes Store to view video or listen to audio developed by independent creators or media outlets such as ESPN, *The Onion*, and *The New York Times*. **Figure 29–4** shows an online directory of podcasts.

VOCABULARY
podcatcher

feed

FIGURE 29–4   Podcasts

- The Web contains several types of file-sharing sites, including those for sharing photos, music, and video. When you share files, you post them on a Web site to make them available to other users. To do so, you usually use a peer-to-peer (P2P) network, which connects computers directly instead of through a central server. **Figure 29–5** shows the home page of Shutterfly, a peer-to-peer site for sharing photographs.

FIGURE 29–5 Peer-to-peer media-sharing site

- A *news feed* (also known as a Web feed) is a data format for providing users with frequently updated content. Content distributors such as media outlets syndicate news feeds so that users can subscribe to them. Similar to a podcast, news-related information is usually delivered using the RSS family of formats (see **Figure 29–6**). You can receive a news feed through your browser or with a dedicated feed reader program.

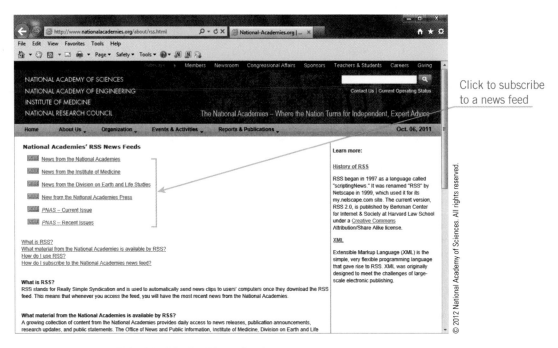

FIGURE 29–6   News feed

3-3.2.2

Searching for Information on the Web

When searching online, one of the primary tools you can use to find information is a *search engine*. You use a search engine to search for *keywords*. Search engines are automated indexes, so you might find that your search results include information that is irrelevant, but you will learn how to refine your search in this lesson. You can use general search engines and special-purpose search engines.

No single tool indexes or organizes the entire Web. When using an online search tool, you are searching and viewing data extracted from the Web. This data has been placed into the search engine's database. It is the database that is searched—not the Web itself. This is one reason you often have different results when you use different search engines.

You search the Internet to find answers to questions and information on any topic that interests you. The following are just a few examples of the types and availability of online data:

- You need to do some research for a paper due in your continuing education class next week.

- Your grandfather is losing his hearing and has asked you to help him find some information on hearing aids.

- You plan to take a trip to Mexico this summer and would like to get information on some of the best places to stay.

In addition to search engines, you can find online information using other tools, including the following:

- *Indexes*, also called *directories*, are Web sites that are organized by categories. Some examples of online directories include Libdex, which is a worldwide index of library catalogs, libraries, and books; Project Gutenberg online books, which contains a listing of over 35,000 free books on the Web; the National Geographic index; technical indexes; and dozens of others.

- *Link lists* are collections of links on a particular topic. You can find hundreds of link list sites on a variety of topics throughout the Internet. Most link lists, such as the site shown in **Figure 29–7**, contain a search engine, which you use to find information on the site.

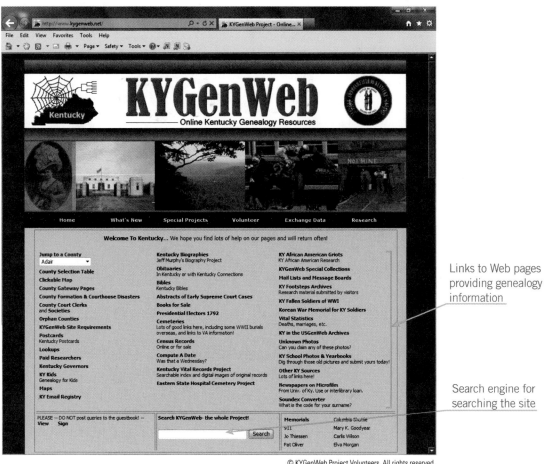

Links to Web pages providing genealogy information

Search engine for searching the site

FIGURE 29–7   Genealogy link list

▶ **VOCABULARY**
shared bookmark

■ A *shared bookmark* is a form of collaborative information sharing that lets users organize and share favorites, or bookmarks. Also called social bookmarking, you use this technology to store, organize, search, and manage a collection of links to Web pages. Many libraries use this process to provide lists of informative links on various topics. Delicious (*delicious.com*) was one of the pioneer Web sites in this technology (see **Figure 29–8**).

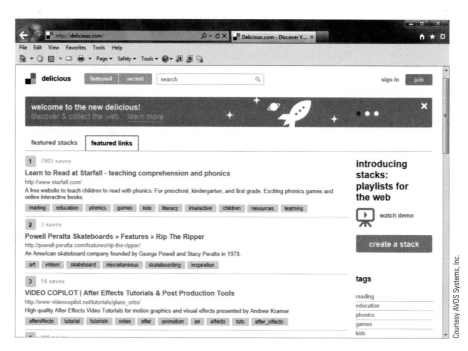

FIGURE 29–8   Social bookmarking site

Besides using one of these tools to search the Web, you can use the links on Web pages to discover content on other Web sites. For example, blogs often contain links. A typical blog generally combines text, images, and links to other blogs, Web pages, and other related media. Many Web sites, including social networking sites, also contain links within their content. Clicking a link can transfer you to a new Web site page or open another Web page within the same site. Other online content, such as a traditional Web site, an informational site, or government sites, generally contains links within the content. **Figure 29–9** shows an example of the Internal Revenue Service Web site, which contains numerous links.

Links for downloading files

Links to news articles

Links to online applications

FIGURE 29–9 Internal Revenue Service Web site

Using a Search Engine

As the Internet continues to expand and more pages are added, effective searching requires new approaches and strategies. When you use a search engine such as Google, the more specific your keywords, the more likely you will find what you want. To make your keywords more specific, you can use phrases, math symbols, Boolean operators, and wildcards. These tools help you refine a search when it generates too many links or links to the wrong type of information.

3-3.2.3

Phrase Searching

If you want to search for words that appear next to each other, then *phrase searching* is your best choice. When you enter a phrase within quotation marks, the search engine matches those words that appear adjacent to each other and in the order you specify. For example, if you are searching for baseball cards, enter the phrase "baseball cards" in quotation marks. The results contain Web sites with the words "baseball" and "cards" next to each other. Without the quotation marks, the search engine finds Web pages that contain the words "baseball" and "cards" anywhere within each page.

If you are searching for more than one phrase, you can separate phrases or proper names with a comma. To find Mickey Mantle baseball cards, for example, enter "baseball cards", "Mickey Mantle." It is always a good idea to capitalize proper nouns because some search engines distinguish between upper- and lowercase letters. On the other hand, if you capitalize a common noun such as "Bread," you find fewer Web pages than if you entered "bread."

> **VOCABULARY**
> **phrase searching**

▶ VOCABULARY
math symbol
Boolean logic

Search Engine Math

Math symbols are another available option to make keywords more specific and narrow your search results. You can use math symbols such as plus (+) and minus (–) to enter a formula that filters out unwanted listings. For example:

- Insert a plus sign (+) before words that should appear on the page (also called an inclusion operator).
- Insert a minus sign (–) before words that you do not want to appear (also called an exclusion operator).

Suppose you are making cookies for a party and want to try some new recipes. Your keywords are "+cookie+recipes." Only pages that contain both words would appear in your results. Now suppose that you want recipes for chocolate cookies. Your keywords are "+cookie+recipes+chocolate." The results display pages with all three words.

To take this a step further, suppose you do not like coconut, so you do not want any recipes that contain the word "coconut." Use the minus (–) symbol to reduce the number of unrelated results. Enter the search phrase as "+cookie+recipes+chocolate–coconut." This tells the search engine to find pages that contain "cookie," "recipes," and "chocolate" and then to remove any pages that contain the word "coconut." To extend this idea and to find chocolate cookie recipes without coconut and honey, your search phrase would be "+cookie+recipes+chocolate–coconut–honey." Subtract terms you do not want to find to produce better results. Nearly all of the major search engines support search engine math. You can also use math symbols with most directories.

Boolean Searching

Recall that when you search for a topic on the Internet, you are not going from server to server and viewing documents on that server. Instead you are searching databases. **Boolean logic** is another way that you can search databases. This logic works on a similar principle as search engine math but has a little more power. Boolean logic consists of three logical operators:

- AND
- NOT
- OR

Returning to the cookie example, suppose you want only cookie recipes, not Web pages about cookies in general or about recipes for other food. Search for "cookies AND recipes." The more terms you combine with AND, the fewer pages you find. If you want chocolate cookie recipes without coconut, you would search for "cookies AND recipes AND chocolate NOT coconut."

You can use OR logic to search for similar terms or concepts. If you do want to find Web pages about cookies in general or recipes for other food, you can search for "cookies OR recipes." In contrast to the AND operator, the more terms you combine in a search with OR logic, the more results you receive from your search. You can combine OR with AND to produce sophisticated results. For example, search for "cookies AND recipes OR chocolate" to retrieve results containing one term or the other or both.

Some search engines assist you with your logical search through the use of forms. For example, look for a hyperlink labeled *Advanced Search* or *Advanced Options* on a search engine's main page to open an advanced search form. Using this form, you can add words and phrases to include and to omit topics. Some search engines do not support Boolean logic, but most do provide a form that allows searching to be refined with filters or specific criteria. Some advanced search forms also provide options to specify a time period, a language, and other options. In Step-by-Step 29.1, you use Google's search engine to search for the cookie recipe.

Step-by-Step 29.1

1. Start your Web browser as you normally do, and then open **google.com**.

2. In the Search box, type **cookies AND recipes AND chocolate**, and then press **Enter** to display the basic search results. See **Figure 29–10**. Note the number of Web pages found. Your results might differ.

Search term entered

Number of Web pages found

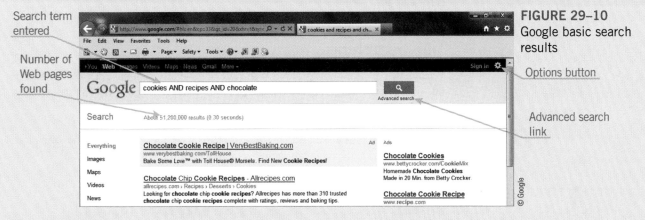

FIGURE 29–10
Google basic search results

Options button

Advanced search link

3. Click the **Advanced search** link to display the Advanced Search page. If an Advanced search link does not appear on your results page, click the **Options** button in the bar at the top of the page and then click **Advanced search**.

4. In the any of these unwanted words text box, type **coconut**. The Advanced Search page should look similar to **Figure 29–11**.

Minus symbol

Complete search term

Search for Web pages that contain all three words

Exclude Web pages that contain this word

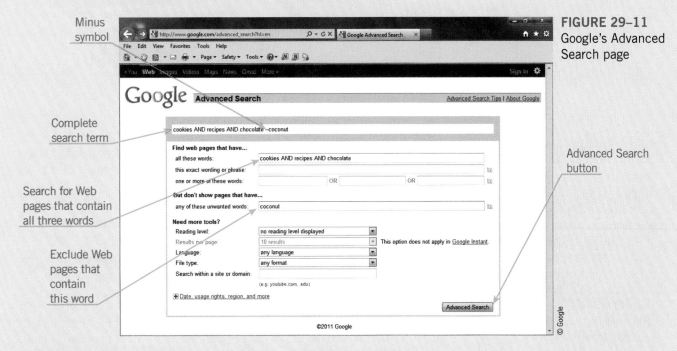

FIGURE 29–11
Google's Advanced Search page

Advanced Search button

5. Click the **Advanced Search** button. Note the number of pages the search engine finds, which should be much less than it found with the first search.

6. Leave your browser open for the next Step-by-Step exercise.

Wildcard Searching

▶ VOCABULARY
wildcard character
related search

The * symbol, or asterisk, is considered a *wildcard character*. If you do not know the spelling of a word or you want to search for plurals or variations of a word, use the wildcard character. For example, if you want to search for "baseball cards and Ichiro Suzuki," but you're not sure how to spell Ichiro, enter the search term using a wildcard—"baseball cards" and "I* Suzuki."

Some search engines permit the * only at the end of the word; with others you can insert the * at the end or beginning. Some search engines do not support wildcard searches.

Title Searching

When a Web page author creates a Web page, it generally contains an HTML title. The title is contained within the Web page HTML code and entered between title tags:

`<Title>Internet Tutorials</Title>`

When you visit a Web site, the title appears in the tab at the top of the Web page. In **Figure 29–12**, the page tab includes the name of the Web page.

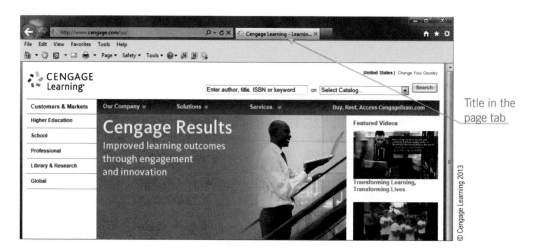

Title in the page tab

FIGURE 29–12   Web page title in the page tab

ABOVE AND BEYOND

Google streamlines typical searches on its Search Features page (*www.google.com/intl/en/help/features.html*). For example, you can search for current local weather conditions, sports scores, and stock quotes. You can also search for information available only within your zip code, such as movie show times or travel details such as flight status and maps.

Many major search engines allow you to search within the HTML document for the title of a Web page, which is called a title search. If you did a title search for "skateparks," most likely one of your results would be the page shown in **Figure 29–12**. Not all search engines support title searches.

Other Search Features

Another feature provided by several search engines is a *related search*. These are preprogrammed queries or questions suggested by the search engine that often lead to other Web pages containing similar information. A related search can improve your odds of finding the information you are seeking. Several search engines offer this feature, although they may use different terminology. Look for terms such as "similar pages," "related pages," or "more pages like this." All of these terms mean basically the same thing. Many search engines list search terms at the bottom of the search results that are related to the search term you entered to help you refine your search, as shown in **Figure 29–13**.

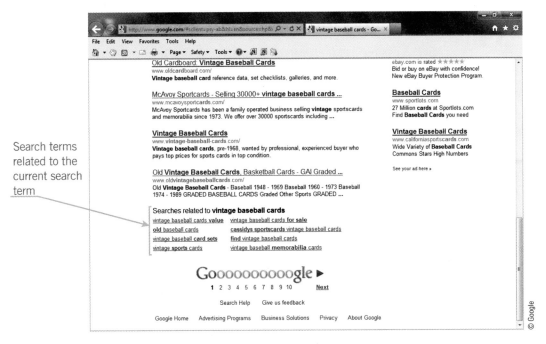

Search terms related to the current search term

FIGURE 29–13   Related searches list in Google

You can also set other search options to sort results. For example, sorting by date provides the most recent information on a particular topic. Google's Advanced Search window provides an option to sort by date. Located at the bottom of the Advanced Search window is a link (+Date, usage rights, region, and more). Clicking the plus sign expands the Advanced Search text box and displays a search option related to date. See **Figure 29–14**.

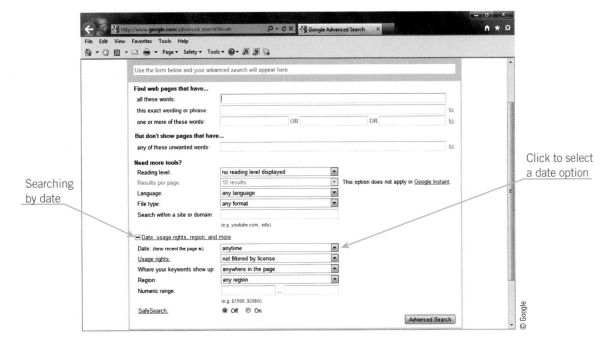

Searching by date

Click to select a date option

FIGURE 29–14   Searching by date

3-3.2.4
3-3.2.5

Evaluating the Quality of Internet Information

Anyone can publish information of any type on the Internet—factual or false, true or incorrect. The Internet does not enforce rules or quality controls about content. Therefore, you should not accept everything as accurate. The following guidelines include criteria for determining the quality of Internet information:

- *Relevance and reliability*: When considering whether to use the content of a Web page, ask yourself the following questions to assess the relevance and reliability of the information. Does the information on the site meet the needs of your research? Is the purpose of this Web site stated? Is the information accurate? Is the information deep enough? Has the information been reviewed? Does the information come from a source that can be trusted? Is the information current? Do not accept any information presented on the Internet at face value. The source of the information should be clearly stated, whether it is original or borrowed from somewhere else.

- *Page layout*: The overall layout of the page also is important. Is the site organized and well designed? The page should be free of spelling and grammatical errors. Even if the page appears to contain valuable information, misspelled words and incorrect grammar can be warning signs that the information itself is not completely reliable.

- *Validity and bias*: Be sure you understand the agenda of the site's owner. Is the purpose of the site to sell a product or service? Is it trying to influence public opinion? As you read through the information, pay close attention to determine whether the content covers a specific time period or point of view or whether the content is broader. To determine the validity of the information, check other resources such as books or journals at the local library that contain similar information.

- *Writing style*: The style of writing and the language used can also reveal information about the quality of the site. If the style is objective, the chances are the information is worthy of your attention. However, if it is opinionated and subjective, you may want to reconsider using the site for gaining information. Ideas and opinions supported by references are additional signs of the value of the site.

- *Coverage*: Is the information presented on the site sufficient for your particular purpose? Or will you also need to access other sites to complete your requirements?

Evaluating Web Sites

The Internet contains Web sites on every imaginable topic and come from sources around the world. When accessing a Web site, remember that even professional-looking Web sites can contain inaccurate or misleading information. Unlike most traditional information media (books, magazines, and newspapers, for example), no independent authority has to approve the content on a Web site before it is published. As with any other document, you must evaluate the nature and source of the information. Keep the following information in mind as you evaluate Web sites:

- Institutional sites such as for a school, nonprofit organization, or government should clearly state their mission. You should also be able to verify that the site represents the organization by contacting a representative by phone or e-mail.

- Blogs generally represent the views and beliefs of the author or owner. Information might be skewed based on the owner's personal experiences and preferences, so you may or may not agree with information contained on the blog.

- A wiki can contain entries from any numbers of users. An entry could be from an expert or from a lay person. No qualifications or expertise is required for the person contributing to the wiki.

Cengage Learning provides guidelines for evaluating Web pages at *http://college.cengage.com/english*. See **Figure 29–15**.

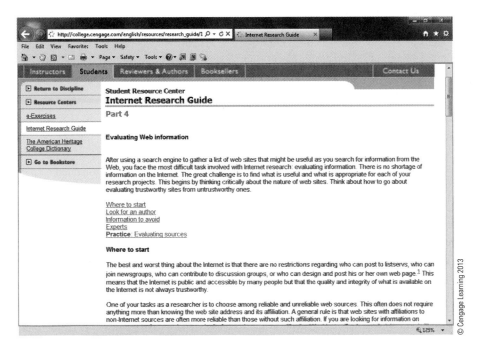

FIGURE 29–15   Criteria for evaluating Web pages

Ask the following questions before using a Web site as a source of reliable information:

- Do you consider that the information is accurate?
- Is there an option to communicate with the Web site author?
- Does the site contain external links? If so, to what sites does it link? Do the linked sites contain valuable information that enhances your knowledge or do they contain information of personal opinions and beliefs?
- How does the Web site rank among similar sites? Use a search engine such as Google to search for a major term central to the purpose of the site, and then evaluate the ranking results.
- How does the Web site information compare with other resources, such as professional journals, books, and other offline sources?

Observing Intellectual Property Laws

For the most part, information displayed on a Web site is easy to copy. Often you can select the text or graphics that you want to copy, use your browser's Copy command, and then paste the content into another document. You can also display a page on your monitor and print the entire page. The ease with which information can be copied, however, does not mean that users have the right to do this.

Most sites have copyright protections. *Copyright* is the exclusive right, granted by law for a certain number of years, to make and use literary, musical, or artistic work, which is considered intellectual property. Even if the copyright notice isn't displayed prominently on the page, someone wrote or is responsible for the creation of the content on a Web page. This means that you cannot use the information as your own. You must give credit to the person who created the work.

ABOVE AND BEYOND

Many other libraries and schools publish guidelines for evaluating Web content. Use your favorite search engine to search for how to evaluate Web content to find criteria and explanations.

3-3.2.6

▶ **VOCABULARY**
copyright

If Internet content, such as a music file, is copyrighted, it cannot be copied without the copyright holder's permission. To do so is a violation of copyright laws. Violating these laws can lead to criminal charges for theft as well as civil lawsuits for monetary damages.

A company's logo or other graphic information may be protected as a **trademark**, which means much the same thing as copyright but relates specifically to visual or commercial images rather than text or intellectual property. In addition, processes and business methods may be protected by patents, which guarantee the inventor exclusive rights to the process or method for a certain period of time.

Copyright and patent laws do provide certain exceptions to the general prohibition against copying. If copyright or patent protection has lapsed on certain material, then it is considered to be in the **public domain** and is available for anyone to copy or use. Also, the law allows for the fair use of properly identified copyrighted material that is merely a small part of a larger research project, for instance, or cited as part of a critique or review.

Citing Internet Resources

You must cite Internet resources used in reports and other documents. In an academic setting, claiming someone else's words as your own is **plagiarism**. You must give proper credit to any information you include in a report that is not your original thought. Providing credits and citations also provides the reader of the document with information about additional research. You can find general guidelines for citing electronic sources in the MLA Handbook for Writers of Research Papers, published by the Modern Language Association. The Chicago Manual of Style is another source for this information.

Following are some samples of citing Internet resources as suggested in the MLA Handbook for Writers of Research Papers:

- *Online journal article*: Author's last name, first initial. (date of publication or "NO DATE" if unavailable). Title of article or section used [Number of paragraphs]. Title of complete work. [Form, such as HTTP, CD-ROM, E-MAIL]. Available: complete URL [date of access].

- *Online magazine article*: Author's last name, first initial. (date of publication). Title of article. [Number of paragraphs]. Title of work. [Form] Available: complete URL [date of access].

- *Web sites*: Name of site [date]. Title of document [Form] Available: complete URL [date of access].

- *E-mail*: Author's last name, first name (author's e-mail address) (date). Subject. Receiver of e-mail (receiver's e-mail address).

▶ **VOCABULARY**

trademark

public domain

plagiarism

Respecting Others

The Web site Wikipedia defines *libel* as follows: "In law, libel (for written words) is the communication of a statement that makes a claim, expressly stated or implied to be factual, that may give an individual, business, product, group, government or nation a negative image." The Internet does not relieve anyone of the burden of ensuring that information they publish is true. If someone publishes information about another person or organization and it is not true, they can be sued for libel and forced to pay compensation for any damages they caused. Treating others with respect is just as important online as it is in other environments. These same guidelines apply to online bullying and harassment.

▶ **VOCABULARY**
libel

Online Responsibilities

Responsibilities for your behavior online are the same as in an academic or similar environment. Information that you publish online should be as accurate and timely as possible. Some other suggestions to be considered follow:

- Use common sense as to what you publish online; the content and tone should be appropriate for the intended audience.
- Behave online the way you would behave in your daily life.
- Indicate if a statement is fact or your opinion. If it is your opinion, provide backup information or links to supportive documents. Opinions should be presented in a respectful format.
- Include contact information.
- Update your information on a regular basis.
- Do not berate or harass others.

TECHNOLOGY CAREERS

Web Content Writer or Producer

If you like to work with Web pages, consider a career as a Web content writer or producer. Writers often create press releases, articles, and journal entries for company blogs. You need to be familiar with how search engines work so that your Web pages appear in search results. You also need to be proficient with HTML, particularly with writing and formatting text and adding links and keywords to a page. Web producers often work with other media such as video or audio and coordinate those sources into a Web site. For example, a Web producer might work for a television network and integrate TV show content into a Web site.

To produce Web content, you need to have training in writing, editing, and graphic design as well as Web site design and maintenance. In some cases, you work with Web content using a content management system (CMS), which is software that helps you create, edit, manage, and publish content in a consistent format and organization. You might also need to use Web analytics, which are tools for tracking visitors to a Web site and determining whether the site meets your business objectives.

SUMMARY

In this lesson, you learned:

- You typically create content for the Internet by publishing it on a Web page and providing links for navigation. Viewers visit your site and interact with the information you provide. Web 2.0 technology lets you invite Web page viewers to contribute information to a site or exchange information, messages, and files with other viewers.

- When searching online, one of the primary tools you can use to find information is a search engine. You use a search engine to search for keywords.

- Keywords describe the information you are trying to locate. Most search engines support keyword searches. Use double quotation marks around a set of words for phrase searching.

- Use the plus and minus signs for including or excluding words within a search. Boolean searches use the three logical operators OR, AND, and NOT.

- Many search engines offer advanced search options that let you filter search results with specific criteria. Use the * symbol for wildcard searching.

- To evaluate Web sites, consider relevance and reliability, page layout, validity and bias, writing style, and coverage.

- Cite any information that you use from the Internet. The MLA style is widely used for citing electronic resources.

■ REVIEW QUESTIONS

TRUE / FALSE

Circle T if the statement is true or F if the statement is false.

T　F　**1.** A related search can improve your odds of finding the information you are seeking.

T　F　**2.** You are required to have a license before you can post anything online.

T　F　**3.** Some search engines assist you with your logical search through the use of forms.

T　F　**4.** Spelling and grammatical errors on a Web page should not affect a user's opinion of a site.

T　F　**5.** If you are searching for more than one phrase, you can separate phrases or proper names with a period.

MULTIPLE CHOICE

Select the best response for the following statements:

1. Boolean logic consists of _____ operator(s).

    A. one

    B. three

    C. two

    D. four

2. You can use _____ on Web pages to search for content on other Web sites.

    A. links

    B. podcatchers

    C. bookmarks

    D. feeds

3. A _____ is a collection of multimedia files.

    A. blog

    B. Boolean

    C. podcast

    D. meta feed

4. A news _____ is a data format for providing users with frequently updated content.

    A. feed

    B. bookmark

    C. post

    D. project

5. Blogs generally represent the views and beliefs of the _____.

    A. author

    B. teacher

    C. president

    D. visitors

FILL IN THE BLANK

Complete the following sentences by writing the correct word or words in the blanks provided:

1. In an academic setting, claiming someone else's words as your own is _____.

2. To subscribe to a podcast requires that you use a software program called a(n) _____.

3. Facebook is an example of a(n) _____ _____ site.

4. When using a search engine, you put a(n) _____ sign before words that should appear on a Web page (also called an inclusion operator).

5. To use _____ _____ with a search engine, you enter two or more words within quotation marks.

■ PROJECTS

PROJECT 29–1

3-3.2.6

An article by Tim Tompkins, located at *www.cs.rpi .edu/academics/courses/fall00/ethics/papers/tompkt .html*, discusses hardware and software liability. The article begins with the following statement: "Often a piece of hardware or software will come with a license agreement that states that the creator is not liable for any damages that may result from the use of their product." Access and read the article and then answer the following questions:

1. Do you agree or disagree that the developer should be responsible for his or her development of hardware or software products? Explain your answer.

2. What are the three levels of loss described in this article?

3. Should hardware and software liability be treated the same or differently? Explain your answer.

PROJECT 29–2

3-3.2.4
3-3.2.5

Evaluate the quality of Web sites you research. Complete the following:

1. Choose a technology topic to research on the Internet, such as cloud computing, Web 2.0, computer ethics, the Deep Web, or green computing. Using the techniques you learned in this lesson, search for Web sites related to your topic.

2. Print the home pages of the first two sites that you find.

3. Using the information you studied in this lesson, evaluate the quality of the content on each site.

4. Report your findings by comparing and contrasting the reliability and validity of the two sites in a short report.

PROJECT 29–3

3-3.2.3

Using the advanced search option provided by search engines can produce valuable results. Complete the following:

1. Use a search engine such as Google, Yahoo!, or Bing to search for Web pages about your favorite restaurant in your area. Note the number of results.

2. Narrow the search to eliminate the Web pages containing a certain keyword, such as lunch or soup. Note the number of results.

3. Narrow the search to include Web pages posted within the last 24 hours. Note the number of results.

4. Save the most recent page as a text file in your assignments folder if your instructor gives you permission to do so.

5. Link to at least five of the other pages in your search results list and use the information you find to create a one-page report that includes at least one graphic or excerpted text that you have saved or copied from a related Web page. Cite the Internet resource appropriately.

6. In the report, mention what search engine you used, how many results you found with each search, and how you narrowed the search.

■ TEAMWORK PROJECT

3-3.2.2

You have been assigned to work as a group on a science project. The Web site located at *http:// all-science-fair-projects.com/project1435_121.html* has a number of popular science projects.

Working in a group with two other students, decide which project you would be interested in researching. Next, create a search strategy form that you can use to search the Internet to find information about the topic. Within the form, list possible search tools and ways in which to search. Include the URLs for any suggested search engines or directory Web sites and for the Web pages that include the most relevant information. Explain for what part of the project you would use each Web page. Make a copy of the form for each student in your group, and then individually use the form to find information about the topic. Meet as a group again and compare the information you found. Create a summary copy of the form that includes the findings for all group members. Did everyone find similar information, exactly the same information, or different information when you did your searches? Include the names of all participants who contributed to the project.

CRITICAL THINKING

With a partner, use the Internet to locate information on computer pioneers. Use as many different types of Web sites as possible to gather your information. Select at least two computer pioneers and then, with your partner, use Microsoft PowerPoint to create a presentation. Within your presentation, intersperse slides showing what search techniques you used to locate the information for each pioneer. Also indicate the type of the Web site where you found information. Example: Slide 1 lists the Web site or sites where you located the information for Slide 2 and indicates that one site is a wiki and another is a news feed. Slide 3 lists the Web site or sites where you located the information for Slide 4, and so on.

3-3.2.1
3-3.2.2

ONLINE DISCOVERY

Select a topic of your choice to research on the Web. Be as specific as possible in the topic you choose—for example, "Apollo missions" or "national parks in the eastern United States." Search for information using three different search engines. Be sure to use exactly the same search techniques (such as keywords, Boolean operators, or related searches) for each search. Create a table with a separate column for each search engine. Then, under the column headings, list the top five sites that the search engine locates. Determine which engine provided you with the highest-quality results.

3-3.2.4

JOB SKILLS

An online identity includes a name and other characteristics used online, such as the user name and description used for a social networking site. Before hiring a new employee, many employers search the Internet for information about the job candidate. Do you think it's a good idea to have an online identity with your real name before you begin a job search? Using a search engine, research the topic of online identity. List four pros and four cons to using your real name in your online identity.

LESSON 30

Technology and Society

■ OBJECTIVES

Upon completion of this lesson, you should be able to:

- Use computers at work, school, and home.
- Use computer technology in everyday life.
- Use technology to transform traditional processes.
- Identify assistive technologies.

■ DATA FILES

You do not need data files to complete this lesson.

■ WORDS TO KNOW

business-to-business (B2B)

business-to-consumer (B2C)

business-to-government (B2G)

critical thinking

digital cash

electronic commerce
(e-commerce)

keyless entry system

online learning

telecommuting

Technology has changed and continues to change every aspect of life—from home to school to the workplace. These changes are swift and dramatic. A little more than 25 years ago, IBM hired Paul Allen and Bill Gates to create an operating system for a new PC, which was the beginning of Microsoft Corporation. About 15 years ago, Google and PayPal were founded, and early versions of the Web browsers Internet Explorer and Netscape Navigator were released. MySpace was founded in 2003 with YouTube following in 2005. Clearly, the trend of electronic innovation affecting daily life is bound to continue.

3-4.1.1

Using Computers at Work, School, and Home

It is becoming increasingly difficult to find employment that does not require some knowledge of computers. If you do not have a working knowledge of or exposure to technology, you most likely will feel the effects on your career options. Technology today is integrated into almost every facet of life and influences how you work, use computers at home, and learn about the world outside your doors.

This lesson discusses how computers facilitate and enhance your everyday activities.

Collecting Information

The Internet and the Web are the major forms of technology affecting your life today. Using the Internet is a fast and easy way to find the information you need. At home and at work, if you need to find the telephone number of a local company or order a pizza for lunch, you can use the computer to search for and find the data. Store this information on your hard disk using software such as Windows Live Mail or Microsoft Outlook.

Not so long ago, if a science teacher gave the class a project to find out how antibiotics work, the students would go to the library and do the research. In most of today's classrooms, the students go to the Internet and visit a Web site such as the ScienceProject.com Web site to collect this information. See **Figure 30–1**.

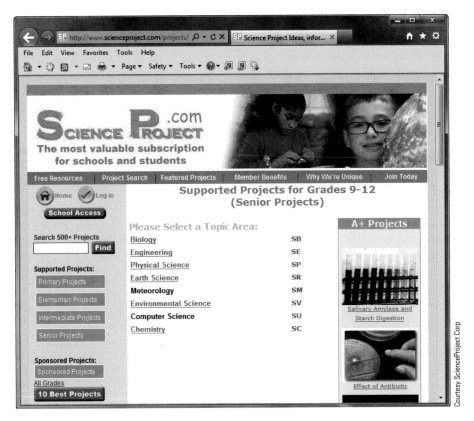

Courtesy ScienceProject Corp

FIGURE 30–1   *ScienceProject.com* Web site

Organizing Information

Computer software helps you organize information. You can use databases and spreadsheets to arrange and calculate data in a variety of ways. After entering data into a spreadsheet, you can format, sort, and chart the data. If you are in the working world, the company you work for most likely uses spreadsheets for statistical data, tax information, or financial reporting. At home, you might use a spreadsheet to track a personal budget, list a collection of items such as baseball cards, and maintain expenses for income tax purposes. At school, spreadsheets are integrated into courses on mathematics, business, and personal finance, to name only a few.

You use a database program to organize and sort data. For example, a database might contain a table with fields for data such as name, address, city, state, and zip code. You can sort the data by any of these fields, whether they contain text or numbers.

Evaluating Information

In addition to using spreadsheet applications to calculate numeric data, you can use spreadsheets to ask what-if questions and evaluate information. Spreadsheets contain mathematic and trigonometry functions as well as statistical functions such as Average, Count, Maximum, Minimum, and Percentile. Arranging data in tables, charts, and lists helps you see patterns or trends in the data and evaluate it by comparing one set of calculated results to another (see **Figure 30–2**).

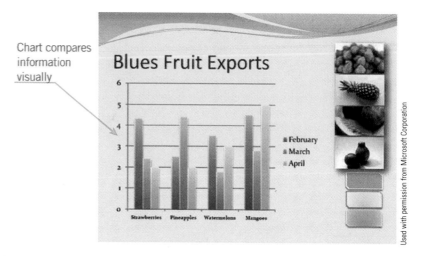

FIGURE 30–2   Evaluating information

Communicating Information

When computers are connected through a network or the Internet, they can exchange information instantaneously. Technology provides communication options such as e-mail, instant messaging, blogs, and social Web sites such as Facebook and Twitter.

Increasing Productivity

Access to the Internet and the Web can increase your productivity by providing online access to multiple resources, including communication with experts and specialists. Applications, such as those discussed in this and previous lessons, also can enhance output and productivity.

Collaborating with Others and Solving Problems

You can take advantage of Web services to supplement project-based learning. With this dynamic approach, you explore real-world problems and challenges. Using online communities, you can collaborate with other people all over the world who might otherwise never meet or know of each other. The exchange and sharing of ideas on a global basis helps you see a problem from different viewpoints. One type of online collaboration is crowdsourcing, which combines the collective effort of many people to complete a task. To perform valuable but labor-intensive research, the University of Buffalo is using crowdsourcing to record the water levels of local streams, an effort that benefits scientists, fishing enthusiasts, and the local community. See **Figure 30–3**.

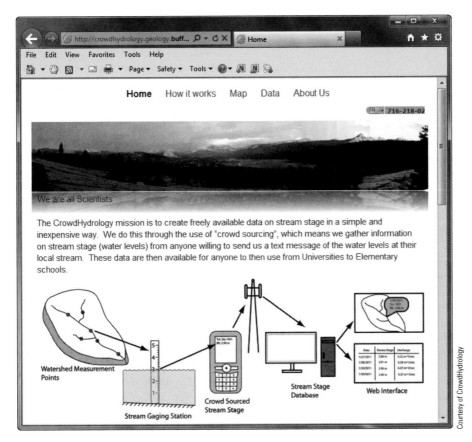

FIGURE 30–3   University of Buffalo's CrowdHydrology site

Creating Communities

Online communities and social networking sites such as Facebook and MySpace have been discussed in previous lessons. This type of Web site provides an opportunity to socialize with others who have common interests. The Wikipedia Web site provides a list of major active social networking Web sites at *http://en.wikipedia.org/wiki/List_of_social_networking_websites*. For example, Flickr is an online community where people share photos, reviews, comments, and photography information. See **Figure 30–4.**

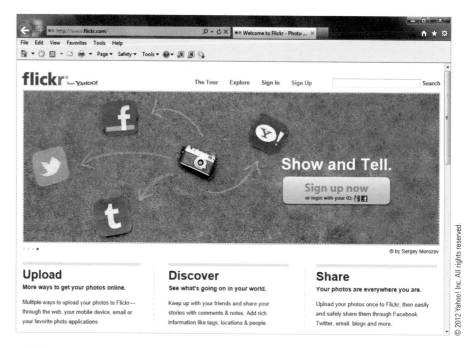

FIGURE 30–4   Flickr home page

Facilitating Learning

You can use the Internet as a resource for learning and discovering new facts and information. As mentioned previously, however, you should not take all online information at face value. Be sure to carefully evaluate and verify the source and the information itself.

Many textbooks published today have an associated Web site where students can access Web-based projects, find study aides to accompany the text, and do homework. Look in the front pages of a textbook that recently has been published to see if there is a Web site that accompanies it. It is even possible for students using a particular textbook to open an online version of the textbook with a password provided by their instructor. This can lighten the load in your backpack as you travel back and forth to school.

Promoting Creativity

Integrating technology in the classroom provides you with an opportunity to demonstrate your inventiveness, individuality, and creativity. Modern technology provides tools you can use to create a range of artistic work that can be published for a real audience anywhere in the world. Project-based collaborations can further enhance creative learning and problem solving (see **Figure 30–5**).

FIGURE 30–5   Project team collaboration

Supporting Critical Thinking

When searching for information on the Internet, you need to use critical thinking. *Critical thinking* can mean "consisting of a mental process of analyzing or evaluating information," "the process of evaluating propositions or hypotheses and making judgments," or "showing or requiring careful analysis before judgment." When reading information online, particularly pages that persuade you to buy or do something, evaluate the information critically, analyze the point of view and motivations, and wait to act until you have gathered and considered all the information.

▶ **VOCABULARY**
critical thinking

ABOVE AND BEYOND

Want to find out more about electronic commerce? The Library of Congress provides a Web page at *www.loc.gov/rr/business/ecommerce/inet-business.html* with links to other sites that explain how to do business online.

Facilitating Daily Life

Electronic commerce, or *e-commerce*, means conducting business on the Internet. It primarily refers to purchasing and selling products or services on the Internet or through other computer networks. Commercial Web sites let you conduct business online. You can access electronic catalogs, select goods, store them in a digital cart or bag, and then check out by paying with a credit card or online account. Organizations provide more than goods online. For example, if you need tickets for the basketball playoffs or an upcoming concert, you can purchase the tickets online, order a program, and in some cases select your seats.

Local, state, and national government Web sites provide access to many services. For example, many local government agencies provide Web sites where you can pay your water bill, renew your driver's license, and sign up for municipal services. Perhaps you need a tax form—the Internal Revenue Service site provides all types of forms and other services such as how to check on your refund and how to file forms electronically (see **Figure 30–6**).

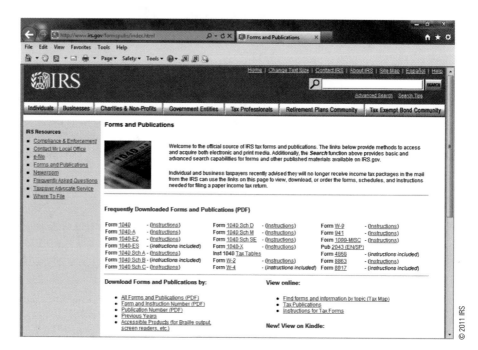

FIGURE 30–6   Forms on the Internal Revenue Service Web site

3-4.1.2

Using Computer Technology in Everyday Life

You probably perform day-to-day activities without thinking about computers and how they affect your life. In fact, using desktop and laptop computers represents only a fraction of your interactions with computer technology. This section discusses how computers are used in daily life.

Automated Teller Machines

Almost everyone with a bank account now takes advantage of the convenience of automated teller machines (ATMs) to deposit or withdraw money. These automated banking machines are located at most banks but are also in supermarkets, convenience stores, restaurants—even at the ballpark or museum. They allow you to do your banking almost anywhere, anytime. Banker's hours from 9:00 a.m. to 5:00 p.m. are definitely a thing of the past (see **Figure 30–7**).

FIGURE 30–7   Automated teller machine

You might not even need to get cash from an ATM for your shopping. Electronic checks and debit cards are making cash more obsolete every day. If you swipe your ATM card or debit card through the machine at the cashier's station at your local store and then enter your personal identification number (PIN), information about your account is transferred to the store's computers and the amount of your purchase is deducted from your checking or savings account.

ABOVE AND BEYOND

ATMs are usually computers running the Windows XP operating system.

Credit Card and Other Commerce Systems

Many people no longer carry large sums of money while traveling. They prefer to use ATM or credit cards. The magnetic strip on the back of the card increases efficiency. When you travel, using a card helps you keep track of your travel expenses. If you lose a credit card or an ATM card, it can be canceled immediately, whereas if your money is lost or stolen, the chances of recovery are very small.

A security concern on the Internet, however, is the theft of credit card information stored electronically. Because the Internet makes transactions so quick and easy, credit card numbers that fall into the wrong hands can cause major problems for cardholders. Although effective encryption technologies keep credit card numbers secure, you can make yours even more secure by following simple precautions. Purchase items only from Web sites that you know are reputable and trustworthy. Read and understand the privacy and consumer-protection policies of online companies before you buy. Be sure that any credit card information is transmitted in a secured, encrypted mode.

Credit card information is not the only personal information you should protect. Take the same precautions whenever you are asked to disclose anything personal, such as to market research companies. For example, avoid providing your telephone number on Web forms. It usually is not a required field even for online purchases. Disclose only what you think is legitimately necessary for the intended purpose. Do not provide personal information to unknown parties. Use code names when appropriate to protect your identity and personal security.

Automated Industrial Processes

The use of computerized robots on assembly lines and in other industrial processes has expanded production capabilities in the manufacturing world. Some automated systems are equipped with vision technology. Performance is precise, measurements are exact, and production is increased. Most manufacturing companies report that after they install automated systems, they realize a high return on investment (see **Figure 30–8**).

© Baloncici / Shutterstock.com

FIGURE 30–8   Industrial robot

Point-of-Sale Systems

A terminal used for electronic processing of payment transactions in a retail outlet is called a point-of-sale (POS) system. When the cashier scans a product you purchase, the pricing comes from a centralized database thousands of miles away. If you use a frequent buyer card, the POS system might record information about your purchase so that you receive coupons or other promotions for similar items. Many of the POS systems include a complete accounting, inventory, and management system. The POS in **Figure 30–9** contains an onscreen menu.

PRNewsFoto/Samsung Electronics

FIGURE 30–9   POS system

Weather Predicting and Reporting Systems

Several weather-prediction software tools are available. Numerical weather-prediction programs are used by most professional meteorologists. In most programs, the user can select the map output or the model output statistics option. The output statistics model allows the user to customize the output for particular locations.

Global Positioning Systems

A global positioning system (GPS), combined with cell phone technology, can provide location information and directions. A GPS also can be a communications device for a driver who needs help or has been in an accident.

Embedded Computers in Appliances and Equipment

Though you might not see them, embedded computer systems play an important role in your daily life. An embedded computer is a special-purpose computer system incorporated into other devices such as automobiles, appliances, and mechanical equipment. Also defined as a single-purpose system, an embedded computer is designed to perform one or a few dedicated tasks within a device or appliance.

Newer cars, for example, have embedded computers that control systems such as ignition timing and antilock brakes. This is accomplished by using input from a number of built-in sensors. (See **Figure 30–10**.) Cars are also available with built-in GPSs, which are controlled by embedded computers.

FIGURE 30–10   Car with an embedded computer

Almost every home has appliances with embedded computers. Any appliance that has a digital clock, for instance, has a small embedded microcontroller that displays the time. Other examples of appliances and mechanical devices with embedded computers are microwaves, refrigerators, cell phones, MP3 players, compressors, propellers, and water pumps.

Security Systems

Many cars today include a remote keyless system and even a remote keyless ignition system. Pressing a button opens or locks the doors. Pressing another button starts the car. *Keyless entry systems* are also available for entrance doors to houses, businesses, and other buildings. Most of these systems include a keypad. To open the lock, you press a button on a remote control device or enter a combination on the keypad.

Some security systems require more sophisticated user identification. Biometrics, for example, applies statistics to biology. A biometric device can match patterns stored in a database with a person's iris, retina, voice, fingerprint, or handprint to confirm or deny someone's identity (see **Figure 30–11**).

ABOVE AND BEYOND

Some high-end refrigerators include computers embedded in their doors with a touchscreen display that lets you use applications for checking the weather, playing music, connecting with family and friends, and displaying a personal appointment calendar. The refrigerator itself is connected to your home wireless network to provide Internet access.

▶ **VOCABULARY**
keyless entry system

FIGURE 30–11   Biometric security

Using Technology to Transform Traditional Processes

3-4.1.3

The integration of personal computers and Internet services has transformed many of the traditional procedures and methods in business, education, and government. This section discusses these transformations.

E-Commerce

You probably have read about the Industrial Revolution and how it affected our world. The Internet economy is being compared to the Industrial Revolution. As mentioned earlier, e-commerce, which means having an online business, is changing the way the world does business.

According to Internet World Stats (*www.internetworldstats.com/stats.htm*), more than two billion people are connected to the Internet. Internet speed will continue to increase as more people add fiber optics, cable modems, or digital subscriber lines (DSL). All of this activity and high-speed connection indicate more online businesses. Analysts at eMarketer (*www.eMarketer.com*) found that total online sales in 2010 were more than $150 billion. The Center for Research in Electronic Commerce at the University of Texas indicates that out of the thousands of online companies, most are not the big Fortune 500 companies—they are smaller businesses.

Using e-commerce, you can buy and sell just about any product through the Internet. Many people hesitate before making online purchases because they fear someone will steal their credit card numbers. However, *digital cash* is a technology designed to ease those fears. The digital cash system allows you to pay by transmitting a number from one computer to another. The digital cash numbers are issued by a bank and represent a specified sum of real money; each number is unique. When you use digital cash, no one can obtain information about you. As an alternative, some credit card companies provide a virtual account option.

▶ **VOCABULARY**
digital cash

Electronic commerce also has generated a number of new jobs and new categories of jobs, which could influence your future career. Some examples include Webmasters, programmers, network managers, graphic designers, and Web developers. You might also consider starting an online business for yourself. People with imagination and ambition discover that the greatest source of wealth is their ideas.

Business Connections

Business-to-business (B2B) describes e-commerce transactions between businesses, such as between a company and a supplier. This includes the online exchange of products, services, or information. ***Business-to-consumer (B2C)*** describes online transactions between businesses and consumers. A third category is ***business-to-government (B2G)***, which includes transactions between businesses and governmental agencies.

Retail businesses often use radio-frequency identification (RFID) tags, which are small electronic devices that identify and track goods from the point of delivery or manufacturing to the point of sale, similar to a bar code. Unlike bar codes, however, scanners can read information from RFID tags from several feet away. Businesses use RFID to improve the efficiency of inventory tracking and management. Governments are using them in passports and in transportation, such as electronic toll collection on highways and in mass transit passes.

Media

In the past, the distribution of media was primarily through newspapers, magazines, television, and radio. The Internet opened a new category of communications media. Media can be distributed by anyone who has an Internet connection. Music, video, audio, pictures, text—all can be distributed online through e-mail, blogs, Web sites, and other types of Internet distribution channels.

Online Learning

For some time, people have been able to obtain their education via distance learning methods. Earlier nontraditional methods include television and correspondence courses that are completed through the mail. In the last few years, the Internet has become a way to deliver ***online learning***. At the elementary and secondary school levels, the Department of Education supports an initiative called the Star Schools Program. This program provides online education to millions of learners annually.

▶ **VOCABULARY**

business-to-business (B2B)

business-to-consumer (B2C)

business-to-government (B2G)

online learning

◗ **ABOVE AND BEYOND**

Project Gutenberg was one of the earlier educational uses of the Internet. It began as a text-based project by Michael Hart in 1971, before the Web even existed. More than 36,000 books, mostly older works of literature in the public domain in the United States, are available to download at *www.gutenberg.org*.

Imagine being able to complete high school from home, take enrichment classes, or complete a career-training program. Online learning Web sites such as Ed2Go make virtual learning possible. See **Figure 30–12**.

FIGURE 30–12   Online learning

Learning management system programs help teachers deliver online courses. These programs are an integrated set of Web-based teaching tools that provide guidance and testing for the student. Three of the more popular of these learning management systems are Blackboard, Moodle, and Angel.

Robotics

ABOVE AND BEYOND

Honda Motor Company created a humanoid robot called Asimo that can walk, recognize and respond to verbal commands, and manipulate objects. Go to *http://world.honda.com/ASIMO* to see Asimo and learn more about Honda's robotics program.

When you think of robotics, you might think of humanoid robots such as those in Star Wars. In real life, however, robotic design did not originally take this path. Robots have been used mostly in assembly plants, often doing dangerous or repetitive tasks, which has transformed industrial processes. More recently, some specialized robots have been developed that do have a humanoid appearance, and robot devices such as NASA's Mars Rovers Spirit and Opportunity, and Jason, the robotic submarine operated by Woods Hole Oceanographic Institute, allow exploration of hostile environments unsafe for humans. See **Figure 30–13**.

Courtesy NASA/JPL-Caltech

FIGURE 30–13   NASA Mars Rover Spirit

Telecommuting

VOCABULARY
telecommuting

Many employers allow their employees to work from home. This arrangement is called *telecommuting*. It involves using communications technology to keep the employee connected to the office. Telecommuting has many advantages for both the employer and the employee. It saves traveling time and expense, and it allows the employee to work at a time that is convenient. Projects and other relevant information can be shared through e-mail and other online distribution options. As with in-house employees, companies transfer telecommuting employees' pay directly to their bank on a regular basis. Insurance and other employment-related activities are handled automatically online.

Online Communities

Online communities, also known as social networks, virtual communities, and e-communities, enable groups of people to interact online through a communications media rather than face-to-face. Social and professional groups use this type of communication to exchange ideas around various topics and to share personal information. Facebook (see **Figure 30–14**) and Flickr were two of the earlier virtual communities.

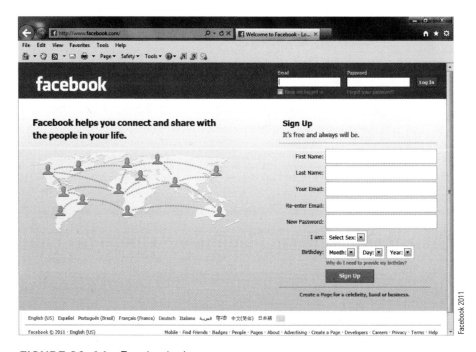

FIGURE 30–14   Facebook sign-up page

Some of the more popular social networks today include Yahoo! Groups (see **Figure 30–15**) and Google Groups (see **Figure 30–16**).

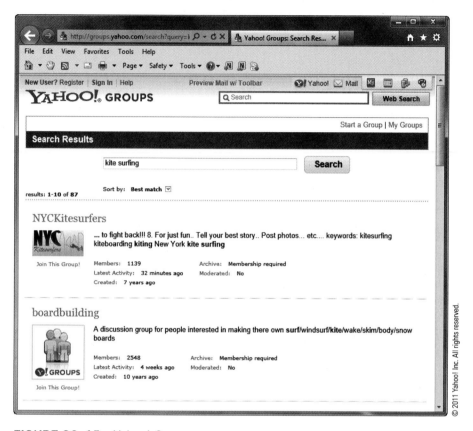

FIGURE 30–15   Yahoo! Groups

FIGURE 30–16   Google Groups

Disaster Recovery

Hurricanes, tornadoes, and other recent disasters have increased awareness of the need for disaster recovery planning for communities, cities, and states. The content of a disaster recovery plan and online resources will vary, based on the location and potential hazards. A segment of the plan, however, should include options for electronic communications, such as a Web site that is updated periodically, e-mail availability, and available resources and locations where help can be provided.

Identifying Assistive Technologies

3-4.1.4

Many of today's technologies can be used to support those who are physically challenged and economically disadvantaged. This section describes some of these technologies.

Assistive Technologies for the Physically Challenged

People around the world can communicate with each other almost instantaneously. Advances in technology affect how you are treated for illnesses and injuries, how cars are manufactured and how they work, even how the meter reader calculates your water bill.

Computers are working behind the scenes to assist in most endeavors. For example, computer programs make it possible to predict dangerous weather and warn people in time to prepare for storms. Electronic devices help disabled people communicate, become more mobile, and participate in activities. For example, telecommunications device for the deaf (TDD) technology allows hearing-impaired people to use a telephone, "smart" buses can lower steps to allow people with disabilities to board the bus or provide a lift for a wheelchair, and personal computers offer accessibility options that permit people with many types of disabilities to work and communicate more easily.

Several adaptive software options are also available for people with vision challenges. These software options follow:

- Screen readers that provide alternative sensory guidance for computer navigation
- Scanning and reading software
- Internet browser readers that read HTML pages
- Braille translators (see **Figure 30–17**)
- Other voice-recognition or text-to-speech applications such as talking checkbooks

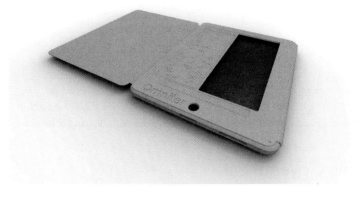

Courtesy of Jayson D'Alessandro

FIGURE 30–17   Braille translator

Electronic Learning

Education today is no longer confined to the classroom, which might be difficult for the physically challenged to access. E-learning and online courses are offered throughout the world by public and private education institutions. Many educational institutions also offer public service and noncredit courses at reduced fees, which is especially helpful to the disadvantaged.

The Federal government provides a number of free educational resources such as those at *http://free.ed.gov* (see **Figure 30–18**). In many cities and towns, local community centers and libraries also provide free or inexpensive educational opportunities. The Discovery Channel (*discovery.com*) and the Learning Channel (*tlc.discovery.com*) have educational resources on topics ranging from animals to global warming.

FIGURE 30–18   Electronic learning resources

Public Service

Computer and Internet technology also provide public services to the community. For example, libraries often include Internet-connected computers for patrons to use to conduct online job searches, access government Web sites, or find general information. These services are especially helpful to the economically disadvantaged. Weather and news applications can also display on-screen alerts to notify the public about weather or other types of events, which can be helpful to those with hearing disabilities.

Electronic Government

All states and most cities have a Web site that provides information about the city or state. In **Figure 30–19**, for instance, the New York City Department of Transportation Web site contains information resources, news and events, services, and key topics.

A bar at the top of the page provides links for residents, business, and visitors, among others. A menu bar on the left provides information for motorists, pedestrians, and bicyclists, for example.

FIGURE 30–19   NYC Department of Transportation Web site

TECHNOLOGY CAREERS

Simulation Analyst

Simulation analysts and consultants work with all types of companies of any size. Their primary job is to investigate different options to determine which would be the best for a particular situation. For instance, health care company administrators might want to implement a new system for filing and processing insurance claims. Before spending a huge amount of money, they might hire a simulation analyst to determine which system would best meet their needs. A bank planning a new system to process checks may hire an analyst to do simulation modeling of what the system might and might not do.

Some necessary skills include the ability to see detail in a system and to be a good technical writer. The person should be a logical thinker and have good analytical skills. A good memory is an additional asset. Opportunities and the need for simulation analysts are increasing. One of the reasons for the increase is that more and more companies are applying simulation to a larger variety of problems.

As a consultant, you would probably do some traveling. Consulting fees are usually quite generous, with some simulation analysts making as much as $75,000 or more per year. You might find some analysts with only a two-year degree, but generally you need at least a bachelor's degree in computer information systems or computer engineering.

SUMMARY

In this lesson, you learned:

- Computers are used in different areas of work, school, and home to collect, organize, evaluate, and communicate information; increase productivity, collaborate with others, and facilitate learning and daily life.

- Desktop and laptop computers represent only a fraction of interaction with computer technology. Embedded computers in automobiles, appliances, and mechanical equipment, for example, are more prevalent. These computers are programmed to perform a specific task within the equipment.

- Traditional processes for banking, news delivery, and education have been transformed due to e-commerce, online news content, and online learning.

- Robotics and other automated systems have increased the efficiency of manufacturing and production.

- Online communities provide communication links for people who share similar interests. They also bridge geographical boundaries between people. Online learning and other learning opportunities are available through the Internet.

- New jobs and new job categories related to the Internet and electronic commerce are being developed. People can telecommute and collaborate globally using e-mail, networks, and automated systems.

- Electronic communication is used to distribute disaster information.

- Technologies such as voice recognition software are available for the blind.

- Local, state, and national governments can provide access to information for the economically disadvantaged.

REVIEW QUESTIONS

TRUE / FALSE

Circle T if the statement is true or F if the statement is false.

T   F   **1.**   The Internet and the Web are the major forms of technology affecting your life today.

T   F   **2.**   The exchange and sharing of ideas on a global basis can help you see a problem from different viewpoints.

T   F   **3.**   B2B e-commerce transactions are between businesses and consumers.

T   F   **4.**   Employees who work primarily on the telephone are called telecommuters.

T   F   **5.**   An embedded computer is designed to perform one or a few dedicated tasks within a device or appliance.

MULTIPLE CHOICE

Select the best response for the following statements.

1. When someone works from home, it is called _____.

   A. homework   C. telecommuting

   B. electronic working   D. B2E

2. _____ can read information from RFID tags from several feet away.

   A. B2B   C. E-mail

   B. Electronic waves   D. Scanners

3. Manufacturers use computerized robots on assembly lines because robots _____.

   A. are precise   C. increase production

   B. take exact measurements   D. all of the above

4. Purchasing tickets online, ordering a program, and selecting your seats is an example of _____.

   A.   simulation   C.   digital cash

   B.   virtual reality   D.   e-commerce

5. Almost every home has appliances with _____ computers.

   A.   GPS   C.   embedded

   B.   active   D.   biometric

FILL IN THE BLANK

Complete the following sentences by writing the correct word or words in the blanks provided.

1. _____ applies statistics to biology.

2. When you use _____ cash, unauthorized people cannot obtain information about you.

3. A terminal used for electronic processing of payment transactions in a retail outlet is called a(n) _____ system.

4. B2G includes transactions between _____ and _____.

5. _____ _____ is showing or requiring careful analysis before judgment.

■ PROJECTS

PROJECT 30–1

3-4.1.1

Many government, nonprofit, and commercial Web sites provide online learning opportunities. Complete the following:

1. Start your Web browser, and then go to the Intel Web site at the following address: *http://educate.intel.com/en/DesignDiscovery/ImplementationExamples/student_projects.htm.*

2. Review the student projects on the site, select one of the projects, and then read its description.

3. Use your word-processing software and prepare a one-page report on what you learned. Copy and paste at least two images from this Web site or from another Web site that is applicable to your report. Create a PowerPoint presentation and share your project with your class.

PROJECT 30–2

3-4.1.3

Social networking Web sites were discussed briefly in this lesson.

1. Access the list of social networking Web sites at *http://en.wikipedia.org/wiki/List_of_social_networking_websites.*

2. Select at least three of the Web sites listed on the Wikipedia site. Review each of the selected Web sites and then write a paragraph of at least 150 words describing the main features of each of your three selected Web sites. Would you be likely to return to this Web site for additional research? Explain why or why not.

PROJECT 30–3

3-4.1.4

Online local, national, and state government Web sites were discussed in this lesson. Complete the following:

1. Use the Internet to locate a government Web site that applies to your community or city.

2. Evaluate the Web site and write a review of what is contained on the Web site.

3. Comment on what you found the most helpful and informational. Also identify what is missing from the Web sites you examined.

■ TEAMWORK PROJECT

3-4.1.3

Your instructor has assigned to you and a team member a project relating to the global economy and electronic commerce. You and your partner are to prepare a report on what information you would need to know before setting up an e-commerce Web site. Create a PowerPoint presentation and present it to your class.

CRITICAL THINKING

Congratulations on your new job at Global Pharmaceuticals. Assume that your supervisor has asked you to research and prepare a report on biometric security measures. After you thoroughly research this project, recommend a specific method to your supervisor. Create a report listing the method you selected, describe how it works, and explain why you selected it. Submit your report to your instructor.

3-4.1.2

ONLINE DISCOVERY

Most dentists today use computers in one way or another. For instance, instead of viewing a film of an x-ray, you can view it on a computer screen. Some dentists use a sonic device to clean teeth. Use search engines to see what you can discover about how dentists are using computers. Prepare a presentation and share it with the class.

JOB SKILLS

Because nearly all jobs involve interacting with others, including your colleagues, supervisors or managers, clients or customers, and suppliers, knowing how to hold an effective meeting is a job skill that can help you get ahead. Research the best ways to hold a business meeting and then create a document listing the steps you should take before, during, and after a meeting to make sure it is successful. Identify when you can use computer technology to perform a step.

LESSON 31

Computer Safety and Ethics

■ OBJECTIVES

Upon completion of this lesson, you should be able to:

- Maintain a safe computing environment.
- Prevent computer-related injuries.
- Identify security risks.
- Set access restrictions.
- Understand workplace privacy.
- Avoid e-commerce problems.
- Protect privacy on the Internet.
- Use the Internet safely and legally.
- Practice responsibility as a computer user.

■ DATA FILES

You do not need data files to complete this lesson.

■ WORDS TO KNOW

browser hijacking

brute force attacks

hacking

hardware firewall

keylogger

private key

public key

repetitive strain injury (RSI)

sniffer

spyware

strong password

Transport Layer Security (TLS)

While using computers and the Internet offers unrivaled access to commerce, entertainment, and information, it also exposes you to breaches in security, privacy, and ethics. This lesson explores the risks of computing and the measures you can take to minimize those risks. In addition, this lesson examines software threats and how to restrict access to your files and data. As a computer user, you have certain responsibilities that govern your use of technology, including following guidelines and policies, exercising ethical conduct online, and maintaining a safe work environment.

3-4.2.1

Maintaining a Safe Computing Environment

Make sure you use a computer in a way that supports your comfort, health, and safety. Whether you use a desktop computer provided by your school or other organization, a notebook computer at home or in an outdoor café, or a smart phone when you are on the go, pay attention to your posture, lighting, and activity level. For example, sitting in the same position for long periods of time causes muscle fatigue and discomfort. Staring at a computer screen can cause eye strain. Be sure to change your position often as you use a computer to encompass a range of motion and sight. Arrange the computer area so that you can work comfortably.

Using a notebook computer introduces risks not associated with desktop computers. Avoid setting a notebook computer directly on your lap or on a soft, flexible surface such as a cushion, which might obstruct air vents and cause the computer to overheat. Use a cooling pad to keep air flowing around the notebook and the battery or AC adapter.

Tablet PCs are light and portable, which allows users to change position frequently. If buttons and other controls are easy to access with natural hand and finger movements, tablet users can also avoid computer-related injuries (discussed next). Some tablet users, however, use poor posture when typing on a tablet, which puts them at risk for neck and shoulder pain.

Review product safety guidelines provided with your computer or any other electronic device. For example, if you need to connect your computer to a power source using a plug that has a third pin for grounding, make sure you insert it only into a grounded outlet. If you are maintaining computer equipment yourself, pay attention to icons and other symbols that warn about the hazards of electrical shock, excessive heat, or sharp edges.

The Occupational Safety and Health Administration (OSHA) provides guidelines for using and purchasing computer equipment. See *www.osha.gov* for more information.

3-4.2.2

▶ **VOCABULARY**
repetitive strain injury (RSI)

Preventing Computer-Related Injuries

When you use a computer, take precautions to avoid chronic physical maladies such as eyestrain, back problems, and *repetitive strain injury (RSI)*, which can result when a person makes too many of the same motions over a long period of time. Ergonomic design adapts equipment and the workplace to fit the worker and can help prevent RSIs, which can develop over time and eventually lead to long-term disability. Having a well-designed work area, using ergonomic furniture, maintaining good posture, and changing positions throughout the day are effective ways to minimize these types of injuries. Avoid or minimize eyestrain by using a high-resolution monitor, providing adequate and properly positioned lighting, and taking regular breaks to allow eye muscles to relax. See **Figure 31–1**.

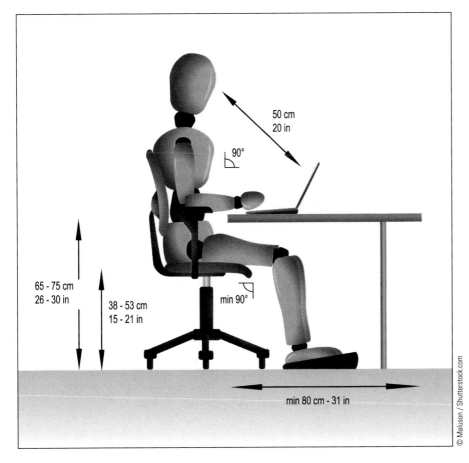

FIGURE 31–1   Ergonomic workstation

> **ABOVE AND BEYOND**
>
> RSIs are common in people who use computers or play video games frequently. Repeated motions can strain and irritate joints and the tendons and muscles around them. Take frequent breaks, stretch, and remain relaxed rather than tense while you work to help prevent these kinds of injuries.

Identifying Security Risks

Most innovations in computer technology introduce new security risks. Wireless networking, for example, is popular because it provides many benefits to computer users. However, it also creates serious risks to data and services if the network is not properly secured.

For example, your next-door neighbor can easily use your broadband connection if it is not password protected. This normally does not cause harm or damage to your network, but it could slow down your Internet access. In other instances, you could be charged for actual usage, which would mean additional costs.

An unauthorized user could also tap into your connection for illegal or criminal activity. If the unauthorized user is part of the network and is working behind a gateway device, any activity coming from the intruder could appear to be coming from your computer, meaning you could be held responsible for the illegal activity.

An intruder could connect directly to your computer, bypassing any firewalls. Once connected, the intruder can scrutinize your computer for personal data such as tax records and other personal information. The intruder could use a *sniffer*, a program that hackers use to capture user names and passwords on a network. To access an unsecured wireless connection, a hacker needs only a computer with a wireless network card and eavesdropping software that can be downloaded free from the Internet.

IC³
3-4.2.3

▶ **VOCABULARY**
sniffer

Using Network Protection

Almost all routers and access points have a factory-set administrator password, which is often a common word such as "password." Some devices do not have a default password at all. When setting up your wireless network, your first step should be to change the default password and then write it down so that you can refer to it if needed. Second, turn on some form of encryption. Several forms of encryption technologies are available. You need to select the one that works best with your wireless network devices. Turn off the network during extended periods when you are not using it.

Computer Hacking

Computer *hacking* involves invading someone else's computer, usually for personal gain or the satisfaction of defeating a security system. Hackers usually are computer experts who enjoy having the power to invade someone else's privacy. They can steal, change, or damage data stored on a computer. It is estimated that hacking causes millions of dollars of damage each year, along with the theft of important and valuable data.

Most servers have built-in security features, but they need to be turned on and configured. Firewalls are essential. If the network is small, a software firewall is sufficient. If the network is large, however, a *hardware firewall* that controls the computers from one point should be implemented. This type of firewall is more secure and easier to monitor.

Avoiding Data Loss

One ever-present threat to a computer system is an electrical power failure. Electricity not only provides the power to operate a computer but is the medium a computer uses to store data. An unexpected power outage can wipe out any data that has not been properly saved. One easy way to avoid data loss is to save frequently. Most software programs provide an option that can be set to save data periodically in the background. For instance, suppose you are working on a 10-page report. If your computer loses power, you lose your work. However, if your software is set to save on a regular basis, such as every 10 minutes, then you can retrieve at least a portion of your report.

To safeguard computer systems against power outages, secure electric cords so that people cannot accidentally disconnect or trip over them. Recall from Lesson 3 that another option is to install an uninterruptible power supply, usually a battery that provides power if the normal current is interrupted. You should also plug surge suppressors into electric outlets to protect against power spikes, which can damage computer hardware and software.

▶ **VOCABULARY**

hacking

hardware firewall

QUICK TIP

The FBI has a cybercrime branch that concentrates in particular on Internet fraud, including identity theft. See *www.fbi.gov/about-us/investigate/cyber/cyber* for more information.

Even saved data can be lost or corrupted by equipment failure, software viruses or hackers, fire or flood, or power irregularities. To protect your data, you should back up important files regularly. Also recall from Lesson 3 that backing up files entails saving them to removable disks or another independent storage device that can be used to restore data if your primary system becomes inaccessible. Because hard drives are mechanical devices, they all fail eventually, preventing access to the data they store. A hard disk crash can result in a catastrophic loss of data if it occurs on a critical system and the files have not been backed up properly. To back up data, home users can plug external hard drives into computers or use a Web site that provides an online backup service for a minimal price. **Figure 31–2** shows the Tools tab in the Properties dialog box for a hard drive. You click the Back up now button to back up files on a Windows 7 computer.

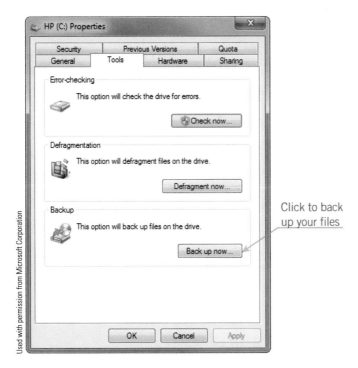

FIGURE 31–2   Using Windows 7 to back up files

Your backup procedures should place a priority on files that would be difficult or impossible to replace or reconstruct if you lost them, such as your data files. Secure backup procedures used by large organizations include a regular schedule for backing up designated files and a means of storing backup files off-site so that they will survive intact if the main system is destroyed either by natural disaster or by criminal acts.

3-4.2.4

Safeguarding Data Against Software Threats

Recall from Lesson 27 that a virus is a program that has been written, usually by a hacker, to corrupt data on a computer. The virus is attached to a file (such as a document or program file) and spreads from one file to another after the program is executed. Often, you can inadvertently run the virus program by opening an e-mail message or attachment. To protect against viruses, you should use strong passwords, download and install the latest security updates for your operating system, and use an up-to-date antivirus program, as shown in **Figure 31–3**.

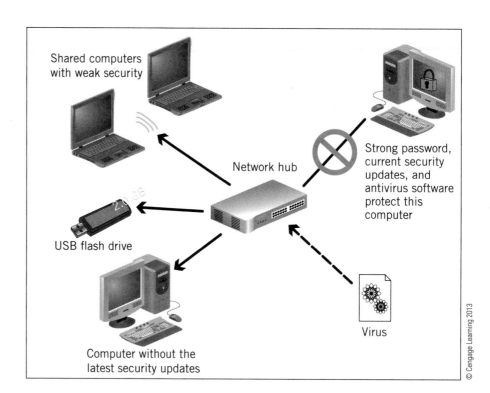

FIGURE 31–3   Protecting against viruses

▶ **VOCABULARY**

strong password

brute force attack

A *strong password* is both complex and secure—it contains numbers, letters, and special characters that do not include personal information such as name or birth date. In addition, strong passwords contain at least eight characters, and at least one letter, number, and special character (such as @ , $, * , or ?).

Strong passwords are more resistant to *brute force attacks*, also called dictionary attacks, which use a script or program to log on to an account using hundreds of words or phrases stored in a dictionary file.

Other types of software threats include worms and keyloggers. Recall from Lesson 27 that a worm makes many copies of itself, resulting in the consumption of system resources that slows down or actually halts tasks, and doesn't have to attach itself to other files to infect your computer. A *keylogger* is a malicious program that records keystrokes. For example, a keylogger might record your keystrokes to keep track of the Web sites you visit, the user names and passwords you enter, and private information such as credit card and account numbers. Because they can aid identity theft, keyloggers are a particularly dangerous type of harmful software.

Worms can spread *spyware*, also called adware and privacy-invasive software, which is software installed surreptitiously on a personal computer. The goal is to collect information about the user, the user's browsing habits, and other personal information. Spyware can significantly slow the performance of your computer, display annoying pop-up ads, and change system settings. Hackers often use spyware to control your browser, a practice called *browser hijacking*. The spyware might replace your home page with another, often to increase the number of visits to the replacement page, which can boost advertising revenue. Spyware is also discussed in the "Protecting Privacy on the Internet" section later in this lesson.

To guard against software threats, be sure to use an antivirus program to regularly scan your system for harmful software and to scan files before you open them (see **Figure 31–4**).

▶ **VOCABULARY**
keylogger

spyware

browser hijacking

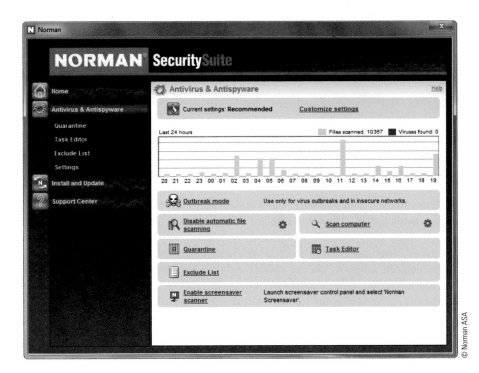

FIGURE 31–4 Antivirus protection

You can also use antispyware software such as Windows Defender to protect your system against spyware (see **Figure 31–5**). Make sure you use reputable antispyware programs—some spyware disguises itself as antispyware to gain access to your system.

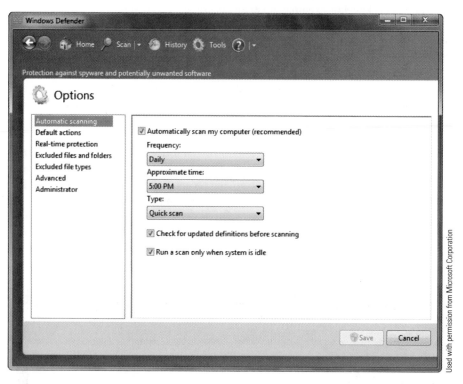

FIGURE 31–5 Windows Defender

3-4.2.5

Setting Access Restrictions

System administrators and users often restrict access to files, storage devices, computers, networks, the Internet, or specific Internet sites. They do so to protect data and other users.

Most organizations use hardware firewalls and other methods to protect data. These devices, however, do not protect data from employees. For instance, competition among companies for a government contract or a bid on new business can encourage some employees to share information with competitors. At universities and other educational institutions, final exams and other files are copied and shared. Malicious tampering can also result in data loss. A disgruntled employee can willfully delete vital records and other important data.

Protecting children from unsuitable Web sites is also a concern for parents, teachers, libraries, and other areas where children have computer access. Software is available that lets you monitor computer usage, including Web sites, e-mail messages, social networks, instant messaging and chats, and applications. Some programs keep track of keystrokes typed and even create screenshots to monitor Web site visits. When using this type of protection and this type of program, it is recommended that protecting users be balanced with preserving privacy.

Understanding Workplace Privacy

3-4.2.6

If you work for a company that provides you with e-mail services, the information you send is available to the company; in fact, it is the company's property. It can be accessed from backup copies the company's e-mail system makes and preserves.

Generally, any information gathered from a company's computer system is company property and not an individual worker's personal property. The employee normally has no right to personal privacy regarding those issues. The company has a right to access any data on their computers and use it for its legitimate purposes. If the company monitors its Internet logs, for instance, and discovers that an employee has been spending time visiting Web sites that bear no relation to work-related duties, it can discipline the employee. Similarly, if an employee uses a company computer in a way that harms the company—contracting a computer virus through unauthorized activities, for example, or allowing hackers into the company's system—he or she can be disciplined or fired. Likewise, the same laws apply to educational institutions. Any information stored on a computer in an educational facility is school property.

Many organizations have computer or network usage policies that provide guidelines for using the organization's systems ethically, professionally, and legally. Before you access the Internet, send e-mail, exchange files, or otherwise use a computer at school or work, make sure you are familiar with the usage policies.

Avoiding E-Commerce Problems

3-4.2.7

E-commerce issues and safety measures were discussed in detail in Lesson 30. This section recaps how to avoid possible hazards of e-commerce and provides information on how sensitive data is encrypted.

Before providing personal information or credit card information on an e-commerce or similar site, first verify that the site is secure. Several companies such as VeriSign (*verisign.com*), GoDaddy (*godaddy.com*), Network Solutions (*networksolutions.com*), and others provide a *Transport Layer Security (TLS)* or Secure Sockets Layer (SSL) certificate for e-commerce sites, sites that process sensitive data, and sites that require privacy and security requirements. See **Figure 31–6**.

▶ **VOCABULARY**
Transport Layer Security (TLS)

Online merchants can purchase SSL certificates from vendors such as Network Solutions

FIGURE 31–6   SSL certificates

TSL and SSL technology encrypts sensitive information by establishing a private communication channel. Data transmitted through this channel is encrypted during transmission. An SSL certificate consists of a ***public key*** and a ***private key***. The public key encrypts information and the private key deciphers the information.

The Federal Trade Commission (FTC) offers the following guidelines on its Web site (*www.ftc.gov*) to make sure your e-commerce transactions are secure and to protect your private information:

- *Use a secure browser*: Make sure you are using the most current version of your browser because contemporary browsers have the most up-to-date encryption features. When submitting your purchase information, look for security indicators such as a padlock icon in the browser's status bar and the "https" protocol in the Address bar. Internet Explorer versions 7 and later also display secure Web sites using a green Address bar.

- *Check privacy policies*: Before you provide any personal financial information to a Web site, look for and read the site's privacy policy. A link to the privacy policy is often listed at the bottom of the home page.

- *Keep personal information private*: Don't provide personal information such as a password, bank account number, or credit card number unless you know who is collecting the information and how they'll use it. Give payment information only to businesses you know and trust.

> **▶ VOCABULARY**
> **public key**
>
> **private key**

3-4.2.8

> **ABOVE AND BEYOND**
>
> Safe ways to pay for online purchases include using a perishable credit card, which assigns a credit card number to an online purchase or online merchant only for a specific amount of time. You can also use third-party payment services such as PayPal. You set up and fund an online account and make payments from that account without exposing your real credit card or bank account information. E-wallets are a type of online account you can maintain for small purchases, such as magazine subscriptions.

Protecting Privacy on the Internet

The amount of personal information available online for the average computer user is astonishing. The major source of revenue for some companies comes from gathering information about consumers and other computer users to create databases and sell or trade this information to others.

Any time you submit information on the Internet, it is possible for this information to be gathered by many persons and used for various situations. Information can also be gathered from online data regarding school, banking, hospitals, insurance, and any other information supplied for such everyday activities.

Much of the information gathered and sold results in your name being added to mailing lists. These lists are used by companies for marketing purposes. Junk e-mails are used for the same purpose. Information regarding one's credit history is also available to be sold.

Phishing, introduced in Lesson 27, is a type of computer fraud that attempts to steal your private data. A hacker tries to fool you into providing information such as user names, passwords, and bank account numbers. Hackers do so by posing as a trustworthy entity in an electronic communication such as an e-mail or text message. Typical phishing messages come from social networking sites, auction sites, banks, and the IRS. The message directs you to enter details at a fake Web site that looks identical to the legitimate one. See **Figure 31–7**.

FIGURE 31–7   Phishing message

Cookies and Spyware

You might be surprised at how much information cookies and spyware track about your computer use. Cookies, as you may remember, are small files that are created when you visit a Web site, stored on your computer, and then accessed again the next time you visit the same site. They may make it easier for you to use the Web site when you return, but they may also provide the Web site owner with information about you and your computer, and they often take up disk storage space that you might want to use for other data. It's a good idea to clean up the unnecessary cookies on your computer frequently with a utility program designed for that purpose.

Spyware does not have any redeeming qualities. As mentioned earlier, spyware not only tracks your Web habits, it can even take over control of your computer and direct you to Web sites you have not chosen to visit. Spyware can be harmful as well as annoying. The FTC Web site includes a page advising consumers how to lower the risk of spyware infection (see **Figure 31–8**). Firewalls consisting of hardware and software features can protect your computer from unauthorized spyware programs.

FIGURE 31–8   Avoiding spyware infection

Securing Data

You secure data to protect it from harm or destruction from natural causes, accidents, and intentional damage. It is not always evident that some type of computer crime or intrusion has occurred. Therefore, you need to set up safeguards for each type of risk. It is the responsibility of a company or an individual to protect their data.

The best way to protect data is to effectively control the access to it. You might need a password to log on to a computer system or to specific parts of it (see **Figure 31–9**). Companies often establish password-protected locations on hard drives and networks so that certain people have access to some areas but not to others. To maintain secure passwords, you or the system administrator should change them frequently so that people who no longer need access cannot continue to use the passwords. The challenge is to create strong passwords that are easy for you to remember but difficult for anyone else to decipher. If you write down a password, keep it in a secure place and do not share it with anyone else. Unauthorized access is much more likely to be caused by people who gain access through a written or shared password than by anyone guessing your user name and password.

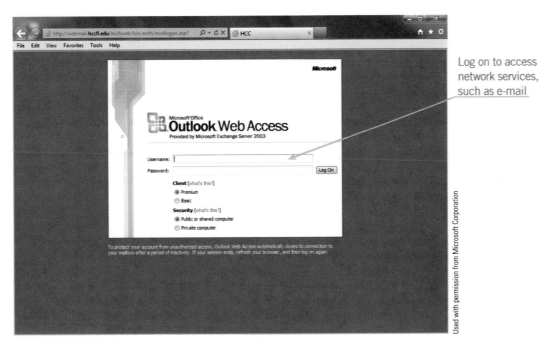

Log on to access network services, such as e-mail

FIGURE 31–9   Signing in with a user name and password

Some other privacy considerations follow:

- The security and privacy of personal information on the Internet is improving all the time. It is still necessary, however, to take precautions to protect both personal and business-related information. Use code names instead of real names. This also applies to protecting personal or family information in public places as well.

- When communicating on a forum, blog, or social network or other similar Internet-related sites, use an alias.

- Verify that you have logged off a computer used in a public place such as a public library, a school, or other similar institutions.

Using the Internet Safely and Legally

3-4.2.9

The Internet makes widespread publication of information easy. It also creates the potential for huge damages if the information turns out to be false. The ease of obtaining information from the Internet and of publishing information on the Internet can contribute to legal problems. Just because information is available on a Web site does not mean that anyone can copy it and claim it as their own, even non-copyrighted information. That is plagiarism. The Internet does not relieve an author of responsibility for acknowledging and identifying the source of borrowed material. Likewise, the Internet does not relieve you of the burden of ensuring that information you publish is true. If someone publishes information about another person or organization and it is not true, they can be sued for libel and forced to pay compensation for any damage they caused.

Nearly all schools, government agencies, companies, libraries, and other similar institutions have written policies and guidelines regarding Internet usage. These policies protect the organization as well as the user. If these policies are not readily available, ask a system administrator or other employee for a copy of the policy.

Additional information on safe use of computers can be found on numerous Web sites, in books and magazines, and in other similar media. The Department of Justice and other government agencies provide resources for Internet safety (see **Figure 31–10**).

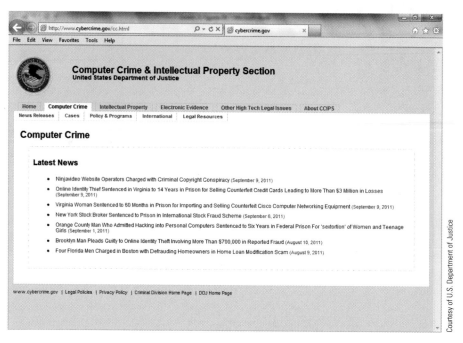

FIGURE 31–10   Resources for Internet safety

3-4.2.10

Practicing Responsibility as a Computer User

It is your responsibility to stay informed about changes and advancements in computer technology, product upgrades, and virus threats. If you have a computer, you must keep your antivirus protection up to date. You can find out how to do this at the Web site of your antivirus program provider; you can also find updates and bulletins about software and hardware at company Web sites.

ETHICS IN TECHNOLOGY

Ethical Questions for Computer Users

Computer technology, especially in the form of Internet use and social networking, introduces ethical questions that were not concerns before computer usage was widespread. For example, should social networking sites sell information about their members? Should you be able to copy software, music, or movies without payment? Is there a so-called digital divide between communities that have computer technology and those that do not? If so, is society obligated to decrease or remove that divide by making sure computer technology is available to everyone?

To help answer these questions, professional societies and organizations create and pledge to follow ethical guidelines for developing and using computing technology. For example, the Association for Computing Machinery (ACM) publishes the ACM Code of Ethics and Professional Conduct (*www.acm.org/about/code-of-ethics*), the IEEE publishes the IEEE Code of Ethics (*www.ieee.org/about/corporate/governance/p7-8 .html*), and the Computer Ethics Institute publishes the Ten Commandments of Computer Ethics (*http:// computerethicsinstitute.org/publications/tencommandments.html*). Overall, the ethical guidelines are principles that computer developers and users should follow to prevent harm to others, which is the basis for any type of ethics.

As a responsible computer user, keep in mind that you can lead by example when you recycle products such as used computer paper and ink cartridges. In addition, old computer hardware such as monitors can create an environmental hazard if disposed of improperly. Consider asking your school or business to donate unneeded computer hardware to charitable organizations that refurbish it and provide it to individuals and organizations that would otherwise be unable to take advantage of computer technology. Before the computer is donated, however, the data on the hard drive should be backed up and then deleted from the hard drive. In addition, your knowledge and experience using computers is a commodity you can share generously. Community centers, schools, and other organizations welcome knowledgeable volunteers to serve as tutors to help other people learn how to use computers effectively.

SUMMARY

In this lesson, you learned:

■ Make sure you use a computer in a way that supports your comfort, health, and safety. When you use a computer, take precautions to avoid chronic physical maladies such as repetitive motion injuries, eyestrain, and back problems that can arise over time. Ergonomic design, which adapts equipment and the workplace to fit the worker, can help to prevent repetitive strain injuries.

■ When setting up your wireless network, your first step should be to change the default password to protect access to the network.

■ Computer hacking involves invading someone else's computer, usually for personal gain or the satisfaction of defeating a security system.

■ To avoid data loss, you can use techniques and devices for preventing power interruptions. You can also devise and follow a regular procedure for backing up your data.

■ A virus is a program that has been written, usually by a hacker, to corrupt data on a computer. The virus is attached to a file and spreads from one file to another when the program is executed.

To protect your computer against virus damage, use up-to-date antivirus software, download and install security updates for your operating system, and avoid opening files sent via e-mail from people you do not know.

■ System administrators and users often restrict access to files, storage devices, various computers, networks, the Internet, or specific Internet sites.

■ If you work for a company that provides you with e-mail services, the information you send is available to the company and is the company's property.

■ TSL and SSL technology enables encryption of sensitive information by establishing a private communication channel. Data transmitted through this channel is encrypted during transmission.

■ Nearly all schools, government agencies, companies, libraries, and other similar institutions have written policies and guidelines regarding Internet usage.

■ LESSON REVIEW

TRUE / FALSE

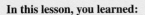

Circle T if the statement is true or F if the statement is false.

T   F   **1.**   The Internet makes widespread publication of information easy.

T   F   **2.**   Changing positions when working with computers is an effective way to minimize repetitive stress injury.

T   F   **3.**   Contemporary browsers do not have up-to-date encryption features.

T   F   **4.**   Spyware has many redeeming qualities.

T   F   **5.**   A strong password contains numbers, letters, and special characters that do not include personal information such as name or birth date.

MULTIPLE CHOICE

Select the best response for the following statements:

1. _____ are small files created when you visit a Web site.

   A. Public keys   C. Cookies

   B. Sniffers   D. Crumbs

2. Most organizations use _____ and other methods to protect data.

   A. firewalls   C. Trojan horses

   B. hackers   D. viruses

3. Strong passwords are more resistant to _____ than other types of passwords.

   A. Transport Layer Security (TLS)   C. brute force attacks

   B. browser hijacking   D. firewalls

4. Even saved data can be lost or corrupted by _____ .

   A. viruses   C. hackers

   B. fire   D. all of the above

5. _____ is a type of computer fraud that attempts to steal your private data.

   A. Phishing   C. Spyware

   B. SSL   D. Keylogging

FILL IN THE BLANK

Complete the following sentences by writing the correct word or words in the blanks provided:

1. A strong _____ is both complex and secure.

2. You can avoid or minimize _____ by using a high-resolution monitor.

3. A(n) _____ is a program that hackers use to capture usernames and passwords on a network.

4. The practice of using spyware to control a user's browser is called _____ .

5. Two technologies that encrypt sensitive information sent online are _____ and _____ .

■ PROJECTS

PROJECT 31–1

3-4.2.4

As described in this lesson, the Internet makes widespread publication of information easy. The ease of obtaining information from the Internet and of publishing information on the Internet can contribute to legal problems.

1. Access the FTC Web site at *www.ftc.gov/bcp/edu/microsites/ spyware/index.html.*

2. Play the Beware of Spyware game on this site and click any related links.

3. Prepare a report on what you learned. Include information on how to avoid spyware.

PROJECT 31–2

3-4.2.7

SSL and TLS certificates were discussed briefly in this lesson. Use Google or another search engine for additional information on SSL and TSL certificates. Then use your word-processing software to describe the certificates. Answer the following questions:

1. What is TLS? How does it differ from SSL?

2. What are certificates?

3. How can you tell if you have a secure TLS or SSL connection when you are online? What does it mean to have a TLS or SSL connection?

4. Which technology is more secure, TLS or SSL?

PROJECT 31–3

3-4.2.9

As mentioned in this lesson, many organizations provide guidelines for using their computers and networks. Complete the following:

1. Access the Dorchester County Library Web site at *www.dcl.lib. sc.us/accept.htm*.

2. Read the Conditions of Use and Wireless Access sections.

3. Use your word-processing program to respond to the following questions:
   - Which three rules do you think are the most important and why?
   - Which three rules do you think are the least important and why?
   - Do you agree with the guidelines contained in these rules? Explain your answer.

4. Locate two similar Web pages that list rules for using a library's computers. List their Web site addresses. How do their guidelines compare to the Dorchester Library Web site?

TEAMWORK PROJECT

3-4.2.8

Work with a team to learn more about Web cookies. In this project, you and your team members research this topic and then create a PowerPoint presentation based on this topic. Additionally, include at least one related graphic on each slide.

Slide 1: Define Web cookies.

Slide 2: What's good about cookies?

Slide 3: What's bad about cookies?

Slide 4: How can you get rid of cookies?

Slide 5: How are cookies used for Internet shopping?

Share your presentation with your class.

CRITICAL THINKING

Wikipedia contains a Web site dedicated to Internet privacy. Access this Web site located at *http://en.wikipedia.org/wiki/Internet_privacy* and review the information contained on the site. Then use your word-processing software to answer the following questions:

1. What did you find that was most beneficial for you personally? Describe why you consider this beneficial.

2. Describe the "levels of privacy" as defined in this article.

3. What are evercookies?

3-4.2.8

4. How can posting photographs online lead to privacy concerns?

ONLINE DISCOVERY

Social networking online is a recent technology that has become very popular. Research this technology and then prepare a report that defines a social networking site. List at least four examples of social networking sites, and then discuss why this technology has become so popular. Select one site (other than Facebook or MySpace) and describe the differences between the site you selected and Facebook or MySpace. Other than Facebook and MySpace, list at least five other social networking sites and provide a short description of each site.

JOB SKILLS

As emphasized throughout this book, computing technology changes rapidly. You can enhance your value as a job candidate or employee by staying informed about changes and advancements in technology.

Brainstorm some ways you can keep up with technology changes, and then list at least five ways using a format suitable for a resume or job evaluation form.

3-4.2.10

MODULE 3 REVIEW

Living Online

■ REVIEW QUESTIONS

TRUE / FALSE

Circle T if the statement is true or F if the statement is false.

T F **1.** Almost every home has appliances with embedded computers.

T F **2.** When searching for information on the Internet, you need to use critical thinking.

T F **3.** Computer hacking involves invading someone else's computer.

T F **4.** You can receive a news feed through your browser.

T F **5.** Protecting credit card information is a security concern on the Internet.

T F **6.** If you cannot download or view an e-mail attachment, this could be due to the size of the attachment.

T F **7.** Backing up data regularly, such as once a week, is not important for the home user.

T F **8.** Organizations rarely use firewalls to protect data.

T F **9.** If you want to search online for words that appear next to each other, you should not use phrase searching.

T F **10.** Routing is the process of selecting paths in a network along which to send network traffic.

T F **11.** Electronic communication is the technology that enables computers to communicate with each other and other devices.

T F **12.** If you are searching for information and want to search for plurals or variations of a word, use the wildcard character.

T F **13.** The terms World Wide Web, Web, and Internet are interchangeable because all three refer to the same technology.

T F **14.** The Internet and the Web have their own terminology.

T F **15.** When computers are connected through a network or the Internet, they cannot exchange information until the main switch is turned on.

MULTIPLE CHOICE

Select the best response for the following statements:

1. In 1994, _____ cofounded Netscape Communications.

   A. Bill Gates   C. Steve Jobs

   B. Marc Andreessen   D. Steve Wozniak

2. A(n) _____ identifies a computer or Web site on the Internet.

   A. ISP   C. domain

   B. cache   D. stem

3. A(n) _____ is a network designed for the exclusive use of people within an organization.

   A. client/server   C. extranet

   B. intranet   D. wide area network (WAN)

4. _____ consists of three logical operators: AND, OR, and NOT.

   A. Boolean logic   C. File Transfer Protocol (FTP)

   B. Encryption   D. Meta logic

5. _____ are the rules that govern the transfer of data and ensure that information created by one system can be interpreted and read by another.

   A. Public keys   C. Algorithms

   B. Protocols   D. User agents

6. A _____ is a collaborative Web site that can be edited by anyone with access.

   A. virus   C. wiki

   B. sniffer   D. cookie

7. _____ is the programming language used to create Web pages.

   A. SSL   C. HTML

   B. HTTP   D. ARPANET

8. A _____ is a Web site that hosts programs you can access with your browser.

   A. Web app   C. wiki

   B. portal   D. blog

9. A(n) _____ is an electronic document that verifies the identity of a person or company.

   A. password   C. bookmark

   B. archive   D. digital certificate

10. A DNS server translates a(n) _____ into a domain name such as *networksolutions.com*.

    A. public key   C. private key

    B. IP address   D. HTTP address

11. _____ tracking and recording helps you keep track of visited Web sites.

    A. Record   C. History

    B. Reverse   D. Forward

12. When you access the Internet using a browser, the browser is the _____ you use to access any available server in the world.

    A. hub   C. proxy server

    B. node   D. client

13. You use _____ services to send messages in real time.

    A. Voice over IP (VoIP)   C. peer-to-peer network

    B. instant messaging   D. newsgroup

14. In 2004, the phrase _____ was coined to refer to Web sites where users can modify the content.

    A. Web 2.0   C. Web 3.0

    B. Internet 2.0   D. Active X 2.0

15. _____ is a format originally developed to syndicate news articles online.

    A. Secure Sockets Layer (SSL)   C. Really Simple Syndication (RSS)

    B. Digital subscriber line (DSL)   D. Rich Text Format (RTF)

FILL IN THE BLANK

Complete the following sentences by writing the correct word or words in the blanks provided.

1. A(n) _____ _____ consists of three parts: the user name, the @ symbol, and the user's domain name.

2. The _____ is made up of many services, including File Transfer Protocol (FTP) and e-mail.

3. E-mail _____ automatically sort(s) your incoming messages according to rules you set up.

4. After you find an ISP, you must install some type of _____ software so you can connect to the Internet.

5. Downloadable audio broadcasts are known as _____.

6. In a client/server network, the server manages network resources; in a(n) _____ network, all of the computers are equal.

7. A(n) _____ is a program that has been written to corrupt data on a computer.

8. In browsers such as Internet Explorer, the _____ displays the URL of the active Web page.

9. Purchasing and selling products or services on the Internet is called _____.

10. A(n) _____ is a document, image, video, or other file that you can send with an e-mail message.

11. A(n) _____ is a group of two or more computers linked together.

12. _____ _____ are Web sites that allow real-time communication so you can exchange messages with others through the computer.

13. A terminal used for electronic processing of payment transactions in a retail outlet is called a(n) _____ system.

14. _____ was the first graphical browser.

15. A(n) _____ covers a large geographical area and can contain communication links across metropolitan, regional, or national boundaries.

■ PROJECTS

PROJECT 3–1

1. Start your Web browser and create a folder in your Favorites list. Give the folder a name of your choice, such as *Project 1 Sites*.

2. Use a search engine of your choice to find information on the following topics:

    ■ Popular Web browsers

    ■ Viruses

    ■ Protecting online privacy

3. Save the most informative Web site addresses to your Favorites folder.

4. Write a paragraph describing what you found on each of the topics.

5. Save the document with a filename of your choice, and then print the documents if instructed to do so. Close all open files.

PROJECT 3-2

Technology has considerably changed the way people with physical challenges live their daily lives. Complete the following:

1. Use the Internet and other sources to research how technology will continue to serve people with physical challenges such as blindness or low vision, hearing problems, cognitive disorders, and physical disabilities.

2. Prepare a report identifying and describing at least two new technologies that will affect people with physical challenges.

PROJECT 3-3

1. Go to one of the Web sites you found in Project 3–1.

2. Evaluate the Web site using the list of questions provided in Lesson 29 that you should ask before using a Web site as a source of reliable information.

3. Prepare a one-page report on the design and quality of content you found at this site. Be sure to address all the criteria provided in the questions listed in Lesson 29.

SIMULATION

JOB 3-1

The human resources manager at your company has asked you to help her create a training presentation for employees about responsible computer use. The presentation should cover topics such as computer security, Internet use, and proper disposal of printouts and storage media that are no longer needed. She wants you to provide information on the following:

- Backing up data
- Using passwords to access company computers
- The company's policy on employee use of the Internet
- Appropriate ways to safely dispose of discarded paper, used CDs, and other computer waste

Search the Web for examples of employee handbooks to see how other companies address these issues. Or, interview the human resource managers of some local companies and ask them about their policies on these issues. Then create a slide presentation that explains your company's policies, how the policies can be followed effectively by employees, and any consequences that can result from failing to follow the policies.

JOB 3-2

You have noticed that many students in your computer classes are having difficulty selecting appropriate electronic resources for their term papers and citing the selected sources. They are spending hours surfing the Internet to locate legitimate information. As a result, you have asked your instructor if you could develop and give a presentation on the criteria for evaluating electronic resources. Use the information in this module and other sources to develop a five- to six-slide presentation.

APPENDIX A

A Comprehensive Guide to IC³

IC3 - MODULE 1: COMPUTING FUNDAMENTALS

STANDARDIZED CODING NUMBER	OBJECTIVES & ABBREVIATED SKILL SETS	PAGE
OBJECTIVE 1.1	**Identify types of computers, how they process information, and the purpose and function of different hardware components**	
IC³-1 1.1.1	Identify different types of computer devices	Mod1-6– Mod1-10
IC³-1 1.1.2	Identify the role of the central processing unit (CPU) including how the speed of a microprocessor is measured	Mod1-10, Mod1-12
IC³-1 1.1.3	Identify concepts related to computer memory (measurement of memory, RAM, ROM)	Mod1-16– Mod1-18
IC³-1 1.1.4	Identify the features and benefits (storage capacity, shelf-life, size, etc.) of different storage media	Mod1-18– Mod1-23
IC³-1 1.1.5	Identify the types and purposes of standard input and output devices on desktop or laptop computers	Mod1-30– Mod1-39
IC³-1 1.1.6	Identify the types and purposes of specialized input devices (cameras, scanners, game controllers, etc.)	Mod1-39– Mod1-44
IC³-1 1.1.7	Identify the types and purposes of specialized output devices (printers, projectors, etc.)	Mod1-45– Mod1-46
IC³-1 1.1.8	Identify how hardware devices are connected to and installed on a computer system	Mod1-46– Mod1-49
IC³-1 1.1.9	Identify factors that affect computer performance	Mod1-49– Mod1-50

OBJECTIVE 1.2		Identify how to maintain computer equipment and solve common problems relating to computer hardware	
IC³-1	1.2.1	Identify the importance of protecting computer hardware from theft or damage	Mod1-58– Mod1-59
IC³-1	1.2.2	Identify factors that can cause damage to computer hardware or media (environmental factors, magnetic fields, etc.)	Mod1-59– Mod1-61
IC³-1	1.2.3	Identify how to protect computer hardware from fluctuations in the power supply, power outages and other electrical issues (such as use of computers on different electrical systems)	Mod1-62
IC³-1	1.2.4	Identify common problems associated with computer hardware	Mod1-63– Mod1-66
IC³-1	1.2.5	Identify problems that can occur if hardware is not maintained properly	Mod1-72
IC³-1	1.2.6	Identify maintenance that can be performed routinely by users	Mod1-73– Mod1-88
IC³-1	1.2.7	Identify maintenance that should ONLY be performed by experienced professionals, including replacing or upgrading internal hardware (especially electrical) components (such as processors or drives) that are not designed to be user accessible	Mod1-88
IC³-1	1.2.8	Identify the steps required to solve computer-related problems	Mod1-94– Mod1-100
IC³-1	1.2.9	Identify consumer issues related to buying, maintaining, and repairing a computer	Mod1-101– Mod1-104
OBJECTIVE 2.1		Identify how software and hardware work together to perform computing tasks and how software is developed and upgraded	
IC³-1	2.1.1	Identify how hardware and software interact	Mod1-110– Mod1-114
IC³-1	2.1.2	Identify the difference between an operating system and application software	Mod1-114– Mod1-118
IC³-1	2.1.3	Identify issues relating to software distribution (licenses, upgrades, etc.)	Mod1-119– Mod1-123
OBJECTIVE 2.2		Identify different types of application software and general concept relating to application software categories	
IC³-1	2.2.1	Identify fundamental concepts relating to word processing (reviewing, editing, formatting, etc.)	Mod1-128– Mod1-130
IC³-1	2.2.2	Identify fundamental concepts relating to spreadsheets (worksheets, formulas and functions, sorting data, etc.)	Mod1-131– Mod1-134
IC³-1	2.2.3	Identify fundamental concepts relating to presentation software (slides, graphics, animation, etc.)	Mod1-134– Mod1-138
IC³-1	2.2.4	Identify fundamental concepts relating to databases (records, fields, tables, queries, reports, forms, etc.)	Mod1-138– Mod1-141

IC³-1	2.2.5	Identify fundamental concepts relating to graphic and multimedia programs (drawing, painting, graphic file formats, etc.)	Mod1-142–Mod1-145
IC³-1	2.2.6	Identify fundamental concepts relating to education and entertainment programs (games, audio, video, virtual reality, etc.)	Mod1-146
IC³-1	2.2.7	Identify the types and purposes of different utility programs (virus, disk maintenance, backup, etc.)	Mod1-146–Mod1-147
IC³-1	2.2.8	Identify other types of software (Web-browsing, project management, group collaboration, etc.)	Mod1-147–Mod1-148
IC³-1	2.2.9	Identify how to select the appropriate application(s) for a particular purpose, and problems that can arise if the wrong software product is used for a particular purpose.	Mod1-148
IC³-1	2.2.10	Identify how applications interact and share data.	Mod1-149
OBJECTIVE 3.1		**Identify what an operating system is and how it works, and solve common problems related to operating systems**	
IC³-1	3.1.1	Identify the purpose of an operating system.	Mod1-154
IC³-1	3.1.2	Identify different operating systems (Windows, Mac OS, Linux, etc.)	Mod1-154–Mod1-158
IC³-1	3.1.3	Identify that a computer user may interact with multiple operating systems while performing everyday tasks such as:	Mod1-158–Mod1-159
IC³-1	3.1.4	Identify the capabilities and limitations imposed by the operating system including levels of user rights (administrative rights, etc.) which determine what a user can and cannot do (install software, download files, change system settings, etc.)	Mod1-160
IC³-1	3.1.5	Identify and solve common problems related to operating systems	Mod1-161–Mod1-164
OBJECTIVE 3.2		**Use an operating system to manipulate a computer's desktop, files and disks**	
IC³-1	3.2.1	Shut down, restart, log on and log off the computer	Mod1-170–Mod1-173
IC³-1	3.2.2	Identify elements of the operating system desktop	Mod1-173–Mod1-176
IC³-1	3.2.3	Manipulate windows (maximize, minimize, close, etc.)	Mod1-176–Mod1-177
IC³-1	3.2.4	Start and run programs	Mod1-177–Mod1-178
IC³-1	3.2.5	Manipulate desktop folders and icons/shortcuts	Mod1-179
IC³-1	3.2.6	Manage files (identify file types and properties, sort files, move and copy files, find files, etc.)	Mod1-179–Mod1-185
IC³-1	3.2.7	Identify precautions one should take when manipulating files	Mod1-185–Mod1-187
IC³-1	3.2.8	Solve common problems associated with working with files (files that are difficult to find, corrupted files, etc.)	Mod1-187

OBJECTIVE 3.3	Identify how to change system settings, install and remove software	
IC³-1 3.3.1	Display control panels/system preferences	Mod1-192– Mod1-197
IC³-1 3.3.2	Identify different control panel/system preference settings	Mod1-197
IC³-1 3.3.3	Change simple settings (date and time, audio volume, etc.)	Mod1-197– Mod1-202
IC³-1 3.3.4	Display and update a list of installed printers	Mod1-203– Mod1-205
IC³-1 3.3.5	Identify precautions regarding changing system settings	Mod1-205
IC³-1 3.3.6	Install and uninstall software	Mod1-206– Mod1-209
IC³-1 3.3.7	Identify and troubleshoot common problems associated with installing and running applications	Mod1-211– Mod1-212

IC3 - MODULE 2: KEY APPLICATIONS 2010 STANDARD

STANDARDIZED CODING NUMBER	OBJECTIVES & ABBREVIATED SKILL SETS	PAGE
OBJECTIVE 1.1	**Be able to start and exit an application, identify and modify interface elements, and use sources of online help**	
IC³-2 1.1.1	Start and exit a Windows style application	Mod2-4, Mod2-5, Mod2-9, Mod2-32–Mod2-33, Mod2-240, Mod2-339
IC³-2 1.1.2	Identify on-screen elements common to applications (e.g., toolbars, Ribbon, document windows)	Mod2-10–Mod2-11, Mod2-13–Mod2-14, Mod2-16, Mod2-32–Mod2-33, Mod2-240
IC³-2 1.1.3	Navigate around open files using scroll bars, keyboard shortcuts, and Go To command	Mod2-10–Mod2-11, Mod2-32, Mod2-50–Mod2-52, Mod2-55, Mod2-59–Mod2-60, Mod2-242–Mod2-243, Mod2-262, Mod2-266, Mod2-268, Mod2-339–Mod2-340, Mod2-364–Mod2-365
IC³-2 1.1.4	Display and use onscreen command buttons	Mod2-16, Mod2-19, Mod2-32–Mod2-33
IC³-2 1.1.5	Change views	Mod2-5, Mod2-32–Mod2-33, Mod2-44–Mod2-45, Mod2-58–Mod2-60, Mod2-245, Mod2-272, Mod2-342
IC³-2 1.1.6	Change magnification level	Mod2-48–Mod2-49, Mod2-58–Mod2-60, Mod2-245, Mod2-266, Mod2-272, Mod2-342, Mod2-364
IC³-2 1.1.7	Display options for changing application defaults (e.g., where files are stored, print and AutoSave options)	Mod2-16, Mod2-32, Mod2-38, Mod2-42, Mod2-60

IC^3-2 1.1.8	Identify and prioritize help resources, including online help, printed documentation, and external help resources	Mod2-26–Mod2-27, Mod2-33–Mod2-34
IC^3-2 1.1.9	Use automated help, including navigating help resources and employing logical search strategies	Mod2-26–Mod2-27, Mod2-33–Mod2-34, Mod2-60, Mod2-366
OBJECTIVE 1.2	**Perform common file-management functions**	
IC^3-2 1.2.1	Create files	Mod2-36, Mod2-58, Mod2-172–Mod2-173, Mod2-179, Mod2-199, Mod2-201–Mod2-202, Mod2-346–Mod2-347, Mod2-364
IC^3-2 1.2.2	Open files within an application and from the desktop, identify extensions associated with applications	Mod2-5, Mod2-18–Mod2-19, Mod2-32, Mod2-339, Mod2-364–Mod2-365
IC^3-2 1.2.3	Switch between open documents	Mod2-5, Mod2-32
IC^3-2 1.2.4	Save files in specified locations/formats	Mod2-24, Mod2-32, Mod2-40, Mod2-58, Mod2-172–Mod2-173, Mod2-243, Mod2-293, Mod2-339
IC^3-2 1.2.5	Close files	Mod2-9, Mod2-24, Mod2-32, Mod2-245, Mod2-345, Mod2-364–Mod2-365
IC^3-2 1.2.6	Identify and solve common problems relating to working with files (e.g., product or version incompatibility, AutoSave recovery options)	Mod2-23, Mod2-33, Mod2-38–Mod2-39
OBJECTIVE 1.3	**Perform common editing and formatting functions**	
IC^3-2 1.3.1	Insert text and numbers into a file	Mod2-39–Mod2-40, Mod2-58–Mod2-59, Mod2-65, Mod2-254
IC^3-2 1.3.2	Perform simple editing (e.g., select, cut, copy, paste, and move information)	Mod2-62–Mod2-63, Mod2-65, Mod2-68–Mod2-69, Mod2-78, Mod2-96–Mod2 -99, Mod2-157, Mod2-254, Mod2-270, Mod2-303, Mod2-308, Mod2-313, Mod2-332, Mod2-345
IC^3-2 1.3.3	Use the Undo, Redo and Repeat commands	Mod2-67, Mod2-96–Mod2-97, Mod2-254, Mod2-353

IC³-2	1.3.4	Find and/or Find and Replace information	Mod2-71–Mod2-72, Mod2-74, Mod2-96
IC³-2	1.3.5	Check spelling	Mod2-76–Mod2-77, Mod2-96, Mod2-99, Mod2-347
IC³-2	1.3.6	Perform simple text formatting, including using Format Painter	Mod2-80–Mod2-81, Mod2-84, Mod2-93, Mod2-96–Mod2-98
IC³-2	1.3.7	Insert pictures and other objects into a file, including clip art, drawn objects, text art, and images created in another application	Mod2-209–Mod2-231, Mod2-234–Mod2-237, Mod2-368, Mod2-374, Mod2-376, Mod2-379
OBJECTIVE 1.4		**Perform common printing/outputting functions**	
IC³-2	1.4.1	Format a document for printing	Mod2-90–Mod2-91, Mod2-97, Mod2-112, Mod2-136, Mod2-272, Mod2-276, Mod2-364–Mod2-365
IC³-2	1.4.2	Preview a file before printing	Mod2-90–Mod2-91, Mod2-97–Mod2-98, Mod2-112, Mod2-136, Mod2-276
IC³-2	1.4.3	Print files, specifying common print options	Mod2-112, Mod2-114, Mod2-117, Mod2-137
IC³-2	1.4.4	Manage printing and print jobs	Mod2-114, Mod2-137
IC³-2	1.4.5	Identify and solve common problems associated with printing (e.g., printer, connection, print setting issues)	Mod2-119, Mod2-137
IC³-2	1.4.6	Output documents in electronic format, including PDF, fax, e-mail attachment, and Web content	Mod2-120, Mod2-122–Mod2-124, Mod2-135, Mod2-177, Mod2-202, Mod2-293
IC³-2	1.4.7	Identify issues related to outputting files in electronic format	Mod2-120, Mod2-122–Mod2-124, Mod2-137
OBJECTIVE 2.1		**Be able to format text and documents, including the ability to use automatic formatting tools**	
IC³-2	2.1.1	Change spacing options	Mod2-84, Mod2-97
IC³-2	2.1.2	Indent text	Mod2-87, Mod2-97
IC³-2	2.1.3	Display the ruler	Mod2-87, Mod2-97, Mod2-148
IC³-2	2.1.4	Use tabs	Mod2-87, Mod2-97

IC³-2	2.1.5	Insert and delete a page break or section break	Mod2-90–Mod2-91, Mod2-97, Mod2-204, Mod2-234
IC³-2	2.1.6	Display non-printing characters and identify on-screen formatting information, including breaks and paragraph, tab, and indent markers	Mod2-41–Mod2-42, Mod2-87, Mod2-204, Mod2-234, Mod2-236
IC³-2	2.1.7	Create and modify single- and multi-level bulleted and numbered lists	Mod2-89, Mod2-96
IC³-2	2.1.8	Insert symbols/special characters	Mod2-192–Mod2-193, Mod2-201
IC³-2	2.1.9	Insert, modify, and format page numbers	Mod2-184–Mod2-185
IC³-2	2.1.10	Create, modify, and format headers and footers	Mod2-184–Mod2-185, Mod2-201
IC³-2	2.1.11	Create, modify, and apply styles	Mod2-179, Mod2-182, Mod2-200
IC³-2	2.1.12	Create and modify columns	Mod2-204, Mod2-234, Mod2-237
IC³-2	2.1.13	Work with tables, including creating, inserting, and editing data in a table	Mod2-140, Mod2-148, Mod2-156–Mod2-157, Mod2-163, Mod2-167–Mod2-170
IC³-2	2.1.14	Modify table structure	Mod2-142–Mod2-148, Mod2-167–Mod2-170
IC³-2	2.1.15	Format tables, including sorting data	Mod2-150–Mod2-162, Mod2-167–Mod2-170
IC³-2	2.1.16	Identify common uses for word processing and identify elements of a well-organized document	Mod2-4, Mod2-34, Mod2-36, Mod2-59, Mod2-81, Mod2-140, Mod2-161, Mod2-170, Mod2-177, Mod2-187, Mod2-194, Mod2-200–Mod2-201, Mod2-204, Mod2-207, Mod2-236
OBJECTIVE 2.2		**Be able to use word-processing tools to automate processes such as document review, security, and collaboration**	
IC³-2	2.2.1	Use language tools	Mod2-78, Mod2-96
IC³-2	2.2.2	Insert and modify data elements into a document, including footnotes and endnotes	Mod2-187, Mod2-189–Mod2-191, Mod2-200–Mod2-201

IC³-2	2.2.3	Use tools that support collaborative creation and editing of documents	Mod2-102, Mod2-106, Mod2-109–Mod2-110, Mod2-120, Mod2-124, Mod2-127–Mod2-130, Mod2-135–Mod2-136
IC³-2	2.2.4	Protect a document from unauthorized viewing or modification	Mod2-120, Mod2-127–Mod2-130, Mod2-135–Mod2-136
OBJECTIVE 3.1		**Be able to modify worksheet data and structure and format data in a worksheet**	
IC³-2	3.1.1	Identify how a table of data is organized in a spreadsheet	Mod2-240, Mod2-243, Mod2-262–Mod2-264, Mod2-270–Mod2-271, Mod2-298, Mod2-300, Mod2-313, Mod2-319–Mod2-321
IC³-2	3.1.2	Identify the structure of a well-organized, useful worksheet	Mod2-242, Mod2-249–Mod2-250, Mod2-262–Mod2-264, Mod2-270–Mod2-271, Mod2-298–Mod2-300, Mod2-319–Mod2-320
IC³-2	3.1.3	Insert and modify data	Mod2-247, Mod2-249, Mod2-254, Mod2-256–Mod2-257, Mod2-262–Mod2-264, Mod2-279
IC³-2	3.1.4	Modify table structure	Mod2-251–Mod2-254, Mod2-262–Mod2-264, Mod2-271, Mod2-279, Mod2-281, Mod2-298, Mod2-300, Mod2-319–Mod2-321
IC³-2	3.1.5	Identify and change number formats, including the Number, Currency, Date and Time, Percentage, and number of decimal places	Mod2-282, Mod2-297–Mod2-299
IC³-2	3.1.6	Apply borders and shading to cells	Mod2-285, Mod2-287–Mod2-288, Mod2-297–Mod2-299
IC³-2	3.1.7	Specify cell alignment	Mod2-279, Mod2-281, Mod2-297

IC³-2	3.1.8	Apply table AutoFormats	Mod2-287–Mod2-288, Mod2-297–Mod2-298
IC³-2	3.1.9	Specify worksheet/workbook-specific print options, including page breaks, print area, repeating rows and columns, and headers and footers	Mod2-272, Mod2-274, Mod2-276, Mod2-297–Mod2-298
IC³-2	3.1.10	Identify common uses of spreadsheets, as well as elements of a well-organized, well-formatted spreadsheet	Mod2-34, Mod2-279, Mod2-285, Mod2-299–Mod2-300, Mod2-319–Mod2-321
OBJECTIVE 3.2		**Be able to sort data, manipulate data using formulas and functions, and create simple charts**	
IC³-2	3.2.1	Sort worksheet data	Mod2-291, Mod2-297–Mod2-298
IC³-2	3.2.2	Filter data	Mod2-291, Mod2-298
IC³-2	3.2.3	Demonstrate an understanding of absolute vs. relative cell references	Mod2-305, Mod2-332
IC³-2	3.2.4	Insert arithmetic formulas into worksheet cells	Mod2-302–Mod2-303, Mod2-313, Mod2-331–Mod2-333
IC³-2	3.2.5	Demonstrate how to use common worksheet functions (e.g., SUM, AVERAGE, MIN, MAX, COUNT)	Mod2-306–Mod2-308, Mod2-310, Mod2-312 Mod2-331–Mod2-334
IC³-2	3.2.6	Use AutoSum	Mod2-306–Mod2-308, Mod2-332
IC³-2	3.2.7	Insert and modify formulas and functions	Mod2-302–Mod2-303, Mod2-306–Mod2-308, Mod2-310, Mod2-312, Mod2-332
IC³-2	3.2.8	Identify common errors people make when using formulas and functions	Mod2-315–Mod2-317
IC³-2	3.2.9	Insert and modify simple charts in a worksheet	Mod2-319–Mod2-321, Mod2-323–Mod2-326, Mod2-332–Mod2-333, Mod2-335
IC³-2	3.2.10	Draw conclusions based on tabular data or charts in a worksheet	Mod2-285, Mod2-299–Mod2-300, Mod2-319–Mod2-321, Mod2-325–Mod2-326, Mod2-333–Mod2-335

OBJECTIVE 4.1	Be able to create and format simple presentations	
IC³-2 4.1.1	Manage slides	Mod2-344–Mod2-345, Mod2-364–Mod2-365
IC³-2 4.1.2	Add information to a slide	Mod2-246–Mod2-347, Mod2-350, Mod2-352–Mod2-353, Mod2-355, Mod2-364, Mod2-368, Mod2-374, Mod2-376, Mod2-379, Mod2-383, Mod2-386, Mod2-388, Mod2-397–Mod2-399
IC³-2 4.1.3	Change slide view	Mod2-342, Mod2-345–Mod2-347, Mod2-355, Mod2-364–Mod2-365
IC³-2 4.1.4	Change slide layout	Mod2-352–Mod2-353, Mod2-364–Mod2-365
IC³-2 4.1.5	Modify a slide background	Mod2-349–Mod2-350, Mod2-364
IC³-2 4.1.6	Assign transitions to slides	Mod2-381, Mod2-397–Mod2-398
IC³-2 4.1.7	Change the order of slides in a presentation	Mod2-344–Mod2-345, Mod2-364
IC³-2 4.1.8	Identify different ways presentations are distributed (e.g., printed, projected to an audience, distributed over networks or the Internet)	Mod2-391–Mod2-394, Mod2-399
IC³-2 4.1.9	Create different output elements (e.g., speaker's notes, handouts, Web page)	Mod2-346–Mod2-347, Mod2-391–Mod2-394, Mod2-398–Mod2-399
IC³-2 4.1.10	Preview the slide show presentation	Mod2-358, Mod2-365, Mod2-397
IC³-2 4.1.11	Navigate an on-screen slide show	Mod2-358, Mod2-365, Mod2-379, Mod2-397
IC³-2 4.1.12	Identify common uses of presentation software as well as effective design principles for simple presentations	Mod2-34, Mod2-338, Mod2-346–Mod2-347, Mod2-349–Mod2-350, Mod2-352–Mod2-353, Mod2-355, Mod2-365–Mod2-366, Mod2-368, Mod2-399

IC3 - MODULE 3: LIVING ONLINE

STANDARDIZED CODING NUMBER	OBJECTIVES & ABBREVIATED SKILL SETS	PAGE MAPPING
OBJECTIVE 1.1	**Identify network fundamentals and the benefits and risks of network computing**	
IC³-3 1.1.1	Identify that networks (including computer networks and other networks such as the telephone network) transmit different types of data	Mod3-4– Mod3-5
IC³-3 1.1.2	Identify benefits of networked computing	Mod3-6
IC³-3 1.1.3	Identify the risks of networked computing	Mod3-7– Mod3-8
IC³-3 1.1.4	Identify the roles of clients and servers in a network	Mod3-9
IC³-3 1.1.5	Identify networks by size and type	Mod3-9– Mod3-12
IC³-3 1.1.6	Identify concepts related to network communication (high-speed, wireless, etc.)	Mod3-13– Mod3-15
IC³-3 1.1.7	Identify fundamental principles of security on a network, including authorization, authentication, and wireless security issues	Mod3-16– Mod3-18
OBJECTIVE 2.1	**Identify different types of electronic communication/collaboration and how they work**	
IC³-3 2.1.1	Identify the different methods of electronic communication/ collaboration and the advantages and disadvantages of each	Mod3-24
IC³-3 2.1.2	Identify how unique users are identified with communication services such as instant mail, text messaging, online conferencing, and social network sites	Mod3-24
IC³-3 2.1.3	Identify the major components of electronic communication (user agents, servers, communication, and protocols)	Mod3-25
OBJECTIVE 2.2	**Identify how to use an electronic mail application**	
IC³-3 2.2.1	Identify how electronic mail identifies a unique e-mail user by e-mail address, including:	Mod3-26
IC³-3 2.2.2	Identify the components of an electronic mail message or instant message	Mod3-26
IC³-3 2.2.3	Identify when to use different electronic mail options	Mod3-26– Mod3-27
IC³-3 2.2.4	Read and send electronic mail messages	Mod3-31– Mod3-34, Mod3-35
IC³-3 2.2.5	Identify ways to supplement a mail message with additional information	Mod3-31, Mod3-33, Mod3-35– Mod3-37

IC³-3 2.2.6	Manage attachments	Mod3-38– Mod3-40
IC³-3 2.2.7	Manage mail	Mod3-27– Mod3-30, Mod3-34
IC³-3 2.2.8	Manage addresses	Mod3-31
IC³-3 2.2.9	Identify the purpose of frequently used mail-configuration options (automatic signature, blocking messages, etc.)	Mod3-41, Mod3-66, Mod3-68
OBJECTIVE 2.3	**Identify the appropriate use of different types of communication/collaboration tools and the "rules of the road" regarding online communication ("netiquette")**	
IC³-3 2.3.1	Identify appropriate uses for different communication methods (e-mail, instant messages, teleconference, syndication, etc.)	Mod3-48– Mod3-49
IC³-3 2.3.2	Identify the advantages of electronic communication	Mod3-49– Mod3-50
IC³-3 2.3.3	Identify common problems associated with electronic communication (lost connection, delivery failure, junk mail, etc.)	Mod3-52– Mod3-64
IC³-3 2.3.4	Identify the elements of professional and effective electronic communications (audience, purpose, reply option, etc.)	Mod3-64– Mod3-65
IC³-3 2.3.5	Identify appropriate use of e-mail attachments and other supplementary information	Mod3-65– Mod3-66
IC³-3 2.3.6	Identify issues regarding unsolicited e-mail ("spam") and how to minimize or control unsolicited mail	Mod3-67
IC³-3 2.3.7	Identify effective procedures for ensuring the safe and effective use of electronic communication (virus checking, netiquette, encryption, etc.)	Mod3-68
OBJECTIVE 3.1	**Identify information about the Internet, the World Wide Web and Web sites and be able to use a Web browsing application**	
IC³-3 3.1.1	Understand the difference between the Internet (a worldwide network of computers) and the World Wide Web (a set of linked pages containing information and applications that uses the Internet to facilitate online communications)	Mod3-74– Mod3-75
IC³-3 3.1.2	Identify terminology related to the Internet and the World Wide Web (domain, HTML, IP address, URL, wiki, etc.)	Mod3-75– Mod3-79
IC³-3 3.1.3	Identify different items on a Web page (graphics, video, hyperlinks, etc.)	Mod3-80
IC³-3 3.1.4	Identify different types of Web sites and the purposes of different types of sites (commercial, academic, portals, etc.)	Mod3-81– Mod3-83
IC³-3 3.1.5	Navigate the Web using a browser (by specifying a URL or IP address, using hyperlinks, using the browser's Forward and Back buttons and address bar, etc.)	Mod3-84– Mod3-89

IC³-3	3.1.6	Reload/Refresh the view of a Web page	Mod3-89
IC³-3	3.1.7	Show a history of recently visited Web sites, navigate to a previously visited site and delete history of visited sites	Mod3-89–Mod3-90
IC³-3	3.1.8	Find specific information on a Web site	Mod3-91–Mod3-92
IC³-3	3.1.9	Manage Bookmarked sites/Favorite sites	Mod3-92–Mod3-94
IC³-3	3.1.10	Copy appropriate elements from a Web site to another application (such as copying text or media to a word processing document or presentation or copying data to a spreadsheet)	Mod3-96–Mod3-98
IC³-3	3.1.11	Download a file from a Web site to a specified location	Mod3-94–Mod3-96
IC³-3	3.1.12	Print information from a Web site or Web page	Mod3-96–Mod3-98
IC³-3	3.1.13	Identify settings that can be modified in a Web browser application (security, privacy, default home page, etc.)	Mod3-87, Mod3-98–Mod3-100
IC³-3	3.1.14	Identify problems associated with using the Web (pop-up ads, required add-ins, security issues, etc.)	Mod3-60, Mod3-100–Mod3-101, Mod3-151–Mod3-160
OBJECTIVE 3.2		**Understand how content is created, located and evaluated on the World Wide Web**	
IC³-3	3.2.1	Identify ways content is created on the Internet (blogs, wikis, social networking sites, etc.)	Mod3-106–Mod3-110
IC³-3	3.2.2	Identify ways of searching for information	Mod3-110–Mod3-113
IC³-3	3.2.3	Use a search engine to search for information (using effective key words, refining a search, etc.)	Mod3-113–Mod3-118
IC³-3	3.2.4	Identify issues regarding the quality of information found on the Internet, including relevance, reliability, and validity	Mod3-118–Mod3-119
IC³-3	3.2.5	Identify how to evaluate the quality of information found on the Web	Mod3-118–Mod3-119
IC³-3	3.2.6	Identify responsible and ethical behaviors when creating or using online content (copyright, plagiarism, etc.)	Mod3-119–Mod3-121
OBJECTIVE 4.1		**Identify how computers are used in different areas of work, school and home**	
IC³-3	4.1.1	Identify how information technology and the Internet are used at work, home, or school to collect, organize, evaluate, and communicate information, increase productivity, etc.	Mod3-126–Mod3-132
IC³-3	4.1.2	Identify that traditional desktop and laptop computers represent only a fraction of the computer technology people interact with on a regular basis (ATMs, point-of-sale systems, security systems, etc.)	Mod3-132–Mod3-136

IC³-3 4.1.3	Identify how computers and the Internet have transformed traditional processes (e-commerce, online learning, etc.)	Mod3-137–Mod3-143
IC³-3 4.1.4	Identify technologies that support or provide opportunities to the physically challenged and disadvantaged	Mod3-143–Mod3-145
OBJECTIVE 4.2	**Identify the risks of using computer hardware and software and how to use computers and the Internet safely, ethically and legally**	
IC³-3 4.2.1	Identify how to maintain a safe working environment that complies with legal, health, and safety rules	Mod3-150
IC³-3 4.2.2	Identify injuries that can result from the use of computers for long periods of time	Mod3-150–Mod3-151
IC³-3 4.2.3	Identify risks to personal and organizational data (theft, data loss, etc.)	Mod3-151–Mod3-153
IC³-3 4.2.4	Identify software threats (viruses, spyware, etc.)	Mod3-154–Mod3-156
IC³-3 4.2.5	Identify reasons for restricting access to files, storage devices, computers, networks, the Internet or certain Internet sites	Mod3-156
IC³-3 4.2.6	Identify the principles regarding when information can or cannot be considered personal, including the difference between computer systems owned by schools or businesses that may have rules and guidelines as to who owns data stored on the system, and computers owned by individuals where the owner of the computer has control over his or her own data	Mod3-157
IC³-3 4.2.7	Identify how to avoid hazards regarding electronic commerce	Mod3-157–Mod3-158
IC³-3 4.2.8	Identify how to protect privacy and personal security online (to avoid fraud, identity theft and other hazards)	Mod3-158–Mod3-161
IC³-3 4.2.9	Identify how to find information about rules regarding the use of computers and the Internet	Mod3-161–Mod3-162
IC³-3 4.2.10	Identify how to stay informed about changes and advancements in technology	Mod3-162
IC³-3 4.2.11	Identify how to be a responsible user of computers (recycling, backing up, sharing knowledge. etc.)	Mod3-163

GLOSSARY

A

absolute cell reference   A reference that does not change when the formula is copied or moved to a new location.

active cell   A selected cell in an Excel worksheet.

active window   The window currently in use. The title bar of the active window is always darker (or displayed in a different color) to distinguish it from other open windows that may be visible in a tiled or cascaded screen.

ActiveX   A set of rules developed by Microsoft for Windows that controls Windows applications that are downloaded from the Internet and then run in a browser.

adapter card   See *expansion card*.

Address Book   Part of most e-mail programs; used to keep a list of contacts and their e-mail addresses.

administrative rights   Permission to make changes on a computer system.

administrator account   A collection of information that determines which files you can access and which settings you use.

algorithm   A set of clearly defined, logical steps that solve a problem.

alignment   How text is positioned between the left and right margins.

animation   Special visuals or sound effects added to text or an object.

Appearance and Personalization category   Control Panel tools that provide options to personalize the desktop by selecting a new color scheme, changing the background, and adjusting the screen resolution.

application file   A file that is part of an application program, such as a word-processing program, a graphics program, and so on.

application software   Also called productivity software; helps you perform a specific task such as word processing or performing calculations on spreadsheets.

application window   The main window that serves as the primary interface between the user and the application.

archive   To save or transfer data to a storage device or folder for the purpose of saving space or organizing the data.

argument   A value, a cell reference, a range, or text that acts as an operand in a function formula; it is enclosed in parentheses after the function name.

arithmetic/logic unit (ALU)   The part of the central processing unit that performs arithmetic computations and logical operations.

ascending order   Alphabetical order from A to Z, or numerical order from lowest number to highest number.

attachment   A document, image, figure, or other file that you can attach to an e-mail message.

audio input   The process of inputting sound into the computer.

AutoShape   A predesigned drawing object, such as a star, an arrow, or a rectangle.

B

Backstage view   A feature that provides quick access to common tasks for managing documents, such as saving, opening, and printing.

backup   Procedures that place a priority on files that would be difficult or impossible to replace or reconstruct if they were lost, such as a company's financial statements, important projects, and works in progress.

banner   A headline that spans the full width of the page, such as the title for newsletter columns.

beta testing   A process that releases commercial software in development to a cross-section of typical users who evaluate the program and report any problems or "bugs" in the software before it is released to the public.

binary   Computer code that contains only 1s and 0s.

biometric security measure   An authentication method that examines a fingerprint, a voice pattern, or the iris or retina of the eye; these must match the entry that originally was stored in the system for an employee to gain access to a secure area.

biometrics   A technique or device that examines a fingerprint, voice pattern, or the iris or retina of the eye.

BIOS ROM   A chip containing instructions to start the system when you turn on a computer.

bit   In binary, a bit represents a zero or one.

bitmapped graphics Images created with a matrix of picture elements (pixels).

blog An abbreviated version of the term "Web log"; a journal maintained by an individual or a group and posted on a Web site for public viewing and comment.

boilerplate text Content that you frequently use in documents.

Boolean logic Way to search databases; consists of three logical operators—AND, NOT, OR.

browser hijacking A program or practice that takes control of your browser without your knowledge.

brute force attack An attack that uses a script or program to log on to an account using hundreds of words or phrases stored in a dictionary file. Also called a *dictionary attack*.

building blocks Document parts that are already designed and formatted.

bundleware Software included with the purchase of a new computer.

business-to-business (B2B) E-commerce transactions between businesses, such as between a company and a supplier.

business-to-consumer (B2C) E-commerce transactions between businesses and consumers.

business-to-government (B2G) Online transactions between businesses and governmental agencies.

byte A byte is another word for character; generally represented by eight bits.

C

cable management A technique or kit that gathers cables together and stores them so they are not a hazard.

cable modem A device that uses coaxial cable to send and receive data.

case sensitive When entering a password, the upper- and lowercasing of the letters must be identical to the casing of the letters in the assigned password.

cell reference Identifies the column letter and row number in a worksheet (for example: A1 or B4).

cell style A set of predefined formats you can apply to some of the worksheet data.

cell One intersection of a row and a column in a table or worksheet.

central processing unit (CPU) The brains of the computer; also known as the microprocessor.

character styles Styles that provide text formats such as font name, font size, font color, bold, italic, underline, borders, and shading.

chart A graphic representation of worksheet or table data.

circuit board A thin plate or board that contains electronic components.

client A computer that uses the services of another program.

client/server network Computer configuration in which one or more computers on the network acts as a server.

clip art A graphic that is ready to insert in a document.

Clipboard A temporary storage place in your computer's memory that is shared among all the Office applications.

Clock, Language, and Region category Control Panel tools to change the language your system uses or the date, time, or time zone.

collating Printing all the pages in one copy of a document before printing the next copy so that the printed pages are automatically arranged in the proper order as they print.

column heading The letter at the top of the column in a worksheet.

comment An electronic note that the author or a reviewer adds to a document; it is not part of the text but is viewable in the margin or in a separate pane, and it can be printed with the document.

communications channel A link from one computer to another through which data can be transmitted.

complex formulas Excel formulas containing more than one operator.

computer system Hardware, software, and data working together.

Computer window A utility program designed to help you find, view, and manage files easily and effectively.

computer An electronic device that receives, processes, and stores data and produces a result.

conditional formatting Applies designated formats to cells when the cell value meets specified conditions (criteria).

Contact Group A collection of information you create to send the same e-mail message to a group.

Control Panel A program accessed from the Windows Start menu that provides specialized features used to change the way Windows looks and behaves.

control unit The part of the central processing unit that controls the flow of information through the processor.

cookie Small text file created by some Web pages when you visit the site that may include information about your preferences for the Web page; cookie files are stored on your computer.

copyright The exclusive right, granted by law for a certain number of years, to make and dispose of literary, musical, or artistic work.

corona wire Wire used to generate a field of positive charges on the surface of the drum and the paper.

critical thinking   The process of evaluating propositions or hypotheses and making judgments.

crop   To cut off portions of a graphic that you do not want to show.

cursor   A vertical blinking line in the document window that indicates the location where new text and data will be entered.

D

data file   A file you create when working with an application program.

data theft   Removing data from a computer without authorization.

data type   A field property in Access that determines the type of data a database field can store.

data   Information entered into the computer to be processed that consists of text, numbers, sounds, and images.

database   A collection of related information organized for rapid search and retrieval.

database server   A computer that stores databases and database management systems.

datasheet   A database table that stores subject-based data; the primary object in a database.

decoding   The process of translating the instruction into signals the computer can execute.

default   (1) A setting that is automatically used unless another option is chosen. (2) In any given set of choices, the choice that is preselected, the selection that is in effect when you open an application, or the settings established during the installation process.

defragmentation   A utility that reduces the amount of fragmentation by physically organizing the contents of the disk to store the pieces of each file contiguously.

descending order   Alphabetical order form Z to A, or numerical order from highest number to lowest number.

desktop computer   A personal computer that typically fits on a physical desktop.

desktop publishing   The process of creating a document using a computer to lay out text and graphics.

digital camera   A camera that takes and stores photographs as digital files.

digital cash   Allows someone to pay by transmitting a number from one computer to another.

digital certificate   An electronic document similar to an ID card.

digital subscriber line (DSL)   An Internet connection technology that provides for the transfer of information to a computer at a high-speed bandwidth over ordinary copper telephone lines.

directory   A container for files and other directories. Windows 7 generally uses the term *folder*, while operating systems such as Linux use the term *directory*.

document management server   A central location for storing, managing, and tracking files.

document template   A file that contains document settings, content, and formats that are available only to documents based on that template.

document window   The area in an application window where you enter new text and data or change existing text and data.

domain   A name or other attribute that identifies a computer or Web site on the Internet.

drag-and-drop editing   Using the mouse to drag selected content from the existing location and then dropping the selected content in a new location.

drawing canvas   A frame-like boundary between a drawing and the rest of the document that keeps your shapes together as one object.

drawing objects   Shapes, curves, and lines to create your own graphic.

driver   A small program that instructs the operating system on how to operate specific hardware.

dual-core processor   A single chip that contains two separate processors.

duplex printing   Printing on both sides of the paper.

E

Ease of Access category   Control Panel tools to adjust hardware and operating system settings for users with vision, hearing, and mobility disabilities.

edit   Modify or adapt and make revisions or corrections.

electronic commerce (e-commerce)   Business conducted over the Internet.

electronic mail (e-mail)   Transmission of electronic messages over networks.

e-mail address   A three-part address you use to send someone a message on a network.

embedded chart   A chart created on the same sheet as the data used in the chart.

embedded computer   A computer that performs specific tasks and can be found in a range of devices such as digital watches, traffic lights, automobiles, household appliances, and system controllers for high end medical equipment.

embedded operating system   Similar in principle to operating systems such as Windows or Linux, embedded operating systems are smaller and generally less capable than desktop operating systems.

emphasis effects   Settings used to draw attention to an object that is already visible on a slide in a PowerPoint presentation.

emulation card   A card that provides the ability for the computer to run a program that was designed for a different operating system.

encryption   A standard method for encoding data.

entrance effects   Settings used to control how an object enters onto a slide in a PowerPoint presentation.

entry   Data entered in a datasheet cell.

ergonomic keyboard   A keyboard that allows for a more natural positioning of your arms and hands.

execution cycle (E-cycle)   The amount of time it takes the central processing unit to execute an instruction and store the results in RAM.

exit effects   Settings used to control how an object leaves a slide in a PowerPoint presentation.

expansion slot   Opening on the motherboard where an expansion board, also called an *adapter card*, can be inserted.

extranet   A network configuration that allows selected outside organizations to access internal information systems.

F

feed   A data format used for providing users with frequently updated content. Also known as a *news feed* or *Web feed*.

fetching   The process of obtaining a program instruction or data item from RAM.

field name   A label that helps identify the field.

field properties   Definitions of the characteristics of and behavior of a database field.

field   In Access, a single piece of database information, such as a first name, a last name, or a telephone number; in Word, an indication of a location in which variable text or data can be inserted.

file   A collection of information saved as a unit.

file allocation table (FAT)   A special log on a disk that labels each track and its location on the disk.

file compatibility   The ability to open and work with files without a format conflict.

file extension   Three or four characters automatically added to the filename when the document is saved; a period separates the filename and the extension, which identifies the type of file.

file properties   Characteristics that help you locate and organize files.

file server   A computer that stores remote programs and data files that are shared by a set of designated users.

file system   Determines the way an operating system stores files on disk.

File Transfer Protocol (FTP)   Internet standard that allows users to download and upload files with other computers on the Internet.

filter   (1) To screen for data matching specified criteria. (2) A process that can be used to cut down on or eliminate most junk mail.

firewall   A combination of hardware and software that creates a buffer between an internal network and the Internet to prevent unauthorized access.

FireWire   Also known as IEEE 1394 and IEEE 1394b. The IEEE 1394 bus standard supports data transfer rates of up to 400 Mbps

first line indent   Formatting in which only the first line of the paragraph is indented.

flowchart   A diagram that shows different paths a program will take depending on what data is inputted.

folder   A means for organizing files into manageable groups.

font   The design of the typeface.

footer   Information and/or graphics that print in the bottom margin of the page.

form   A database object which provides a convenient way to enter, edit, and view data from a table.

Format Painter   A Microsoft Office feature used to quickly copy and apply font and paragraph formatting as well as some basic graphic formatting, such as borders, fills, and shading.

format   To change the appearance of the text or of the whole document.

formula   The equation using numbers and cell references to perform calculations such as addition, subtraction, multiplication, and division.

fragmentation   Files that are not stored in contiguous clusters, but rather are divided into subparts and stored in different disk locations. It takes longer for a disk drive to access fragmented files than unfragmented files.

fraud   Something intended to deceive; deliberate trickery intended to gain an advantage.

freeze   To lock a row or column to keep an area visible as you scroll through the worksheet.

function formula   A special formula that names a function instead of using operators to calculate a formula.

G

gadget   A small program such as a clock or calendar.

geographic imaging   Technology to change imagery of the Earth's surface into valuable information.

global template   A file that contains document settings that are available to all documents.

graphics Items other than text, such as digitized photographs, scanned images, and pictures.

gridlines Boundary lines in a table used for layout purposes; they display on the screen, but they do not print.

H

hacker Expert computer user who invades someone else's computer either for personal gain or simply for the satisfaction of being able to do it.

hacking Invading someone else's computer.

handheld operating system Operating system for mobile devices.

hanging indent Formatting in which the first line of text begins at the left margin and all other lines of the paragraph hang, or are indented, to the right of the first line.

hard copy A printed copy of a document.

hard disk A data storage unit inside a computer that can store a large quantity of data (60GB or more).

Hardware and Sound category Control Panel tools to manage hardware devices such as printers, the mouse, and the keyboard.

hardware firewall A device that controls computers from one point.

hardware The tangible, physical equipment that can be seen and touched.

header Information and/or graphics that print in the top margin of the page.

header row Column headings or field names at the top of columns in a table or data source.

hidden file A file like any other except it is not displayed in a folder window.

hoax An attempt to deceive an audience into believing that something false is real.

home page First page that is displayed when a browser is launched.

hub A junction where information arrives from connected computers or peripheral devices and is then forwarded in one or more directions to other computers and devices.

humidity Moisture in the air that can cause computers to short circuit, resulting in the loss of data and damage to hardware.

Hypertext Markup Language (HTML) Protocol that controls how Web pages are formatted and displayed.

Hypertext Transfer Protocol (HTTP) Protocol that defines how messages are formatted and transmitted over the Web.

I

I-beam The mouse pointer shape (which looks like a capital letter I) when the mouse is positioned within the document window.

icon A graphic image or symbol that represents applications (programs), files, disk drives, documents, embedded objects, or linked objects.

incremental search A search that returns matches for the string of characters in the document as you type; as the search text is augmented, the matched in the document change.

indent A space inserted between the margin and where the line of text appears.

index A Web site organized by categories.

information The output produced by a computer after it processes data.

inkjet printer A type of printer that uses a nonimpact process. Ink is squirted from nozzles as they pass over the media.

input Data or instructions, which must be entered into the computer and then stored temporarily or permanently on a storage media device.

inputting The process of using an input device to enter data.

Insert mode In this default text entry mode, when you enter new text in front of existing text, the existing text shifts to the right to make room for the new text.

insertion point A vertical blinking line in the document window that indicates the location where new text and data will be entered.

instant messaging A form of electronic communication that allows you to send and receive text messages in "real time" from friends and colleagues who are currently online.

instruction cycle (I-cycle) The amount of time it takes the central processing unit to retrieve an instruction and complete the command.

Internet Protocol (IP) address A numerical addressing system that uniquely identifies computers and networks linked to the Internet.

Internet service provider (ISP) An organization or company that provides connectivity to the Internet through a telecommunications line or wireless system.

Internet The largest network used as a communication tool.

intranet A network designed for the exclusive use of computer users within an organization that cannot be accessed by users outside the organization.

J

Jump List A collection of links that provides quick access to files and data.

junk e-mail See *spam*.

K

keyboard   Common input device for entering numeric and alphabetic data into a computer.

keyless entry system   A system in which to open a lock, you press a button on a remote control device or enter a combination on the keypad.

keylogger   A malicious program that records keystrokes.

keyword   A word that describes the information the user is trying to locate.

L

landscape orientation   A page layout in which the content of the document is formatted with the long edge of the page at the top.

laptop computer   See *notebook computer*.

laser printer   A printer that produces images using the same technology as copier machines.

libel   A claim that creates a negative image of an individual, business, product, group, government, or nation.

link list   A collection of links on a particular topic.

linked styles   Styles that provide either text or paragraph formats, depending on the content that is selected when the style is applied.

Linux   A variant of the UNIX operating system.

Linux PC   A standard personal computer that runs the Linux operating system.

local area network (LAN)   A series of connected personal computers, workstations, and other devices, such as printers or scanners, within a confined space, such as an office building.

logic bomb   Computer virus triggered by the appearance or disappearance of specified data.

M

Mac OS X   The Macintosh operating system.

machine cycle   The combination of the instruction cycle and one or more execution cycles.

Mail Setup   Tools you use to create e-mail accounts and directories, change settings for Outlook files, and set up multiple profiles of e-mail accounts and data files.

mainframe computer   A large, powerful computer used for centralized storage, processing, and management of very large amounts of data.

maintenance   Tasks you perform to keep equipment in working order.

manual column break   A command inserted by the user to adjust where a column ends.

manual line break   A paragraph marker inserted by the user to force a line break at a specific location and thereby create a new paragraph.

manual page break   A command inserted by the user to force a page break at a specific location.

margin   The blank space around the edges of the page.

markup   The revision marks and comments that display in a document.

math symbol   The plus or minus sign used to filter out unwanted hits when searching online.

mathematical function   A function that performs calculations that you could perform using a scientific calculator.

memory   Where data is stored on the computer's motherboard.

merging cells   Combining multiple cells by removing the boundaries between the cells, usually done to create a title or informational text over multiple columns.

metadata   Data that describes other data.

minimized   The state in which an application is still running, but the application window is no longer displayed on the screen.

mixed cell reference   A cell reference that contains both relative and absolute references.

mobile device   An electronic device that fits into the palm of your hand, such as a calculator, smart phone or other cell phone, electronic organizer, or handheld game.

modem   Communications hardware device that facilitates the transmission of data.

monitor   The display device on a computer, which includes the screen and the housing for its electrical components.

motherboard   A circuit board that contains all of the computer system's main components.

motion paths   Settings used to create a path for an object to follow on a PowerPoint slide.

mouse   A pointing device that serves as a faster, more effective alternative to the keyboard in communicating instructions to the computer.

multicore processor   An expanded chip that provides for more than two separate processors.

multimedia   The use of text, graphics, audio, and video in some combination to create an effective means of communication and interaction.

N

netiquette   A combination of the words net and etiquette, refers to good manners and proper behaviors when communicating through electronic media.

Network and Internet category Control Panel tools that help you connect to and view a network and network computers and devices, sync with other computers, and perform other networking tasks.

network drive A disk drive located on another computer or server that provides space you can use for data storage.

network license A type of license that gives the organization the right to install a program on a server which can be accessed by a specific number of computers.

news feed See *feed*.

node A device on the network.

Normal template (Normal.dotm) A file containing default styles and customizations that determine the structure and page layout of a document.

notebook computer A small, portable personal computer.

notification area The right side of the Windows taskbar.

O

object linking and embedding (OLE) A technology developed by Microsoft that lets you create a document or object in one program and then link and/or embed that data into another program.

object A discrete item that provides a description of virtually anything known to a computer.

online learning Classes and other educational opportunities provided on the Internet.

open To load a file into an application.

operand A number or cell reference.

operating system (OS) System software that provides an interface between the user or application program and the computer hardware.

operator A symbol that indicates the mathematical operation to perform with the operands.

optical storage device A device that enables the computer to give the user the results of the processed data.

order of evaluation The sequence used to calculate the value of a formula.

outcrop Add extra white space around a graphic.

output Data that has been processed into a useful format.

Overtype mode In this text entry mode, new text replaces existing characters.

P

packet A unit of data sent across a network. When a large block of information is sent, it is broken up into smaller data packets that are sent separately and then reassembled in their original order at the other end.

Palm OS An operating system that runs on Palm mobile devices and other third-party devices.

paragraph styles Styles that provide both text formats and paragraph formats such as line spacing, text alignment, indentation, and tab stops.

patch Software applied over software that you already have installed.

path The route the operating system uses to locate a document; the path identifies the disk and any folders relative to the location of the document.

peer-to-peer (P2P) network Computer architecture in which all of the computers on a network are equal and there is no computer designated as the server.

personal computer (PC) A microcomputer designed for use by one person at a time.

phishing A type of personal information scam.

phrase searching Searching for words that appear next to each other.

ping A DOS command that tests connectivity and isolates hardware problems and any mismatched configurations.

placeholder text Provides guidance for adding text, pictures, tables, or charts to fields.

plagiarism Claiming someone else's words as your own.

plug and play Technology that allows a hardware component to be attached to a computer so that it is automatically configured by the operating system, without user intervention.

podcast A method of publishing files (primarily audio) to the Internet that can be streamed or downloaded for playback on a computer or a personal digital audio player.

podcatcher A program that checks a feed for new content on a regular basis, and then downloads the podcast to your specified device.

pointing device Device, such as a mouse or trackball, that allows the user to select objects on the screen.

points The units of measure for fonts. The larger the point number, the larger the font size. (One inch equals approximately 72 points.)

port An interface to which a peripheral device attaches to or communicates with the system unit.

Portable Document Format (PDF) A format developed by Adobe Systems designed to preserve the visual appearance and layout of each page and enable fast viewing and printing.

portal A Web site that features useful content, but also contains links to other sites.

portrait orientation A page layout in which the content of the document is formatted with the short edge of the page at the top.

power spike A short, fast transfer of electrical voltage, current, or energy.

presentation The document file in PowerPoint.

presentation software Software that is used to create and edit information to present in an electronic slide show format.

primary key Unique identifier of each record in an Access table.

print queue A feature that shows information about documents that are waiting to print.

printer A device that produces a paper or hard copy of the processing results.

private key The part of encryption process that deciphers an encoded certificate.

problem solving A systematic approach of going from an initial situation to a desired situation.

Program Compatibility Wizard A Windows 7 tool for changing the compatibility settings for a program.

Programs category Control Panel options to install, change, or remove software and Windows components; see a list of installed software; control access to certain programs; and add gadgets to the desktop.

proxy server A server that acts as an intermediary between a user and the Internet.

public domain Information or content to which copyright protection does not apply and that is available for anyone to copy.

public key The part of encryption process that encodes a certificate.

Public Switched Telephone Network (PSTN) The world's collection of interconnected commercial and government-owned voice-oriented systems.

pyramid scheme An illicit business model where profits are based on the investor's ability to recruit other individuals who are enrolled to make payments to their recruiters. Generally, neither a product nor service is delivered.

Q

query A database object which enables you to locate multiple records matching specified criteria.

Quick Tables Built-in tables with sample data and table formats.

R

random access memory (RAM) Computer location where instructions and data are stored on a temporary basis. This memory is volatile.

range A group of adjacent cells selected in a worksheet; all cells in a range touch each other and form a rectangle.

RDF Summary A format originally developed to facilitate the syndication of news articles.

read-only document Users can open and view the document, but they are not able to make any changes to the document.

read-only memory (ROM) Permanent storage; instructions are burned onto chips by the manufacturer.

record A group of related fields in a database, such as all the contact information for an individual.

Recycle Bin A holding area for files and folders before their final deletion from a storage device.

related search Preprogrammed queries or questions suggested by the search engine.

relational database A database in which information is organized into separate subject-based tables, and the relationship of the data in one or more tables is used to bring the data together.

relative cell reference A cell reference that will be adjusted relative to the formula's new location when a formula is copied or moved to a new location.

remote storage A storage device used to extend disk space on a server and to eliminate the addition of more hard disks or other storage devices.

repetitive strain injury (RSI) An injury that can result when a person makes too many of the same motions over a long period of time.

report A database object which allows you to organize, summarize, and print all or a portion of the data in a database.

resizing Stretches or shrinks the dimensions of a graphic.

reverse printing Reverses the order of the pages so that the last page prints first.

Ribbon A banner in the Office Fluent user interface that organizes commands in logical groups presented on tabs.

router A device that directs traffic on a network by dividing data into smaller packets that travel by different routes and then are reassembled at their destination.

row heading The number at the left of the row in a worksheet.

S

save To store a document on a disk or other storage medium.

scanner An input device that can change images into codes for input to the computer.

ScreenTip   A small window with descriptive text that displays when you position the mouse pointer on a command or control in the application window.

scroll   To move text and content vertically or horizontally on a display screen when searching for a particular section, line, option, and so on.

search engine   A tool that allows you to enter a keyword to find sites on the Internet that contain information you need.

section break   A formatting code that divides the document into multiple sections and controls the section formatting of the text that precedes it.

section   An area within a document that can have its own separate page formats.

sector   A division on magnetic media used for storing digital information.

Secure Sockets Layer (SSL)   A protocol for managing the security of message transmissions on the Internet.

seek time   The time it takes for a read/write head to move to a specific data track; one of the delays associated with reading or writing data on a computer disk drive.

select   To point to an object and then press and release the primary mouse button. Also to identify blocks of text or objects you want to edit.

server   A computer that handles requests for data, e-mail, file transfers, and other network services from other computers (clients).

server operating system   High-end programs designed to provide network control and include special functions for connecting computers and other devices into a network.

service pack   A collection of updates, fixes, or enhancements to a software program delivered as a single file.

shared bookmark   A form of collaborative information sharing that lets users organize and share favorites, or bookmarks. Also called *social bookmarking*.

sheet tab   A tab in the horizontal scroll bar to provide quick and easy access to a worksheet.

shortcut   A pointer to an application or document file; double-clicking the shortcut icon opens the actual item to which the shortcut is pointing.

shortcut menu   A list of the command options most commonly performed from the current window display.

signature   Text or graphics added to the end of outgoing e-mail messages.

single-user license   A license that gives you the right to install software on a single computer.

sizing handles   Small circles and squares on the borer of a graphic or object indicating that it is selected.

slide layout   The arrangement of placeholders on a slide.

slide master   The main slide that stores information about the theme and layouts of a presentation.

slide pane   The area in the presentation window that contains the slide content.

slide transitions   Settings that determine how a slide is introduced as you move from one PowerPoint slide to another in Slide Show view.

SmartArt graphics   Built-in, predesigned, and formatted layouts which you can use to illustrate concepts and ideas.

sniffer   A program that hackers use to capture IDs and passwords on a network.

social bookmarking   See *shared bookmark*.

social networking site   An online community that provides interaction for groups of people who share a similar interest or activity.

soft copy   A digital copy of data.

soft page break   A page break that is automatically inserted when you fill a page with text or graphics.

software   Intangible set of instructions that tells the computer what to do.

Software as a Service (SaaS)   A software delivery method where an application is licensed for use as a service. The software is provided to customers on demand through the Internet, an intranet, or through a network.

software development   The multistep process of designing, writing, and testing computer programs.

software license   A license that gives you permission to use a program.

software piracy   The illegal copying or use of computer programs.

solid-state storage   A nonvolatile, removable medium that uses integrated circuits.

spam   Unsolicited commercial e-mail that is sent to many people at the same time to promote products or services; also called *junk e-mail*.

sparkline   A tiny chart embedded in a cell that provides a visual representation of data.

special-purpose computer   A computer used to control another device.

split   To divide a worksheet into two panes.

splitting cells   Converting a cell into multiple cells by adding cell boundaries.

spreadsheet   A grid of rows and columns into which you enter text data (i.e., surnames, cities, states) and numerical data (i.e., dates, currency, and percentages).

spyware Software installed surreptitiously on a personal computer, with the goal of collecting information about the user, the user's browsing habits, and other personal information.

startup program A program that runs when a computer system starts.

statistical function A function that describes large quantities of data.

storing Writing computer data to memory.

strong password A password that is complex and secure—it contains numbers, letters, and special characters that do not include personal information such as name or birth date. In addition, strong passwords contain at least eight characters, and at least one letter, number, and special character.

style A set of formatting characteristics that you can apply to characters, paragraphs, tables, and numbered and bulleted lists.

subfolder A folder within another folder.

supercomputer The largest and fastest type of computer, capable of storing and processing tremendous volumes of data.

support agreement A list of services specifically designed to provide assistance to a company or organization.

surge suppressor A device that protects against power spikes.

system administrator A user who has an administrator account.

System and Security category Control Panel tools that include settings for a variety of system tasks, such as backup and restore, systems options, power options, and Windows Update.

system file An essential file necessary for running Windows or another operating system.

System Restore A Windows tools that creates and saves restore points on a regular basis.

system settings A collection of settings that affect an entire computer.

system software A group of programs that coordinate and control the resources and operations of a computer system.

T

T-1 line A type of fiber-optic telephone line that can transmit up to 1.544 megabits per second or can be used to transmit 24 digitized voice channels.

table A datasheet that stores subject-based data. It is the primary object in an Access database.

table style A set of predefined formats that you can apply to all the worksheet data.

tablet PC A personal computer similar in size and thickness to a notepad on which you can take notes using a stylus or digital pen on a touch screen.

tagging The practice of adding keywords to content to simplify searching.

telecommuting Using communications technology to keep an employee connected to the office.

teleconferencing Telecommunications service in which parties in remote locations can participate via telephone in a group meeting.

template A file that affects the basic structure of a document and contains document settings such as fonts, line spacing, margins, and page layout.

text box A drawing object that enables you to add text to artwork.

text editor A basic word-processing application.

text messaging Using a cell phone or other mobile device to send and receive written messages.

time bomb Computer virus that does not cause its damage until a certain date or until the system has been booted a certain number of times.

toggle To alternate between the off and on states by repeating a procedure, such as clicking a button.

touchpad A pointing device you can use instead of a mouse. These devices sense the position of your finger and then move the pointer accordingly.

track Where an electromagnetic read/write head stores or retrieves data on a disk.

trackball A pointing device that works like a mouse turned upside down; the ball is on top of the device.

trademark Similar to a copyright, but relates specifically to visual or commercial images rather than text or intellectual property.

Transport Layer Security (TLS) A protocol for managing the security of message transmissions on the Internet.

trigger An instruction that will start a sound effect or animation segment on a PowerPoint slide.

Trojan horse Computer virus that does something different from what it is expected to do.

troubleshooting Analyzing problems to correct faults in the system.

U

Uniform Resource Locator (URL) Address that tells the browser where to locate a Web page.

uninterruptible power supply (UPS) A battery power source that provides electric current during a power outage.

Universal Serial Bus (USB)   Standard for computer ports that support data transfer rates of up to 12 million bits per second.

UNIX   Operating system developed by AT&T. It is considered portable, meaning it can run on just about any hardware platform.

update   A collection of files for updating released software that fixes bugs or provides enhancements.

upgrade   Replacing software with a newer or better version to bring the system up to date or to improve its characteristics.

urban legend   A story which at one time could have been partially true, but has grown from constant retelling into a mythical yarn.

USB flash drive   A small removable data storage device.

useful life   The estimated time period that an asset, such as computer equipment, will be of use to the owner.

User Accounts and Family Safety category   Control Panel tools that let you change user accounts and passwords, change a user's mail profile, and change your Windows password.

user agent   A software application installed on the local PC, network, or Web, such as e-mail, text message, and instant messaging programs.

utility software (utility program)   Systems software that performs tasks related to managing the computer's resources, file management, diagnostics, and other specialized chores.

V

value   The text and numbers contained in a worksheet cell.

vector graphics   Graphics that use points, lines, curves, and shapes based on mathematical equations to represent images.

virus   A computer program that is written to cause corruption of data.

W

warranty   A written guarantee that a product or service meets certain specifications.

Web 2.0   Web sites where users can modify the content.

Web application (Web app)   An application without platform constraints or installation requirements that is accessed through a Web browser over a network such as an intranet or the Internet.

Web cache   A temporary storage area on your computer for collecting online data.

Web feed   See *feed*.

Web server   A computer that houses and delivers Web pages.

wide area network (WAN)   Computer network that covers a large geographical area. Most WANs are made up of several connected LANs.

wiki   A collaborative Web site that can be edited by anyone with access.

wildcard characters   The asterisk (*) and question mark (?) characters used to represent unknown characters in a search for filenames, words, or phrases.

WiMAX   A recent wireless technology that can deliver maximum speeds of up to 7 Mbps to your cell phone, hom computer, or car. Stands for Worldwide Interoperability for Microwave Access.

Windows Embedded CE   An operating system designed for devices such as digital cameras, security robots, intelligent appliances, gaming devices, GPS, and set-top boxes.

Windows Live Mail   E-mail software provided with Windows Live.

Windows Phone   A version of the Windows operating system that runs on smart phones and other types of mobile computers.

wireless Internet service provider (WISP)   An ISP that provides connection speeds more than 30 times faster than dial-up connections—from 384 Kbps to 2.0 Mbps.

wireless keyboard   A keyboard that uses radio or infrared frequencies to connect to a computer rather than a cable.

wireless LAN (WLAN)   A variation of a LAN that uses no physical wires.

word wrap   A feature by which Word automatically wraps the text to the next line.

WordArt graphics   A feature that enables you to transform text into a graphic.

word-processing software   Software used to prepare text documents such as letters, reports, flyers, brochures, and books.

workbook   Where worksheets are stored; a workbook contains one or more worksheets.

worksheet   A spreadsheet in Excel, consisting of a grid of rows and columns formatted to contain numbers, text, and formulas.

worm   Computer virus that makes many copies of itself, resulting in the consumption of system resources that slows down or actually halts tasks.

X

XML Paper Specification (XPS)   A format developed by Microsoft designed to preserve the visual appearance and layout of each page and to enable fast viewing and printing.

INDEX

Index